Physical Anthropology

Physical Anthropology

Ninth Edition

Philip L. Stein
Los Angeles Pierce College

Bruce M. Rowe
Los Angeles Pierce College

Boston   Burr Ridge, IL   Dubuque, IA   Madison, WI   New York   San Francisco   St. Louis
Bangkok   Bogotá   Caracas   Kuala Lumpur   Lisbon   London   Madrid   Mexico City
Milan   Montreal   New Delhi   Santiago   Seoul   Singapore   Sydney   Taipei   Toronto

The McGraw·Hill Companies

Higher Education

PHYSICAL ANTHROPOLOGY

Published by McGraw-Hill, a business unit of The McGraw-Hill Companies, Inc., 1221 Avenue
of the Americas, New York, NY, 10020. Copyright © 2006, 2003, 1999, 1996, 1993, 1989,
1982, 1978, 1974 by The McGraw-Hill Companies, Inc. All rights reserved. No part of this
publication may be reproduced or distributed in any form or by any means, or stored in a
database or retrieval system, without the prior written consent of The McGraw-Hill Companies,
Inc., including, but not limited to, in any network or other electronic storage or transmission, or
broadcast for distance learning.

Some ancillaries, including electronic and print components, may not be available to customers outside the
United States.

This book is printed on acid-free paper.

1 2 3 4 5 6 7 8 9 0 QPD/QPD 0 9 8 7 6 5

ISBN   0-07-299483-5

Editor in Chief: *Emily Barrosse*
Publisher: *Phillip A. Butcher*
Senior Sponsoring Editor: *Kevin Witt*
Developmental Editor: *Larry Goldberg*
Senior Marketing Manager: *Daniel M. Loch*
Managing Editor: *Jean Dal Porto*
Lead Project Manager: *Susan Trentacosti*
Art Director: *Jeanne Schreiber*
Text and Cover Designer: *Srdjan Savanovic*
Art Manager: *Robin Mouat*
Illustrators: *John and Judy Waller, Kirstin Mount*
Photo Research Coordinator: *Natalia C. Peschiera*
Photo Researcher: *Mary Reeg*
Cover Credit: © *Tom McHugh/Photo Researchers, Inc.*
Media Project Manager: *Michele Borrelli*
Associate Media Producer: *Christie Ling*
Associate Production Supervisor: *Jason I. Huls*
Composition: *10/12 Times Roman by Techbooks/GTS–York, PA Campus*
Printing: *45# Scholarly Matte, Quebecor World Dubuque Inc.*

Credits: The credits section for this book begins on page C and is considered an extension of the copyright page.

Library of Congress Control Number: 2005927936

The Internet addresses listed in the text were accurate at the time of publication. The inclusion of a website
does not indicate an endorsement by the authors of McGraw-Hill, and McGraw-Hill does not guarantee the
accuracy of the information presented at these sites.

www.mhhe.com

To our families and in the memory of
Eleanor Frances Blumenthal Rowe Michael
Barbara Stein Akerman
Arnold L. Freed, M.D.
Sidney G. Stein
Rae Stein

Brief Contents

Contents

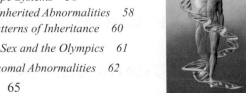

Chapter 7

THE LIVING PRIMATES   146

Chapter 8

COMPARATIVE STUDIES: ANATOMY AND GENETICS   176

Chapter 9

NONHUMAN PRIMATE BEHAVIOR   212

Chapter 10

HUMAN BEHAVIOR IN PERSPECTIVE   238

Chapter 11

THE RECORD OF THE PAST   260

Chapter 12

THE EARLY PRIMATE FOSSIL RECORD AND THE ORIGINS OF THE HOMININS   288

Chapter 13

THE EARLY HOMININS   316

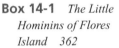

Chapter 14

EARLY SPECIES OF THE GENUS *HOMO*   352

Preface

WHY WE WROTE THE BOOK

We began working on the first edition of this book over 34 years ago. At that time, all the other introductory physical anthropology texts reflected the personal research interests of each of the book's authors. We, as teachers, decided to write a book that covered the field of physical anthropology in a balanced and unbiased way. We also decided to write a book for the general education student, but at the same time provide an excellent background in physical anthropology for students who wanted to go into anthropology in the future.

In this Ninth Edition, we have remained true to our initial approach. We have not concentrated on areas of our own interest. Instead, we have written a text that provides a truly balanced approach based on the most recent information available. We also have presented competing views on various topics such as ideas on the evolution of modern hominins. These contrasting presentations serve to show students that physical anthropology is a dynamic field of study, with concepts competing for acceptance.

We also have remained true to our goal of writing a book for students. Our book shows a concern for the student in a number of ways. We have made sure to write in a manner that does not assume previous knowledge. We explain all concepts carefully. We have made an effort to make complex topics as easy to understand as possible. Yet we have not simplified topics to the point of inaccuracy. Throughout the text, we have consistently tried to show the complexity of topics in a systematic and understandable way. Reviewers have unanimously praised the book as being well written and well suited for the intended audience.

FEATURES OF THE BOOK

In this new edition of *Physical Anthropology* we continue to share our love of discovery with students. Every concept is carefully explained and illustrated, guiding students step by step through difficult material. We have learning aids in each chapter (see below) as well as a new supplemental Online Learning Center (see below).

This text maintains its emphasis on three important themes: first, that anthropology is a holistic discipline; second, that human beings are an integral part of nature; and third, because humans depend on learned behavior, our maintenance of a balance with nature can be strengthened by an understanding of our evolutionary past. As always, we use the most current data to unravel the mystery of the evolution of humankind and examine the dynamic relationship between humans and their environment.

Each chapter of the book guides the student along with a number of study aids that we designed in an effort to make the book easy to use. Every chapter begins with a chapter outline to let the student know in general terms what is to come. This is followed by a number of questions that the student should keep in mind and be able to answer after reading the chapter. Chapters are organized by first-, second-, and third-degree headings to help the student see the relationship of the chapter topics to each other. Rather than having one large summary at the end of the chapter, each section begins with a first-degree heading and ends with a section summary. Each chapter is illustrated with numerous line drawings and photographs. We also have increased the number of charts and tables in this edition and have updated the numerous maps. There are boxes in each chapter on cutting-edge information, controversies within the field, topics of historical interest, and information from fields other than anthropology that relate to the chapter's topics. All technical terms are bolded, and there is both an in-chapter glossary in the margins of the book and an end-of-text glossary. Each chapter has marginal icons that direct the student to the Online Learning Center. The end of each chapter has study questions, critical thinking questions, annotated suggested readings, and suggested websites.

WHAT IS NEW IN THE NINTH EDITION?

Physical anthropology is a dynamic field. We have updated all the chapters on the basis of new information. This is seen most clearly in the chapters on the fossil record of human evolution. In fact, as the book was going to press, it was announced that a new hominin species had been discovered in Indonesia, characterized by small stature and small cranial capacity and dated at 18,000 B.P. (Chapter 15). We have added questions to the chapter openings that give the student a preview of the important concepts found in each chapter.

The major design change made in this edition is the addition of full color. In previous editions we had color inserts and two-color illustrations. Now almost all the illustrations are in full color. Although the illustrations have been chosen for their instructive value, we hope that they are an aesthetically appealing addition to the book. More specific additions and changes in this edition are listed below:

Chapter One—Investigating the Nature of Humankind. The sections on scientific thinking, "creation-science," and intelligent design were revised. The box on the Scopes trial was revised, and a new box has been added on William "Strata" Smith.

Chapter Two— The Study of Heredity. We have expanded the information on twin studies and clarified the section on the principle of segregation. We rewrote the box on Gregor Mendel and added to the box "Facts about DNA." The section on hemoglobin and sickle-cell anemia has been moved to Chapter 5.

Chapter Three—The Modern Study of Human Genetics. We updated the material on molecular genetics, rewrote and updated much of the section called "The Control of Human Biological Evolution," and added a section on stem cell research and new material on cloning.

Chapter Five—Natural Selection and the Origin of Species. We expanded the section on kin selection and the section on hemoglobin and sickle-cell anemia. A new box on the meaning of the word *evolution* has been added.

Chapter Seven—The Living Primates. We adopted a new classification of the primates that reflects current thinking about taxonomy and primate evolution. Because of the new taxonomy, we have followed the current practice of replacing *hominid* with the term *hominin* to refer to humans and their predecessors that lived after the split from a common ancestor with the apes. The chapter includes an extensive reorganization of the descriptions of major groups of primates. We also added a box on color vision.

Chapter Eight— Comparative Studies of Anatomy and Genetics. The chapter includes new illustrations that blend tables and pictures. Sections on comparative cytogenetics and molecular biology have been updated and reorganized.

Chapter Nine—Nonhuman Primate Behavior. We have updated the box on the behavior of the Coquerel's dwarf lemur and the material on the social behavior of chimpanzees.

Chapter Ten—Human Behavior in Perspective. We rewrote the material on the human band and added a new section on demographics and life history. We also rewrote the section titled "Skepticism about Ape-Language Studies" to show more clearly why what the apes are doing (in terms of sign language) is not really language. We discuss the significance of the FOXP2 gene to the evolution of language in a new box.

Chapter Eleven—The Record of the Past. The geological time scale was recalibrated, using the latest available radiometric dates.

Chapter Twelve—The Early Primate Fossil Record and the Origin of the Hominins. With the discovery of very old hominin fossils, the gap is closing between the oldest hominins and the apelike fossils. Therefore, the material on the oldest hominins was moved from Chapter 13 to Chapter 12. We also discuss recently discovered fossils.

Chapter Thirteen—The Early Hominins. All new significant fossil finds are described and discussed. We rewrote and reorganized the material on the evolution of human social and cultural behavior.

Chapter Fourteen—Early Species of the Genus *Homo*. All the new significant fossil finds that fall into the time period covered by this chapter have been included and discussed. We added new discussions of the evolution of human social organization and cultural potentials.

Chapter Fifteen—The Evolution of *Homo sapiens*. As in Chapters 13 and 14, new significant fossil finds are discussed. As in Chapter 14, we discuss the further evolution of social and cultural potentials that evolved in the time period covered by this chapter.

Chapter Sixteen—The Biology of Modern *Homo sapiens*. We moved the discussion of Gloger's, Allen's, and Bergmann's rules from Chapter 17 to this chapter.

Chapter Seventeen—The Analysis of Human Variation. We did a major rewrite of the concept of "race" in which we discuss in more detail why race is a social construct with little biological validity. There is a new section titled "Race as Illusion." We added the most recent genomic data and a new section on why the medical profession still uses racial categories in research and diagnosis.

Chapter Eighteen—The Modern World. We added a section on global warming and one on terrorism, including the possible use of dirty bombs.

SUPPLEMENTS

For the Student

Student's Online Learning Center—This free Web-based student supplement features the following helpful tools at www.mhhe.com/stein9:

- Chapter objectives, outlines, and overviews.
- PowerPoint lecture notes.
- Self-quizzes (multiple choice and true/false questions with feedback indicating why an answer is correct or incorrect).
- Essay questions.
- Key terms.
- Vocabulary flashcards.
- Interactive exercises.
- Internet activities.
- Audio glossary.
- Anthropology Supersite with tutorials, breaking needs, and other features.
- PowerWeb: Anthropology is a password-protected website that includes current articles from *Annual Editions,* weekly updates with assessment, informative and timely world news, refereed Web links, research tools, student study tools, interactive exercises, and much more.

FOR THE INSTRUCTOR

Instructor's Manual/Test Bank—This indispensable instructor supplement features chapter outlines, chapter summaries, learning objectives, media and film suggestions, and a complete and extensive test bank with over a thousand test questions.

Instructor's Disk—This computerized disk contains

- An electronic version of the instructor's manual.
- An easy-to-use computerized testing program that is available for both Windows and Macintosh computers.
- A complete set of chapter-by-chapter PowerPoint lecture slides.

Instructor's Online Learning Center—Password-protected access to important instructor support materials and downloadable supplements such as

- The instructor's manual.
- PowerPoint lecture slides.
- Links to professional resources.
- A message board.

PowerWeb: Anthropology—A password-protected website that offers professors a turnkey solution for adding the Internet to a course. It includes current articles from *Annual Editions,* curriculum-based materials, weekly updates with assessment, informative and timely world news, refereed Web links, research tools, student study tools, interactive exercises, and much more.

PageOut—Designed for the instructor just beginning to explore Web options, this technology supplement allows even novice computer users to create a course website with a template provided by McGraw-Hill.

Videotapes—A wide variety of videotapes from the *Films for the Humanities and Social Sciences* series are available to adopters of the text.

As a full-service publisher of quality educational products, McGraw-Hill does much more than just sell textbooks. The publisher has created and published an extensive array of print, video, and digital supplements for students and instructors. This edition of *Physical Anthropology* includes an exciting supplements package. Orders of new (versus used) textbooks help us defray the cost of developing such supplements, which is substantial. Please consult your local McGraw-Hill representative for more information on any of the supplements.

Philip L. Stein
Bruce M. Rowe

Philip L. Stein

Los Angeles Pierce College

Philip L. Stein has been teaching continuously at Pierce College since 1964. He received his BA in Zoology and MA in Anthropology from UCLA in 1961 and 1963, respectively. He has held a variety of positions at Pierce College, both as an instructor and as an administrator. He is currently the Chair of the Department of Anthropological and Geographical Sciences. He has contributed articles and chapters and has made presentations on the teaching of physical anthropology, including "The Teaching of Physical Anthropology," in C. Kottak, et al. (eds.), *The Teaching of Anthropology: Problems, Issues, and Decisions* (Mountain View, CA: Mayfield, 1996), pp. 183–188, and "Teaching Anthropology in the Community College," in A. S. Ryan (ed.), *A Guide to Careers in Physical Anthropology* (Westport, CT: Bergin & Garvey, 2002), pp. 43–51. He has just completed *The Anthropology of Religion, Magic, and Witchcraft* (Allyn & Bacon, 2005) with his daughter, Rebecca Stein, an instructor at Los Angeles Valley College. Professor Stein is a fellow of the American Anthropological Association and a member of the American Association of Physical Anthropologists and other professional organizations. He is active in the Society for Anthropology in Community Colleges, in which he served as President in 1995–96.

Bruce M. Rowe

Los Angeles Pierce College

Bruce M. Rowe is Professor of Anthropology at Los Angeles Pierce College, where he has taught since 1970. In addition to teaching physical and cultural anthropology courses, he teaches sociology and linguistics classes. He has coauthored eight previous editions of *Physical Anthropology* and two editions of *Physical Anthropology: The Core.* Professor Rowe also has authored five editions of *The College Survival Guide: Hints and References to Aid College Students* and is the coauthor of *A Concise Introduction to Linguistics* (with Diane P. Levine). Professor Rowe has received numerous awards for teaching. He is a fellow of the American Anthropological Association and a member of the American Association of Physical Anthropologists and the Society for Anthropology in Community Colleges.

Acknowledgments

David Abrams,
Sacramento City College

Leslie Aiello,
University College, London

Clifton Amsbury

James Baker,
Okanagan College

Robert L. Blakely,
Georgia State University

Rita Castellano,
Los Angeles Pierce College

Russell L. Ciochon,
University of Iowa

Glenn C. Conroy,
Washington University School of Medicine

Elena Cunningham,
Queen College

Mildred Dickerman

Daniel Evett,
Cornell University

Marc Feldsman,
Portland State University

Robin Franck,
Southwestern College

Everett L. Frost,
Eastern New Mexico University

Janet O. Frost,
Eastern New Mexico University

Douglas R. Givens,
St. Louis Community College

Glenn A. Gorelick,
Citrus College

Philip G. Grant

Joseph Guillotte III,
University of New Orleans

Van K. Hainline,
Citrus College

Mark E. Harlan

C. C. Hoffman,
University of Nevada, Reno

Cheryl Sorenson Jamison,
Indiana University

L. Lewis Johnson,
Vassar College

Gail Kennedy,
University of California, Los Angeles

Karen Kovac

Andrew Kramer,
University of Tennessee, Knoxville

William Leonard,
University of Florida

Diane P. Levine,
Los Angeles Pierce College

Leonard Lieberman,
Central Michigan University

Mary Jean Livingston,
Wayne County Community College

Jonathan Marks,
University of California, Berkeley

James H. Mielke,
University of Kansas

Anne Morton,
Finger Lakes Community College

Edward E. Myers

Crystal Patil,
Ohio State University

Robert L. Pence,
Los Angeles Pierce College

Louanna Pettay,
California State University, Sacramento

Gary D. Richards,
University of California, Berkeley

Peter S. Rodman,
University of California, Davis

Irwin Rovner,
North Carolina State University

Jeffrey H. Schwartz,
University of Pittsburgh

Paul W. Sciulli,
Ohio State University

Robert Shanafelt,
Florida State University

J. Richard Shenkel,
University of New Orleans

Richard J. Sherwood,
University of Wisconsin, Madison

Paul E. Simonds,
University of Oregon

Sandra L. Snyder

William A. Stini,
University of Arizona

Soheir Stolba,
American River College

Linda L. Taylor,
University of Miami

Mayl L. Walek,
North Carolina State University

Tim White,
University of California, Berkeley

We also would like to acknowledge the dedicated work of the people at McGraw-Hill. We want to give special acknowledgment to Director and Publisher Phil Butcher, who has guided us through most of the editions of this book, and to our editor Kevin Witt.

A textbook in Physical Anthropology is full of bones, fossils, stones, and other physical things, in addition to important, complex concepts. A good set of photographs and line drawings is essential for successful mastery of the material. This ninth edition is the first that has been published in full color. This has given us the opportunity to revisit all of the illustrations. We did not simply replace black-and-white photos with colored ones, but searched for the best and most useful photos possible. This was a grand undertaking, and we were assisted by many exceptionally talented people. We want to thank these people here: Art manager Robin Mouat; illustrators John Waller, Judy Waller, and Kirstin Mount; photo research coordinator Natalia Peschiera; and photo researcher Mary Reeg. We also want to thank the rest of the book team for their efforts: Developmental editor Larry Goldberg; project manager Susan Trentacosti; designer Srdjan Savanovic; production supervision Jason Huls; media project manager Michele Borrelli; media producer Christie Ling; and marketing manager Dan Loch.

Special appreciation goes to our families—especially Carol Stein and Christine L. Rowe, for their encouragement and help, and the representative of the second generation, Rebecca Stein, for taking on the task of preparing the Student's Online Learning Center and the Instructor's Disk.

List of Boxes

Chapter-Opening Literary Credits

Chapter 1

E. Mayr, *What Evolution Is* (New York: Basic Books, 2001), p. 275. Courtesy Perseus Books Group.

Chapter 2

T. Dobzhansky, "Mendelism, Darwinism, and Evolution," *Proceedings of the American Philosophical Society* 109 (1965), p. 205.

Chapter 3

International Human Genome Sequencing Consortium, "Initial Sequencing and Analysis of the Human Genome," *Nature* 409 (2001), p. 914.

Chapter 4

R. A. Fisher, *The Genetical Theory of Natural Selection* (Oxford: Clarendon Press, 1930), p. 22.

Chapter 5

C. Darwin, *On the Origins of Species* (London: J. Murray, 1859), p. 61.

Chapter 6

From James Burke, *The Day the Universe Changes* (Boston: Little, Brown, 1985), pp. 240–241.

Chapter 7

D. R. Swindler, *Introduction to the Primates* (Seattle: University of Washington Press), p. 3. Reprinted by permission of University of Washington Press.

Chapter 8

Reprinted from *An Introduction to Human Evolutionary Anatomy* by Leslie Aiello and Christopher Dean, p. 1. Copyright 1990, with permission of Elsevier.

Chapter 9

R. A. Hinde, "Can Nonhuman Primates Help Us Understand Human Behavior?" in B. B. Smuts et al. (eds.), *Primate Societies* (Chicago: University of Chicago Press, 1987), p. 413. © 1986 by The University of Chicago.

Chapter 10

A. Alland, Jr., *To Be Human* (New York: Wiley, 1980), pp. 621–622. Courtesy of Alexander Alland, Jr.

Chapter 11

Reprinted by permission of the publisher from *Life History of a Fossil: An Introduction to Taphonomy and Paleoecology* by Pat Shipman, p. 3, Cambridge, Mass.: Harvard University Press. Copyright © 1981 by the President and Fellows of Harvard College.

Chapter 12

R. L. Ciochon and D. A. Etler, "Reinterpreting Past Primate Diversity" in R. S. Corruccini and R. L. Ciochon (eds.), *Integrative Paths to the Past* (Englewood Cliffs, NJ: Prentice-Hall, 1944), p. 37.

Chapter 13

D. C. Johanson and M. A. Edey, *Lucy: The Beginnings of Humankind* (New York: Simon & Schuster, 1981), pp. 20–21. Copyright © 1981 by Donald C. Johanson and Maitland A. Edey. Reprinted by permission of Simon & Schuster, Inc.

Chapter 14

E. Trinkaus and P. Shipman, *The Neandertals: Changing the Image of Mankind* (New York: Knopf, 1992), p. 419.

Chapter 15

P. Mellers and C. Stringer (eds.), *The Human Revolution* (Princeton, NJ: Princeton University Press, 1989), p. ix.

Chapter 16

T. Dobzhansky, *Mankind Evolving* (New Haven, CT: Yale University Press, 1962), p. 20.

Chapter 17

M. Root, "The Use of Race in Medicine as a Proxy for Genetic Differences," *Philosophy of Science* 70 (2003), p. 1174. Published by The University of Chicago Press. Copyright 2003 by Philosophy of Science Association. All rights reserved.

Chapter 18

A. E. Stevenson, Farewell Speech to the United Nations, July 1965.

Summary

Blood studies have traditionally been important to anthropology because they provide a relatively easy way to study genetically controlled variability in human populations. They also play an important role in forensic science. A large number of polymorphic blood proteins are found in blood that are inherited in known Mendelian patterns. The best-known system of blood proteins is the ABO system, which consists of three basic blood antigens.

About 16,000 inherited traits have been recognized in humans. Phenylketonuria is an example of an abnormality that is inherited as a simple recessive; achondroplastic dwarfism, on the other hand, is inherited as a simple dominant. Not all patterns of inheritance follow these simple Mendelian rules. Many apparent exceptions, in reality complexities, are summarized in Table 3.4.

One distinctive pattern of inheritance occurs when the gene in question is located on the X chromosome. Since males inherit only one X chromosome from their mothers and a Y chromosome from their fathers, genes on the X chromosome are not paired as they are in females. Because of their distinctive inheritance pattern, X-linked traits are relatively easy to identify, such as the example of hemophilia.

A number of abnormalities are not due to single genes but to errors in the number and structure of chromosomes. Such errors, when they involve autosomes, tend to lead to major abnormalities. Individuals with errors in the number of sex chromosomes do survive with varying degrees of problems.

translocation Form of chromosomal mutation in which segments of chromosomes become detached and reunite to other nonhomologous chromosomes.

ACCESSIBLE, STUDENT-FRIENDLY WRITING STYLE. This text is written for *students* using a balanced approach, based on the latest research in the field of physical anthropology. All concepts are carefully explained in a systematic and understandable way.

FULL-COLOR TEXT WITH OUTSTANDING VISUALS. This newly designed ninth edition contains striking photographs and illustrations in brilliant color. This brand-new look brings the world of physical anthropology to life by presenting the material in a more accessible and exciting format for both students and instructors. The numerous color photographs and illustrations help readers visualize the concepts discussed in the text.

Figure 8.1 *(continued)*

Brachyteles arachronides

(e) New World semibrachiation
The animal suspends itself under a branch by its arms and prehensile tail. Found among spider monkeys, howler monkeys, wooly monkeys.

Alouatta palliata

(f) Slow climbing
The animal moves slowly and cautiously without leaping. Found among lorises, potto.

Loris tardigradus

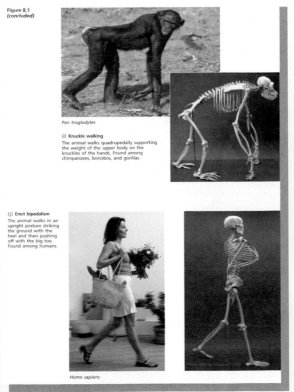

Figure 8.1 *(concluded)*

Pan troglodytes

(i) Knuckle walking
The animal walks quadrupedally supporting the weight of the upper body on the knuckles of the hands. Found among chimpanzees, bonobos, and gorillas.

(j) Erect bipedalism
The animal walks in an upright posture striking the ground with the heel and then pushing off with the big toe. Found among humans.

Homo sapiens

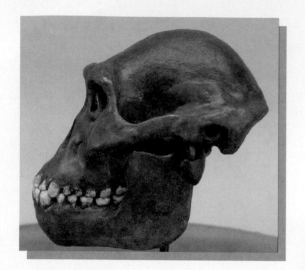

MCGRAW-HILL FOSSIL IMAGE BANK.

This image bank shows students *views of casts of key fossils* studied in the course and covered in the text. Students see various angles of the fossil and then answer questions regarding where the fossil was found, the significance of the fossil's structure, and how it compares to other fossils in the gallery.

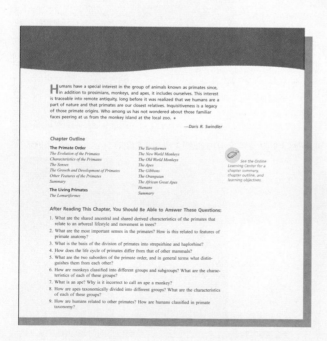

STUDY AIDS IN EVERY CHAPTER.

Each chapter begins with a chapter outline to let students know in general terms what is to come. This outline is followed by chapter-specific questions that set objectives for the student and guide student learning. The chapter headings are clearly structured, and each main section ends with a section summary.

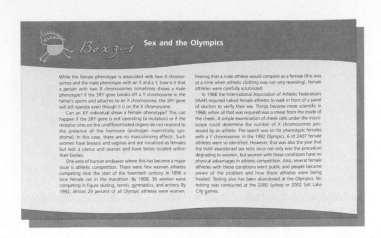

DYNAMIC BOXES.
Boxes presenting cutting-edge information, controversies in the field, and topics of historical interest enhance every chapter of the ninth edition.

Box 3-1   **Sex and the Olympics**

While the female phenotype is associated with two X chromosomes and the male phenotype with an X and a Y, how is it that a person with two X chromosomes sometimes shows a male phenotype? If the *SRY* gene breaks off a Y chromosome in the father's sperm and attaches to an X chromosome, the *SRY* gene will still operate even though it is on the X chromosome.

Can an XY individual show a female phenotype? This can happen if the *SRY* gene is not operating (a mutation) or if the receptor sites on the undifferentiated organs do not respond to the presence of the hormone (androgen insensitivity syndrome). In this case, there are no masculinizing effects. Such women have breasts and vaginas and are socialized as females but lack a uterus and ovaries and have testes located within their bodies.

One area of human endeavor where this has become a major issue is athletic competition. There were few women athletes competing near the start of the twentieth century. In 1896 a lone female ran in the marathon. By 1908, 36 women were competing in figure skating, tennis, gymnastics, and archery. By 1992, almost 29 percent of all Olympic athletes were women.

Fearing that a male athlete would compete as a female (this was at a time when athletic clothing was not very revealing), female athletes were carefully scrutinized.

In 1966 the International Association of Athletic Federations (IAAF) required naked female athletes to walk in front of a panel of doctors to verify their sex. Things became more scientific in 1968, when all that was required was a smear from the inside of the cheek. A simple examination of cheek cells under the microscope could determine the number of X chromosomes possessed by an athlete. The search was on for phenotypic females with a Y chromosome. In the 1992 Olympics, 6 of 2407 female athletes were so identified. However, that was also the year that the IAAF abandoned sex tests since not only was the procedure degrading to women, but women with these conditions have no physical advantages in athletic competition. Also, several female athletes with these conditions went public and people became aware of the problem and how those athletes were being treated. Testing also has been abandoned at the Olympics. No testing was conducted at the 2000 Sydney or 2002 Salt Lake City games.

KEY TERMS.
Technical terms are bold where first defined in the text, and these terms are repeated in a running marginal glossary within each chapter. In addition, the ninth edition contains a comprehensive end-of-book glossary to enhance student mastery of the concepts in physical anthropology.

altruism Behavior characterized by self-sacrifice that benefits others.

kin selection A process whereby an individual's genes are selected for by virtue of that individual's increasing the chances that his or her kin's genes are propagated into the next generation.

inclusive fitness An individual's own fitness plus his or her effect on the fitness of any relative.

coefficient of relatedness A measurement of the degree of genetic relationship or the number of shared genes between two individuals.

and the colorful peacock have a high degree of fitness since they produce a larger number of offspring than other individuals.

Biologists noted in their studies of animal behavior that most behaviors can be explained in terms of increased fitness. Nevertheless, there exists a set of behaviors that actually reduce the fitness of the individual. How can such features evolve? For example, some animals will postpone breeding in order to assist their parents in raising the next generation. Because of this assistance, a greater number of the parents' offspring will survive (Figure 5.9). Also, an animal will share a limited food supply with another animal, thus reducing the food available to it. There are many situations in which animals behave in ways that contribute to the survival of other members of the community, sometimes placing themselves at a disadvantage. This type of behavior is known as **altruism.**

In 1964, W. D. Hamilton (1936–2000) proposed the concept of **kin selection.**[5] Simply put, fitness can be seen in terms of maximizing the number of genes passed on to the next generation. Biologically related individuals share a certain number of their genes. Thus, if an animal behaves in a way that causes the fitness of a relative to increase, this will, in effect, increase the number of the first individual's genes in the next generation. We use the term **inclusive fitness** when we combine the fitness of an individual with a proportion of the fitness of kin sharing many of the same genes.

Hamilton developed a mathematical statement of kin selection: $rb > c$. In this formula, b is the fitness benefit to those affected by the behavior, while c is the fitness cost to the individual who is doing the behavior. Thus, altruistic behavior will evolve in situations where the benefit is greater than ($>$) the cost. However, a key factor is the closeness of the relationship. The letter r stands for the **coefficient of relatedness,** which is a measure of the proportion of genes that are shared. Table 5.1 gives the coefficient of relatedness for a number of representative relationships. When we take this coefficient of relatedness into account, we see that the closer the relationship, the greater the cost that will be tolerated.

Table 5.1 Coefficient of Relatedness

Relationship	r
Parent and child	0.5
Full siblings	0.5
Grandparent and grandchild	0.25
Uncle/aunt and nephew/niece	0.25
First cousins	0.125
Nonrelatives	0.0

[5] W. D. Hamilton, "The Evolution of Social Behavior," *Journal of Theoretical Biology*, 7 (1964), pp. 1–52.

WEBSITE ICONS. Marginal website icons direct the reader to Internet activities on the Online Learning Center that accompanies the text. Visit the Online Learning Center at **www.mhhe.com/stein9** for comprehensive resources for both students and instructors.

See the Online Learning Center for an Internet Activity on the primate order.

arboreal Living in trees.

THE PRIMATE ORDER

The order Primates contains approximately 238 species. It includes a number of well-known kinds of animals—monkeys, apes, and humans—as well as less well known animals, such as lemurs and tarsiers. Generally speaking, primates are tropical animals, commonly found in the tropical rain forests of Central and South America, Africa, and southern and southeastern Asia. A few species have moved into more temperate habitats. Two examples are monkeys living at high altitudes in the Himalayas and monkeys surviving winter snows in Japan. One species, *Homo sapiens*, occupies a large percentage of the earth's terrestrial habitats.

For the most part primates are **arboreal** animals. However, some species have adapted to a semiterrestrial way of life on the open savanna grasslands and semidesert regions of Africa. A few species have taken up an urban lifestyle, coexisting with *H. sapiens*. The latter species has become a specialized terrestrial animal.

Primates are generally vegetarian, eating a variety of plant foods such as fruits, leaves, flowers, bark, and sap. However, many primate diets also include insects and small animals such as lizards and birds, and two species systematically hunt and eat meat.

Living primates generally possess large brains; flattened nails instead of claws, at the very least on the big toes; grasping thumbs and big toes; and eye sockets that are encircled by a postorbital bar and convergence of the eye sockets on the front of the face, facing forward.

See the Online Learning Center for additional study questions.

Study Questions

1. What does the field of taphonomy tell us about the development of the fossil record? Why is fossilization a relatively rare event?
2. Why are some animals better represented in the fossil record than others? What are the various "sampling errors" found in the fossil record?
3. Although the fossil record is fragmentary, paleontologists are able to reconstruct a great deal about once-living animals. Describe some of the types of information that can be deduced from fossil evidence.
4. Species are defined in terms of reproductive isolation. Since evidence for this cannot be inferred from the fossil record, how does the paleontologist handle the concept of prehistoric species?
5. Individual fossils that were considered representatives of different species have sometimes turned out to belong to a single species. What factors are responsible for variation within species as represented in the fossil record?
6. Distinguish between relative dating and chronometric dating. What are some examples of each type of dating method?
7. Geological events often have a profound influence on the evolution of living organisms. Briefly describe the impact of continental drift on the evolution of plants and animals.

Critical Thinking Questions

1. How can we be confident that certain events took place millions of years ago when no one was around to see them? We reconstruct fossil and archaeological events through inference based on geological and paleontological evidence. What evidence is there that convinces us that now-extinct forms really did live millions of years ago?

END-OF-CHAPTER RESOURCES. As in previous editions, every chapter contains end-of-chapter study questions, critical thinking questions, and suggested readings and websites.

Supplements

ONLINE RESOURCES for *students and instructors*—including the McGraw-Hill Fossil Image Bank—are available on the text-specific **Online Learning Center** at **www.mhhe.com/stein9.** For students, this website features Internet exercises, self-quizzing, interactive activities, and **PowerWeb.** PowerWeb for *Physical Anthropology* gives students password-protected, course-specific articles with assessments from current research journals and popular press articles, refereed and selected by Physical Anthropology instructors.

For instructors, this dynamic website also features a detailed Instructor's Manual (under password protection), as well as answers to the student questions in the Fossil Image Bank.

INSTRUCTOR RESOURCE CD-ROM.

For instructors only, this free CD-ROM contains the Instructor's Manual and Test Bank, along with a modifiable Computerized Test Bank and over 110 PowerPoint slides tied to the text. In addition, the IRCD contains a link to the Fossil Image Bank along with an answer key for the student questions.

Physical Anthropology

Investigating the Nature of Humankind

Charles Darwin's study at Down House.

E volution is not merely an idea, a theory, or a concept, but is the name of a process in nature, the occurrence of which can be documented by mountains of evidence that nobody has been able to refute. . . . It is now actually misleading to refer to evolution as a theory, considering the massive evidence that has been discovered over the last 140 years documenting its existence. Evolution is no longer a theory, it is simply a fact. ●

—*Ernst Mayr (1904–2005)*

Chapter Outline

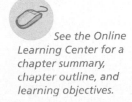
See the Online Learning Center for a chapter summary, chapter outline, and learning objectives.

After Reading This Chapter, You Should Be Able to Answer These Questions:

1. What are the main areas of interest in physical anthropology, and how does physical anthropology relate to the other subfields of anthropology?

2. What is meant by the term *scientific thinking,* and how does scientific thinking differ from religious thinking?

3. Generally speaking, the average European before the fifteenth century viewed the world much differently than does a modern person employing scientific thinking. In what ways were earlier views of the world different from those of most people in the scientific community today?

4. What are the historical events mentioned in this chapter that led to the changing view of the world? Specifically, what were the contributions of Nicolaus Copernicus, Carolus Linnaeus, Georges-Louis Leclerc de Buffon, Jean-Baptiste de Lamarck, Charles Lyell, William Smith, Jacques Boucher de Crèvecoeur de Perthes, Louis Pasteur, Charles Darwin, and Alfred Russel Wallace?

5. What is the concept of intelligent design, and what are the arguments against it?

"We have now seen that man is variable in body and mind; and that the variations are induced, either directly or indirectly, by the same general causes; and obey the same general laws, as with the lower animals."[1] These words were revolutionary for Charles Darwin's time. Darwin's message was that humans, like all animals, were not specially created and that human characteristics arise from the actions of the same natural forces that affect all life.

Darwin is thought to have been a great discoverer of new facts and ideas, and indeed he was. On the other hand, Darwin's ideas, like all ideas, were formed, nurtured, and brought to maturity in the context of particular intellectual backgrounds. The things we think, the relationships we see, and the very process of creativity are determined, in part, by our cultural environment. The knowledge that a person has at any one time represents the accumulation of information and ideas from his or her whole lifetime and from the people who lived in times past. The theory of evolution was not developed by one person. It was part of a chain of intellectual events, each link being necessary to the continuity of that chain.

One of the disciplines that studies the theory of evolution is physical anthropology. We will begin our voyage of discovery by exploring the field of physical anthropology and its place in the world of anthropology.

THE WORLD OF PHYSICAL ANTHROPOLOGY

anthropology The broad-scope scientific study of people from all periods of time and in all areas of the world. Anthropology focuses on both biological and cultural characteristics and variation as well as biological and cultural evolution.

physical anthropology A branch of anthropology concerned with human biology and evolution.

The anthropologist is an explorer in pursuit of answers to such questions as: What is it to be human? How did humans evolve? What is the nature of humankind? **Anthropology** is such a broad discipline, however, that it is divided into several subfields or branches. One of the oldest subfields is that of **physical anthropology,** which includes the study of human biological evolution, the process of biological change by which populations of organisms come to differ from their ancestral populations.

Studies of Physical Anthropology

Physical anthropology is a very diverse field. Some areas of interest lie within the realm of biology and medical science; others are more tuned to cultural anthropology and archaeology.[2]

Anthropologists who specialize in the study of growth and development and anatomy often are found in departments of anatomy and health sciences and schools of medicine. These investigators frequently conduct research on human populations in various parts of the world, allowing them to compare different modern populations. For example, physical anthropologists might study the growth patterns of children growing up at high altitude in the Peruvian Andes Mountains. Other anthropologists study a wide range of health-related topics such as nutrition, disease, and aging.

A focal area of study in physical anthropology is the study of evolution. Anthropologists join with their colleagues in biology in the study of evolutionary theory. Anthropologists are particularly interested in the reconstruction of human and nonhuman primate evolution. Key evidence in these studies is the evidence provided through the fossil record (paleontology) and through analysis of cultural remains (archaeology). Paleontology and archaeology join to create the study of paleoanthropology (Figure 1.1).

A major key in understanding evolutionary processes is an understanding of the mechanisms of heredity—the field called genetics. Many anthropologists are active in studying topics in many subfields of genetics, including human and primate genetics. More recently the comparative study of DNA, the heredity material, has created the field of molecular evolution, which has brought forth new understandings about the relationships among contemporary organisms.

---

[1] C. Darwin, *The Descent of Man,* 2nd rev. ed. (London: J. Murray, 1874), p. 47.

[2] For further information about the diversity of disciplines within physical anthropology, see C. W. Wienker and K. A. Bennett, "Trends and Developments in Physical Anthropology," *American Journal of Physical Anthropology* 87 (1992), pp. 383–393. (See also Table 18–3.)

Figure 1.1 The Study of the Past Paleoanthropologists Jack Fisher, Glynn Isaac, and Desmond Clark excavate a test pit in the Ituri Forest of Zaire.

As we will see later, the critical unit of evolution is the population, a group of closely related organisms. Anthropologists carefully document the characteristics of extant human populations in a number of ways. From these studies, we can learn about how different human populations adapt to their environments. The study of human variation is especially important in our shrinking world as more and more people from diverse parts of the world economically and politically influence one another.

Many physical anthropologists specialize in the study of the fossil record or in skeletal remains found in an archaeological context. For these reasons, anthropologists have become very interested in the biology of the skeleton. As a result, some anthropologists are employed in forensic anthropology, a branch of forensic science. Often found in coroners' offices, forensic anthropologists analyze skeletal remains from criminal scenes to determine biological factors about the individual, such as sex and age at death, as well as to determine the probable cause of death.

See the Online Learning Center for an Internet Activity on the American Anthropological Association.

The members of the animal kingdom most closely related to humans in an evolutionary sense are the primates, a group of animals that include the living prosimians, monkeys, apes, and humans in addition to a wide variety of now-extinct forms. Many anthropologists are in the field studying primate behavior and ecology while others are in the lab working on problems in primate anatomy and evolution (Figure 1.2).

Physical Anthropology in the World of Anthropology

Physical anthropology is one of four main branches of the study of people; the others are cultural anthropology, archaeology, and linguistics. Many anthropologists see applied anthropology as a fifth field. While traditionally anthropologists are trained in all four of the main fields and see anthropology as a holistic discipline, in recent years, the discipline of anthropology has become more and more diverse and specialized, and many new anthropologists are given minimal training outside their own specializations. This has become very much the case in physical anthropology.

Figure 1.2 The Study of Primates Primatologist Dian Fossey discusses the fine points of photography with some of her subjects. Her life is recounted in the book and the movie *Gorillas in the Mist*. The Dian Fossey Gorilla Fund International

Box 1-1 **The Branches of Anthropology**

PHYSICAL ANTHROPOLOGY

The study of human biological evolution with an interest in the interaction between human behavior, the physical environment, and biology.

Some Areas of Concentration within Physical Anthropology

Human genetics: The study of the processes of inheritance and inherited variation.

Primate paleontology: The search for and study of the fossil evidence of primate (humans are primates) evolution. The term *paleoanthropology* is used when the emphasis is strictly on humans and human ancestors. Paleoanthropology also includes the study of archaeological evidence.

Primatology: The study of the living nonhuman primates, which include prosimians, monkeys, and apes.

Human biological variation: The study of the genetic and other biological variation among different groups of people.

Human growth and development: The study of gender and group differences in growth and development and the study of how patterns of growth and development have changed over time.

Human ecology: The study of people's relationships to their environments.

Osteology: The study of the skeleton.

Forensic anthropology: The application of anthropological knowledge, especially of the skeleton, to criminal investigations. Such knowledge, popularized on such television programs as *CSI* and *The New Detectives,* is used for identifying bodies and determining the cause of death.

CULTURAL ANTHROPOLOGY

The study of all aspects of human behavior from a comparative perspective.

Some Areas of Concentration within Cultural Anthropology

Ethnography: The study of an individual culture that results in a written description of that culture.

Ethnology: The cross-cultural study of culture. Although cultural anthropologists study individual cultures, the focus of cultural anthropology is to develop a broad understanding of human nature through the analysis and comparison of individual ethnographies. The goal is to discover human universals and the range of human behavioral variation.

Cultural anthropologists believe in a holistic approach; that is, in order to know about any subsystem of a culture, say, religion, you need to know about all areas of that culture (kinship, politics, economics, concepts of health and disease, and so on). Yet many cultural anthropologists, keeping holism in mind, specialize in a subsystem of human behavior. So within cultural anthropology some of the specializations are:

Comparative religion: The study of magic, witchcraft, and religion.

Kinship studies: The study of how people see themselves as related to others.

Economic anthropology: The study of how goods and services are distributed within and between societies.

Political anthropology: The study of the distribution and use of power and authority within and between societies.

Medical anthropology: The study of attitudes and practices dealing with health and illness.

Urban anthropology: The study of city life from an anthropological prospective.

ARCHAEOLOGY

Although some archaeologists study contemporary cultures, most attempt to reconstruct and describe cultures of the past. Archaeologists study artifacts, the manufactured objects made by humans to perform a variety of tasks, the context in which the artifacts are found, and the physical environment.

---

cultural anthropology
The study of the learned patterns of behavior and knowledge characteristic of a society and of how they vary.

culture Learned, nonrandom, systematic behavior and knowledge that can be transmitted from generation to generation.

Cultural anthropology is the study of human social organization and culture. A central concept in cultural anthropology is that of **culture.** Culture is learned, transmittable behavior that employs the use of symbols, such as words. Cultural behavior, the focus of Chapter 10, is the main way by which humans adjust to their environments.

Archaeology is the study of the material remains of human activity, artifacts, and the context in which they are found. Both artifacts and their context are used to reconstruct how different cultures have adjusted to varying situations through time and to explain stability and change. Although some archaeologists study contemporary societies, most archaeologists study the cultures of the past. **Anthropological linguistics** examines the history,

Some Areas of Concentration within Archaeology

Area-of-the-world emphasis: Some archaeologists are interested in a particular area of the world. This includes New World archaeology and Old World archaeology. Yet, within these two broad areas, there might be more specific interest. A New World archaeologist, for instance, might specialize in the Southwestern United States.

Time-period emphasis: Some archaeologists are interested in studying the recent past, say, Native American culture of a hundred or so years ago. Others are interested in the remote past, such as the first stone tools that were produced more than two million years ago.

Cultural resource management (CRM): Today, in many government jurisdictions, an environmental impact study is required before any construction can begin. Usually an element of such a study is an archaeological survey of the proposed construction site. If archaeological evidence is found, excavation of the site might have to be completed before construction proceeds. The majority of archaeologists in the United States do cultural resource management studies.

Underwater archaeology: The study of shipwrecks and other underwater sites.

Archaeologists who deal with cultures that did not have writing are called **prehistoric archaeologists,** whereas those who supplement their research with written records are called **historical archaeologists. Classical archaeologists** specifically study Old World civilizations and often are trained in the area of art, the classics, or Near Eastern studies.

ANTHROPOLOGICAL LINGUISTICS

Anthropological linguistics is the comparative study of the structure of and relationship between world languages. It also is concerned with the evolution of human language capacity and the role of language in the general evolution of the human species.

Some Areas of Concern within Anthropological Linguistics

Ethnolinguistics: The study of the interrelationship of language to the general culture. Ethnolinguists are interested in such questions as: Does the language one speaks influence thought? If it does, to what degree does that influence extend? How does language encode and transmit cultural, emotional, and symbolic meaning and values?

Sociolinguistics: Sociolinguistics is the study of the degree and form of social variation in the use of language between different genders, age groups, ethnic groups, occupation groups, and other social classifications.

Language acquisition studies: The study of how children learn language.

The study of the structure of language: Some anthropological linguists emphasize the study of *phonology* (the sound systems of language), *morphology* (words, their structure and history), *syntax* (structures larger than words, such as clauses, phrases, and sentences), or *semantics* (the study of meaning).

Historical linguistics: This is the study of language change and the relationship of one language to another.

APPLIED ANTHROPOLOGY

Applied anthropology is the practical application of anthropological knowledge from any subfield of anthropology to real-world concerns. Within physical anthropology, forensic investigation would be an example of applied physical anthropology. Some cultural anthropologists work for international development agencies with the goal of using funds for such development in an efficient and humane way based on anthropological knowledge of the population that is being helped. Environmental impact studies would be an example of applied anthropology done by archaeologists. Anthropological linguists might help with the development of language teaching programs. These are just a few examples of applied anthropology.

function, structure, and physiology of one of people's most definitive characteristics—language. **Applied anthropology** is concerned with the application of anthropological ideas to current human problems (Box 1-1).

While many physical anthropologists work closely with biologists and other related specialists, physical anthropologists are keenly aware of the special nature of the human species. Herein lie the special emphasis and approach of the physical anthropologist. For example, a biologist who is studying human populations may note that one population has a higher frequency of dark skin than another. The biologist's approach is to describe this variation, perhaps by investigating the genetic mechanisms that led to the differentiation. An anthropologist goes one step further: he or she attempts to discover cultural conventions that may be keeping the dark-skinned populations from interbreeding with the light-skinned ones. For instance, cultural

archaeology The scientific study of the past and current cultures through the analysis of artifacts and the context in which they are found.

anthropological linguistics The study of language in cross-cultural perspective; the origin and evolution of language.

applied anthropology A branch of anthropology devoted to applying anthropological theory to practical problems.

conventions involving concepts of beauty, class distinctions, kinship considerations, economic relationships, and so on, all affect breeding patterns. In other words, the physical anthropologist takes note of the fact that culture both builds upon and modifies biology.

Conclusion

This text deals with many issues about the nature of humanity, a very complex and difficult topic. There are no simple answers to the many questions that are raised in this book. The purpose of the book is to provide a basic understanding of humans, their evolution, and their place in nature. We cannot promise that all your questions about people will be answered; in fact, we can promise that they will not. A great deal has been learned about human nature over the centuries, especially in the last century and a half, yet anthropology is still a dynamic subject. With each publication of a research project, new information is added to our knowledge of humanity. In other words, data that are needed to answer crucial questions about the human species are still being uncovered.

Why study anthropology? Because anthropology provides empirical knowledge about the human condition. On one level, this serves to feed our curiosity about ourselves. However, anthropological studies also provide data useful to the fields of medicine, environmental maintenance, urban planning, education, and so forth. Anthropology also attempts to provide a profile of human potentials and limitations. For instance, it explores the question of whether humans are violent by nature.

THE NATURE OF SCIENCE

The physicist investigating the relationship between time and space, the chemist exploring the properties of a new substance, the biologist probing the mysteries of the continuity of life, and the anthropologist searching for human origins share a common trait—curiosity. This is not to say that nonscientists are not curious; most people possess curiosity. The scientist, however, uses scientific reasoning as a specific method to delve into enigmatic problems.

Unfortunately, science often is misunderstood. The multiplication of our knowledge in medicine and technology has led to the idea that science can cure all and explain all and that only enough time, money, and intelligence are needed. In truth, science cannot provide all the answers. In fact, many phenomena are not even subject to scientific explanations.

Science also has been attacked as a cause of most contemporary problems. It is said to be responsible for depersonalizing the individual, for stripping creativity from human behavior, and for creating massive threats to the species through the development of nuclear power, insecticides, and polluting machinery. If we analyze the situation, we can see that the people who developed computers did not intend to debase humankind, nor did those who introduced mass production wish to crush creativity. It is what society, policy makers especially, does with scientific achievements that makes them social or antisocial. There is nothing inherently good or bad about science.

science A way of learning about the world by applying the principles of scientific thinking, which includes making empirical observations, proposing hypotheses to explain those observations, and testing those hypotheses in valid and reliable ways; also refers to the organized body of knowledge that results from scientific study.

empirical Received through the senses (sight, touch, smell, hearing, taste), either directly or through extensions of the senses (such as a microscope).

hypothesis An informed supposition about the relationship of one variable to another.

Scientific Thinking

Just what is **science?** Here is where the dictionary fails, for science is not something that can be easily defined. It is an activity, a search, and a method of discovery that results in a body of knowledge.

The first step in science is to determine what one plans to study. The next step is to make observations about the subject of the study. These observations must be **empirical** observations. By *empirical* we mean that we must be able to experience the object of study through our senses, although instruments such as a microscope or an electronic sensing device often extend our senses.

Hypotheses and Testing Hypotheses A **hypothesis** is a tentative answer to a question posed about an observation. A hypothesis, however, is not any explanation. It must be logical and testable; that is, there must be an objective way to find out if the hypothesis is correct or incorrect. Another way of stating this is that there must be some way to prove that the hypothesis is not true, although the result may show that the hypothesis is indeed correct.

In testing a hypothesis, one looks at the factors that characterize the observation; these factors are called **variables.** A variable is any factor or property of a phenomenon that may be displayed in different ways or values. For example, the volume of the brain case, the part of the skull that houses the brain, is a variable. It may measure 400 cubic centimeters in one animal and 1300 cubic centimeters in another—it can vary. For a variable to be the subject of a scientific study, we must be able to measure it precisely. Different people measuring the same variable must arrive at the same value.

variable Any property that may be displayed in different values.

A hypothesis can be a statement about the relationship of one variable to another. Is one variable independent of the other variable, does one variable cause another variable to change, or does a third variable cause the two variables to change in a systematic way? For example, one might hypothesize that as the average size of the human brain increased through time, so did the complexity of technology. Brain size is one variable, and technological complexity is a second variable. The hypothesis proposes a direct relationship between the two variables: As one increases, so does the other. While this particular hypothesis proposes a relationship between two variables, it does not propose that one variable causes the other to occur.

Once proposed, the hypothesis must be tested against reality. One way to do this is to test the predictive value of the hypothesis by comparing it to all known data gathered from nature. In the above example, we could measure brain case size in fossil skulls and count the number of certain types of stone tools found in association with each skull. If, upon analysis, we find that as the average size of the brain case increases, so does the number of tool types, we have identified one line of evidence that supports the validity of the hypothesis. New discoveries will either support the hypothesis or contradict it.

A second way to test a hypothesis is through experimentation. An **experiment** compares one situation with a second situation in which one variable has been altered by the experimenter. For instance, a geneticist could formulate a hypothesis about the function of a specific unit of inheritance. The geneticist could then conduct an experiment in which he or she rendered that unit inactive in one group of test subjects and left it alone in another group of test subjects. Analysis of the resulting data (observations) provides evidence of the validity of the hypothesis, disproves the hypothesis, or leads to a modification of the hypothesis. Experiments must be repeatable, and the validity of the original experiment depends on whether, when repeated, it yields the same results as did the initial experiment.

experiment A test of the predictive value of a hypothesis. A controlled experiment compares two situations in which only one variable differs.

A third possible way to test a hypothesis is to compare one phenomenon to other phenomena to determine relationships between them. The phenomena can be just about anything—rocks, stars, languages, living organisms. Although we cannot experiment directly with things that existed only in the past, we can compare living organisms to each other and look for patterns that indicate past evolutionary events and relationships. Comparative studies of anatomy have shown that chimpanzees and humans are more closely related to each other than humans are to monkeys. However, humans and monkeys are anatomically more closely related to each other than humans are to dogs. In Chapter 8, we will discuss comparative studies of genetics and biological molecules. In Chapters 9 and 10, we will talk about comparative behavioral studies. Scientists do comparative studies of embryos, comparative studies of psychology, and comparative studies of physiology as well.

After a number of studies exploring the relationships of all the variables have been completed, we might develop some generalizations. For instance, we might suggest that an increase in the volume of the brain case is correlated with a whole range of behaviors that differentiate earlier humanlike populations from later ones. Each of these new hypotheses would have to be tested by some research design. Each test might reveal hidden variables that will disprove or modify the original and related hypotheses. This hypothesis-test-hypothesis-test cycle is a self-corrective feature of science. Scientists realize that results are never final.

theory A step in the scientific method in which a statement is generated on the basis of highly confirmed hypotheses and used to generalize about conditions not yet tested.

Theory Science is cumulative. After many tests have been conducted on a set of similar hypotheses with confirming results, a **theory** may be proposed. For example, the testing of thousands of hypotheses on the reasons for progressive change in anatomy and behavior has led to great confidence in the theory of evolution.

Theory is a frequently misunderstood term. Many nonscientists equate theory with *hypothesis* or *speculation*. In popular usage to say that something is "just a theory" means that it is just a vague and possibly erroneous sort of fact.

In reality, a scientific theory is a statement of extremely high validity—usually some general law or principle. The distinction between fact and theory is often subtle. For example, that evolution has occurred is a fact (see the opening quote). The mechanisms, such as natural selection, that explain how and why evolution has occurred constitute a theory. The validity of evolution as a fact has not been an issue in science for well over a hundred years, but the theories that explain the mechanisms of evolutionary change are still very much discussed and are important areas of ongoing research.

Science and Religion

The theologian deeply involved in an interpretation of scriptures, the bereaved individual looking to scripture to explain death, and the shaman dancing for rain are putting their trust in traditional doctrines that, for the most part, they do not question. In contrast, the biologist examining cell structure, the anthropologist studying death rituals, and the meteorologist investigating the weather rely on methods and techniques that are aimed at producing new information and validating or correcting old explanations. Thus, they build a body of knowledge from which accurate predictions about natural occurrences can be made. The credibility of scientific conclusions is based on the concepts of accuracy, validity, and reliability; belief in religious doctrines is based on faith.

Scientists can attempt to answer only some questions; others cannot be subjected to scientific inquiry and are therefore not in the domain of empirical or objective research. For example, science cannot deal with the question of the existence of an omnipotent force. In order for an experiment to be carried out, a **control,** a situation that differs from the situation being tested, must be possible. If a phenomenon is present always and everywhere, how can its absence be tested?

control In the experimental method, a situation in which a comparison can be made between a specific situation and a second situation that differs, ideally, in only one aspect from the first.

Scientists do not claim that their conclusions are final. They realize that their statements are only as good as the data they have and that new information may alter their concepts. A religious belief can change in response to personal interpretation and public opinion, but such interpretation or new information is not necessarily linked to new empirical facts. To a believer, his or her religious belief or faith is taken as being absolutely true, whereas at no time is a scientific statement considered totally and irrefutably correct.

The scientific approach has been consciously and consistently used in Western societies since the 1600s; however, it is not just the industrial societies that practice science. All people make conclusions on the basis of experiments and observations. The phenomena that they can treat in this way make up their objective knowledge; the more mysterious facets of life are treated religiously or magically. For example, the Trobriand Islanders of the Pacific do two types of fishing: one in the shallow coastal pools and the other far out at sea. The first type is safe and is undertaken by men, women, and children; the second, filled with the unknown, is dangerous and is considered a male activity. Since shallow fishing is undertaken with regularity, time is spent making observations of fish behavior and experiments are performed on how best to catch the prey. Nothing is done religiously or magically to protect the fishing party. The story is different with deep-sea fishing. Men occasionally do not return from the expeditions, and so elaborate rituals are performed to appease or appeal to the gods of the unpredictable seas.

In conclusion, a scientific statement asserts the natural causality of phenomena. One thing happens because of preceding events that led up to it. Things happen and conditions exist because of the physical, chemical, biological, behavioral, and/or cultural and social characteristics of the thing in question and the context in which it is found. Religious or magical statements assert causality beyond the natural; when natural causality cannot be determined or is not sought, spiritual causality is often assumed.

Summary

Science is the activity of seeking out reliable explanations for phenomena. Science is also the search for order and a method for discovery. The result of the activity of science is a body of empirical knowledge that can be used to better understand the universe and to predict the processes, structure, form, and function of natural occurrences. Scientific thinking provides a systematic method of investigation and includes the identification of variables, hypothesis formation, and tests of the validity of the hypothesis and of postulating theories. All scientific statements are tentative. It is because new evidence is always possible that a scientific statement can never be completely proved.

   The scientist and the theologian are both interested in giving answers. However, the scientist proceeds by testing questions about the nature of empirical observation, whereas the theologian consults the philosophy of his or her particular religion and interprets the meaning of that philosophy for a particular situation. Scientific statements are never considered absolute, but at any one time religious doctrine is. All people have a body of scientific knowledge, but for the things they fear or cannot understand in an empirical way, religion and magic provide a measure of comfort and assurance.

VIEWS ON THE ESSENCE OF HUMANS, NATURE, AND TIME

Although there were many variations in the early ideas about the universe, they were often the opposite of those embodied in present evolutionary theory. These old ideas had to be challenged before a new concept of reality could arise.

First among the early views was the idea of human superiority, or **anthropocentricity.** This belief was that the earth is the center of the universe and that all the celestial bodies revolve around it. Humans placed themselves on a pedestal, believing that God provided the animals and plants for people's use and fancy. The similarities that people observed between humans and animals and among various animal species were seen as reflecting the design of the Creator. Many people believed that certain shapes and forms are pleasing to God and that God therefore used these as models for all creations.

People of that era, as well as many people today whose beliefs are based on a literal interpretation of the Bible, thought that life had been formed from nonlife at the will of the Creator. Some believed that this process of creation continued even after the original six days of Genesis. This concept is known as **spontaneous generation,** whereby living organisms could arise from nonliving material. People also believed that once a type of organism is created, its descendants will remain **immutable,** in the same form as the original, from generation to generation.

The original creation, as described in Genesis, supposedly took place a few thousand years before the Greek and Roman empires. Archbishop James Ussher of Armagh, Ireland (1581–1656), used the generations named in the Bible to calculate that the earth's creation took place at 9 A.M. on October 23, 4004 B.C. The idea of a spontaneously created and static life, a life brought into being only 6000 years ago, is directly counter to modern evolutionary theory. The development of evolutionary theory depended on an increasing disbelief in these old ideas.

Questioning the Old Ideas

What a shock it must have been to European scholars of the sixteenth century when Nicolaus Copernicus (1473–1543) showed conclusively that the earth was not the center

See the Online Learning Center for an Internet Activity on the history of evolutionary theory.

anthropocentricity The belief that humans are the most important elements in the universe.

spontaneous generation An old and incorrect idea that complex life forms could be spontaneously created from nonliving material.

immutable Unchanging.

Figure 1.3 Carolus Linnaeus (1707–1778)
Portrait of Carolus Linnaeus painted in 1737 in a Lapp costume. A Swedish naturalist and botanist, he established what became the modern method of naming the living world.

of the universe and was not even the center of the solar system! This was but one of a series of revelations that were to bombard the old ideas.

A tired, lost sea captain who was fearful that he was going to fall off the edge of the earth might have been both elated and confused at the greeting he received from an exotic people living on a shore that he thought could not possibly exist. The Age of Exploration, which began for Europeans in the late 1400s with the voyages of explorers such as Christopher Columbus and Vasco de Gama, revealed variations of life not dreamed of before. By 1758, 4235 species of animals were cataloged. Today, more than 1,750,000 species are known. During the Age of Exploration, strange animals never mentioned in the Bible were seen by Europeans for the first time. Naturalists were overwhelmed by the quantity of new discoveries and the problems of organizing this rapidly growing wealth of data.

Carolus Linnaeus's Classification   Although all cultures classify plants and animals into some kind of scheme, it was not until the seventeenth and eighteenth centuries that comprehensive written classifications were made. The Swedish naturalist Carolus Linnaeus (1707–1778) succeeded in classifying every animal and plant known to him into a system of categories (Figure 1.3). This type of classification is absolutely necessary for a scientific understanding of the relationship of one plant or animal to the next. Yet at first it reinforced traditional ideas. Linnaeus saw each category as fixed and immutable, the result of divine creation.

Linnaeus's scheme became important to modern biological sciences for many reasons. First, it imposed order on nature's infinite variation. Linnaeus saw that the analysis of anatomical structures could be used to group plants and animals into categories. The most specific groups included organisms that were very much alike, whereas the more general levels encompassed the specific groups, thereby representing a wider range of variation. Linnaeus wrote that the first order of science is to distinguish one thing from the other; his classification helped do just that.

Second, although Linnaeus considered organisms to be immutable, paradoxically his classification provided a means for "seeing" changes and possible ancestral relationships. Scientists wondered if similar organisms were related by common ancestry. If two or more types had a common origin but were now somewhat different, it followed that evolution must have occurred. Linnaeus, who had been so emphatic about the idea of unchanging species, began in later life to question this concept of fixity. He had observed new types of plants resulting from crossbreeding, and he had decided that perhaps all living things were not immutable.

Third, Linnaeus included people in his classification. Although he did not contend that humans are related to other animals, his placement of humans in this scheme was sure to raise the question.

Could Nature Be Dynamic?   Many people in the eighteenth century were intrigued with the rapidly increasing information brought to the fore by exploration. Not only were new varieties of plants and animals being discovered, so were new people. Who were the Native Americans, the Polynesians, the Africans? Were they human, or were they part human and part ape? Credible answers to these and other questions could not be supplied by traditional explanations.

The effect of exploration in guiding people to new realities was intensified by the great revolutions of the eighteenth and nineteenth centuries. These revolutions included technological changes in the industrial age as well as political upheavals, such as the American and French revolutions. Technological and political developments that brought about major social changes created an atmosphere in which the idea of immutability could be questioned. If people could change their social systems so rapidly, if human life could be so dynamic, then perhaps so was nature. It was in the late eighteenth century that the first modern theories of organic evolution emerged.

Early Evolutionary Ideas

Georges-Louis Leclerc, Comte de Buffon (1707–1788), a contemporary of Linnaeus, proposed many major points that Darwin would later include in *On the Origin of Species.* Buffon recognized the tendency of populations to increase at a faster rate than their food supply, hence the struggle for survival. He noted the variations within species and speculated on methods of inheritance. He questioned spontaneous creation. He also challenged the church's dating of the earth, proposing that the earth is much older than 6000 years. Buffon's importance was diminished by his lack of conciseness, but he might have been vague and apologetic about his thoughts for fear of being considered a heretic.

Although Buffon was one of the first people to scientifically investigate evolution, it was left to Jean-Baptiste de Lamarck (1744–1829) to articulate a systematic theory of evolution as an explanation of organic diversity. Lamarck, who coined the word *biology,* used the previous nonevolutionary idea that organisms could be ranked in a progressive order, with humans at the top. He envisioned evolution as a constant striving toward perfection and believed deviations were due to local adaptations to specific environments.

Lamarck is remembered by many for his explanation of the cause of these deviations. He proposed that an organism acquired new characteristics in its lifetime by virtue of using or not using different parts of its body. Lamarck believed that frequent use of a part of the body improved it whereas the lack of use of a body part weakened it, in some cases to the point where it disappeared altogether. This is called the **principle of use and disuse.** For instance, if an animal constantly had to stretch its neck to get at food in the branches of a tree, its neck would get longer. If the trees were to get taller, the animal would then have to stretch more, and its neck would get longer still. This was Lamarck's explanation of the giraffe. He believed that a trait, once acquired, would be passed on to the next generation. This concept is known as the **principle of acquired characteristics.**

Lamarck's importance lies in his proposal that life is dynamic and that there is a mechanism in nature that promotes ongoing change. The method of change he suggested, however, is incorrect. Acquired characteristics are not transmitted to offspring. A person who is very muscular as a result of lifting weights will not be more likely to have a muscle-bound child (Figure 1.4).

Lamarck, like so many famous people of science, was a synthesizer. He combined previously existing notions (such as Linnaean classification and the idea of acquired characteristics) into a new system with new meaning. Although the details of his ideas are incorrect, his emphasis on change gave support to the thoughts of those investigators who would ultimately discover accurate explanations for the changes he proposed.

Catastrophism The work of Lamarck and other early evolutionists, along with increasing evidence that changes had occurred in the living world, prompted thinkers to attempt to reconcile the traditional view of a divinely created changeless world with new evidence and ideas. The French scholar Georges Cuvier (1769–1832) is known for developing the idea called the theory of **catastrophism.** Cuvier

principle of use and disuse Concept popularized by Lamarck that proposes that parts of the body that are used are often strengthened and improved, whereas parts of the body that are not used become weak and ultimately may disappear.

principle of acquired characteristics Concept, popularized by Lamarck, that traits gained during a lifetime can then be passed on to the next generation by genetic means; considered invalid today

catastrophism Idea that the earth has experienced a series of catastrophic destructions and creations and that fossil forms found in each layer of the earth are bounded by a creation and destruction event.

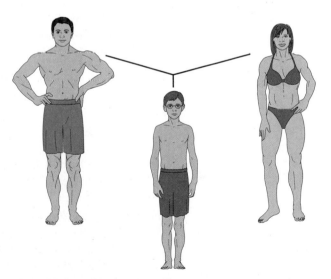

Figure 1.4 Inheritance of Acquired Characteristics
Today biologists do not believe that the increase or decrease in the size or strength of parts of the body due to use or disuse is transmitted to offspring. For example, if a couple lift weights and become muscular, their newly acquired physical condition will not be passed on genetically to their offspring.

Figure 1.5 Charles Lyell (1797–1875) The main purpose of his book *Principles of Geology* was to establish the principle of uniformitarianism, as the book's subtitle indicates: "Being an attempt to explain the former changes of the earth's surface, by reference to causes now in operation."

recognized the fact that as we dig down into the earth, we see different assemblages of plants and animals. In many cases, specific layers of flora and fauna seem to be almost totally replaced by new types overlying them. Cuvier believed that the living organisms represented in each layer were destroyed by a catastrophic event and that the next set of plants and animals represented a new creation event. Although Cuvier did not construct his ideas to bolster a literal interpretation of the Bible, others saw the last catastrophic event as the biblical flood.

According to the proponents of catastrophism, not all plants and animals need be destroyed by a cataclysmic event. For instance, the animals that were collected by Noah survived the flood. Also, Cuvier believed that catastrophes could be localized. Organisms that survived in an area not affected by the cataclysm could then migrate into the areas left vacant by the catastrophe.

Today evolutionists reject the ideas of divinely created organisms and divinely orchestrated catastrophes. However, just as Linnaeus's classification, originally conceived to explain traditional religious concepts, has become a major tool for modern biologists, some of Cuvier's ideas are still present in the work of modern evolutionary theorists. As with Linnaeus's ideas, Cuvier's ideas have been expanded upon and reinterpreted in nonreligious terms. For instance, some modern researchers see catastrophic events, such as the effects of meteorites that hit the earth, as the catalysts of major evolutionary events, such as mass extinctions of plants and animals and ensuing rapid evolutionary changes in some of the surviving populations. However, other evolutionists do not view catastrophic events as primary causes of evolutionary change. They see large-scale evolution as being the result of the gradual accumulation of small changes over time. This idea of gradual modification of a species is the basic thesis of Darwin's model of evolution. Before we discuss Darwin, however, we turn to a scientist who directly influenced him.

What Is the Age of the Earth?

By the early nineteenth century, masses of new data had been gathered that threw doubt on traditional interpretations. Charles Lyell (1797–1875) synthesized this new information in a textbook, *Principles of Geology,* the first of three volumes being published in 1830 (Figure 1.5). In it he popularized the principle of **uniformitarianism,** first proposed by James Hutton (1726–1797), which was a main prerequisite to the development of a credible evolutionary theory. The principle of uniformitarianism states that physical forces, such as wind, rain, heat, cold, moving water, volcanism, and earthquakes, that are at work today altering the earth were also in force, working in the same way, in former times. Therefore, "the present is the key to the past."

Lyell also realized that, as they operate today, the processes resulting in physical alteration of the earth would require very long periods of time to form the layers of the earth known as **strata** (Figure 1.6). Therefore, it could be inferred that the large number and often great thickness of strata formed in the past must have taken a long time to develop. This inference also challenged biblical chronology because it showed that the earth's age was many times greater than previously thought. In popularizing the theory of uniformitarianism, Lyell also was setting the stage for a theory of the evolution of the living world.

uniformitarianism Principle that states that physical forces working today to alter the earth were also in force and working in the same way in former times.

strata Layers of sedimentary rocks.

William Smith (1769–1839), who was nicknamed "Strata Smith," had found that each stratum was characterized by distinct fossils that could be used to indicate the age of strata. In 1815, he released the first geological maps of English strata (Box 1-2).

Charles Lyell also studied fossil plants and animals that were embedded in the various strata. These and other similar investigations suggested that the earth is extremely old and that life had existed in various forms, some now extinct, for hundreds of centuries. Lyell himself did not become convinced of the antiquity of living things until later in his life when, in his text *The Antiquity of Man* (1863), he supported Charles Darwin's theory of natural selection.

Humans before Adam and Eve?

Fossils of extinct forms of plants and animals had been known long before Lyell's time, and many valid interpretations had been made. However, as often happens, the evidence was more frequently viewed in terms of predispositions and the special interests of the observer; it was not analyzed critically. For instance, early proponents of catastrophism believed that extinct animals were creatures "who did not make the Ark." After Lyell's systematic investigation, some scientists began at last to speculate on the idea of a more dynamic world. Yet the notion of prehistoric people was still heresy. Were not all people descendants of Adam and Eve?

In the early 1800s, Jacques Boucher de Crèvecoeur de Perthes (1788–1868) made a systematic attempt to demonstrate the existence of a prehistoric period. While digging on the banks of the Somme River in southwestern France, he discovered that many stones were not made of the same material as the walls of the pit in which they were uncovered. In addition, the stones had obviously been shaped into specific forms (Figure 1.7). Other people also had observed these types of rocks. They considered them to be "figured stones" of an unknown origin or "lightning stones," petrified lightning cast to the earth by God during thunderstorms. Boucher de Crèvecoeur de Perthes was convinced that they were made by ancient people. To back up this conviction, he collected what he thought was an immense amount of evidence to support his case. He submitted his report in 1838 to various scientific societies, where it was rejected. Not until 20 years later, a year before the publication of Darwin's *On the Origin of Species*, were his conclusions accepted.

By the time of Darwin, the notions of anthropocentrism, immutability, and a date of 4004 B.C. for the earth's origin had been altered or reversed. For most of the scientific community, the final discrediting of spontaneous creation would have to wait until the time of the French chemist Louis Pasteur (1822–1895). Pasteur, who had developed the pasteurization process and vaccinations against anthrax and rabies, also disproved spontaneous creation.

Figure 1.6 Stratigraphy The Grand Canyon shows the various strata that have accumulated over millennia.

Figure 1.7 Lower Paleolithic Hand Ax This Acheulean hand ax is from the site of Clacton-on-Sea, England. The 450,000-year-old tool was found associated with the butchered remains of now extinct species of elephant, horse, rhinoceros, bison, and deer.

Box 1-2

William "Strata" Smith

William Smith (1769–1839) was born at a time when the earth was believed to be less than 6,000 years old, an age consistent with that calculated by Bishop James Ussher in 1658. Since the entire world was thought to have been created by God, it followed that strange and unusual objects often found embedded in the earth—objects that today we call minerals, crystals, fossils, and so forth—were created at the same time as the rest of the earth.

However, many of those objects curiously resembled living creatures and parts of creatures. Those fossils were referred to as figured stones because they were clearly composed of a mineral—they were a type of rock that nevertheless resembled something that was once living. Many people of the day saw those figured stones as special creations of God, created in place within the ground. During the eighteenth and nineteenth centuries, figured stones were avidly collected and placed in curio cabinets in fine houses and museums.

Toward the end of the eighteenth century, knowledge of the earth and of figured stones had increased dramatically, and scholars began to realize that certain types of figured stones were always found in particular layers or in certain types of soils. To explain this distribution, scholars took the huge step of proposing that those objects were the real remains of once-living creatures. While some of the remains resembled creatures living at the time, which must have been caught up in the mud and eventually transformed into stone, others resembled creatures that clearly were nothing like anything living on the face of the earth in the eighteenth century. Religious fundamentalists and others explained this observation by referring to Noah's flood or the "Noachian Deluge." The remains of extinct animals were simply those which did not make it to the ark and thereby perished.

William Smith, of humble origins, was a surveyor by trade. He became involved with coal mining and the surveying of routes for the canals that were being constructed all over England as an inexpensive way to get the coal from mine to market. In descending into coal mines, Smith observed what miners knew but, since they were for the most part illiterate, did not write about. The earth underground existed in layers, and each layer could be distinguished by specific characteristics such as texture, color, and the types of fossils embedded within it. Smith noticed that those layers *always* occurred in the same order in every mine he explored. Later, when cutting though hills and excavating tunnels for canals, he noticed the same pattern of layers. His studies of these layers, or strata, gave him his nickname "Strata".

A fact of great importance was that the layers sloped in a very characteristic fashion. As a result different layers appeared on the surface of the earth in certain areas. If a layer on the surface could be recognized, one immediately would know what layers lay beneath—a valuable piece of information for someone looking for coal.

Smith's observations eventually led to the publication of the first geological map of England in 1815, a feat that earned him an important place in history. The documentation of the presence of large numbers of strata, each produced by recognizable processes that look long periods of time to occur, helped established the ancient age of the earth and presented evidence of earlier forms of life in the past. Today the study of strata, or stratigraphy, is a fundamental part of the study of archaeology and paleontology.

Source: S. Winchester, *The Map That Changed the World: William Smith and the Birth of Modern Geology* (New York: HarperCollins, 2001).

See the Online Learning Center for an Internet Activity on Charles Darwin.

Darwin's Voyage of Discovery

It was Charles Darwin (1809–1882) who proposed a compelling theory for the mechanism of organic evolution that accurately synthesized the available evidence (Figure 1.8). At the age of 22, Darwin was invited to accompany a scientific investigation on the ship HMS *Beagle*. On December 27, 1831, the *Beagle* sailed from Plymouth, England, on what was to be a five-year voyage of discovery. Darwin spent much of the five years confined on the small ship, which measured 90 feet in length and less than 25 feet at the widest point. He was one of 74 aboard.

The purpose of the voyage was to chart the southeastern coast of South America and to calculate an accurate fixing of longitude around the world. It was the role of the voyage in Darwin's life, however, that made it one of the most famous journeys in history. On this voyage Darwin gained new insights into the origin of coral reefs, described in detail fauna and flora, and studied fossilized animals.

In the Andes, Darwin found seashells in rocks at 3962 meters (13,000 feet), and in Valdivia, Chile, he experienced a devastating earthquake that elevated the shore by several feet. These and other experiences showed how dynamic the earth is. He realized that the tops of mountains once had been under the sea and that coastlines could be significantly altered by earthquakes.

Throughout his trip, Darwin witnessed the great diversity in nature. His five-week visit to the Galápagos Islands, a volcanic group of islands some 965 kilometers (600 miles) west of Ecuador, possibly provided a major stimulus for his most famous contribution to science: the concept of natural selection. It was there that he observed giant tortoises, seagoing lizards, ground finches, and other animals that showed variations related to differences in the different island habitats. Ultimately he hypothesized that environmental forces acted to weed out those individuals whose characteristics were not as well suited to a particular situation.

Darwin was not the only person who was developing a theory of evolution based on species adaptation to the environment. As often happens in science, two or more people came up with basically the same conclusion simultaneously. In the summer of 1858, Darwin must have got quite a jolt when he received an essay from Alfred Russel Wallace (1823–1913), another naturalist, with whom he had been corresponding (Figure 1.9). Wallace had come up with basically the same ideas Darwin had been working on for two decades. Both men received credit for their work at a meeting of the Linnaean Society in 1858. Because Darwin was the first to publish his work, in his book *On the Origin of Species* in 1859, he has since received most of the credit for modern evolutionary theory.

Darwinian Natural Selection

The concept of **natural selection** emerged from the analysis of the observations made and specimens collected by Charles Darwin on his voyage. Natural selection is the process of favoring or weeding out individuals with different characteristics from a population. Those individuals that are well-suited for their environment will be "favored" in the sense that they will pass on their heritable attributes to the next generation at a higher rate than will individuals not as well suited to the environment.

Darwin noted that within any group of plants or animals there existed much variability. Each offspring of a pair of sexually reproducing adults is unique. (Exceptions include identical twins and the results of cloning.) While the majority of organisms resemble some type of average or norm, there will always be individuals that are smaller or larger, are lighter or darker, or possess some unique features compared with the average.

Darwin also realized that all living creatures have the capacity to reproduce in great numbers. For example, if one pair of houseflies bred in April and all eggs hatched and in turn lived to reproduce, by August the total number of houseflies descending from the original pair would be 191,010,000,000,000,000,000. Of course, in real life, not all eggs do hatch, and not all individuals that are born live to reproduce. However, the numbers of individuals born or hatched tend to be vast.

Figure 1.8 Charles Darwin (1809–1882) The 1250 copies of the first printing of his book *On the Origin of Species* sold out on the day of its issue on November 24, 1859. Darwin's concept of natural selection has been firmly established as a hallmark of modern biological science.

Figure 1.9 Alfred Russel Wallace (1823–1913) In June 1858, Charles Darwin received an essay from Wallace outlining a concept of natural selection very much like his own. On July 1, a joint presentation of writings by Darwin and Wallace were read at the meeting of the Linnean Society in London. The presentations received little attention at the time.

natural selection Differential fertility and mortality of variants within a population.

See the Online Learning Center for an Interactive Exercise on natural selection.

The consequence to humans of this rapid increase in number was noted by Thomas R. Malthus (1766–1834) in his *Essay on the Principles of Population.* Malthus wrote that the human population is growing at a faster rate than food production, and famine and economic chaos would result as the population grew and food resources dwindled. In general, populations have the potential of dramatically increasing in numbers. However, such growth is limited by such factors as space, food, predators, and disease.

Because of limitations in population growth, Darwin concluded that only a proportion of animals that are born live to reproduce. Since individuals differ from one another, those individuals who possess features that increase the chance of surviving are likely to pass on these features to the next generation. On the other hand, organisms with traits that reduce the chance of successfully reproducing are less likely to pass on these traits. Thus, populations of organisms changed through time as those features that contributed to survival were inherited by future generations.

Darwin's Finches: A Case of Natural Selection Darwin believed that natural selection operated over extremely long periods of time. Therefore, natural selection could not be directly observed, although it could be deduced through the study of the end products or through individuals that have been fossilized. Darwin believed that his logic was sound—natural selection had to be occurring, but at a pace that was impossible to observe within the human life span.

Contemporary field biologists, however, have discovered many situations where natural selection is operating on a time scale that can be observed during the professional lifetime of the investigator. One such case involves the finches found on the Galápagos Islands. These birds, studied by Charles Darwin on his voyage, are today called Darwin's finches.

Finches are songbirds that belong to the same family as sparrows and canaries. Darwin observed several species of finches that had beaks of different sizes and shapes and generally ate different foods. Finches with large, powerful beaks could break open hard seeds that other finches could not. One variety of finch had a short, thick beak; its diet consisted mainly of leaves, buds, blossoms, and fruits. Another finch had a long, straight beak; it subsisted mainly on nectar from the prickly pear cactus (Figure 5.14).

Darwin believed that competition led to diversity in animal and plant types. For example, the small-beaked birds could not compete for hard seeds with the birds that had more powerful beaks. Unless the birds with smaller beaks possessed characteristics that would allow them to exploit a different segment of the habitat, they might become extinct.

Darwin was impressed by the fact that animals on the Galápagos Islands had "cousins" on the South American mainland. He postulated that since these volcanic islands were younger than the mainland, the animals must have originated on the mainland. He then reasoned that as members of the original population became isolated from each other, they evolved differently, depending on the local environment.

In 1973, biologists Peter and Rosemary Grant arrived on the very small island of Daphne Major in the Galápagos, where they began a study that would involve several of their students and would last over three decades. Out of this work would come direct proof that natural selection did indeed occur in a real-life situation.[3]

Daphne Major is a small island of about 100 acres, small enough to be studied intensively. The Grants studied two species of finch that lived on the island: the medium ground finch and the cactus finch (Figure 1.10). Eventually all the finches on the island were captured and released. They were carefully weighed and measured and then photographed; colored rings placed on their legs ensured that the investigators were able to identify each and every bird in the field. Newborn chicks were examined and banded before they left the nest. Their habitats were also carefully studied, and available food supplies were quantified.

---

[3] P. R. Grant, *Ecology and Evolution of Darwin's Finches* (Princeton, NJ: Princeton University Press, 1986); J. Weiner, *The Beak of the Finch* (New York: Knopf, 1994).

(a)   (b)

Figure 1.10 Darwin's Finches (a) The medium ground finch, *Geospiza fortis,* and (b) the cactus finch, *Geospiza scandens.*

No rain fell on Daphne Major between mid-1976 and early 1978. Because of the lack of water, fewer seeds were produced and the small, soft seeds that were the preferred food for the ground finches soon disappeared. What was left were the larger, harder seeds that were very difficult to eat. In this situation, birds with larger and more powerful beaks had a distinct advantage. For example, it is very difficult to reach the four to six seeds within the hard fruit of *Tribulus.* On the average, the large ground finch is able to crack the fruit in about 2 seconds and within an additional 7 seconds is able to eat all the seeds. On the other hand, the smaller ground finch takes about 7 seconds to get into the fruit and another 15 seconds to eat the one or two seeds it can wrestle out of the shell. The smaller bird is using more energy to get less food than the larger bird.

Not surprisingly, a large number of birds died as a result of the drought. Of the 1200 medium ground finches living on the island at the beginning of 1977, only 180 remained at the end of that year—only 15 percent of the birds survived. The rest had died primarily of starvation. However, when the Grants measured the beaks of the surviving medium ground finches, they discovered that the survivors had an average beak size that was 4 percent greater than the size found before the start of the drought. Since beak size is to a large extent inherited, this increased beak size also characterized the new generation of birds born after the end of the drought. Clearly, natural selection had produced an increase in average beak size.

Evolution and Anti-Evolution Movements

On departing from Plymouth in 1831, the captain of the *Beagle,* Robert Fitzroy, presented Charles Darwin with a gift. That gift, a copy of the newly published *Principles of Geology* by Charles Lyell, influenced the development of Darwin's ideas and was the source of some heated debates between Darwin and Fitzroy, a religious fundamentalist. Had Fitzroy read the book, he may never have given it to Darwin.

After the voyage, Lyell became Darwin's friend. In 1859, Lyell recommended that a partial disclaimer of sorts be added to *On the Origin of Species,* one that would recognize the role of the "Creator" in evolution. The book was first published on November 24, 1859, with no disclaimer; it sold out its first printing that same day. *On the Origin of Species* became the focus of a controversy between those who believed in the divine creation of life (creationists) and those who believed in a natural origin of life (evolutionists).

"Creation-Science" Darwin's concept of natural selection has survived the scrutiny of 150 years of biological study to become one of the foundations of modern biological science.

Yet for various reasons that lie outside the realm of science, there are those who feel that the concept of evolution must be disproved in favor of a creationist interpretation. In recent times creationists modified an old strategy. They labeled the concept of the divine creation of life a scientific view, and the term **creation-science** was born.

creation-science The idea that scientific evidence can be and has been gathered for creation as depicted in the Bible. Mainstream scientists, many religious leaders, and the Supreme Court discount any scientific value of "creation-science" statements.

Beginning early in the twentieth century, attempts were made by some state legislatures to mandate the teaching of creationism as an alternative explanation of the diversity of life. Some statues actually outlawed the teaching of evolution. Perhaps one of the most famous of those laws was the Butler Act passed in 1925 by the Tennessee legislature. The legal challenge to this law was embodied in the Scopes trial, which is described in Box 1-3.

Creation-science advocates began to sue teachers and school districts to force them to teach creation-science alongside evolutionary theory. They also put pressure on publishers to deemphasize evolution in biology textbooks. Under such pressure, several states passed "balanced-treatment acts," which required that teachers present "scientific" evidence for creation along with the teaching of evolution. Because it ultimately came before the United States Supreme Court, the 1981 Balanced Treatment Act of Louisiana became one of the most important of those acts. On June 19, 1987, the Supreme Court, by a vote of 7 to 2, declared the Louisiana act, and therefore all others like it, unconstitutional. In the majority decision the justices wrote:[4]

> The Act impermissibly endorses religion by advancing the religious belief that a supernatural being created humankind. The legislative history demonstrates that the term "creation-science," as contemplated by the state legislature, embraces this religious teaching. The Act's primary purpose was to change the public school science curriculum to provide persuasive advantage to a particular religious doctrine that reflects the factual basis of evolution in its entirety. Thus, the Act is designed either to promote the theory of creation science that embodies a particular religious tenet or to prohibit the teaching of a scientific theory disfavored by certain religious sects. In either case, the Act violates the First Amendment.

Although many biologists believed that creation-science advocates had been dealt a coup de grâce to their legal battle to establish laws that would prohibit or cripple the teaching of evolution, creationists developed other strategies. For example, in 1999 the Kansas State School Board created a media uproar by voting to reject parts of the national teaching standard dealing with evolution and other scientific principles. The school board did not ban the teaching of evolution, but it removed it as a topic in state competency tests. The implication was that evolution should not be considered factual. This decision received both media ridicule and criticism from scientific organizations, including the National Academy of Sciences, which had issued the national teaching standard. The voters in Kansas elected a new school board, and on February 14, 2001, the board restored evolution as a central part of the curriculum and rejected all suggestions to decrease and downgrade the coverage of evolutionary theory in the classroom. However, similar challenges to the teaching of evolution continue to be lodged in several states.

Intelligent Design   Today, the battleground has shifted away from "creation-science" to an approach called **intelligent design (ID) theory.** Modern intelligent design theory is a new version of an old idea that preceded the publication of *On the Origin of Species* by over half a century. In 1802, Reverend William Paley (1743–1805) published *Natural Theory: Evidence of the Existence and Attributes of the Deity, Collected from the Appearances of Nature.* Paley argued that one would have to conclude that something as complex as a watch had to have been made by a watchmaker intent on making a watch. By analogy, life, which is much more complex than any watch, also must have been made by some intelligent force intent on creating life.

intelligent design theory An essentially religious explanation of the world that assumes the existence of a supernatural force that is responsible for the great complexity of life on earth today.

Although there is some variation in its presentation, proponents of intelligent design theory appear to be willing to accept a long history of life on earth and the operation of

---

[4] U. S. Supreme Court, *Edwards v Aguillard,* 1987, pp. 589–594.

In the early part of the twentieth century many American theologians, as well as much of the public, had reconciled the concept of natural selection and evolution with their religious beliefs. Yet in some quarters there was still strong opposition to what was referred to as Darwinism. As the century progressed, opposition from religious institutions grew, and by the early 1920s, many southern states were considering legislation designed to remove the teaching of evolution from the public school curriculum and textbooks.

The growing opposition to Darwinism was a response to the growing influence of Christian fundamentalism in the United States. Author Richard Antoun describes fundamentalism in general "as an orientation to the modern world . . . that focuses on protest and change and on certain consuming themes: the quest for purity, the search for authenticity, totalism and activism, the necessity for certainty (scripturalism), selective modernization, and the centering of the mythic past in the present."[1]

In 1925, the state of Tennessee passed and signed into law the Butler Act. This was the strongest law up to that time, one that made the teaching of evolution illegal and subject to criminal prosecution. The American Civil Liberties Union (ACLU) quickly saw the danger of the Butler Act and similar proposed legislation to public education and science in the United States. The ACLU developed a simple strategy: create a test case in Tennessee where the defendant would be judged guilty, a foregone conclusion since the defendant would have taught evolution in the classroom in defiance of the law. They would then appeal the ruling to the Tennessee Supreme Court and then to the United States Supreme Court, where the law probably would be ruled unconstitutional. In 1925 the ACLU placed a notice in the *Chattanooga Times*: "We are looking for a Tennessee teacher who is willing to accept our services in testing this law in the courts. Our lawyers think a friendly test case can be arranged without costing a teacher his or her job. Distinguished counsel have volunteered their services."[2]

Soon thereafter a group of prominent citizens in the small town of Dayton decided that they could use a little publicity for the town and decided to offer up a test case. They recruited a young science teacher, John T. Scopes, a friend of one of the prosecuting attorneys. Scopes taught physics, math, and football but had substituted for an absent biology instructor, using a textbook that contained a chapter on evolution. John Scopes was quickly indicted by a special session of the grand jury and released without bond.

One of the most well-known proponents of anti-Darwinism laws was William Jennings Bryan. Bryan had entered Congress in 1890, where his charismatic speaking ability and stands on the issues of the day gave him the title the "Great Commoner." He was nominated as the Democratic candidate for president in 1896, 1900, and 1904. In 1912 he became President Woodrow Wilson's secretary of state, but he eventually resigned in protest of administration policies. Bryan remained in the public eye as an energetic and popular public speaker and author and soon became an important spokesman for the anti-evolution movement.

Always on the lookout for an issue to gain publicity, Bryan offered to join the team prosecuting John Scopes, even though he had not practiced law for 30 years. Seeing the opportunity for even more publicity for the town, the local prosecution attorneys readily accepted the offer. The noted defense attorney from Chicago Clarence Darrow offered to join the defense. Thus, what the ACLU hoped would be a simple test case whose main purpose was to provide a stepping-stone to a review of the Tennessee law by the Supreme Court had become the trial of the decade.

The trial began on July 10, 1925. Bryan's role was to give the closing argument, which he had carefully prepared and was to be one of his greatest speeches. He did not know that the defense planned to waive closing arguments and thereby prevent Bryan from delivering his speech.

The prosecution's case took about one hour to present as it was quickly established that Scopes had taught about evolution in the classroom. The defense began by calling the first of several scientists to testify about the validity of evolution. The prosecution objected: The trial was about whether Scopes had taught evolution, not about the validity of the law. The jury was dismissed while the first scientist was examined, after which the judge ruled that all evidence regarding the validity of the law was inadmissible and that the testimony of the scientists would not be presented to the jury.

Then came the most dramatic part of the trial as the defense called Bryan as an expert on the Bible. Bryan agreed to this over the objections of his fellow prosecutors, and the jury once again was sent out. It is generally conceded that Darrow got the better of Bryan, whose testimony was ruled inadmissible. Since the defense was not permitted to call its expert witnesses, Darrow asked the court to instruct the jury to find the defendant guilty, a task that took the jury nine minutes to accomplish. Scopes was fined $100.

During the following year the case was appealed to the Tennessee Supreme Court, which ruled the law to be constitutional. However, it also overturned the conviction on a technicality, thereby preventing the case from being appealed to the United States Supreme Court.

Largely because of the highly successful play and movie *Inherit the Wind,* a fictionalized account of the Scopes trial, the trial has entered the annals of American folklore. It served to articulate the growing rift between those who accept the principles of evolution and the creationists.

[1] R. T. Antoun, *Understanding Fundamentalism: Christian, Islamic and Jewish Movements* (Walnut Creek: AltaMira Press, 2001), p. 2.

[2] "Plan Assault on State Law on Evolution," *Chattanooga Daily Times,* May 4, 1925, p. 5.

Source: E. J. Larson, *Summer for the Gods: The Scopes Trial and America's Continuing Debate over Science and Religion* (Cambridge, MA: Harvard University Press, 1997).

some evolutionary processes, but only the evolution of small changes over short periods of time. Although disguised as a scientific alternative to evolution, ID predicates the existence of a supernatural force—the designer—who is responsible for the great complexity of life on earth today. And that intelligent force, the designer, was God. Because of its reliance on a supernatural or divine power, it is essentially a religious and not a scientific explanation. (However, some advocates for ID say that it is not a religious idea because the designer may not have been God but an alien life form.)

irreducible complexity
Concept that there exists processes and structures that are too complex to have arisen through evolutionary mechanisms but must have arisen by work of a "designer."

The core idea of intelligent design theory is that the great complexity of structure and biochemical and physiological processes found in living organisms cannot be explained on the basis of the natural process of evolution. Of course one may argue that the lack of a natural explanation refers to our present ignorance, and those seemingly complex processes in living organisms will someday be understood, just as other ideas were considered to be unknowable in the past. To answer this argument, ID proponents have introduced the concept of **irreducible complexity.** This refers to processes that are so complex that they could not have arisen step by step as postulated by an evolutionary interpretation. This is seen by the "fact" that if one takes away any element of the process, the whole process fails to function.

Well before the current evolution–intelligent design debate, Charles Darwin addressed this issue. The human eye is a very complex organ. Yet Darwin pointed out that early predecessors to the human eye and other complex eyes—those without lenses, for example—might have simply helped animals position themselves in relationship to light. Modern scientists have found such primitive light-sensing organs in living animals as well as in fossil organisms that appear to represent what might also have been transitional forms to the modern complex eye.

See the Online Learning Center for an Internet Activity on intelligent design and the evolution of the eye.

Evolutionary biologists also point out that many complex biological systems exhibit major imperfections or design flaws that should not be present if a divine intelligence were responsible for that design. Design flaws can best be explained as the natural outcome of gradual modification through time through natural selection rather than as the handiwork of a divine force. One example of such a design flaw is the fact that the retina of the human eye is constructed with blood vessels and nerve fibers overlaying the surface that receives the light, so that light that enters the eye must pass through these structures before hitting the retina. The passage of these nerves through the retina to the optic nerve on the back side of the retina results in a blind spot.

It should be pointed out that creation-science does not single out evolutionary theory. Most proposed laws and regulations influence virtually all modern scientific disciplines. For instance, intelligent design also is used to explain the origin of the universe instead of the Big Bang Theory and to replace the scientific explanation of the structure and pattern of arrangement of the elements as represented on the periodic table.[5]

Evolutionary Theory after Darwin: The Synthetic Theory

The basic concepts of Darwin's theory of evolution remain the cornerstone of modern evolutionary theory, yet much has been added to this base. Darwin, Wallace, and other naturalists of their day did not have an accurate picture of inheritance. They therefore were not sure of how characteristics were passed on from generation to generation or how new characteristics might arise. Progress in this area began to be made by Gregor Mendel, who will be discussed in the next chapter. Mendel discovered the basic laws of heredity, which he published in 1868.

Mendel's work began to answer basic questions of inheritance. Since Mendel's time, our knowledge of genetics has grown enormously. In the 1930s, population geneticists began

---

[5] For a more detailed discussion of the responses that evolutionists have to creationist arguments see J. Rennie, "15 Answers to Creationist Nonsense," *Scientific American* (July 2002), pp. 78–84.

to explain, in mathematical and statistical terms, how evolution could be seen as a change in the genetic composition of populations. From the 1970s through the 2000s, dramatic new discoveries about the genetic material (DNA and RNA) have allowed us to see evolutionary processes that occur at the molecular level. In addition, advances in the study of embryology, paleontology, animal behavior, and other disciplines all have contributed to a modern understanding of evolution. Because this understanding is based on a synthesis of information from diverse fields, it is sometimes called the **synthetic theory of evolution.**

synthetic theory of evolution The theory of evolution that fuses Darwin's concept of natural selection with information from the fields of genetics, mathematics, embryology, paleontology, animal behavior, and other disciplines.

Summary

Evolutionary theory has been shown to be a valid and reliable explanation of basic questions about life. Modern evolutionary theory grew out of a European intellectual climate. Before the nineteenth century, most Europeans saw humans as the superior center of a world populated by spontaneously created organisms that did not change once created. Each of these ideas fell in the light of new knowledge gathered by hundreds of scholars, including Copernicus, Linnaeus, Buffon, Lamarck, Lyell, Boucher de Crèvecoeur de Perthes, Darwin, Wallace, and Mendel. Darwin's concept of natural selection has fused with Mendel's concept of genetics; to this mixture new ingredients continue to be added, including concepts about the genetics of populations. Also, ideas of what embryos, fossils, and animal behavior can tell us about the past have become part of what is called the synthetic theory of evolution.

Key Terms

anthropocentricity, *11*
anthropological
    linguistics, *6*
anthropology, *4*
applied anthropology, *7*
archaeology, *6*
catastrophism, *13*
control, *10*
creation-science, *20*
cultural anthropology, *6*
culture, *6*

empirical, *8*
experiment, *9*
hypothesis, *8*
immutable, *11*
intelligent design
    theory, *20*
irriducible complexity, *22*
natural selection, *17*
physical anthropology, *4*
principle of acquired
    characteristics, *13*

principle of use and
    disuse, *13*
science, *8*
spontaneous generation, *11*
strata, *14*
synthetic theory of
    evolution, *23*
theory, *9*
uniformitarianism, *14*
variable, *9*

Study Questions

1. The development of the evolutionary concept was part of the general changes that were occurring in Western society from the fifteenth through nineteenth centuries. How were such historical events as the discovery of North America and the American Revolution related to the development of the theory of evolution?

2. What were some of the concepts about human nature and the relationship between humans and nature that had to change before an evolutionary concept could develop?

See the Online Learning Center for additional study questions.

3. How does the idea of "catastrophism" differ from Darwin's concept of natural selection?

4. Who were some of the scholars who contributed to the development of evolutionary ideas? What did each contribute to that development?

5. Darwin, Wallace, and other naturalists of the nineteenth century did not have an accurate notion of one aspect of modern evolutionary theory. What element of modern theory was missing from their writings? Who began to provide accurate analyses of this missing element?

6. What is meant by the phrase "the synthetic theory of evolution"?

7. Many antievolutionists believe that since science does not have answers for all questions, scientific conclusions are not necessarily correct. This attitude reflects a failure to understand the nature of science. What is the general nature of scientific thinking? In what way is science "self-correcting"?

8. In what way does a scientific statement differ from a doctrine?

Critical Thinking Questions

1. One of the criticisms levied against evolution is that no one has ever seen one kind of animal evolve into another. Although natural selection has been seen to occur in a small-scale situation, such as the case of the finches of Daphne Major, the time frame for the evolution of new species is far greater than the human life span. However, it is possible to infer the evolutionary history of living species by using facts of anatomy, DNA analysis, and the fossil record. We make conclusions as to facts from inference all the time in our normal, everyday activities. Give some examples.

2. The development and acceptance of evolutionary theory in the nineteenth century was very much a product of the political, economic, and intellectual changes of that time. Discuss how the development of the industrial revolution set the stage for the development and acceptance of the concept of evolution.

3. Scientific thinking is based on the application of the scientific method of empirical observation and experimentation to formulate ideas about reality. Religion is generally based on the acceptance of ideas based on faith found in religious writings and the interpretations made by religious practitioners. Do you think that there is any possibility of a philosophical combination of science and religion into one concept of reality?

Suggested Readings

Alters, B. J., and S. M. Alters. *Defending Evolution in the Classroom: A Guide to the Creation/Evolution Controvery.* Sudbury, MA: Jones and Bartlett, 2001. The authors provide a detailed and thoughtful account of the creationist movement and how teachers can deal with the subject of evolution in the classroom.

Browne, J. *Charles Darwin: The Origins and After—The Years of Fame.* New York: Knopf, 2002. The story of the publication of *On the Origin of Species* and the events that followed.

Darwin, C. *On the Origin of Species by Means of Natural Selection, or the Preservation of Favored Races in the Struggle for Life.* London: J. Murray, 1859. Many editions have been produced of this classic, including a 1967 facsimile of the first edition.

Desmond, A., and J. Moore. *Darwin: The Life of a Tormented Evolutionist.* New York: Warner, 1991. This biography of Darwin makes use of newly available sources and places Darwin and his ideas in the context of Victorian science and society.

Eldredge, Niles. *The Triumph of Evolution and the Failure of Creationism.* New York: Freeman, 2000. Niles Eldredge, of the American Museum of Natural History, presents a well-thought-out discussion of evolutionary theory and how evolution successfully accounts for the diversity of life on our planet.

Giere, R. N. *Understanding Scientific Reasoning,* 4th ed. Fort Worth: Holt, Rinehart and Winston, 1996. This book explains scientific thinking by using examples of scientific discoveries and everyday events.

Gould, S. J. *Time's Arrow Time's Cycle.* Cambridge, MA: Harvard University Press, 1987. The author discusses the historical development of the concept of deep time in geology, including a discussion of Charles Lyell's contributions.

Lyell, C. *Principles of Geology,* 3 vols. London: J. Murray, 1830–1833; rpt. New York: Johnson Reprint, 1969. This was the first geology "textbook," and it influenced Darwin's perceptions of nature.

Mayr, E. *What Evolution Is.* New York: Basic Books, 2001. This is an introduction to evolution by one of the most important evolutionary biologists of the twentieth century.

Milner, R. *The Encyclopedia of Evolution.* New York: Facts on File, 1990. This is a very useful encyclopedia with entries on important people and concepts.

Pennock, Robert T. *Tower of Babel: The Evidence against the New Creationism.* Cambridge, MA: MIT Press, 1999. Philosopher Robert Pennock explores and critiques the ideas of creationism.

Pennock, Robert T. *Intelligent Design and Its Critics: Philosophical, Theological, and Scientific Perspectives.* Cambridge, MA: MIT Press, 2002. This sequel to *Tower of Babel* is an anthology of articles by creationists and responses by their critics. Pennock concludes with an essay on why creationism should not be taught in schools.

Raby, P. *Alfred Russel Wallace: A Life.* Princeton, NJ: Princeton University Press, 2001. A biography of the other naturalist who developed the idea of natural selection.

Rayan, A. S. *A Guide to Careers in Physical Anthropology.* Westport, CT: Bergin & Garvey, 2002. Each chapter, written by someone in the field, discusses various careers pursued by physical anthropologists.

Rudwick, M. J. S. *Georges Cuvier, Fossil Bones, and Geological Catastrophes: New Translations and Interpretations of Primary Text.* Chicago: University of Chicago Press, 1997. This volume includes a translation of Cuvier's papers and corrects misconceptions about his ideas and motivations.

Scott, E. C. *Evolution vs. Creationism.* Westport, CT: Greenwood Press, 2004. The executive director of the National Center for Science Education surveys the evolution versus creationism controversy.

Young, D. *The Discovery of Evolution.* Cambridge, England: Cambridge University Press, 1991. Richly illustrated by many historical photographs and drawings, this volume traces the development of evolutionary theory. It is an excellent introduction to evolution for the new student.

In addition to books, the journals and magazines listed below consistently have materials useful to physical anthropology students. The following are popular magazines:

American Scientist

Archaeology

BioScience

Discover

National Geographic

Natural History

Science News

Scientific American

Smithsonian

The following are scientific journals:

American Anthropologist

American Journal of Human Biology

American Journal of Physical Anthropology

American Journal of Primatology

Annals of Human Biology and Human Ecology

Current Anthropology

Evolutionary Anthropology

Human Biology

Human Evolution

Journal of Animal Behavior

Journal of Forensic Science

Journal of Human Evolution

Nature

Science

Suggested Websites

About Darwin:
www.aboutdarwin.com

American Anthropological Association:
www.aaanet.org

The Charles Darwin Foundation for the Galápagos Islands:
http://darwinfoundation.org

History of evolutionary theory from the University of California Museum of Paleontology:
www.ucmp.berkeley.edu/history/evolution.html

The writings of Charles Darwin on the Web:
http://pages.britishlibrary.net/charles.darwin

Chapter 2

The Study of Heredity

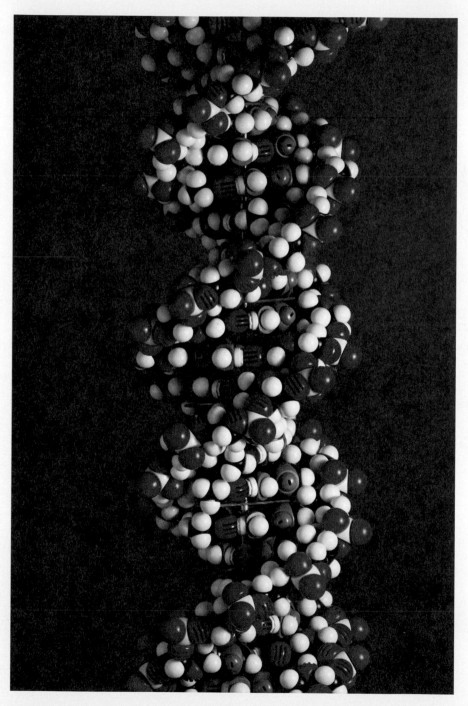

Model of the molecule deoxyribonucleic acid, the hereditary material.

C harles Darwin, not knowing of Gregor Mendel's work, was making some experiments of his own, which led him within an ace of obtaining results paralleling Mendel's. Whether or not he would have analyzed the results as masterfully as Mendel did is a moot point. •

—*Theodozius Dobzhansky (1900–1975)*

Chapter Outline

Discovering the Mechanisms of Heredity
Problems in the Study of Heredity
The Work of Gregor Mendel
A Model of Genetic Events
What Is a Trait?
Mendelian Inheritance in Humans
Summary

Cytogenetics
The Chromosomes
Cell Division

Reexamining Mendelian Genetics
Summary

The Molecular Basis of Heredity
Molecules of Life
The Nucleic Acids
Protein Synthesis
Summary

See the Online Learning Center for a chapter summary, chapter outline, and learning objectives.

After Reading This Chapter, You Should Be Able to Answer These Questions:

1. What are the principle of segregation and the principle of independent assortment?

2. In what ways did Gregor Mendel's work disprove the blending theory of inheritance and the concept of pangenesis?

3. Are all traits determined completely by inheritance? If not, what other factor might be involved in the expression of a trait?

4. What role do chromosomes play in inheritance?

5. What are the two types of cell division, and what does each one accomplish? How does the process of cell division differ in the two types?

6. In what ways does knowledge of cell division help explain Mendel's findings? In what ways does knowledge of cell division explain why Mendel's principles do not always work in the way he predicted?

7. What is the structure of the genetic material?

8. How does knowledge of the structure of DNA and RNA help us understand the nature of inheritance and the way proteins are manufactured?

Charles Darwin's concept of natural selection explains why variants within a population increase or decrease in number over generations. As we saw in the previous chapter, one of the foundations of natural selection is the observation that populations are variable and that part of this variation is the result of heredity. When a particular individual produces a significantly greater number of offspring than other organisms do, that individual passes on certain traits to the next generation at a greater frequency than other organisms.

Although Darwin recognized the relationship between the processes of inheritance and natural selection, he was never able to define the rules of heredity. He did not discover how new variants, the raw material of natural selection, arise. Nor did he figure out how characteristics are transmitted from generation to generation. Although some of the basic principles of genetics were worked out during Darwin's time, he was unaware of this new knowledge.

This is the first of three chapters on genetics. In this chapter, we will lay out the basic mechanisms of heredity.

blending theory An early and incorrect idea that the inherited characteristics of offspring are intermediate between maternal and paternal genetic characteristics.

pangenesis An early and inaccurate idea that acquired characteristics of the parents are transmitted to their offspring.

DISCOVERING THE MECHANISMS OF HEREDITY

Almost everyone would agree with the statement that children resemble their parents and that distinctive physical traits often characterize family lines. Moving from a simple and obvious statement about family likenesses to an actual determination of the genetic mechanisms involved is a long jump.

Problems in the Study of Heredity

See the Online Learning Center for an Internet Activity on Mendelian genetics.

One early attempt at explaining family resemblances was the idea that hereditary units merge as one might mix two colors of paint. This is known as the **blending theory.** However, if such were the case, traits would be irreversibly changed from generation to generation and would not persist. For example, red paint mixed with white paint yields pink, but both the red and the white colors cease to exist. Neither the red nor the white color can be reconstituted from the pink.

Charles Darwin proposed a mechanism of heredity that we call **pangenesis.** He believed that particles present in the body were influenced by activities of the organism throughout its life. These particles traveled to the reproductive cells through the circulatory system. There they modified the sex cells in such a way that the acquired characteristics of the individual organism could now be passed on to the next generation. This hypothesis did not survive.

Much of the nineteenth-century interest in genetics revolved around the study of human characteristics. However, the study of human heredity is many times more difficult than the study of heredity in other organisms. This is perhaps the main reason so many early biologists failed to discover the underlying principles of genetics.

Figure 2.1 Gregor Mendel (1822–1884)
In 1865, Gregor Mendel presented two lectures before the Natural Science Society of Brünn. Those lectures, published in the following year, presented his conclusions from his experiments with pea plants.

The Work of Gregor Mendel

It is not surprising that the breakthrough in the understanding of heredity took place outside the arena of human genetics. In 1865, a monk by the name of Gregor Mendel (1822–1884) first wrote about many of the principles of heredity (Figure 2.1) (Box 2-1).

In his experiments, Mendel realized that the best traits for the study of heredity were those that are either obviously present or completely absent, rather than those that have intermediate values and must be measured on some type of scale. Mendel chose seven contrasting pairs of characteristics of the common pea plant. Using as large a sample as possible to eliminate chance error, he observed each pea plant separately and kept the different generations apart. The results were quantified and expressed as ratios.

Box 2-1

Gregor Mendel and the Discovery of the Laws of Heredity

Major breakthroughs in scientific knowledge often come from the least expected places. Gregor Mendel's discovery of the laws of heredity was the result of a farmer's son's interest in horticulture and the development of new hybrids for horticultural purposes. His work took place in a context of increasing interest in the application of science to the practical issues of farming.

Because he was of humble origins, Mendel's only opportunity to get an education was to join the church. He became a monk at a monastery in Brünn, in what is now Brno, Czech Republic. Mendel's order encouraged teaching and research, and when it became apparent after his ordination that his skills as a parish priest were limited, the abbot of the monastery encouraged Mendel to further his education at the university in Vienna. His science education was well rounded and included work in mathematics. Perhaps it was his mathematical view of the world that led Mendel to see in his data things that other experimenters of that time failed to see.

Mendel began his work on pea plant hybridization in 1856, a task that lasted eight years. He selected the pea plant because the structure of the flower was such that he could control fertilization easily. The traits he studied were clear-cut, never showing up in an intermediate form. He selected seven characteristics: shape of ripe seed (round or wrinkled), color of seed albumen (variation of yellow or green), color of seed coat (white or gray), shape of ripe pod (smooth or wrinkled), color of unripe pod (green or yellow), position of flowers (distributed along the main stem or bunched at the end of the stem), and length of stem (tall or dwarf). The color of the seed coat is associated with the color of the flower: the white seed coat with white color and the gray seed coat with violet color.

At the conclusion of his experiments Mendel presented two lectures to the Natural Science Society of Brünn on February 8 and March 8, 1865. They were subsequently published in 1866 in the proceedings of the society. Mendel sent several copies to distinguished scientists, including Charles Darwin. Darwin, who was pondering the problem of heredity, never read the lectures. In the printing process several pages were printed on the same large piece of paper and then folded and bound, with the folds between the pages uncut. The reader would have had to cut the pages with a knife—Darwin's copy remained uncut. In any case, Mendel's work was one of many studies that were conducted on plant hybridization at that time. Mendel's heavy use of mathematics would have deterred all but the most motivated reader. In wasn't until the start of the twentieth century that his conclusions were rediscovered along with the record of his experiments and conclusions.

Sources: A. F. Corcos and J. V. Monaghan, *Gregor Mendel's Experiments on Plant Hybrids: A Guided Study* (New Brunswick, NJ: Rutgers University Press, 1993); R. M. Henig, *The Monk in the Garden: The Lost and Found Genius of Gregor Mendel, the Father of Genetics* (Boston: Houghton Mifflin, 2000).

In the first series of experiments, Mendel started with **true-breeding** plants. These are plants that have been bred only with plants of the same kind and show the same traits over many generations. Mendel cross-pollinated true-breeding plants that produced only violet flowers with true-breeding plants that produced only white flowers. Those original plants made up the parental, or P_1, generation.

true-breeding Showing the same traits without exception over many generations.

Next, Mendel grew plants from the seeds produced by the parental plants. These were plants of the first filial, or F_1, generation. He observed that plants of the F_1 generation produced only violet flowers; he observed no white flowers or flowers of intermediate color, such as pink. These F_1 plants are termed **hybrids.** The hybrid plant produced violet flowers, as did one of the parental plants, yet it differed from the true-breeding parents in having one parent that produced flowers unlike its own, in this case white.

hybrids Individuals that are the result of a cross or mating between two different kinds of parents.

Mendel then allowed the hybrids to self-pollinate to produce the next generation, called F_2. In this generation, he found that some plants produced violet flowers while others produced white flowers. When he counted the number of plants showing each trait, he found that approximately three-fourths of the plants bore violet flowers while one-fourth bore white flowers.

As we saw, the F_1 hybrid plants bore violet flowers only, although these plants had parents with white flowers. When the F_1 generation was self-pollinated, some of the offspring had white flowers. The trait that is seen in the hybrid is said to be **dominant.** The trait that is not seen yet can be passed on in a later cross is termed **recessive.** Mendel noted that violet flowers, tallness, and smooth seeds were dominant features, while white flowers, dwarfness, and wrinkled seeds were recessive.

dominant The trait that is seen in the hybrid is said to be dominant.

recessive The trait that is not seen in the hybrid is said to be recessive.

The fact that the F_1 generation produced *only* violet flowers and the F_2 generation produced violet *and* white flowers showed that the blending theory was erroneous. No plant with pink flowers appeared in the F_1 generation, and in the F_2 generation white flowers reappeared. This confirmed the fact that the genetic unit for white flower color had not blended but had persisted without having been altered in any way.

A Model of Genetic Events

model A representation of a phenomenon on which tests can be conducted and from which predictions can be made.

segregation In the formation of sex cells, the process in which paired hereditary factors separate, forming sex cells that contain either one or the other factor.

A **model** is a representation of an object or an ideal. It is a simplified representation of a real-world phenomenon. Models help us test hypotheses, make predictions, and see relationships. The model may be a diagrammatic representation of some phenomenon, a statistical description, or a mathematical formula. For instance, the mathematical formula $A = \pi r^2$ allows us to predict exactly how a change in the radius of a circle will affect the area of that circle.

Models act as summaries of the known characteristics of a phenomenon. They provide a means of testing hypotheses about the phenomenon by measuring the effect of one element (variable) of the model on other elements. Gregor Mendel was not aware of the physical or chemical realities of the hereditary mechanism, but he did develop a model to explain what he had observed.

Principle of Segregation Mendel concluded that the hereditary factors maintain their individuality by not blending with one another. These hereditary factors exist as discrete pairs, and each factor can exist in several varieties. In the formation of the sex cells of plants—pollen and ova—the paired hereditary factors separate, forming sex cells that contain either one factor or the other. For example, the factor that controls the color of the flower exists in two forms, one responsible for violet flowers and the other responsible for white flowers. If a plant contains one of each form, one for violet and one for white, the paired factors will separate during the process of sex cell production, forming sex cells with either one factor for violet or one factor for white, but not both. This is now known as the principle of **segregation.**

Thus, Mendel reasoned that in the parental generation, the violet-flowered plant produces sex cells that carry the factor for violet flowers only, while the white-flowered plant produces sex cells that carry the factor for white flowers only. The hybrid develops from the union of two sex cells, one carrying the unit for violet color and one carrying the unit for white color. The hybrid therefore contains a pair of units—one for violet color and the other for white. Why, then, is the flower on the hybrid plant not pink, a mixture of violet and white? Mendel reasoned that in this case only one of the factors—that for violet color—is seen in the hybrid, while the other—that for white color—is not. The one that is seen is said to be *dominant.* The one that is not seen in the hybrid is said to be *recessive.*

When the hybrid produces sex cells, the two units segregate, producing sex cells of two types. Half the sex cells carry the unit for violet flowers, while the other half carry the unit for white flowers. When fertilization takes place, four different combinations may occur in the new plants. Some F_2 plants may inherit two units for violet flowers; others may inherit two units for white flowers; and still others may inherit one unit for violet flowers and one unit for white flowers (this last combination can occur in two ways: violet-white or white-violet). Since the violet-violet, violet-white, and white-violet combinations all produce violet flowers, three out of every four plants yield violet flowers. Only the white-white combination (one out of every four plants) produces white flowers. This experiment is illustrated in Figure 2.2.

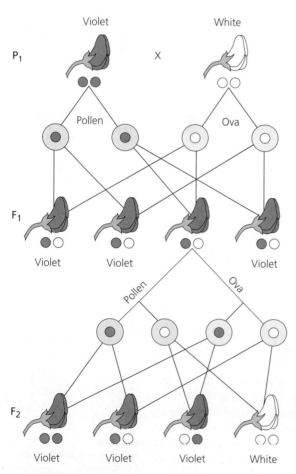

Figure 2.2 Segregation In the formation of sex cells, the hereditary factors separate, forming sex cells that contain either one factor or the other. Individual sex cells combine at fertilization, producing new combinations of hereditary units.

To test his hypothesis, Mendel planned another experiment. He predicted the results before beginning, and he managed to predict them correctly. He crossed an F_1 hybrid with a true-breeding, white-flowered plant. This is called a **back cross.** Figure 2.3 shows the result of this experiment.

Principle of Independent Assortment Mendel next studied the simultaneous inheritance of more than one trait. For example, he crossed a normal-stature (tall) plant bearing violet flowers with a dwarf plant bearing white flowers. The F_1 hybrid was a tall plant with violet flowers. When the F_1 hybrids were crossed, four distinct types of offspring resulted: tall plants with violet flowers, tall plants with white flowers, dwarf plants with violet flowers, and dwarf plants with white flowers, with the frequencies of $\%_{16}$, $\%_{16}$, $\%_{16}$, and $\%_{16}$, respectively. The explanation for these results is seen in Figure 2.4.

From these data, geneticists formulated the principle of **independent assortment,** which states that the inheritance patterns of differing traits are independent of one another. Whether a plant is tall or dwarf is unrelated to whether that plant bears violet or white flowers.

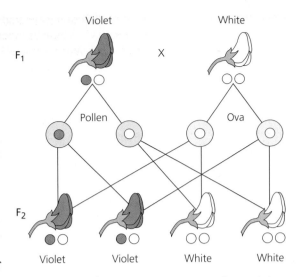

Figure 2.3 Back Cross The hybrid violet-flowered plant is crossed with the true-breeding white-flowered parent. One-half of the offspring bear violet flowers, while one-half bear white flowers.

What Is a Trait?

An organism's observable or measurable characteristics make up its **phenotype.** Whether the organism is a pea plant or a human being, the phenotype includes, among other things, physical appearance, internal anatomy, and physiology.

back cross The process of crossing a hybrid with its homozygous recessive parent.

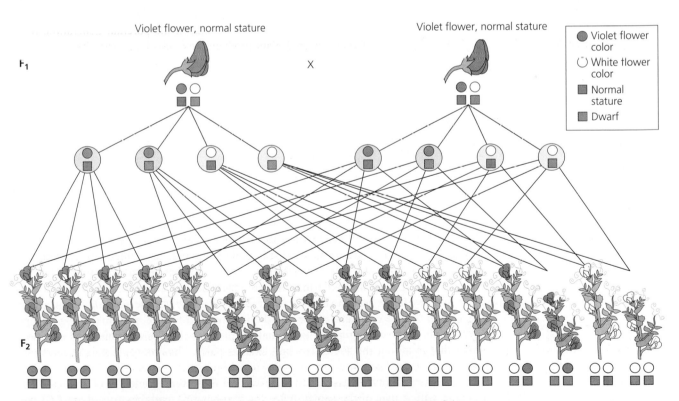

Figure 2.4 Independent Assortment The inheritance of flower color is independent of the inheritance of stature. Since the hereditary factors for flower color segregate independently of those for stature, four different kinds of sex cells are produced. These sex cells will combine at random into 16 different genotypes in the offspring.

independent assortment A Mendelian principle that states that differing traits are inherited independently of each other.

phenotype The observable and measurable characteristics of an organism.

trait One aspect of the phenotype.

genotype The genetic constitution of an individual.

environment Everything external to the organism.

monozygotic twins Identical twins: derived from a single zygote.

zygote A fertilized ovum.

dizygotic twins Fraternal twins; twins derived from separate zygotes.

In describing the phenotype of a person, we can observe certain features, such as skin color, eye color, hair color and texture, and general body build. We also can measure such traits as stature, head circumference, nose width, and arm length. Various physiological traits, such as the rate of glucose metabolism, also can be analyzed. Even personality and intelligence can be investigated. The result of these examinations is a profile of the individual's total phenotype. A **trait** is but one aspect of the phenotype—a particular hair texture, an allergy, a blood type.

Determining the Influence of the Environment The phenotype results from the interaction of an individual's **genotype** and the **environment.** The genotype is the individual's specific genetic constitution; the environment includes everything that is external to the individual, including sunlight, nutrition, and disease. A trait can be the result of the interaction of many genetic and environmental factors.

Many traits are determined solely by heredity—blood type, for example. Other traits are determined by the environment—a pierced ear or a dyed head of hair. Most features, however, are influenced by both genetic and environmental factors. It is the task of the investigator to determine the relative influence of genetic and environmental factors in the development of specific traits.

One method of estimating the environmental influence on a particular trait in humans is studying twins. Identical, or **monozygotic twins,** which are derived from a single fertilized ovum, or **zygote,** share identical genotypes. On the other hand, fraternal, or **dizygotic twins** are derived from separate zygotes; they have genotypes that differ to the same extent as those of brothers and sisters who are not twins. Monozygotic twins are always of the same sex, while dizygotic twins can be of the same sex or different sexes.

Since monozygotic twins share the same heredity, it follows that differences in their phenotypes are due entirely to the effects of the environment. On the other hand, differences between dizygotic-twin partners are due to both genetic and environmental factors. Therefore, we can use twin data to estimate the importance of genetic versus environmental factors with respect to a given trait.

We can look at several traits in a series of monozygotic twins who were separated at birth. If one twin possesses a particular trait and the other twin always shows the same trait, that trait is probably due to the expression of an allele with little or no environmental influence. However, if the incidence of the same trait in both members of a set of separated monozygotic twins is low, say, only 15 percent, the genetic influence is probably slight if it exists at all. It is when the percentage of identical expression of a trait in both members of a set of identical twins is high, but not 100 percent, that both genetic and environmental factors are suspected to be at work.

Mendelian Inheritance in Humans

genes Sections of the genetic material that have specific functions.

alleles Alternative forms of a gene.

homozygous Having two like alleles of a particular gene: homozygous dominant when the allele is dominant and homozygous recessive when the allele is recessive.

homozygous dominant Having two dominant alleles of the same gene.

A number of human characteristics are inherited in a simple Mendelian manner. One of these is the form of the human earlobe. Some individuals have earlobes that are characterized by the attachment of the lower part directly to the head. Other people have free-hanging earlobes.

The hereditary units that determine earlobe type and other features are called **genes.** Genes occur in alternative forms termed **alleles.** The gene for earlobe type occurs in two forms. We will write the gene using the letter *E* and distinguish the two alleles by using the uppercase *E* for the dominant allele and the lowercase *e* for the recessive allele. *E* represents the allele for free-hanging earlobes, and *e* represents the allele for attached earlobes. Remember that in all but the sex cells genes exist as pairs. Thus the gene pair for earlobes can exist as *EE, Ee,* or *ee.*

What are the phenotypes associated with each of these three genotypes? Studies show that a person with a pair of the same alleles for free-hanging earlobes (genotype *EE*) has free-hanging earlobes, while a person with a pair of the same alleles for attached earlobes (genotype *ee*) has attached earlobes. These people are said to be **homozygous.** This means that they have two alleles of the same kind. The former is **homozygous dominant;** the latter

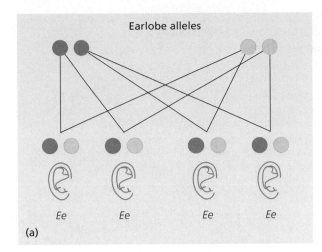

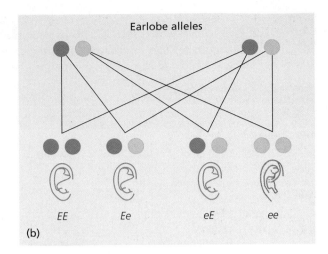

Figure 2.5 The Inheritance of Earlobe Type (a) All of the offspring of a homozygous dominant and a homozygous recessive parent will be heterozygous. (b) The offspring of two heterozygous parents could be (*EE*) homozygous dominant (two dominant alleles), (*Ee* and *eE*) heterozygous (one dominant and one recessive allele), or (*ee*) homozygous recessive (two recessive alleles).

is **homozygous recessive.** What about a person with the genotype *Ee*? An individual with the genotype *Ee* is said to be **heterozygous,** which means that he or she has two different alleles. Since the allele for free-hanging earlobes (*E*) is dominant, it is expressed in the heterozygous phenotype, whereas the recessive allele (*e*) is not. The heterozygous individual therefore possesses free-hanging earlobes (Figure 2.5).

While persons with different earlobe types cannot be mated in the lab, couples of certain phenotypes can be located and their children can be studied. Three basic types of matings are found: free hanging × free hanging, free hanging × attached, and attached × attached. But those with free-hanging earlobes can be either homozygous (*EE*) or heterozygous (*Ee*). The different mating types and their offspring are listed in Table 2.1.

An Example of Independent Assortment Several other traits can be used to demonstrate Mendelian inheritance in humans. An example is the ability to taste the organic chemical **phenylthiocarbamide (PTC).** This ability is tested by having people chew a piece of paper soaked in a concentrated PTC solution. Most people experience a definite bitter taste, but the percentage of such individuals varies widely in human populations from 35 percent in a population in India to over 98 percent among the Papago, a Native American group living in Arizona.[1] The ability to taste PTC is controlled by a dominant allele.

What happens when we look at the inheritance of two traits, PTC tasting and the shape of earlobes? We will examine the results of a mating between two individuals who are heterozygous for both traits. By using the letter *T* to represent the gene for PTC tasting, we can express the mating as *TtEe* × *TtEe*.

In the production of sex cells, the *T* and *t* segregate, as do the *E* and *e*. The segregation of the *T* and the *t* is totally independent of the segregation of the *E* and the *e*. Therefore, four kinds of sex cells will result. Some will carry the *T* and the *E*; others will carry the *T* and the *e*, the *t* and the

homozygous recessive
Having two recessive alleles of the same gene.

heterozygous Having two different alleles of a particular gene.

phenylthiocarbamide (PTC) An artificially created substance whose main use is in detecting the ability to taste it; ability to taste PTC is inherited as a dominant.

Table 2.1 Possible Combinations and Offspring for a Trait with Two Alleles

Mating Type	Offspring		
	EE	*Ee*	*ee*
EE × *EE*	X		
EE × *Ee*	X	X	
EE × *ee*		X	
Ee × *EE*	X	X	
Ee × *Ee*	X	X	X
Ee × *ee*		X	X
ee × *EE*		X	
ee × *Ee*		X	X
ee × *ee*			X

[1] R. Lewis, "The Bitter Truth about PTC Tasting," *The Scientist,* 17 (June 2, 2003), p. 32.

Table 2.2 Independent Assortment: Possible Genotypes and Phenotypes from a Mating between Two Individuals Heterozygous for Two Traits, PTC Tasting and Earlobe Type

		Offspring						
	TE		*Te*		*tE*		*te*	
TE	*TTEE*	taster–free-hanging lobe	*TTEe*	taster–free-hanging lobe	*TtEE*	taster–free-hanging lobe	*TtEe*	taster–free-hanging lobe
Te	*TTEe*	taster–free-hanging lobe	*TTee*	taster–attached lobe	*TtEe*	taster–free-hanging lobe	*Ttee*	taster–attached lobe
tE	*TtEE*	taster–free-hanging lobe	*TtEe*	taster–free-hanging lobe	*ttEE*	nontaster–free-hanging lobe	*ttEe*	nontaster–free-hanging lobe
te	*TtEe*	taster–free-hanging lobe	*Ttee*	taster–attached lobe	*ttEe*	nontaster–free-hanging lobe	*ttee*	nontaster–attached lobe

Summary of Phenotypes	Frequency of Phenotypes
9 taster–free-hanging lobe	$9/16$
3 taster–attached lobe	$3/16$
3 nontaster–free-hanging lobe	$3/16$
1 nontaster–attached lobe	$1/16$

E, or the *t* and the *e*. The sperm and the ova combine at random. A *TE* sperm may fertilize a *TE, Te, tE,* or *te* ovum, or a *Te* sperm may fertilize a *TE, Te, tE,* or *te* ovum. The same is true for the other two types of sperm. Table 2.2 shows the 16 different combinations that can occur. Four different phenotypes are observed: taster–free hanging, taster–attached, nontaster–free hanging, and nontaster–attached. Since the inheritance of earlobe shape and that of PTC tasting are independent events, the four different phenotypes will occur in the frequencies of $9/16$, $3/16$, $3/16$, and $1/16$, respectively.

Summary

Because of the lack of control over matings, the small size of families, the long generation span, the difficulties in determining what part of a trait is genetic as opposed to environmental, and problems of measurement and quantification, human beings have not been easy subjects for genetic research. The basic principles of heredity were worked out using nonhuman organisms.

The hereditary units are called genes. Genes occur in alternative forms called alleles. A genotype consisting of two dominant alleles is said to be homozygous dominant, while a genotype consisting of two recessive alleles is said to be homozygous recessive. A genotype consisting of two different alleles is said to be heterozygous.

Through careful experimentation with the common pea plant, Gregor Mendel was the first scientist to discover the basic principles of heredity. From his data, he formulated two principles based on a model of genetic events. The principle of segregation states that in the formation of sex cells, the hereditary factors separate, forming sex cells that contain either one or the other of the paired factors. The principle of independent assortment states that the inheritance patterns of differing traits are independent of one another. At the most basic level, these principles are universal among all living organisms, including the human species.

CYTOGENETICS

The principles of genetics were outlined by Gregor Mendel as an attempt to explain the results of his observations on the production of pea plants. Yet his model was not grounded in the reality of biology since he was unaware of the biological nature of the genetic material. After 1900, biologists began to experiment on the genetics of other organisms, primarily maize and the fruit fly. It rapidly became apparent that the genetic material resided within the nucleus of the cell.

Cytology is the branch of science that specializes in the biology of the cell. This term is derived from *cyto,* meaning "cell." The study of the heredity mechanisms within the cell is called **cytogenetics,** the subject of this section.

The **cell** is the basic unit of all life. In fact, cells are the smallest units that perform all the functions that are collectively labeled "life." These include taking in energy and excreting waste; using and storing energy; combining nutrients into substances for growth, repair, and development; adapting to new situations; and, perhaps the most important of all, reproducing new cells.

The great variety of cells all share several structural characteristics (Figure 2.6). A cell is bounded by a **plasma membrane** that allows for the entry and exit of certain substances and maintains the cell's integrity. A **nucleus** in the cell is contained within its own **nuclear membrane.** The material between the nuclear membrane and the cell membrane is called the **cytoplasm.**

The Chromosomes

When a cell begins to divide, long ropelike structures become visible within the nucleus. Because these structures stain very dark purple, they are called **chromosomes**—*chroma* means "color" and *soma* means "body." Viewed under the microscope, a single chromosome is seen to consist of two strands—the **chromatids.** These chromatids are held together by a structure called the **centromere.**

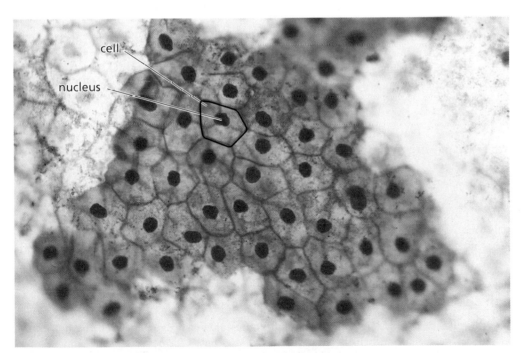

Figure 2.6 Human Cells Most living organisms are either single cells or are made up of cells. Here is a picture of human skin cells as they appear under a microscope. The nuclei appear dark because they have been stained with a purple dye. The chromosomes, which contain the genetic material, are found within the nuclei.

---

cytology The study of the biology of the cell.

cytogenetics The study of the heredity mechanisms within the cell.

cell The smallest unit able to perform all those activities collectively called life. All living organisms are either one cell or composed of several cells.

See the Online Learning Center for an Internet Activity on cells.

plasma membrane A structure that binds the cell but allows for the entry and exit of certain substances.

nucleus A structure found in the cell that contains the chromosomes.

nuclear membrane A structure that binds the nucleus within the cell.

cytoplasm Material within the cell between the plasma membrane and the nuclear membrane.

chromosomes Bodies found in the nucleus of the cell that contain the hereditary material.

chromatids Strands of a replicated chromosome. Two chromatids are joined together by a centromere.

centromere A structure in the chromosome holding the two chromatids together; during cell division, it is the site of attachment for the spindle fibers.

Figure 2.7 Human Chromosomes The genetic material is contained within bodies known as chromosomes. Pictured here is a complete set of 46 chromosomes obtained from a white blood cell from a normal human female.

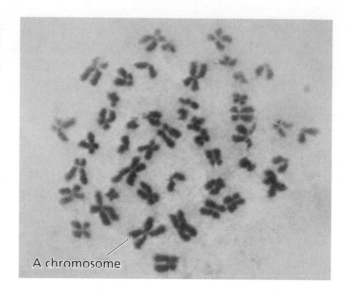

A chromosome

karyotype The standardized classification and arrangement of chromosomes.

homologous chromosomes Chromosomes of the same pair containing the same genes but not necessarily the same alleles.

sex chromosomes The X and Y chromosomes. Males usually have one X and one Y chromosome; females usually have two X chromosomes.

X chromosome The larger of the two sex chromosomes. Females usually possess two X chromosomes; males usually possess one X and one Y chromosome.

Y chromosome The smaller of the two sex chromosomes. Females usually possess no Y chromosome; males usually possess one X and one Y chromosome.

autosomes Chromosome other than sex chromosomes.

See the Online Learning Center for an Interactive Exercise on cell division.

Figure 2.7 is a photograph of chromosomes prepared from a human blood sample. The chromosomes have been stained by a special process that produces a pattern of bands so that individual chromosomes can be identified.

Much information can be obtained from an image of chromosomes. First, the chromosomes can be counted. Different organisms are characterized by specific chromosome numbers per cell. For example, the Indian fern has the highest number, with 1260 chromosomes; the roundworm has only 2. More typical numbers of chromosomes are found in dogs (78), humans (46), cats (38), and the fruit fly (8).

Second, not all chromosomes are alike; they differ in relative size and in the position of the centromere. In some, the centromere is centered, and so the "arms" of the chromosomes are of equal length; in others, the centromere is off center, and so the arms are of unequal length. Thus, it is possible to classify and identify chromosomes. Each chromosome in an image can be cut out and arranged in a standardized representation known as a **karyotype.**

Looking at the karyotypes in Figure 2.8, we can see that all the chromosomes, with one exception, exist as pairs. The chromosomes that make up a pair are called **homologous chromosomes.** Homologous chromosomes have the same shape and are of the same size. They also carry the same genes, but they may carry different alleles for certain genes.

The **sex chromosomes** of the male, however, are not homologous. While the normal female possesses two homologous sex chromosomes, the **X chromosomes,** the male has only one X chromosome, which pairs with a different type, the **Y chromosome.** In both sexes, there are 22 pairs of nonsex chromosomes, referred to as **autosomes.** These autosomal pairs are numbered from 1 to 22. The 23rd pair consists of the sex chromosomes.

Cell Division

The physical basis of Mendelian genetics becomes clear when we observe the movement of chromosomes during cell division. There are two basic forms of cell division: mitosis and meiosis. **Mitosis** is the process by which a one-celled organism divides into two new individuals. In a multicellular organism, mitosis results in the growth and replacement of body cells. **Meiosis,** on the other hand, is specialized cell division that results in the production of sex cells, or **gametes.**

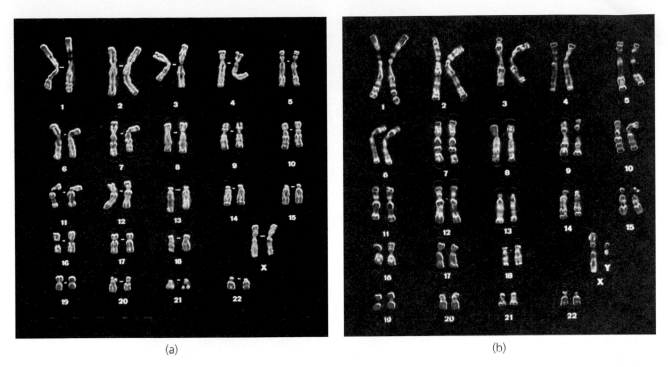

(a)   (h)

Figure 2.8 Human Karyotypes Karyotypes of (a) a normal female and (b) a normal male. In both sexes, there are 22 pairs of nonsex chromosomes or autosomes and a pair of sex chromosomes. The autosomal pairs are numbered from 1 to 22.

Mitosis The events of mitosis follow each other in a continuous fashion. Various studies show that it takes 30 to 90 minutes for one complete mitotic division in humans, depending on the type of cell. Some cells, such as skin cells, are constantly being replaced, and so they divide often. On the other hand, nerve cells usually stop dividing at birth or shortly thereafter. In order to make the events of this process clear, mitosis is divided into several arbitrary phases defined by specific landmark events. The phases of mitosis are listed in Table 2.3 and are illustrated in Figure 2.9.

Meiosis Meiosis differs from mitosis in many ways. Meiosis takes place only in specialized tissue in the testes of the male and in the ovaries of the female. Meiotic division results in the production of *gametes,* which are the sperm in the male and the ova in the female.

A significant feature of meiosis is the reduction in chromosome number from 46 to 23. If a sperm and an ovum each contained 46 chromosomes, the cell resulting from the fertilization of an ovum by a sperm would have 92 chromosomes. In the next generation, there would be 184 chromosomes, and so on. Instead, meiosis in humans produces gametes with 23 chromosomes each. When fertilization takes place, the number of chromosomes remains constant at 46. The events of meiosis are described in Table 2.4 and are illustrated in Figure 2.10.

Sperm and Ova Production **Spermatogenesis,** or sperm production, begins in the average American male at 12 to 13 years of age and usually continues throughout life. However, the onset of spermatogenesis is variable, not only among individuals but also among the averages for different populations. The male normally produces millions of sperm at any one time.

Oogenesis, or ova production, is different. The beginnings of the first division of meiosis occur within the ovaries during fetal development, between the fifth month and seventh month after conception. These cells remain in metaphase I until they are stimulated, beginning at puberty, by certain hormones to complete their development.

mitosis Form of cell division whereby one-celled organisms divide and whereby body cells divide in growth and replacement.

meiosis Form of cell division occurring in specialized tissues in the testes and ovaries that leads to the production of gametes or sex cells.

gamete A sex cell produced by meiosis that contains one copy of a chromosome set (23 chromosomes in humans). In an animal with two sexes, the sex cell is either a sperm or an ovum.

spermatogenesis Sperm production.

oogenesis The production of ova.

Table 2.3 The Stages of Mitosis

To make the events of mitosis clear, mitosis can be divided into a number of arbitrary phases. These phases are diagrammed in Figure 2.9.

Interphase

Interphase is the period between successive mitotic divisions. Interphase is divided into three stages, labeled G_1, S, and G_2. The cell increases in size during the G_1 phase, replication of the DNA occurs during the S stage, and processes associated with the preparation for mitosis occur during the G_2 stage. Chromosomes appear as an undifferentiated mass.

Prophase

Prophase is the first stage of mitosis. The chromosomes become visible as threadlike structures; they then become shorter and thicker. At this point, each chromosome is made up of two strands, each called a **chromatid,** that are connected by the **centromere.** The two **centrioles,** located within the **centrosomes,** move apart and end up at opposite poles of the nucleus. Protein structures called **kinetochores** form on each side of the centromere. The nuclear membrane begins to break down.

Prometaphase

The structure known as the **spindle** forms during prometaphase. The spindle is formed of several units and includes the poles, radiating microtubules called **asters,** and fibers. The kinetochores, each associated with a chromatid, attach to the spindle. The chromosomes begin to migrate to the **metaphase plate** or central plane of the cell.

Metaphase

At metaphase, the chromosomes line up at the metaphase plate.

Anaphase

In anaphase, the chromatids separate at the centromere, resulting in two separate chromosomes. Each chromosome now consists of a single chromatid. Each chromatid of a pair is pulled by the kinetochore spindle fibers to an opposite pole.

Telophase

In telophase, new nuclear membranes appear around the two groups of chromosomes as the spindle disappears. The cell then divides to form two new cells.

---

polar bodies Cells that develop in oogenesis that contain little cytoplasm and do not develop into mature ova.

ovulation The point during the female reproductive cycle, usually the midpoint, when the ovum has matured and breaks through the wall of the ovary.

The first meiotic division is different in the female than in the male. In the female, the spindle does not form across the center of the cell; instead, it forms off to one side. During cell division, one nucleus carries the bulk of cytoplasm. This is also true of the second meiotic division. Thus, a single large ovum and two very small cells, the **polar bodies,** are produced from the one original cell. The large ovum contains enough nutrients to nourish the embryo until the embryo implants itself in the wall of the uterus.

Oogenesis is cyclical. The length of the cycle is highly variable, not only within the female population but also in the same female at different times of her reproductive life. The median length of the cycle among American women between the ages of 20 and 40 ranges from 26.2 to 27.9 days. Ninety percent of the cycle lengths range from a low of 21.8 days to a high of 38.4 days.[2]

At the midpoint of the cycle, the ovum has matured and breaks through the wall of the ovary. This event is known as **ovulation.** In contrast to the great quantity of sperm produced by the male, only one ovum is usually produced during each cycle by the average human female.

---

[2] A. E. Treloar et al., "Variations of the Human Menstrual Cycle through Reproductive Life," *International Journal of Fertility,* 12 (1967), pp. 77–126.

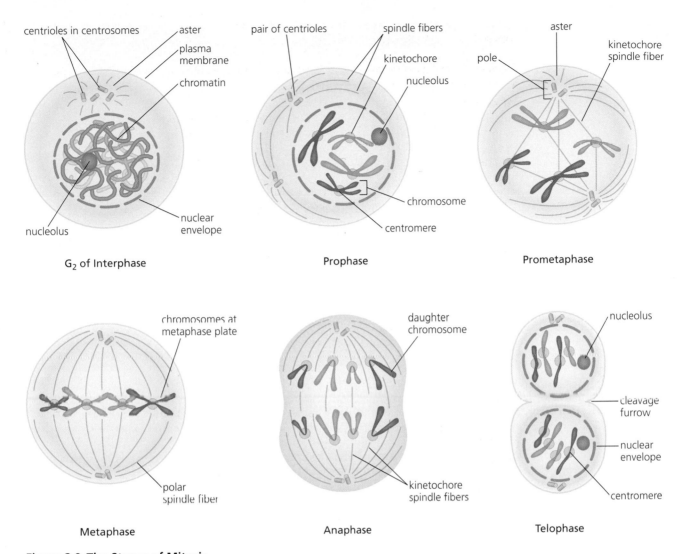

Figure 2.9 The Stages of Mitosis

Fertilization must take place soon after ovulation. In nonhuman mammals, sexual receptivity is related to the ovarian cycle. The female comes into **estrus,** the period of sexual receptivity, around the time of ovulation. Unlike the case with other mammals, sexual receptivity in the human female is not linked to the periodic occurrence of ovulation. This will be discussed in Chapter 10.

estrus Time period during which the female is sexually receptive.

Reexamining Mendelian Genetics

The details of cell division can help us understand Mendelian genetics. Mitosis is merely a copying of the genetic material, but in meiosis, the physical reality of Mendel's principles of segregation and independent assortment can be observed.

Each individual cell contains 23 pairs of chromosomes. One member of each pair is obtained from the mother, and one from the father. When the individual then produces gametes, the paired chromosomes will separate during the first meiotic division; this is

Table 2.4 The Stages of Meiosis

To make the events of meiosis clear, meiosis can be divided into a number of arbitrary phases. These events are diagrammed in Figure 2.10.

Prophase I

In prophase I, the chromosomes become visible as they contract and thicken. Homologous chromosomes (members of a pair) come together, and crossing-over may occur.

Metaphase I

In metaphase I, the paired chromosomes line up at the metaphase plate across the center of the cell.

Anaphase I

In anaphase I, the paired chromosomes separate and are pulled to opposite poles by spindle fibers.

Telophase I

In telophase I, a nuclear membrane forms around each set of chromosomes and the cell divides. Each new cell now has one representative of each homologous pair, 23 chromosomes in humans. Each chromosome is still made up of two chromatids.

Prophase II

In prophase II, the cell prepares to undergo a second division.

Metaphase II

In metaphase II, the chromosomes line up at the metaphase plate.

Anaphase II

In anaphase II, the chromatids separate at the centromere, resulting in two separate chromosomes. Each chromosome, now consisting of a single chromatid, is pulled by the kinetochore spindle fibers to opposite poles.

Telophase II

In telophase II, new nuclear membranes appear around the two groups of chromosomes as the spindle disappears. The cell then divides to form two new cells.

Spermatogenesis

In spermatogenesis, or sperm production, the products of meiosis are four cells called **spermatids.** Each spermatid becomes a sperm.

Oogenesis

In oogenesis, or ova production, the cell divides unevenly in meiosis. In the first division of meiosis, the cell divides into one large cell that contains the bulk of the cytoplasm of the original cell and a small cell called a polar body. The large cell then begins the second division of meiosis, again dividing unevenly into a large cell and a small polar body. The polar bodies eventually disintegrate.

segregation. Therefore, each gamete will contain only one of each pair and, hence, only the alleles on those particular chromosomes.

When two genes exist on different chromosomes, the inheritance of each gene is independent of the other. As the chromosomes line up in meiosis, the individual chromosomes can orient in different patterns, as we will see below. This explains Mendel's observations of independent assortment.

As one meiotic division follows another, gamete after gamete is produced, yet each individual gamete is unique, consisting of a particular set of chromosomes. As the 23 chromosomes line up in meiosis, they can recombine into several configurations.

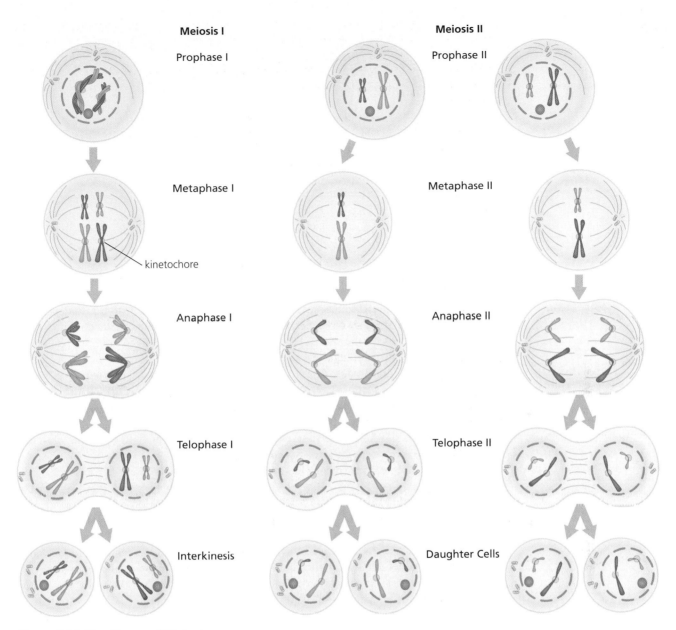

Figure 2.10 The Stages of Meiosis

Let us assume that, in Figure 2.11, the chromosomes with dominant alleles are inherited from the mother (*A, B*) and those with the recessive alleles are inherited from the father (*a, b*). When you are looking at two pairs, they can be oriented in two basic patterns: both paternal chromosomes can lie on one side and the maternal chromosomes on the other, or one of each can lie on each side. From this, four types of gametes are produced, as shown in Figure 2.11. When all 23 chromosome pairs are considered, there are 8,324,608 possible combinations.

Linkage Early studies of inheritance revealed the fact that Mendel's principle of independent assortment does not always work. Traits determined by genes carried on different chromosomes do behave in the way he described, but if different genes are on the same

linkage Association of genes on the same chromosome.

crossing-over The phenomenon whereby sections of homologous chromosomes are interchanged during meiosis.

recombination New combinations of alleles on the same chromosome as a result of crossing-over.

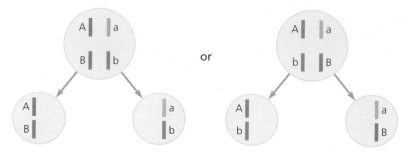

Figure 2.11 Independent Assortment The chromosomes can orient themselves in two different ways, resulting in four distinct combinations of alleles.

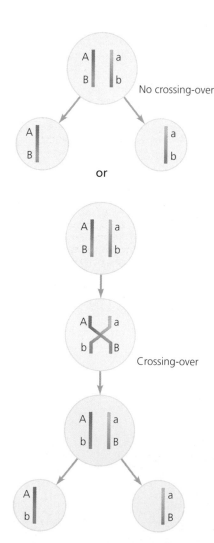

Figure 2.12 Linkage Genes located on the same chromosome will be inherited as a unit, except when crossing-over occurs.

chromosome, they tend to remain together in the formation of gametes. Interestingly, some of the seven traits Mendel studied in the pea plant are located on the same chromosome, but in his experiments demonstrating independent assortment, he by chance chose pairs of traits located on separate chromosomes.

Genes on the same chromosome are said to be linked, and the phenomenon is called **linkage.** Theoretically, if two genes are linked, only two types of gametes are produced instead of the four predicted by the principle of independent assortment. However, during meiosis, genetic material is often exchanged between homologous chromosomes inherited from an individual's father and mother; this event is called **crossing-over.** In this way, new combinations of alleles can arise with alleles that are located on the same chromosome, a process known as **recombination.**

As we can see in Figure 2.12, crossing-over provides a mechanism whereby new combinations of alleles can arise among genes that exist on the same chromosome. The farther apart two genes are on a chromosome, the greater the chance that they will cross over. This may be because there are more points between genes at which the chromosome can break and then reunite. As a result, each individual chromosome within each gamete may contain genetic material from both parents. Variation among gametes is the rule. The variations that result among living individuals form the basic raw material for the operation of natural selection.

Sex Linkage The X and Y chromosomes are not homologous; each has genes unique to it. Genes on the Y chromosome are said to be **Y-linked,** whereas genes on the X chromosome are said to be **X-linked.** Because of this nonhomogeneity, inheritance of traits carried on the X and Y chromosomes does not follow the simple Mendelian pattern.

The Y chromosome is small and carries few genes. (The *SRY* gene that determines the male sex in humans is discussed in Chapter 3.) The story is different with the X chromosome. Over 500 genes are known to lie on it, and more is known about the X chromosome than about any of the other chromosomes. The inheritance of X-linked genes differs from classical Mendelian inheritance in one important way. Males inherit X-linked genes only from their mothers. Therefore, if the mother is heterozygous, a son will inherit one or the other allele from his mother, but he will not inherit an allele for this gene from his father. A deleterious recessive allele will always be expressed since the carrier state cannot exist in a male. A daughter, of course, will inherit both an allele from her mother and an allele from her father (Figure 3.4). An example of an X-linked gene will be given in the next chapter.

Summary

Stimulated by Mendel's work, early geneticists began to search for the physical reality of the gene. Their work led them to the cell and to those small bodies within the nucleus of the cell, the chromosomes.

By means of special techniques, chromosomes can now be routinely observed through the microscope. Each chromosome consists of two strands, the chromatids, held together by the centromere. For a particular species, there is a characteristic chromosome number, which in humans is 46.

There are two basic forms of cell division. Mitosis is the division of body cells, while meiosis is the production of gametes—sperm and ova—which takes place in the ovaries and testes. Detailed studies of the behavior of the chromosomes during cell division have provided a physical explanation for Mendelian genetics.

Deeper probing of the mechanisms of inheritance has shown that Mendel's principles do not always apply. This is not because they are wrong but because the real hereditary mechanisms are very complex. For example, some traits are inherited on the sex chromosomes, and so their pattern of inheritance differs from the patterns seen by Mendel.

Y-linked Refers to genes on the Y chromosome.

X-linked Refers to genes on the X chromosome.

atoms The building blocks of matter.

molecules Units composed of two or more atoms linked by a chemical bond.

carbohydrates Organic compounds composed of carbon, oxygen, and hydrogen; include the sugars and starches.

lipids Class of compounds that includes fats, oils, and waxes.

proteins Long chains of amino acids joined together by peptide bonds (a polypeptide chain).

amino acids Molecules that are the basic building block of proteins.

THE MOLECULAR BASIS OF HEREDITY

The previous section focused on the behavior of chromosomes as a means of explaining and expanding the observations of Mendel. However, the chromosome is not the gene itself. What is the gene, and how does it operate? To answer this question and others, we must turn to an examination of the chemical nature of the hereditary material.

All substances are composed of **atoms,** the basic building blocks of matter. Of the 92 kinds of atoms that occur in nature, 4 are found in great quantity in living organisms: carbon, hydrogen, oxygen, and nitrogen. Others that play extremely important roles, but are less common, include calcium, phosphorus, sulfur, chlorine, sodium, magnesium, iron, and potassium (Table 2.5).

Atoms can join to form **molecules,** which can vary tremendously in size depending on the number of atoms involved. The molecules found in living organisms are usually of great size because carbon atoms form long chains that can consist of hundreds or thousands of atoms and often include rings of five or six carbon atoms. Other kinds of atoms are attached to the carbon backbone.

Molecules of Life

Most of the molecules found in living organisms fall into four categories: carbohydrates, lipids, proteins, and nucleic acids. The **carbohydrates,** include the sugars and starches. **Lipids** include the fats, oils, and waxes.

Some of the most important molecules of the body are **proteins.** Proteins include muscle fibers, enzymes, and hormones. An understanding of the protein molecule is essential in comprehending the action of the genes. Proteins are long chains of basic units known as **amino acids.** All 20 basic amino acids share a common subunit, which contains carbon, oxygen, hydrogen, and nitrogen.

Table 2.5 Common Elements in Living Organisms

Element	Approximate Composition of Human Body, by Weight (%)
Oxygen	65.0
Carbon	18.5
Hydrogen	9.5
Nitrogen	3.3
Calcium	1.5
Phosphorus	1.0
Others	1.2

peptide bond A link between amino acids in a protein.

polypeptides Chains of amino acids.

nucleic acids The largest of the molecules found in living organisms; they are composed of chains of nucleotides.

nucleotide The basic building block of nucleic acids; a nucleotide is composed of a five-carbon sugar (either ribose or deoxyribose), a phosphate, and a base.

ribose A five-carbon sugar found in RNA.

deoxyribose A five-carbon sugar found in the DNA molecule.

phosphate unit A unit of the nucleic acid molecule consisting of a phosphate and four oxygen atoms.

Attached to this subunit are various groups of atoms that define the specific amino acid. These groups range from single hydrogen atoms to very complicated groups containing several carbon atoms. The end of one amino acid can link up with an end of another, forming a **peptide bond.** Short chains of amino acids are called **polypeptides.** A protein forms when several polypeptide chains join together.

Proteins are further complicated by other bonds. These bonds can involve sulfur and hydrogen and can lead to a folding, looping, or coiling of the protein molecule. The three-dimensional structure of proteins is important in determining how they function.

The Nucleic Acids

Early in the twentieth century, biologists debated whether the gene is in fact a protein or a nucleic acid. It was soon determined that it was the latter.

Nucleic acids are the largest molecules found in living organisms. Like the proteins, the nucleic acids are long chains of basic units. In this case, the basic unit is a **nucleotide.** The nucleotide itself is fairly complex, consisting of three lesser units: a five-carbon sugar, either **ribose** or **deoxyribose;** a **phosphate unit;** and a **base.** The bases fall into two categories, **purines** and **pyrimidines,** both containing nitrogen. The purine consists of two connected rings of carbon and nitrogen atoms; the pyrimidine consists of a single ring.

The nucleic acid based on the sugar ribose is called **ribonucleic acid (RNA).** The nucleotides that make up the RNA contain the following bases: the purines **adenine** (A) and **guanine** (G) and the pyrimidines **uracil** (U) and **cytosine** (C). The nucleic acid based on the sugar deoxyribose is called **deoxyribonucleic acid (DNA).** DNA also contains adenine, guanine, and cytosine, but in place of uracil is found the pyrimidine **thymine** (T) (Figure 2.13).

The DNA Molecule As with the proteins, the three-dimensional structure of the nucleic acids can be critical in understanding how the molecule works. The basic structure of DNA consists of a pair of extremely long chains composed of many nucleotides lying parallel to

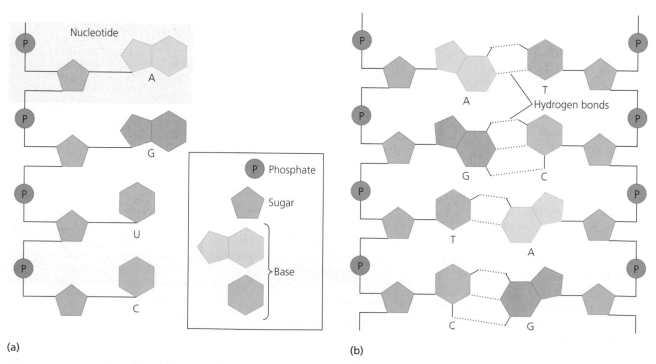

(a)

(b)

Figure 2.13 Structure of the Nucleic Acids (a) Short segment of RNA molecule. Note the presence of the base uracil and the absence of thymine. (b) Short segment of DNA showing four varieties of bases. Each base is joined to a deoxyribose molecule, and each deoxyribose molecule is held in the chain by phosphate molecules.

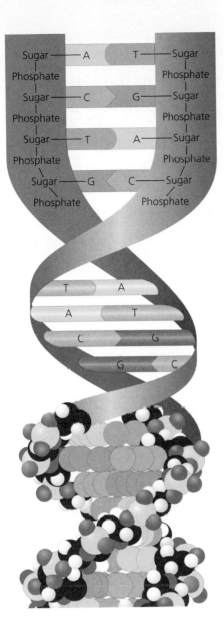

Figure 2.14 The DNA Molecule This illustration shows different representations of the DNA molecule. Note that adenine and thymine are always across from each other, as are guanine and cytosine. A sugar molecule (deoxyribose) bonds with each base, and each sugar bonds to a phosphate. This sugar–phosphate–sugar–phosphate arrangement forms the "backbone" of the DNA molecule.

base A subunit of a nucleotide that makes up the DNA and RNA molecules: adenine, cytosine, guanine, thymine, uracil.

purines Bases found in nucleic acids that consist of two connected rings of carbon and nitrogen; in DNA and RNA, adenine and guanine.

pyrimidines Bases found in nucleic acids that consist of a single ring of carbon and nitrogen; in DNA, thymine and cytosine; in RNA, uracil and cytosine.

ribonucleic acid (RNA) A type of nucleic acid based on the sugar ribose; exists in cells as messenger RNA and transfer RNA.

adenine One of the bases found in DNA and RNA; a purine.

guanine One of the bases found in the DNA and RNA molecules; a purine.

uracil One of the bases found in RNA; a pyrimidine.

cytosine One of the bases found in the DNA and RNA molecule; a pyrimidine.

deoxyribonucleic acid (DNA) A nucleic acid that controls the structure of proteins and hence determines inherited characteristics; genes are portions of the DNA molecule that fulfill specific functions.

thymine One of the bases found in DNA, a pyrimidine.

complementary pairs Sets of two nucleotides, each on a different polynucleotide chain, that are attracted to each other by a chemical bond. In DNA, adenine and thymine, and cytosine and guanine, form complementary pairs.

one another. The units are linked in such a way that a backbone of sugar and phosphate units is formed with the bases sticking out. The chains are connected by attractions between the hydrogen atoms of the two bases. Since the distance between the two chains must be constant, one of the two bases must be a pyrimidine, and the other a purine. Two pyrimidines would be too narrow, and two purines too wide. In addition, because of the nature of the bonding, bonding can take place only between an adenine and a thymine and between a cytosine and a guanine. These are said to be **complementary pairs.**

In 1953, James D. Watson and Francis H. C. Crick (1916–2004) proposed a model for the three-dimensional structure of DNA.[3] DNA consists of two long chains wound around each other, forming a double helix, with a complete turn taking 10 nucleotide units (Figure 2.14 and Box 2-2).

[3] J. D. Watson and F. H. C. Crick, "Molecular Structure of Nucleic Acids: A Structure for Deoxyribose Nucleic Acid," *Nature* 171 (1953), pp. 737–738.

Box 2-2   **Facts about DNA**

James Watson and Francis H. C. Crick received a Nobel Prize in 1954 for their work on decoding the structure of DNA.

A human cell contains at least two meters of DNA.

All of this DNA is packaged into a nucleus that is about five microns (5/1000 millimeter) in diameter.

A human gene can contain over a hundred million base pairs; the entire human genetic code is made up of about 3 billion base pairs.

Because the sequence of base pairs can occur in any order, genetic variability is virtually unlimited.

Ninety-eight percent or more of human DNA is noncoding; it does not code for the production of proteins.

Although some scientists have called noncoding DNA "junk DNA," it appears that this is a misleading label. Although we do not know a lot about it, it appears that it may have important regulatory and other functions and helps determine the differences between people and between species.

The same basic genetic code applies to all life on earth; that is, the same codons code for the same amino acids in all life from bacteria to humans.

The DNA sequences that control for specific proteins are about 99 percent the same for chimpanzees, gorillas, and humans.

The percentage of the human genome that is functionally identical in any two humans is about 99.99999 percent.

Genetic information can be transmitted from cell to cell within an organism or from one generation to the next without being encoded in a nucleotide sequence. This type of information transmission is called epigenetic inheritance. Geneticists are studying how it works.

---

mitochondria Bodies found in the cytoplasm that convert the energy in the chemical bonds of organic molecules into ATP.

adenosine triphosphate (ATP) The main fuel of cells. ATP is manufactured by the mitochondria.

mitochondrial DNA (mtDNA) A double-stranded loop of DNA found within the mitochondria; there can be as few as one or as many as a hundred mitochondria per cell, and each mitochondrion possesses between 4 and 10 mtDNA loops.

nuclear DNA (nDNA) DNA found within the nucleus of the cell.

See the Online Learning Center for an Interactive Exercise on DNA structure and replication.

Mitochondrial DNA Not all DNA is found within the nucleus of the cell. A small amount is found in the cytoplasm in structures known as **mitochondria.** Mitochondria convert the energy in the chemical bonds of food into **adenosine triphosphate (ATP).** ATP is the main fuel of cells.

Mitochondrial DNA (mtDNA) is a double-stranded loop of DNA. There can be one or many mitochondria per cell. Each mitochondrion possesses between 4 and 10 mtDNA loops. Cells with high energy demands, such as muscle cells, have high numbers of mitochondria.

Human mitochondrial DNA codes for 37 genes. Twenty-four of those genes encode RNA molecules that aid in protein synthesis. The remaining 13 genes encode proteins that function in cellular respiration that provides energy for the cells. Estimates vary as to the number of genes coded in **nuclear DNA (nDNA).** Current estimates lie between 20,000 and 40,000 genes. Viewed another way, nDNA contains about 3 billion base pairs, whereas mtDNA has only 16,569 base pairs.

The inheritance of the genes in mtDNA does not follow Mendelian principles. Mitochondrial DNA is inherited only from one's mother. The mitochondria of the zygote are supplied by the cytoplasm of the ovum; the sperm does not contribute mitochondria.

Replication of DNA At the end of mitosis and meiosis, each chromosome is composed of a single chromatid that will eventually replicate itself to become double-stranded again. A chromatid is basically a single DNA molecule. In molecular terms, the DNA molecule has the ability to replicate itself to become two identical molecules.

In replication, the bonds holding the complementary pairs together are broken and the molecules come apart, with the bases sticking out from the sugar–phosphate backbone. Individual nucleotides of the four types (ultimately obtained from the digestion of food) are found in the nucleus, and the bases of these nucleotides become attracted to the exposed bases on the chain, forming complementary pairs. Thus, a nucleotide with an adenine becomes attracted to a thymine, and so on. When the nucleotides are in place, they bond to one another (Figure 2.15).

The Genetic Code In order for the DNA molecule to function as the hereditary material, there must be a method by which information is stored in the DNA molecule. Remember, there are four bases that can be arranged in several ways. In the following hypothetical example, the DNA backbone of sugar and phosphate units is indicated by a single line, the bases by letters on the line:

<u>C T C G G A C A A A T A</u>

The above sequence codes for amino acids. Each amino acid is determined by specific three-base units called **codons.** This code has been broken and is given in Table 2.6. Thus, the sequence in the above example would code for the amino acids glutamic acid–proline–valine–tyrosine.

codons Sequences of three bases on the DNA molecule that code a specific amino acid or other genetic function.

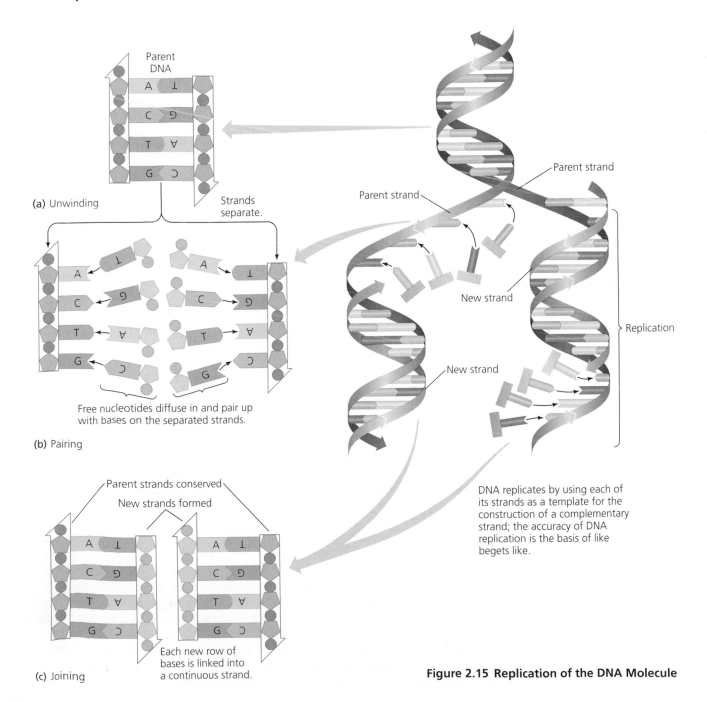

(a) Unwinding

Strands separate.

Free nucleotides diffuse in and pair up with bases on the separated strands.

(b) Pairing

Parent strands conserved

New strands formed

Each new row of bases is linked into a continuous strand.

(c) Joining

Parent strand

Parent strand

New strand

New strand

Replication

DNA replicates by using each of its strands as a template for the construction of a complementary strand; the accuracy of DNA replication is the basis of like begets like.

Parent DNA

Figure 2.15 Replication of the DNA Molecule

Table 2.6 The Genetic Code

Amino Acid	Codons*
Alanine	CGA, CGG, CGT, CGC
Arginine	GCA, GCG, GCT, GCC, TCT, TCC
Asparagine	TTA, TTG
Aspartic acid	CTA, CTG
Cysteine	ACA, ACG
Glutamic acid	CTT, CTC
Glutamine	GTT, GTC
Glycine	CCA, CCG, CCT, CCC
Histidine	GTA, GTG
Isoleucine	TAA, TAG, TAT
Leucine	AAT, AAC, GAA, GAG, GAT, GAC
Lysine	TTT, TTC
Methionine	TAC
Phenylalanine	AAA, AAG
Proline	GGA, GGG, GGT, GGC
Serine	AGA, AGG, AGT, AGC, TCA, TCG
Threonine	TGA, TGG, TGT, TGC
Tryptophan	ACC
Tyrosine	ATA, ATG
Valine	CAA, CAG, CAT, CAC

* The code is given in terms of the nucleotide sequence in the DNA molecule. In addition, there are specific codons signaling the beginning and end of a sequence.

Protein Synthesis

See the Online Learning Center for an Interactive Exercise on protein synthesis.

ribosomes Small spherical bodies within the cytoplasm of the cell in which protein synthesis takes place.

messenger RNA (mRNA) Form of RNA that copies the DNA code in the nucleus and transports it to the ribosome.

transfer RNA (tRNA) Within the ribosome, a form of RNA that transports amino acids into the positions coded in the mRNA.

The blueprint for a specific protein is located in the DNA molecule within the nucleus of the cell or the mitochondria. The actual production of proteins by the joining of specific amino acids in a specific sequence takes place within the mitochondria for genes encoded by mtDNA. For genes encoded by nDNA, protein production also occurs in the cytoplasm in extremely small, spherical bodies known as **ribosomes.** How is the information transmitted from the nDNA to the ribosomes?

The carrier of the information is **messenger RNA (mRNA).** This molecule copies the sequence of base pairs from the nDNA molecule. A segment of DNA that contains the code for a particular polypeptide chain unwinds, leaving a series of bases on the DNA chain exposed. Nucleotide units of RNA, which are found in the nucleus, are attracted to the complementary bases on the nDNA chain; the adenine of the RNA is attracted to the thymine on the nDNA, the guanine to the cytosine, the cytosine to the guanine, and the uracil of RNA (remember, uracil replaces thymine) to the adenine on the nDNA.

After the nucleotide units are in place, they link together and the newly formed messenger RNA leaves the nDNA molecule as a unit. A molecule of mRNA is considerably shorter than a molecule of nDNA, since the mRNA contains the code of a single polypeptide chain.

In the ribosome is another form of RNA, called **transfer RNA (tRNA)** (Figure 2.16). The tRNA is extremely short, consisting in part of a series of three nucleotide units. The three bases form an anticode for a particular amino acid; that is, if the code on the mRNA is ACG, the code on the tRNA consists of the complementary bases, UGC. Attached to the tRNA is the amino acid being coded.

The tRNA moves in and lines up opposite the appropriate codon on the mRNA molecule. For example, GUA is the code for valine on the mRNA, and so the tRNA that carries the amino acid valine will have the base sequence CAU. After the amino acids are brought into their proper positions, they link together by means of peptide bonds and the polypeptide chain moves away from the mRNA and tRNA.

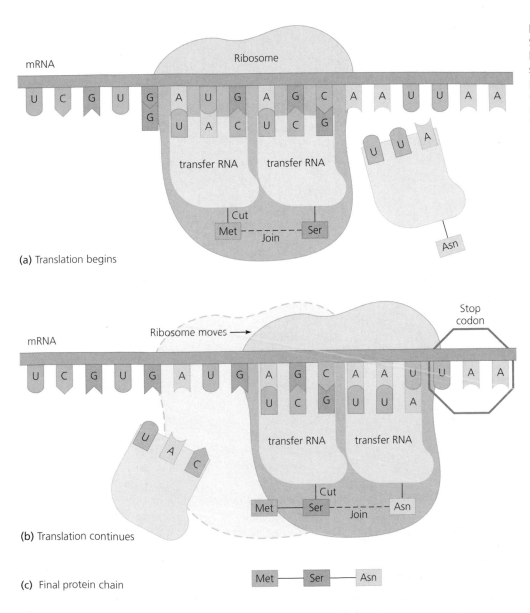

(a) Translation begins

(b) Translation continues

(c) Final protein chain

Met ——— Ser ——— Asn

Figure 2.16 Protein Synthesis in the Ribosome This is a highly simplified representation of protein synthesis. A start codon on the mRNA (AUG) signals the beginning of the production of a protein as a tRNA molecule brings the amino acid methionine into place. A second tRNA brings the second amino acid (serine, in this example) into place based on the code on the mRNA. The methionine and serine form a polypeptide bond as the first tRNA molecule is ejected. This process continues as more amino acids are linked. A code on the mRNA (stop codon) indicates that the protein is finished. The entire protein is now free of the RNA and is used by the body in the way specific to the type of protein that it is. (Asn stands for the amino acid asparagine.)

Summary

Processes like inheritance can be understood on many levels. In the years after Mendel proposed his model for inheritance, scientists began investigating the chemical nature of genetic transmission. Their examinations revealed that the genetic material is a nucleic acid, DNA. DNA controls cell activities and hence determines inherited physical characteristics. DNA, which has the ability to replicate itself, is also the mechanism through which one generation passes its characteristics on to the next.

The information contained in the DNA molecule is coded by the arrangement of base pairs. The information on the nuclear DNA molecule is transmitted by messenger RNA to the ribosome, the site of protein manufacture, where transfer RNA functions to bring the appropriate amino acids into position.

On the molecular level, a gene is a segment of the DNA molecule that codes for a particular functioning protein or segment of a protein. When random changes occur in this code, they increase genotypic variation by creating "new" alleles. The various alleles of a particular gene are simply slight variants in the code itself.

Key Terms

adenine, *46*
adenosine triphosphate (ATP), *48*
alleles, *34*
amino acids, *45*
atoms, *45*
autosomes, *38*
back cross, *33*
base, *46*
blending theory, *30*
carbohydrates, *45*
cell, *37*
centromere, *37*
chromatids, *37*
chromosomes, *37*
codons, *49*
complementary pairs, *47*
crossing-over, *44*
cytogenetics, *37*
cytology, *37*
cytoplasm, *37*
cytosine, *46*
deoxyribonucleic acid (DNA), *46*
deoxyribose, *46*
dizygotic twins, *34*
dominant, *31*
environment, *34*
estrus, *41*
gamete, *38*

genes, *34*
genotype, *34*
guanine, *46*
heterozygous, *35*
homologous chromosomes, *38*
homozygous, *34*
homozygous dominant, *34*
homozygous recessive, *35*
hybrids, *31*
independent assortment, *33*
karyotype, *38*
linkage, *44*
lipids, *45*
meiosis, *39*
messenger RNA (mRNA), *50*
mitochondria, *48*
mitochondrial DNA (mtDNA), *48*
mitosis, *38*
model, *32*
molecules, *45*
monozygotic twins, *34*
nuclear DNA (nDNA), *48*
nuclear membrane, *37*
nucleic acids, *46*
nucleotide, *46*
nucleus, *37*
oogenesis, *39*
ovulation, *40*

pangenesis, *30*
peptide bond, *46*
phenotype, *33*
phenylthiocarbamide (PTC), *35*
phosphate unit, *46*
plasma membrane, *37*
polar bodies, *40*
polypeptides, *46*
proteins, *45*
purines, *46*
pyrimidines, *46*
recessive, *31*
recombination, *44*
ribonucleic acid (RNA), *46*
ribose, *46*
ribosomes, *50*
segregation, *32*
sex chromosomes, *38*
spermatogenesis, *39*
thymine, *46*
trait, *34*
transfer RNA (tRNA), *50*
true-breeding, *31*
uracil, *46*
X chromosome, *38*
X-linked, *44*
Y chromosome, *38*
Y-linked, *44*
zygote, *34*

See the Online Learning Center for additional study questions.

Study Questions

1. Describe the concepts of segregation and independent assortment. In what ways do these concepts differ?

2. Many people take the term *dominant* to mean that an allele is common. However, dominance and recessiveness have nothing to do with frequency. What, precisely, do these two terms signify?

3. Why have the major breakthroughs in the understanding of the mechanisms of heredity been made with bacteria, plants, and nonhuman animals, such as fruit flies and mice, rather than with humans?

4. An individual's phenotype results from the interaction of the genotype and the environment. How does a geneticist proceed to demonstrate the relative importance of these two factors for a specific trait?

5. How does the process of meiosis tend to confirm Mendel's observations of segregation and independent assortment? Is independent assortment an unbroken rule, or are there exceptions?

6. In what ways does oogenesis differ from spermatogenesis? Because of these differences, does the mother's genetic contribution differ from that of the father? In what way?

7. An important feature of meiosis is the reduction in chromosome number. What is the significance of this reduction?

8. In terms of the chemical structure of DNA, what is the gene? Is the concept of the gene a valid one?

9. What is mitochondrial DNA? How does it differ from nuclear DNA?

Critical Thinking Questions

1. Gregor Mendel discovered the principles of segregation and independent assortment. Which of these principles does linkage violate? Why? Is linkage responsible for results that are different from those predicted by this Mendelian principle? Does this violation of Mendel's principle mean that Mendel was wrong?

2. Charles Darwin embraced the concept of pangenesis as his hypothesis for explaining inheritance. How did Gregor Mendel disprove the concept of pangenesis?

3. Today we think of a gene as a segment of DNA that codes for a particular protein or part of a protein. Since a DNA segment that corresponds to a gene can be hundreds or thousands of nucleotide pairs long, mutations can develop through changes in several locations, or loci, on the DNA chain. Geneticists today recognize that a particular genetic abnormality may result from one of many errors at several locations. How would this affect our discussion of Mendelian genetics?

Suggested Readings

Henig, R. M. *The Monk in the Garden.* Boston: Houghton Mifflin, 2000. This is a biography of Gregor Mendel. The book also tells of the origins of the science of genetics.

Lewin, B. *Genes,* 8th ed. Upper Saddle River, NJ: Prentice Hall, 2004. This is a popular introductory text on general genetics. It presents an encyclopedic treatment of genetics and as such is an excellent reference book.

Lewis, R. *Human Genetics: Concepts and Applications.* New York: McGraw-Hill, 2001. This is a general introduction to all areas of human genetics.

Orel, V. *Gregor Mendel: The First Geneticist.* New York: Oxford University Press, 1996. This is an analysis of Mendel's life and work. It discusses the attitudes that his contemporaries had about his experiments.

Watson, J. D., et al. *Molecular Biology of the Gene,* 5th ed. Menlo Park, CA: Benjamin/Cummings, 2004. This work, written by five researchers and teachers, including one of the discoverers of the structure of DNA, gives a detailed discussion of DNA and gene structure.

Suggested Websites

MendelWeb (classic papers, plant science, and data analysis):
www.netspace.org/MendelWeb/

Primer on Molecular Genetics:
www.ornl.gov/hgmis/publicat/primer/intro.html

Chapter 3

The Modern Study
of Human Genetics

The Human Genome Project is but the latest increment in a remarkable scientific program whose origins stretch back a hundred years to the rediscovery of Mendel's laws and whose end is nowhere in sight. In a sense, it provides a capstone for efforts in the past century to discover genetic information and a foundation for efforts in the coming century to understand it. •

—International Human Genome Sequencing Consortium (2001)

Chapter Outline

Medical Genetics
Blood-Type Systems
Human Inherited Abnormalities
Other Patterns of Inheritance
Chromosomal Abnormalities
Summary

Genetics and Human Affairs
Genetics and Medicine
The Control of Human Biological Evolution
Summary

Advances in the Molecular Study of Genetics
What Is a Gene?
The Human Genome
Summary

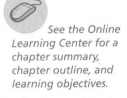
See the Online Learning Center for a chapter summary, chapter outline, and learning objectives.

After Reading This Chapter, You Should Be Able to Answer These Questions:

1. What have been some of the contributions of genetics to medicine?

2. Why was the discovery and description of the mode of inheritance of the ABO blood-type system important? How does the mode of inheritance of the ABO blood-type system differ from that of the characteristics Mendel studied in the pea plant?

3. How is pedigree analysis used to study the mode of inheritance of genetically determined or genetically influenced characteristics?

4. The ABO blood-type system exemplifies one way in which the inheritance of genetic characteristics deviates from Mendelian genetics. What are other deviations from Mendelian genetics?

5. What are the two basic types of chromosomal abnormalities?

6. What is Tay-Sachs disease? Can it be prevented?

7. Currently, some genetic diseases can be tested for and medically managed. What are some ways in which currently experimental techniques in medical genetics might be used in the future to deal with genetic disease?

8. In molecular terms, what is a gene?

The modern study of genetics began in 1900 when several scholars uncovered the same basic mechanisms of heredity that were first suggested by the experiments of Gregor Mendel. From that beginning emerged a period of experimentation using laboratory plants and animals that could be bred in large numbers. From those experiments, many of the details and complexities of genetics came to light.

It was clear that most new information about how genetics works would come from experimentation. Yet there was always a special interest in human heredity. In the nineteenth century, Sir Francis Galton (1822–1911) was encouraged by the writing of his cousin, Charles Darwin. Galton published in 1869 a study entitled *Hereditary Genius,* in which he attempted to show that human intellectual talents were inherited.

In 1902, a physician, Archibald Garrod, wrote a paper in which he demonstrated that the human disease **alcaptonuria** appeared to be inherited as a simple recessive. This was the first demonstration of Mendelian inheritance in humans. From that beginning, investigators have cataloged today approximately 16,000 inherited traits in humans.

MEDICAL GENETICS

The rapid development of the science of genetics in the twentieth century was the result of the application of the scientific method using plants and animals whose breeding could be controlled. Nevertheless, there was always a great interest in the application of genetic principles to humans. The focus of much of that interest was in the arena of medical genetics, the subject of this section.

Blood-Type Systems

In 1900, the same year Mendel's experiments were being rediscovered, Karl Landsteiner at the University of Vienna discovered the existence of important differences among red blood cells. These differences are due to variations found in particular molecules that are composed of a protein linked with a sugar and are located on the surface of the red blood cells. These variations are the basis of the ABO blood-type system. Its discovery led to the development of safe blood transfusions and an understanding of the cause of certain medical conditions. Blood types also became an important tool in the study of human variation.

There are many different molecules in human blood that occur in several forms. They are said to be **polymorphic,** from *poly,* meaning "many," and *morph,* "structure."

Through blood transfusions and occasional mixing of maternal and fetal blood at birth, molecules can be introduced into the blood of a person whose blood naturally lacks them. The body reacts to these foreign molecules by producing or mobilizing **antibodies,** whose role is to destroy or neutralize foreign substances that have entered the body. An entity that triggers the action of antibodies is known as an **antigen.** An antigen can be a toxin, foreign protein, or bacterium. Antigen–antibody reactions are of great medical significance and help define differences in blood proteins that exist in humans.

The ABO Blood-Type System The best-known set of blood antigens is the **ABO blood-type system.** This system consists of two basic antigens, which are called simply antigens A and B. The antigens are large molecules found on the surface of red blood cells. Other antigens do exist in the system, and the actual situation is more complex than is presented here.

There are four phenotypes in the ABO system, depending on which antigens are present. Type A indicates the presence of antigen A, while type B shows the presence of antigen B. Type AB indicates the presence of both antigens; type O indicates the absence of both antigens.

In our examples in Chapter 2, we looked at genes that possess two alleles. However, **multiple alleles** frequently occur. The inheritance of ABO blood types involves three alleles, which we will write as I^A, I^B, and i. Two of these alleles are dominant with respect to i: I^A results in the production of the A antigen, and I^B in the production of the B antigen. In relationship to each other, alleles I^A and I^B are said to be **codominant** in that an $I^A I^B$ individual produces both antigens. The allele i is recessive and does not result in antigen production.

---

alcaptonuria A recessive enzyme deficiency that results in an accumulation of homogentisic acid, a normal product of the breakdown of phenylalanine and tyrosine. Urine of affected individual turns dark upon exposure to air.

polymorphic The presence of several distinct forms of a gene or phenotypic trait within a population.

antibodies Proteins manufactured by the body to neutralize or destroy an antigen.

antigen A substance that stimulates the production or mobilization of antibodies. An antigen can be a foreign protein, toxin, bacterium, or other substance.

ABO blood-type system A blood-type system that consists of two basic antigens, A and B. Blood type O is the absence of both antigens.

See the Online Learning Center for an Interactive Exercise on the ABO blood-type system.

multiple alleles A situation in which a gene has more than two alleles.

codominant The situation in which, in the heterozygous condition, both alleles are expressed in the phenotype.

Table 3.1 Phenotypes and Genotypes of the ABO Blood-Type System

Type	Antigen	Antibody	Genotype
A	A	Anti-B	$I^A I^A, I^A I$
B	B	Anti-A	$I^B I^B, I^B I$
O	—	Anti-A, Anti-B	II
AB	A, B	—	$I^A I^B$

The ABO system is unusual in that the antibodies are present before exposure to the antigen. Thus, type A individuals have anti-B in their blood. Furthermore, an AB individual has neither antibody, while an O individual has both. The various genotypes and phenotypes are summarized in Table 3.1.

Because of the presence of antibodies in the blood, blood transfusions can be risky if the blood is not accurately typed and administered. If, for example, type A blood is given to a type O individual, the anti-A present in the recipient's blood will agglutinate all the donor's type A cells entering the recipient's body. **Agglutination** refers to a clumping together of red cells, forming small clots that may block blood vessels.

Table 3.2 shows the consequences of various types of blood transfusions. Blood type O often is referred to as the universal donor because the entering O cells lack antigens of this system and therefore cannot be agglutinated. However, type O blood does contain anti-A and anti-B, which can cause damage in an A, B, or AB recipient. Although such damage is minimal, since the introduced antibodies become diluted and are rapidly absorbed by the body tissues, the safest transfusions are between people of the same blood type.

Other Blood-Type Systems Another major blood-type system, which is a great deal more complex than the ABO system, is the **Rh blood-type system.** This blood-type system is also polymorphic and has multiple alleles resulting in many antigens. The inheritance of Rh blood type and that of ABO blood type are independent of one another, an example of independent assortment.

In the United States and Europe, a problem arises with respect to one of the antigens, Rh_0. About 15 percent of the people in this population lack this antigen; these people, who are homozygous recessive, are said to be Rh-negative (Rh−).

Although Rh compatibility can cause problems in transfusion, it is of greater interest as the cause of **erythroblastosis fetalis, a hemolytic** (blood-cell-destroying) **disease** affecting 1 out of every 150 to 200 newborns. The problem occurs when an Rh-negative mother carries an Rh-positive fetus. At birth, Rh antigens in the fetal blood can mix with the maternal blood, causing the production of the antibody anti-Rh in the mother's blood. Although the first few pregnancies usually do not present any danger to the fetus, eventually the anti-Rh levels in the mother's blood become fairly high. At this point, if the anti-Rh comes into contact with the fetal bloodstream, it can cause destruction of the fetal blood cells (Figure 3.1). Today the development of anti-Rh antibodies can be prevented medically.

agglutination A clumping together of red blood cells in the presence of an antibody.

Rh blood-type system A blood-type system consisting of two major alleles. A mating between an Rh− mother and Rh+ father may produce the hemolytic disease erythroblastosis fetalis in the infant.

erythroblastosis fetalis A hemolytic disease affecting unborn or newborn infants caused by the destruction of the infant's Rh+ blood by the mother's anti-Rh antibodies.

hemolytic disease Disease involving the destruction of blood cells.

Table 3.2 Results of Blood Transfusions

	Donor			
Recipient	A	B	O	AB
A	−	+	(+)	+
B	+	−	(+)	+
O	+	+	−	+
AB	(+)	(+)	(+)	−

+ indicates heavy agglutination of donor's cells. (+) indicates no agglutination of donor's cells, but antibodies in donor's blood may cause some agglutination of recipient's cells. − indicates no agglutination of donor's or recipient's cells.

**Figure 3.1
Erythroblastosis
Fetalis**

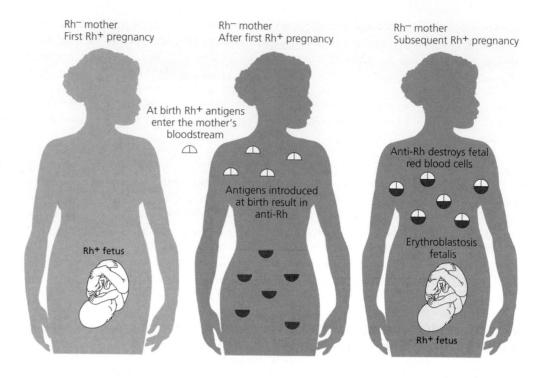

Rh⁻ mother
First Rh⁺ pregnancy

Rh⁻ mother
After first Rh⁺ pregnancy

Rh⁻ mother
Subsequent Rh⁺ pregnancy

At birth Rh⁺ antigens
enter the mother's
bloodstream

Antigens introduced
at birth result in
anti-Rh

Anti-Rh destroys fetal
red blood cells

Rh⁺ fetus

Erythroblastosis
fetalis

Rh⁺ fetus

The Use of Blood Types in Forensic Science There are many other blood-type systems that are known for human blood, including the MNSs, Diego, P, Lutheran, Kell, Lewis, Duffy, Kidd, Auberger, Sutter, and Xg. Because each of these systems consists of many diverse antigens, the probability of two persons having an identical combination of antigens is small. If a blood sample is found at a crime scene, it is often possible to determine which of the many blood antigens are present. The particular combinations of blood types in the blood sample, for example, can be compared with the blood types found in blood on the accused person's clothing to see if they are the same.

Of course, it is possible for two people to have the identical combination of blood types. The probability of this occurring can be calculated if the frequency of the occurrence of particular blood types is known in the population. However, a failure to match two blood samples can be used to prove conclusively that they did not come from the same person.

The use of blood proteins in criminal identification is enhanced by the fact that the A, B, and other antigens are found in most cells of the body in some individuals and are secreted in body fluids such as saliva, often found at crime scenes. The ability to secrete A and B antigens is determined by the dominant **secretor allele.** About 80 percent of the American people are secretors.

secretor allele Dominant allele that controls the presence of the ABO antigens in body secretions such as saliva.

Human Inherited Abnormalities

In 1966, Victor A. McKusick's first edition of *Mendelian Inheritance in Man* listed 1487 inherited human traits. By 2005, the number of known inherited characteristics had reached 15,991.[1] Due to recent advances in determining the genetic nature of traits, our knowledge of genetics is exploding, with new genetic traits being discovered almost daily. Still, the known number of genetically influenced or controlled traits represents only a small percentage of the number of genes that have been estimated to exist in humans. Since genetic research is costly, most studies of human genes have focused on inherited abnormalities and have been motivated by the hope that cures or treatments can be found. As a result, most of the known inherited traits are abnormalities.

---

[1] Number of entries on April 16, 2005. Online Mendelian Inheritance in Man, OMIM. McKusick-Nathans Institute for Genetic Medicine, John Hopkins University (Baltimore, MD), and National Center for Biotechnology Information, National Library of Medicine (Bethesda, MD), 2000. www.ncbi.nlm.nih.gov/.

The majority of genetic abnormalities are caused by the interaction of genes and the environment. Although the role of the environment in these situations is difficult to determine, many abnormalities are primarily the result of the action of the genotype. Some of the better-known ones, listed in Table 3.3, are the result of the inheritance of a simple dominant or recessive allele.

Many inherited abnormalities involve errors in metabolism. One of the best known of these is **phenylketonuria (PKU),** an abnormality inherited as a recessive. PKU involves an error in the enzyme phenylalanine hydroxylase, which is responsible for the conversion of the amino acid phenylalanine to tyrosine.

A child with PKU is unable to convert phenylalanine into tyrosine. Not only does this result in an inadequate supply of tyrosine, the levels of phenylalanine build up in the blood. As this buildup progresses, the excess phenylalanine is broken down into toxic by-products. These by-products usually cause, among other things, severe brain damage and mental retardation. This defect occurs in about 1 out of 100,000 live births among northern Europeans and in lower frequencies in most other populations. PKU accounts for about 1 percent of all admissions to mental institutions.

Another type of genetic abnormality is one that leads to an anatomical problem; an example is **achondroplastic dwarfism.** An achondroplastic dwarf is a person whose head and trunk are of normal size but whose limbs are quite short. In contrast with PKU, this abnormality results from the inheritance of a dominant allele. A person heterozygous (*Dd*) for this gene would be a dwarf. A homozygous dominant (*DD*) individual is usually stillborn or dies shortly after birth; a normal person is homozygous recessive (*dd*).

The Study of Pedigrees Studies of human genetics are often after-the-fact studies; that is, after a child with PKU has been born, an attempt is made to reconstruct the matings that

phenylketonuria (PKU) A genetic disease, inherited as a recessive, brought about by the absence of the enzyme responsible for the conversion of the amino acid phenylalanine to tyrosine; phenylalanine accumulates in the blood and then breaks down into by-products that cause severe mental retardation in addition to other symptoms.

achondroplastic dwarfism Form of dwarfism in which the individual's head and trunk are of normal size but the limbs are quite short; inherited as a dominant.

Table 3.3 Some Human Genetic Abnormalities

Abnormality	Symptoms	Inheritance	Incidence	
Cystic fibrosis	Excessive mucus production, digestive and respiratory failure, reduced life expectancy.	Recessive	1/3300	(European Americans)
Albinism	Little or no pigment in skin, hair, and eyes.	Recessive	1/200	(Hopi Indians)
Tay-Sachs disease	Buildup of fatty deposits in brain, blindness, motor and mental impairment, death in early childhood.	Recessive	1/3600	(Ashkenazi Jews)
Beta-thalassemia	Anemia due to abnormal red blood cells, bone and spleen enlargement.	Recessive	1/30	(Greek and Italian Americans)
Sickle-cell anemia	Sickling of red blood cells, anemia, jaundice; fatal.	Codominant	1/400	(African Americans)
Achondroplastic dwarfism	Heterozygotes display long bones that do not grow properly, short stature, other structural abnormalities; homozygotes stillborn or die shortly after birth.	Dominant	1/9100	(Danes)
Familial hypercholesterolemia	High levels of cholesterol, early heart attacks.	Dominant	1/500	(general U.S. population)
Huntington's disease	Progressive mental and neurological damage leading to disturbance of speech, dementia, and death.	Dominant	4–7/100,000	(general U.S. population)

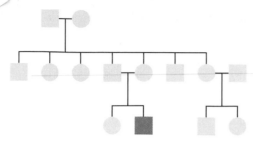

Figure 3.2 Pedigree of PKU Phenylketonuria is inherited as a recessive trait. Individuals with PKU are shown in orange. Note that neither of his parents has the disease; they are both carriers.

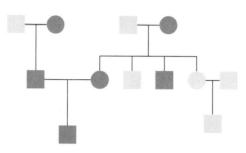

Figure 3.3 Pedigree of Dwarfism This type of dwarfism is inherited as a dominant trait. Dwarfs are shown as the darker color. Note that the trait occurs in every generation.

pedigree A reconstruction of past mating in a family, expressed as a diagram.

have already occurred. Such a reconstruction is called a **pedigree.** In the pedigree in Figure 3.2, the males are indicated by squares, the females by circles. Matings are indicated by horizontal lines, while descent is shown by vertical lines. Individuals with the trait in question are dark in color. As you examine the pedigree in Figure 3.2, note that the trait is infrequent. The parents of the PKU child are normal, since a PKU individual generally does not reproduce. Therefore, it can be assumed that the parents are heterozygous for the trait while the affected individual is homozygous recessive.

Now let us compare this pedigree of a recessive trait with that of a dominant trait. Figure 3.3 shows a pedigree of achondroplastic dwarfism. Note that all dwarf children have at least one parent who is also a dwarf. Since the abnormality is the result of a dominant allele, it is expressed in the heterozygous individual. A mating between two nondwarfs produces nondwarf children only.

You might think that a good way to identify the mode of inheritance from a pedigree is to look for the characteristic Mendelian proportions, but such proportions are rarely found. The size of families is too small to provide a large enough sample. Although the data from several families can be pooled, this requires specific mathematical procedures.

Other Patterns of Inheritance

The basic principles of genetics as worked out by Gregor Mendel are seen in all living organisms. However, the inheritance of many traits does not follow these basic patterns. In fact, because the actual modes of inheritance are usually more complex, traits inherited in the basic Mendelian pattern are the exception rather than the rule. We have already examined the case of multiple alleles and codominance in our discussion of ABO blood types. These and other deviations from Mendel's rules are summarized in Table 3.4.

Table 3.4 Some Deviations from Mendelian Genetics

Deviation	Definition	Example
Environmental influences	Nongenetic factors that influence the phenotype.	Dyed hair color.
Polygenic inheritance	A specific trait is influenced by more than one gene.	Stature.
Codominance	Both alleles are expressed in the heterozygous genotype.	In sickle-cell anemia, the heterozygous genotype produces both hemoglobin A and S.
Multiple-allele series	Three or more alleles exist for a specific gene.	In the ABO blood-type system, the four major blood types are determined by three alleles.
Modifying gene	One gene alters the expression of another gene.	One gene controls whether a person who has inherited the alleles for cataracts will get cataracts.
Regulatory genes	Genes that initiate or block the activities of other genes.	Genes that control aging.
Incomplete penetrance	The situation in which an allele that might be expected to be expressed is not.	A person who inherits the alleles for diabetes may not express the symptoms of the disease.
Sex-limited trait	A trait expressed in only one sex.	A beard in a male.
Pleiotropy	A single allele may affect an entire series of traits.	Sickle-cell anemia may cause blindness, stroke, kidney damage, etc.

Box 3-1 **Sex and the Olympics**

While the female phenotype is associated with two X chromosomes and the male phenotype with an X and a Y, how is it that a person with two X chromosomes sometimes shows a male phenotype? If the *SRY* gene breaks off a Y chromosome in the father's sperm and attaches to an X chromosome, the *SRY* gene will still operate even though it is on the X chromosome.

Can an XY individual show a female phenotype? This can happen if the *SRY* gene is not operating (a mutation) or if the receptor sites on the undifferentiated organs do not respond to the presence of the hormone (androgen insensitivity syndrome). In this case, there are no masculinizing effects. Such women have breasts and vaginas and are socialized as females but lack a uterus and ovaries and have testes located within their bodies.

One area of human endeavor where this has become a major issue is athletic competition. There were few women athletes competing near the start of the twentieth century. In 1896 a lone female ran in the marathon. By 1908, 36 women were competing in figure skating, tennis, gymnastics, and archery. By 1992, almost 29 percent of all Olympic athletes were women.

Fearing that a male athlete would compete as a female (this was at a time when athletic clothing was not very revealing), female athletes were carefully scrutinized.

In 1966 the International Association of Athletic Federations (IAAF) required naked female athletes to walk in front of a panel of doctors to verify their sex. Things became more scientific in 1968, when all that was required was a smear from the inside of the cheek. A simple examination of cheek cells under the microscope could determine the number of X chromosomes possessed by an athlete. The search was on for phenotypic females with a Y chromosome. In the 1992 Olympics, 6 of 2407 female athletes were so identified. However, that was also the year that the IAAF abandoned sex tests since not only was the procedure degrading to women, but women with these conditions have no physical advantages in athletic competition. Also, several female athletes with these conditions went public and people became aware of the problem and how those athletes were being treated. Testing also has been abandoned at the Olympics. No testing was conducted at the 2000 Sydney or 2002 Salt Lake City games.

Y-Linkage and the Determination of Sex Since male progeny inherit the Y chromosome, all males inherit the Y-linked genes. Y linkage, however, is difficult to distinguish from a **sex-limited gene**. These genes behave as if they were on the Y chromosome, but they are actually carried on an autosome and are expressed only in the male. The most significant gene that is found on the Y chromosome is the one that establishes the sex of the individual.

Most people accept the fact that people are born either as female or male. However, we need to distinguish between different kinds of sex. **Phenotypic sex** refers to how an individual's phenotype is viewed and is based on a person's sex organs and secondary sexual characteristics. Sometimes an individual's phenotypic sex is ambiguous. **Chromosomal sex** refers to the number of X and Y chromosomes. However, some individuals are born with abnormal numbers of sex chromosomes, as we will see later in this chapter. **Genetic sex** refers to the presence of the gene that determines sex. This gene, called *SRY* (**S**ex-determining **R**egion **Y** chromosome), is located on the Y chromosome.

A human embryo develops a set of generalized organs and tubes that will eventually turn into the sex organs. Between the fifth and seventh weeks of development, the *SRY* gene, if present, produces a chemical that influences the undifferentiated **gonad** (sex organ) to become a testis. Once the testis begins to develop, it will produce testosterone that will turn the other structures into the male sex organs. If this does not occur by the 13th week, the gonad begins to develop into an ovary, and under the influence of ovarian hormones, the tubes will develop into female structures (see Box 3-1).

X-Linked Abnormalities In the last chapter, we saw that genes that are found on the X and Y chromosomes show a distinctive pattern of inheritance. Here we study an example of an X-linked abnormality. **Hemophilia** is a recessive X-linked trait that is characterized by excessive bleeding due to a faulty clotting mechanism (Figure 3.4).

During the nineteenth and twentieth centuries, hemophilia occurred with some frequency in the royal houses of Europe. The disease probably originated with Queen Victoria of England, because all the people involved are descended from her. None of her ancestors

See the Online Learning Center for an Internet Activity on sex determination and intersex individuals.

sex-limited gene Non-sex-linked allele that is expressed in only one of the sexes.

phenotypic sex The sex that a person is judged to be, based on his or her physical appearance. Phenotypic sex may not correspond to chromosomal sex.

chromosomal sex The number of X and Y chromosomes a person has. The chromosomal sex of a person with two X chromosomes is a female. The chromosomal sex of a person with one X and one Y chromosome is a male.

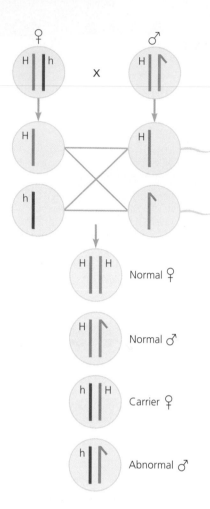

♀   ♂

X

H H   Normal ♀

H   Normal ♂

h H   Carrier ♀

h   Abnormal ♂

Figure 3.4 The Inheritance of Hemophilia The recessive allele for hemophilia, identified by the letter *h*, is located on the X chromosome but not on the Y. This is an example of the X-linked pattern of inheritance.

had the disease, but of Queen Victoria's nine children, two daughters were carriers, three daughters were possible carriers, and one son (Leopold) had the disease. These people brought the disease into the royal families of England, Spain, Russia, and probably Germany (Figure 3.5).

A famous case of the relationship of hemophilia to history involved Alix, granddaughter of Victoria, who married the future czar of Russia, Nicholas II, and became known in Russia as Alexandra. She had four daughters and one son, Alexis, who was a hemophiliac. Historians have suggested that the preoccupation of Nicholas and Alexandra with their son's disease brought them under the control of Rasputin and hastened the overthrow of their government.

Chromosomal Abnormalities

Besides abnormalities in specific genes, problems occur with chromosomes. The processes of mitosis and meiosis are precise, yet errors do occur. Such errors lead to **chromosomal aberrations,** which consist of two types: abnormal chromosome number and abnormal chromosome structure.

Abnormal Chromosome Number A common error of meiosis is that of **nondisjunction.** When two members of a chromosome pair move together to the same pole instead of to opposite poles, nondisjunction has occurred. This leads to abnormal chromosome numbers in the second-generation cells. Thus, two second-generation cells are formed: one contains 22 chromosomes, and the other has 24. The union of a gamete having the normal complement of 23 chromosomes with a gamete having an abnormal number of chromosomes will produce a zygote with either an extra or a missing chromosome. For example, if a sperm with 24 chromosomes fertilizes an ovum with 23, the zygote will have 47 chromosomes.

What phenotype is found in an individual developing from a zygote with an abnormal karyotype? Figure 3.6a shows a karyotype of an individual with 47 chromosomes, one too many. Since the extra chromosome is a number 21, a fairly small chromosome, a relatively small number of genes are involved. Figure 3.6b shows a child with this karyotype; the condition is called **Down syndrome** or **trisomy** 21. (The term *trisomy* refers to the presence of three chromosomes instead of a pair, in this case three chromosome 21s.)

Down syndrome is characterized by a peculiarity in the eyefolds, short stature with stubby hands and feet, and congenital malformations of the heart and other organs. Perhaps the most significant feature is mental retardation. Down syndrome is not rare. The risk of giving birth to a Down syndrome child increases with the age of the mother and perhaps the father (Table 3.5).

More common than nondisjunctions of autosomes are extra or missing sex chromosomes. Among these are such abnormal sex chromosome counts as X– **(Turner syndrome),** XXY **(Klinefelter syndrome),** XXX, and XYY (Table 3.6). While these individuals have a higher survival rate than do infants with extra or missing autosomes, possessors of abnormal sex chromosome numbers often show abnormal sex organs and abnormal secondary sexual characteristics, sterility, and sometimes mental retardation.

Structural Aberrations of Chromosomes In addition to abnormal numbers of chromosomes due to nondisjunction, several types of structural abnormalities can occur. Structural abnormalities are the result of breaks in the chromosome.

Deletion occurs when a chromosome itself breaks and a segment of it that is not attached to the spindle fails to be included in the second-generation cell. The genetic

genetic sex In humans, male sex is determined by the presence of the *SRY* gene, which is located on the Y chromosome. Persons who lack the Y chromosome, and hence the *SRY* gene, or who possess an abnormal allele of the *SRY* gene, are genetically female.

gonad General term used for an organ that produces sex cells; the ovary and testis.

hemophilia A recessive X-linked trait characterized by excessive bleeding due to a faulty clotting mechanism.

chromosomal aberration Abnormal chromosome number or chromosome structure.

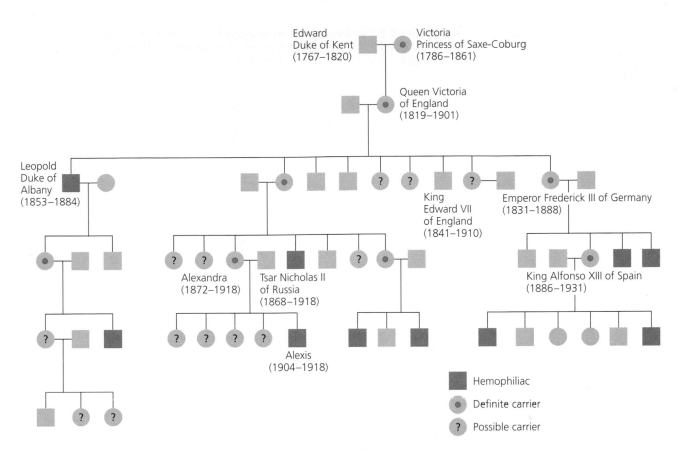

Figure 3.5 Hemophilia in Queen Victoria's Family Queen Victoria's pedigree.

material on the deleted section is "lost." **Duplication** is the process whereby a section of a chromosome is repeated. **Inversion** occurs when parts of a chromosome break and reunite in a reversed order. No genetic material is lost or gained, but the position of the alleles involved is changed. **Translocation** is the process whereby segments of chromosomes become detached and then reattach to other nonhomologous chromosomes.

nondisjunction An error of meiosis in which the members of a pair of chromosomes move to the same pole rather than moving to opposite poles.

Down syndrome Condition characterized by a peculiarity of eyefolds, malformation of the heart and other organs, stubby hands and feet, short stature, and mental retardation; result of extra chromosome 21.

trisomy The state of having three of the same chromosome, rather than the normal pair. For example, trisomy 21, or Down syndrome, is a tripling of chromosome number 21.

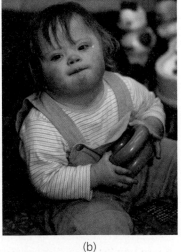

(a)　　　　　　　　　　　　　　　(b)

Figure 3.6 Down Syndrome (a) Karyotype of Down syndrome. Note the extra chromosome 21. (b) Girl with Down syndrome. Down syndrome is characterized by a peculiarity in the eyefolds, short stature with stubby hands and feet, congenital malformations of the heart and other organs, and significant mental retardation.

See the Online Learning Center for an Internet Activity on Down syndrome.

Turner syndrome Genetic disease characterized by 45 chromosomes with a sex chromosome count of X–; phenotypically female, but sterile.

Klinefelter syndrome A sex-chromosome count of XXY; phenotypically male, tall stature, sterile.

deletion A chromosomal aberration in which a chromosome breaks and a segment is not included in the second-generation cell. The genetic material on the deleted section is lost.

duplication Chromosomal aberration in which a section of a chromosome is repeated.

inversion Form of chromosome aberration in which parts of a chromosome break and reunite in a reversed order. No genetic material is lost or gained, but the positions of the involved alleles are altered.

Table 3.5 Incidence of Chromosomal Abnormalities in Newborn Infants

Maternal Age, Years	Incidence of Down Syndrome	Incidence of Any Chromosomal Abnormality
20	1/1667	1/526
30	1/952	1/384
35	1/385	1/192
40	1/106	1/66
45	1/30	1/21

Source: Data from E. B. Hook, "Rates of Chromosomal Abnormalities at Different Maternal Ages," *Obstetrics and Gynecology,* 58 (1981), pp. 282–285, and E. B. Hook et al., "Chromosomal Abnormality Rates at Amniocentesis and in Live-Born Infants," *Journal of the American Medical Association,* 249 (1983), pp. 2034–2038.

Abnormal chromosome numbers and structural aberrations account for a significant number of defects in newborns and a large number of spontaneous abortions (miscarriages). About 50 percent of the miscarriages in the United States are due to chromosomal abnormalities. Approximately 1 in 118 live births is accompanied by a chromosomal abnormality. One way of preventing what is very often a tragedy is to identify the abnormality before birth. Karyotypes can be made from the fetal cells found in the amniotic fluid; if chromosomal abnormalities are seen, the early fetus can be aborted. The procedure is recommended to all mothers over 35 years of age as a means of identifying fetuses having Down syndrome or other chromosomal abnormalities.

Table 3.6 Some Examples of Abnormal Chromosome Numbers

Type	Incidence	Phenotype
Autosomal Abnormalities		
Trisomy 13 (Patau syndrome)	1/15,000	Severely malformed; about 5% survive to first birthday. Small head, sloping forehead, cardiac and other defects.
Trisomy 18 (Edward syndrome)	1/7500	Growth and developmental retardation; death usually before 6 months.
Trisomy 21 (Down syndrome)	1/800	See text for description.
Sex-Chromosome Abnormalities		
47, XXY (Klinefelter syndrome)	1/500 males	Phenotypically male. Sterile, small penis, breast enlargement in 40% of cases, average IQ scores.
45, X– (Turner syndrome)	1/2000 females	Phenotypically female. Variable characteristics. Short stature, relatively normal IQ scores, small chin, webbing of neck in 50% of cases, shield-shaped chest, cardiovascular disease in 35% of cases, affectionate, sterile.
47, XYY (Jacob syndrome)	1/1000 males	About 96% apparently normal, phenotypically male, fertile. Some delayed language development and cognitive problems, taller than average, and bad acne.
47, XXX (triple-X)	1/1000 females	Phenotypically female. Some impairment of intellectual development in about two-thirds of cases, suggested increase in risk for schizophrenia, sometimes menstrual disorders and early menopause.

Source: Data from R. Lewis, *Human Genetics,* 4th ed. (Boston: McGraw-Hill, 2001), pp. 210–214.

translocation Form of chromosomal mutation in which segments of chromosomes become detached and reunite to other nonhomologous chromosomes.

Summary

Blood studies have traditionally been important to anthropology because they provide a relatively easy way to study genetically controlled variability in human populations. They also play an important role in forensic science. A large number of polymorphic blood proteins are found in blood that are inherited in known Mendelian patterns. The best-known system of blood proteins is the ABO system, which consists of three basic blood antigens.

About 16,000 inherited traits have been recognized in humans. Phenylketonuria is an example of an abnormality that is inherited as a simple recessive; achondroplastic dwarfism, on the other hand, is inherited as a simple dominant. Not all patterns of inheritance follow these simple Mendelian rules. Many apparent exceptions, in reality complexities, are summarized in Table 3.4.

One distinctive pattern of inheritance occurs when the gene in question is located on the X chromosome. Since males inherit only one X chromosome from their mothers and a Y chromosome from their fathers, genes on the X chromosome are not paired as they are in females. Because of their distinctive inheritance pattern, X-linked traits are relatively easy to identify, such as the example of hemophilia.

A number of abnormalities are not due to single genes but to errors in the number and structure of chromosomes. Such errors, when they involve autosomes, tend to lead to major abnormalities. Individuals with errors in the number of sex chromosomes do survive with varying degrees of problems.

GENETICS AND HUMAN AFFAIRS

Perhaps no other area of scientific discoveries affects human affairs more profoundly than that of genetics. In the future, the direct manipulation of the genetic material may prevent or cure genetic disease, extend life span, and allow children to be created "to order." Already, advances in genetics have sparked heated debates over the ethics of manipulating the human **genome,** the totality of genes located within a gamete. In the paragraphs below, we will discuss how our knowledge of genetics, and ultimately our ability to manipulate the genetic material, has had and might have an impact on human affairs.

genome All of the genes carried by a single gamete.

Genetics and Medicine

A hundred years ago a pediatric ward in a large hospital would have been populated by children with many infectious diseases. These diseases largely have been eradicated or controlled through major breakthroughs in the development of immunization and antibiotics. A hundred years ago a disease with a genetic cause would have accounted for a very small percentage of hospitalized children. Today diseases of genetic cause or influence have become the subject of a great amount of medical research. Here we examine one such illness, Tay-Sachs disease, as an example of the nature and treatment of children tragically born with diseases and abnormalities of genetic origin.

Tay-Sachs disease
Enzyme deficiency of lipid metabolism inherited as a recessive; causes death in early childhood.

Tay-Sachs disease is a metabolic abnormality caused by an abnormal **enzyme.** In this case, the enzyme is hexaminidase A, which occurs within the brain cells. Absence of the normal enzyme, which occurs in homozygous recessive individuals, permits the buildup of lipid material in the brain cell, leading to cell death. Appearing normal at birth, the child develops symptoms at about six months of age, and death occurs a few years later.

enzyme A molecule, usually a protein, that makes a biochemical reaction happen or speeds up a slow chemical reaction. It is not itself altered in the reaction.

A person who possesses a recessive abnormal allele in the heterozygous condition is said to be a **carrier.** Ashkenazi Jews of central and eastern European origin have a high

carrier A person who possesses a recessive allele in the heterozygous condition.

frequency of Tay-Sachs carriers, about 1 in 27, compared with the general population, in which the carrier rate is about 1 in 250. Such elevated frequencies of particular genetic abnormalities are common, and some abnormalities are found in all populations. For example, **cystic fibrosis,** one of the more common genetic diseases, has its highest frequency among people of northern European origin. An elevated frequency of Tay-Sachs carriers has also been identified in a French-Canadian population and in a Cajun population from Louisiana.

When a disease occurs at an elevated frequency in a specific population, an agency may conduct an educational screening program for carriers. Screening is especially effective for Tay-Sachs disease because the test is very accurate and relatively inexpensive. Screening programs have reduced dramatically the incidence of Tay-Sachs disease among Ashkenazi Jews.

How does screening reduce the frequency of a genetic disease? For a child to have Tay-Sachs disease, both parents must be carriers. If screening shows that both are carriers, several options are open. The parents may choose to have no children; they may try to adopt children; or if the woman does become pregnant, she may choose to undergo **amniocentesis,** which is a medical procedure in which a sample of **amniotic fluid** from the womb is removed and used to determine the presence of abnormal genes in the fetus. In the latter case, if it is determined that she carries an affected child, the parents could elect to abort the fetus.

Unfortunately, because most people do not know of Tay-Sachs disease or falsely believe that it is exclusively a Jewish disease, they do not seek testing. As a result, most of the recent cases of Tay-Sachs disease are among non-Jews.

Probabilities of Inheriting a Specific Genetic Disease If both members of a couple are carriers of Tay-Sachs disease, what is the probability of their having an affected child? A carrier has one normal allele and one abnormal one, and so each parent in our example has the genotype *Tt*. The mating is represented as *Tt* × *Tt*. Since the disease is caused by a recessive allele, the affected individual has the genotype *tt* (homozygous recessive). Because the alleles *T* and *t* have an equal chance of being included in any sex cell, half the father's sperm carries the *t* allele, as will half the mother's ova.

What is the probability of two carriers producing a Tay-Sachs child? For a child to inherit the disease, he or she must inherit a recessive allele from each parent. The probability of inheriting a *t* from a specific parent is ½. What about inheriting a *t* from both parents? The answer to this question is based on the statistical principle that the probability of the occurrence of two independent, random events is the product of the events' separate probabilities. Inheriting the recessive allele from the father is independent of inheriting the allele from the mother. Thus, the answer to our question is ½ × ½, or ¼.

When we take population data and individual mating probabilities into consideration, we can calculate the overall probability of having a Tay-Sachs child. In the Ashkenazi Jewish population, the incidence of carriers is ¹⁄₂₇. The chance that two carriers will mate is ¹⁄₂₇ × ¹⁄₂₇, or ¹⁄₇₂₉. Since the probability of two carriers producing a Tay-Sachs child is ¼, the probability of a Tay-Sachs child for any people from this population is ¹⁄₇₂₉ × ¼, or ¹⁄₂₉₁₆. Until recently, this was the actual rate of such births; but as mentioned earlier, because of screening programs, the percentage is much lower today.

Genetic Counseling When a person suspects that he or she or a relative has a genetic disease or abnormality, that person might seek genetic counseling. Or a couple who has already conceived a child with an abnormality may go to the genetic counselor to seek information about the probability of conceiving another child with a genetic defect. A **genetic counselor** is someone who advises prospective parents or an affected individual of the probability of having a child with a genetic problem.

In many cases, members of a specific cultural or ethnic group that is characterized by a high frequency of some inherited disease might wish to know what the chances are that they are carrying the abnormal allele. This is the case for Tay-Sachs disease among Ashkenazi Jews. As further examples, African Americans and certain other people show a

---

cystic fibrosis A recessive genetic abnormality that affects the production of mucus in the lungs.

See the Online Learning Center for an Internet Activity on Tay-Sachs Disease.

amniocentesis A medical technique in which amniotic fluid is removed for study of the fetus.

amniotic fluid The fluid surrounding the fetus.

See the Online Learning Center for an Internet Activity on genetic counseling.

genetic counselor A medical professional who advises prospective parents or a person affected by a genetic disease of the prob-ability of having a child with a genetic problem.

high frequency of the blood disorder sickle-cell anemia (Chapter 5); Mediterranean peoples display a high frequency of another blood disorder, beta thalassemia; the general northern European population has a high rate of cystic fibrosis (a respiratory disease); and Inuit ("Eskimos") have a high frequency of kushokwin (a protein disease). In fact, elevated frequencies of particular genetic abnormalities characterize most human populations.

For many diseases, the inheritance pattern is more complex than in Tay-Sachs or cystic fibrosis. In these cases, a genetic counselor must construct a pedigree to determine the probability of a concerned individual's being a carrier or having an allele or alleles for a specific genetic problem. A genetic counselor can work out probabilities only for genetic disorders with a known mode of inheritance, and the validity of a probability calculation is dependent on how much information is known about the client's kin.

The Control of Human Biological Evolution

Techniques for improving the human gene pool are referred to as **eugenics.** The simplest eugenic methods involve the control of breeding. **Negative eugenics** is any process whereby some people are prevented from mating. The people involved are usually labeled undesirable by some group or government. The converse is **positive eugenics** for encouraging certain people to mate. Adolf Hitler practiced both positive and negative eugenics. He encouraged and sometimes forced people he called "members of the superrace" to mate with each other in breeding camps. He discouraged others from mating in the most extreme way possible—he had them killed. These practices bestowed a sinister connotation on the word *eugenics.*

Today, new eugenic methods aim first to eliminate deleterious genes and eventually to alter the human genome. Methods now on the horizon go well beyond changing the frequency of alleles in a population by controlling conceptions and matings. The hope of most eugenic researchers is the actual altering of the genetic material to produce a healthier person. The industrial or experimental technology to do this is called **genetic engineering.** A few of the things that may be applied to human genetic engineering in the near future are discussed in this section.

Regulatory Genes First identified in the 1960s, a **regulatory gene** codes for a protein that acts as a switch for a structural gene or another regulatory gene. A structural gene codes for specific polypeptide chains that make up protein molecules such as insulin. A regulatory gene either allows the second gene to express itself or shuts it down. So, for example, the gene that codes for insulin can be turned on or off by its regulatory gene.

Genetic diseases that result from the faulty action of a regulatory gene may be managed by treatment that leads to turning the gene either on or off. As we discover what chemicals affect what genes, regulation may be controlled. For instance, it is believed that aging is controlled by regulatory genes and that the aging process could be arrested if the cytoplasmic products that influence the aging regulatory genes could be controlled.

Restriction Enzymes In 1973, scientists discovered that certain types of enzymes, called **restriction enzymes,** could be used to "cut" the DNA at specific sites. This has enabled scientists to cut out specific genes, which can then be spliced into a different organism. For instance, the human gene for insulin has been spliced into the genetic system of a bacterium. The resulting bacterial progeny produced human insulin, which is marketed under the name "Humulin."

Artificial Genes In 1976, it was announced that a completely **artificial gene,** used to replace a defective gene in a virus, had been synthesized. Will we be able to manufacture genes that will make us have more endurance, be resistant to disease, and be more intelligent? Perhaps these "designer genes" will be the wave of the future.

Cloning and Stem Cell Research "Humulin" was made possible, in part, by cloning. **Cloning** is the process of producing a group of genes, cells, or whole organisms that have the same genetic constitution. Once the human gene for insulin was introduced into bacteria

See the Online Learning Center for an Internet Activity on prenatal genetic testing.

eugenics The study of the methods that can improve the inherited qualities of a species.

negative eugenics Method of eliminating deleterious alleles from the gene pool by encouraging persons with such alleles not to reproduce.

positive eugenics Method of increasing the frequency of desirable traits by encouraging reproduction by individuals with these traits.

See the Online Learning Center for an Internet Activity on genetic engineering.

genetic engineering The altering of the genetic material to create specific characteristics in individuals.

regulatory gene A segment of DNA that functions to initiate or block the function of another gene.

restriction enzyme Enzyme used to "cut" the DNA molecule at specific sites; used in recombinant DNA technology.

artificial gene A gene that is made in a laboratory and used in place of a defective or undesirable gene.

cloning The process of asexual reproduction in an otherwise multicellular animal.

by recombinant DNA techniques, repeated mitosis in the bacteria continued to produce the same gene over and over again. The gene originated from a body (somatic) cell, not from a sex cell.

Whole organisms can be cloned. In fact, a type of cloning has been done with plants for years. In 1952, a tadpole became the first animal to be cloned. In 1996, a lamb named Dolly was the first mammal to be cloned from adult body cells. Since that time several other mammals have been cloned, including sheep, goats, cows, mice, pigs, cats, and rabbits. Between 1998 and 1999, Dolly gave birth to four normal noncloned offspring. Although they possess the same genotype, such clones are not exact duplicates of the donor since environmental factors both before and after birth are responsible for much variation.

Dolly, who prematurely aged and had developed arthritis at 5½ years of age, was euthanized in 2003 at 6 years old, which is about half the normal life span for sheep. She was put down because of a lung disease she might have caught from being with other sheep. Although Dolly's health problem might not have been due to the fact she was cloned and although hundreds of other apparently healthy mammals have been cloned since 1996, Dolly's early death sent up a red flag about attempts to clone a human.

Cloning of nonhuman mammals might affect humans in many ways. In 2003, the U.S. Food and Drug Administration (FDA) approved the use of cloned animals for food. In the future cloned animals may be genetically altered to, for instance, make their meat leaner. Over 40 genetically altered plants such as soybeans, sugar beets, corn, tomatoes, and cantaloupes have been approved for commercial use in the United States, whereas other nations have banned their use. Plants might be altered to make them resistant to insects, resistant to disease, or tolerant of cold or drought and to have improved nutritional characteristics. There are numerous questions about the safety of genetically manipulated foods and vaccines.

embryonic stem cells Undifferentiated cells from an embryo with the potential to become any type of adult specialized cells.

Another aspect of cloning is the possibility of cloning tissue and individual organs from human **embryonic stem cells.** These are cells extracted from an ovum five days after fertilization. They can be induced to develop into virtually any type of tissue or organ. A person with medical needs would have some of his or her own cells used to create an embryo. The cloned cells would then be used to produce a needed tissue or organ. It is hoped that this therapeutic cloning some day will be able to provide tissue and organs that would not be rejected by the body to treat heart disease, cancer, Alzheimer's disease, and other medical problems. In the future genetically modified and cloned animals might provide human tissue and organs for medical use.

There are numerous technical, ethical, and political issues involved with cloning, stem cell research, and other types of genetic manipulation. From a technical point of view cloning is still inefficient. It took 277 attempts to clone Dolly and 947 attempts before the first cloned mouse was produced. The ethical and political concerns are too numerous to cover comprehensively here, but they include the concern that genetic manipulation is "playing God" and is unnatural, that cloned individuals would not have a soul, and that genetic methods could be used to create classes of individual such as superwarriors.

gene therapy A genetic-engineering method in which genetic material is manipulated in ways that include removing, replacing, or altering a gene.

Gene Therapy **Gene therapy** involves detecting a genetic defect and correcting it by replacing the DNA sequence that causes the defect with the correct DNA sequence. The first successful gene therapy was performed in 1990. White blood cells of a four-year-old girl suffering from ADA deficiency, an immune deficiency disease, were modified with normal DNA and transfused back into her.

Other successful gene therapies followed, but several patients have developed cancers. This brought about a reexamination of gene therapy techniques. Yet many researchers in this area believe that gene therapy will be a common medical practice sometime in the early part of the twenty-first century.

Consequences of Genetic Engineering Any modification of human genetic material is controversial. Some ethical implications of genetic engineering are discussed in Box 3-2. Here, we will mention two possible biological problems with genetic engineering. The first is the reduction of variability within a population.

There are numerous ethical concerns that are being ushered into our consciousness due to our growing knowledge of human genetics. Some of those concerns revolve around the question of who will be able to take advantage of the medical techniques that result from this knowledge. For instance, there is hope that in the future more and more genetic diseases will be treated or even cured. Yet in twenty-first-century America, millions of people do not have health insurance and cannot afford basic medical care. In the future, will only the wealthy profit from what might be very expensive management of genetic diseases? A genetically engineered drug for cancer, first used in 2001, costs $25,000 a year.

Another concern is that of privacy. We are developing the ability to predict for which diseases a person may be at risk in his or her lifetime. If this information is available to insurance companies, health and life insurance might be denied or be very expensive. Knowing that insurance might be denied, people might avoid having tests to determine if they are at risk for genetic diseases or genetically influenced conditions. In turn, those people who do not have these tests done may not be able to take advantage of medical treatments in time to save their lives. These issues have been debated in the United States Congress for many years. In 2005, the Senate passed a bill that would prevent potential employers from denying employment based on genetic information. The bill would prevent insurance companies from refusing to issue insurance policies or raising premiums based on genetic testing results. The Bush administration supports the bill. As this book goes to press, the House of Representatives is considering a similar bill.

Imagine a situation where, by using eugenic means, we could eliminate the allele for a recessive genetic disease through detection of heterozygotes. This is a fine goal. However, as we will discuss in detail in Chapter 5, people who are heterozygous for the sickle-cell allele have considerable protection from malaria. Other heterozygous genotypes seem to provide protection from other diseases, even if the homozygous recessive condition causes severe illness or death. The paradox is that by eliminating the genetic disease, we might be eliminating protection from some other factor.

A second possible biological negative consequence is the fact that a gene can have more than one effect on the phenotype. An engineered change of one gene may have effects on the individual far beyond those that are intended, and some of those effects might be deleterious.

Although our knowledge of genetics has increased geometrically since the beginning of the twentieth century, there is still much that we do not know. One of the things about which we know little is the multiple effects of genes and the effect of genes on each other.

Summary

Genetics may be one of the most important concerns of people in the twenty-first century. In the previous century, we learned about the mode of inheritance of many recessive and dominant genetic abnormalities as well as ones with more complex patterns of inheritance. The field of genetic counseling has grown as our knowledge of human genetics has expanded.

Already geneticists can, in a limited way, manipulate the human genome. In the future, human cloning, gene therapy, and other forms of genetic engineering may become common practices to cure genetic abnormalities, create children with specific characteristics, and allow couples to have special types of children, such as clones of themselves. Political, ethical, philosophical, and biological concerns about eugenics will no doubt fill the pages of newspapers, magazines, and journals for decades to come.

ADVANCES IN THE MOLECULAR STUDY OF GENETICS

The advent of high-tech methods of analyzing nucleic acids has allowed for rapid and accurate recording of the genetic code. This has led to a better understanding of what a gene is as well as providing insights into evolutionary relationships between species and relationships among members of the same species.

What Is a Gene?

We can examine this question in the light of studies of the structure and function of the hereditary material, the DNA molecule. The concept of the gene was originally developed as part of a model to explain the mechanisms of heredity when the actual physical and chemical nature of the hereditary material was unknown.

A gene is a biological unit of inheritance; it is a section of DNA that has a specific function. That function could be the coding of a particular protein, a polypeptide chain; or it could be a regulatory function, that is, controlling of the activity of other genes. In the first situation, the 438 nucleotides that code for the structure of the hemoglobin beta chain can be thought of as a gene.

Linkage Maps Because of the distinctive inheritance pattern of X-linked traits, geneticists have identified many genes that reside on the X chromosome. In the 1950s, geneticists identified the first human autosomal genes that are associated on the same chromosome. Such sets of genes are called **linkage groups.** Genes located close together on the same chromosome tend to be inherited together since crossing-over seldom occurs between them. Genes located far apart on large chromosomes, however, behave as if they were on separate chromosomes, since crossing-over occurs frequently between them. Thus they recombine according to the principle of independent assortment.

Crossing-over data can be used to determine the linear order of genes in a linkage group. Since the frequency of crossing-over is proportional to the distance between genes on a chromatid, genes that are farther apart will cross over more frequently.

The next step is to associate linkage groups with specific chromosomes. Small chromosomal aberrations are often associated with unusual inheritance patterns. These can be used to determine the location of specific autosomes on a specific chromosome. Today we know that cystic fibrosis is located on chromosome 7, sickle-cell anemia on chromosome 11, phenylketonuria on chromosome 12, and Tay-Sachs disease on chromosome 15.

The next stage is the development of a physical map. A physical map includes specific features of the chromosome and the banding patterns that develop when the chromosome is treated with certain dyes. These features are then associated with specific genes and DNA sequences called gene markers. The first physical maps were published in 1992. By 1993, simple physical maps were produced for all human chromosomes. Figure 3.7 is a map of the X chromosome.

The Human Genome

As we saw in Chapter 2, the genetic material, DNA, communicates information through a code. Computer scientists as well as biologists appreciate the elegance of the DNA code. Some futurists envision computer storage devices based on codes at the molecular level. The words in this text, maintained on a hard disk in the authors' office, might some day actually be coded in the computer of the future by artificial DNA or a molecule like it.

Geneticists today are actively studying the genetic code in order to understand how the code works. In 1977, researchers developed the first efficient methodology for determining the sequence of nucleotides or base

linkage groups Sets of genes that are found on the same chromosome.

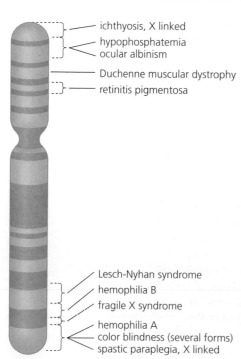

ichthyosis, X linked
hypophosphatemia
ocular albinism
Duchenne muscular dystrophy
retinitis pigmentosa

Lesch-Nyhan syndrome
hemophilia B
fragile X syndrome
hemophilia A
color blindness (several forms)
spastic paraplegia, X linked

Figure 3.7 Gene Map of X Chromosome

Ninety-eight years after the rediscovery of Mendel's principles of segregation and independent assortment and two years before the first draft of the human genome was completed, essentially the entire genetic code of an animal was decoded for the first time. Although few humans feel akin to that animal, the methods used to determine its genetic code have proved useful to the Human Genome Project. The animal is *Caenorhabditis elegans*, one of a group of small invertebrates known as nematodes or roundworms. Its DNA sequence is made up of about 97 million base pairs representing about 19,000 genes. More than 40 percent of the proteins coded by those genes match known genes in humans.

Just as Mendel's discovery of the basic principles of genetics was the jumping-off point for understanding more complex principles of genetics, the decoding of the DNA sequence in *C. elegans* is providing new strategies useful in other genome projects. It also is providing a method of comparison that will help gauge what genes are common to all or most organisms.

This landmark achievement helped usher in a new world of bioinformatics. Bioinformatics is the analysis of biological information using computer and statistical techniques. In its genomic application, researchers in bioinformatics are developing methods to search genome databases quickly, to compare the genomes of different organisms, and to construct hypotheses that predict DNA sequences in organisms whose DNA sequences have not been completed. Many of the applications of bioinformatics can only be imagined at this time.

One of the most comprehensive genomic databases is KEGG (*Kyoto Encyclopedia of Genes and Genomes*). As of February 7, 2005, KEGG had computer databases for 233 organisms. Most of these organisms are bacteria, but there are also databases for several animals whose sequences where decoded after *C. elegans*. These animals include humans (*Homo sapiens*), the chimpanzee (*Pan troglodytes*), the house mouse (*Mus musculus*), the Norway and brown rat (*Rattus norvegicus*), the chicken (*Gallus gallus*), the zebrafish (*Danio rerio*), the Japanese pufferfish (*Fugu rubiripes*), the malaria-carrying mosquito (*Anopheles gambiae*), the fruit fly (*Drosophila melanogaster*), the sea squirt (*Ciona intestinalis*), and a nematode related to *C. elegans* (*Caenorhabditis briggsae*). Each year more and more genomes are being decoded. In 1995, the only genome sequences that had been decoded were those of two types of bacteria. Between January 2003 and February 2005, the genomes of more than 124 organisms were decoded in draft or final form.

Sources: The C. elegans Sequencing Consortium, "Genome Sequence of the Nematode C. elegans: A Platform for Investigating Biology," *Science*, 282 (1998), pp. 2012–2017; Kyoto Encyclopedia of Genes and Genomes, www.genome.ad.jp/kegg.

---

pairs in a strand of DNA. Almost immediately, biologists began to ponder the possibility of determining the base pair sequence for all human genes. Although in 1977 such a dream appeared technologically light-years away, by the second half of the 1980s, molecular biologists were beginning to think that such a project was feasible.

It is estimated that the entire human genome contains about three billion base pairs or nucleotides. In the mid-1980s, biologists estimated that one technician could sequence 100,000 base pairs a year, which meant that it would take 30,000 person-years to sequence the entire human genome. The cost was established at $3 billion. Out of this early interest came the Human Genome Project. In 1988, the National Center for Human Genome Research was established by the National Institutes of Health. The first director, from 1988 through 1992, was James Watson, who, with Francis Crick, had first determined the structure of DNA in 1953. The project formally began in 1990 and was seen as a 15-year effort. A private corporation, Celera Genomics, head by Craig Venter, and the publicly funded Human Genome Project, headed by Francis Collins, jointly announced the completion of the first draft in June 2000, five years ahead of schedule.

What will the sequencing of the human genome contribute to society? From a metaphysical point of view, it will change many people's view of humanity's place in nature. Previously most sources stated that the human genome contained about 100,000 genes. Now it appears that there might be fewer than 30,000 genes that code for human proteins. This puts us closer to the number of genes in the genome of the roundworm, *Caenorhabditis elegans* (see Box 3-3).

An understanding of the genomes of different organisms will force a rethinking about the complexities of evolution and how subtle differences in the genome can have enormous

See the Online Learning Center for an Internet Activity on the Human Genome Project.

Box 3-4
DNA Fingerprinting

In the 1880s, Sir Francis Galton, a cousin of Charles Darwin, reported that no two people could have the same fingerprint pattern. Since that time the use of fingerprint analysis has played a central role in criminal investigation. In 1984, the British geneticist Alex Jeffreys developed another powerful identification tool—DNA fingerprinting. Many state governments and the federal government are considering legislation that would require that all felons be genetically fingerprinted in the same way that they are required to be fingerprinted. Since its development DNA fingerprinting has been used to both convict and exonerate hundreds of criminal suspects. For example, between 1992 and May 2004, one organization alone was responsible for proving the innocence of 144 inmates jailed for a variety of charges, including rape and murder.[1]

DNA fingerprinting relies on the analysis of the genetic material itself. Except for identical twins, each person's genetic code is unique. DNA analysis can be done using blood, skin, hair, saliva, or semen that is left at a crime scene. In this way, an individual can be identified or excluded as the culprit.

The method involves the use of enzymes to break up the DNA recovered at the crime scene and the DNA obtained from the suspect. The DNA fragments are then separated in an electric field, producing a specific pattern. These patterns are the "fingerprints" that can then be compared.

The area of controversy in the courtroom today revolves around the probability that a particular fingerprint is unique.

Since forensic scientists do not analyze the entire genome of an individual, it is theoretically possible for two people to show the same pattern. The probability of this occurring with today's methods varies from 1 in 100,000 to 1 in 100 million. More complex methods being developed will reduce this probability to about zero.

DNA fingerprinting is used for more than criminal investigation. In some circumstances it can be used to identify victims of disasters and unidentified bodies. It is also used in determining paternity and for historical studies. In 1998, DNA testing was used to help determine who the ancestors of Thomas Jefferson were and whether he had children by one of his slaves, Sally Hemings. The researchers concluded that he most likely had at least one child and maybe more with Sally.[2] However, some researchers believe that it was not Thomas Jefferson who fathered one or more of Sally Hemings's children, but one of his relatives.[3] DNA fingerprinting methods are also used to test for the presence of specific alleles and in genetic engineering research.

[1] The Innocence Project at http://www.innocenceproject.org.

[2] E. A. Foster, et al., "Jefferson Fathered Slave's Last Child," *Nature,* 396 (1998), pp. 27–28.

[3] "Thomas Jefferson and Sally Hemings: A Brief Account, February 2003," www.monticello.org/plantation/hemingscontro/hemings-jefferson_contro.html.

---

phenotypic consequences. In genetic terms, humans are very similar to the rest of the living world. A better understanding of the minute differences between us and the rest of the animal world will help us understand our connection to the rest of the living world as well as our uniqueness. An understanding of animal genomes will help us understand the most basic questions about life, including: How do genes interact with each other? How do mutations occur? How does DNA repair itself? How are proteins manufactured?

In a more down-to-earth vein, an understanding of the human genome will contribute to society's health by permitting the identification, and ultimately the treatment and perhaps cure, of genetically based disease, both physical and behavioral. A greater understanding of the human genome also will lead to an ever-more-reliable forensic use of DNA analysis (see Box 3-4).

Developing from the Human Genome Project is a new academic and commercial discipline, **bioinformatics.** This field combines knowledge from computer science, mathematics, and genomic sequencing to form a discipline focused on the analysis of genetic information and the practical use of that information.

bioinformatics A new discipline dedicated to the analysis of genetic information and the practical use of that information.

The Human Genome Project is not without controversy. Some people ask if we should undertake the task of mapping the human genome. What would be the consequences? A complete human gene map would lead to improved diagnosis of hereditary diseases and the development of new drugs for genetic abnormalities. The mapping of the human genome also could lead to ethical dilemmas and abuses. Whose genome should be taken as prototypically human? Would only the rich be able to take advantage of the health benefits gained from the new technology? And who would control the technology? Control of the human genome could lead to the engineering of specific types of humans and could create an elitist society. Yet work continues on the project, with the proponents believing that the benefits of its success will far outweigh any problems it creates.

Summary

Today, a gene is seen as a section of DNA that has a specific function, such as the coding of a particular protein. Geneticists have been able to identify the location of specific genes on specific chromosomes. Such mapping has been accomplished through linkage studies and identification of specific DNA sequences with specific genes.

One of the most ambitious scientific ventures of the past decade is the Human Genome Project, the mapping of the entire human genome. On the one hand, such knowledge is seen as crucial for research on genetic disease. On the other hand, the project has critics who point to numerous ways that the information obtained could be used in unethical and elitist ways.

Key Terms

ABO blood-type system, *56*
achondroplastic dwarfism, *59*
agglutination, *57*
alcaptonuria, *56*
amniocentesis, *66*
amniotic fluid, *66*
antibodies, *56*
antigen, *56*
artificial gene, *67*
bioinformatics, *72*
carrier, *65*
chromosomal aberration, *62*
chromosomal sex, *61*
cloning, *67*
codominant, *56*
cystic fibrosis, *66*
deletion, *62*

Down syndrome, *62*
duplication, *63*
embryonic stem cells, *68*
enzyme, *65*
erythroblastosis fetalis, *57*
eugenics, *67*
gene therapy, *68*
genetic counselor, *66*
genetic engineering, *67*
genetic sex, *61*
genome, *65*
gonad, *61*
hemolytic disease, *57*
hemophilia, *61*
inversion, *63*
Klinefelter syndrome, *62*
linkage groups, *70*

multiple alleles, *56*
negative eugenics, *67*
nondisjunction, *62*
pedigree, *60*
phenotypic sex, *61*
phenylketonuria (PKU), *59*
polymorphic, *56*
positive eugenics, *67*
regulatory gene, *67*
restriction enzyme, *67*
Rh blood-type system, *57*
secretor allele, *58*
sex-limited gene, *61*
Tay-Sachs disease, *65*
translocation, *63*
trisomy 21, *62*
Turner syndrome, *62*

Study Questions

1. Why are studies of the genetics of blood types of more use to anthropologists than are studies of IQ or skin color?
2. What is meant by the term *multiple alleles*?
3. How does Y-linked and X-linked inheritance differ from autosomal inheritance?
4. What is the difference between phenotypic sex, chromosomal sex, and genetic sex?
5. What is a common error of meiosis, and to what type of problems does this error lead?
6. In what ways can human genetics be purposefully altered? What might be possible in the future?

See the Online Learning Center for additional study questions.

7. The book discusses two possible negative effects of eugenics. What are they? Can you think of other possible negatives of eugenics? What are the positive aspects of eugenics?

8. What is the Human Genome Project? What methods do the scientists working on this project use to accomplish their goals?

Critical Thinking Questions

1. Today there are many medical tests that can determine if a person has a particular genetic abnormality before the onset of symptoms. Huntington's disease is characterized by neurological degeneration, and the symptoms first appear in the patient's 30s. The disease is fatal. An infant is tested and found to have Huntington's disease, although the symptoms will not show themselves until middle age. What would you do with this information? Would you tell the child? When would you tell the child?

2. In November 2001, human embryos were cloned for the first time. One of the possible applications of this technology is to produce replacement tissue and organs for people who might need them and to do research on human diseases such as heart disease and Parkinson's disease. The reaction to this cloning was mixed. Some greeted the news with high expectations of major medical breakthroughs in the near future. Others saw it as immoral manipulation of nature. The detractors also saw it as creating life in order to destroy it (during experimentation some cells would die). What do you think about experimenting with human embryos, genetic manipulation of genetic materials, and other eugenic techniques?

3. What is a gene? Is a person simply the totality of his or her genes? Why are people and all living things more than just a collection of chemicals? Or are they just that?

Suggested Readings

Lewin, B. *Genes,* 8th ed. Upper Saddle River, NJ: Prentice-Hall, 2004. This is a popular introductory text on general genetics. It presents an encyclopedic treatment of genetics and, as such, is an excellent reference book.

Read, A. P., and T. Strachen. *Human Molecular Genetics,* 2nd ed. New York: John Wiley, 2000. This text covers molecular genetics up to the recent developments in eugenics and the Human Genome Project.

Silver, L. M. *Remaking Eden: Cloning and Beyond in a Brave New World.* New York: Avon/Weidenfeld and Nicoson, 1998. This book tells what can currently be done with genetic engineering and what might be possible later in the twenty-first century. It also discusses the ethical, political, and practical concerns people have about genetic engineering.

Watson, J. D., et al. *Molecular Biology of the Gene,* 5th ed. Menlo Park, CA: Benjamin/Cummings, 2003. This two-volume set, written by five researchers and teachers, including one of the discoverers of the structure of DNA, gives a detailed discussion of DNA and gene structure.

Suggested Websites

March of Dimes Fact Sheets (information on various birth defects and genetics): **www.modimes.org; see Birth Defects and Genetics**

National Institutes of Health: **www.nih.gov**

Tay-Sachs Information and Links: **www.ntsad.org/t-sachs.htm**

Chapter 4

Population Genetics

Amish family, Pennsylvania.

The object is to combine certain ideas derived from a consideration of . . . a population of organisms, with the concepts of the factorial scheme of inheritance, so as to state the principle of Natural Selection in the form of a rigorous mathematical theorem. •

—R. A. Fisher (1890–1962)

Chapter Outline

A Model of Population Genetics
Populations
Genetic Equilibrium
Using the Genetic-Equilibrium Model
Summary

Mechanisms of Evolutionary Change
Mutations

Genetic Drift, Population Bottlenecking,
*   and the Founder Principle*
Gene Flow
Nonrandom Mating
Differential Fertility
Summary

See the Online Learning Center for a chapter summary, chapter outline, and learning objectives.

After Reading This Chapter, You Should Be Able to Answer These Questions:

1. In evolutionary terms, what is a population?
2. What is genetic equilibrium? Can a population ever be in genetic equilibrium?
3. What are some of the uses of the Hardy-Weinberg equilibrium model?
4. The chapter discusses five major mechanisms of evolutionary change. What are they?
5. What does it mean when we say that mutations are random? What causes mutations? Mutations are the main source of which biological phenomenon?
6. What are the differences between genetic drift, population bottlenecking, and the founder principle?
7. How does gene flow change the gene pool of a population?
8. In what ways is mating nonrandom? How does nonrandom mating change the gene pool?
9. In the simplest terms, what is natural selection?

In 1930, Ronald A. Fisher published a book that evaluated Darwin's theory in terms of mathematics and statistics. In *The Genetical Theory of Natural Selection,* Fisher described equations that showed how genetic diversity within populations allows more possibilities for adapting to environments.

Up to this point, we have been concerned mainly with the mechanisms of heredity in the individual and in family groups. Evolution, however, occurs in reproductive populations. This chapter focuses on the dynamics of populations and various mathematical principles that measure genetic changes in populations.

A MODEL OF POPULATION GENETICS

The individual is not the unit of evolution, although a person does change over time. An individual gets taller and heavier, and perhaps his or her hair changes color; other changes occur that are variously labeled "growth," "development," and "decline." Yet although an individual today is not the same individual he or she will be tomorrow, that person is not evolving. Likewise, evolution is not a case of people producing offspring different from themselves, for no two individuals, whether contemporaries or living at different times and whether related or unrelated, are exactly alike. Variation is not evolution.

Populations

reproductive population A group of organisms capable of successful reproduction.

reproductive isolating mechanism A mechanism that prevents reproduction from occurring between two populations.

The unit of evolution is the **reproductive population.** The reproductive population can be defined as a group of organisms potentially capable of successful reproduction.

Successful reproduction requires sexual behavior culminating in copulation, fertilization, normal development of the fetus, and production of offspring that are normal and healthy and capable of reproducing in turn. A number of conditions, called **reproductive isolating mechanisms,** can prevent closely related populations from exchanging genes by preventing successful reproduction. Examples of such mechanisms include geographical barriers, such as a river or a mountain range. Others involve anatomical and behavioral characteristics. Several types of reproductive isolating mechanisms are discussed in Chapter 5.

Of course, successful reproduction of a population requires a rate of reproduction sufficient to sustain the population. As we saw in Chapter 1, Thomas R. Malthus pointed out that although a population has the potential for very rapid growth, environmental factors can severely limit the number of individuals that survive. The number of individuals produced each generation must be great enough to compensate for deaths due to accident, predation, disease, and so on. However, the rate of reproduction cannot be so great that the population will increase to the point at which it can no longer be supported by its food sources or other elements in the environment. In other words, a successful reproductive rate is one that maintains a balance between population size and the potentials and limitations of the environment.

species The largest natural population whose members are able to reproduce successfully among themselves but not with members of other species.

The largest reproductive population is the **species.** The members of a species are potentially capable of successful reproduction among themselves but not with members of other species. Species can be broken down into smaller reproductive populations, which are to some degree and often temporarily isolated from one another.

Describing a Population Just as one can speak of the phenotype of an individual, one also can speak of the phenotype of a population. Since a population is made up of varied individuals, such a description must be handled statistically. For example, one can calculate the average stature for a population and the variation from that average. It is also possible to calculate the percentage of blood type O, blue eyes, red hair, and so on, and emerge with a statistical profile.

As stated earlier, no two individuals are ever alike; the possible combinations of alleles are staggering. Nevertheless, the frequency of alleles in a population may remain relatively constant over many generations. What we have are individuals being formed out of a pool of genes that can be combined in an almost infinite number of ways. New combinations do not necessarily change the frequencies of any allele in the next generation (Figure 4.1).

The sum of all alleles carried by the members of a population is known as the **gene pool.** Since a population is made up of many individuals, each represented by a unique genotype, a gene pool is described in statistical terms. The frequency of alleles in the gene pool can be calculated with formulas that will be discussed in a moment. Since each body cell has the same genetic components, each individual can be thought of as contributing one of those cells to the gene pool. From these cells, the genes can be extracted and tallied.

For example, if the alleles for PTC tasting in a population are tallied, the result may be that 41.3 percent of them are dominant (*T*) and 58.7 percent are recessive (*t*). Further examination may reveal that 17.1 percent of the genotypes that emerge from the gene pool of PTC alleles are homozygous dominant, whereas 48.4 percent are heterozygous and 34.5 percent are homozygous recessive. A complete statistical description of the genotype of a population would require that we know the frequency of every allele in the gene pool.

Genetic Equilibrium

Before we discuss the mechanisms of evolution, evolution must first be defined in terms of populations. **Evolution** can be defined as a significant change in the gene pool of a population. For example, if the frequency of the allele *T* changes from 41.3 percent to 42.1 percent, we can say that the population has evolved.

A population is evolving if the frequencies of its alleles are changing. It is not evolving if these frequencies remain constant, a situation termed **genetic equilibrium.** Since several factors can bring about frequency changes, it is best to begin with a consideration of genetic equilibrium and then to follow with a separate consideration of each factor that brings about change.

A Model of Genetic Equilibrium In building a model of genetic equilibrium, we can simplify things by considering a hypothetical gene. We will assume that this gene occurs as two alleles, *A* and *a*, each with a frequency of ½. The symbol *f* will be used to indicate "frequency of." Therefore, we can write our example as follows: $f(A) = ½$ and $f(a) = ½$. If these are the only alleles for this gene, the frequencies must add up to 1, or unity. This gives us the formula

$$f(A) + f(a) = ½ + ½ = 1$$

If the frequencies of the alleles are each ½, what are the frequencies of the different individual genotypes? As we saw in the last chapter, the probability of two independent events both occurring is the product of their separate probabilities. Therefore, if $f(A) = ½$, it follows that $f(AA) = ½ \times ½ = ¼$. Thus, one-fourth of the population is homozygous dominant.

Similarly, $f(Aa) = 2 \times ½ \times ½ = ½$. Why the number 2? Because we are including two separate cases, *Aa* and *aA*. While the origin of the alleles differs in each, the genotype is the same. We must then add the two cases together. Therefore, one-half the population is heterozygous. Finally, $f(aa) = ½ \times ½ = ¼$; one-fourth of the population is homozygous recessive.

Now suppose the individuals within this population mate at random. The possible matings are *AA* × *AA*, *AA* × *Aa*, *AA* × *aa*, *Aa* × *Aa*, *Aa* × *aa*, and *aa* × *aa*. Three of the six

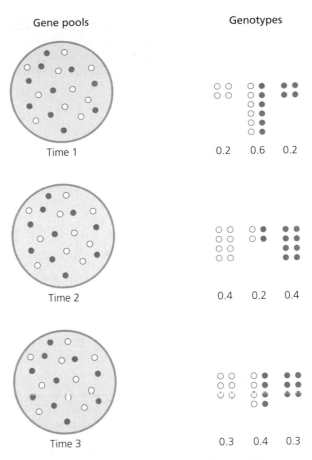

Gene pools   Genotypes

Time 1   0.2   0.6   0.2

Time 2   0.4   0.2   0.4

Time 3   0.3   0.4   0.3

Figure 4.1 The Gene Pool Even though the allele frequencies remain constant, in this case 10 white and 10 colored, the genotype frequencies can differ through time.

gene pool The sum of all alleles carried by the members of a population.

evolution Change in the frequencies of alleles within a gene pool of a population over time.

genetic equilibrium A hypothetical state in which a population is not evolving because the allele frequencies remain constant over time.

Table 4.1 Frequencies of Mating Types

Mating Type	Frequency
AA × AA	¼ × ¼ = ¹⁄₁₆
AA × Aa	2 × ¼ × ½ = ¼
AA × aa	2 × ¼ × ¼ = ⅛
Aa × Aa	½ × ½ = ¼
Aa × aa	2 × ½ × ¼ = ¼
aa × aa	¼ × ¼ = ¹⁄₁₆
Total	1

matings can be accomplished in two ways; for example, $AA \times Aa$ also could be $Aa \times AA$. To simplify matters in each of these three cases, the two situations will be combined (added) as one mating.

How frequent is each of the mating types? To find out, one multiplies the frequencies of each genotype. For example, the frequency of the first type, $AA \times AA$, is ¼ × ¼ = ¹⁄₁₆. In the case in which mating types can be accomplished in two ways, the separate frequencies must be added together. This is why the number 2 must be included. The frequencies of the mating types are shown in Table 4.1; note that the frequencies add up to 1.

Since we are interested in seeing how the frequencies of the alleles change between generations, the next step is to calculate the frequency of offspring produced. Table 4.2 presents a series of calculations showing the contribution of each mating type to the next generation. The first case, $AA \times AA$, occurs one-sixteenth of the time and therefore produces one-sixteenth of all the offspring. Since all these offspring are AA, we can say that this mating type contributes ¹⁄₁₆ AA children to the next generation, as shown in the AA column in Table 4.2.

The second case, $AA \times Aa$, accounts for one-fourth of all matings, and therefore this mating type produces one-fourth of all the offspring. Of these offspring, one-half are AA and one-half are Aa. Since ½ of ¼ is ⅛, ⅛ is placed in the AA column and ⅛ in the Aa column. The same procedure is followed for calculating the contributions of the other mating types.

Next, we add up the numbers in each column. We see that one-fourth of the total offspring are AA, one-half Aa, and one-fourth aa. In other words, the relative frequencies of the varying genotypes have remained unchanged from the previous generation. The population is therefore in genetic equilibrium.

The Hardy-Weinberg Equilibrium In the above example the frequency of each genotype within the population remained unchanged. However, the fact that populations *do* change is what makes this model important. By being able to specify under what conditions a static situation would exist, we can see, measure, and analyze change.

Certain conditions must be assumed for a population to remain in genetic equilibrium. Mutation must not be taking place. The population must be infinitely large so that change does not occur by chance. Individuals from a neighboring population must not introduce alleles into the population. Mating must take place at random, that is, without any design or propensity of one kind for another. These matings must be equally fertile; that is, they must produce the same number of viable offspring. In other words, natural selection must not be occurring. Deviation from equilibrium shows that one or a combination of these conditions is not being met.

See the Online Learning Center for an Interactive Exercise on Hardy-Weinberg equilibrium.

Table 4.2 Contributions of Mating Types to the Next Generation

Mating Type	Frequency	Offspring		
		AA	Aa	aa
AA × AA	¹⁄₁₆	¹⁄₁₆		
AA × Aa	¼	⅛	⅛	
AA × aa	⅛		⅛	
Aa × Aa	¼	¹⁄₁₆	⅛	¹⁄₁₆
Aa × aa	¼		⅛	⅛
aa × aa	¹⁄₁₆			¹⁄₁₆
Total		¼	½	¼

Table 4.3 Algebraic Derivation of Hardy-Weinberg Equilibrium

Allele	Frequency	Genotype	Frequency of Genotype in Population
A	p	AA	p^2
a	q	Aa	$2pq$
		aa	q^2

Offspring Resulting from Random Matings

Parents	Frequency of Mating Types	Frequency of Offspring		
		AA	Aa	aa
$AA \times AA$	$p^2 \times p^2 = p^4$	p^4	—	—
$AA \times Aa$	$2 \times p^2 \times 2pq = 4p^3q$	$2p^3q$	$2p^3q$	—
$AA \times aa$	$2 \times p^2 \times q^2 = 2p^2q^2$	—	$2p^2q^2$	—
$Aa \times Aa$	$2pq \times 2pq = 4p^2q^2$	p^2q^2	$2p^2q^2$	p^2q^2
$Aa \times aa$	$2 \times 2pq \times q^2 = 4pq^3$	—	$2pq^3$	$2pq^3$
$aa \times aa$	$q^2 \times q^2 = q^4$	—	—	q^4

$$f(AA) = p^4 + 2p^3q + p^2q^2 = p^2(p^2 + 2pq + q^2) = p^2(1) = p^2$$
$$f(Aa) = 2p^3q + 2p^2q^2 + 2p^2q^2 + 2pq^3 = 2pq(p^2 + pq + pq + q^2) = 2pq(1) = 2pq$$
$$f(aa) = p^2q^2 + 2pq^3 + q^4 = q^2(p^2 + 2pq + q^2) = q^2(1) = q^2$$

In the discussion above, we simplified matters by taking a simple example. However, in the real world, not all pairs of alleles exist in the frequencies of ½ and ½. Now we want to generalize the calculations to fit all possible allele frequencies.

The calculations for genetic equilibrium were first made independently by Godfrey Hardy and Wilhelm Weinberg in 1908 and are known as the **Hardy-Weinberg equilibrium.** This equilibrium can be developed algebraically (Table 4.3). This results in the following general formula for the Hardy-Weinberg equilibrium:

$$p^2 + 2pq + q^2 = 1$$

In this formula, $p = f(A)$ and $q = f(a)$. Therefore, $p^2 = f(AA)$, $2pq = f(Aa)$, and $q^2 = f(aa)$.

Hardy-Weinberg equilibrium A mathematical model of genetic equilibrium: $p^2 + 2pq + q^2 = 1$.

Using the Genetic-Equilibrium Model

The assumptions necessary for this formula have already been listed: no mutation, infinite population size, no introduction of genes from neighboring populations, random mating, and equal fertility. Since these conditions can never hold true for any population, the Hardy-Weinberg formula defines a model that can be used to test hypotheses about gene pools and the evolutionary forces that work on them.

While no populations are actually in genetic equilibrium, some do come close. For the sake of illustration, we will first look at a hypothetical population that is large; we will focus on a trait that does not play a role in mate selection and does not influence fertility or survival to any known degree. That trait is PTC tasting, which was discussed in Chapter 2.

PTC Tasting In taking a random survey of a hypothetical population, we find that out of 1000 individuals tested, 640 are tasters and 360 are nontasters. What are the frequencies of the two alleles, and how many tasters are carriers of the recessive allele?

In our population, 360 out of 1000 individuals, or 36 percent, are nontasters, and hence homozygous recessive or *tt*. We can set up the equation $f(tt) = q^2 = 0.36$, where q^2 is the proportion of homozygous recessive individuals and 0.36 is the decimal equivalent of $^{360}/_{1000}$. If $q^2 = 0.36$, then $q = 0.6$ (0.6 being the square root of 0.36). If $q = 0.6$, then p

must equal 0.4, since $p + q = 1$. Therefore, 40 percent of the alleles in the gene pool are the dominant T, while 60 percent are the recessive t.

The numbers obtained through our calculations may be surprising at first. The majority of individuals are tasters, yet the majority of alleles are for nontasting. This means that a large number of the recessive alleles are found in the heterozygous individuals and are therefore not expressed in the phenotype.

What proportion of the population consists of heterozygous tasters (carriers)? The answer is $2pq$, or 48 percent ($2 \times 0.4 \times 0.6$). Only 16 percent ($p^2 = 0.4 \times 0.4$) are homozygous dominant tasters, and 36 percent are nontasters.

Phenylketonuria In England, approximately 1 out of every 40,000 children is born with the metabolic abnormality PKU.[1] Several questions may be asked: How frequent is the defective allele in the gene pool? What is the probability that an individual in the population will be a carrier? What is the probability that two normal individuals mating at random will have a child with PKU?

This example is not a case of genetic equilibrium, since the assumptions for genetic equilibrium are not being met. For example, until recently, children with PKU did not grow up and reproduce. However, we can assume genetic equilibrium and use the Hardy-Weinberg formula to estimate the answers to these questions.

If the rate of abnormality is 1 child out of 40,000, the relative frequency of the trait is $\frac{1}{40,000}$, or 0.000025 (0.0025 percent). Therefore, $f(kk) = q^2 = 0.000025$, so $q = 0.005$. This means that 0.5 percent of the gene pool is k, while 99.5 percent ($p = 0.995$) is the normal allele K.

What is the probability of being a carrier? The answer is $2pq$, which equals 0.00995 ($2 \times 0.995 \times 0.005$), which is rounded off to 0.01. Therefore, approximately 1 percent of the members of the population are carriers, which is 1 out of 100 individuals. This is a large number, especially when we realize that only 1 out of 40,000 actually has the disease.

What is the probability that two persons mating at random will have a PKU child? The probability of being a carrier is 0.01, so the probability of two persons being carriers is 0.01×0.01, or 0.0001. If both are carriers, one out of every four of their children is expected to have the defect. When 0.0001 (the probability that both will be carriers) is multiplied by $\frac{1}{4}$ (the probability that two carriers will have a PKU child), the answer is 0.000025, or $\frac{1}{40,000}$.

It is apparent from the PKU example that populations contain reservoirs of deleterious alleles hidden in the heterozygous condition. In fact, estimates show that every person is carrying an average of three to five recessive alleles that in a homozygous condition would lead to death or disablement. The term **genetic load** refers to the totality of recessive **lethal** alleles in a population; these are alleles that bring about death before reproductive age. The expression of this genetic load is responsible for the presence of many harmful genetic abnormalities in human populations.

Demonstrating Genetic Equilibrium The Hardy-Weinberg formula also can be used to show if a population is in genetic equilibrium with respect to a particular trait. With this information, we can gain some idea of the impact of the forces of evolutionary change on the population. We can take as an example a hypothetical population with the following genotypic frequencies: $f(AA) = 0.34$, $f(Aa) = 0.46$, and $f(aa) = 0.20$. To find the frequency of A, we add the frequency of the AA individuals, who contribute only A alleles to the gene pool, and one-half the frequency of the Aa individuals, since only one-half of their alleles are A. Therefore, $f(A) = p = f(AA) + \frac{1}{2}f(Aa) = 0.34 + 0.23 = 0.57$. Since $p = 0.57$, $q = 0.43$.

genetic load The totality of deleterious alleles in a population.

lethals Alleles that bring about premature death.

---

[1] The incidence of PKU in England ranges between 2 and 6 per 100,000; $\frac{1}{40,000}$ falls within this range. See T. A. Munro, "Phenylketonuria: Data of 47 British Families," *Annals of Eugenics* 14 (1947), pp. 60–88.

To determine whether this population is in genetic equilibrium with respect to this gene, we take the calculated allele frequencies and calculate the expected frequencies of the genotypes. Thus, the expected frequencies are

$$f(AA) = p^2 = (0.57)^2 = 0.325$$

$$f(Aa) = 2pq = 2 \times 0.57 \times 0.43 = 0.490$$

$$f(aa) = q^2 = (0.43)^2 = 0.185$$

When these are compared with the observed frequencies, they do not agree. The amount of disagreement between the expected and observed frequencies may or may not be statistically significant. (Methods exist for determining significance, but they will not be discussed here.) Therefore, our population is not in genetic equilibrium with respect to this gene.

Summary

The unit of evolution is the reproductive population. Such a population is described, in statistical terms, as having both a phenotype and a genotype. The genotype of a population is referred to as the gene pool. The gene pool is composed of all the alleles carried by the members of a population. As the frequencies of alleles within the gene pool change, the population evolves. Conversely, if the allele frequencies remain constant, the population does not evolve; it is said to be in a state of genetic equilibrium. Genetic equilibrium, however, can be only a hypothetical state.

By using the Hardy-Weinberg formula, we can measure the strength of evolutionary forces by making comparisons between the hypothetical situation of no change and observed situations of change. Also, the formula can be used to calculate the frequencies of specific alleles and specific genotypes, such as carriers, within a population.

MECHANISMS OF EVOLUTIONARY CHANGE

In the model of a population in genetic equilibrium, the frequencies of the alleles in the gene pool remain constant. Such a population is not evolving. However, in order to have genetic equilibrium, five requirements must be met: no mutation, infinite population size, absence of alleles being introduced from neighboring populations, random mating, and equal fertility. Since no natural population meets these requirements, it follows that all populations must be evolving.

From the five conditions that must be met for genetic equilibrum to occur, we can list the various mechanisms that bring about evolutionary change. The first is mutation. Next is finite population size, which is responsible for three mechanisms of evolutionary change: genetic drift, population bottlenecking, and the founder principle. The movement of alleles into a population from neighboring populations is termed gene flow. Nonrandom mating occurs in several forms, as we will soon see. And finally, and to many, the most important are differential fertility rates, another way of saying natural selection.

See the Online Learning Center for an Interactive Exercise on mutations.

Mutations

A **mutation** is any alteration in the genetic material. A **point mutation** is a change at a particular point on the DNA molecule. Chromosomal aberrations are changes in the number or structure of chromosomes.

mutation An alteration of the genetic material.

point mutation An error at a particular point on the DNA molecule.

Mutations are chance events. Organisms do not sense a change or potential change in the environment and then "decide to" mutate; nor are there innate mechanisms that can provide predictions of what future environmental conditions will be like. Mutations arise with no design, no predetermined reason or purpose; in other words, they are random.

Mutations bring about new alleles. When new alleles occur in body cells, the effect may be insignificant unless, of course, it causes a medical problem such as a cancer that can have a direct effect on the viability of the organism. However, when the mutation occurs in the sex cells and brings about new alleles in the ova and sperm, it can change the gene pool since the mutation can be passed on to the next generation. Mutation is the ultimate source of all variation within the gene pool. It creates variability rather than directly bringing about evolutionary change.

Mutations as Random Events What is the probability that a chance alteration of the genetic code will be advantageous to the organism? Imagine that a Shakespearean sonnet is being transcribed into Morse code. Suppose that in the process a dot is selected at random and replaced with a dash. What is the probability that this change will improve the poem? Most likely, the change will result in a misspelled word; it might even change the word and, hence, the meaning.

However, although most new mutations are harmful, a few may be neutral and even fewer actually may be beneficial. The latter mutations are responsible for maintaining variation within the genotype of a population by introducing new alleles into the gene pool. Even though most beneficial mutations do not bring an immediate advantage to the population, they may become important later, when environmental conditions change or the population migrates into new areas.

How Do Mutations Occur? A mutation may be a **spontaneous mutation,** that is, one that occurs in response to the usual conditions within the body or environment, or it may be an **induced mutation** brought about by human agents. In both cases, some factor is actively causing the mutation to occur. The exact cause of any specific mutation usually cannot be determined, although in experimental situations, various agents can be shown to increase the frequency of the occurrence of mutations.

Geneticists believe that many point mutations result from mistakes in the replication of the DNA molecule. For example, consider the replication of a polypeptide that includes the codon ATA, which codes for the amino acid tyrosine. If an incorrect complementary base were incorporated into the DNA molecule, the new codon might read AAA, which codes for phenylalanine. As a result, phenylalanine replaces tyrosine, a substitution that may greatly alter the functioning of the protein.

Once the substitution has occurred, the new codon would be the basis for replications of additional DNA, all with the same error. We would refer to the altered genetic code as a mutation. Not all substitutions produce phenotypic changes. All but two amino acids are coded by more than one codon, and so some mutations can be genetically neutral. For example, if the codon ATA mutated to ATG, there would be no change in the amino acid since both codons code for the same amino acid, in this case tyrosine.

The factors that initiate spontaneous mutations are for the most part unknown. It was once thought that background radiation from the general environment accounted for the majority of the observed spontaneous mutations, but most geneticists now believe that this is not true. Naturally occurring chemicals and fluctuations in temperature may account for many spontaneous mutations.

The story is different for induced mutations. In 1927, H. J. Muller demonstrated that mutations could be induced in fruit flies by using x-rays.[2] In fact, the increase in the frequency of mutations was directly proportional to the increase in the dosage of radiation (Figure 4.2). This discovery increased the awareness of the dangers of artificial radiation

spontaneous mutation
Mutation that occurs spontaneously, that is, in response to the usual conditions within the body or environment.

induced mutation
Mutation caused by human-made conditions.

---

[2] H. J. Muller, "Artificial Transmutation of the Gene," *Science* 66 (1927), pp. 84–87.

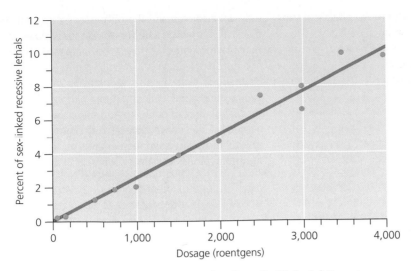

Figure 4.2 Effects of Radiation on the Genetic Material X-ray dosage and frequency of sex-linked recessives induced in fruit fly spermatozoa.

from medical or occupational exposure and nuclear fallout. The U.S. National Academy of Sciences has concluded that there is no safe level of radiation, such as x-rays.

There are other kinds of **mutagens,** mutation-causing factors. Certain chemicals added to foods, compounded in medicines, or poured into the atmosphere or waters are known to cause mutations, cancers, or other adverse effects in human populations. Since many substances that are commonly used are suspect, it is important that they be fully investigated. In addition, certain viruses are known to cause mutations.

When mutations do occur, they may have no effect on the phenotype of the organism, as is the case, for example, when the mutant allele is a recessive. On the other hand, mutations can produce phenotypic alterations that range from extremely subtle to drastic. If mutations occur in body cells, cell death and abnormal development, including cancer, could result. A single chance mutation taking place in a skin cell, for example, may have virtually no effect on the phenotype, yet the same isolated mutation taking place in a sex cell may have a significant effect on the individual conceived from that sex cell. Such a mutation may result in potentially valuable characteristics, abnormal conditions, or even inviable gametes.

How frequent are mutations? Although mutation rates vary from trait to trait, most estimates for mutations that occur in sex cells are about 2 to 12 in every 100,000 gametes per generation per gene. When the large number of genes per gamete is considered, the probability of a particular gamete carrying at least one new mutation is about ½. Since many of these new mutations are recessive, they probably will not cause any problems in the immediate offspring.

Genetic Drift, Population Bottlenecking, and the Founder Principle

The model of genetic equilibrium is mathematical and assumes an infinitely large population, but natural populations are not infinitely large. When we deal with small populations, we often see changes in gene frequencies that are due to chance effects.

Sampling Error Political polls that predict the winners of elections can serve as examples of **sampling error.** Imagine it is election time, and you have been hired by a candidate to predict the winner. Because of time and money limitations, you cannot possibly reach all 100,000 eligible voters, and so you decide to take a sample.

The first question is: How large must the sample be to represent the population adequately? If you ask only 10 people, they might all be voting for the same person by pure chance. Maybe

mutagens Factors—such as radioactivity, chemicals, and viruses—that are capable of causing mutations.

See the Online Learning Center for an Internet Activity on the mechanisms of evolutionary change.

sampling error In population genetics, the transmission of a nonrepresentative sample of the gene pool over space or time due to chance.

Table 4.4 Sampling Error in a Set of Actual Trials

Possible Combinations for 10 Throws		Times Combination Thrown	
Heads	Tails	Number	Percent
10	0	0	0
9	1	0	0
8	2	3	3
7	3	7	8
6	4	23	26
5	5	23	26
4	6	13	15
3	7	12	14
2	8	5	7
1	9	1	1
0	10	0	0
		87	100

they are relatives and the only ones voting for this candidate! If you take a sample of 100 individuals, the predictive value of the poll might be increased. Here, too, you must protect against bias by not polling people who might be inclined toward one candidate because of their ethnic background, financial situation, party affiliation, and so forth. One way of achieving an unbiased sample is by randomly polling an adequate-sized sample. The actual size of a representative sample depends on the variation within the population. Statistical formulas can be used to determine what sample size is needed to ensure that predictions will be within a desired level of accuracy.

One more, slightly different example can be used: flipping coins. Since the odds of landing heads are ½, we would expect that one-half of the flips will always be heads. Thus, if you flip a coin 10 times, you would expect 5 heads; 100 times, 50 heads; and 1000 times, 500 heads. Yet if the coin is flipped the suggested number of times, the results might deviate from the predicted situation. If, for example, you flip the coin 10 times, you *might* end up with 5 heads, but any number from 0 to 10 is possible. Furthermore, if you flip the coin 10 times repeatedly, the number of heads will fluctuate from series to series (Table 4.4). If a large number of flips, say, 1000, are performed, not only will you come closer to the ideal probability of ½ heads, but the fluctuations from one series to another will not be as dramatic (Table 4.5).

Genetic Drift As the genes in a gene pool are being passed from one generation, we are, in effect, taking a sample. Just as with a sample of voters or coins, all the possibilities may not be represented. If the gene pool is large, and hence the number of matings great, the odds are high that the new gene pool will be fairly representative of the old one. If the gene pool is small, however, the new pool may deviate appreciably from the old. Such chance deviation in the frequency of alleles in a population is known as **genetic drift.**

genetic drift The situation in a small population in which the allelic frequencies of the F₁ generation will differ from those of the parental generation due to sampling error.

Figure 4.3 plots the change of allele frequency through time as the result of genetic drift. Note that the fluctuations appear to be random. However, when the allele frequency is high, there is a strong possibility that it will reach 100 percent, with the alternate allele disappearing from the population.

population bottlenecking A form of sampling error in which a population is reduced in size, which in turn reduces variability in the population. The population that descends from the reduced population is therefore less variable than the original population.

Population Bottlenecking Another form of sampling error occurs as the result of **population bottlenecking.** This happens when a population is reduced to a small size for some reason, such as a natural disaster. The initial reduction in the size of the population causes a reduction in variation because of the probability that some variants will be lost by chance as individuals are lost from the population. As the reduced population reproduces, the variability of ensuing populations is less than the variation that existed before the bottlenecking took place.

Naoyuki Takahata and several other population geneticists have proposed that a population bottleneck occurred in the evolution of *Homo* sometime during the last 400,000 years. This would explain why there is less genetic variation among humans worldwide than the genetic variation found among geographically close individuals of other species such as chimpanzees. The proposed bottleneck might have reduced the number of reproducing humans from about 100,000 to 10,000 individuals. Much of the diversity of the original population could have been lost by chance. The new population of 10,000 individuals would then have given rise to new generations of descendants with reduced variation. Not everyone agrees with this explanation for the relative lack of genetic

Table 4.5 Population Size in a Set of Actual Trials

Number of Throws	Number of Heads Expected	Number of Heads Observed	Deviation from Expected (%)
250	125	118	5.6
500	250	258	3.2
1000	500	497	0.6

Box 4-1

The Case of the Island of the Colorblind

The island of Pingelap is a small coral atoll in the Eastern Caroline Islands in the western Pacific. Around the year 1775, a typhoon struck the island. Since the height of the island does not exceed 10 feet above sea level, the destruction of the land, the people, and their food supply was devastating. Prior to the typhoon the island had a population of about 1000 people; fewer than 20 individuals survived. Today the population of Pingelap has grown back to about 1000 people.

The Pingelapese are noteworthy among geneticists because of their high incidence of **achromatopsia, or total color blindness.** People suffering from achromatopsia lack cones or possess nonfunctioning cones in the retina of the eye. The cones are responsible for color vision and for seeing fine detail. Persons with this abnormality see in black and white, have difficulty seeing in bright daylight, exhibit jerky movements of the eye, and are prone to the development of cataracts. Achromatopsia is an extremely rare autosomal recessive genetic abnormality. Its frequency averages between 1 in 20,000 to 1 in 50,000 throughout the world. However, among the Pingelapese, between 1 in 10 and 1 in 25 suffer from this trait.

Population bottlenecking occurs when some factor, such as a natural disaster, rapidly reduces the size of a population. The new smaller population is rarely a random sample of the original, larger population. Geneticists believe that prior to the 1775 typhoon, the recessive allele was very rare—perhaps only one copy of the allele existed. The small population that existed following the typhoon and its aftermath must have included at least one carrier, thought, perhaps, to be the king of the island. The person or persons carrying the allele for achromatopsia who survived the typhoon survived by chance, not because achromatopsia conveyed selective advantage. Today about 30 percent of the population are carriers. This high frequency of the defective allele explains the large number of people with total color blindness found on the island today.

Sources: M. D. O'Neill, "Linkage Reported for Total Color Blindness in the Pingelapese," *American Journal of Human Genetics* 64 (1999), pp. 1679–1685; and O. Sachs, *The Island of the Colorblind* (New York: Knopf, 1997)

---

diversity in modern human populations. For example, some statisticians believe that a population of 10,000 is still too large to be an effective bottleneck (Box 4-1).

Founder Principle Another form of sampling error in populations is the **founder principle,** which may occur when a segment of a population migrates to another area. The migrating group represents a sample of the original, larger population, but this sample is probably not a random representation of the original group. For instance, it may be made up of members of certain family groups whose gene frequencies vary considerably from the average of the original population. If the migrant population settles down in an uninhabited area or

founder principle
Situation in which a founding population does not represent a random sample of the original population; a form of sampling error.

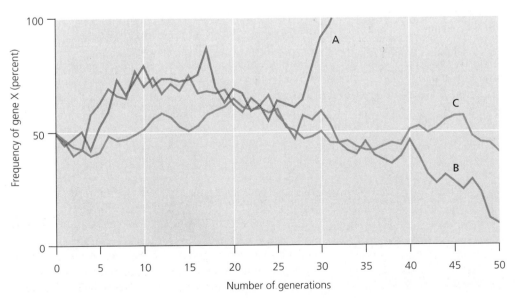

Figure 4.3 Genetic Drift This diagram traces genetic drift in three hypothetical populations, beginning with an allele frequency of 50 percent for 50 generations. Population A consists of 50 individuals, population B consists of 100 individuals, and population C consists of 250 individuals. Note that the frequency shows the greatest fluctuations in the smallest population, where the frequency actually reaches 100 percent.

Box 4-2   The Case of Mad King George

History is shaped, in part, by the existence and activities of great men and women. Yet these persons are biological beings, and their lives are partly shaped by illness. In turn, illness influences history. For example, one might say that the success of the American Revolution hinged on an abnormal gene.

Porphyria is a genetic abnormality that has plagued the British royal family, including Mary Queen of Scots. But perhaps the most famous member of the royal family with the disease was George III, the king who ruled during the American Revolution.

Porphyria results from an abnormally low production of hemoglobin. Symptoms include sensitivity to sunlight, abdominal pain, wine-colored urine, paralysis in the limbs, and development of psychiatric symptoms, and may lead to convulsions, coma, and death. The cause of this disease is the absence or nonfunctioning of an enzyme that is responsible for a step in the breakdown of hemoglobin in the blood.

George III (1760–1820) suffered from a rather severe form of the disease. George's symptoms first appeared in 1765, and from 1811 to his death in 1820 he became progressively insane and blind. His disease affected the decisions he made in regard to unhappy American colonists. In 1811, the Prince of Wales took the throne from George III.

Porphyria is found in a relatively high frequency in South Africa, where it is the most common occurring single-gene abnormality. Since some medicines cause serious symptoms in porphyria patients, many South African hospitals routinely test for the presence of porphyria.

The early European settlers in South Africa were Dutch. This was a predominantly male population, and so women were occasionally sent to South Africa to become wives. One such woman was a Dutch orphan from Amsterdam named Ariaantje Adriaansse. When she arrived in South Africa in 1688, she married Gerrit Janz van Deventer. Geneticists believe that Ariaantje possessed the abnormal allele for porphyria. Among their descents today, who are found in both the "white" and "colored" populations, are thousands of persons suffering from this disease.

The founder principle refers to the fact that a migrant population is not a random sample of the population from which it came due to sampling error. While porphyria was a rare disease in Holland, it became a fairly common disease in South Africa because one migrant from Amsterdam, joining a relatively small founder population, carried the allele to South Africa.

---

restricts mating to itself, it may become the founder population for the larger population that will develop from it (Figure 4.4). The migrant population may also ultimately merge with other populations, or it may become extinct.

The Xavante of the Amazon Basin provide an example of the founder principle. The Xavante live in villages with average populations of several hundred individuals. When a village becomes too large, it divides into two villages, each with 100 to 200 people. Consequently, the breeding size of each new village is smaller than that of the original village. The split into two villages is largely along family lines. Since family members stay together, and many do not mate because of the incest taboo, the effective breeding size of the population is even smaller; that is, the number of potential mates is reduced even further from what we may assume from the size of the population alone. Therefore, the fission of the original village leads to the establishment of new populations that may by chance statistically differ from each other in terms of gene frequencies (Box 4-2).

Figure 4.4 Founder Principle The founders of the new population represent a nonrandom sample of the original population.

○ = 1/2   ● = 1/2

○ = 1/4   ● = 3/4

Gene Flow

Movement of people into areas that are already occupied may serve to introduce new alleles into the population; this is termed **gene flow.** For example, travelers may bring a previously absent allele to a population.

An introduced allele is analogous in effect to a mutation. If the new allele gives its possessor some advantage, this allele will tend to spread through the population in subsequent generations. Gene flow may alter the effects of genetic drift, since alleles lost or reduced in frequency by chance may be reintroduced into a population by newcomers. Also, gene flow usually has a homogenizing effect. The process generally makes two or more populations more similar to each other than would be the case if gene flow did not occur between them.

Note that the terms *gene flow* and *migration* are not synonymous. Gene flow refers to the transfer of alleles into different gene pools, whereas migration connotes a permanent or long-term move to another area. Thus, one person could migrate but contribute no alleles to his or her new population, but a male could go on even a short trip and disperse his genes through his sperm. Soldiers, traveling businesspersons, and others have produced gene flow without actually migrating.

gene flow The process in which alleles from one population are introduced into another population.

Nonrandom Mating

The statistical model of genetic equilibrium calls for random mating. If matings were truly random, the probability of mating with any one individual of the opposite sex would be the same as the probability of mating with any other individual. In reality, mating is not truly random. When you choose a mate, very definite biases contribute to the choice—factors such as physical appearance, education, socioeconomic status, religion, and geographical location.

There are two basic types of nonrandom matings that will be discussed here. The first is **consanguineous mating,** which refers to mating between relatives; the second is **assortative mating,** which involves preference for or avoidance of certain people for physical and/or social reasons.

consanguineous mating Mating between biological relatives.

assortative mating Preference for or avoidance of certain people as mates for physical or social reasons.

Consanguineous Mating Consanguineous mating is mating between relatives. For most American and European societies, mating between close relatives is now rare. In the not-too-distant past, it was more common for close relatives, such as first cousins, to marry. Charles Darwin married his first cousin, and Albert Einstein's second wife was his first cousin. In some societies, however, consanguineous mating is not only common but preferred.

Many societies have cultural patterns of preferential marriage with a particular relative. **Cross-cousin preferential marriage** is one common type. In this system, an example of your preferred marriage partner is your mother's brother's child or your father's sister's child, who in each case is your first cousin. Yet marriage may be prohibited between you and your mother's sister's child or father's brother's child. Cousin marriage is quite common in many parts of the world. For example, in Saudi Arabia, Kuwait, and Jordan more than 50 percent of marriages are consanguineous, most commonly between the children of brothers.

cross-cousin preferential marriage Marriage between a person and his or her cross-cousin (father's sister's child or mother's brother's child).

Marriages also occur between second and third cousins, as well as between other types of relatives, such as uncle and niece. In fact, a preferential marriage that is considered repulsive to most Western societies, brother–sister marriage, was common for the royalty of several societies, including Hawaiians and ancient Egyptians. Some scholars believe that Cleopatra was the offspring of a brother–sister marriage and was at one time married to her brother.

What are the effects of consanguineous matings on a gene pool? Such matings have little effect on common alleles, but their effect on rare alleles is a different story.

Earlier we looked at the genetics of phenylketonuria (PKU). In our population approximately 1 percent ($1/100$) are carriers. We concluded that if two people mate at random, the probability of having a child with the disease is 1 in 40,000. What happens when the two individuals are first cousins?

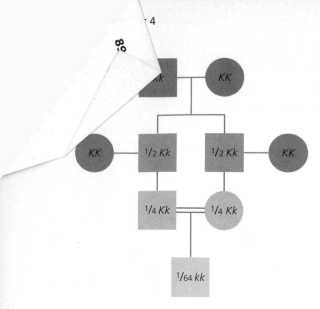

Figure 4.5 Cousin Mating See explanation in text.

First cousins are individuals who share one of their grandparents. Let us begin with an example in which we are looking at a man whose paternal grandfather is known to be a carrier for this trait. This means that his odds of also being a carrier are not $1/100$ but $1/4$ assuming Grandma and all other individuals in the pedigree are *KK* (Figure 4.5). If this individual, with a $1/4$ probability of being a carrier, marries a nonrelative with no known PKU in her pedigree, the probability of having a child with PKU is $1/4 \times 1/100 \times 1/4$, or $1/1600$. However, if he marries a first cousin who has the same carrier grandmother, the odds fall to $1/64$.

However, it is unlikely that we know that Grandma is a carrier. In the case of PKU this probability is $1/100$. Therefore, the probability of a grandchild having the trait is actually $1/64 \times 1/100$, or $1/640$. (Of course, we are simplifying the problem by assuming all others to be *KK*. We could take into account the probability of their being *Kk* as $1/100$.) A probability of $1/640$ is much higher than a probability of $1/40,000$ of two unrelated people mating and having a PKU child.

Consanguineous matings increase the probability of homozygous recessive genotypes. In the example above, the probability of producing a homozygous recessive individual is $62\frac{1}{2}$ times greater if first cousins mate than it is if random mating occurs. In fact, some recessive alleles are so rare that the probability of a carrier mating with another carrier at random is just about zero. Some recessive abnormalities are known only from inbred family groups.

The result of consanguineous matings in a population is a reduction in the number of heterozygous individuals and an increase in the number of homozygous individuals. If the homozygous recessive genotype is deleterious, the frequency of the abnormality will increase. Since natural selection can then act upon the abnormal homozygous recessive individuals, there could result a net decrease in the frequency of the allele in the population.

Not all inbreeding is the result of preferential marriage. In a small society, it may be impossible to find a mate who is not a relative. Because of this, the effects of consanguineous marriages and genetic drift are often operating together in the same population, as seen in Box 4-3.

Assortative Mating In the United States, consanguineous matings are not common. Nevertheless, mating is far from random. Deviation from random mating stems from the fact that Americans choose spouses because of particular physical traits and by certain cultural conventions that they learn from parents, friends, and the mass media. *Assortative* mating means that people with certain phenotypes tend to mate more or less often than would be expected if matings were random.

Assortative mating influences gene combination in the F_1 generation. The failure of particular individuals to mate because they are not selected as mating partners would prevent certain alleles (such as those causing mental retardation) from being passed on to the next generation's gene pool. Preferences for particular phenotypes might increase the probability that certain gene combinations will be represented in the gene pool of the next generation. For instance, if a tall individual selected as a mate another tall individual, extremely tall offspring might then appear in the next generation, thus bringing about new variation in the population.

Charles Darwin recognized the fact that mating is not a random affair and that differences in physical characteristics influence the probability of an individual mating at all. He referred to this phenomenon as sexual selection; it will be discussed more fully in Chapter 5.

Differential Fertility

The model of genetic equilibrium assumes that all matings are equally fertile, but this is obviously not the case. Some couples have three children, others one, and still others no

The Amish are a series of small populations that have remained socially isolated for religious and cultural reasons. There are Amish settlements in 23 states and Ontario, Canada, but the most studied group consists of the 20,000 or so Amish of Lancaster County, Pennsylvania. The Amish are one of several religious isolates that are ideal for population studies. They are a strictly defined, closed group with good genealogical records, high nutritional and health standards, and good medical care. Almost all the Amish are at the same socioeconomic level, and they tend to have large families.

Most of the Amish of Lancaster County are the descendants of a founder population of about 200 pre–Revolutionary War ancestors who migrated to Pennsylvania from Europe between 1720 and 1770. Because of the small population size, most available mates are related to some degree, although first-cousin marriages are prohibited.

The Amish represent the results of the founder effect, genetic drift, and consanguineous mating. They have a fairly high frequency of some rather rare alleles, such as the one responsible for Ellis–van Creveld syndrome.

The **Ellis–van Creveld syndrome** is characterized by dwarfism, extra fingers on the hand, and, often, congenital malformations of the heart. The syndrome is quite rare, found in about 1 in 60,000 live births in the general population. Yet among the Amish of Lancaster the frequency is 1 in 200 live births. All the patients with this trait are descendants of Samuel King and his wife, who came to the area in 1744. One was probably a carrier of this rare recessive allele.

Many such isolates, like the Amish, have been studied by students of human evolution. Besides showing a higher incidence of several rare recessive traits, these populations also show allele frequencies for traits such as blood type that differ from the frequencies of the surrounding population. For example, among the Dunkers, a group of 3500 individuals in Pennsylvania descended from German ancestors who migrated to America beginning in 1719, more than 44 percent are of blood type M. This compares with a frequency of 29 percent for blood type M found in the present-day populations of the United States and West Germany. Since there is no evidence that these blood-type frequencies are due to natural selection, they are most likely due to the founder principle and/or genetic drift.

children at all. This means that the contribution to the gene pool of the succeeding generation varies from couple to couple.

V. A. McKusick presents some interesting figures.[3] He estimates that more than half of all zygotes never reproduce: 15 percent are lost before birth, 3 percent are stillborn, 2 percent are lost in the neonatal period, 3 percent die before maturity, 20 percent never marry, and 10 percent marry but remain childless.

Except for identical twins, each zygote is a unique genotype, representing a unique assortment of alleles, a particular combination that will never occur again. Why do more than half of these fail to reproduce at all? Because of some inherited abnormality, many are lost either before or after birth. Others never mate because they are institutionalized. Some die in wars or accidents. Many mate but never have children because of medical problems. And some do not mate or marry, or they marry but choose to have no children.

Of the 47 percent of the original combinations that do reproduce, reproductive rates vary. Some have only one child, others a dozen. What factors determine the differences in fertility? Some are medical, such as blood-type incompatibility, but many are cultural. For instance, many couples today restrict their families to one or two children because of ecological or economic concerns; others believe, on religious grounds, that salvation lies in high fertility. The point is that the next generation is the result of the reproductive activities of the parental generation.

What we have been talking about is natural selection, the heart of the theory of evolution. Natural selection is the fact that certain individuals tend to have more offspring than do other individuals and therefore make a greater contribution to the gene pool of the next generation. Factors that result in greater fertility, *if genetically determined,* will be passed on to the next generation with greater frequency. Factors that result in lowered fertility or higher mortality, such as genetic abnormality, will tend to be eliminated.

---

[3] V. A. McKusick, *Human Genetics,* 2nd ed. (Englewood Cliffs, NJ: Prentice Hall, 1969), p. 167.

As a final note, it should be emphasized that the mechanisms of evolution—mutation, drift, gene flow, founder principle, genetic bottlenecking, nonrandom mating, and natural selection—work *together* to create net change. For instance, natural selection would have nothing to "select" for or against if the variability provided by mutation were not present.

Summary

Natural populations are not in genetic equilibrium because various mechanisms bring about changes in allele frequency. Mutations, the ultimate source of genetic variability, provide one way in which the predicted frequencies deviate from observed frequencies. Since mutations are usually deleterious to the individual, they rarely "catch on." Their importance lies in providing a potential for adapting to new situations.

Random genetic drift is another factor in evolutionary change. With genetic drift, by chance alone, not all alleles in a population will be represented proportionally in the next generation. The smaller the population, the more pronounced this effect. According to the founder principle, a new population based on a small sample of the original population may show distinctive gene frequencies. Population bottle-necking may dramatically alter gene frequencies due to a sudden drop in the size of a population. Again, the smaller the sample, the greater the potential deviation from the original group. Sampling error is in part responsible for much of the physical variation in different human populations.

Gene flow can bring new alleles into a population, where they may be adaptive and increase in frequency. Gene flow also acts to make populations genetically more similar to each other.

The genetic-equilibrium model assumes random mating, but individuals consciously choose mates for myriad reasons. For example, they may prefer to marry a relative in order to keep power and wealth within the family, or they may want to mate with someone with green eyes for personal aesthetic reasons. Nonrandom mating leads to changes in gene frequencies from generation to generation.

Differential fertility, or natural selection, is a powerful force of evolutionary change. This topic will be a major focus of the next chapter.

Key Terms

assortative mating, *89*
consanguineous mating, *89*
cross-cousin preferential marriage, *89*
evolution, *79*
founder principle, *87*
gene flow, *89*
gene pool, *79*
genetic drift, *86*

genetic equilibrium, *79*
genetic load, *82*
Hardy-Weinberg equilibrium, *81*
induced mutation, *84*
lethal, *82*
mutagens, *85*
mutation, *83*
point mutation, *83*

population bottlenecking, *86*
reproductive isolating mechanism, *78*
reproductive population, *78*
sampling error, *85*
species, *78*
spontaneous mutation, *84*

Study Questions

See the Online Learning Center for additional study questions.

1. Why do we define evolutionary change in terms of changes in relative gene frequencies rather than in terms of changes in phenotype?

2. Genetic equilibrium is a state that never actually exists. Why can it not exist in a real population?

3. What is meant by the term *sampling error?* What types of sampling errors can occur in the reproduction of populations?

4. Cousin marriage is illegal in some states. Does mating between cousins produce more abnormal children than mating between nonrelatives? What genetic factors are involved?

5. What role does mutation play in evolutionary change? Could evolution occur without mutation?

6. Insecticide is sprayed on an insect population. A small percentage of the insects survive because of a mutation that allows them to "neutralize" the toxin. Did the mutation arise because the insect population needed it to? Explain.

7. In what way does natural selection affect a gene pool? How does natural selection interact with other forces of evolution to create changes in the gene pool?

8. Do you believe that the course of human evolution can be predicted? If so, why and how? If not, why not?

Critical Thinking Questions

1. The Hardy-Weinberg equilibrium assumes that none of the evolutionary factors we discussed in the chapter are working on a population. We know that this condition cannot actually exist; that is, evolutionary factors such as mutation and natural selection always operate on populations. Why is the Hardy-Weinberg equilibrium concept still an important tool in population genetics?

2. The forces of evolution are working on all populations. What are some factors in modern industrial countries that affect human populations in terms of mutation rates, natural selection, gene flow, mating patterns, and sampling error?

3. Human mating patterns are profoundly influenced by social customs, especially those that control the selection of a marriage partner. Patterns of preferential marriage exist in many societies along with rules that determine who one can and cannot marry. For example, the rule of exogamy is that a marriage partner must come from outside a particular social group, for example, a clan. On the other hand, endogamy means that a marriage partner must come from inside a particular social group, for example, a caste. In some societies these rules are very strict and exceptions are rare. In American society similar rules may exist, but as pressures or tendencies rather than ironclad rules. Describe some of these pressures and tendencies.

Suggested Readings

Bowler, P. J. *Evolution: The History of an Idea,* rev. ed. Berkeley: University of California Press, 1989. This book outlines the history of evolutionary theories. Its final chapter looks at modern debates about evolutionary theory, including the ideas of creationists.

Futuyma, D. J. *Evolutionary Biology,* 3rd ed. Sunderland, MA: Sinauer Associates, 1998. This book provides one of the best discussions of population genetics available.

Griffiths, A., et al. *An Introduction to Genetic Analysis,* 7th ed. New York: Freeman, 2000. This is a general introduction to genetics with excellent chapters on population genetics. There are numerous solved exercises.

Hartl, D. L., and A. Clark. *Principles of Population Genetics,* 3rd ed. Sunderland, MA: Sinauer Associates, 1998. This is a popular introduction to population genetics.

Volpe, E. P., and P. Andrew. *Understanding Evolution,* 6th ed. New York: McGraw-Hill, 2000. This is a short introduction to evolutionary theory with a good overview of population genetics.

Suggested Websites

Human Biology: Population Genetics Web Pages
www.people.virginia.edu/~rjh9u/popgenes.html

Population Biology Simulations
http://darwin.eeb.uconn.edu/simulations/simulations.html

Recessive Disease Calculator
www.perinatology.com/calculators/recessive.htm

Natural Selection and the Origin of Species

A marine iguana on the Galápagos Islands, visited by Charles Darwin on his trip aboard the HMS *Beagle*.

have called this principle, by which each slight variation, if useful, is preserved, by the term of Natural Selection. ●

—*Charles Darwin (1809–1882)*

Chapter Outline

Natural Selection

The Variability of Populations
Environment, Habitat, and Niche
The Mechanisms of Natural Selection
Types of Natural Selection
Natural Selection in Humans
Natural Selection and Sickle-Cell Anemia
Sexual Selection
Kin Selection
Summary

The Origin of Species

The Evolution of Subspecies
The Evolution of Species
Specialized and Generalized Species
Rates of Speciation
Some Basic Concepts in Evolutionary Theory
Summary

See the Online Learning Center for a chapter summary, chapter outline, and learning objectives.

After Reading This Chapter, You Should Be Able to Answer These Questions:

1. What is natural selection, and what is its role in the evolution of populations?
2. What do anthropologists mean by the term *fitness*?
3. What are the three types of natural selection?
4. What is sexual selection, and what role does it play in evolution?
5. What is kin selection, and what role does it play in evolution?
6. What is a subspecies? How do subspecies evolve into separate species?
7. What are the two ideas about the tempo or rate of evolutionary change?
8. What are the differences between a specialized species and a generalized species?
9. What do we mean by competition, preadaptation, adaptive radiation, and extinction?

Box 5-1   **The Importance of Words**

Charles Darwin never used the word *evolution* in the first edition of *On the Origin of Species,* which was published in 1859. The closest he came was in the very last words in the book.[1]

There is grandeur in this view of life, with its several powers, having been originally breathed into a few forms or into one; and that, whilst this planet has gone cycling on according to the fixed law of gravity, from so simple a beginning endless forms most beautiful and most wonderful have been, and are being, evolved.

The reason for this is that words have histories and their meanings change over time. In 1859 the word *evolution* did not correspond to Darwin's concept of natural selection. Instead, he chose to use the phrase "descent with modification."

In the mid-nineteenth century the word *evolution* had two meanings. Its technical meaning was derived from the work of the German biologist Albrecht von Haller, who coined the word in 1744 from the Latin *evolvere,* "to unroll." Von Haller proposed that residing within the ovum (some preferred the sperm) was a perfectly formed miniature human being, or homunculus, which, through the reproductive process, developed into a human infant. That human infant would in turn possess ova (or sperm) also containing homunculi for the next generation. It logically followed that the ova of Eve (or the sperm of Adam) contained, preformed, all human beings that would ever exist on the earth. If all human beings were preformed for all time, how could people change through "descent through modification"?

The term *evolution* also had a more general meaning in 1859. Many scholars accepted the idea that change did occur but thought that it did so in a progressive fashion. For example, they believed that the complexity of human societies changed from simple hunting groups to civilizations through a natural process that always moved in the direction of increasing complexity. Darwin, in contrast, realized that change moved an organization to a better adaptation to its habitat, which might involve greater complexity but also might not. In other words, charge was not necessarily in the direction of greater complexity.

In the latter half of the nineteenth century the technical meaning used by von Haller was no longer considered valid, and through Darwin's influence many scientists came to realize the true meaning of Darwin's ideas about evolution. In later editions of *On the Origin of Species,* the term *evolution* began to appear.

[1] C. Darwin, *On the Origin of Species by Means of Natural Selection, or the Preservation of Favoured Races in the Struggle for Life* (London: Murray, 1859), pp. 489–490.

Source: S. J. Gould, *Ever Since Darwin: Reflection in Natural History* (New York: Norton, 1977), pp. 34–45.

Evolution is change. Scientists theorize that life began to form more than 3½ billion years ago. Eventually, unicellular organisms evolved, followed by multicellular organisms. From this early life, millions of species evolved, some becoming extinct without leaving descendants, others evolving into species that populate the world today.

The biological evolution that leads to the propagation and diversity of life occurs on at least two levels. What is sometimes called "small-scale" biological evolution, or **microevolution,** is any change in the frequency of alleles within the gene pool of a population, which we examined in the last chapter. These microevolutionary changes occur through several mechanisms, including mutation, gene flow, genetic drift, and, the subjects of the first part of this chapter, natural selection, sexual selection, and kin selection.

The second level of biological evolution is often referred to as "large-scale" evolution, or **macroevolution.** This is the subject of the second part of this chapter. Macroevolution leads to the evolution of new species and larger categories of life.

microevolution "Small-scale" evolution; genetic changes within a population over time.

macroevolution "Large-scale" evolution; the evolution of new species and higher categories.

See the Online Learning Center for an Internet Activity on natural selection.

NATURAL SELECTION

We will now revisit the concept of natural selection, which we already have encountered in Chapters 1 and 4. Natural selection remains one of the central concepts in modern evolutionary theory. Charles Darwin first wrote about natural selection in 1842, but most people did not learn of it until 1859, when Darwin presented the concept in his book *On the Origin of Species.* Darwin had collected an enormous amount of facts in the areas of geology, biogeography, biology, animal husbandry, paleontology, and other fields. He presented his data in a way that ultimately convinced the scientific world of the validity of the concept of natural selection (Box 5-1).

Natural selection is one of the processes that act to change the frequency of alleles in a population. Darwin and others observed that individuals within a population produce far more offspring than is necessary to replace themselves. He also observed that these populations are variable. Environmental factors such as predators, disease, lack of food, competition over mates, and lack of space will tend to eliminate or reduce the genetic contribution (the number of offspring) of those individuals who do not have the characteristics that allow them to cope with these pressures.

Darwin contrasted natural selection with **artificial selection.** Artificial selection is the deliberate breeding of domesticated plants and animals. It is similar to natural selection except that it is controlled by humans. People have probably been selectively breeding animals for at least 13,000 years. Darwin believed that if people could select for thicker wool in sheep, speed in horses, or docile temperaments in dogs, then the pressures imposed on natural populations could similarly, although not deliberately, bring about changes as well.

artificial selection The deliberate breeding of domesticated animals or plants.

The Variability of Populations

All populations, including humans, display variability. Some of this variability is clearly observable: color, size, and shape, for example. Other differences are observable only through dissection or microscopic and biochemical analysis.

Humans are polymorphic. Polymorphism refers to the presence of several distinct forms with frequencies greater than 1 percent within a population. An example of this would be the presence of individuals with A, B, AB, and O blood types within a population (Chapter 3).

We can easily observe variation of phenotypes among human populations in different parts of the world; this is the subject of Chapter 17. Even among siblings from a single family, there are differences in physical features, blood types, and psychological patterns. Some of these differences vary with sex and age; others are influenced by the cultural or natural environment; and many, such as blood type, are totally inherited.

Environment, Habitat, and Niche

We have referred to the role of the environment in natural selection. The environment, in its most general sense, is anything and everything external to a particular entity. The environment of a specific red blood cell includes other red blood cells, white blood cells, and the plasma. A person's environment would include such things as clothing, furniture, air temperature, trees, and flowers, as well as other people.

This concept of environment is very broad. Therefore, it is often useful to think in terms of the physical environment, biological environment, and cultural environment. The **physical environment** refers to the inanimate elements of the surroundings, such as sunlight, the atmosphere, and soil. The living elements around us—the trees, grass, birds, and insects, for example—are more specifically referred to as the **biological environment.** The **cultural environment** contains the products of human endeavor, such as tools, shelters, clothing, toxic wastes, and even social institutions.

Sometimes we want to talk about the environmental factors immediately surrounding an organism. This is the **microenvironment.** For example, a particular organism may live in only a certain species of tree and may occupy space on only the end branches of those trees.

A term related to environment is **habitat;** habitat is defined as the place in which an organism lives. Examples of habitats are tropical rain forests, deserts, freshwater marshes, and tundra. Some authors also employ the concept of **microhabitat,** which is a more specific "address" for an organism, such as the upper story of the tropical rain forest.

In the study of natural selection, we are concerned with the specific environmental factors surrounding a specific organism. Yet environment is not enough, for different organisms have evolved different strategies for survival in each specific microhabitat. A useful concept in evolutionary studies is that of **ecological niche.**

physical environment The inanimate elements that surround an organism.

biological environment The living elements surrounding the organism.

cultural environment The products of human endeavor, including technology and social institutions surrounding the organism.

microenvironment A specific set of physical, biological, and cultural factors immediately surrounding the organism.

habitat The place in which a particular organism lives.

microhabitat A very specific habitat in which a population is found.

ecological niche The specific microhabitat in which a particular population lives and the way that population exploits that microhabitat.

This chart shows the spatial distribution of seven species of African arboreal monkeys in relationship to diet and three different activities. Each species occupies a specific niche that is defined in terms of space and how that space is used.

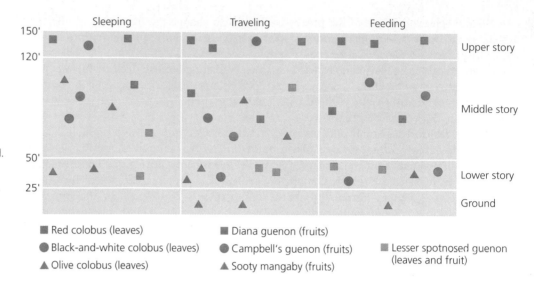

■ Red colobus (leaves)   ■ Diana guenon (fruits)

● Black-and-white colobus (leaves)   ● Campbell's guenon (fruits)   ■ Lesser spotnosed guenon (leaves and fruit)

▲ Olive colobus (leaves)   ▲ Sooty mangaby (fruits)

A niche, or ecological niche, refers first to the specific microhabitat in which a particular population lives. Sometimes the microhabitat is extremely narrow and includes a very specific set of environmental factors. Other times the niche is very broad in that the organism can function under a wide range of environmental factors.

The term ecological niche also includes the anatomical, physiological, and behavioral methods by which the organism exploits physical space and its relationship to other organisms. Two animals may occupy the same physical area, but one consuming leaves and the other fruits or one being active at night and the other active during the day are occupying different niches (Figure 5.1).

The Mechanisms of Natural Selection

As we saw in the last chapter, individuals in a population differ from one another in terms of their fertility rates, that is, the number of offspring they produce. Possessors of some phenotypes live to reproduce and do so to varying degrees; possessors of other phenotypes either die before reproductive age or live but do not reproduce. Numerous factors, both environmental and genetic, account for these differences in fertility rate.

Sometimes it is possible to identify a specific factor that brings about differences in fertility rates. For example, in Chapter 1 we looked at Darwin's finches on the island of Daphne Major. The medium ground finches show much variability in the sizes of their beaks. Differences in beak size, often a matter of only a few millimeters, are related to the ability of the bird to process seeds of particular size and hardness.

Changes in the climate profoundly affect the numbers and types of seeds that are available for finches to eat. During the 1976–1978 drought, Peter and Rosemary Grant documented the fact that small soft seeds rapidly disappeared, leaving only relatively large hard seeds to eat. Since only the birds with the larger beaks were able to handle the larger seeds effectively, these birds survived; birds with smaller beaks died. It has been estimated that about 80 percent of beak size is due to heredity. Therefore, when the rains came again, the surviving birds, which were those with the larger beaks, began to breed. The new generation of birds had beaks that were about 4 percent larger than the average beak size that existed before the drought.

selective agent Any factor that brings about differences in fertility and mortality.

selective pressure Pressure placed by a selective agent on certain individuals within the population that results in the change of allelic frequencies in the next generation.

Selective Agents Any factor that brings about a difference in fertility among members of a population is termed a **selective agent.** A selective agent places **selective pressure** on certain individuals in the population, resulting in a change in the frequency of alleles in the next generation. In the case of Darwin's finches, differences in the size and hardness of seeds were selective agents. (Of course, plants also are subject to natural selection. The lack of rainfall was a selective agent bringing about differences in fertility and mortality among seed-producing plants.)

An example of a selective agent in a human population is the smallpox virus. If a population is exposed to the virus, some individuals will acquire the disease and die, others will develop mild cases, and still others will not contract the disease at all. Environmental factors such as exposure, hygiene, age, diet, and stress play major roles in determining who gets the disease and the severity of the disease. Research suggests that certain biochemical factors, such as ABO blood types, also play a role in determining who acquires smallpox. Thus, possessors of certain phenotypes will have a higher death rate than others; a high mortality rate is directly related to a low fertility rate. Only those who survive will be available to transmit their genes to the next generation.

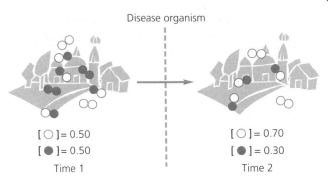

Figure 5.2 Disease as a Selective Agent Disease can bring about different survival rates among the possessors of different genotypes, hence changing the allele frequencies in the gene pool.

Selective agents act upon the phenotype of the members of the population. Only those individuals who survive the smallpox epidemic will be able to reproduce. If the factor that has enabled the organism to survive is determined genetically, these genes, passed on to the next generation, will aid in the survival from smallpox in the next generation. On the other hand, if the characteristic that led to survival is determined solely by an environmental factor, natural selection will not occur. Of course, the majority of phenotypic traits have both genetic and environmental components. Therefore, smallpox as a selective agent ultimately operates to produce a subsequent gene pool that is more resistant (better adapted) to the disease environment (Figure 5.2).

Finally, an environmental factor that may cause death but does not "select" one phenotype over another is not a selective agent. For example, an earthquake occurs in a rural region and 100 out of a population of 10,000 individuals die. If an individual survived because of luck, such as by chance being in an earthquake-proof building at the time of the earthquake, we cannot say that that person was selected for in terms of natural selection. Only if some factor determined or influenced by genes is selected for is natural selection taking place.

Fitness Individuals within a population reproduce at different rates. There are three primary reasons for this. The first is survival. Obviously, if an individual dies at an early age, the number of progeny he or she will produce will be dramatically reduced since that individual will have less time to reproduce. Of course, if the individual dies before puberty, that person will not reproduce at all.

A second reason for differences in reproductive rates is success at mating. Charles Darwin termed this *sexual selection,* a topic that will be discussed later in this chapter. Again, it is fairly obvious that if an individual fails to mate for one of several reasons, that individual's reproductive rate will be low or nonexistent. The third reason for differences in fitness is that individuals who do survive and mate will produce varying numbers of offspring.

The reasons for these differences in reproductive rates include both biological and environmental factors. An individual's reproductive rate will be different in different habitats. As a simple example, take an animal that is light-colored. In one habitat, where the ground is light in color, that animal will blend in and will be less likely to become someone's dinner. However, if the same animal moves to an area where the ground is dark—a lava flow, for example—it will stand out and probably will not survive for long.

The term that is often used to refer to differences in reproductive rates is **fitness.** An individual who is highly fit is an individual who, for whatever reason, has a large number of offspring in a particular habitat and thereby passes on a large amount of genetic material to the next generation. It follows that an individual who has low fitness has few if any offspring. Of course, the reproductive rates of most individuals fall somewhere between the two extremes.

fitness Measure of how well an individual or population is adapted to a specific ecological niche as seen in reproductive rates.

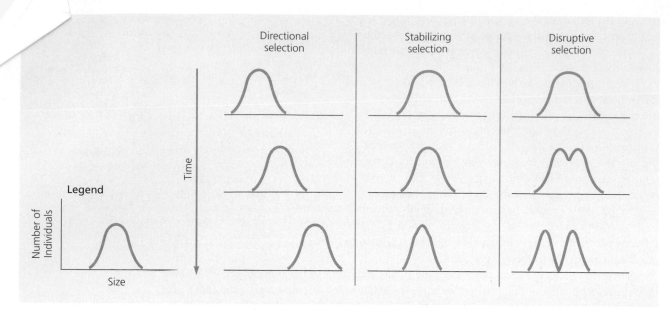

Figure 5.3 The Types of Natural Selection Three recognized types of natural selection exist because different parts of the range of variation have different reproductive rates.

The concept of fitness applies to all living things. With humans, however, it is important to remember that the term *fitness* does not refer to characteristics that a particular society values. A highly educated and wealthy citizen who has no children has a fertility rate of zero.

Types of Natural Selection

directional selection A type of natural selection characterized by a generation-after-generation shift in a population in a specific direction, such as toward larger body size. In this example, individuals with smaller body size are being selected against.

stabilizing selection A type of natural selection characterized by a generation-after-generation shift in a population in the direction of the average (mean) individual, such as, for example, toward average body size. In this example, individuals with small and large body size are being selected against.

We can examine the range of variation within a population. The different types of selection occur because different parts of the range of variation have different reproductive rates. Biologists generally recognize three types of natural selection (Figure 5.3). In all three cases, we start by looking at the distribution of variability—beak size in finches, for example—and observe where on the distribution curve selection is operating. In other words, where on the variation curve do we find significant differences in fertility rate?

Returning to the medium ground finch on Daphne Major, we observe that one end of the variability curve is being negatively impacted during the drought. That is, finches with small beaks are dying from starvation because they are unable to process the large, hard seeds that were the only seeds remaining. (The investigators actually measured the beaks of dead birds found on the island.) As a result, the mean of the curve showing variation in the next generation shifted toward larger beaks. This is called **directional selection** because the mean of the variation is moving each generation in a particular direction.[1]

Another situation is where natural selection selects against organisms at both ends of the curve; those individuals near the mean have the higher fertility rate. This often is found in populations that exist in stable habitats. An example is birth weight in humans. Human infants that are lighter or heavier than average do not survive as well as do those of average weight. This is termed **stabilizing selection.**

---

[1] One would expect that over time, the beaks of finches on Daphne Major would be getting larger and larger. However, directional selection actually favors smaller beaks during times of heavy rains. The end result is an oscillation of the mean back and forth over time.

The third type of natural selection is **disruptive selection.** Here, natural selection favors both extremes; individuals near the mean have the lower fertility rate. Diversity increases, and sometimes the population actually fragments into two new populations.

disruptive selection
A type of natural selection characterized by a generation-after-generation shift in the population away from the average individual, such as, for example, toward both larger and smaller body size. In this example, individuals with average (mean) body size are being selected against.

Natural Selection in Humans

Charles Darwin believed that natural selection progressed so slowly that it would be impossible to see. Yet today, biologists have documented over 100 cases of natural selection occurring in nature within a time frame that can be studied by human investigators. Natural selection also is occurring in human populations. Because of the long time between generations, however, examples of selection in human populations are not as easy to document as they are in birds, for example. Yet several studies based on indirect evidence have dealt with what might be real, but subtle, examples.

Selection against Simple Dominant and Recessive Alleles The least complicated case of natural selection is that involving total selection against a simple dominant abnormality that affects all persons who inherit the defective allele and is lethal before reproductive age. Since the trait affects all individuals with the allele equally and results in death before reproductive age, selection will eliminate the allele in the next generation. Because none of the individuals with the abnormality will reproduce, the appearance of the trait in the next generation will be due only to new mutations.

Natural selection acts much more slowly against a recessive trait. Only homozygous recessive individuals are affected by selection. Heterozygous individuals will carry the allele to the next generation. For example, persons with Tay-Sachs disease always die as children, but carriers survive to adulthood and have normal reproductive rates. Since the carriers act as a reservoir for defective alleles, the allele will tend to be eliminated, but much more slowly than will a dominant trait with the same fitness (Figure 5.4).

Natural Selection and the ABO Blood Types Differences in blood-type frequencies exist in different populations. For example, in a population in India, 35.38 percent of the members were of blood-type B; 33.21 percent were type O; 24.55 percent were type A; and 6.86 percent were type AB. This contrasts strongly with a Kwakiutl Indian population from British Columbia, Canada, in which 67.74 percent of the members were of type O and 32.27 percent were type A. Types B and AB were totally absent.[2]

Why should these differences exist within and between populations? Until relatively recent times, all people lived in small groups. Group differences developed from group to group because of genetic drift. Likewise, when a small group migrated from one group to establish a new population, differences developed because of the founder principle. However, evidence suggests that natural selection also played a role in the evolution of the ABO blood-type system.

In Chapter 1 we saw the relationship between phenotype and environment in the case of Darwin's finches, in which an increase in beak size was associated with drought conditions. We may speculate that there are associations between the various blood types and environmental factors,

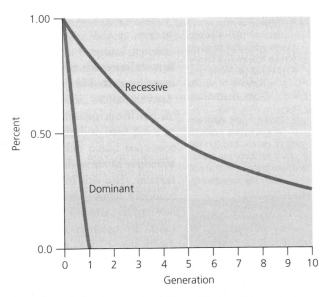

Figure 5.4 Selection against Rare Alleles This graph shows the rate at which frequencies of rare alleles are reduced by natural selection. One line shows a dominant abnormality, and the other a recessive one. In both cases, the frequencies begin at 1 percent, and selection is complete. Assume no new mutations.

[2] A. E. Mourant et al., *The Distribution of the Human Blood Groups and Other Polymorphisms,* 2nd ed. (London: Oxford University Press, 1976).

erythrocyte Red blood cell found in blood that lacks a nucleus and contains the red pigment hemoglobin.

hemoglobin Protein in red blood cell that carries oxygen to and carbon dioxide from body tissues.

hemoglobin A (HbA) Normal adult hemoglobin whose globin unit consists of two alpha and two beta chains.

hemoglobin A$_2$ (HbA$_2$) Normal adult hemoglobin whose globin unit consists of two alpha and two delta chains; hemoglobin A$_2$ is found in small quantities in normal human blood.

fetal hemoglobin (HbF) Normal form of hemoglobin, also known as *fetal hemoglobin,* that consists of two alpha and two gamma polypeptide chains; hemoglobin F is found in the fetus and early infant, and is gradually replaced by hemoglobin A.

hemoglobin S (HbS) An abnormal variant of hemoglobin A that differs from the latter in having a single amino acid substitution on the beta chain; know as *sickle hemoglobin.*

thus helping to explain the blood-type polymorphisms. One major environmental factor is the diseases that affect individuals of different blood types with different frequencies and severities.

Of particular interest are the associations between different blood types and the major epidemic diseases that have played major roles in world history. For example, people with blood type O seem to have higher rates of infection and higher mortality rates in association with plague, cholera, and tuberculosis, while those with blood type A have higher mortality rates with regard to smallpox and malaria. Thus, for example, a smallpox epidemic moving through a region will dramatically change the relative frequencies of blood types A and O as a result of differences in mortality and, hence, reproductive rates. There are many other associations of particular blood types and diseases.

Natural Selection and Sickle-Cell Anemia

Blood is a very complex tissue that includes, among other items, **erythrocytes,** or red blood cells. Packed into the erythrocytes are millions of molecules of the protein **hemoglobin.** There are several forms of normal hemoglobin. The most common is **hemoglobin A (HbA).** Others include **hemoglobin A$_2$ (HbA$_2$)**, which is found in small amounts in adult human blood, and **fetal hemoglobin (HbF),** which is found in the fetus but usually disappears within the first year after birth. These hemoglobins differ somewhat in the ability to carry oxygen. Hemoglobin also exists in many abnormal forms, the best known of which is **hemoglobin S (HbS),** whose presence is the cause of the inherited illness **sickle-cell anemia.**

Sickle-cell anemia is caused by the presence of hemoglobin S (HbS) within the red blood cells. This disease is characterized by periodic episodes during which the red blood cells become distorted and rigid, with some assuming the shape of a sickle (Figure 5.5). These abnormal cells clog the minute capillaries by forming small clots; cells located beyond the clots are deprived of oxygen and die. Depending on the location of the clots, they may cause heart failure, stroke, blindness, kidney damage, and other serious physical injuries.

The genetics of sickle-cell anemia is quite simple. The individual homozygous for HbA is normal, while the person homozygous for HbS has abnormal hemoglobin and the potential for developing the disease sickle-cell anemia. The heterozygous individual has a mixture of normal and abnormal hemoglobin but very rarely has symptoms related to HbS. Such an individual is said to have the **sickle-cell trait.** This is an example of codominance.

The precise molecular structure of HbS has been known for quite some time. The hemoglobin molecule consists of four heme units and a **globin.** The globin, in turn, consists of a

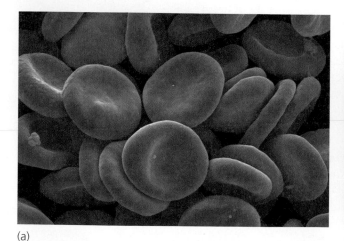

(a)

(b)

Figure 5.5 Normal and Sickled Erythrocytes The electron microscope reveals the distinctive shape of (a) normal erythrocytes and (b) sickled erythrocytes.

pair of alpha chains and a pair of beta chains. In HbS the alpha chains are normal; the defect is found in the beta chains. Out of the 146 amino acids that make up each beta chain, the sixth from the beginning of the molecule is incorrect: instead of glutamic acid, which is found in HbA, the amino acid valine is present in HbS. The rest of the chains are the same.

The codons that code for glutamic acid and valine differ in only one base pair. One code for glutamic acid is CTT, while one code for valine is CAT. There are 146 amino acids in the chain, coded by 438 nucleotides. A mistake in only one produces an abnormal hemoglobin with these drastic consequences.

Sickle-Cell Anemia as an Example of Natural Selection The fitness of the individual with sickle-cell anemia is effectively zero. Therefore, as we would expect, natural selection is operating to eliminate the allele Hb^S in many areas, such as the United States. Nevertheless, populations in many parts of Africa, southern Europe, and the Middle East have very high Hb^S allele frequencies, as high as approximately 0.20. This means that as many as 36 percent of the individuals in these populations have the sickle-cell trait or sickle-cell anemia. The high frequency for Hb^S is startling, especially when we remember that the frequency of the allele for PKU, also a deleterious recessive, is only 0.01 or less in all populations for which data are available. What factors are responsible for the high frequency of Hb^S?

The British geneticist Anthony Allison was one of the first to realize that the high frequencies of Hb^S are found in areas characterized by high incidences of falciparum malaria.[3] The distribution of hemoglobin S (seen in Figure 5.6) correlates highly with that of malaria. This suggests that the heterozygote, with both hemoglobin A and hemoglobin S, is relatively resistant to malaria and has a higher fitness than does either homozygous type. This increased resistance has been confirmed.

Malaria involves parasites that, at one stage of their complex reproductive cycle, reproduce in the red blood cell. The malaria parasite cannot infect cells that contain hemoglobin S. The fitness of the anemic individual is low because of the effects of sickle-cell anemia. The fitness of the individual homozygous for hemoglobin A in malarial areas is depressed because malaria has such a high mortality rate and because malaria often leaves the victim sterile.

The fitness of the heterozygote, however, is relatively high because of lower mortality from malaria. Thus, the heterozygote has the greatest probability of surviving, reproducing, and contributing the most genetic material to the next generation. Yet because the heterozygote produces a certain proportion of children with the disease, the death rate from sickle-cell anemia may be high in areas where the allele is plentiful.

Disease organisms are important environmental factors. Some anthropologists believe that malaria as it is known today did not exist in Africa before the development of farming some 10,000 years ago. This cultural change caused an opening of the forest and the creation of stagnant pools of water in which mosquitoes, which are the carriers of the malarial parasites, reproduced. As the rate of malaria increased, so did mortality. A population in a malarial environment has several possible fates. It may die off when the mortality rate is so great that the population is no longer large enough to maintain itself; on the other hand, a chance mechanism for survival might save the population.

Most likely, sickle-cell anemia already existed, but before the rise of malaria, the frequency of the allele Hb^S would have been low because of the low fitness of the anemic individual. With the increase and spread of malaria, the fitness of the heterozygote became greater than the fitness of the homozygous $Hb^A Hb^A$ individual, and the frequency of the allele Hb^S increased. Today, population fitness in malarial areas is balanced between mortality due to malaria and mortality due to sickle-cell anemia. The combined death rate is lower than the rate would be for mortality due to malaria alone if the sickle-cell allele did not exist. This situation, in which the heterozygous individual is best fit, is one form of **balanced polymorphism.**

sickle-cell anemia
Disorder in individuals homozygous for hemoglobin S in which red blood cells will develop into rigid, misshapen forms that clog capillaries, resulting in anemia, heart failure, and many other symptoms.

sickle-cell trait The condition of being heterozygous for hemoglobin A and S, yet the individual usually shows no abnormal symptoms.

globin A constituent of the hemoglobin molecule; in hemoglobin A, the globin consists of two alpha and two beta polypeptide chains.

balanced polymorphism Maintenance of two or more alleles in a gene pool as the result of heterozygous advantage.

---

[3] A. C. Allison, "Protection Afforded by Sickle-Cell Trait against Subtertian Malarial Infection," *British Medical Journal* 1 (1954), pp. 290–294.

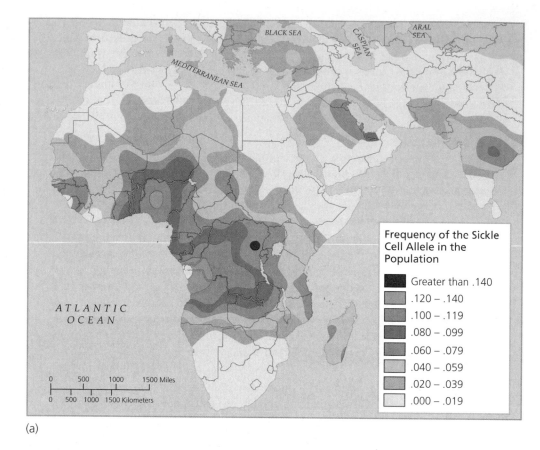

(a)

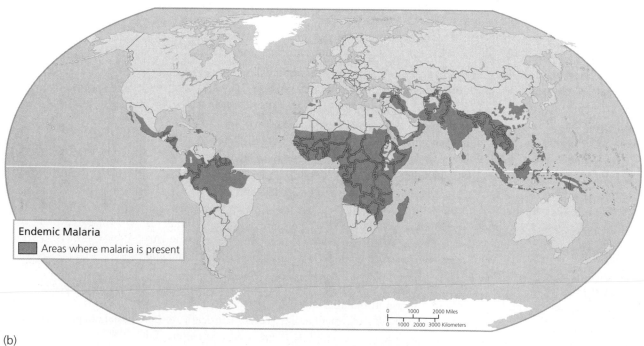

(b)

Figure 5.6 Distribution of (a) the Sickle Cell Allele and (b) Endemic Malaria

Balanced polymorphism is a condition for which two or more alleles are maintained in a population by natural selection. Selection produces an equilibrium so that allele frequencies remain the same from generation to generation. Heterozygote advantage, as seen in the case of sickle-cell anemia, is the simplest type of balanced polymorphism. In such a case, if the frequency of the sickle-cell allele decreases, more people who are homozygous for Hb^A are born, and there is increased selection against the Hb^A allele. If the frequency of the Hb^S allele increases, more individuals homozygous for that allele are born, and there is increased selection against the Hb^S allele. If the heterozygote is more fit than either homozygous condition, this produces a balance–counterbalance system that keeps the frequencies of alleles stable.

Several other genetic conditions are associated with the distribution of malaria. They include **hemoglobin C** in northwestern Africa and the **thalassemias** found in a wide area, including the Mediterranean areas of Europe and Africa, through southern Asia, and Indonesia.

Sexual Selection

Natural selection is, in part, about access to resources. Animals that are more successful at finding and processing food, for example, are more likely to survive and produce the greater numbers of offspring. In natural selection, both males and females are competing for access to resources such as food and space. However, the situation for females and males differs significantly when it comes to reproduction.

Among mammals in general, an individual female makes a major investment in each of her offspring in terms of pregnancy, nursing, and protecting the newborn infant. This is often accomplished without any assistance from the male, although, in many species, males do play important roles in the rearing of offspring. The reproductive success of a female, that is, the number of offspring the female produces in her lifetime, is limited by her access to resources such as food and a good hiding place for her young. All females do generally mate. Thus, differential access to males as mates is not a factor in female reproductive success.

The situation is different for males. A particular male can produce offspring with a number of females. The reproductive success of a male, that is, the number of offspring a male can sire and, ultimately, the number of genes he can pass on to the next generation, is determined by the number of females with which he mates. Therefore, the male's reproductive success is limited by his access to females, resulting in competition among males for females. Characteristics that increase the success of a male in competing for females will increase in frequency over time; this is called **sexual selection.**

Intersexual Selection Evolutionary biologists recognize two forms of sexual selection. The first is **intersexual selection,** selection for traits that make males more attractive to females. This occurs when females consistently select as mates males with particular features that are unique to males. Of course, as in natural selection, sexual selection will occur only if the trait selected is inherited.

There are many kinds of intersexual selection. Females often prefer as mates males with traits that confer direct benefit on the female. These traits include those that enable the male to more successfully protect offspring, provide food, or defend the territory where the offspring are kept.

For example, in many species, males will first establish territories as a prelude to competing for females. Females will be attracted to males with large safe territories; the presence of such territories will increase the probability of her offspring surviving.

Another kind of trait that appears to be favored by sexual selection is that which enables the female to distinguish male genetic quality. Many male mammals and birds are characterized by conspicuously colored body parts. Often there is a direct correlation between the brightness of a patch of fur or feathers and the health of the animal. For example, parasites often result in a dulling of an animal's coat. Parasite infestation is also affected, to a degree,

hemoglobin C An abnormal variant of hemoglobin A that differs from the latter in having a single amino acid substitution on the beta chain at the same position as the substitution producing hemoglobin S.

thalassemia Absence or reduction of alpha- or beta-chain synthesis in hemoglobin; in the homozygous condition (thalassemia major), a high frequency of hemoglobin F and fatal anemia occurs; in the heterozygous condition (thalassemia minor), it is highly variable but usually occurs with mild symptoms.

See the Online Learning Center for an Interactive Exercise on sexual selection.

sexual selection Selection that favors characteristics that increase reproductive success, usually due to male competition or female mate choice.

intersexual selection A form of sexual selection; selection for traits that make males more attractive to females.

Figure 5.7 Intersexual Selection The male peacock displays his brightly colored plumage in an attempt to attract the attention of the female in the foreground.

intrasexual selection A form of sexual selection. Selection for characteristics that make males better able to compete with one another for sexual access to females.

sexual dimorphism Differences in structure between males and females of the same species.

by the animal's genotype. By favoring a brightly colored male, females are selecting as mates the more healthy animals.

Intersexual competition sometimes leads to an exaggeration of male traits. The classic example is the large and colorful tail of the peacock (Figure 5.7). Female preference for large, brightly colored tails, related to the health status of the male, has led, through time, to extremely large, colorful tails. Yet such tails have a downside. A bird endowed with such a large, bright phenotype will be easily seen by predators and have difficulty flying. Perhaps the fact that such males are able to survive means that they possess the right genes for survival.

Intrasexual Selection The second form of sexual selection is **intrasexual selection.** In this case, males directly compete with one another, with the winner enjoying sexual access to the females. Males will engage in fights and displays directed toward one another. Ultimately, one male will drive the other males away and will take possession of the female or females. The females do not have any choice in the matter. Therefore, sexual selection favors those traits that increase the probability of a male winning the battle with other males.

Success in fights often depends on greater general size and the evolution and enlargement of special anatomical features for fighting such as large canine teeth and large horns, tusks, and antlers. In many mammalian species, males are significantly larger than are females, and males often exhibit distinct physical features. This phenomenon is referred to as **sexual dimorphism.** For example, male orangutans are considerably larger than females, and, in one subspecies, they also possess a flange of flesh around the face (Figure 5.8).

Figure 5.8 Intrasexual Selection Among the orangutans, the adult male, seen here on the left, is much larger than the adult female, seen on the right. This is an example of sexual dimorphism.

Sexual Selection in Humans The demonstration of sexual selection in humans is difficult. The heart of the problem is the issue of what aspects of human behavior are genetically determined and what aspects are the results of culture. With the exception of a very small number of genetic abnormalities that include very specific behavioral symptoms, scholars have yet to identify any normal behavior pattern that is clearly inherited. On the other hand there is evidence that some behavioral patterns do have genetic components.

Many scholars are interested in the issue of biological influence on human behavior and the role of natural selection in human behavior. This is in large part the discipline of **evolutionary psychology.** It should be pointed out that this research is very controversial and has more than its share of critics. We do not have room in these pages for a rigorous critique of these ideas, but they should be taken simply as suggestions and an area for future research.

evolutionary psychology
The study of the role of biology and natural selection on human behavior.

David M. Buss led a major cross-cultural study on the subject of mate choice.[4] In this study, Buss and his colleagues interviewed 9474 individuals from 33 countries on six continents and five islands. In the interviews, each individual was questioned about characteristics desired in a mate.

Some traits on the list showed great variation from culture to culture. These are probably the result of cultural tradition, that is, learned behavior. An example is the importance of chastity in a mate. In some societies, including China, India, Indonesia, and Iran, great importance was placed on chastity. In contrast, many Western European societies, including Sweden, Finland, and West Germany, responded that chastity was irrelevant or unimportant.

See the Online Learning Center for an Internet Activity on evolutionary psychology.

A number of traits showed great differences between male and female subjects. In general, males in all societies appear to value appearance in a potential mate more than do females. Females appear to value to a greater degree than males educational background, emotional stability, favorable social status, and intelligence. Such sex differences are fairly consistent among the various cultures.

Buss believes that the differences between what males and what females are looking for in potential mates are examples of sexual selection. Males tend to prefer females who will reproduce successfully. Fertility in women is highest in their early 20s and steadily declines until menopause. A male seeking to maximize his reproductive success would be expected to favor women in their early 20s along with physical features that are associated with youth, features that men consider to be associated with beauty. Although men express their preference in terms of beauty, in effect, men are exhibiting preferences for women with the highest probability of reproductive success.

On the other hand, Buss tells us that women prefer mates who are able to provide resources for them and their children, since resources (such as food, shelter, access to health care, and so forth) will maximize their reproductive success. Beauty is not as critical an issue in selecting a mate. More important are factors associated with financial success, social status, and education. Older males can be quite fertile, and most older males are clearly established in their careers and social status.

Kin Selection

Both natural selection and sexual selection can be seen in terms of reproductive success for the individual. The finch with the larger beak that can process food during a drought and a colorful peacock that is more successful than his fellows at attracting a female will have relatively high reproductive rates. In the first case, the finch succeeds through survival; in the second case, the peacock succeeds by successfully attracting a female. Fitness has been defined in terms of the number of offspring produced by the animal. The large-beaked finch

---

[4] D. M. Buss et al., "International Preferences in Selecting Mates," *Journal of Cross-Cultural Psychology* 21 (1990), pp. 5–47; D. M. Buss and D. P. Schmitt, "Sexual Strategies Theory: An Evolutionary Perspective on Human Mating," *Psychological Review* 100 (1993), pp. 204–232.

Figure 5.9 Kin Selection In kin selection an individual's genes are selected for by virtue of that individual's increasing the chances that his or her kin's genes will be propagated into the next generation. This illustration shows an older sibling (right) that stays near the nest and assists its parents in raising its younger siblings. By so doing, it is helping to increase the probability of the offspring surviving and hence the probability of its genes being represented in the next generation's gene pool. In a like manner, members of a human family that cooperate in the protection of the relatives with whom they share alleles are increasing the fitness of those shared alleles.

altruism Behavior characterized by self-sacrifice that benefits others.

kin selection A process whereby an individual's genes are selected for by virtue of that individual's increasing the chances that his or her kin's genes are propagated into the next generation.

inclusive fitness An individual's own fitness plus his or her effect on the fitness of any relative.

coefficient of relatedness A measurement of the degree of genetic relationship or the number of shared genes between two individuals.

and the colorful peacock have a high degree of fitness since they produce a larger number of offspring than other individuals.

Biologists noted in their studies of animal behavior that most behaviors can be explained in terms of increased fitness. Nevertheless, there exists a set of behaviors that actually reduce the fitness of the individual. How can such features evolve? For example, some animals will postpone breeding in order to assist their parents in raising the next generation. Because of this assistance, a greater number of the parents' offspring will survive (Figure 5.9). Also, an animal will share a limited food supply with another animal, thus reducing the food available to it. There are many situations in which animals behave in ways that contribute to the survival of other members of the community, sometimes placing themselves at a disadvantage. This type of behavior is known as **altruism.**

In 1964, W. D. Hamilton (1936–2000) proposed the concept of **kin selection.**[5] Simply put, fitness can be seen in terms of maximizing the number of genes passed on to the next generation. Biologically related individuals share a certain number of their genes. Thus, if an animal behaves in a way that causes the fitness of a relative to increase, this will, in effect, increase the number of the first individual's genes in the next generation. We use the term **inclusive fitness** when we combine the fitness of an individual with a proportion of the fitness of kin sharing many of the same genes.

Hamilton developed a mathematical statement of kin selection: $rb > c$. In this formula, b is the fitness benefit to those affected by the behavior, while c is the fitness cost to the individual who is doing the behavior. Thus, altruistic behavior will evolve in situations where the benefit is greater than ($>$) the cost. However, a key factor is the closeness of the relationship. The letter r stands for the **coefficient of relatedness,** which is a measure of the proportion of genes that are shared. Table 5.1 gives the coefficient of relatedness for a number of representative relationships. When we take this coefficient of relatedness into account, we see that the closer the relationship, the greater the cost that will be tolerated.

Table 5.1 Coefficient of Relatedness

Relationship	r
Parent and child	0.5
Full siblings	0.5
Grandparent and grandchild	0.25
Uncle/aunt and nephew/niece	0.25
First cousins	0.125
Nonrelatives	0.0

[5] W. D. Hamilton, "The Evolution of Social Behavior," *Journal of Theoretical Biology*, 7 (1964), pp. 1–52.

Summary

Variability is inherent in all populations. The human species is polymorphic, and natural selection operates upon this variability. Natural selection can be seen as differences in reproductive rates among the variants within the population. Possessors of some genotypes reproduce to varying degrees, while others leave behind no offspring. Since the possessors of different genotypes produce differing numbers of offspring, their contribution to the next generation differs, and this brings about changes in the gene pool. Individuals or populations with higher survival or fertility rates are said to be better fitted to the environment in which they live. Still, a genotype that is fit in one environment may lose some or all of its fitness in a new one; the converse is also true.

There are three types of natural selection: directional selection, stabilizing selection, and disruptive selection. All of them are seen as eliminating those individuals from the population who are not fit or are less fit than others in the population. In contrast is kin selection, whereby an individual contributes to his or her reproductive success by acting in a manner that allows his or her kin to be reproductively successful.

Still another type of selection is sexual selection. Intersexual selection selects for traits that make males more attractive to females. Intrasexual selection involves males competing with one another, with the successful individuals contributing genes to the next generation.

THE ORIGIN OF SPECIES

Microevolution is the process of establishing and eliminating alleles from a population through such processes as natural selection and genetic drift. It is small-scale evolution that can be seen occurring in living populations, as in the case of Darwin's finches. Thus far we have been discussing microevolution.

See the Online Learning Center for an Internet Activity on speciation.

Macroevolution, the subject of this section, addresses the evolution of new species and higher categories such as genera and families. It is evolution, which in part is the cumulative effect of microevolutionary change, that takes place over many generations and can be inferred from fossil and other types of evidence.

The Evolution of Subspecies

All natural populations of plants and animals vary. For instance, within your community, your classroom, and your family, there are obvious differences in physical appearance in addition to less easily observed differences in such traits as blood type and resistance to disease.

Likewise, small natural populations vary. These local populations or **demes** are groups of organisms of the same species that live together, exploit the same habitat, and mate most frequently with one another. As a result, individuals within the deme tend to resemble one another more closely than they do individuals living in adjacent demes.

demes Local breeding populations; the smallest reproductive populations.

Demes, however, do not exist in isolation. Members of one deme, sometimes all the adult members of one sex, will leave the deme of their birth, often at puberty, and join a neighboring deme. When the newcomer mates with members of the new deme, new alleles are effectively transferred from one deme to another. This is gene flow (Figure 5.10).

As a result of gene flow, nearby demes resemble one another more closely than do demes farther away. This can be illustrated by a map showing the distribution of demes of a particular kind of animal. When we plot a particular feature, its frequency appears to

Box 5-2   Social Darwinism

What famous person who lived in the nineteenth century coined the phrase "survival of the fittest"? When asked, many students assertively answer: Charles Darwin. Actually, the phrase was coined by the English philosopher Herbert Spencer (1820–1903), who was greatly influenced by Darwin's ideas. In many of his works, including *First Principles* (1862) and *Principles of Ethics* (1879–1893), Spencer attempted to apply his own and Darwin's notions of biological evolution to psychology, sociology, and other social sciences. The application of the principles of biological evolution to explain topics such as social inequalities became known as social Darwinism.

Spencer and other proponents of social Darwinism viewed social life as a competitive struggle for power, wealth, and general well-being among individuals and nations. Using this concept, Europeans of the nineteenth century could argue that their dominant position in the world was the result of natural superiority that resulted from natural selection. The Asian, African, Polynesian, and other peoples that Europeans ruled or subdued at the time were seen as belonging to earlier and more primitive stages of evolution. Likewise, the social inequalities among individuals within European society were thought to be variations on which natural selection acted. The prosperous were seen as being "fit," while the poor and powerless were seen as "unfit" individuals against whom natural selection would select.

Spencer and other social Darwinists, including the American sociologist William Graham Sumner (1840–1910), believed that government should do nothing to aid the poor or sick. Modern social Darwinists assert that programs such as food stamps, aid to families with dependent children, and free public health clinics would interfere with the natural weeding out of unfit people and thereby weaken society. Or, said in reverse, a laissez-faire approach to social inequalities would lead to a natural cleansing of a population and hence would lead to a society and a world better adapted to environmental pressures. In the United States and Europe, social Darwinism has been used to justify discriminatory actions against women, nonwhites, and various ethnic groups. It must be noted, however, that Charles Darwin was not a social Darwinist; at least, he avoided any discussion of the social implications of his ideas.

Scientific studies on human populations have not supported the tenets of social Darwinism. It appears that it is discrimination and the ideas of superiority, as well as differential access to natural resources, that produce most inequalities. The fact that some societies are more powerful than others and that some individuals within a society do not have equal access to necessities and luxuries is due to social history. When populations or classes of people within societies are freed from discriminatory practices, they can reach the same levels of wealth, power, and education as those groups which traditionally define themselves as superior.

---

clinal distribution
A distribution of frequencies that show a systematic gradation over space; also called continuous variation.

subspecies Interfertile groups within a species that display significant differentiation among themselves.

change as a function of distance. This systematic change in the frequency of a trait as one moves in a given direction is referred to as a **clinal distribution.**

In reality the distribution of demes is seldom regular across the landscape. Subtle differences in environment, such as typography, microclimate, and plant life, will create subtle differences in ecological niche. Also, there are various hindrances and barriers to gene flow—a patch of desert or a fast-flowing river. Whether there are complete barriers or more subtle influences that slow down gene flow, groups of demes develop distinctive features that separate them from other groups of demes. Individuals within groups may be, on the average, larger, different in color, or different in body shape. Such distinct segments of a species are referred to as **subspecies.** Yet in spite of the differences that exist between

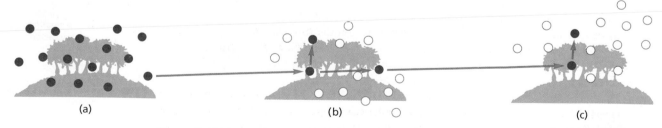

(a)   (b)   (c)

Figure 5.10 Gene Flow An individual from population a moves to an adjacent island and breeds with members of population b. His or her alleles become a part of the gene pool of population b. a descendant of the original individual moves to another island and breeds with members of population c. Thus, alleles from population a are ultimately introduced into population c.

subspecies, all members of all subspecies that make up the species are capable of successful reproduction.

Of course, physical barriers to gene flow may be very minor or even nonexistent, and variation among demes may be more or less continuous from one end of a range to another. Yet groups of demes at opposite ends of the range may appear distinct, and thus they may be defined as separate subspecies. It is difficult to draw a dividing line where one subspecies ends and another begins.

The Evolution of Species

The development of subspecies usually occurs when some factor is present that prevents or hinders gene flow between groups of demes. The simplest example is **geographical isolation** (Figure 5.11). If a particular animal is not capable of crossing bodies of water, for example, the change in the course of a river that now cuts across an area occupied by the species will create two groups of demes, one on either side of the river. Inability to swim prevents gene flow from occurring, leaving each group to evolve its own unique characteristics and to evolve into two distinct subspecies.

Once gene flow between two subspecies has ceased, two subspecies will continue to evolve independently, as various mechanisms, such as genetic drift and natural selection, operate differently in the two populations. Also, new alleles may arise in one subspecies and not in the other through mutation. If the genetic differences between the subspecies become great enough, members of the two subspecies will no longer be capable of successful reproduction with each other even if the barrier is later removed. Consequently, the two groups may begin as two distinct subspecies and eventually evolve into two distinct species.

Geographical Isolation Geographical isolation is a primary initiator of the evolution of new species in animals. It is the process in which members of a population become separated by barriers that prevent the interchange of genes. Such barriers include large bodies of water, mountain ranges, and deserts. Isolation allows descended populations to develop in an undisturbed manner, without the infusion of genes from another closely related population. **Speciation,** the evolution of new species, occurs when the separated populations have evolved characteristics that successfully prevent reproduction between them even if the geographical barriers are later lifted. Species that occupy mutually exclusive geographical areas are called **allopatric species** (Figure 5.12a).

Speciation may result from spatial isolation more subtle than major geographical barriers. Organisms may adapt to narrowly defined ecological niches. Within a tropical forest, for example, the tops of trees present microhabitats that may be quite different from those on the tree trunks or near the ground. In such cases, speciation may take place because of spatial isolation within a relatively small area.

Mutation, drift, nonrandom mating, and selection operate to bring about speciation in isolated populations. The probability that the *same* mutation will occur, or that mutations will occur in the same sequence, in two different isolated populations is effectively zero. Different mutations create different potential genotypes.

Also, alleles can recombine in an almost infinite number of ways, which is important since a particular allele can have differing selective advantages in the context of variable genotypes. Since each isolated population contains unique gene combinations, new combinations may arise by chance, providing some selective advantage to the population.

In addition, no two habitats are identical. Therefore, separate populations are subject to different selective pressures. The genetic systems of separated populations tend to adapt to

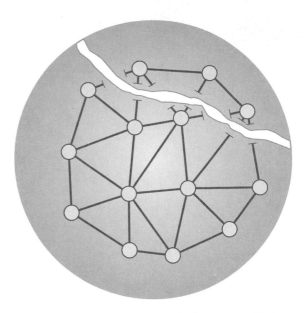

Figure 5.11 First Step in Speciation Geographical isolation of two groups of demes prevents gene flow between them. Small circles represent demes, and connecting lines between them represent gene flow.

geographical isolation Form of reproductive isolation in which members of a population become separated from another population through geographical barriers that prevent the interchange of genes between the separated populations.

speciation An evolutionary process that is said to occur when two previous subspecies (of the same species) are no longer capable of successful interbreeding; they are then two different species.

allopatric species Species occupying mutually exclusive geographical areas.

Figure 5.12 Allopatric and Sympatric Species (a) Allopatric species occupy mutually exclusive geographical areas. (b) Sympatric species live in the same area, but they are prevented from successful reproduction by a reproductive isolating mechanism.

sympatric species
Different species living in the same area but prevented from successfully reproducing by a reproductive isolating mechanism.

ecological isolation Form of reproductive isolation in which two closely related species are separated by what is often a slight difference in the niches they occupy.

seasonal isolation Form of reproductive isolation in which the breeding seasons of two closely related populations do not correspond.

sexual isolation Form of reproductive isolation in which one or both sexes of a species initiate mating behavior that does not act as a stimulus to the opposite sex of a closely related species.

mechanical isolation Form of reproductive isolation that occurs because of an incompatibility in structure of the male and female sex organs.

the changing environments. In fact, they must, or else they will become extinct. The new populations also represent different sectors of the parental population because of the founder principle, and so they are somewhat different from each other from the very beginning.

Reproductive Isolating Mechanisms Spatial isolation initiates speciation, but once speciation has taken place, the related species may come to reside within the same region. Such species are called **sympatric species** (Figure 5.12b). Eight reproductive isolating mechanisms serve to separate closely related species living side by side.

Ecological isolation is the circumstance in which two closely related populations are separated by what is often a slight difference in the niches they occupy. Some species are adapted to such extremely narrow niches that minor differences, such as variations in soil conditions, can effectively separate them, even when they are living next to each other.

Seasonal isolation occurs when the breeding seasons of two closely related populations do not correspond. For example, a male from one species whose breeding season is in April will not mate with a female from another species whose breeding season is in June.

Sexual isolation is the condition in which an incompatibility in behavior prevents mating between individuals of closely related populations. For instance, one or both sexes of a species may initiate mating by a pattern of behavior that acts as a stimulus to the other sex of its own species but does not act as a stimulus to the opposite sex in a closely related species. The stimuli might take the form of specific visual signals, such as the mating rituals of certain birds or the light signals sent out by male fireflies. The member of the opposite sex responds only to the signal characteristic of its group. Incompatibility in auditory stimuli, such as calls, and chemical stimuli, such as the release of odoriferous substances, also can act as behavioral isolating mechanisms.

Mechanical isolation occurs because of an incompatibility in the structure of the male and female sex organs. In some cases, copulation is attempted, but no sperm is transferred.

Ecological, seasonal, sexual, and mechanical reproductive isolating mechanisms are **premating mechanisms** that prevent species from exchanging sperm and ova. In **postmating mechanisms,** gametes are exchanged but either no offspring result or the offspring that do result are inviable, are sterile, or have reduced fertility. Premating mechanisms are less wasteful than postmating mechanisms, since in the former gametes are not used, but in the latter they are.

Gametic mortality is the process by which sperm are immobilized and destroyed before fertilization can take place. This occurs if antibodies in the genital tract of the female kill the sperm or if sperm cannot penetrate the membrane of the egg. The term **zygotic mortality** describes the situation in which fertilization occurs but development ceases soon after.

Hybrid inviability occurs when a mating between two species gives rise to a fertile hybrid that does not leave any offspring. This process is not well understood, but the lack of success of the hybrid may depend on its inability to compete effectively with nonhybrid individuals. In other words, the hybrid may not be as well adapted as the nonhybrid parents, or it may not display appropriate mating behavior. These adaptive and behavioral limitations may prevent the production of progeny.

Hybrid sterility occurs when the hybrid of two species is sterile. The classic example is the hybrid of the horse and the donkey, the mule, which, with few exceptions, is incapable of reproduction.

Specialized and Generalized Species

A species is **specialized** when it exhibits little variation. Thus, it can tolerate little change in its particular niche. A specialized species may not be able to move into new niches, even when the environmental conditions are similar, and may not be able to compete successfully with other populations.

An example of an extremely specialized animal in terms of diet is the Australian koala, which eats almost exclusively the leaves of eucalyptus trees. The many species of eucalyptus evolved toxins that prevent many animals, especially insects, from eating their leaves. However, koalas evolved a highly specialized digestive system in which bacteria break down those toxins and thus were able to occupy niches that were occupied by few other animals. However, there is a price to pay for such specialization in that the koala cannot process many other types of food. The distribution and proliferation of these trees therefore determine the distribution of the animal. Any change in tree population, due to a change in climate or in human use, will affect the koala population.

Because a specialized species can tolerate little change in its ecological niche, its ability to disperse is limited. However, as long as the habitat remains stable, a specialized species will be highly competitive toward less specialized species in its habitat. It will experience a high degree of reproductive success.

A **generalized species** exhibits a greater variability than does a specialized species and can survive in a variety of ecological niches. Humans are perhaps the most generalized of all species. Humans' variability is also expressed in terms of cultural patterns. Through their cultural ingenuity, human populations can adjust to environments such as the extreme cold of the Arctic and the heat and humidity of the tropics by making tools and building appropriate shelters. Now, with the development of life-support systems, people can live for extended periods under the sea and in outer space. This ability to move into a variety of habitats has been responsible for the great dispersal of humans over the earth. Perhaps in the future it will be responsible for their dispersal throughout the solar system.

Because of people's lack of precise environmental requirements, and because of their ability to adjust culturally, geographical barriers have had little chance to isolate human populations effectively. Since gene flow has been continuous, speciation has not occurred among humans. People are, of course, not the only generalized animals. In fact, *generalized* and *specialized* are relative terms. At one end is the extremely specialized koala and at the other the very generalized *Homo sapiens*. Within these limits are varying degrees of generalization and specialization.

We have been using the concepts of generalization and specialization to refer to the relationship between a population and its niche, but we also can use these terms to label specific characteristics displayed by the members of populations. For instance, the human

premating mechanism A form of reproductive isolation that prevents mating from occurring.

postmating mechanism Any form of reproductive isolation that occurs after mating.

gametic mortality Form of reproductive isolation in which sperm are immobilized and destroyed before fertilization can take place.

zygotic mortality Form of reproductive isolation in which fertilization occurs but development stops soon after.

hybrid inviability Form of reproductive isolation in which a mating between two species gives rise to a hybrid that is fertile but nevertheless does not leave any offspring.

hybrid sterility Form of reproductive isolation in which a hybrid of two species is sterile.

specialized species A species closely fitted to a specific niche and able to tolerate little change in that niche.

generalized species Species that can survive in a variety of ecological niches.

Humans are one of the most ecologically generalized species, primarily because of human culture, which allows for flexible responses to diversity and environmental change. Humans also display some biological variation—polymorphisms, for example—that evolve in response to natural selection.

Eugenics is the study of various methods that can improve the inherited qualities of a species. Nevertheless, in some instances, eugenic programs could have a very negative effect on the human population by reducing genetic variability.

A major question is: What traits should be eliminated? Genetic abnormalities that lead to an early death, extremely low intelligence, and severe skeletal abnormalities will probably never have any advantages in future generations. However, what about certain mild metabolic defects or blood disorders that could conceivably have beneficial effects if the environment should change? Also, alleles that are deleterious in the homozygous state may confer adaptive advantage in the heterozygote.

A classic example of this situation is the relationship between sickle-cell anemia and malaria. Sickle-cell anemia is often a lethal trait, bringing about disability and early death, yet the presence of this deleterious allele in the heterozygous individual brings about a resistance to malaria, a resistance also found in the homozygous individual. Many other examples exist of alleles that, although disadvantageous in the homozygous recessive state,

bring about a greater adaptation in the heterozygous than in the homozygous normal individual (balanced polymorphism). In 1987, the carrier rate for cystic fibrosis, a fatal lung disease, was found to be higher than expected; one explanatory proposal is that the heterozygous individual has some selective advantage that has not yet been identified.

Imagine a situation whereby, by using eugenic means, we could eliminate the allele for sickle-cell anemia through detection of heterozygotes. This is a fine goal. What would happen, though, if the techniques for controlling malaria become ineffective? Because of the disappearance of the sickle-cell allele, the population would lack the protection from malaria conferred by this allele. This is not far-fetched, since the major means of controlling malaria is to destroy the disease-carrying mosquito with insecticides such as DDT. Already, large populations of mosquitoes have evolved resistance to DDT. If malaria became a threat again and the sickle-cell allele no longer existed, the population would be less fit in the new malarial environment than it was in the old one.

As the situation changes, what was at one time advantageous (the sickle-cell trait) might become disadvantageous, but conceivably it could become advantageous again. Also, new diseases can evolve; if certain types of people are deleted from the population through eugenics, it later might turn out that they were the people who carried the immunity to the new disease.

hand is generalized in that it can be used for many purposes, such as carrying objects and manufacturing tools. The foot, on the other hand, is specialized in that it is used for basically one thing, locomotion. What is important here is that the relative specialization or generalization of a specific trait may make that trait more or less important for survival than another trait. Generally, the more specialized anatomical, physiological, or behavioral features an animal has, the more specialized the total phenotype will be.

Specialization can lead not only to speciation but also to evolutionary dead ends. The more specialized an animal becomes, the less likely it will be to move into new niches; hence, the animal has less chance of encountering the isolation necessary for further speciation to occur. When a species becomes so specialized in a particular niche that it cannot tolerate change, it is in greater danger of extinction than a more generalized species is. If eucalyptus trees die out, so will koalas. On the other hand, if one of the environments that a particular group of humans occupies becomes unlivable, other environments will support this group.

Rates of Speciation

The rates at which speciation occurs are difficult to determine, and the fossil record is of little help. First, it is difficult or impossible to know when reproductive isolating mechanisms came into being. How is one to know from bones if differences in mating behavior existed between two morphologically similar populations?

Second, even if isolating mechanisms could be observed in the fossil record, they develop in too short a time for the points at which differentiation takes place to be noticed. Reproductive isolating mechanisms might develop quickly, but a fossil sequence most likely consists of forms that lived thousands of years apart.

Although rates of speciation cannot be measured effectively, we can infer that they are dependent on internal and external factors. Internal factors include such things as point mutations, chromosome changes, and other genetic factors that may lead to the development of reproductive isolating mechanisms. External factors include the types of barriers to gene flow, the types of new ecological niches available, and so forth.

We may assume that related populations that have low mutation rates, that live in homogeneous environments without physical barriers, and that are not under great selective pressure may remain basically stable and not develop sufficient differences for speciation. It follows that high mutation rates, strong selective pressures, differing ecological niches, and separation by geographical barriers may provide the necessary conditions for rapid speciation.

The Tempo of Evolutionary Change There are two general views on the tempo of evolutionary change. **Phyletic gradualism** sees evolution as a slow process characterized by gradual transformation of one population into others. In 1972, paleontologists Niles Eldridge and Stephen Jay Gould (1941–2002) proposed a different scheme, called **punctuated equilibrium.**[6]

The phyletic gradualism model of evolution assumes that the rate of evolutionary change is relatively slow and constant most of the time. The fossil record, however, reveals what appear to be shifts in the pace of evolutionary change within specific lineages. An evolutionary line that has been very "conservative" for millions of years may seem to suddenly undergo a rapid burst of evolutionary change. Evolution may proceed quickly when a population enters a new habitat, but as the population adapts to its new niche, the rate of evolution will slow.

These shifts in the tempo of evolution are seen as an illusion by phyletic gradualists. Such shifts in tempo are explained as reflections of imperfections in the fossil record, caused by such things as changing conditions for fossilization and cycles of erosion.

The punctuated equilibrium model is consistent with the data from the fossil record. Eldredge and Gould propose that a large population may become fragmented into several new populations by geographical isolation or migration. New populations, now peripheral to the main population, would initially differ from the main population because of the founder effect. In addition, these peripheral populations would be small and therefore subject to the effects of genetic drift. Some researchers believe that in small peripheral populations, genetic drift is a much stronger evolutionary force than has previously been proposed in most microevolutionary models. Thus, natural selection and genetic drift may differ in their importance in microevolution and macroevolution in different populations (Figure 5.13).

Other genetic events could be responsible for relatively rapid evolutionary shifts. Among these would be chromosomal mutations such as translocations and inversions. Another possibility involves regulatory genes. A regulatory gene initiates or blocks the activities of another gene. Mutations in regulatory genes may play an important role in speciation. Such mutations would not affect the coding for a polypeptide chain, but they might change the timing of the production of that structural unit or block its production altogether.

Some Basic Concepts in Evolutionary Theory

We will conclude this chapter by looking at some concepts that will prove useful in later chapters. They are competition, preadaptation, adaptive radiation, and extinction.

Competition Animal populations are able to expand into new geographical regions and occupy some of the ecological niches that exist in those regions. However, the ability to adapt to new niches varies from an extremely limited potential in some populations to an almost unlimited, expansive ability in others. The major factors influencing this capability include the nature of the geographical barriers, the amount of change a group of organisms can tolerate, and the mode or modes of dispersal, that is, the ability of the organism to "get around."

See the Online Learning Center for an Internet Activity on punctuated equilibrium.

phyletic gradualism The idea that evolution is a slow process with gradual transformation of one population into another.

punctuated equilibrium A model of evolution characterized by an uneven tempo of change.

---

[6] N. Eldredge and S. J. Gould. "Punctuated Equilibria: An Alternative to Phyletic Gradualism," in T. J. M. Schopf (ed.), *Models in Paleobiology* (San Francisco: Freeman, Cooper, 1972), pp. 82–115.

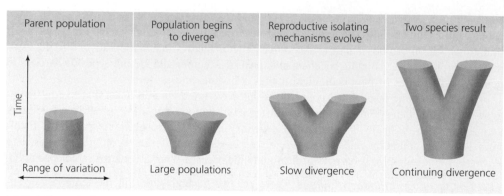

Parent population	Population begins to diverge	Reproductive isolating mechanisms evolve	Two species result

Range of variation

Large populations

Slow divergence

Continuing divergence

(a) Phyletic gradualism

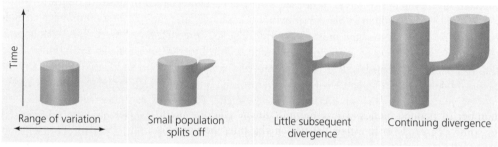

Range of variation

Small population splits off

Little subsequent divergence

Continuing divergence

(b) Punctuated equilibrium

Figure 5.13 Phyletic Gradualism and Punctuated Equilibrium Charles Darwin and other proponents of phyletic gradualism see evolution as a slow process whereby one species diverts and differentiates into different species, each different from each other and the original species. Niles Eldredge and Stephen Jay Gould proposed the concept of punctuated equilibrium whereby one population fragments into more than one new population. The populations that "bud" off of the main population are small and become peripheral to the mother species. The small fragmented populations evolve rapidly, while the mother population changes little.

competition The situation in which two populations occupy the same or parts of the same niche.

Of course, an important factor that influences movement of a population into a new niche is whether another population of a different species is already present. When two populations occupy the same or parts of the same niche, they are said to be competing with one another. **Competition** does not necessarily mean that individuals belonging to the two species physically fight one another. It simply means that they eat the same food, seek out the same sleeping places, or are active at the same time of day.

When two populations are competing in the same niche, differences in anatomy, physiology, or behavior may give one population the edge. For example, a population that is able to gain access to food at the expense of the other population will be able to maintain itself in the niche. The other population will die out, move, or—an important factor in speciation—adapt to another or a more restricted niche. Thus, if one population's diet includes fruits, leaves, and occasionally insects and another population's diet consists of fruits and leaves only, the first might increase its intake of insects. This population may ultimately become primarily insectivorous in its habits.

preadaptation The situation in which a new structure or behavior that evolved in one niche is by chance also suited, in some cases better suited, to a new niche.

Preadaptation Populations entering new geographical regions often occupy niches not found in their original area. These populations will not be totally adapted to the new niches, since the selective pressures characteristic of these new niches would not have been operating on them. Nevertheless, many populations, or individuals within a population, may already have evolved characteristics that prove to be adaptive in the new situation. The term **preadaptation** refers to the potential to adapt to a new niche. Organisms do not adapt because they need to but because by chance they have the potential to adapt.

A classic example of preadaptation is the evolution of flight in birds. Ever since the discovery in Germany of an ancient bird in 1861, named *Archaeopteryx,* most paleontologists have seen a connection between modern birds and the dinosaurs. Perhaps one of the most specialized traits in modern birds is feathers, structures that are found on no other contemporary animal. Flight is a complicated method of locomotion, and the anatomy for flight could not have simply arisen in place. The evolution of feathers was not a response to any anticipated need for flight.

Two well-preserved dinosaur fossils have been discovered in Liaoning Province, in northeastern China, dated between 135 and 120 million years old.[7] These dinosaurs possessed feathers! The two new dinosaur species are *Protarchaeopteryx,* named after *Archaeopteryx,* and *Caudipteryx,* meaning "tail-feather." The feathers are identical to those of modern birds in structure, and include both down-like and vaned, barbed feathers located on the arms and legs, body, and tail. Nevertheless, these two animals were definitely not birds, and, from an analysis of their anatomy, they were clearly not capable of flight. For what purpose did feathers originally evolve? Some possibilities include camouflage, display, or perhaps insulation. The presence of feathers, however, made the later evolution of avian flight possible.

Adaptive Radiation Movement into new ecological niches depends on many factors. First, there has to be physical access to the new niche; physical barriers may limit an organism's chance for dispersal. Second, the habitats in which the individuals live must provide a variety of niches. A lowland animal living in a valley surrounded by high mountains has immediate access to a diversity of adjacent altitudinal niches. In contrast, a flatland animal population, while perhaps finding it easier to move more extensively, may encounter only a limited number of flatland niches. Third, the individuals entering the new niche must be preadapted to some degree. Fourth, either the new niche must be unoccupied or the entering individuals must be able to compete successfully with other populations already existing in the niche.

A generalized species is usually able to survive in a variety of habitats. Its members may spread into new ecological niches to which they are preadapted and form new populations. Over time, these populations will take on distinctive characteristics as they become more closely adapted to their new niches. Subspecies will form, and in many cases, new species will emerge. The evolution of new species is most likely to occur in certain situations: when a species enters an uninhabited environment or one in which competition does not exist (as in the example below) or when a species develops new anatomical or physiological adaptations that allow it to compete successfully in a variety of niches. Such a proliferation of new species is called an **adaptive radiation.**

A classic example of adaptive radiation is the case of the finches of the Galápagos Islands, where a single mainland species evolved into 13 new species upon reaching the islands (Chapter 1) (Figure 5.14). Another important example is the case of primates on the island of Madagascar where, isolated from monkeys and apes, earlier primates evolved into a number of forms found nowhere else—lemurs, indris, and aye-ayes. We will look at these primates in Chapter 7.

Extinction While evolution is constantly bringing about the development of new species, other species are disappearing. When pressures develop in an environment, natural selection does not always bring about new adaptations. In many cases, the organisms involved simply do not have the potential to adapt. Because they are too specialized and are not preadapted to the new situation, they become extinct.

Extinction can occur in another way. As a species evolves, there is a point at which a species can be considered to be significantly different from its ancestral species. At this point, paleontologists may give it a new species name. The ancestral species becomes extinct not by dying off but by evolving into something else.

Extinction is not an unusual event. Extinctions of the past far outnumber the total number of species that are living today. Humans, through their technology, have increased the rate of extinction. Humans use guns to kill animals and bulldozers to destroy their habitats.

See the Online Learning Center for an Internet Activity on adaptive radiation in Darwin's finches.

adaptive radiation The evolution of a single population into a number of different species.

extinction The disappearance of a population.

---

[7] J. Qiang et al., "Two Feathered Dinosaurs from Northeastern China," *Nature* 393 (June 25, 1998), pp. 753–761; K. Padian and L. M. Chiappe, "The Origin of Birds and Their Flight," *Scientific American,* February 1998, pp. 38–47; and J. Ackerman, "Dinosaurs Take Wing," *National Geographic* 194 (July 1998), pp. 74–99.

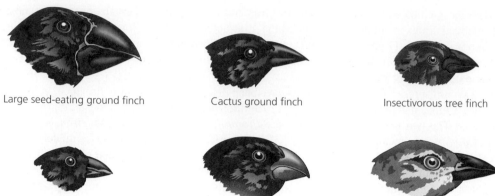

Large seed-eating ground finch   Cactus ground finch   Insectivorous tree finch

Small seed-eating ground finch   Vegetarian tree finch   Woodpecker finch

Figure 5.14 Darwin's Finches The diverse bill forms represent adaptations to different niches, an example of an adaptive radiation.

Although there is usually competition between organisms over particular niches, wherein some of the competitors are displaced, no large animals can compete successfully with *Homo sapiens* for any habitat. (Interestingly, those organisms that do compete successfully with humans are small forms, such as mice, flies, and disease organisms.) Therefore, the give-and-take, the periods of change and reestablishment of new balances, and the derivation of new types do not generally occur when people take over an environment.

Summary

Macroevolution includes those processes responsible for the evolution of species and higher taxa. The local reproductive population is the deme, and the forces of evolution operate to bring about changes in gene frequencies within the gene pools of demes. Since different demes of the same species occupy slightly different habitats, selective pressures may differ from deme to deme.

When demes or groups of demes become reproductively isolated, subspecies may develop. The elimination of gene flow between demes, which is usually the result of some type of geographical barrier, allows for the accumulation of different mutations within each deme. These accumulations and gene-frequency changes, generated within and restricted to each deme, ultimately make successful reproduction between the demes impossible. Over time, these populations may become distinct species, called allopatric species.

Sympatric species are closely related species that have come to reside in the same general geographical area. Yet gene flow is effectively prevented by one of several reproductive isolating mechanisms: ecological isolation, seasonal isolation, sexual isolation, mechanical isolation, gametic mortality, zygotic mortality, hybrid inviability, and hybrid sterility.

Populations within a species will tend to disperse into new regions where they occupy similar ecological niches, but these new niches can never be identical to the original ones. Certain individuals within the population may possess preadapted variations that increase their adaptation in the new niche. When a population enters an area in which it has no competition, or when a population evolves new anatomical or physiological adaptations, speciation may be quite rapid. This rapid proliferation of species is an adaptive radiation. However, if populations unable to compete in their original niche do not adapt to new or changing niches, extinction may result.

Key Terms

adaptive radiation, *119*	generalized species, *115*	physical environment, *99*
allopatric species, *113*	geographical isolation, *113*	postmating mechanism, *114*
altruism, *110*	globin, *104*	preadaptation, *118*
artificial selection, *99*	habitat, *99*	premating mechanism, *114*
balanced polymorphism, *105*	hemoglobin, *104*	punctuated equilibrium, *117*
biological environment, *99*	hemoglobin A(HbA), *104*	seasonal isolation, *114*
clinal distribution, *112*	hemoglobin A$_2$ (HbA$_2$), *104*	selective agent, *100*
coefficient of relatedness, *110*	hemoglobin C, *107*	selective pressure, *100*
competition, *118*	hemoglobin S(HbS), *104*	sexual dimorphism, *108*
cultural environment, *99*	hybrid inviability, *115*	sexual isolation, *114*
demes, *111*	hybrid sterility, *115*	sexual selection, *107*
directional selection, *102*	inclusive fitness, *110*	sickle-cell anemia, *104*
disruptive selection, *103*	intersexual selection, *107*	sickle-cell trait, *104*
ecological isolation, *114*	intrasexual selection, *108*	specialized species, *115*
ecological niche, *99*	kin selection, *110*	speciation, *113*
erythrocyte, *104*	macroevolution, *98*	stabilizing selection, *102*
evolutionary psychology, *109*	mechanical isolation, *114*	subspecies, *112*
extinction, *119*	microenvironment, *99*	sympatric species, *114*
fetal hemoglobin (HbF), *104*	microevolution, *98*	thalassemia, *107*
fitness, *101*	microhabitat, *99*	zygotic mortality, *115*
gametic mortality, *115*	phyletic gradualism, *117*	

Study Questions

1. What is meant by the statement that evolution is based on variation within the population and within the niche?

2. What is the difference between microevolution and macroevolution?

3. Often the fitness of a particular trait and the nature of the selective pressures within a population are not obvious. What selective pressures are operating on hemoglobin S in a malarial environment?

4. What are the different types of selection discussed in this chapter? How does kin selection differ from other forms of selection?

5. What is meant by the term *sexual selection?* Does sexual selection operate in human populations?

6. Speciation follows geographical isolation. What occurs genetically after a population becomes geographically isolated? What factors other than geography serve to isolate populations?

7. Contrast the phyletic gradualism model of evolution with the punctuated equilibrium model.

8. What differentiates a generalized from a specialized species?

9. There are two types of extinction. What are they?

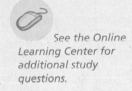

See the Online Learning Center for additional study questions.

Critical Thinking Questions

1. In the nineteenth century many scholars applied the biological concept of natural selection to human society. Unemployment, poverty, criminal behavior, and so forth, were thought to be biologically based, and death from disease and starvation was nature's way of eliminating such individuals from society. This argument was used against various social welfare programs. What are some of the major fallacies of such reasoning?

2. The concept of predestination is an element of most world religions. Does this have any application to biological evolutionary theory? Or is the idea of predestination contrary to modern evolutionary theory?

3. Why is necessity not the "mother of invention" in evolutionary terms?

Suggested Readings

Bowler, P. J. *Evolution: The History of an Idea,* 3rd ed. Berkeley: University of California Press, 2003. This book outlines the history of evolutionary theories. Its final chapter looks at modern debates about evolutionary theory, including the ideas of creationists.

Buss, D. M. *The Evolution of Desire: Strategies of Human Mating,* rev. ed. New York: Basic Books, 2003. This is a report of David Buss's study of mate selection in 37 societies.

Edelstein, S. J. *The Sickled Cell: From Myths to Molecules.* Cambridge, MA: Harvard University Press, 1986. This book details the history and nature of sickle-cell anemia.

Jones, D. *Physical Attractiveness and the Theory of Sexual Selection.* Ann Arbor: Michigan Museum of Anthropology Publications, 1996. This is a study of human sexual selection. The book includes a discussion of research in five human societies.

Maitland, A. E., and D. C. Johanson. *Blueprints: Solving the Mystery of Evolution.* Oxford: Oxford University Press, 1991. Written by a journalist and a well-known paleoanthropologist, this book is an extremely readable introduction to evolutionary theory. It tells the story of how evolutionary and genetic ideas developed through time.

Mayr, E. *What Evolution Is.* New York: Basic Books, 2002. One of the best-known modern evolutionary theorists discusses his ideas about evolution and the origin of species.

Volpe, E. P., and P. Andrews. *Understanding Evolution,* 6th ed. New York: McGraw-Hill, 2000. This is a short introduction to the theory of evolution and population genetics.

Wright, R. *The Moral Animal.* New York: Vintage Books, 1994. A very readable introduction to evolutionary psychology.

Suggested Websites

Center for Evolutionary Psychology at University of California Santa Barbara: **www.psych.ucsb.edu/research/cep/**

Speciation in Progress (the example of *Ensatina escholtz,* a lungless salamander): **www.santarosa.edu/lifesciences/ensatina.htm**

Chapter 6

People's Place in Nature

Cover page of *Systema Naturae*, 1735, by Carolus Linnaeus, which set forth the form of the classification of animals still in use today.

It was to reveal the divine design that a young Swedish naturalist called Carl von Linné (generally known by his pen-name of Linnaeus) began the first great catalogue of animals and plants which culminated in the publication in 1752 of *Philosophia Botanica,* written in Latin, in which he classified all plants according to class, genus, and species. . . . In his view the universe was static and atemporal, unchanged since it had first been created by God. He was interested only in the number, figure, proportion and situation of the organisms he classified, because these data were essential if the full complexity of God's design were to be revealed. Linnaeus conceived of a perfectly balanced nature, advocating zoos with cages each containing one pair of each type of animal, separated from other types, without interaction between them. According to him such a zoo would reproduce conditions as they had been on earth immediately after Creation. ●

—James Burke

Chapter Outline

Taxonomy
Linnaeus's Classification
The Taxonomic Hierarchy
The Basis of Modern Taxonomy
Determining Evolutionary Relationships
Cladistics
Summary

People and the Animal World
The Animal Kingdom
The Phylum Chordata
The Vertebrates
The Mammals
Summary

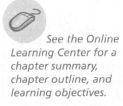

See the Online Learning Center for a chapter summary, chapter outline, and learning objectives.

After Reading This Chapter, You Should Be Able to Answer These Questions:

1. What is taxonomy? What were Linnaeus's contributions to taxonomy?

2. On what philosophical principle was Linnaean taxonomy based? On what principle or principles is modern biological taxonomy based?

3. What do the terms *convergence* and *parallelism* refer to?

4. What is the difference between homologous features and homoplastic features? What are the four kinds of homoplasy?

5. What is cladistics?

6. What are some of the distinguishing features of animals compared with plants, chordates compared with other animal phyla, vertebrates compared with other chordates, and mammals compared with other vertebrates?

7. On what basis are mammals divided into subgroups? What is the relationship of the primates to the other kinds of mammals?

Humans are animals. They are part of a great diversity of living things, all of which share certain basic traits. Within the depths of the cell, biochemical mechanisms are remarkably similar wherever they are found. Yet, upon this base, life has evolved into an amazing variety of forms.

Early naturalists, including Carolus Linnaeus, viewed the complexity of life as a manifestation of the divine design that revealed itself at the creation. Although Linnaeus's view was a far cry from the vision of evolutionary change published by Charles Darwin over 100 years later, the classification of the living world was an important step in the development of such a theory. Classification provided biologists with a system for discussing, comparing, and contrasting living forms. This chapter discusses biological classification and looks at how humankind is related to the rest of the animal kingdom.

TAXONOMY

All human societies attempt to put order into their world. To understand the nature of living things and their diversity, people sort this diversity into a manageable number of categories. These categories can then be related to one another.

Ordering is one of the first steps in science, and the scientist is involved in the development of classification schemes. If we are to consider variability scientifically, we must precisely define the units of study and how they are related to one another. A system of organizing data is a **classification.** The science of classifying organisms into different categories is known as **taxonomy.**

Linnaeus's Classification

The most significant early attempt to order the living world was that of the Swedish naturalist Carolus Linnaeus (1707–1778) (Figure 1.3). Although fundamental differences exist in theory, the system developed by Linnaeus is the basis of the system of classification used in modern biology.

The basic unit of classification in Linnaeus's scheme is the species, which Linnaeus considered to be a unit of creation, unchanging and distinct through time. His task was to define all the species known to him and classify them. In his 10th edition of *Systema Naturae,* published in 1758, he listed 4235 animal species. Today, over one million animal species have been described in scientific journals (Box 6-1).

Binomial Nomenclature Linnaeus realized that a given animal is often known by different names in different parts of the world. Indeed, the same kind of animal often has several names in the same language. For these reasons, he decided to give species new Latin names. He chose Latin not only because it was the language of science but also because it was unchanging and politically neutral.

Eighteenth-century scientists wrote long descriptions for each known kind of plant and animal. In compiling his list, Linnaeus recorded each form in a simple two-word shorthand. These notations became the basis of his **binomial nomenclature.** In this system, each species is known by a **binomen,** or a two-part name. For example, Linnaeus gave the human species the name *Homo sapiens. Homo* is the generic name, or the name of the **genus** to which humans belong. A genus is a group of similar species. This name is always capitalized, and no two genera (plural of *genus*) in the animal kingdom can have the same name. The second name is the specific name. The specific name is never capitalized, and it must always appear in association with the generic name. The generic and specific names are always in italics or underlined. Thus, humans belong to the genus *Homo* and the species *Homo sapiens.*

The Classification of Species According to Linnaeus, the characteristics of each animal species were the result of creation and a reflection of the divine plan. Variations within a species did exist, but these variations were considered irrelevant. The basic unit of study was actually the divine blueprint, or **archetype,** of a particular species.

classification A system of organizing data.

taxonomy The science of classifying organisms into different categories.

See the Online Learning Center for an Internet Activity on Linnaeus.

binomial nomenclature A system of naming species that uses a double name such as *Homo sapiens.* The first name alone names the genus; both names used together name the species.

binomen A two-part name given to a species; the first name is also the name of the genus. An example of a binomen is *Homo sapiens.*

genus A group of closely related species.

archetype The divine plan or blueprint for a species or higher taxonomic category.

Box 6-1

The Diversity of Life

The typical urban American student is probably aware of only a very small number of animal species. The first that come to mind are those we keep as pets, including the familiar dogs and cats and the less familiar tropical fish, turtles, and parrots. Perhaps more significant are those urban species about which we would rather not think: rats, spiders, flies, and cockroaches. William Jordan describes several animal species that have made notable adaptations to an urban lifestyle in the suburbs of Los Angeles: the opossum, coyote, skunk, crow, parrot, alligator lizard, argentine ant, cellar spider, and feral cat.[1] Yet the totality of urban fauna is rather limited.

Moving to a larger venue, we may ask: How many animals worldwide have been identified and named by biologists? Not surprisingly, this list is a great deal longer. Yet most of the animals on this list are known only from a few specimens in a dusty museum drawer or a drawing in a technical scientific journal. This state of affairs makes it extremely difficult to arrive at an accurate estimate of the number of animal species that do exist on earth. Estimates vary tremendously, and many biologists agree that the number of animal species described and named may be only a fraction of the species that actually exist.

Biologist Edward O. Wilson ponders this question over 10 years ago.[2] As a result of his search, he estimated that 1,032,000 animals are described and named. If we examine the number of animals in each of the categories seen in the figure, we observe that the vast number of known animal species are the arthropods, the phylum that includes the beetles, spiders, ants, and butterflies. And of the animal species yet to be discovered, the vast majority will probably turn out to be the arthropods living in the world's tropical rain forests. Biologists are very concerned about the rapid destruction of the rain forests that is destroying tens of thousands, if not millions, of unknown animal species, some of which could have a major impact on human survival and the quality of human life.

And what of the mammals, the group of animals to which we belong? Only about 4000 mammals are known, and except for a few small forms, most mammals have been named and described.

[1] W. Jordan, "New Eden, City of Beasts," in *Divorce among the Gulls* (San Francisco: North Point Press, 1991), pp. 70–100.

[2] E. O. Wilson, *The Diversity of Life* (Cambridge, MA: Belknap Press, 1992).

Number of Living Animal Species Currently Known
(According to Major Group)

Animals: Total species, 1,032,000

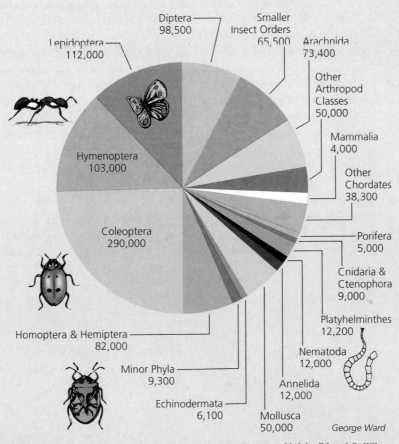

Linnaeus noted that some species are more alike than others; monkeys resemble humans quite closely, and humans resemble dogs more than they do fish. Scientists of the eighteenth century believed that these similarities in structure were due to similarities in archetype. To study the similarities between animal forms, and to classify them on this basis, was to reveal the divine plan.

Archetypes were found on different levels. Each species had an archetype. Because humans and monkeys shared a great many features, Linnaeus placed them in a common group on the basis of these similarities. The archetype for the group Primates was simply a less specific blueprint than the archetype for the individual species. Going one step further, Linnaeus placed humans, monkeys, dogs, horses, and others into an even larger group, Mammalia. Here again, an archetype existed, but with even more generalized specifications.

The Taxonomic Hierarchy

The species is the basic unit of classification. Similar species are placed in a common genus. A genus is an example of a **taxon** (plural, *taxa*), which is a group of organisms at any level of the taxonomic hierarchy.

Taxa above the level of genus are often referred to as the **higher taxa.** The existing system of classification contains five main higher taxa: **family, order, class, phylum,** and **kingdom.** A family contains similar-appearing genera; an order is a group of similar-appearing families; and so forth. Linnaeus saw this classification as a hierarchical system of categories that nested within larger categories. As we go higher in the hierarchy, each succeeding level is defined by more generalized characteristics. Because the higher taxa encompass so much variation, the included species have fewer characteristics in common.

Humans belong to the species *Homo sapiens* and the genus *Homo.* Although the genus *Homo* contains only one living species, it includes several extinct species such as *Homo erectus.* The genus *Homo* is part of the family Hominidae, which also includes extinct genera such as *Ardipithecus, Australopithecus,* and *Paranthropus,* as well as the great apes. The family Hominidae belongs to the order Primates, as do the monkeys and prosimians. The order Primates, in turn, is part of the next higher taxon, the class Mammalia. Other examples of mammals are dogs, cattle, whales, elephants, and bats. The class Mammalia is included in the phylum Chordata, which also encompasses birds, reptiles, amphibians, and fish. Finally, the chordates belong to the kingdom Animalia, which includes all animal forms.

The seven taxonomic levels, however, are not sufficient for a complete and satisfactory classification. The prefixes *super-, sub-,* and *infra-,* as well as additional taxa such as the tribe, are used to create additional levels. Thus, there can be a superfamily, a suborder, an infraclass, and so on. Table 6.1 presents a detailed classification of the species *Homo sapiens.*

See the Online Learning Center for an Internet Activity on the taxonomic hierarchy.

taxon A group of organisms at any level of the taxonomic hierarchy. The major taxa are the species and genus and the higher taxa: family, order, class, phylum, and kingdom.

higher taxa Taxa above the genus level, such as family, order, class, phylum, and kingdom.

family Major division of an order, consisting of closely related genera.

order Major division of a class, consisting of closely related families.

class Major division of a phylum, consisting of closely related orders.

phylum Major division of a kingdom, consisting of closely related classes; represents a basic body plan.

kingdom A major division of living organisms. All organisms are placed into one of five kingdoms: Monera, Protista, Fungi, Planti, and Animalia.

Table 6.1 The Classification of *Homo sapiens*

KINGDOM: Animalia
PHYLUM: Chordata
SUBPHYLUM: Vertebrata
CLASS: Mammalia
SUBCLASS: Theria
INFRACLASS: Eutheria
ORDER: Primates
SUBORDER: Anthropoidea
SUPERFAMILY: Hominoidea
FAMILY: Hominidae
SUBFAMILY: Homininae
TRIBE: Hominini
GENUS: *Homo*
SPECIES: *Homo sapiens*

The Basis of Modern Taxonomy

Biologists no longer think of species as fixed units of creation. A species is a population whose members are able to reproduce successfully among themselves but are unable to reproduce with members of other species. The species is a dynamic unit, constantly changing through time and space; a species living at one point in time may be quite different from its descendants living tens of thousands of years later. Segments of a species may develop into subspecies and, finally, may form a separate species. Species are not defined by physical similarities per se but rather on the criterion of their reproductive success. Species are classified into higher taxonomic levels on the basis of their evolutionary relationships.

Today the system devised by Linnaeus is still used; however, it is based on demonstrated evolutionary relationships rather than similar appearance. Thus a family, for example, consists of several genera that are shown to be related to one another, that is, to have a common ancestor. However, as we will see later in this chapter, some biologists feel that the Linnaean system does not accurately reflect the evolutionary basis of modern classification.

Determining Evolutionary Relationships

Phylogeny refers to the evolutionary history of species. Since the development of classifications depends on the knowledge of evolutionary relationships among taxa, this section will discuss some of the problems in determining these evolutionary relationships.

phylogeny The evolutionary history of a population or taxon.

Homologous Features A comparison of two different animals may reveal many anatomical correspondences. In the reconstruction of a phylogeny, the taxonomist looks for structural correspondences that are the result of inheritance from a common ancestor. These are known as **homologies** or homologous features.

Evolution is irreversible. If we examine a series of changes in the genetic code, the probability that it will evolve back into the exact code from which it came is effectively zero. Specific anatomical traits may appear to evolve into an ancestral condition, but such similar appearances are superficial. An anatomical trait, however, can disappear or evolve further into something else. Furthermore, new structures do not simply appear from nowhere; they evolve from preexisting structures.

homologies Similarities due to inheritance from a common ancestor.

Figure 6.1 shows the forelimbs of a series of vertebrates. Externally, these forelimbs are quite different and serve different functions: manipulating objects, running, flying, and swimming. Yet all are derived from the same basic structure found in a common ancestral form. While the whale flipper reminds one of a fish fin, upon dissection the derivation of

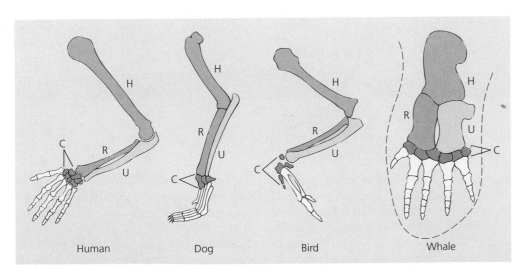

Human   Dog   Bird   Whale

Figure 6.1 Vertebrate Forelimbs Homologous bones in the forelimbs of four vertebrates are (H) humerus, (U) ulna, (R) radius, and (C) carpals. Homologies are similarities resulting from inheritance from a common ancestor.

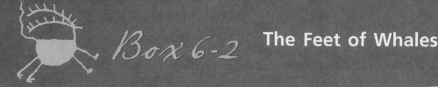

Box 6-2   The Feet of Whales

One of the great mysteries of evolution was the origin and evolution of the whales. Whales belong to the order Cetacea, which includes the dolphins, the porpoises, and the many species of whales. They are highly successful and specialized mammals, but until recently the lack of transitional forms in the fossil record was used to question the validity of evolution. A very small percentage of the creatures than once lived are ever found as fossils. The odds of finding fossils from the middle of a rapidly evolving lineage are very small; this is why transitional forms are rare in the fossil record. This is especially true for whales, in whose rapid evolution, the transition from land to sea took only 8 million years. Yet in the last two decades paleontologists have uncovered a surprisingly large number of whale fossils, and the prehistory of the whales is becoming clear.

The earliest known ancestors of the whales, the Pakicetidae, did not live in the sea at all but were land mammals whose fossils have been found in Pakistan and India, dating back to around 50 million years ago (Figure b). Dated at 49 million years ago are the Ambulocetidae, which moved both on land and in shallow seas, where they ambushed prey in the manner of a modern crocodile (Figure c). By 41 million years ago we find a series of whales whose fossils are known from Egypt and the eastern United States. Those animals, which included the Basilosaurids, measured up to 60 feet in length yet still had functioning hind limbs that included a flexible knee and toes (Figure d, *Dorudon*, closely related to the Basilosaurids). Those legs could not have been used in locomotion. One suggestion is that they assisted the animal in positioning itself for sexual activity. By 40 million years ago the oldest modern whales appeared.

There is some debate about the origins of the cetaceans. Some believe that the order evolved from a carnivorous hoofed animal of the order Artiodactyla, which includes even-toed hoofed forms such as cows, pigs, camels, and deer. DNA evidence suggests that whales may have shared a common ancestor with the modern hippopotamus.

Source: Research Program of the Thewissen Lab, http://darla.neoucom.edu/DEPTS/ANAT/ Thewissen.html.

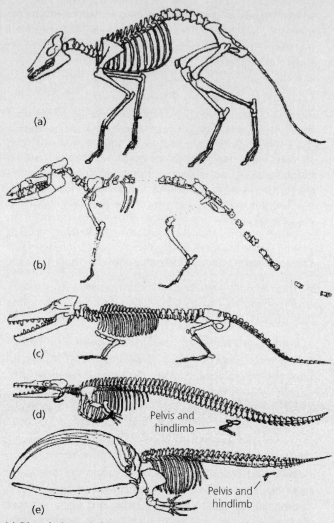

(a) *Diacodaxis,* a primitive even-toed hoofed mammal; (b) *Pakicetus,* an early terrestrial cetacean: (c) *Ambulocotus,* an early amphibious cetacean; (d) *Dorudon,* an early fully aquatic cetacean; (e) *Balaena,* a recent whale. Drawings not to scale.

Source: From Christian de Muizon, "Waliking with Whales," *Nature* 413 (2001), p. 259 (www.nature.com). Courtesy of Christian de Muizon.

---

the flipper becomes obvious. It is an elaboration of the basic structure of the forelimb of a four-footed land vertebrate (Box 6-2).

Homoplastic Features It is, of course, possible for structures in two different species to be similar without being homologous. Such similarities are said to be **homoplastic.** Homoplasy can come about in four different ways: convergence, parallelism, analogy, and chance.

Convergence refers to similar developments in less closely related evolutionary lines. Figure 6.2 shows a gray wolf, a Tasmanian wolf, and a sperm whale. If a biologist had to classify these animals based on their evolutionary relationships, what criteria would be used?

homoplastic Referring to similarities that are not homologous. Homoplasy can arise from parallelism, convergence, analogy, and chance.

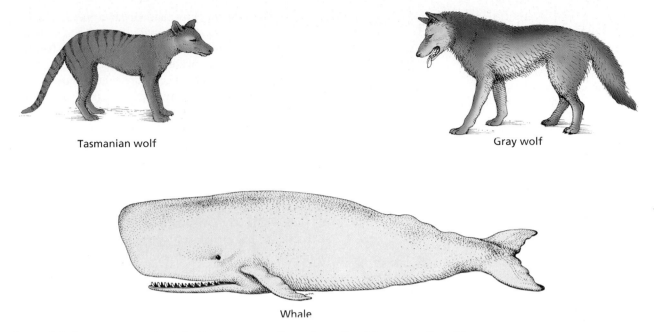

Tasmanian wolf

Gray wolf

Whale

Figure 6.2 Convergence The similarities between the Tasmanian wolf and the gray wolf result from convergent evolution. Actually, the gray wolf is more closely related to the whale.

A comparison of gray and Tasmanian wolves shows similarity in body size and shape, type of dentition, and diet   but it also shows great differences as well. The gray wolf and the sperm whale are both placental mammals. In these species, the fetus is nourished through a placenta until birth. The placenta is an example of an ancestral structure found in many descendant species. In contrast, the Tasmanian wolf, which is thought to be extinct today, is a marsupial, or pouched mammal, like the kangaroo. The absence of the placenta in the marsupials is evidence of a more distant relationship since the marsupials diverged from the mammalian line before evolution of the placenta.

The complex method of fetal nourishment characterized by the placenta is more indicative of a close evolutionary relationship than are size and shape. Yet the similarities seen in the gray wolf and the Tasmanian wolf are striking. They are due to the fact that similar selective pressures can bring about similar adaptations in divergent evolutionary lines; this is convergence. (For another example of convergence, see Figure 6.11.)

A special case of convergence is **parallelism.** In parallelism the common ancestry did provide initial commonalities that gave direction to a parallel evolution in the two lines. For example, while the common ancestor of the monkeys of the New World (Central and South America) and the monkeys of the Old World (Africa, Europe, and Asia) evolved in Africa, the evolution of monkeys in the New World and Old World occurred independently of one another. Many similarities between these two major groups of monkeys arose independently in the two hemispheres but from a common premonkey ancestor (Figure 6.3).

Another type of homoplasy occurs when two structures are superficially similar in very distantly related forms. For example, the wing of a bat and that of an insect are superficially similar and serve the same function—flying; however, there is no common relationship. Such similarities are called **analogies** (Figure 6.4). Of course, similarities also can arise by chance.

Cladistics

An important approach to the theory of classification is **cladistics.** This term comes from the word **clade,** which refers to a set of species descended from a particular ancestral species. The practitioner of cladistics looks for homologous features. A major concern in this search is how far back in time the homologies first appeared.

convergence
Nonhomologous similarities in different evolutionary lines; the result of similarities in selective pressures.

parallelism Homoplastic similarities found in related species that did not exist in the common ancestor; however, the common ancestor provided initial commonalities that gave direction to the evolution of the similarities.

analogies Structures that are superficially similar and serve similar functions but have no common evolutionary relationship.

cladistics A theory of classification that differentiates between shared ancestral and shared derived features.

clade A group of species with a common evolutionary ancestry.

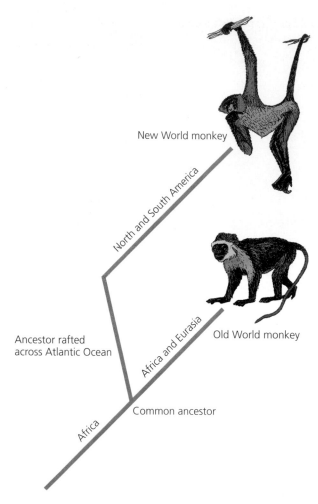

Figure 6.3 Parallelism Old World and New World monkeys had a common origin in Africa. After rafting to South America, the New World monkeys evolved along lines similar to those of Old World monkeys because of the common origin and similarities in ecological niches.

In cladistics, homologies that appeared recently and are therefore shared by a relatively small group of closely related taxa are called **shared derived (synapomorphic) features.** Homologies that first appeared a longer time ago and are shared by a larger group of species are called **shared ancestral (symplesiomorphic) features.** The task of the taxonomist is to identify which features are shared derived and which are shared ancestral and to separate both of these types from features that are **uniquely derived (autapomorphic)** in a particular species or group of species.

Conducting a cladistic analysis is relatively straightforward. Let us say that we wish to determine evolutionary relationships among three species. These are species A, B, and C in Figure 6.5. We include in our analysis several other species that are closely related to the three in question; these additional species are called an **outgroup.** Features that appear in all or most of the species including the outgroup (A through F in Figure 6.5) are assumed to be shared ancestral features. (It is possible for a particular shared ancestral feature to be absent from a particular species because the feature has disappeared in that species.) Features that are found in the original set of species (A, B, and C) but not in the outgroup are assumed to be shared derived features.

From a cladistic analysis, a **cladogram** can be drawn that graphically presents the evolutionary relationships among the species (or other taxa) being studied (Figure 6.6). While such a diagram appears to convey an evolutionary history, the time element is not present. Thus, the cladogram, while depicting relationships among taxa, does not depict temporal relationships (Box 6-3).

See the Online Learning Center for an Internet Activity on cladistics.

shared derived (synapomorphic) feature
A recently appearing homology that is shared by a relatively small group of closely related taxa.

shared ancestral (symplesiomorphic) feature Compared with shared derived features, a homology that did not appear as recently and is therefore shared by a larger group of species.

Figure 6.4 Analogy The wings of the butterfly, the bird, and the bat are analogous structures. They serve the same function, flying, but were independently evolved in different evolutionary lines.

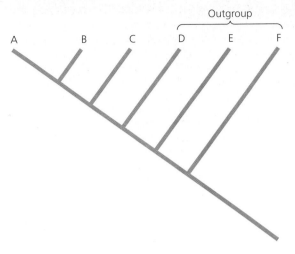

Outgroup

A   B   C   D   E   F

Figure 6.5 Cladogram This cladogram shows the relationships between species based on shared ancestral features.

uniquely derived (autapomorphic) feature A feature that is unique to a particular species.

outgroup Species used in a cladistic analysis that are closely related to the species being studied and are used to differentiate between shared derived and ancestral derived features.

cladogram A graphic representation of the species, or other taxa, being studied, based on cladistic analysis.

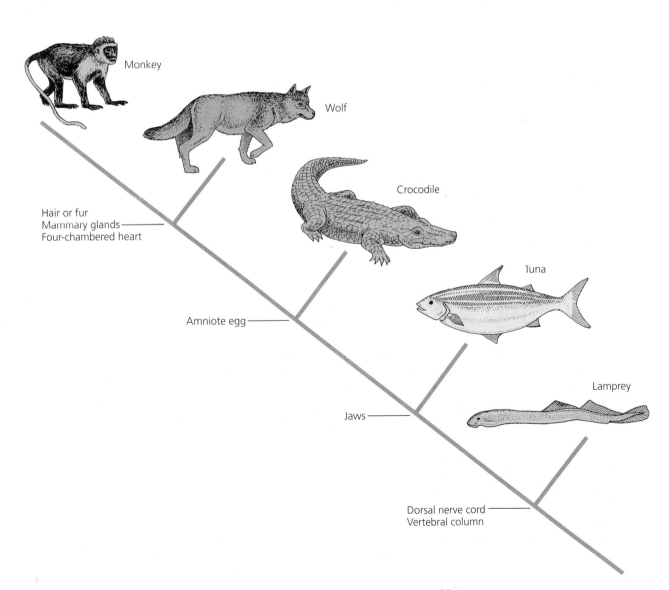

Monkey

Wolf

Crocodile

Tuna

Lamprey

Hair or fur
Mammary glands
Four-chambered heart

Amniote egg

Jaws

Dorsal nerve cord
Vertebral column

Figure 6.6 Cladogram This cladogram shows the relationships among representatives of five vertebrates. Each branch point is defined by one or more newly evolved shared derived features.

Box 6-3 Linnaean Systematics in the Twenty-First Century

Historically the system of naming and classifying species that was developed by Linnaeus is based on a nonevolutionary view of the biological world. With the development of evolutionary theory in the nineteenth century, biologists chose to keep the form of the Linnaean system and reinterpreted the hierarchical system of ever-more-inclusive levels or ranks in an evolutionary manner. Thus the stability of the system was maintained.

The Linnaean system is based on the demonstration of homologies, the inference of common origin based on anatomical similarities. With the growth of cladistics, biologists have come to a different view of the relationship of living organisms in terms of clades or evolutionary lineages. Now, as an outcome of the growth of cladistics, some biologists would like to reinvent a system of classification based on the demonstration of clades. In addition, some biologists are concerned that the Linnaean system cannot adequately handle the dramatic increase in the total number of named species, which is expected to increase astronomically with the ap-plication of genome analysis to the identification of species and subspecies. A new system of classification has been proposed called the "PhyloCode." In this system organisms would not be grouped into ranks, such as genera, families, and orders. Instead they would be defined in terms of clades. Species names might be shortened or even replaced by a numeric designation.

Needless to say, there is a great deal of opposition to the new proposal on both practical and theoretical grounds. The Linnaean system, in use for over 250 years, has provided stability in the naming and classifying of living organisms. Perhaps some type of hybrid system can be developed. Meanwhile, a draft of the proposed PhyloCode has been distributed for study and comment.

Sources: J. Withgott, "Is It 'So Long, Linnaeus'? (Carolus Linnaeus' Classification of World Organisms)," *BioScience,* August 2000; E. Pennisi, "Linnaeus' Last Stand," *Science* 291 (2001), pp. 2304–2307. The draft of the PhyloCode can be found on the Internet at www.ohio.edu/phylocode.

Summary

Central to the scientific study of the diversity of life is a system of ordering data, which is known as classification; the science of classifying organisms into different categories is known as taxonomy. In 1758, Linnaeus published the 10th edition of his classification of the living world; the form of this classification is still used today. Linnaeus gave all living species a binomial name, or binomen, and placed species in genera, genera in families, and so forth up the taxonomic hierarchy. Species were seen as unchanging, divinely created units, each of which had an archetype, or divine blueprint. Similar-looking animals were placed in categories based on increasingly generalized archetypes.

Modern taxonomists think of the species as a dynamic unit defined in terms of reproductive success. Evolutionary relationships between species can be deduced on the basis of structural similarities that are the result of inheritance from a common ancestor; such similarities are known as homologies. On the other hand, structures in two different animals can be similar without being homologous; such similarities are said to be homoplastic. Homoplasy can come about in several different ways. Independent evolution of similarities in related species is referred to as parallelism. Convergence refers to developments that arise in divergent evolutionary lines when similar selective pressures cause similar adaptations. Two structures can be superficially similar in two or more species unrelated to common ancestry; such similarities are called analogies. Similarities also can come about by chance. In cladistics, a distinction is made between homologies that have appeared recently and are shared by a relatively small group of species or taxa (shared derived features) and homologies that first appeared a much longer time ago and are shared by a relatively large group of species or taxa (shared ancestral features).

PEOPLE AND THE ANIMAL WORLD

The Animal Kingdom

The first step in the classification of organisms is to divide them into large, basic units known as *kingdoms.* It was once thought that all organisms could be placed in either the plant kingdom or the animal kingdom. Today, however, taxonomists realize that many forms, such as unicellular organisms, bacteria, and fungi, do not fit neatly into either of these two groups; they are placed in other kingdoms, bringing the total number of kingdoms to five (Table 6.2).

Members of the animal kingdom differ from plants in a number of ways. Animals are incapable of synthesizing food from inorganic materials; they must obtain their nutrients by consuming other organisms. Animals are composed of specialized kinds of cells. They are highly mobile and have contracting fibers such as muscles. Most respond quickly to changes in their environment because they have nerves and special sensing organs.

The animal kingdom is divided into several units known as *phyla,* with each phylum representing a basic body plan. Biologists recognize about 36 animal phyla. Most familiar animals belong to the following nine phyla (examples of animals in each are given in parentheses): Porifera (sponges), Cnidaria (jellyfish, sea anemones), Platyhelminthes (planaria, tapeworms), Nematoda (roundworms), Mollusca (snails, scallops, octopuses), Annelida (earthworms), Echinodermata (starfish), Arthropoda (spiders, butterflies, crayfish), and Chordata (fish, reptiles, birds, mammals).

The Phylum Chordata

Humans belong to the phylum Chordata. **Chordates** include such forms as the tunicates, fish, amphibians, reptiles, birds, and mammals. It is instructive to compare this phylum with another, such as the phylum Arthropoda. Figure 6.7 compares a grasshopper, an arthropod, with an *Amphioxus,* a small, ocean-dwelling chordate.

A distinctive feature of the chordates is the presence of an internal skeleton. Part of this skeleton is a cartilaginous rod, called the **notochord,** that runs along the back of the animal. In all chordates, the notochord is present in the embryonic stage, but in most chordates, it is replaced by the spine in the adult. In the grasshopper (arthropod), the skeleton is external; the animal has no notochord.

In chordates, a single, hollow nerve cord lies on top of the notochord (**dorsal** to the notochord). In the arthropods, the nerve cord is double and solid, and it is located on the **ventral,** or bottom, side of the animal. In addition, all chordates have **gill slits** at some time in their life history. Although gills do not actually develop in humans, structures that appear in the human embryo are thought by embryologists to be possible precursors to gill slits.

The Vertebrates

The phylum Chordata includes the subphylum Vertebrata, which includes most of the animals within the phylum. There are seven living classes of vertebrates: the jawless

See the Online Learning Center for an Internet Activity on the domains of life.

chordates Members of the phylum Chordata; chordates are characterized by the presence of a notochord, a dorsal, hollow, single nerve cord, and gill slits at some point in the life cycle.

notochord A cartilaginous rod that runs along the back (dorsal) of all chordates at some point in their life cycle.

dorsal Toward the top or back of an animal.

ventral The front or bottom side of an animal.

gill slits Structures that filter out food particles in nonvertebrate chordates and are used for breathing in some vertebrates.

Table 6.2 The Five Kingdoms of Life

KINGDOM: Animalia (sponges, earthworms, grasshoppers, shellfish, starfish, reptiles, mammals)
KINGDOM: Planti (pine trees, flowering plants)
KINGDOM: Fungi (mushrooms)
KINGDOM: Protista (unicellular organisms)
KINGDOM: Monera (bacteria, blue-green algae)

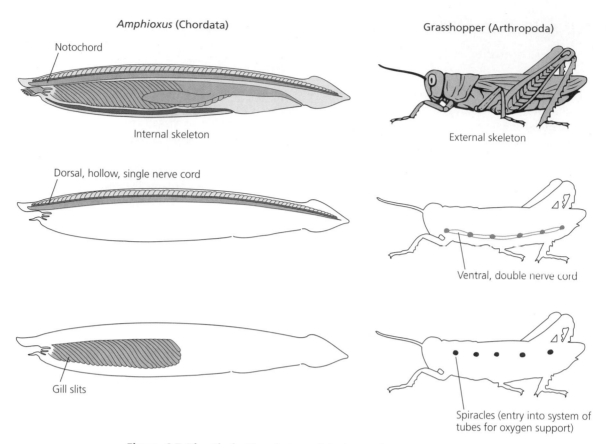

Amphioxus (Chordata)

Notochord

Internal skeleton

Dorsal, hollow, single nerve cord

Gill slits

Grasshopper (Arthropoda)

External skeleton

Ventral, double nerve cord

Spiracles (entry into system of tubes for oxygen support)

Figure 6.7 The Phyla Chordata and Arthropoda The major characteristics of the phylum Chordata are contrasted with those of the phylum Arthropoda.

vertebrates, the sharks and rays, the bony fish, the amphibians, the reptiles, the birds, and the mammals (Table 6.3).

The early **vertebrates** were similar in many ways to *Amphioxus,* but in place of a notochord, a true vertebral column, or spine, developed. The early vertebrates were filter feeders. Because they lacked jaws, they swam with open mouths; by forcing water into their mouths and out through their gills, they filtered out food particles.

vertebrates Members of the subphylum Vertebrata; possess a bony spine or vertebral column.

Table 6.3 The Classification of the Chordates

PHYLUM: Chordata
  SUBPHYLUM: Tunicata (tunicates)
  SUBPHYLUM: Cephalochordata (*Amphioxus*)
  SUBPHYLUM: Vertebrata
    CLASS: Agnatha (lampreys, hagfish)
    CLASS: Chondrichthyes (sharks, rays)
    CLASS: Osteichthyes (perch, herring, salmon)
    CLASS: Amphibia (frogs, salamanders)
    CLASS: Reptilia (turtles, lizards, snakes)
    CLASS: Aves (robins, vultures, ostriches, penguins)
    CLASS: Mammalia (dogs, elephants, whales, gorillas)

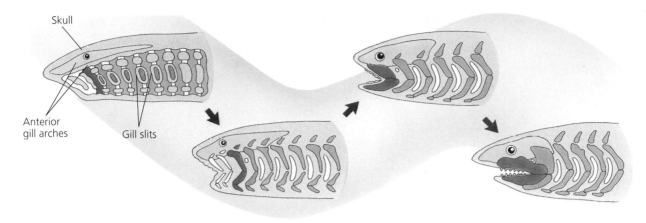

Skull

Anterior
gill arches

Gill slits

Figure 6.8 Evolution of the Jaws The vertebrate jaw evolved from the anterior (front) gill arches of early jawless vertebrates.

A major event in vertebrate evolution was the evolution of jaws. New structures do not simply arise from nothing; they develop as modifications of preexisting structures. The jawless vertebrates have skeletal elements, **gill arches,** that support the gill slits. In the early fish, the first gill arches enlarged to become a primitive jaw (Figure 6.8).

While filter feeding restricted the jawless vertebrates to very small food particles, the evolution of jaws enabled them to prey on one another and to proliferate. Today, these jawed vertebrates are represented by the cartilagenous fish, the sharks and rays, and the bony fish.

The Land Vertebrates The ancestors of the land vertebrates were freshwater bony fish capable of coping with drought conditions, which were common at the time. Periodically, lakes and streams dried up or became small ponds of stagnant water. These vertebrates had lungs for supplementing their oxygen supply in oxygen-deficient water.

The origin of land vertebrates also depended on the evolution of legs. Unlike the fish of today, these early fish had bony elements in their fins. The constant drying up of lakes and streams gave a local selective advantage to these fish which could move overland from one pond to the next.

Land vertebrates did not arise because there was opportunity on land. Organisms do not evolve structures to meet the requirements of new potential habitats. No fish ever lifted its head out of the water, surveyed the land, and decided that since the land was devoid of competition and food was plentiful, it would then evolve lungs and limbs. The structures that make life on land possible evolved as adaptations to aid the fish in *water* under drought conditions. In retrospect, it appears as if the population evolved new adaptations in order to enter new niches on land. In reality, the evolution of new adaptations for life in water merely allowed the animal to adapt to new terrestrial habitats, an example of preadaptation.

The earliest land vertebrates were the amphibians. Amphibians, however, were tied to the water. Most needed to keep their skin moist, especially to aid in breathing through the skin, and all had to lay their eggs in water. This prevented an extensive exploitation of terrestrial habitats.

A life spent totally on land was made possible by changes in the breathing apparatus, which increased the efficiency of the lungs; a waterproof skin; and the **amniote egg.** The amniote egg may have evolved as a method of protecting eggs in water; but once it had developed, reproduction on land became possible.

The embryo in an amniote egg develops within a shell. Fertilization must take place inside the body of the female before the shell is formed. Within the shell, several membranes develop from embryonic tissue (Figure 6.9).

gill arches Skeletal elements supporting the gill slits in nonvertebrate chordates and some vertebrates.

amniote egg An egg with a shell and several internal membranes, which made reproduction on land possible.

Figure 6.9 Amniote Egg The embryo is contained inside a fluid-filled amnion. The chorion lies just beneath the shell and acts as a surface for oxygen absorption. The yolk sac provides nutrients. The allantois is where waste material is deposited.

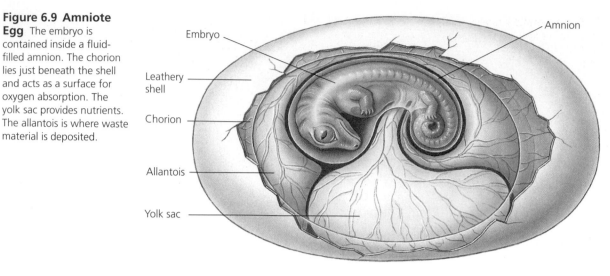

With the development of the amniote egg, vertebrates were no longer tied to the water. The earliest true land vertebrates were the reptiles. From this radiation evolved the dinosaurs and modern reptiles, as well as the birds and mammals.

The Mammals

See the Online Learning Center for an Interactive Exercise on the characteristics of mammals.

The reptilian group from which the **mammals** ultimately emerged appeared very early in the reptilian radiation 220 million years ago. These early mammallike reptiles did not resemble modern reptiles; from the beginning, they showed marked mammalian features and soon evolved into true mammals. The mammals coexisted with a variety of animals, including the dinosaurs, throughout most of their history. With the demise of the dinosaurs, mammals became the dominant form of large terrestrial animal.

The Regulation of Body Temperature A lizard sleeps through the cold desert night in an underground shelter. When it senses the warmth of the sun, it emerges into the daylight and suns itself. At last it is ready to perform the activities of the day. Yet when the desert sun is high, the lizard must seek shelter, for it cannot function in the desert's fierce heat.

A cold wind is blowing down the mountainside, yet the mouse wakes up before dawn. In the dark, safe from most of its enemies, it forages for food. Unlike the lizard, the mouse can function in the cold of night or in the fierce heat of day.

Contemporary reptiles are said to be "cold-blooded," while mammals are described as "warm-blooded," but these terms are far from descriptive since the body temperature of a lizard may be as high as that of a mammal. The primary distinction between the body temperatures of reptiles and mammals lies in the source of the body heat. Reptiles derive most of their body heat from outside their bodies. Reptiles can and do maintain a high and constant body temperature, but they accomplish this primarily through behavior. During the cold of the night, the lizard seeks a relatively warm underground burrow; in the early morning, the animal suns itself on a rock; and during the heat of the day, it finds the shade of a plant or rock. This method of maintaining relatively constant temperature is termed **behavioral thermoregulation.** To maintain a constant temperature, the reptile must vary its activity with changes in the environment.

Like the lizard, the mouse also maintains a relatively high, constant body temperature. Unlike the lizard, however, mammals are **homeothermic;** that is, mammals can control their body temperature through physiological means and can maintain a high body temperature largely independent of the environmental temperature. This is accomplished by the ability to generate body heat internally and by special physiological and anatomical mechanisms for regulating body temperature. This means that mammals can maintain a relatively constant,

mammals Members of the class Mammalia, a class of the subphylum Vertebrata, that are characterized by a constant level of activity independent of external temperature and by mammary glands, hair or fur, heterodonty, and other features.

behavioral thermoregulation Using behavior, such as avoiding or seeking sources of heat, to regulate body temperature.

homeothermic The ability to control body temperature and maintain a high body temperature through physiological means.

Figure 6.10 Mammalian Jaws and Teeth The jaws and teeth of a mammal are compared with those of a reptile (a snake). The mammal pictured is a hypothetical generalized placental mammal. The teeth are (I) incisors, (C) canines, (P) premolars, and (M) molars.

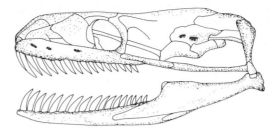

Snake

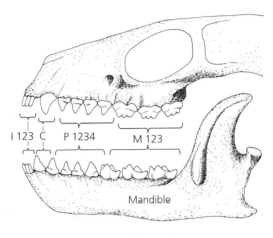

Mammal

high level of activity with a fair degree of independence from the constraints of environmental temperature.

Homeothermy requires a complex of interrelated features such as the evolution of regulating mechanisms in the brain, the growth of fur or hair to provide a layer of insulation, and the development of sweat glands to allow cooling of the body if necessary. In addition, it requires a reliable and fairly large intake of food. A snake may eat once every other week. It simply swallows an entire animal, which then dissolves slowly in the digestive juices in its stomach; the bones and fur are excreted. Mammals do not swallow animals whole. Instead, meat-eating mammals tear their prey into small pieces, and plant eaters bite off small amounts that they then chew into small pieces.

Some Additional Characteristics of the Mammals Mammals are characterized by **heterodont** dentition, the regional differentiation of teeth (Figure 6.10). Unlike reptiles, whose teeth are all simple, pointed structures **(homodont),** mammals evolved different types of teeth—incisor, canine, premolar, and molar—that serve the different functions of tearing, piercing, and chewing. Mammals have two sets of teeth **(diphyodonty),** the deciduous teeth and the permanent teeth; reptilian teeth are continuously replaced **(polyphyodonty).**

The lower teeth of the mammals are embedded in one bone on either side of the lower jaw, or mandible, which is a solid structure able to take the stresses of chewing. The reptilian lower jaw is composed of six bones, while the mammalian lower jaw or **mandible** is composed of two bones that are often fused into a single structure. Two of the reptilian jawbones have been transformed into middle-ear bones, giving mammals three bones in the middle ear in contrast to the single bone in reptiles. While the eardrum, or **tympanic membrane,** is found near the surface of the body in reptiles, the mammalian tympanic membrane and middle ear are encased in bone.

Many other anatomical features in mammals aid in dealing with terrestrial habitats. These include the **diaphragm,** which is a muscle lying beneath the lungs that functions in breathing; the **hard palate,** which separates the nasal from the oral cavity and permits the animal to breathe and chew at the same time; and the **four-chambered heart,** which allows for more complete separation of oxygenated and deoxygenated blood than in reptiles. These and other characteristics of the mammals are listed in Table 6.4.

Mammalian Reproduction and Behavior One of the most important aspects of mammalian reproduction is that the offspring develop inside the mother. The embryo and fetus are not exposed to the outside environment. This ensures a higher chance of survival for the fetus, which means that fewer young are required to maintain the population.

Behavioral changes are as important as anatomical and physiological changes. Newborn mammals cannot obtain their own food; they are nourished by taking milk from their mothers' **mammary glands.** The ability of the mother to produce a high-quality, dependable food also increases the mammalian infant's chances of survival. The care given the young by the mother and often by the father is equally important. Among some mammals, adults other than the parents care for infants. Unlike many reptilian young, who often never see their parents, mammalian young develop close bonds with their mothers and sometimes their fathers and siblings.

heterodont Dentition characterized by regional differentiation of teeth by function.

homodont Situation in which all teeth are basically the same in structure, although they may differ in size, as is found in reptiles.

diphyodonty Having two sets of teeth, the deciduous and the permanent teeth.

polyphyodonty The continuous replacement of teeth such as found in reptiles.

mandible The bone of the lower jaw; contains the lower dentition.

tympanic membrane The eardrum.

Table 6.4 Some Characteristics of the Mammals

Homeothermy (constant body temperature through physiological mechanisms of thermoregulation)

Fur or hair provides a layer of insulation

Sweat glands permit cooling of the body

Heterodont dentition (regional differentiation of teeth)

Diphyodonty (two sets of teeth: deciduous and permanent)

Bone growth occurs in growth plates between the diaphysis and epiphyses of the bone

Saliva includes the digestive enzyme ptyalin, which initiates the digestive process in the mouth

Lower teeth embedded in one bone on either side of the lower jaw

Three bones in the middle ear

Eardrum, or tympanic membrane, and middle ear are encased in bone

Diaphragm functions in breathing

Hard palate separates the nasal from the oral cavity

Four-chambered heart allows efficient separation of oxygenated and deoxygenated blood

Offspring usually develop inside the mother

Newborns nourished from their mothers' mammary glands

Care is given to the young by the mother and often by the father and other adults

Much of mammalian behavior is learned

Improvements in the nervous system and elaboration of the brain

---

diaphragm A muscle that lies beneath the lungs. When the diaphragm contracts, the volume of the lungs increases, causing a lowering of pressure within the lungs and movement of air from the outside into the lungs. When the diaphragm relaxes, air is expelled from the lungs.

hard palate The bony roof of the mouth that separates the mouth from the nasal cavity, permitting the animal to breath and chew at the same time.

four-chambered heart A heart that is divided into two sets of pumping chambers, effectively separating oxygenated blood from the lungs from deoxygenated blood from the body.

mammary glands Glands found in mammalian females that produce milk.

prototherian Referring to mammals belonging to the subclass Prototheria; monotremes or egg-laying mammals.

Bonding and protection of offspring not only function to protect the offspring but also make the transmission of learned behavioral patterns possible. To a large extent, mammals also adjust to their niches through behavior. In contrast to insect behavior, which is basically innate, much of mammalian behavior is learned. Behavioral adjustments can thereby change rapidly, even within a single generation, in response to changing environmental pressures. Anatomical adaptations, such as improvements in the nervous system, including the elaboration of the brain, are important in creating the potential for behavioral adjustments.

Classification of the Mammals The mammals belong to the class Mammalia, which is divided into two subclasses containing three groups that correspond to the three major kinds of mammals. The subclass Prototheria consists of the egg-laying mammals; the pouched mammals and the placental mammals belong to the subclass Theria.

Prototherian mammals, also known as the **monotremes,** include only two living forms, the platypus and the echidna (Figure 6.11). These animals lay eggs but also produce milk. In most ways, they possess both reptilian and mammalian characteristics, and for this reason some taxonomists consider them to be mammallike reptiles. Modern mammals did not evolve from prototherianlike ancestors. They represent a branch of the mammalian class that evolved a number of distinctive traits after the monotremes had branched off the main mammalian evolutionary line.

The **therian** mammals, which produce live young, can be divided into two infraclasses. The infraclass Metatheria contains the **marsupials,** or pouched mammals (Figure 6.12). Most of them live in Australia, although the opossums are a well-known North American group. They differ from other mammals in many ways but most importantly in method of reproduction. Metatherian offspring are born while they are still fetuses. The fetus then crawls into the mother's pouch or fold, where it continues to develop and mature.

The remainder of the mammals, and by far the largest number of species, belong to the infraclass Eutheria. These are the **placental mammals.** Their young remain inside the mother, nourished by the **placenta,** until they reach an advanced state of development. The placenta is an organ that develops from fetal membranes. It penetrates the lining of

Figure 6.11 The Echidna (*Tachyglossus aculeatus*) This is an example of a prototherian mammal. The spines on the body resemble those of the porcupine, a placental mammal, yet they have a different internal structure. This is an example of convergent evolution.

Figure 6.12 Eastern gray kangaroo (*Macropus giganteus*) This female, shown with a joey in her pouch, is an example of a metatherian mammal, or marsupial.

monotremes Member of the subclass Prototheria of the class Mammalia; the egg-laying mammals.

therian Referring to mammals belonging to the subclass Theria; the "live-bearing" mammals including the marsupials and placental mammals.

marsupial A member of the infraclass Metatheria of the class Mammalia; young are born at a relatively less-developed stage than in placental mammals. After birth, the young attaches to a mammary gland in the pouch, where it continues to grow and develop.

placental mammal Member of the infraclass Eutheria of the class Mammalia; mammal that forms a placenta.

placenta An organ that develops from fetal membranes that functions to pass oxygen, nutrients, and other substances to and waste material from the fetus.

the uterus where the placental blood vessels come into close contact with the mother's blood. Oxygen, nutrients, and other substances pass from the mother's bloodstream into that of the fetus. Waste material passes in the opposite direction.

The Relationship of Primates to Other Mammals Today there are 18 (some count more) living orders of placental mammals, which are listed in the classification in

Figure 6.13 Evolutionary Relationships among the Mammals See text for explanation.

Source: M. J. Novacek, "Mammalian Phylogeny: Shaking the Tree," *Nature* 356 (1992), 121–125 (www.nature.com). Courtesy of M. J. Novacek.

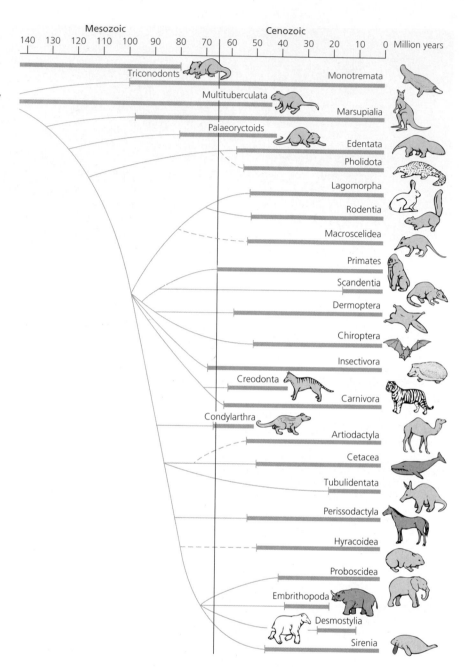

Table 6.5. Since the major subject of physical anthropology is humans, we are most interested in the order Primates, which is the subject of the next several chapters.

The traditional classification of taxa is based on the analysis of anatomy and paleontology. More recently, molecular and chromosome data have been considered, and this has led to many discussions about the relationships among various groups of animals, such as the orders of placental mammals. Although there is no consensus on this issue, Figure 6.13 shows one attempt, based on molecular data, to picture the relationship among the mammalian orders.[1]

Some biologists place the order Primates in a superorder named Archonta. The Archonta includes the primates along with the Scandentia (tree shrews), the Dermoptera (flying lemurs), and the Chiroptera (bats).

---

[1] M. J. Novacek, "Mammalian Phylogeny: Shaking the Tree," *Nature* 356 (1992), pp. 121–125.

Table 6.5 The Classification of the Mammals

CLASS: Mammalia
  SUBCLASS: Prototheria
      ORDER: Monotremata (platypuses, echidnas)
  SUBCLASS: Theria
   INFRACLASS: Metatheria
     ORDER: Marsupialia (kangaroos, koalas, opossums)
   INFRACLASS: Eutheria
     ORDER: Insectivora (shrews, hedgehogs, moles)
     ORDER: Macroscelida (elephant shrews)
     ORDER: Scandentia (tree shrews)
     ORDER: Chiroptera (bats)
     ORDER: Dermoptera (flying "lemurs")
     ORDER: Edentata (armadillos, anteaters, tree sloths)
     ORDER: Pholidota (pangolins)
     ORDER: Primates (lemurs, tarsiers, monkeys, apes, humans)
     ORDER: Rodentia (squirrels, beavers, mice, porcupines)
     ORDER: Lagomorpha (rabbits, hares)
     ORDER: Cetacea (whales, porpoises, dolphins)
     ORDER: Carnivora (dogs, bears, cats, hyenas, seals)
     ORDER: Tubulidentata (aardvarks)
     ORDER: Perissodactyla (horses, rhinoceroses, tapirs)
     ORDER: Artiodactyla (pigs, camels, deer, cattle, hippopotamuses)
     ORDER: Proboscidea (elephants)
     ORDER: Sirenia (sea cows, dugongs)
     ORDER: Hyracoidea (hyraxes, conies)

This classification is based upon that of E. H. Colbert and M. Morales, *Evolution of the Vertebrates,* 4th ed. (New York: Wiley-Liss, 1991), pp. 434–437. The classification of other authors may differ. For example, many zoologists place the seals and walruses into their own order, the Pinnipedia. The Cetacea and Chiroptera each is often divided into two orders instead of one. Copyright © 1991 Wiley-Liss. This material is used by permission of Wiley-Liss, Inc., a subsidiary of John Wiley & Sons, Inc.

Summary

People belong to the animal kingdom. This large group of organisms is divided into several phyla that represent basic body plans. The phylum Chordata is characterized by a notochord; dorsal, hollow nerve cord; and gill slits. In the largest subphylum of chordates, the vertebrates, the notochord is replaced by a vertebral column in the embryo. One group of early vertebrates gave rise, through the refinement of lungs and limbs, to the first land vertebrates, the amphibians. With the evolution of the amniote egg, reproduction was no longer tied to water. This evolutionary development resulted in the great reptilian radiation, which included a line of reptiles that were mammal-like. Through a long evolutionary history, these reptiles ultimately gave rise to the mammals.

The mammals are a class of vertebrates. They are characterized by homeothermy and endothermy, heterodont dentition, mammary glands, and complex patterns of learned behavior. The mammals have radiated into 20 living orders. Included in one of these orders, the order Primates, are people.

Key Terms

amniote egg, *137*

analogies, *131*

archetype, *126*

behavioral
thermoregulation, *138*

binomen, *126*

binomial nomenclature, *126*

chordates, *135*

clade, *131*

cladistics, *131*

cladogram, *132*

class, *128*

classification, *126*

convergence, *130*

diaphragm, *139*

diphyodonty, *139*

dorsal, *135*

family, *128*

four-chambered heart, *139*

genus, *126*

gill arches, *137*

gill slits, *135*

hard palate, *139*

heterodont, *139*

higher taxa, *128*

homeothermic, *138*

homodont, *139*

homologies, *129*

homoplastic, *130*

kingdom, *128*

mammals, *138*

mammary glands, *139*

mandible, *139*

marsupial, *140*

monotremes, *140*

notochord, *135*

order, *128*

outgroup, *132*

parallelism, *131*

phylogeny, *129*

phylum, *128*

placenta, *140*

placental mammals, *140*

polyphyodonty, *139*

prototherian, *140*

shared ancestral
(symplesiomorphic)
feature, *132*

shared derived
(synapomorphic)
feature, *132*

taxon, *128*

taxonomy, *126*

therian, *140*

tympanic membrane, *139*

uniquely derived
(autopomorphic)
feature, *132*

ventral, *135*

vertebrates, *136*

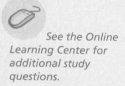

*See the Online
Learning Center for
additional study
questions.*

Study Questions

1. Although the form of Linnaeus's system of biological classification is still in use, the concept of classification has changed considerably. In what ways does the theory of taxonomy of the eighteenth century differ from that of the twenty-first century?

2. One line of evidence for evolutionary relationships is homologous structures. How does the taxonomist distinguish between two similar structures that are truly homologous and those that are the result of convergent evolution?

3. What is the theoretical basis of the cladistic approach?

4. Each animal phylum represents a basic body plan. What features characterize the phylum Chordata? Can these features be identified in humans?

5. What selective pressures operating on the water-dwelling bony fish resulted in a preadaptation for life on land?

6. What major adaptations have been largely responsible for the success of the mammals at the expense of the reptiles?

7. What is the basis of the division of mammals into prototherian, metatherian, and eutherian categories?

Critical Thinking Questions

1. Throughout most of European history, humans were seen as being distinct from animals. Modern evolutionary theory sees humans as part of a phylogenetic tree, as having evolved from nonhuman forms. Do you believe that humans are so distinct from the rest of the animal kingdom that they should not be classified as animals? What case can you make for this argument? Or do you think that humans and human characteristics represent homologies that are the result of evolutionary diversion from nonhuman ancestors and therefore humans are rightfully called animals? What argument can you make for this point of view?

2. Many comic books feature reptilian-like creatures that have evolved human intelligence. Why is it unlikely that a humanlike creature would evolve in the class Reptilia?

Suggested Readings

Colbert, E. H., et al. *Evolution of the Vertebrates,* 5th ed. New York: Wiley-Liss, 2002. This book presents the history of the vertebrates, including the fossil record and a survey of living forms.

Koerner, L. *Linnaeus: Nature and Nation.* Cambridge, MA: Harvard University Press, 1999. This is a biography of the Swedish botanist Carolus Linnaeus, who developed the form of the system of biological classification used today.

Mayr, E. *The Science of the Living World.* Cambridge, MA: Harvard University Press, 1997. One of the twentieth century's preeminent biologists discusses the nature of science, biology, and evolution.

Nielsen, C. *Animal Evolution: Interrelationships of the Living Phyla.* New York: Oxford University Press, 1995. This book provides a detailed cladistic analysis of animal species, including the primates.

Radinsky, L. B. *The Evolution of Vertebrate Design.* Chicago: University of Chicago Press, 1987. A well-written and easily understood book on the evolution of vertebrate anatomy.

Tudge, C. *The Variety of Life: A Survey and a Celebration of All the Creatures That Have Ever Lived.* New York: Oxford University Press, 2000. This volume presents a classification and survey of the living world, including living and extinct forms.

Suggested Websites

Introduction to cladistics from the Museum of Paleontology, University of California, Berkeley:
www.ucmp.berkeley.edu/clad/clad1.html

The Phylogeny of Life (an exploration of life):
www.ucmp.berkeley.edu/alllife/threedomains.html

Tree of Life (information on phylogenetics and biodiversity):
http://tolweb.org/tree/phylogeny.html

Chapter 7

The Living Primates

Japanese macque, *Macaca fuscata*

Humans have a special interest in the group of animals known as primates since, in addition to prosimians, monkeys, and apes, it includes ourselves. This interest is traceable into remote antiquity, long before it was realized that we humans are a part of nature and that primates are our closest relatives. Inquisitiveness is a legacy of those primate origins. Who among us has not wondered about those familiar faces peering at us from the monkey island at the local zoo. •

—*Daris R. Swindler*

Chapter Outline

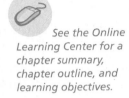

See the Online Learning Center for a chapter summary, chapter outline, and learning objectives.

After Reading This Chapter, You Should Be Able to Answer These Questions:

1. What are the shared ancestral and shared derived characteristics of the primates that relate to an arboreal lifestyle and movement in trees?

2. What are the most important senses in the primates? How is this related to features of primate anatomy?

3. What is the basis of the division of primates into strepsirhine and haplorhine?

4. How does the life cycle of primates differ from that of other mammals?

5. What are the two suborders of the primate order, and in general terms what distinguishes them from each other?

6. How are monkeys classified into different groups and subgroups? What are the characteristics of each of these groups?

7. What is an ape? Why is it incorrect to call an ape a monkey?

8. How are apes taxonomically divided into different groups? What are the characteristics of each of these groups?

9. How are humans related to other primates? How are humans classified in primate taxonomy?

In 1758, Linnaeus classified humans together with the monkeys and apes into the same category, Primates. Since then, many people have attempted, as Richard Passingham says, to "put animals back in their proper place."[1] Different rationales have been posited to put distance between humans and the other primates—for that matter, all animals—but today biologists no longer debate the issue.

Humans *are* primates; they share with other primates many basic primate characteristics. This perhaps explains the tremendous fascination people have for monkeys and apes in zoos. Anthropologists, too, are fascinated by primates. Studies of their natural history, behavior, and anatomy provide important clues for the reconstruction and understanding of human evolutionary history.

This is the first of several chapters that examine the relationship of humans to their nonhuman primate relatives. This chapter defines what a primate is and then surveys the animals that make up this order.

THE PRIMATE ORDER

The order Primates contains approximately 238 species. It includes a number of well-known kinds of animals—monkeys, apes, and humans—as well as less well known animals, such as lemurs and tarsiers. Generally speaking, primates are tropical animals, commonly found in the tropical rain forests of Central and South America, Africa, and southern and southeastern Asia. A few species have moved into more temperate habitats. Two examples are monkeys living at high altitudes in the Himalayas and monkeys surviving winter snows in Japan. One species, *Homo sapiens,* occupies a large percentage of the earth's terrestrial habitats.

For the most part primates are **arboreal** animals. However, some species have adapted to a semiterrestrial way of life on the open savanna grasslands and semidesert regions of Africa. A few species have taken up an urban lifestyle, coexisting with *H. sapiens*. The latter species has become a specialized terrestrial animal.

Primates are generally vegetarian, eating a variety of plant foods such as fruits, leaves, flowers, bark, and sap. However, many primate diets also include insects and small animals such as lizards and birds, and two species systematically hunt and eat meat.

Living primates generally possess large brains; flattened nails instead of claws, at the very least on the big toes; grasping thumbs and big toes; and eye sockets that are encircled by a postorbital bar and convergence of the eye sockets on the front of the face, facing forward.

The Evolution of the Primates

When looking at any group of animals, we ponder how and why the features we observe evolved in the first place. We also need to distinguish between the shared ancestral features that primates have retained from their nonprimate ancestors and the shared derived features that evolved in the subsequently evolving primate line. Of course, different groups of primates are characterized by their own unique derived features.

Several hypotheses have been proposed to account for the origin of the primates. Those hypotheses differ largely in the order in which the various features—nails, grasping hands and feet, convergence of the eyes—evolved. The problem is complex because other closely related nonprimate groups also evolved some of the same characteristics.

The various hypotheses suggest that the evolution of these features resulted from (1) leaping patterns of locomotion in which grasping branches was important for climbing and landing, (2) consumption of fruits that grow on the ends of slender branches, (3) insect predation on slender branches in which the primate locates the insect through enhanced vision and then, anchoring itself to a branch with its grasping feet, lunges forward to catch the animal in its grasping hand, and (4) some combination of these factors. All these

arboreal Living in trees.

See the Online Learning Center for an Internet Activity on the primate order.

---

[1] R. Passingham, *The Human Primate* (Oxford: Freeman, 1982), p. 1.

hypotheses emphasize the grasping ability of hands and feet and the enhancement of vision. We will revisit this issue when we examine the early primate fossil record in Chapter 12.

Characteristics of the Primates

Primates are generally arboreal animals, and many of the shared derived features of their anatomy are related to movement in arboreal habitats. Primates have evolved a degree of precision of the hand and foot by which they are able to grasp; a monkey walking along a branch grasps that branch. This grasping ability is also used to manipulate objects in their habitat.

Primates have retained a number of ancestral features that are related to arboreal locomotion. The forelimb structure of the primate corresponds well to the generalized limb structure of early placental ancestors. For example, all primates have retained the clavicle (collarbone), the two separate bones in the lower arm (the ulna and radius) that permit rotation of the lower arm, and five fingers **(pentadactylism).** This arrangement allows a great degree of flexibility in the shoulder, forearm, and hand, which facilitates movement through the trees as well as manipulation.

Flexibility of the primate skeleton is associated with the wide range of locomotor patterns both within and among the various species. The anatomical structures that play major roles in movement and locomotion will be described in more detail in Chapter 8.

As has been mentioned, there are five digits on the hands and feet. These digits are capable of a high degree of independent movement, and the thumb and big toe are separated from the other digits. This permits the grasping of food or a branch. In fact, a grasping big toe is a feature that is found in all primates except *H. sapiens.*

Many but not all primates have a grasping thumb. In many cases the thumb has become truly **opposable.** An opposable thumb is one that can rotate so that the terminal pad of the thumb comes into contact with the terminal pad of one or more of the other digits, providing for the fine manipulation of objects.

The fingers and toes, as well as the palm and sole, are covered with patterns of **epidermal ridges** that form the familiar fingerprint patterns. These ridges make up the **tactile pads.** They provide a friction surface that aids in holding on to objects and branches. They are also endowed with a high concentration of nerve endings. Another feature of the digits is the replacement of pointed claws by flat nails, especially on the big toe.

The Senses

Among terrestrial mammals, the **olfactory** sense, or sense of smell, plays a crucial role. Hunters realize that when they approach an animal such as a deer, the animal is not apt to see them, especially if they freeze when it is looking up, but they had better stalk the animal from downwind to avoid being detected by their smell.

Smells are relatively unimportant in the trees. Most odors hug the ground, and the wind, as it blows through the trees, eliminates their usefulness. Also, the sense of smell does not give an arboreal animal the type of information it needs, such as the exact direction and distance of one branch from another. Thus, in the primates, the sense of smell has diminished; over time, it has proved to have little selective advantage.

In the primates, the nasal structures of the skull are reduced in size and the muzzle or snout is relatively small (Figure 7.1). The olfactory regions of brain, which are associated with the sense of smell, are reduced. Some of the primates have retained a **rhinarium,** a moist, naked area surrounding the nostrils, attached to the upper lip by a **philtrum** (Figure 7.2). These features characterize the **strepsirhine primates** that include the prosimians. Primates without these features are called **haplorhine primates.** They include the monkeys, apes, and humans.

Vision Most primates see both in three dimensions and in color, although the degree of development of color vision varies among different groups of primates (Box 7–1). Color vision helps them distinguish detail, since similar colors, such as various shades of green

pentadactylism
Possessing five digits on the hand and/or foot.

opposable thumb
Anatomical arrangement in which the fleshy tip of the thumb can touch the fleshy tip of all the fingers.

epidermal ridges The pattern of ridges found on the hands and feet that form "fingerprint" patterns. These ridges are richly endowed with nerve endings that are associated with a refined sense of touch.

tactile pads The tips of the fingers and toes of primates; areas richly endowed by tactile nerve endings sensitive to touch.

olfactory Referring to the sense of smell.

rhinarium The moist, naked area surrounding the nostrils in most mammals; absent in most primates.

philtrum A vertical cleft in the center of the upper lip.

strepsirhine primates
Primates, such as lemurs and lorises, that possess a rhinarium and philtrum.

haplorhine primates
Primates, such as monkeys, apes, and humans, that lack a rhinarium and possess a free upper lip.

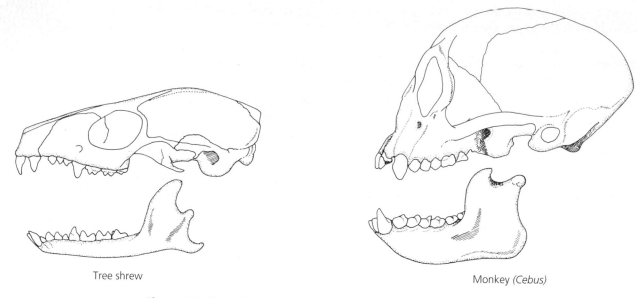

Figure 7.1 The Primate Face The facial skeleton of a monkey (*Cebus*) is compared with that of a tree shrew, a member of the order Scandentia. Note the reduction of the olfactory apparatus and the relatively flat facial skeleton of the monkey.

in a tropical forest, may blend if seen only in black and white. In addition, stationary objects, such as a piece of ripe fruit, stand out in a three-dimensional field.

The primate eye is large, and its **retina** contains two types of cells, **rods** and **cones,** that are sensitive to light. Rods respond to very low intensities of light and are responsible for black-and-white vision. Cones, while not as sensitive to low light intensities, sense color

retina The layer of cells in the back of the eye that contains the cells—rods and cones—that are sensitive to light.

rods Cells of the retina of the eye that are sensitive to the presence or absence of light; function in black-and-white vision.

cones Cells of the retina of the eye; each of the types of cones is sensitive to a specific wavelength of light, thereby producing color vision.

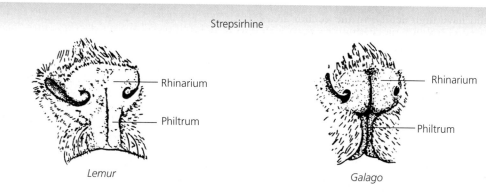

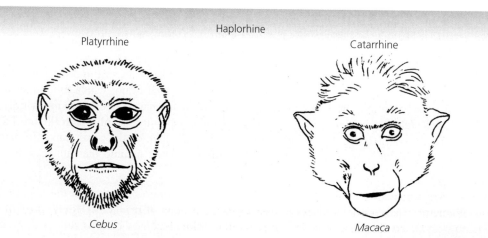

Figure 7.2 Primate Noses The strepsirhine primates, which include the prosimians, have a nose that is characterized by a rhinarium and a philtrum. The haplorhine primates, which include the monkeys, apes, and humans, lack these features. The platyrrhine nose is found in the New World monkeys, while the Old World monkeys, apes, and humans have a catarrhine nose.

Box 7-1
The Advantages of Color Vision

A trip to a paint store demonstrates the enormous range of colors that humans can discriminate. There are different brands of paint, each with numerous shades of red, blue, yellow, orange, green, and other colors. Humans can distinguish between more than 2 million colors.

We see color because of the presence of cells called cones in the retina of the eye. Light-sensitive pigments in the cones are sensitive to different wavelengths of light. While birds have four pigments sensitive to blue, green, red, and ultraviolet light, most primates that evolved in Africa and Asia, including humans, have only three, lacking the cones sensitive to ultraviolet light. This condition is called **trichromacy.** Most other mammals, including most primates in the New World, are characterized by **dichromacy** in that they have pigments for only blue and green and therefore can distinguish fewer colors.

What might be the adaptive significance of trichromacy? One of the earliest explanations is that sensitivity to red helped early arboreal primates pick out ripe red and orange fruit from among the green leaves of the forest. A second explanation is that it allows animals to distinguish the new red leaves on trees and bushes from the older green ones. New leaves are more nutritious and many African and Asian primates eat a lot of leaves, and so the ability to find the more nutritious food would be an advantage. On the other hand, most primates of the New World do not use leaves as their primary source of food, with a few exceptions, such as the howler monkey. The howler monkey does have trichromatic color vision that probably evolved independent of its evolution in the Old World, an example of parallel evolution.

In most mammals, the sense of smell helps a male identify a female who is about to ovulate. Most primates have a reduced ability to sense odors, and many male primates are attracted to females that show visual signs of sexual receptivity. Often the visual cue is a swelling and redness of the sexual skin.

In the final analysis, all three of these explanations are plausible—there is no reason to believe that a characteristic has only one function. Perhaps trichromacy was a preadaptation for the human interest in decoration.

Sources: N. J. Dominy and P. W. Lucas, "Ecological Importance of Trichromatic Vision to Primates," *Nature,* 410 (2001), pp. 363–366; E. R. Liman and H. Innan, "Relaxed Selective Pressure on an Essential Component of Pheromone Transduction in Primate Evolution," *Proceedings of the National Academy of Sciences,* 100 (2003), pp. 3328–3332; and J. Travis, "Visionary Research: Scientists Delve into the Evolution of Color Vision in Primates," *Science News,* 164 (2003), pp. 234–236.

---

and have high acuity. In the central area of the retina is the **macula,** an area consisting of only cones. Within the macula of most primates is a depression, called the **fovea,** that contains a single layer of cones with no overlapping blood vessels. This is the area of greatest visual acuity; it permits the fine visual discrimination characteristic of the primate eye (Figure 7.3).

The eyes, and the eye sockets, have converged on the front of the face, facing forward. As a result, the visual fields seen by each eye overlap extensively, producing a broad **binocular field.** Thus, the brain receives images of the same objects simultaneously from both eyes. This fact is a prerequisite for three-dimensional or **stereoscopic vision.** The evolution of stereoscopic vision is dependent not only on binocular vision but also on significant changes in the optic nerves and the brain.

In the primates, the eye is supported on the side by a **postorbital bar** that forms a complete bony ring around the eye socket (Figure 7.4). This skeletal feature is found in all living primates and in some other mammalian groups. However, the morphological details of the postorbital bar differ among the different mammalian taxa, and the evolution of the postorbital bar in different orders most likely represents a case of convergent evolution.

In some primates, and in other mammal orders, the orbit, the space that contains the eye, is not separated from the

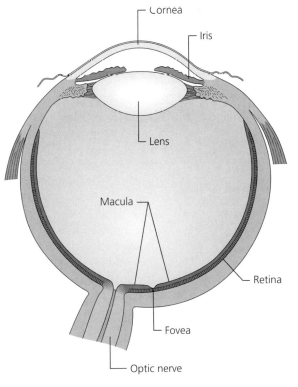

Figure 7.3 The Primate Eye A diagrammatic cross section of the human eye.

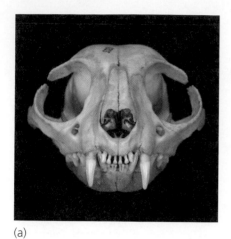 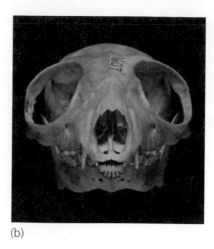 

(a)   (b)   (c)

Figure 7.4 The Eye Socket (a) An eye socket is absent in the cat. (b) While an eye socket is absent in the lemur, the eye is surrounded by a complete bony ring. (c) The monkey skull displays a complete eye socket.

macula The central area of the retina consisting of cones only.

fovea A depression within the macula of the retina of the eye that contains a single layer of cones with no overlapping blood vessels; region of greatest visual acuity.

binocular field The visual field produced by the overlapping of the separate visual fields from each eye when the eyes are located on the front of the face.

stereoscopic vision Visual perception of depth due to overlapping visual fields and various neurological features.

postorbital bar A feature of the skull formed by an upward extension of the zygomatic arch and a downward extension of the frontal bone that supports the eye.

postorbital septum A bony partition behind the eye that isolates the eye from the muscles of the jaw and forms a bony eye socket or orbit in which the eye lies.

prenatal That period of an individual's life cycle from conception to birth.

muscles behind it. In most primates, a bony **postorbital septum** is found behind the eye that isolates it from these muscles and forms a bony socket in which the eye lies.

Primates are highly social animals, and vision plays a key role in primate communication. Unlike dogs, which smell one another on meeting, primates communicate largely through visual stimuli, although vocalizations also play important roles. Facial expression is made possible in many primates by differentiation of the muscles of the face. The facial musculature in other mammals is relatively undifferentiated. Also, unlike other mammals, many primates have an upper lip that is not attached to the upper gum. This allows a wide range of gestures, including the kiss.

The Growth and Development of Primates

The life of an individual can be divided into several phases or periods: **prenatal,** from conception to birth; **infantile,** from birth to the eruption of the first permanent teeth; and **juvenile,** which encompasses the time from the eruption of the first permanent teeth to the eruption of the last permanent teeth. This is followed by the **adult** period. Figure 7.5 shows the relative length of these subdivisions of growth and development in several primate forms.

The primate placenta differs from that of other placental mammals. In most mammals, the blood vessels of the fetus and those of the mother come into close contact, and nutrients and other substances pass through two vessel walls from the maternal to the fetal bloodstream. In the **hemochorial placenta,** which is found in all primates except prosimians, the fetal blood vessels penetrate the lining of the uterus. The uterus undergoes cellular changes, and the fine blood vessels of the mother break down to form a spongy, blood-filled mass. The result is that maternal blood surrounds the fetal blood vessels, and so materials pass through only a single vessel wall in moving from one blood system to the other.

The period of time between conception and birth is known as **gestation.** The primates are characterized by a prolonged gestation. To illustrate this point, we can compare three mammals of similar size: the chimpanzee (a primate), the impala (a hoofed mammal), and the coyote (a carnivore). Gestation is 240 days in the chimpanzee, 191 days in the impala, and 63 days in the coyote. Human gestation is 270 days (Table 7.1).

Besides the lengthened prenatal period, a rapid rate of growth characterizes the human fetus. For example, the orangutan fetus grows at an average rate of 5.7 grams (0.2 ounce) per day, while the rate for the human fetus is about 12.5 grams (0.44 ounce) per day. Because the placenta develops earlier in humans, rapid growth begins soon after conception and remains rapid throughout the gestation process.

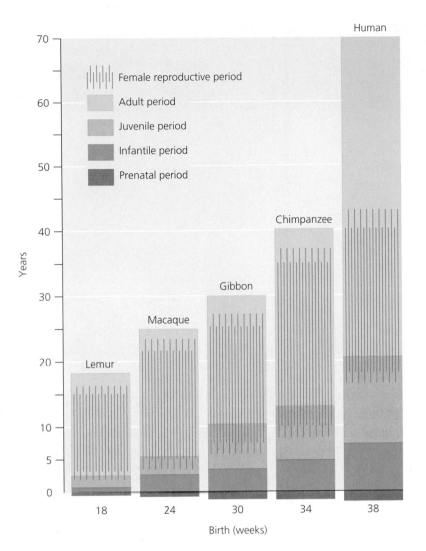

Figure 7.5 The Life Cycles of Primates

Along with a lengthened childhood period is a lengthened life span in general. Primates are relatively long-lived animals. Among mammals, longevity is related to body size, with the larger mammals, in general, living longer than the smaller ones. Yet when other mammals of similar size are compared with primates, the latter tend to exhibit a longer life span. Other life-cycle events also take longer in primates. The age at which the female gives birth to her first offspring is 14 years in the chimpanzee, 2 years in the impala, and 3 years in the coyote. Finally, the life span is approximately 53 years in the chimpanzee, $12\frac{1}{2}$ years in the impala, and 16 years in the coyote.

Other Features of the Primates

Dentition is discussed in detail in Chapter 8, but it should be mentioned here that primate dentition is characterized by fewer teeth than the number found in the ancestral placental mammal. This ancestral form had 44 teeth, whereas many primates, including humans, have only 32. Primate teeth are relatively simple in structure, especially compared with those of grazing animals or carnivores. Features of the skeleton are also discussed in Chapter 8.

Primates are known for their great intelligence. The primate brain is large in relation to the size of the body, and the areas that control complex behavioral patterns are well developed. This permits a great degree of behavioral flexibility. The anatomy of the primate brain is discussed in Chapter 8 and primate behavior in Chapter 9.

infantile That period in an individual's life cycle from birth to the eruption of the first permanent teeth.

juvenile That period in an individual's life cycle that lasts from the eruption of the first to the eruption of the last permanent teeth.

adult The period in an individual's life cycle after the eruption of the last permanent teeth.

hemochorial placenta Type of placenta found in most anthropoids in which materials pass between the maternal and fetal bloodstreams through a single vessel wall.

gestation The period of time from conception to birth.

Table 7.1 Landmarks in the Life Cycle of Primates

Species	Gestation (days)	Age of First Birth (years)	Life Span (years)
Ring-tailed lemur *Lemur catta*	134–138	3	27
Rhesus macaque *Macaca mulatta*	164	4.5	29
Yellow baboon *Papio hamadryas cynocephalus*	175	5.5	40
White-handed gibbon *Hylobates lar*	205	9.3	44
Borneo orangutan *Pongo pygmaeus*	244	12–15	59
Western lowland gorilla *Gorilla gorilla gorilla*	256	9–11	50
Chimpanzee *Pan troglodytes*	240	11.5–15	53
Humans *Homo sapiens*	270	16–20	80–90

Source: Data from N. Rowe, *The Pictorial Guide to the Living Primates* (Charlestown, RI: Pogonias Press, 1996).

Much primate adaptability is the result of learned behavioral adaptations. Most primates live in large social units, usually produce single births, and have a long childhood period; these factors facilitate learning. The social behavior of primates is the topic of Chapter 9.

Summary

The order Primates contains 238 species found throughout the tropical areas of Africa, Asia, and North and South America, although some species have adapted to temperate climates. Most primates are arboreal. Several hypotheses have been put forth to explain the origin of the primates, including emphasis on leaping patterns of locomotion, consumption of fruits growing at the ends of branches, and insect predation.

Living primates are characterized by flexible hands and feet, usually with five digits that end with flattened nails instead of claws. In some cases the thumb is truly opposable. The hands and feet are covered with tactile pads with epidermal ridges that support a refined sense of touch. This flexibility of the hand, along with flexibility in the shoulder and arms, facilitates movement through the trees as well as manipulation of the environment.

The sense of smell is reduced in primates, but the sense of vision is greatly enhanced, being both stereoscopic and in color. The eye sockets are encircled by a postorbital bar, and the eyes converge on the front of the face. We can identify two major groups of primates: The strepsirhine primates have a rhinarium and philtrum in the nasal region, while the haplorhine primates, such as humans, lack these features.

Primates have relatively long gestations, infantile and juvenile periods, and life spans. They possess large brains and are highly intelligent. Living in large social groups, they adapt largely by means of complex, learned behavioral patterns. The major derived characteristics of the primates are summarized in Table 7.2.

Table 7.2 Derived Characteristics of the Primates

Grasping and opposable thumbs	Hands can grasp and hold on to objects. Primates with opposable thumbs are able to manipulate their habitats extensively.
Grasping big toe	With the exception of humans, all primates can grasp and hold on to objects with their feet.
Fingers and toes end in nails	Although some primates have claws on some digits, most have nails on all digits.
Tactile pads	At the ends of fingers and toes are tactile pads that act to create a friction surface for grasping and confer a refined sense of touch.
Reduced sense of smell	The sense of smell is less acute in primates than it is in other mammals.
Enhanced visual sense	Primate eyes are located in the front of the head, which allows for three-dimensional (stereoscopic) vision. Primates also see in color.
Complete eye socket	All living primates have a postorbital bar, and most have a bony postorbital septum that forms a complete bony socket to protect the eye.
Hemochorial placenta	Found in many primates, this is a highly efficient placenta in terms of providing nutrition to the developing fetus.
Prolonged stages of life	Primates have long gestational periods, and all other periods of life are prolonged in comparison with most other mammals.
Primate intelligence	Primates, especially the apes and humans, show a great deal of behavior flexibility and ability to learn from experience.

THE LIVING PRIMATES

Approximately 238 species of primates have been described. This section will follow the classification shown in Table 7.3. In this section, we will discuss representative species in each family in terms of their classification and natural history. More detailed information on behavior, anatomy, and other subjects will be presented in subsequent chapters. The distribution of the primates is seen in Figure 7.6.

The Lemuriformes

The primate order is divided into two suborders, which are divided further into two infraorders. The suborder Prosimii includes the infraorders Lemuriformes and Tarsiiformes.

The Lemuriformes are a diverse group of primates, most of which are **nocturnal** (active at night), with eyes adapted for nocturnal vision. These are strepsirhine primates with a well-developed sense of smell. Their nostrils are surrounded by a rhinarium, and the upper lip is attached to the gums by a philtrum.

Unlike their other fingers and toes, which end in nails, all lemuriformes possess second toes that end in claws. These **grooming claws** are used by the animal in scratching and cleaning its fur. Finally, in most species the lower front teeth, the incisors and canines, are thin and narrow and they project forward horizontally to form a **dental comb.**

Five closely related families of prosimians—the Lemuridae, Lepilemuridae, Cheirogaleidae, Indriidae, and Daubentoniidae—live on the island of Madagascar (Malagasy Republic), which is located about 400 kilometers (250 miles) off the southeast coast of Africa. Primatologists believe that the early ancestors of these animals found their way to the island by rafting across the channel, which was once narrower than it is today, on masses of vegetation. Once on the island, they were isolated from the mainland, and thus they were protected

See the Online Learning Center for an Interactive Exercise on primate taxonomy.

See the Online Learning Center for an Internet Activity on prosimian research at the Duke University Primate Center.

nocturnal Active at night.

grooming claws Claws found on the second toes of prosimians that function in grooming.

dental comb A structure formed by the front teeth of the lower jaw projecting forward almost horizontally; found in prosimians.

Table 7.3 A Classification of the Order Primates

Suborder: Prosimii
    Infraorder: Lemuriformes
        Superfamily: Lemurioidea
            Family: Lemuridae (lemurs, gentle lemurs, ruffed lemurs)
            Family: Lepilemuridae (sportive lemurs)
            Family: Cheirogaleidae (dwarf lemurs, mouse lemurs)
            Family: Indriidae (indri, sifakas, avahis)
            Family: Daubentoniidae (aye-aye)
        Superfamily: Lorisoidea
            Family: Lorisidae (angwantibos, potto, slender lorises, slow lorises)
            Family: Galagidae (galagos)
    Infraorder: Tarsiiformes
        Family: Tarsiidae (tarsiers)
Suborder: Anthropoidea
    Infraorder: Platyrrhini
        Superfamily: Ceboidea
            Family: Cebidae
                Subfamily: Cebinae (capuchin monkeys, squirrel monkeys)
                Subfamily: Aotinae (night monkey, titi monkeys)
                Subfamily: Atelinae (spider monkeys, howler monkeys)
                Subfamily: Pithecinae (uakaris, sakis)
            Family: Callitrichidae
                Subfamily: Callitrichinae (tamarins, marmosets)
    Infraorder: Catarrhini
        Superfamily: Cercopiothecoidea
                Subfamily: Cercopithecinae (macaques, mangabeys, mandrills, baboons, guenons)
                Subfamily: Colobinae (guerezas, langurs, proboscis monkey, snubnosed langurs)
        Superfamily: Hominoidea
            Family: Hylobatidae (gibbons)
            Family: Hominidae
                Subfamily: Ponginae (orangutans)
                Subfamily: Gorillinae (gorillas)
                Subfamily: Homininae
                    Tribe: Panini (chimpanzees, bonobos)
                    Tribe: Hominini (humans)

Source: D. R. Swindler, *Introduction to the Primates* (Seattle: University of Washington Press, 1998), pp. 26–27. The classification of the Hominoidea has been modified.

from the later-evolving monkeys and apes. In isolation and lacking competition from other mammals, the Madagascar lemuriformes were able to move into many diverse niches; this is reflected in their numbers and diversity.

The family Lemuridae includes the lemurs. In general, the small lemurs are nocturnal, solitary, and **omnivorous** and eat a variety of foods. The larger lemurs, including the well-known ringtailed lemur (Figure 7.7), are more **diurnal** (active during the day), live in large social units, and include plant food as a major part of their diet.

Stereoscopic vision is not as well developed in the lemurs as it is in the monkeys and apes. On the other hand, the ringtailed lemur's sense of smell is keen. When it is disturbed, it often rubs its anal region against a tree, a behavior termed **scent marking.** The male ring-tailed lemur has a specialized gland on his forearm that also is used in scent marking.

Because of their nocturnal habits, the sportive lemurs (Lepilemuridae) and the dwarf lemurs (Cheirogaleidae) are not well known. The dwarf lemurs include the pygmy mouse lemur, which is the smallest living primate. The adult weighs about 30.6 grams (1.1 ounce).

omnivorous Eating both meat and vegetable food.

diurnal Active during daylight hours.

scent marking Marking territory by urinating or defecating, or by rubbing scent glands against trees or other objects.

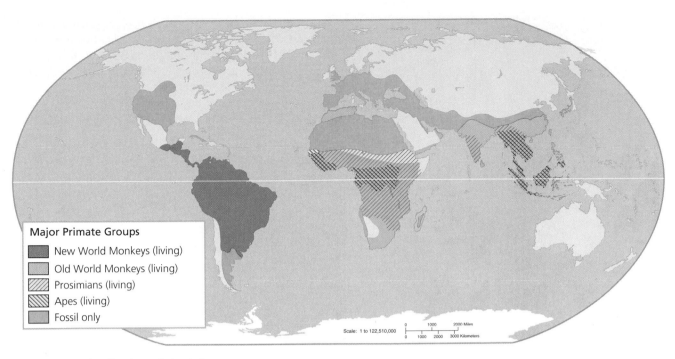

Figure 7.6 Distribution of the Primates

Also living on the island of Madagascar, the family Indriidae consists of the indri, avahi, and sifaka (Figure 7.8). The indri, which is totally diurnal, is the largest of the Madagascar prosimians, weighing about 6.3 kilograms (14 pounds). When they are resting, they cling upright on a vertical branch; when moving, they use their very long legs to leap from branch to branch, maintaining an upright posture. The indri is the only Madagascar prosimian that lacks a tail.

The family Daubentoniidae contains only one species, the aye-aye, now on the verge of extinction (Figure 7.9). The aye-aye was once thought to be a rodent since it has large,

Figure 7.7 Lemuriformes Representative of the family Lemuridae: Ring-tailed lemur, *Lemur catta,* Madagascar. Ring-tailed lemurs have a long tail with alternating bands of white and black rings that is used for visual displays. It has a black pointed muzzle and rhinarium, the moist naked area at the tip of the nose. Its nickname is "cat lemur" because it produces a purring-like vocalization.

Figure 7.8 Lemuriformes Representative of the family Indridae: Coquerel's Sifaka, *Propithecus verreauxi coquereli*, Madagascar. Sifakas have long, powerful hind limbs that they use to leap between trees, using their long tails for balance.

continuously growing front teeth that are separated from the rest of the teeth by a large gap. The hand is characterized by a long, thin middle finger, and all the digits except the big toes end in claws. During the night, the aye-aye uses its front teeth to tear open the outer layers of bamboo or the bark of trees to get at the insects inside; the insect is then extracted with the elongated finger.

The lorises probably have survived competition with the monkeys and apes in Asia and Africa because of their nocturnal habits. The superfamily is divided into two families. The Lorisidae contains species that walk along branches very slowly and deliberately, hand over hand. These animals have very powerful grips, enhanced by the reduction of their index fingers to mere bumps. The lorises live alone or in pairs. Their diet is varied, consisting of fruits, leaves, seeds, birds and birds' eggs, lizards, and insects. The Asiatic members of the subfamily are the slender loris and slow loris; the African members are the potto and angwantibo.

The African family Galagidae includes the galagos, also known as bush babies (Figure 7.10). These are small animals weighing between 65 grams (2.3 ounces) and 1.3 kilograms (3 pounds). Although they show a variety of locomotor patterns, these nocturnal primates are noted for their leaping ability, which is made possible by their elongated legs. This leaping ability enables the animal to move quickly through the branches, searching for and catching insects.

The Tarsiiformes

The tarsiers represent an interesting mosaic of prosimian and anthropoid features (Figure 7.11). Like the lemuriformes, tarsiers possess grooming claws; in fact they have two grooming claws on each foot (on the second and third toes), and their lower jaw is composed of two halves. Like the monkeys and apes, tarsiers lack a dental comb and have a haplorhine nose, where the nostril is surrounded by hairy, dry skin. Their eye socket is partially closed; in this they are intermediate between the lemuriformes and the monkeys and apes. The tarsiers also possess a number of unique features. For example, the tibia and fibula, the two bones of the lower leg, are fused together (this feature is also found in the rabbits and hares).

The tarsiers are placed in their own infraorder, Tarsiiformes, within the suborder Prosimii. This infraorder includes only one family, the Tarsiidae. The five species of tarsier are found on islands in southeast Asia, including Borneo, Sumatra, and the Philippines.

The tarsiers are very small primates. Their name is derived from their elongated tarsal (ankle) bones, which enable them to leap long distances. The tarsiers leap among the thin, vertical saplings near the ground, keeping their bodies in a vertical position. At rest, they press the lower part of their long tails against the tree trunk for support.

Figure 7.9 Lemuriformes Representative of the family Daubentoniidae: Aye-aye, *Daubentonia madagascariensis,* Madagascar. The Aye-aye is the largest nocturnal primate, with both males and females weighing about 2.6 kilograms (5.7 pounds). Like rodents, their incisors grow continuously. It has a long middle finger and bat-like ears. The aye-aye is highly endangered.

Tarsiers are strictly nocturnal. Their eyes have become so large that they cannot be moved by the eye muscles, which have become degenerate. Instead, the animal is capable of turning its head almost 180 degrees to look behind itself. Tarsiers feed on insects and lizards; they do not eat plant food.

The New World Monkeys

The second major division of the order Primates is the suborder Anthropoidea. This suborder includes the primates that are familiar to most people: the New World monkeys, Old World monkeys, small-bodied and great apes, and humans.

The term **monkey** embraces a large number of species found throughout the tropics of the Old World (Africa, Asia, and Europe) and the New World (South, Central, and North America). Although most people see the monkeys as a single group, in reality the monkeys of the Old World and those of the New World are fairly distinct. Many anthropologists theorize that the ancestral monkeys first evolved in Africa. Later, some populations rafted across the Atlantic Ocean to populate the New World. Isolated in their own hemisphere for over 30 million years, each group evolved many unique features. Yet the Old World and New World monkeys, building on the same basic anatomy, retained and evolved many similarities as well. This is an example of parallelism.

The monkeys of the New World belong to the superfamily Ceboidea. These monkeys are easily identified by the **platyrrhine nose,** in which the nostrils are usually separated by a broad nasal partition, or septum, and open facing forward or to the side (Figure 7.2). This nose form contrasts with the nose of the Old World monkeys, apes, and humans. Consequently, the New World monkeys are often referred to as the platyrrhine monkeys and are placed in the infraorder Platyrrhini.

The New World monkeys tend to be smaller than those of the Old World, and they are strictly arboreal. The New World monkeys have three premolars in each quarter of the mouth; some, but not all, have **prehensile tails** that can be used to hang onto branches and even to pick up objects; the thumb is grasping but nonopposable, and in some forms it has disappeared.

The New World monkeys are divided into two families. The first family, the Callitrichidae, includes the marmosets and tamarins (Figure 7.12). Unlike most primates, the marmosets and tamarins possess modified claws on all their digits except the big toes, which bear true nails. They are generally omnivorous and include insects in their diet. The marmosets rely heavily on sap and gums. They use their specialized lower teeth to make holes in the bark of trees to increase the flow of sap to the surface of the bark.

Most New World monkeys belong to the family Cebidae. In contrast to the Callitrichidae, the cebids are larger and have nails on all digits. The larger cebids habitually move and feed while suspended under branches, and many have evolved prehensile tails to aid in suspension.

The cebids are divided into four subfamilies. The subfamily Cebinae includes the small squirrel monkeys and the

Figure 7.10 Lemuriformes Representative of the family Lorisidae: Lesser bush baby or galago, *Galago senegalensis* found throughout equatorial Africa.

monkey Any member of the superfamilies Ceboidea (New World monkeys) and Cercopithecoidea (Old World monkeys).

Figure 7.11 Tarsiiformes Representative of the family Tarsiidae: Philippine tarsier, *Tarsius syrichta*. Tarsiers have the largest eyes compared to body size of any mammals, and their ears resemble those of bats. They have two grooming claws on each foot and an elongated middle finger.

Figure 7.12 New World Monkey Representative of the family Callitrichidae: Golden lion tamarin, *Leontopithecus rosalia*, Brazil. Its common name refers to the golden lion-like mane that surrounds the head. It has claw-like nails all digits except for the big toes and a nonopposable thumb. Because its pelt is valuable, poachers have hunted it to virtual extinction.

well-known capuchin monkeys (Figure 7.13). The subfamily Aotinae includes the titi monkey and the night monkey, the only truly nocturnal anthropoid. The subfamily Pithecinae includes the sakis and uakaris, and the subfamily Atelinae contains the howler and spider monkeys (Figure 7.14). These latter monkeys are noted for their dexterous prehensile tails, which serve as a third "hand." The underside of the lower part of the tail lacks hair and is sensitive to touch.

The Old World Monkeys

Old World monkeys, apes, and humans make up the infraorder Catarrhini. Members of this infraorder are characterized by the **catarrhine nose** in which the nostrils are separated by a narrow nasal septum and open downward (Figure 7.2). The thumb is well developed in most forms and is opposable. The superfamily Cercopithecoidea includes the Old World monkeys.

platyrrhine nose Nose in which nostrils open sideways and are usually separated by a broad nasal septum; characteristic of the New World monkeys.

prehensile tail A tail found in some New World monkeys that has the ability to grasp.

catarrhine nose Nose in which nostrils open downward and are separated by a narrow nasal septum; found in Old World monkeys, apes, and humans.

See the Online Learning Center for an Internet Activity on African primates.

Figure 7.13 New World Monkey Representative of the family Cebidae: White-faced capuchin, *Cebus capucinus*, Costa Rica. The capuchin takes its name from the tuft of hair on the top of its head that resembles the cowl or capuche worn by a Capuchin Franciscan friar. Its prehensile tail is not as effective as a "fifth hand" as in other New World monkey species.

Old World monkeys comprise a large number of species that are spread over Africa and Asia, and they include one small population in Europe. In contrast to the New World monkeys, some Old World monkeys tend to be fairly large. Although many are arboreal, some genera are semiterrestrial. None has a prehensile tail.

The Old World monkeys are divided into two subfamilies. Many members of the subfamily Cercopithecinae exhibit a marked sexual dimorphism, that is, a major difference in size and nonsexual features between sexes. A distinguishing feature of these monkeys is the presence of **ischial callosities** in the anal region of the animal; these calluses are in contact with the branch or ground when the animal sits. The female usually has a **sexual skin** that often turns bright pink or red and sometimes swells when the female is in estrus, the period of sexual receptivity. The Cercopithecinae are omnivorous, and they have **cheek pouches** that open into the mouth and are used for temporary food storage.

Many arboreal and all of the semiterrestrial monkeys of Africa belong to the Cercopithecinae. The many species of guenons and mangabeys are spread throughout the African rain forest, woodland, and savanna habitats (Figure 7.15). The ground-dwelling monkeys of the

Figure 7.14 New World Monkey Representative of the family Cebidae: Black-handed Spider Monkey, *Ateles geoffroyi*, southern Mexico and Central America. Spider monkeys have long limbs and a prehensile long tail. The females have an enlarged clitoris that is visible in this photograph.

ischial callosities A thickening of the skin overlying a posterior section of the pelvis (ischial tuberosity), found in Old World monkeys and some apes.

sexual skin Found in the female of some primate species; skin in anal region that turns bright pink or red and may swell when animal is in estrus.

cheek pouches Pockets in the cheek that open into the mouth; some Old World monkeys store food in the cheek pouch.

Figure 7.15 Old World Monkey Representative of the subfamily Cercopithecinae: De Brazza's monkey, *Cercopithecus neglectus*, Central Africa. The De Brazza monkey has cheek pouches to store food. They have a white muzzle and a long white beard. Note the distinctive color pattern found on the infant.

Figure 7.16 Old World Monkey Representative of the subfamily Cercopithecinae: Adult male gelada, Ethiopia. This male has a long, thick mane and is considerably larger than the female, an example of sexual dimorphism. Both sexes have hairless areas on their chest.

savanna are the baboons. One species, the hamadryas baboon, lives in the semidesert regions of southern Ethiopia, where the baboons sleep at night on cliffs rather than in trees. Baboons are often referred to as the "dog-faced monkeys" because of their well-pronounced muzzles. Associated with the muzzle are large, formidable canine teeth, especially in the adult males. Other African cercopithecoids include the patas monkey, vervet monkey, drill, mandrill, and gelada (Figure 7.16).

The Asiatic representatives of the Cercopithecinae are the macaques; macaques are also found in North Africa and the Rock of Gibraltar. The dozen macaque species live in a great diversity of habitats, including tropical rain forests, savanna, grasslands, semideserts, and even temperate regions with winter snows. The only European monkey is a macaque living on the Rock of Gibraltar.

The other subfamily, the Colobinae, or leaf-eating monkeys, also inhabits both Africa and Asia. The members of this subfamily lack cheek pouches. They are able to digest mature leaves because of the presence of a complex sacculated stomach in which bacterial action is able to break down the cellulose found in leaves.

A major group of leaf-eating monkeys is the langurs of south and southeast Asia (Figure 7.17). One population lives in the Himalayas at elevations up to 3650 meters (12,000 feet). Others are found in very dry habitats, where they can survive because of their ability to digest dry, mature leaves and bark. Other Asiatic forms include the snub-nosed langurs and the proboscis monkey. The African representatives of this subfamily are the colobus monkeys, or guerezas.

The Apes

A child standing in front of an exhibit of chimpanzees may be told to "look at the monkeys," and chimpanzee behavior is often referred to in the popular media as "monkey business." This is very strange to primatologists since apes and monkeys are very different kinds of animals and are quite easy to tell apart. Apes are not monkeys!

apes A common term that includes the small-bodied apes (the gibbon and siamang) and the great apes (the orangutan, chimpanzee, bonobo, and gorilla).

A simple distinction between monkeys and **apes** is that monkeys have tails and apes do not. (Of course, there are always exceptions. Two species of monkeys are tailless.) There are also a great many less obvious anatomical traits that differ in the two groups. Most important is the general structure of the body. Monkeys are basically adapted for quadrupedalism, walking on all four limbs. Apes, in contrast, engage in a great deal of suspensory behavior; that is, they frequently suspend themselves under a branch by the arms. This is reflected in differences in anatomy that we will discuss in detail in Chapter 8.

Ape Taxonomy As we saw in the previous chapter, a classification is not merely a convenient way of organizing and keeping track of species. Modern taxonomy is a representation of evolutionary relationships, and species are placed in particular categories on the basis of demonstrated evolutionary ties. The problem is that evolutionary relationships are not always known, and different investigators may present different views or new data and thus different classifications. Nowhere has this been more evident than in the classification of the superfamily Hominoidea (the apes and humans).

The "classic" classification of the primates is based on the work of the biologist George Gaylord Simpson.[2] Simpson's taxonomy of the Hominoidea, shown below, was based on the study of comparative anatomy. The family Hylobatidae was not part of Simpson's original classification but became part of that classification in the 1960s.

Family: Hylobatidae (gibbons)

Family: Pongidae (orangutans, chimpanzees, bonobos, gorillas)

Family: Hominidae (humans)

In some taxonomic systems the Pongidae were divided into the Pongidae, the orangutans, and the Panidae: the gorillas, chimpanzees, and bonobos.

For a very long time evolutionary relationships were inferred from the analysis of homologies as seen in anatomy. In the 1960s primatologists turned their attention to the study of molecular evidence. The early studies, based on comparisons of protein molecules, strongly suggested that the relationship between apes and humans was much closer than it appeared from anatomical data alone. Also, humans share a much closer evolutionary tie with chimpanzees and bonobos than they do with the other apes. This has been confirmed through more recent studies comparing chimpanzee and human genomes (Chapter 8).

These studies have led many primatologists to revise the classification of the primates to reflect the new data. Some have gone so far as to place the chimpanzees in the genus *Homo.* While this may seem extreme to many anthropologists who have been using some version of the Simpson system for years, it is obvious that that taxonomy no longer can be seen as accurate.

One of the major problems in writing this edition of the text has been to decide what classification system of apes and humans to use. After considerable thought, the authors have decided to use a system that reflects modern data yet avoids the extreme act of placing the chimpanzees in the genus *Homo,* although the authors admit that this view may prevail in the near future (Box 7-2). Here is the classification that will be used in this edition:

Family: Hylobatidae (gibbons)

Family: Hominidae

  Subfamily: Ponginae (orangutans)

  Subfamily: Gorillinae (gorillas)

  Subfamily: Homininae

    Tribe: Panini (chimpanzees, bonobos)

    Tribe: Hominini (humans)

Figure 7.17 Old World Monkey Representative of the subfamily Colobinae: Langur, *Presbytis entellus,* India. The Hindi word *langur* means "having a long tail"; these animals have tails up to 107 centimeters (42 inches) long. It also has long fingers and toes with a short but opposable thumb.

[2] G. G. Simpson, "The Principles of Classification and a Classification of Mammals," *Bulletin of the American Museum of Natural History,* 85 (1945), pp. 1–350.

Box 7-2 — Talking about Apes and Humans

The introductory student is likely to find the use of scientific names difficult. While many animals are known by commonly used terms such as lemur and chimpanzee, this is not true for the more obscure animals and animals known from the fossil record. In addition, there are names for higher taxonomic categories such as Anthropoidea and Hominidae. These latter terms are very useful. For example, Anthropoidea is a convenient category that includes the monkeys, apes, and human.

The need for terms to use for groups of animals is reflected in the use of names that are based upon the scientific names. These nontechnical forms of scientific names are used throughout this book in discussions of both living and fossil primates. Therefore, the following table might prove useful. However, many publications, even some fairly recently published ones, still use an older form of terminology that uses the nontechnical names in a somewhat different way. (For example, some authors use *hominid* instead of *hominin* to refer exclusively to humans.)

Taxon	Name of Taxon	Nontechnical Form of Name	Living Primates That Are Included
Superfamily	Hominoidea	Hominoid	All apes and humans
Family	Hominidae	Hominid	Great apes and humans
Subfamily	Homininae	Hominine	Chimpanzees, bonobos, and humans
Tribe	Hominini	Hominin	Humans

The Gibbons

The family Hylobatidae includes the gibbons, often referred to as the **small-bodied (lesser) apes.** This is a diverse group consisting of 13 species placed in four genera (Figure 7.18). This diversity is due to the fact that gibbons are distributed through southern China, southeast Asia, and Indonesia. Because they frequently occupy islands or otherwise isolated areas, they have undergone considerable speciation. Many gibbon species are highly endangered, primarily because of habitat loss created by the harvesting of trees from the tropical rain forest for export.

The gibbons are much smaller than the other apes. They are exclusively arboreal and move rapidly through the trees by means of **brachiation.** This form of locomotion involves suspending the body under a branch and rapidly moving hand over hand. This locomotor specialization is reflected in their anatomy. The arms and hands are exceptionally long, while the body and legs are relatively short and compact.

Unlike the other hominoids, gibbons live in small family units consisting of an adult pair and immature offspring. The social behavior of the gibbon is discussed in

Figure 7.18 Small-Bodied Ape Representative of the family Hylobatidae: White-handed gibbon, *Hylobates lar,* Southeast Asia. The white-handed gibbon is a small ape weighing between 4.5–6 kilograms (9.0–13.2 pounds) with long arms and a body generally adapted for swinging through the trees. Males and females are similar in size. They occur in two color phases, black and blond.

(a)   (b)

Figure 7.19 Great Ape Representatives of the family Pongidae: (a) Borneo orangutan, *Pongo pygmaeus pygmaeus,* adult male and juvenile; (b) Sumatran orangutan, *Pongo pygmaeus abelii,* adult male. The word *orangutan* means "man of the forest" in Malay. They spend almost all of their time in trees and have long arms and short legs. Males are considerably larger than females.

Chapter 9. Gibbons are also highly vocal, and their distinctive calls are heard over long distances. The four main types of gibbons, correlated with the four genera, are the dwarf gibbons, hoolock gibbons, crested gibbons, and siamangs.

The Orangutan

We now turn our attention to the family Hominidae, which includes the **great apes** and humans. The hominids are divided into three subfamilies. We will begin with a consideration of the subfamily Ponginae, the orangutans (Figure 7.19).

Although the fossil record shows that orangutans once ranged over a large area of southeast Asia, today they are found only on the Indonesian islands of Sumatra and Borneo. Separated for thousands of years by open seas, the populations on the two islands have developed a number of distinct characteristics. The two island groups are usually classified as subspecies of *Pongo pygmaeus.* Some primatologists today use this designation for the Borneo orangutan, calling the Sumatran form *Pongo abelii.*

The orangutan is a fairly large animal, with the Borneo male weighing, on the average, 77½ kilograms (171 pounds). However, in marked contrast to the male, the female averages only 37 kilograms (81½ pounds), an example of sexual dimorphism. The hair of the Borneo orangutan is long and coarse and is orange, brown, or maroon in color. Males also possess cheek pads and a large throat pouch. When more than one male is present in a particular area, only the dominant male develops this pouch. When the dominant male dies, another male begins to develop a pouch. The Sumatran orangutan is thinner, with a pale red coat; while possessing cheek pads, the males do not develop a throat pouch.

In spite of their size, orangutans are arboreal primates, rarely coming down to the ground. They move slowly through the forest, grabbing on to branches with both hands and feet. Their preferred foods are ripe fruits, and they use their powerful jaws and teeth to rip open large fruits with thick rinds. They eat a variety of other vegetable material, small

small-bodied (lesser) apes The gibbons and siamangs of Asia.

brachiation Hand over hand locomotion along a branch with the body suspended underneath the branch by the arms.

great ape A term that refers to the orangutan from Asia and the chimpanzee, bonobo, and gorilla from Africa.

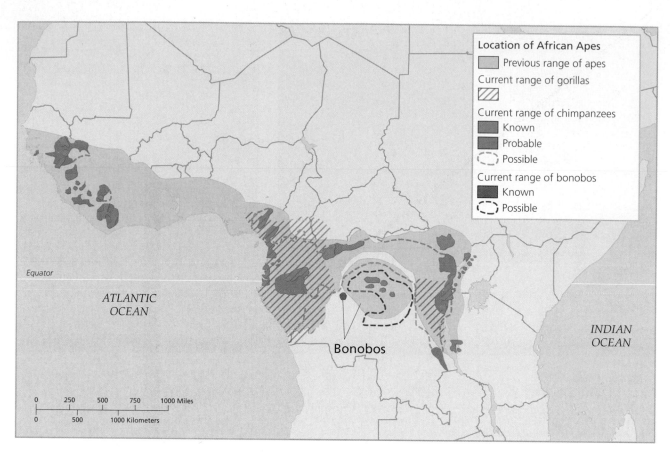

Figure 7.20 Distribution of the African Great Apes

mammals, and insects. Orangutans are essentially solitary animals, and except for a mother and her child, small social groups are encountered infrequently.

Orangutans develop very slowly. Females have their first baby between 12 and 15 years of age. They breed very slowly, having a child only once every 7 or 8 years. This slow reproductive rate makes it very difficult for an orangutan population to recover from episodes of hunting or loss of habitat due to deforestation. In fact, orangutans are disappearing rapidly in the wild, and most experts believe that they will be extinct in the wild within the next 20 years.

The African Great Apes

Charles Darwin wrote, "It is therefore probable that Africa was formerly inhabited by extinct apes closely allied to the gorilla and chimpanzee; and as these two species are now man's nearest allies, it is somewhat more probable that our early progenitors lived on the African continent than elsewhere."[3] Over the years it has become clear that *Homo sapiens* shares a very close relationship to the African great apes—gorillas, chimpanzees, and bonobos—which is why these animals are of such interest to students of human evolution.

The African great apes are placed into two subfamilies. The first is the Gorillinae, the gorillas. The chimpanzees and bonobos are placed into the same subfamily as humans, the Homininae. This latter grouping reflects the extremely close genetic relationship between chimpanzees, bonobos, and humans. The distribution of the African great apes is shown in Figure 7.20.

---

[3] C. Darwin, *The Descent of Man and Selection in Relation to Sex,* 2nd ed. (London: John Murray, 1882), p. 155.

Box 7-3 **The Discovery of the Gorilla**

The nineteenth century was an age of exploration as Europeans learned of new lands, plants, animals, and peoples. These discoveries provided fresh data for the scientists of the time who were developing new ideas to explain the natural world, a world suddenly made more complex. One of those ideas was that of evolution. Throughout the nineteenth century, reports reached Europe of new species of monkeys and apes that provided important clues to the mystery of human origins.

The gorilla was the last of the apes to be discovered by Europeans. Although the largest of the great apes may have been seen by early explorers, "as object of scientific study this ape simply did not exist at the beginning of the nineteenth century, and it was not until the middle of the century that it was definitely described and generally accepted as a new genus of anthropoid ape."[1]

The first scientific account of the gorilla was an article by Thomas Savage in 1847. The creature was named after the "hairy people" or "gorillae" described in the fifth century B.C. by the Carthaginian Hanno, who had sailed along the western coast of Africa. (In all probability, however, Hanno's "gorillae" were monkeys.) Additional studies of the animal followed as bones and preserved specimens were sent to Europe. The first living gorilla seen in Europe was exhibited in England in 1855.

The early accounts of gorilla behavior were based on rumors and stories that were more fanciful than factual. Little was known about the behavior of gorillas in the wild, and that ignorance enabled storytellers to create images of gorillas as large terrifying beasts, exemplified in the movie *King Kong.* As Robert Yerkes wrote in 1929:

> Creature of mystery, the gorilla long played hide and seek in the reports of hunters and naturalists. Even now the name holds peculiar fascination because imaginative descriptions abound. Relatively rare, inaccessible, powerful, reputedly dangerous, difficult to capture, and untamable, it has yielded slowly to human curiosity. For centuries rumors of the existence of such a huge anthropoid, native superstitions, and alarming tales stirred popular and scientific interest.[2]

Today, we have a very different understanding of the natural history and behavior of the gorilla through the studies of several primatalogists, including George Schaller and Dian Fossey. In contrast to the image of King Kong, George Schaller writes: "The gorilla is by nature reserved and shy and, whenever it can possibly do so, it avoids contact with its human neighbors."[3] Dian Fossey's book *Gorillas in the Mist* and the movie of the same name show gorillas as gentle vegetarians characterized by only rare acts of aggression.

[1] R. M. Yerkes, *The Great Apes* (New Haven: Yale University Press, 1929), p. 31.

[2] Ibid., p. 381.

[3] G. B. Schaller, *The Year of the Gorilla* (Chicago: University of Chicago Press, 1964), pp. 101–102.

The Gorilla Gorillas are a group of large primates that are well known to anyone who has ever gone to a zoo. Often portrayed in the media as ferocious beasts, in reality they are relatively gentle, quiet vegetarians. There are three subspecies of gorilla (Box 7-3). Because of the work of Dian Fossey, the film *Gorillas in the Mist*, and numerous articles in *National Geographic*, the mountain gorilla is quite well known, although it is not seen in captivity (Figure 7.21a). This subspecies lives high in the rugged mountains in the border regions of Uganda, Rwanda, and the Democratic Republic of the Congo.

The western lowland gorilla is found in an area stretching from southern Nigeria east and south to the Congo River (Figure 7.21b). This is the familiar animal seen in zoos. The third subspecies is the eastern lowland gorilla, which is found in the lowlands to the west of the mountain gorilla.

Gorillas are quite large animals. The weight of western lowland gorilla males averages 169½ kilograms (374 pounds). However, they show a considerable degree of sexual dimorphism, with the females averaging 71½ kilograms (158 pounds). Gorillas are strictly vegetarian, consuming large quantities of all the parts of many plants, concentrating on the leaves, stems, and roots. They also eat small quantities of insects and other small creatures.

Gorillas, especially smaller ones, readily climb trees, but they spend considerable time on the ground. Their locomotor pattern on the ground is called knuckle walking since they actually bear their body weight on the flexed fingers, with the middle joint hitting the ground. This contrasts with monkeys, which walk on their palms. Gorillas also stand bipedally for short periods of time.

(a)

Figure 7.21 African Great Apes
Representatives of the subfamily Gorillinae:
(a) Mountain gorilla, *Gorilla gorilla beringei;*
(b) Western lowland gorilla, *Gorilla gorilla gorilla.*
Mountain gorillas are the largest of the great apes.
Males and females weigh 160 and 85 kilograms
(353 and 187 pounds) respectively. Western
lowland gorillas are somewhat smaller, with males
and females weighing 140 and 75 kilograms (309
and 165 pounds) respectively. The hair of the
mountain gorilla is longer and thicker than that of
the Western lowland gorilla.

(b)

Gorillas live as long as 50 years. They reproduce slowly. The females give birth to their first offspring between 9 and 11 years of age and have a child approximately every 4 years. Gorillas live in small social groups with one and occasionally two mature silverback (fully adult) males, several females, and their young. The group size varies between 3 and 21 animals.

Gorillas are endangered animals. In addition to habitat loss, the rapidly expanding human population is moving into areas set aside for gorillas, and gorillas are hunted as bush meat. One approach to managing the relationship between gorillas and humans is the establishment of ecotourism. The income derived from tourists coming to see gorillas in the wild provides an incentive to preserve the animal.

The Chimpanzee Perhaps the best-known ape is the chimpanzee. Chimpanzees differ in many ways, including details of facial color, shape and color of beard, shape of head, size, and degree of sexual dimorphism. Most biologists separate chimpanzee populations into three subspecies (Figure 7.22). These are the west African (pale-faced) subspecies, once found in a large area of west Africa from Senegal to Nigeria; the central African (black-faced) subspecies, ranging from Nigeria south to the Congo River; and the east African (long-haired) subspecies, found eastward to Lake Tanganyika. Some biologists recognize a fourth subspecies in western Nigeria and northeastern Cameroon. To complicate the picture further, some biologists suggest that, based on genetic studies, the west African subspecies may be a separate species.

Chimpanzees are considerably smaller than gorillas. Male weight generally ranges from 40 to 60 kilograms (88 to 132 pounds), while female weight ranges from 32 to 47 kilograms ($70^1/_2$ to $103^1/_2$ pounds). Chimpanzee females usually have their first infant at about 14 or 15 years of age and give birth at 5-year intervals. Their life expectancy averages 53 years. One famous movie chimpanzee, Cheeta, who was Tarzan's sidekick in the early Tarzan movies, was 72 years old in 2004.

Chimpanzees inhabit a wide range of habitats, from tropical rain forest, to dry woodlands, to savanna grasslands. Fruit plays an important role in their diet, along with leaves, flowers, and other plant material. This is supplemented with animal food such as insects, grubs, and birds. Some chimpanzee communities regularly hunt and eat meat. Of special interest to anthropologists is the fact that chimpanzees frequently use tools in obtaining and processing food. There is also evidence that particular patterns of behavior are passed on through learning and become characteristic of particular groups. Like the gorillas, chimpanzees are knuckle walkers on the ground but practice a wide variety of locomotor patterns in the trees. Chimpanzees live in large communities that are broken in smaller groups with ever-changing membership. These subjects will be discussed in Chapter 9.

The Bonobo The bonobo is not as familiar to the general public as are chimpanzees and gorillas. Bonobos are closely related to chimpanzees and sometimes are called pygmy chimpanzees even though they are the same size as some chimpanzee subspecies. However, they do have a more slender body build and longer arms than chimpanzees do. Male weight averages 39 kilograms (86 pounds), while female weight averages 31 kilograms (68 pounds). Bonobos are covered with black hair and possess a very characteristic pattern of hair on the top of the head that can be seen in Figure 7.23. They generally have a life span of 40 years. Bonobos reside in tropical rain forests, where they eat a variety of vegetable food supplemented by insects, earthworms, and the like.

See the Online Learning Center for an Internet Activity on chimpanzees and the Jane Goodall Institute.

Bonobo social organization is of interest. They live in larger communities than do chimpanzees, and their social interactions are more easygoing than are those of chimpanzees. They frequently engage in nonreproductive sexual behavior that appears to reduce tensions within the group.

Humans

The final primate we will examine belongs to the species *Homo sapiens*. This species has the greatest distribution of any primate and is found in a great variety of both tropical and temperate habitats. Some groups actually survive in severe high-altitude or Arctic environments. In spite of this worldwide distribution, humans show remarkably little genetic diversity.

(a)

(b)

Figure 7.22 African Great Apes Representative of the subfamily Homininae, tribe Panini: Chimpanzee, *Pan troglodytes*. Populations of chimpanzees are found in many regions of Africa, and these populations show much physical variation. Several subspecies of chimpanzees have been identified. (a) *Pan troglodytes schweinfurthii* from the Gombe Stream Wildlife Research Center, Tanzania, East Africa: a female grooms a male; (b) *Pan troglodytes verus* from Bossou, Guinea, West Africa: a chimpanzee cracks a nut using a stone hammer on a stone anvil.

Figure 7.23 Great Ape
Representative of the subfamily Hominini, Tribe Panini: Bonobo, *Pan paniscus.* Bonobos were once called "pygmy chimpanzees," but they are not particularly smaller than *Pan troglodytes.* Some researchers believe that they are as different from chimpanzees as chimpanzees are from gorillas. Their hair is generally longer, their skull more gracile (delicate), and their limbs more slender than those of the common chimpanzee.

Although there is some physical variation among different groups, there are no biological criteria that can be used to divide this species into any subspecies or races, although many societies construct "races" as social units (Chapter 17).

Homo sapiens is characterized by habitual erect posture and bipedal locomotion, a locomotor pattern that is associated with many significant anatomical changes, including the only nongrasping big toe in the primate order (Chapter 8). There is relatively little hair or fur covering the body. The brain is especially large. Males average 68 kilograms (150 pounds), while female weight averages 55 kilograms (121 pounds). They have exceptionally long childhoods, and females have their first infant at 16 to 20 years of age, although in some populations this occurs much later in life. The life expectancy can be as high as 80 to 90 years.

Unlike other primates, humans are strictly terrestrial. Humans are omnivores and include a very large variety of food sources in their diet. Subsistence activities include hunting, foraging, fishing, and in some cases the domestication of both plants and animals. Their social groups vary tremendously in composition and structure from one area to another. Sometimes they live in small family units consisting of a single male-female pair, but a social group consisting of a single male and several females is very common. However, these family units tend to come together in communities that range from fairly small (35 to 50 individuals) to communities that contain millions of individuals. Their unusual patterns of social behavior will be discussed in more detail in Chapter 10.

Box 7-4 **Vanishing Primates**

Miss Waldron's red colobus monkey is gone! This monkey, once found in the rain forests of Ghana and the Ivory Coast, is the first primate species (or subspecies, according to some) to become extinct.

Today close to half of all known primate species are either endangered or vulnerable in the wild. Leading the list of endangered species are the muriqui and lion tamarin of the Atlantic forests of eastern Brazil, the mountain gorilla of Africa, the 28 species of primates on the island of Madagascar, and the lion-tailed macaque and the snub-nosed monkeys from Asia.

The major threat to primates in the wild is destruction of their habitats, which is occurring primarily in the tropical forests where the vast majority of modern primates live. Because the rapidly increasing human populations in these parts of the world cannot be supported on the traditional agricultural land or in the large cities, vast areas of tropical forest are being converted into farmland and ranchland. Other factors responsible for much of the destruction of the tropical forest are the need for firewood, poor management of industrial logging, and the construction of hydroelectric projects.

In many parts of the world, primates are hunted for food or to procure skins and other body parts. The skins of the black-and-white colobus monkey have been used for rugs, coats, and native headdresses.

Finally, primates are used extensively for scientific research. Although today the importation of primates from the wild has decreased markedly, only a few decades ago thousands of animals were imported for research and the pet trade.

Today, major efforts to preserve the primate fauna have been initiated in many countries. Yet while laws have been passed to promote the conservation of primates, they are often impossible to enforce. The major problem is the exploding population characteristic of many tropical countries. The need to feed and house this expanding population has made it difficult to preserve endangered primate species.

Source: R. A. Mittermeier and D. L. Cheney, "Conservation of Primates and Their Habitats," in B. B. Smuts et al. (eds.), *Primate Societies* (Chicago: University of Chicago Press, 1986), pp. 477–490; International Union for Conservation of Nature and Natural Resources, "The 2003 IUCN Red List of Threatened Species," www.redlist.org.

Summary

This section has described the major groups of living primates, including the lemuriformes, tarsiers, New World monkeys, and Old World monkeys, as well as the apes: the gibbons, orangutan, gorilla, chimpanzee, and bonobo (Box 7-4). In the chapters that follow we will examine their anatomy, behavior, and evolutionary history.

Key Terms

adult, *153*
apes, *162*
arboreal, *148*
binocular field, *152*
brachiation, *165*
catarrhine nose, *160*
cheek pouches, *161*
cones, *150*
dental comb, *155*
diurnal, *156*
epidermal ridges, *149*

fovea, *152*
gestation, *153*
great ape, *165*
grooming claws, *155*
haplorhine primates, *149*
hemochorial placenta, *153*
infantile, *153*
ischial callosities, *161*
juvenile, *153*
macula, *152*
monkey, *159*

nocturnal, *155*
olfactory, *149*
omnivorous, *156*
opposable thumb, *149*
pentadactylism, *149*
philtrum, *149*
platyrrhine nose, *160*
postorbital bar, *152*
postorbital septum, *152*
prehensile tail, *160*
prenatal, *153*

Study Questions

1. What is meant by the idea that adaptability is the primate's way of coping with its habitat? How is this related to the arboreal environment?

2. In what ways can the primate be said to possess a generalized anatomy? In what ways is a generalized anatomy more advantageous than a more specialized one?

3. An animal's awareness of its environment depends on data received through the sense organs. What senses have been refined in the primates? How do the refinements of these senses provide adaptations to arboreal habitats?

4. What are some of the characteristics of the primates that can be considered shared derived (synapomorphic)? What characteristics can be considered shared ancestral (symplesiomorphic)?

5. How does the suborder Prosimii as a group contrast with the suborder Anthropoidea?

6. In what ways have the evolution of New World monkeys and that of Old World monkeys paralleled each other? What features can be used to distinguish between the two groups?

See the Online Learning Center for additional study questions.

Critical Thinking Questions

1. This chapter lists various characteristics of the order Primates. Most of these characteristics can be seen as having evolved in relation to natural selective factors associated with arboreal environments. Humans are primates but are not arboreal. In what ways are the arboreal traits of nonhuman primates preadaptations for the development of the human ability for cultural behavior?

2. Many species of primates are endangered, as are other types of animals. Do you think this loss is important? Why?

3. While it is relatively easy to write an objective description of a particular species of monkey or ape, writing the same type of objective biological description of humans can be a difficult task. Imagine that you are at a zoo and see an exhibit of a group of humans. Objectively describe the characteristics of these humans.

Suggested Readings

Ciochon, R. L., and R. A. Nisbett (eds.). *The Primate Anthology: Essays on Primate Behavior, Ecology, and Conservation from Natural History.* Upper Saddle River, NJ: Prentice Hall, 1998. This volume contains a series of articles that appeared originally in *Natural History.*

De Waal, Frans. *My Family Album: Thirty Years of Primate Photography.* Berkeley: University of California Press, 2003. A series of photographs and commentary.

Fleagle, J. G. *Primate Adaptation and Evolution,* 2nd ed. San Diego: Academic, 1999. The first half of this book is a discussion of the primate order and the various primate taxa.

Martin, R. D. *Primate Origins and Evolution.* Princeton, NJ: Princeton University Press, 1990. This large volume presents a wealth of detailed information about many aspects of the primate order.

Napier, J. R., and P. H. Napier. *The Natural History of the Primates.* Cambridge, MA: M.I.T., 1985. The first five chapters of this book deal with characteristics of the primates, primate origins, anatomy, and behavior. This is followed by profiles of each primate genus, illustrated with black-and-white and color photographs.

Rowe, N. *The Pictorial Guide to the Living Primates.* Charlestown, RI: Pogonias Press, 1996. An exhaustive catalog of all primate species, with photographs and descriptive material.

Sleeper, B., and A. Wolfe. *Primates: The Amazing World of Lemurs, Monkeys and Apes.* San Francisco: Chronicle Books, 1997. This is primarily a book of photographs of primates with brief descriptive material and excellent photographs.

Swindler, D. R. *Introduction to the Primates.* Seattle: University of Washington Press, 1998. This is a comprehensive introduction to the primate order.

Suggested Websites

African Primates at Home (information, photographs, vocalizations):
www.indiana.edu/~primate/primates.html

Duke University Primate Center
www.duke.edu/web/primate

Primate Gallery Archive (pictures, links to information):
http://homepage.mac.com/wildlifeweb/primate/archive.html

Primate Info Net (from the Wisconsin Regional Primate Research Center; lists of primate organizations, information resources):
www.primate.wisc.edu/pin/

Chapter 8

Comparative Studies: Anatomy and Genetics

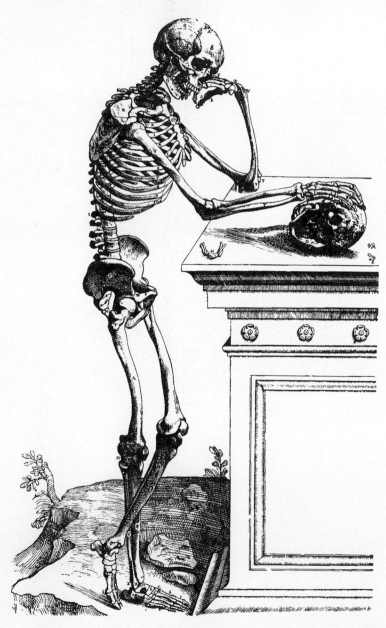

An illustration from *De Humani Corporis Fabrica* (*On the Structure of the Human Body*) by Andreas Vesalius (1514–1564)

In order to interpret the fossils, to determine what hominid fossils were like in life, it is necessary to compare the structure of their fossil bones and teeth to those of humans, apes and other primates. This can help us to determine not only that they were on the human line, but also details about their function, how they moved and what they ate. Only by such analogy with modern humans and non-human primates can we have confidence in our conclusions about the nature of our evolutionary ancestors. ●

—Leslie Aiello and Christopher Dean

Chapter Outline

Comparative Anatomy of Locomotion and Manipulation
Locomotor Patterns among the Primates
Comparative Anatomy of Primate Locomotion
The Hominoid Skeleton
Adaptations for Erect Bipedalism
Comparative Anatomy of the Hand
Summary

Comparative Anatomy of the Skull and the Brain
Positioning of the Skull on the Spine

The Sense Organs
The Evolution of the Brain
Primate Dentition
The Jaw
Summary

Comparative Cytogenetics and Molecular Biology
Comparative Cytogenetics
The Nature of Chromosome Evolution
Comparative Studies of Proteins and DNA
Summary

See the Online Learning Center for a chapter summary, chapter outline, and learning objectives.

After Reading This Chapter, You Should Be Able to Answer These Questions:

1. What are the major patterns of locomotion among the primates?

2. What are the features of the skeleton that distinguish apes from monkeys?

3. What skeletal characteristics related to locomotion does the human skeleton share with the ape skeleton? What skeletal characteristics related to locomotion are unique to the human skeleton?

4. What are the major features of the human hand? How does this hand permit fine manipulation and the manufacture and use of tools?

5. What features of the human skull differentiate it from ape and monkey skulls?

6. What are the significant characteristics of the primate brain? How does the human brain differ from monkey and ape brains?

7. What are the distinguishing features of ape and human teeth and jaws?

8. What can be learned about the evolutionary relationship between organisms through the study of comparative cytogenetics?

9. What are phylogenetic trees and molecular clocks?

The fossil record provides, in a sense, the "hard evidence" of evolutionary history. Yet, as we will see in later chapters, the fossil record is difficult to read because of its fragmentary and incomplete nature. Evolutionary history also can be reconstructed from the study of living primates. New features, anatomical and genetic, do not suddenly arise from nowhere. Instead, they develop gradually as modifications of preexisting structures. By comparing anatomical features, as well as chromosomes, proteins, and DNA, of living primates, anthropologists are able to gain an understanding of the evolutionary relationships among living forms. Such comparisons also allow anthropologists to make educated guesses about the nature of the hypothetical common ancestors of contemporary primates. This chapter will examine these comparative studies.

COMPARATIVE ANATOMY OF LOCOMOTION AND MANIPULATION

Humans are erect bipeds, but they are not the only erect bipeds in the animal kingdom, nor are they the only primates capable of this method of locomotion. Unlike other primates, however, hominins habitually depend on this mode of locomotion. They have evolved many anatomical features that have made efficient and habitual erect bipedalism possible. As we will see in later chapters, these anatomical features evolved over the last 6 million years or more.

Locomotor Patterns among the Primates

Primates exhibit a rather large repertoire of locomotor behaviors. Not only are many patterns found in the order, but a wide range of locomotor patterns may characterize a single species. Figure 8.1 illustrates the major locomotor patterns among primates.

Vertical Clinging and Leaping **Vertical clinging and leaping** is the dominant locomotor pattern of the tarsiers as well as many of the lemuriformes, such as the sifakas and galagos (Figure 8.1a). As the term suggests, the animal rests on a tree trunk in a clinging position, keeping its body in an upright, or **orthograde,** posture. In moving from one tree to another, it uses its long, powerful legs to leap, landing vertically with its hindlimbs on the new trunk. On the ground, the animal either hops or moves bipedally.

Quadrupedalism The basic pattern of locomotion of most terrestrial vertebrates is **quadrupedalism.** The quadruped moves on all four limbs with its body held parallel to the ground, a position known as **pronograde** posture. Different forms of quadrupedalism vary in terms of the relative importance of the hands, feet, and tail in locomotion. These differences reflect the requirements of different habitats. Here we present the five basic forms of quadrupedalism, but they are not always distinct and tend to grade into one another.

In **branch running and walking,** the primate walks, climbs, jumps, and leaps on and among the branches (Figure 8.1b). Since the branches are often small and uneven and tend to move a great deal, arboreal quadrupeds use their hands and feet to grasp the branches as they move along them. Branch runners and walkers are aided in their movement through the trees by legs that are longer than their arms, relatively short limbs that bring their bodies close to the branch for stability, and relatively long fingers and toes to facilitate the grasping of branches.

The more terrestrial quadrupedal primates tend to be larger in size. In **ground running and walking** the animal does not grasp the ground as it would grasp a branch, and it seldom leaps or climbs as it moves along a relatively flat surface (Figure 8.1c). Compared with more arboreal quadrupeds, terrestrial quadrupeds have shorter fingers and toes and their arms and legs are of nearly equal length. Branch and ground runners and walkers form the ends of a continuum, and primates that spend significant amounts of time both on the ground and in the trees often have intermediate anatomical features.

See the Online Learning Center for an Internet Activity on primate locomotion.

vertical clinging and leaping A method of locomotion in which the animal clings vertically to a branch and moves between branches by leaping vertically from one to another. The animal moves on the ground by hopping or moves bipedally.

orthograde Vertical posture.

quadrupedalism Locomotion using four limbs, with hands and feet moving on a surface such as the ground or top of a branch of a tree.

pronograde Posture with the body held parallel to the ground.

branch running and walking A form of quadrupedalism in which the animal is walking along a branch, grasping with both hands and feet.

ground running and walking A form of quadrupedalism that takes place on the ground as opposed to in the trees.

Some arboreal quadrupeds spend a considerable amount of time suspended under branches enabling a primate to reach food below. This pattern is referred to as **semibrachiation.** In **Old World semibrachiation** there is much leaping and hanging using the arms and hands (Figure 8.1d). However, in **New World semibrachiation,** suspension is achieved through the aid of a prehensile or grasping tail (Figure 8.1e). The final form of quadrupedalism is called **slow climbing** which is found in a few lemuriformes that move slowly through the bushes and trees (Figure 8.1f).

Ape and Human Locomotion Ape and human anatomy show many skeletal adaptations for suspensory behavior. The apes display many locomotor patterns that are variants of this type of behavior. Unlike the quadrupeds, the apes maintain an orthograde posture when hanging underneath a branch. The closely related humans have become quite specialized for terrestrial locomotor behavior while maintaining many anatomical features for **suspensory behavior.**

In **true brachiation,** which is characteristic of the gibbons, the body is suspended from above and propelled by arm swinging (Figure 8.1g). The animal moves rapidly hand over hand along a branch while swinging the body. A tail is not involved since all apes lack tails. Gibbons are bipedal on the tops of large branches and on the ground. Brachiators have short, compact bodies and short legs but very long, powerful arms and long hands for hooking onto branches.

The orangutan also spends a great deal of time hanging from branches. The fact that zoo orangutans spend so much time on the ground is usually due to a lack of climbing structures in the exhibit. Being large, they move deliberately, using the feet in the manner of a hand, hence the term **quadrumanous** (Figure 8.1h). When they do walk on the ground, they walk with their hands made into fists.

Chimpanzees, bonobos, and gorillas spend varying amounts of time in trees but move quite well on the ground. However, they differ from the quadrupeds in that they possess elongated arms and hands, and so the body is held at an angle with respect to the ground. In marked contrast with the quadrupeds that walk on the palms of their hands, these apes walk on their knuckles, hence the term **knuckle walking** (Figure 8.1i).

Many primates exhibit **erect bipedalism** over short distances, but only in humans is erect bipedalism the habitual means of locomotion (Figure 8.1j). This method of locomotion is problematic in that the animal faces major challenges in maintaining balance while walking on two hindlimbs in an upright posture. Because of this, humans are perhaps the most specialized of the primates in terms of skeletal anatomy. Humans maintain an orthograde posture while standing and walking. As a human walks, the heel of the foot strikes the ground first; the cycle ends when the individual pushes off with the big toe. This is called the **heel-toe stride.**

Comparative Anatomy of Primate Locomotion

A major topic in early hominin evolution is the origin of erect bipedalism. If hominin and ape locomotor patterns share a common ancestry, evidence should be found by comparing those parts of the anatomy that relate to locomotion. From such an analysis, a hypothetical common ancestor can be reconstructed. In comparing modern forms and the reconstructed ancestor, the evolutionary history of habitual erect bipedalism reveals itself.

This section is not intended as a complete survey of comparative anatomy. Rather, it discusses the method of comparative anatomy and some of the major conclusions of this method. This section focuses on the parts of the skeleton that function in locomotor activities. An introduction to the skeleton, including the identification of the various bones, is presented in the appendix.

The Mammalian Skeleton The basic mammalian skeleton is greatly modified in many mammalian orders. For example, the horse skeleton is adapted for high-speed running

semibrachiation Locomotor pattern involving extensive use of arms and hands in a basically quadrupedal animal.

old world semibrachiation Locomotor pattern involving extensive use of hands, but not the tail, in leaping in a basically quadrupedal animal.

new world semibrachiation Locomotor pattern involving extensive use of hands and prehensile tail to suspend and propel the body in species otherwise quadrupedal.

slow climbing Locomotor pattern in which the animal moves slowly and cautiously without leaping.

suspensory behavior Form of locomotion and posture whereby animals suspend themselves underneath a branch.

true brachiation Hand-over-hand locomotion along a branch with the body suspended underneath the branch by the arms.

quadrumanous Locomotor pattern found among orangutans, who often suspend themselves under branches and move slowly using both forelimbs and hindlimbs.

knuckle walking Semierect quadrupedalism, found in chimpanzees and gorillas, with upper parts of the body supported by knuckles as opposed to palms.

erect bipedalism A form of locomotion found in humans in which the body is maintained in an upright posture on two legs while moving by means of a heel-toe stride.

heel-toe stride Method of progression characteristic of humans where the heel strikes the ground first; the person pushes off on the big toe.

Figure 8.1 Primate Locomotor Patterns

(a) Vertical clinging and leaping The animal, resting in a vertical, clinging position, leaps and lands vertically with its hindlimbs on the new trunk or branch. Found among tarsiers, galagos, sifakas.

Galago senegalensis

(b) Branch running and walking The animal walks, climbs, jumps, and leaps on and among the branches, grasping branches with prehensile hands and feet, with palms down. Found among lemurs, tamarins, saki and titi monkeys, guenons, mangabeys.

Cercopithecus albigena johnstoni

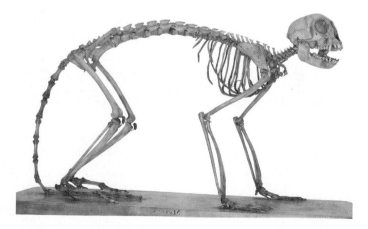

Cercopithecus mona

Papio cynocephalus

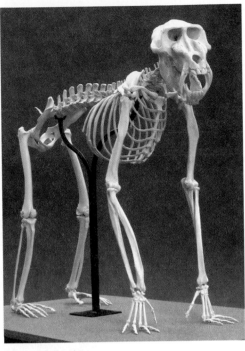

(c) **Ground running and walking**
The animal walks and runs on the ground on the palms of
the hand. Found among baboons, drill, mandrill, gelada.

Mandrillus sphinx

(d) **Old World semi-brachiation**
The animal swings by its
arms without the use of
a prehensile tail. Found
among colobus monkeys,
langurs.

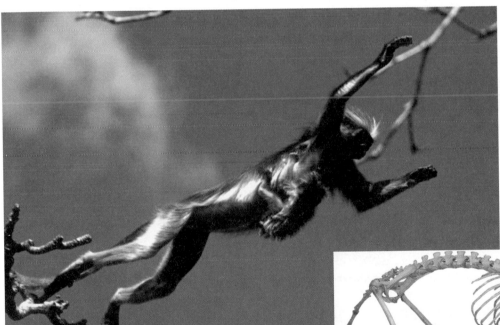

Procolobus kirkii

Colobus polykomos

Figure 8.1 *(continued)*

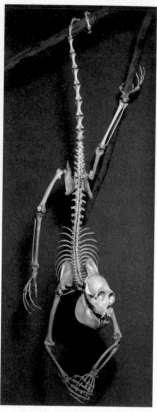

Brachyteles arachronides

(e) New World semibrachiation
The animal suspends itself under a branch by its arms and prehensile tail. Found among spider monkeys, howler monkeys, wooly monkeys.

Alouatta palliata

(f) Slow climbing
The animal moves slowly and cautiously without leaping. Found among lorises, potto.

Loris tardigradus

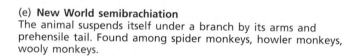

Hylobates lar

(g) True brachiation
The body is suspended under a branch as the animal moves arm over arm. Found among gibbons.

Pongo pygmaeus

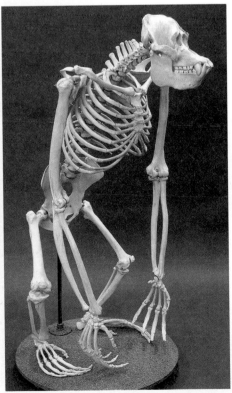

(h) Quadrumanous
The animal moves cautiously through the trees, using feet in the manner of hands. Found among orangutans.

**Figure 8.1
*(concluded)***

Pan troglodytes

(i) **Knuckle walking**

The animal walks quadrupedally supporting the weight of the upper body on the knuckles of the hands. Found among chimpanzees, bonobos, and gorillas.

(j) **Erect bipedalism**

The animal walks in an upright posture striking the ground with the heel and then pushing off with the big toe. Found among humans.

Homo sapiens

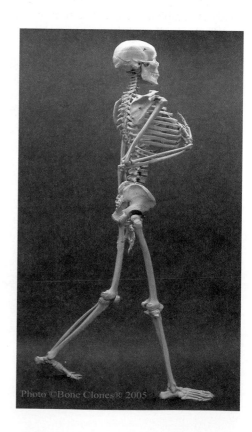

(Figure 8.2). This type of locomotion involves constant jarring of the body and transmits great forces through the limbs to the body. As the horse skeleton has no clavicle, the scapula attaches directly to the rib cage by muscles that absorb the forces generated by running. Of course, flexibility in the shoulder has been lost, but a grass-eating animal running across the plains has little need to lift its forelimb above its head. The radius and ulna in the horse skeleton have fused; four of the five digits on each limb have been lost, and the remaining digit has evolved into a hoof.

In contrast to the horse and most other mammals, the primates have retained a basically generalized skeleton. All primates have retained the clavicle, and most are able to rotate their forearms. With a few exceptions, primates have five fully developed fingers and toes at the end of each limb.

The Hominoid Skeleton

Quadrupedal monkeys carry their bodies parallel to the ground. The spine forms an arch supported by the limbs; the trunk is relatively long and narrow. In contrast to the quadrupedal skeleton, the skeleton of the hominoids (apes and humans), which is frequently carried vertical to the ground, shows a number of contrasting features. The hominoid trunk is relatively short and broad; for example, the spine of the gorilla contains three to four lumbar vertebrae compared with seven in the rhesus monkey. Unlike the monkey's back, the hominoid back does not play an important role in locomotion. The ape body is semivertical to the ground, whereas the human body is completely erect. The back muscles of the hominoids are fairly small, and the spine is relatively inflexible.

Figure 8.3 shows the relative positions of the bones of the shoulder girdle. In a monkey, the scapula lies on the side of the trunk, with the head of the humerus pointing backward. In a hominoid, the long clavicles place the arms well to the side of the body. The clavicles extend backward so that the scapula lies on the back and the head of the humerus points inward.

The socket of the scapula is relatively shallow in humans and apes, permitting a greater degree of rotation of the humerus than occurs in monkeys. Thus, a hominoid can easily hold its

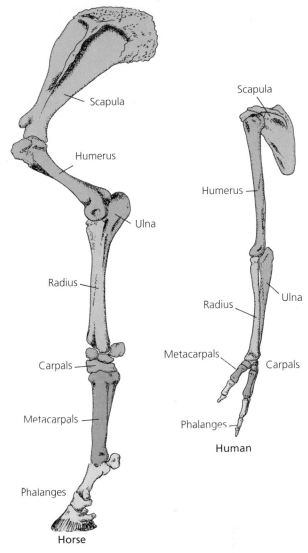

Figure 8.2 Limb Skeletons of a Horse and a Human
While the forelimb of the horse has been highly specialized for running on hard ground, the primate forelimb has remained relatively generalized. Note the fusion of the radius and ulna and the loss of four of the five digits in the horse.

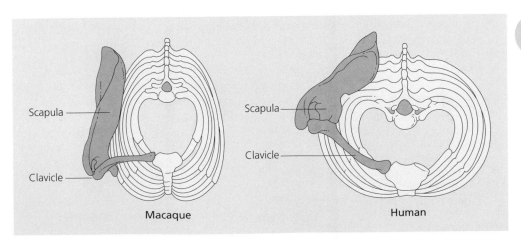

See the Online Learning Center for an Interactive Exercise on the anatomy of humans and chimpanzees.

Figure 8.3 Cross Section of Trunk Note the differences in the shape of the rib cage and the relative positions of the clavicle and scapula.

intermembral index The length of the humerus and radius relative to the length of the femur and tibia.

lumbar curve A curve that forms in the lumbar region of the spine in humans.

gluteus maximus In humans, the largest muscle of the body; acts as an extensor, extending the leg in running and climbing.

gluteus medius Muscle of the pelvis that in monkeys and apes acts as an extensor, but in humans acts as an abductor.

gluteus minimus Muscle of the pelvis that in monkeys and apes acts as an extensor, but in humans acts as an abductor.

extensor A muscle that straightens out the bones about a joint.

arms directly overhead, as when an ape suspends itself from an overhead branch. In addition, hominoids can rotate their forearms to a much greater extent than can monkeys. Humans can rotate their forearms about 160 degrees, allowing them to do pull-ups with the palms either toward the body or away from it.

These are some of the many characteristics common to apes and humans in the shoulder and arm. These features are adaptations to suspensory behavior and suggest that hominins evolved from an ancestor adapted to arboreal locomotion. This does not mean that the ancestor was a specialized brachiator like the modern gibbon, with elongated forearms and fingers; the ancestor may have simply been an animal that engaged in some degree of suspensory behavior and emphasized the arms in locomotion.

The length of the leg in quadrupedal monkeys is nearly the same as or somewhat longer than the arm. The ratio of arms to legs is seen by comparing the **intermembral index.** This index compares the length of two bones in the arm (the humerus and the radius) with the length of two bones in the leg (the femur and the tibia). The equation for calculating the intermembral index is

$$\frac{\text{Length of humerus } + \text{ length of radius}}{\text{Length of femur } + \text{ length of tibia}} \times 100$$

The number that results from this formula provides an indication of the relative proportion of the forelimb and the hindlimb. An index of 100 means that the arms and legs (excluding the hand and foot) are of equal length. An index over 100 indicates longer arms than legs, while an index under 100 means that the legs are longer. Note that this index in the quadrupedal monkeys is nearly or somewhat below 100. On the other hand, apes, with their characteristically elongated arms, typically have intermembral indices above 100. Table 8.1 lists this index for several primates.

Table 8.1 Primate Intermembral Indices

Locomotor Type	Primate	Intermembral Index
Vertical clinging and leaping	Demindoff's bush baby	68
	Verreaux's sifaka	59
	Western tarsier	52
Slow climbing	Angwantibo	89
	Slender loris	93
Branch running and walking	Ring-tailed lemur	70
	Common marmoset	75
	Golden lion tamarin	87
	Common squirrel monkey	79
	White-collared mangabey	83
	Red-tailed guenon	79
Ground running and walking	Olive baboon	97
	Gelada	100
New World semibrachiation	Mantled howler monkey	98
	Black spider monkey	105
Old World semibrachiation	Eastern black-and-white colobus	79
	Hanuman langur	83
	Proboscis monkey	94
True brachiation	Hookock gibbon	129
	Siamang	147
Quadrumanous	Borneo orangutan	139
Knuckle walking	Mountain gorilla	116
	Bonobo	103
	Chimpanzee	103–106
Erect bipedalism	Human	72

Adaptations for Erect Bipedalism

In general, the skeleton of the human trunk, shoulders, and upper limbs shows adaptations to suspensory behavior similar to those found in apes. However, other parts of the human anatomy, particularly the pelvis, leg, and foot, show specializations for erect bipedalism.

A chimpanzee occasionally assumes an upright stance. For the bipedal ape, the major problem is maintaining a balance of the trunk since in an upright position the center of gravity shifts to the front of the pelvis and legs. The chimpanzee must therefore bend the leg at the knee, resulting in an awkward and inefficient form of bipedalism. In humans, habitual erect bipedalism is facilitated by the fact that the knee joint is locked and stabilized when fully extended. The human ankle is also more stable than is that of the ape.

In humans, the position of the skull on top of the spine and the development of curvatures of the spine, especially the **lumbar curve,** have resulted in a trunk balanced over the pelvis. The ilium of the pelvis has become short and broad, which provides the surfaces necessary for the attachment of muscles involved in erect bipedalism. With changes in the shape and position of the ilium, the human sacrum has come to lie in a new position, closer to the point of articulation between the femur and the pelvis than it is in the ape. Consequently, the weight of the trunk is transmitted more directly to the legs (Figure 8.4).

Three muscles having an important role in hominoid stance and movement are the **gluteus maximus, gluteus medius,** and **gluteus minimus.** In the ape, all three act as **extensors,** extending the leg at the hip. In the chimpanzee, the gluteus medius is the largest of the three (Figure 8.5).

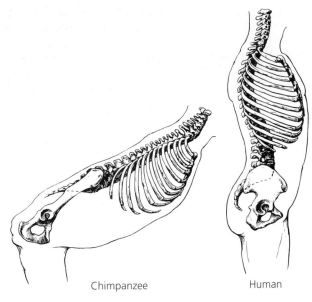

Chimpanzee   Human

Figure 8.4 The Pelvis and Trunk A comparison of the pelvis and trunk in the chimpanzee and human.

See the Online Learning Center for an Internet Activity on human anatomy.

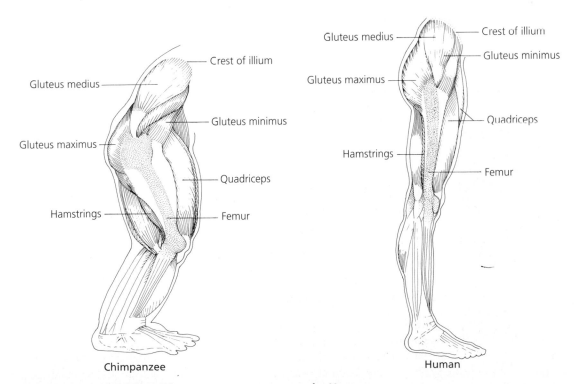

Gluteus medius — — Crest of ilium

Gluteus maximus —

Gluteus minimus

Quadriceps

Hamstrings — — Femur

Chimpanzee

Gluteus medius — — Crest of ilium

— Gluteus minimus

Gluteus maximus —

— Quadriceps

Hamstrings —

— Femur

Human

Figure 8.5 Gluteal Musculature in a Chimpanzee and a Human

abductors Muscles that move a part of the body away from the midline of the body.

brachial index The length of the radius relative to the length of the humerus.

crural index The length of the tibia relative to the length of the femur.

Table 8.2 Average Brachial and Crural Indices in Selected Primates			
Locomotor Type	Primate	Brachial Index*	Crural Index†
Branch running and walking	Geunons	96	98
	Mangabeys	99	86
Ground running and walking	Baboons	104	85
True brachiation	Gibbons	113	88
Quadrumanous	Orangutan	100	92
Knuckle walking	Chimpanzee	93	84
	Gorilla	80	80
Erect bipedalism	Humans	76	83

* Brachial index = Length of radius × 100/length of humerus
† Crural index = Length of tibia × 100/length of femur

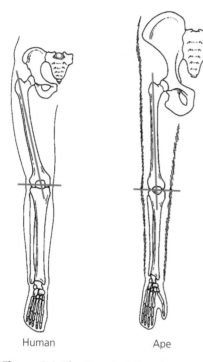

Human   Ape

Figure 8.6 The Hominin Leg In contrast with that of an ape, the human upper leg angles inward, bringing the knees directly under the body.

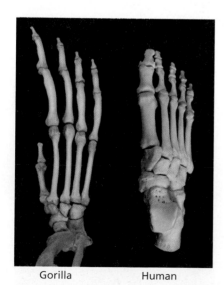

Gorilla   Human

Figure 8.7 Foot Skeletons of a Gorilla and a Human

The modification of the pelvis in human evolution has brought about reorganization of the muscles involved in movements of the leg. In hominins, changes in the structure and orientation of the ilium have resulted in repositioning of the gluteus medius and gluteus minimus. These muscles now act as **abductors,** moving the thigh away from the midline of the body and rotating it laterally as well. Both muscles are responsible for keeping the trunk in a stable, upright position during walking. The gluteus maximus has become a very large muscle and acts as a major extensor of the leg in running and climbing.

The leg and foot have also been modified for erect bipedalism. The leg is long and powerful; the intermembral index is 72. Instead of extending straight down from the pelvis, as in the ape, the human thigh extends down at an angle, bringing the knees close together for better balance (Figure 8.6). There are also important differences in proportions between the upper and lower arms and the upper and lower legs. These proportions are conveniently given by the **brachial index** for the arm and the **crural index** for the leg (Table 8.2). For example, the radius is shorter with reference to the humerus in humans than in apes, where the arm assumes an important role in locomotion.

The foot shows great evolutionary changes and is among the most specialized human features. In other primates, the big toe is well developed and is capable of movements to the side of the foot; this capability allows these primates to grasp with their feet. In contrast, the human foot is fairly inflexible, and an arch has developed. The toes are short, including the big toe, and they are incapable of extensive sideways movement. Thus, humans have only a limited grasping ability; they are not capable of manipulating objects with their feet to the degree found in other primates (Figure 8.7). In walking, the heel hits the ground first and the push of the step-off is on the big toe itself. This is the heel-toe stride. As a result, the human footprint is markedly different from that of an ape.

Comparative Anatomy of the Hand

Hands are complex organs with many functions. In primates they are organs of manipulation as well as sensation since the sense of touch is highly developed. Also, with the exception of humans, hands are organs of locomotion as well. All the locomotor patterns we have studied, except for habitual erect bipedalism, involve the constant use of the hands.

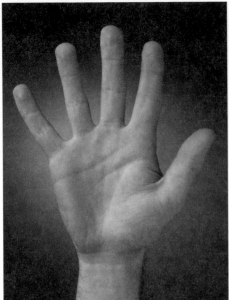

Human   Chimpanzee

Figure 8.8 Hands of a Human and a Chimpanzee

As we already have seen, the primates are characterized by pentadactylism; they have retained the five fingers characteristic of the early placental mammals (Figure 8.8). (In a few species—the spider monkey and the colobus monkey, both semibrachiators—the thumb has been lost.) The palm and fingertips of the primate hand are devoid of hair and are covered with fine epidermal ridges that are richly endowed with nerve endings and are responsible for the highly developed sense of touch. The claws characteristic of many mammals have been replaced with nails.

Most prosimians, tarsiers, and New World monkeys can draw their fingers back against the palm of the hand, facilitating the grasping of branches and other objects. In these primates, movement of the thumb is restricted to the joint between the metacarpal and first phalanges and to the joint between phalanges.

In the Old World monkeys, apes, and humans, the development of a saddle configuration in the joint between the carpal and metacarpal allows the thumb to be directly opposed to the other fingers (Figure 8.9). Humans differ primarily in the degree of movement possible at this joint. The human thumb is able to oppose the other fingers, and so the fleshy tip of the thumb comes into direct contact with the fleshy tips of all the fingers. In the apes, the fingers are elongated, and the metacarpals and phalanges are curved; in humans these bones are straight.

The hand is capable of several types of prehensile functions. In the **power grip,** the animal grabs an object between the palm and the fingers; in this position, much force can be applied (Figure 8.10). All primates are capable of the power grip. More important for fine manipulation of objects is the **precision grip,** where the animal holds an object between the thumb and the fingers. This is made possible by the presence of an opposable thumb. Humans have developed precision handling to a degree not found in other primates.

A major feature of the hominins is their ability to manufacture tools. Evidence for toolmaking comes from two sources. The first is the discovery of stone tools; the earliest archaeological material dates to about 2½ million years ago. It is also very likely that tools made of perishable materials such as wood and vines date back much earlier in time. The second line of evidence is the anatomy of the hand, whose structure permits the fine coordination required for tool manufacture.

power grip A grip in which an object is held between the fingers and the palm with the thumb reinforcing the fingers.

precision grip A grip in which an object is held between one or more fingers with the thumb fully opposed to the fingertips.

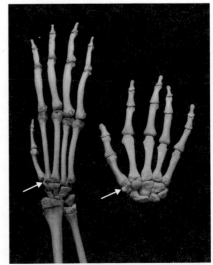

Chimpanzee   Human

Figure 8.9 Hand Skeletons of a Chimpanzee and a Human Arrows point to the joint between the carpal and metacarpal of the thumb. In humans, this joint has a saddle configuration that permits the thumb to be directly opposed to the other fingers.

Figure 8.10 Hand Grips (a) Gorilla holding branch with a power grip; (b) chimpanzee removing debris during grooming using a precision grip.

(a)

(b)

Summary

Primates display a variety of locomotor patterns, not only among the various species within the order but also within a given species itself. Many fundamental locomotor patterns can be identified within the primate order. These include branch running and walking, ground running and walking, New World semibrachiation, Old World semibrachiation, vertical clinging and leaping, true brachiation, quadrumanous locomotion, knuckle walking, and erect bipedalism.

While the skeleton of most mammals, such as the horse, is highly specialized for locomotion, the primate skeleton is relatively generalized. It has retained many traits of the generalized mammal, such as five fingers on all limbs and the clavicle, but some degree of skeletal specialization does exist.

The skeletons of living apes and humans are adapted to suspensory behavior. Some of the skeletal features needed for suspension include a short, broad trunk; fewer lumbar vertebrae in the spine; clavicles that extend backward; a scapula that lies on the back of the trunk, with the head of the humerus pointed inward; a shallow socket on the scapula; and the ability to rotate the lower arm 160 degrees. From studies of the anatomy of the hominoids, many anthropologists have concluded that the common ancestor of humans and apes was an arboreal primate adapted to some degree of suspensory behavior.

Unlike the skeletons of most primates, the human skeleton has become specialized for erect bipedalism. Some modifications that made this possible include the development of the lumbar curve, changes in the shape and orientation of the pelvis, changes in the function of the gluteal musculature, elongation of the leg relative to the arm, and the evolution of a short, stout big toe and an arch of the foot.

One of the most significant characteristics of the hominins is the development of the hand as a fine instrument of manipulation. The primate hand possesses five fingers and fingernails and is covered with fine epidermal ridges. The thumbs of the Old World monkeys, apes, and humans are opposable and thus capable of fine precision handling.

COMPARATIVE ANATOMY OF THE SKULL AND THE BRAIN

The skull is a very complex part of the skeleton, composed in humans of 28 separate bones plus 32 teeth in the adult. A description of the skull and an identification of the individual bones are included in the appendix.

The skull contains the brain and the sense organs for seeing, hearing, tasting, and smelling, as well as the jaws and teeth, the organs of mastication. The structure of the skull reflects its position on the spine and the nature of the animal's diet. This section discusses these points, as well as the structure of the brain itself.

Positioning of the Skull on the Spine

The skull articulates with the spine by the **occipital condyles,** two rounded projections on the cranial base. The occipital condyles are located on the sides of a large hole, the **foramen magnum,** in the cranial base; the spinal cord passes through the foramen magnum to merge with the brain.

Figure 8.11D shows a bottom view of the skulls of a cat and several primates. The occipital condyles on the cat skull are located far to the rear of the skull. This animal is pronograde; the skull attaches directly to the front of the spine, where the powerful **nuchal muscles** keep the head up. A flange, called the **nuchal crest,** develops on the back of the skull that provides the surface area necessary for the attachment of the nuchal muscles.

Apes are characterized by a degree of orthograde posturing. Consequently, the occipital condyles are in a more forward position on the cranial base to articulate better with the top of the spine in a vertical position. In the gorilla, the massive facial skeleton weights the head so that powerful nuchal muscles are needed, hence the presence of a prominent nuchal crest. In humans, the condyles and the foramen magnum lie in a position almost directly in the center of the underside of the skull. With the reduction of the facial skeleton and the enlargement of the brain case, the skull has achieved a good balance on top of the spine. Note the absence of a prominent nuchal crest.

The Sense Organs

Seeing, smelling, and hearing are characterized by special sense organs: the eye, nose, and ear. These organs are, in part, housed within the skull. Therefore, the structure of the skull reflects the nature of these organs. As we learned in Chapter 7, the eyes of most primates are located on the front of the head, allowing for binocular vision. The anthropoid eye is encased within a bony eye socket or orbit (Figure 7.4).

In primates, because of the general reduction in the sense of smell, the nasal region of the skull is relatively small. This results in a general flattening of the face. Associated with the reduction in olfaction is a reduction in the surface area of the nasal membranes and the bony plates that support those membranes.

The organ of hearing, the ear, consists of the external ear, a tube leading to the eardrum, the eardrum itself, the three middle-ear bones, a coiled tube containing the nerve endings that sense the vibrations created by sound, and fluid-filled chambers associated with movement and orientation. Most of the ear is housed within the skull. There is some variation in the structure of the part of the skull that houses the ear, and specialists study how this differs among different groups of primates. However, we will not go into much detail in this introduction.

The architecture of the skull is a reflection of the organization of the brain, teeth, and sense organs. In the primates, the facial skeleton has become relatively small primarily because of the reduction of the sense of smell. This contrasts with the enlargement of the cranium. In lemuriformes, the facial skeleton is located to the front of the brain case, but in

See the Online Learning Center for an Internet Activity on the skull.

occipital condyles Two rounded projections on either side of the foramen magnum that fit into a pair of sockets on the top of the spine, thus articulating the skull with the spine.

foramen magnum A large opening in the occipital bone at the base of the skull through which the spinal cord passes.

nuchal muscle The muscle in the back of the neck that functions to hold the head up. In primates with heavy facial skeletons, the large nuchal muscle attaches to a nuchal crest.

nuchal crest Flange of bone in the occipital region of the skull that serves as the attachment of the nuchal musculature of the back of the neck.

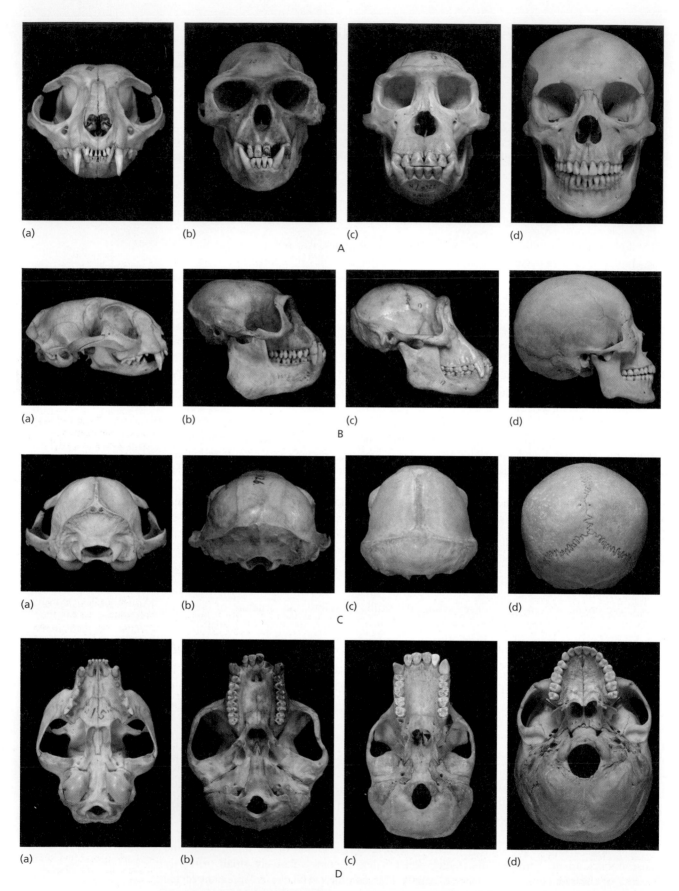

Figure 8.11 Comparative Anatomy of the Skull (A) Front view, (B) side view, (C) back view, and (D) bottom view of the skulls of a (a) cat, (b) monkey (langur), (c) chimpanzee, (d) human. (Not to scale.)

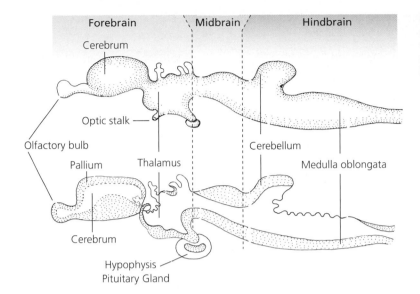

Figure 8.12 The Vertebrate Brain A generalized and schematized representation of the vertebrate brain. The lower figure is a longitudinal section showing differences in the thickness of the brain wall.

anthropoids, and especially in humans, the relatively small facial skeleton has moved below the large brain case. Although the nasal apparatus is reduced in size, the massiveness of the teeth and jaw in some species, such as the baboon and gorilla, results in a **prognathism,** which is a jutting forward of the jaw.

The Evolution of the Brain

The human brain, which allows for the complexity of behavior and culture, is a remarkable organ and is one of the most distinctive features of *Homo sapiens.* The anatomy of the brain is described in the appendix.

The major element of the nervous system in the primitive vertebrate is the single, hollow nerve cord. At the front end of the cord, the primitive brain developed. Here are the sense organs; information gathered by these structures is fed into the brain, which then produces some type of response. The primitive vertebrate brain consists of three swellings in the hollow nerve cord associated with a thickening of walls: the **forebrain, midbrain, and hindbrain.** These swellings established the basic structure of all vertebrate brains, including those of the primates (Figure 8.12).

In early vertebrates, differentiation of each of the three divisions of the brain already had taken place. Three sections make up the forebrain: the thalamus, the cerebral hemispheres, and the olfactory bulbs. The midbrain also developed special structures, including the optic lobes. The cerebellum developed as a large swelling on the hindbrain, with the thick lower portion becoming the medulla oblongata. These are only the major features of the early vertebrate brain, for many other structures were also developing. In the early vertebrates, the paired cerebral hemispheres of the forebrain were smooth swellings; they were associated primarily with the sense of smell.

In the early reptiles the cerebrum enlarged, and a new area, the **neocortex,** appeared as a gray covering on the cerebrum. The neocortex is involved with the association and coordination of various impulses coming from the sense organs and other areas of the brain. The neocortex expanded in the mammals and came to cover the entire cerebrum. Many of the functions that were controlled in the early mammals by other sections of the brain are associated with the **cerebral cortex** in modern mammals. For example, in mammals visual stimuli are received by the cerebral cortex rather than by the optic lobes of the midbrain. Several vertebrate brains are compared in Figure 8.13.

The Primate Brain Many convolutions greatly increase the surface area of the cerebral cortex in the Anthropoidea. In humans, the cerebral cortex covers the olfactory lobes

prognathism A jutting forward of the facial skeleton and jaws.

forebrain The anterior of three swellings in the hollow nerve cord of the primitive vertebrate brain formed by a thickening of the wall of the nerve cord.

midbrain The middle of the three swellings in the hollow nerve cord of the primitive vertebrate brain formed by a thickening of the wall of the nerve cord.

hindbrain The posterior of three swellings in the hollow nerve cord of the primitive vertebrate brain formed by a thickening of the wall of the nerve cord.

neocortex Gray covering on the cerebrum of some vertebrates; site of higher mental processes.

cerebral cortex The "gray matter" of the brain; the center of conscious evaluation, planning, skill, speech, and other higher mental activities.

Figure 8.13 Comparison of Vertebrate Brains Side and top views of four vertebrate brains. Note expansion of the forebrain in the mammals.

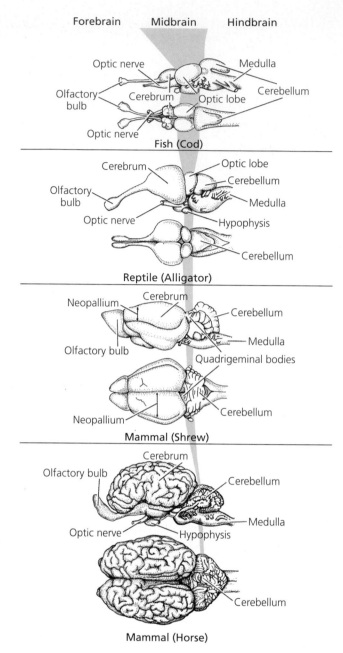

Forebrain   Midbrain   Hindbrain

Fish (Cod)

Reptile (Alligator)

Mammal (Shrew)

Mammal (Horse)

allometric growth
Pattern of growth whereby different parts of the body grow at different rates with respect to each other.

and the midbrain. Areas of the brain concerned with the sense of smell have undergone reductions, while areas associated with vision and the sense of touch have become elaborated.

The evolution of the primate brain is characterized by a general increase in brain size relative to body size. As the size of the body increases, so does the size of various parts of the body. Not all body parts increase at the same rate; some parts of the body, such as the brain, increase at a faster rate. This is the concept of **allometric growth.** In many large animals, the brain is relatively larger than it is in closely related smaller species.

Since humans are large primates, we expect to see a large brain due to allometric growth. The increase in the size of the hominin brain through time, however, is greater than can be explained by allometric growth alone. The increase in brain size over and beyond that which

Box 8-1
Difference in Male and Female Brains: Preference for Toys

Many studies have concluded that the brains of women are generally more bilaterally symmetrical than those of men. This has been correlated with differences in the way men and women process language and differences in other cognitive abilities and motor skills. For more than 99 percent of *Homo sapiens'* tenure on earth, hunting, gathering, and scavenging were the only patterns of subsistence. Men predominantly hunted and scavenged, and women predominantly gathered vegetable foods. Thus, different selective forces, related to the food quest, could have led to many sexual dimorphisms in overall size and shape, fat and muscle composition, and brain function (Chapter 16).

One interesting difference between males and females has to do with preferences for toys. Although toy preference largely results from social learning, that preference might also be the result of differences in the evolution of brain processing in males and females. Researchers have found that male children prefer toys that move, such as balls and trucks, whereas female children prefer dolls and toys with warm colors. One hypothesis used to explain this dichotomy is that the brain of

the male hunter evolved sensitivity to movement because that sensitivity would contribute to success in tracking animals. In contrast, females developed a neurological system sensitive to the features of objects (such as facial features) and to color. Those sensitivities would serve them well as caretakers of children since attention to the features of things would make women more likely than men to pay attention to the nonverbal cues of infants and children, such as facial expressions and vocal pitch. Thus, they could more readily determine the various needs of the children in their care. The greater sensitivity to color would perhaps help women find partially hidden vegetable material while they were gathering and better judge the degree or ripeness or condition of fruits and other vegetable foods.

Sources: Gerianne M. Alexander, "An Evolutionary Perspective of Sex-Typed Toy Preferences: Pink, Blue, and the Brain," *Archives of Sexual Behavior* 32 (2003), pp. 7–14; Roland Kalb, et al., "Sex Differences in Simple Reaction Tasks," *Perceptual and Motor Skills* 98 (2004), pp. 793–802.

---

can be explained by an increase in body size is termed the **encephalization quotient (EQ).** Table 8.3 gives several examples of this measure. Note the tremendous difference between humans and other primates.

The evolution of toolmaking abilities, language, and other human characteristics has affected the evolution of the brain. The cortical areas associated with hand coordination are about three times as extensive in the human brain as they are in the ape brain, and the expansion of the areas concerned with language is even greater.

The cerebral cortex makes possible a level of complex behavior that we call intelligence, which is most highly developed in humans. The cortex also allows for **social intelligence,** through which the knowledge and images that originate in an individual's brain can be transferred by speech (and, in the last 5000 years, writing) to the brains of others. The knowledge of an entire society, which is always greater than the knowledge of any one individual, can be drawn on to meet crises. This is one major factor that differentiates humans from other species.

The Brain Case As the brain enlarges, so does the neurocranium in which the brain is housed. In most mammals, as in the cat, the facial skeleton is relatively large in relation to the brain case, and it is located in front of the brain case. In primates, the brain case is larger than the facial skeleton, and the facial skeleton is partially located underneath the brain case rather than directly in front of it.

encephalization quotient (EQ) A number reflecting the increase in brain size over and beyond that explainable by an increase in body size.

Table 8.3 Encephalization Quotient in Some Primates

Primate	EQ
Tarsier	1.29
Spider monkey	2.33
Rhesus monkey	2.09
Hamadryas baboon	2.35
Gibbon	2.74
Orangutan (male)	1.63
Gorilla (male)	1.53
Chimpanzee (male)	2.48
Human (male)	7.79

Source: H. J. Jerison, *Evolution of the Brain and Intelligence* (New York: Academic, 1973).

Table 8.4 Cranial Capacities of the Living Hominoidea

Primate	Average Cranial Capacity (cubic centimeters)
Gibbon	102
Chimpanzee	399
Orangutan	434
Gorilla	535
Human	1350

Source: P. V. Tobias, "The Distribution of Cranial Capacity Values among Living Hominoids," *Proceedings of the Third International Congress of Primatology, Zurich, 1970,* vol. 1 (Basel: Karger, 1971), pp. 18–35.

social intelligence The knowledge and images that originate in an individual's brain that are transferred by speech (and in the last 5000 years, writing) to the brains of others.

cranial capacity The volume of the brain case of the skull.

endocranial cast A cast of the inside of the brain case.

The volume of the interior of the brain case is the **cranial capacity.** Note that cranial capacity is the volume of the brain case, *not* the size of the brain (Table 8.4). Although the two are close, the brain itself is covered by tissue, nerves, and blood vessels, and so its volume is always less than that of the cranium.

Wide variation in cranial capacity is usually seen within a given species. While we note that the average cranial capacity of modern humans is 1350 cubic centimeters, the nonpathological range runs from about 900 to more than 2000 cubic centimeters. Within this range, there appears to be no correlation between brain size and intelligence. Even between species, the structure and physiology of the brain are more important than its size is.

Since the inside of the brain case does conform roughly to the outside surface of the brain, it can convey some information about the brain itself. Often, a cast is made of the inside of a cranium of a fossil find; the result is an **endocranial cast** like the one in Figure 8.14. From such a cast the relative proportion of the lobes of the brain and other information can be inferred. Remember, however, that this is not a fossil brain but simply a cast of the inside of the brain case.

Primate Dentition

The ingestion of food is a major prerequisite for life in animals and involves the coordination of several parts of the anatomy. In vertebrates, the teeth, jaw, and muscles used for chewing are employed in preparing food for intake into the digestive system of the body. We already have seen that mammals are characterized by heterodonty, the regional differentiation of teeth into different kinds of teeth that serve different functions, and diphyodonty, the development of two sets of teeth, the deciduous dentition (milk teeth) followed by the adult dentition. In general, the primates have retained a fairly unspecialized tooth structure; the reduction in the number of teeth has not progressed to the degree that it has in many other mammalian orders.

Among mammals, we recognize four different kinds of permanent teeth: incisors, canines, premolars, and molars (Figure 8.15). Among primates in general, the incisor tends to be a broad, cutting type of tooth with a rather simple structure; it is often described as "spatulate." The incisors are used to grasp food. Primates that eat fruit use their incisors to tear off small pieces that can then be properly masticated (chewed) by the premolars and molars. Smaller food objects, such as seeds and grasses, are usually passed directly back to

Figure 8.14 An Endocranial Cast An endocranial cast of *Homo erectus,* a fossil hominid from China.

Box 8-2   The Ultrastructure of Tooth Enamel

The development of the scanning electron microscope has made possible the development of comparative studies on a microscopic level. This technology has been used to study tooth enamel, the hard outer layer of the tooth. These studies are exciting because enamel changes very little during the process of fossilization and because teeth are very common in the fossil record. In fact, many extinct species are known by their teeth alone.

Tooth enamel is 96 percent mineral—crystals of apatitic calcium phosphate. These crystals form into rods or prisms that are then assembled into even larger units. Electron microscope studies have shown that the structure of tooth enamel is very regular, yet variations exist among species.

There are three major patterns in the arrangement of prisms. Distinct differences in pattern exist between living hominins and other living and fossil anthropoids. Pattern 1 prisms are found in insectivores and many bats. Pattern 2 prisms are found in most hoofed mammals, rodents, and marsupials. Prisms with pattern 3, often called the "keyhole" pattern, are commonly found in humans. Many subtypes also exist. All three enamel types can be found in the primate order. While pattern 3 is found in human enamel, pattern 2 is found frequently in the enamel of the rhesus monkey, and pattern 1 in the lemurs.

Differences also are found among the various species of hominoids. In general, pattern 3 enamel characterizes the great apes and humans. However, the relative abundance of some of the subtypes differs. A specialist in the microstructure of tooth enamel can distinguish human enamel from chimpanzee and gorilla enamel when viewed with a scanning electron microscope.

Because of variation in structure, pattern differences become a valuable diagnostic tool. Remember that teeth are the most common parts of the skeleton to be preserved in the fossil record. Since teeth are largely composed of minerals, few changes are found in teeth that have been buried in the ground. Analysis of the microstructure of tooth enamel can therefore provide valuable clues as to the evolutionary relationship of a particular fossil tooth and living primate forms.

Sources: A. Boyde and L. Martin, "The Microstructure of Dental Enamel," in D. J. Chivers, B. A. Wood, and A. Bilsborough (eds.), *Food Acquisition and Processing in Primates* (New York: Plenum, 1984), pp. 341–367; T. G. Bromage and M. C. Dean, "Reevaluation of the Age at Death of Immature Fossil Hominids," *Nature* 317 (1985), pp. 525–527; and D. B. Gantt, "Enamel Thickness and Ultrastructure in Hominoids: With Reference to Form, Function, and Phylogeny," in D. R. Swindler and J. Erwin (eds.), *Systematics, Evolution, and Anatomy* (New York: Liss, 1986), pp. 453–475.

---

the chewing teeth. Primates that specialize in this type of diet often have smaller incisors than do the fruit eaters.

The canine is a simple, pointed, curved tooth, usually larger than the other teeth. This tooth serves many functions, such as grasping, stabbing, ripping, and tearing food, and plays a role in defense and displays of dominance. Canines of the Anthropoidea tend to be much larger in males than in females, another example of sexual dimorphism. Canines, highly developed in the terrestrial male baboon, act as a weapon in troop defense.

The premolars and molars are often called the **cheek teeth;** these are the teeth used in chewing. The premolars, or bicuspids in dental terminology, are simple teeth that usually have two **cusps,** or points. In many mammals, including some primates, the premolar either

cheek teeth The premolars and molars.

cusps Points on a tooth.

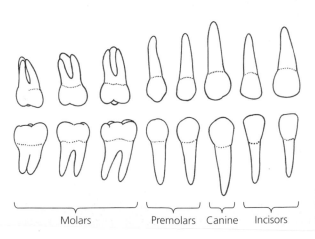

Figure 8.15 Four Types of Primate Teeth Human dentition from half of the upper jaw and half of the lower jaw.

Molars   Premolars   Canine   Incisors

Figure 8.16 Molar Morphology and Diet

Diet	Dentition	Example	Drawing
Frugivorous (fruit-eating)	Low cusps for crushing soft fruits	Spider monkey	
Folivorous (leaf-eating)	Well-developed shearing crests for cutting tough leafy material into small pieces	Langur	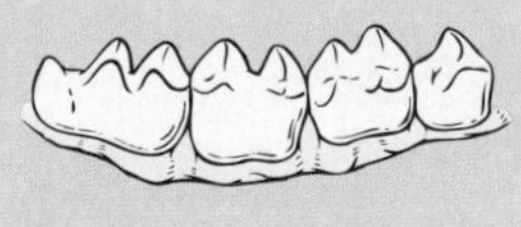
Insectivorous (insect-eating)	Sharp crests for puncturing the outer skeleton of insects	Goeldi's monkey	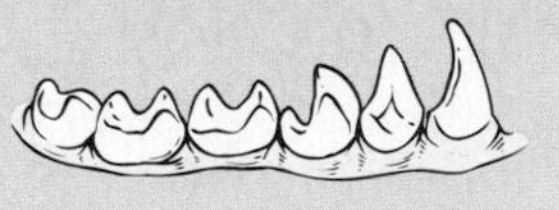

insectivores Animals that eat primarily insects; also members of the mammalian order Insectivora.

frugivores Animals that eat primarily fruits.

folivores Animals that eat primarily leaves.

omnivores Animals that eat a variety of different kinds of food.

has developed additional cusps to become more molarlike or possesses only a single cusp; for this reason, anthropologists do not call the premolars "bicuspids."

The molars are the most complex teeth in structure due to the formation of several cusps and minor cusps, ridges, and valleys. The molars chew and prepare the food for passage to the stomach for digestion. The smaller the food particles, the greater the surface area per unit of volume upon which the digestive enzymes can act.

Some types of foods are more difficult to process than others, and primates tend to specialize in different kinds of diets. Most living primates show three basic dietary adaptations; they may be classified as **insectivores** (insect eaters), **frugivores** (fruit eaters), and **folivores** (leaf eaters). Many primates, such as humans, show a combination of these patterns and are called **omnivores,** which in a few primates includes eating meat. Since the teeth play major roles in the procurement and processing of food, we would expect to find special dental adaptations that are related to the special requirements of various types of diets (Figure 8.16). Once we understand these adaptations in living primates, we can look for similar adaptations in fossil primates, and we can attempt to gain some understanding of their dietary habits.

The ingestion both of leaves and of insects requires that the leaves and the insect skeletons be broken up and chopped into small pieces. The molars of folivores and insectivores are characterized by the development of shearing crests on the molars that function to cut the food into small pieces. Insectivores' molars are further characterized by high, pointed cusps that are capable of puncturing the outside skeleton of insects.

Frugivores, on the other hand, have molar teeth with low, rounded cusps; their molars have few crests and are characterized by broad, flat basins for crushing and mashing the food. Low, rounded cusps also are seen on molars of primates that consume hard nuts or seeds, but these molars also are characterized by very thick enamel.

dental formula Formal designation of the types and numbers of teeth. The dental formula 2.1.2.3/2.1.2.3 indicates that in one-half of the upper jaw and lower jaw there are two incisors, one canine, two premolars, and three molars.

Dental Formulas The types and numbers of teeth are designated in **dental formulas,** some of which are listed in Table 8.5. Since dentition is bilaterally symmetrical, we need only note the numbers and kinds of teeth on one side of the jaw. The teeth of the upper jaw are shown above the line, and those of the lower jaw, below the line. While the notations for the upper and lower jaws are generally the same, there are exceptions. In the formula, the four numbers, separated by dots, are the number of incisors, canines, premolars, and molars, respectively, per quadrant. Paleontologists have reconstructed the dental formula of the common ancestor of living placental mammals as

$$\frac{3.1.4.3}{3.1.4.3}$$

Primate evolution is characterized by a loss of teeth in the dental formula, although the total reduction in tooth number in primates is not as great as that found in some other mammalian orders.

Table 8.5 Adult Dental Formulas of Living Primates

Primate	Dental Formula	Total Number of Teeth
Lemurs	$\dfrac{2.1.3.3}{2.1.3.3}$	36
Indris	$\dfrac{2.1.2.3}{1.1.2.3}$	30
Aye-ayes	$\dfrac{1.0.1.3}{1.0.0.3}$	18
Marmosets	$\dfrac{2.1.3.2}{2.1.3.2}$	32
New World monkeys	$\dfrac{2.1.3.3}{2.1.3.3}$	36
Old World monkeys, apes, and humans	$\dfrac{2.1.2.3}{2.1.2.3}$	32

The different prosimian groups have different numbers of teeth. All the Ceboidea are characterized by three premolars per quadrant; among the ceboids, the cebids have retained three molars while the marmosets and tamarins have two. All the Old World anthropoids have 32 teeth and the dental formula

$$\frac{2.1.2.3}{2.1.2.3}$$

In apes and humans, a further reduction in the dental formula is possible since one or more of the third molars (wisdom teeth) do not develop at all in some individuals. Also, when the third molars erupt, the human jaw is often too small to accommodate them, and the resulting impacted molars require surgical removal.

Ape Dentition Because of a common ancestry, the dentition of the apes and that of the hominins have many traits in common. Even so, each evolutionary line has evolved several distinctive features (Figure 8.17).

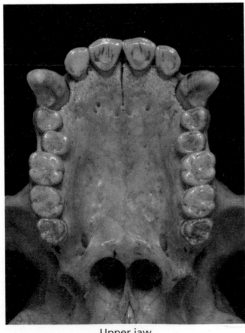

Upper jaw

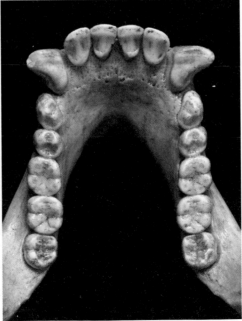

Lower jaw

Figure 8.17 Ape Dentition Note that the premolar and molar teeth of the chimpanzee on each side of the mouth are approximately parallel to each other; there are two diastemata in the dental arcade of both the upper and the lower jaw; and the canine teeth are longer than the other teeth. See the text for other features of ape dentition.

Figure 8.18 Sectorial Premolar In this side view of a chimpanzee mandible, we see a gap or diastema behind the projecting canine and in front of the first premolar. This premolar is elongated and single-cusped, providing a surface that shears against the upper canine that, in chewing, fits into the diastema. This specialized premolar is known as a sectorial premolar.

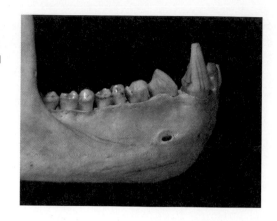

diastema A space between teeth.

dental arcade The tooth row as seen from above.

sectorial premolar Unicuspid first lower premolar with a shearing edge.

Y-5 pattern Pattern found on molars with five cusps separated by grooves, reminiscent of the letter Y.

bilophodont Refers to a form of molar found in Old World monkeys consisting of four cusps with a small constriction separating them into two pairs.

The incisors of the great apes are quite broad and spatula-like, and the upper incisors of these animals are implanted in the jaw at an angle. The canine is large and projecting. When the animal closes its mouth, the canines interlock, each fitting into a space, or **diastema,** in the opposite jaw. In the upper jaw, the diastema is in front of the canine, while in the lower jaw, it is behind the canine. Thus, in chewing, the chimpanzee cannot use the more rotary motion characteristic of hominins. The canines of all great apes show marked sexual dimorphism.

When the mandible of a prosimian is looked at from above, the row of teeth, or **dental arcade,** presents the outline of the letter V. With the evolution of large, projecting canines in the ape, the front of the mandible has broadened so that the ape dental arcade is in the shape of the letter U.

The first lower premolar in the ape is also specialized because the canine in the upper jaw shears directly in front of it. This premolar is larger than the other and has an enlarged cusp. This tooth, known as a **sectorial premolar,** presents a sharpening edge for the canine (Figure 8.18). The cheek teeth, the premolars and molars, are arranged in two straight rows that parallel each other, although they often converge toward the back of the jaw.

The basic structure of the molars in apes is the same as that in humans. The upper molar contains four cusps, and the lower molar has five. The arrangement of the five cusps and the grooves between them suggests a letter Y and therefore is called the **Y-5 pattern** (Figure 8.19). This contrasts with the **bilophodont** molar structure in the monkey, whose lower molar consists of four cusps with a small constriction separating them into two pairs.

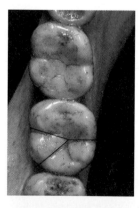

Figure 8.19 The Y-5 Molar Pattern The Y-5 molar pattern is seen here on the lower molars of an adult male chimpanzee. The superimposed lines trace the letter Y lying on its side. This pattern is characteristic of the lower molars of apes and humans.

Modern Human Dentition In the evolution of hominin dentition, the size of the teeth has decreased and the length of the portion of the jaw that holds the cheek teeth has decreased relative to the length of the skull. When viewed from the side, all the teeth are at the same level; the canine is not projecting, and the first lower premolar is not sectorial. As shown in Figure 8.20, the teeth are arranged in a curved, or parabolic, dental arcade with no diastema.

The human incisors, in contrast to those of the ape, are narrower and are implanted vertically in the jaw. Human canines are small, with a spatulate cutting edge; they do not project or interlock, nor do they show much sexual dimorphism. This contrasts markedly with the ape canines, which are pointed, projecting, and interlocking and show great sexual dimorphism. Diastemata associated with the ape canines are absent in humans.

Like the ape molars, the human upper molars have four cusps (although the upper third molar tends to have only three), while the lower molars exhibit the Y-5 pattern. In contrast to ape molars, human molars show more rounded and compacted cusps. These features are due to the fact that hominin teeth have relatively thick enamel (the outer covering of the

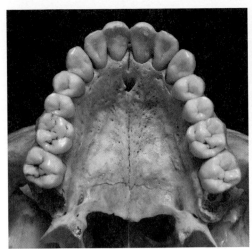

Upper jaw

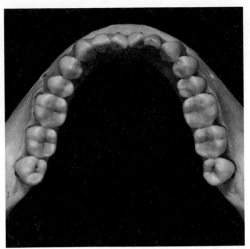

Lower jaw

Figure 8.20 Human Dentition Human dentition contrasts in a number of ways from ape dentition. Note that the premolars and molars of the human are not parallel to each other; there are no diastemata; and the canine teeth are not any longer than the other teeth. See the text for other features of human dentition.

teeth). Thick enamel, characteristic of both living and fossil hominins, is suited to the increased crushing and grinding required in the processing of hard, tough food materials. Most of the apes possess relatively thin enamel.

The permanent teeth normally erupt in a predictable pattern (Chapter 16). Monkeys and apes are similar in that the canine tends to be the tooth that erupts last or next to last. This may be related to the fact that the large, projecting canine can be an effective and dangerous weapon. The monkey and ape canine erupts after the animal has attained full adult size and social status. The human canine erupts before the second and third molars and, in some individuals, may even erupt before one or more of the premolars.

Besides differences in the order of eruption, the time over which the teeth erupt is extended in humans as a consequence of the extended childhood period. Thus, by the time the second molar erupts, the first molar has had the opportunity to be partially ground down by abrasion from some types of food particles. When the third molar erupts, it shows a high relief with its patterns of cusps and valleys, compared with the second molar, which is somewhat ground down, and the first molar, which is ground down even further. This steplike wear pattern in a fossil jaw may be indicative of an extended childhood period.

The reduction in the size of the teeth may be related to the development of tool use and a more meat-oriented diet. The apes, for example, use their large front teeth to break open hard fruits; humans might use a chopping tool held in the hand in the same situation. Another suggestion is that a major function of the large, projecting canine is its role in aggressive displays. With the development of cooperative hunting in human societies, such displays probably no longer occurred. Also, humans use weapons instead of canines for defense.

Remember, however, that use and disuse of a structure during a lifetime does not directly affect the evolution of that structure. The reduction of the canine represents a shift in frequencies from the alleles that produce larger canines to those that produce smaller ones; that is, mutations were originally responsible for creating a range of variation in canine size. When the large canines lost their selective advantage, the smaller canines may have gained some selective advantage; through time, the frequency of large canines gradually decreased.

The Jaw

The modern human jaw is smaller and shorter relative to the skull than is the ape jaw. Since human food is usually cut up or in some way processed into smaller pieces so that it is easier

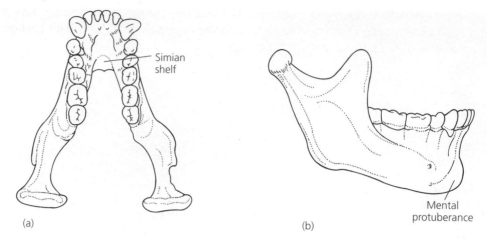

(a)

(b)

Figure 8.21 Simian Shelf and Chin Note (a) the simian shelf in the ape mandible and (b) the chin or mental protuberance on the human mandible.

simian shelf A bony buttress on the inner surface of the foremost part of the ape mandible, functioning to reinforce the mandible.

chin A bony projection of the lower border of the outside of the mandible.

temporalis A muscle of chewing that arises on the side of the skull and inserts on the jaw.

sagittal crest Ridge of bone along the midline of the top of the skull that serves for the attachment of the temporalis muscle.

masseter A muscle of chewing that arises on the zygomatic arch of the skull and inserts on the mandible.

to chew, humans do not need to exert as much pressure when chewing as apes do. In time, of course, fire was used to cook meat, thus tenderizing it.

In the anthropoids, the mandible, or lower jaw, consists of two fused symmetrical halves. In the ape, the forces generated by the jaw in eating are great and the curved front section of the mandible, where the two halves of the mandible have fused, is reinforced internally by a buttress, the **simian shelf.** This shelf rarely occurs in the hominins. In modern humans, the evolution of a small jaw has resulted in a **chin,** or mental protuberance, a product of changes in the growth and development pattern of the jaw (Figure 8.21).

The muscles that operate the jaw also have changed in the course of human evolution, becoming smaller. The **temporalis** muscle arises on the side of the skull and inserts on the jaw (Figure 8.22). In the gorilla, this muscle is very large while the brain case is relatively small, and so a large flange, the **sagittal crest,** develops across the top of the skull, providing the surface area necessary for muscle attachment. The **masseter,** another muscle that functions in chewing, arises on the zygomatic arch of the skull and inserts on the mandible. An animal with large teeth and jaw and, consequently, a large masseter has a robust zygomatic.

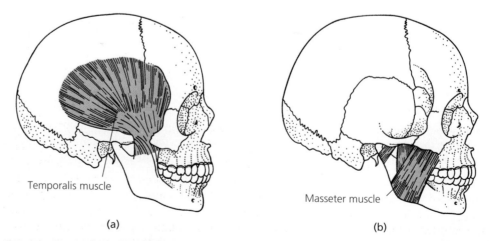

Temporalis muscle

Masseter muscle

(a)

(b)

Figure 8.22 The Muscles of the Jaws The temporalis muscle (a) and masseter muscle (b) as seen on a human skull.

Since the temporalis passes through the opening formed by the zygomatic and the side of the skull, a large temporalis is associated with a flaring zygomatic arch. In modern humans, the zygomatic arch is slender and not flaring.

Summary

The human skull, composed of 28 separate bones plus 32 teeth in the adult, is a very complex part of the skeleton. In primates the occipital condyles are located underneath the skull. In humans, they are positioned almost directly in the center of the skull; this achieves a good balance of the skull atop the spine. In general, the primate facial skeleton is reduced in relationship to the rest of the skull. The nasal apparatus is reduced in size, and the eyes are encased in bony eye sockets located on the front of the skull.

Within the primate order, we see the progressive enlargement of brain volume and development of the cerebral cortex. The human neocortex makes possible higher mental activities. In association with other features, such as bipedalism and manual dexterity, the cerebral cortex allows for social as well as individual intelligence. It is this social intelligence that enables humans as a species to significantly alter the environment. These alterations can be advantageous, as seen in the general increase in comfort and living standards that technology can bring, or devastating, as evidenced by pollution, the effects of war, and depletion of resources.

The increase in the size of the human brain is reflected in the increased volume of the cranium, or brain case. While the average cranial capacity is 1350 cubic centimeters, the range of variation is large. Within normal limits, no correlation between brain size and intelligence exists.

The primates have retained a fairly unspecialized tooth structure. The New World monkeys have three premolars per quadrant of the mouth, and most have a total of 36 teeth. All the Old World anthropoids have only two premolars, for a total of 32 permanent teeth. General characteristics of modern hominin dentition are a reduction in tooth size, lack of a sectorial premolar, a parabolic dental arcade, lack of a diastema and projecting canine, vertical implantation of the incisors, early eruption of the canine, a differential wear pattern of the molars, and thick tooth enamel.

The human jaw is smaller and shorter, relative to the skull, than is the ape jaw, and a chin is present. The muscles that operate the jaw are smaller. The modern human skull always lacks a sagittal crest and is characterized by small or absent brow ridges and a slender, nonflaring zygomatic arch.

COMPARATIVE CYTOGENETICS AND MOLECULAR BIOLOGY

The study of comparative anatomy has its roots deep in the nineteenth century. The museums of that time collected large amounts of skeletal material from both extant and extinct creatures. However, students of comparative anatomy encountered many problems. First, there is a degree of subjectivity in comparing skeletal materials, although many generations of scholars have taken precise measurements and utilized statistical analyses. Second, the phenotype is influenced by environmental factors, and so a particular anatomical feature may represent environmental influence and not genetic continuity with the past. Finally, there is the problem of convergence, in which similarities in selective agents may result in phenotypic similarities among divergent animals.

Table 8.6 Some Chromosome Numbers of Primates

Primate	Family	Chromosome Number
Owl monkey	Cebidae	54
Spider monkey	Cebidae	34
Capuchin monkey	Cebidae	54
Woolly monkey	Cebidae	62
Squirrel monkey	Cebidae	44
Common marmoset	Callitrichidae	46
Red-crowned mangabey	Cercopithecidae	42
Vervet monkey	Cercopithecidae	60
Patas monkey	Cercopithecidae	54
Rhesus monkey	Cercopithecidae	42
Baboon	Cercopithecidae	42
Indian langur	Cercopithecidae	44
White-handed gibbon	Hylobatidae	44
Crested gibbon	Hylobatidae	52
Siamang	Hylobatidae	50
Orangutan	Hominidae	48
Gorilla	Hominidae	48
Chimpanzee	Hominidae	48
Human	Hominidae	46

Source: T. C. Hsu and K. Benirschke, *Atlas of Mammalian Chromosomes,* vol. 10 (Berlin: Springer, 1977), pt. 4.

comparative cytogenetics The comparative study of chromosomes.

comparative molecular biology The comparative study of molecules.

The story began to change with the emergence of **comparative cytogenetics,** the comparative study of chromosomes, and **comparative molecular biology,** the comparative study of the molecules found in living organisms, especially proteins and DNA. These are the topics of this section.

Comparative Cytogenetics

The genetic material within the cell is found in small bodies called chromosomes (Chapter 2). Comparative cytogenetics is the comparative study of chromosomes from the cells of different species of plants and animals. Such studies shed light on the evolutionary relationships and histories of these species.

A species is associated with a characteristic number of chromosomes. In *Homo sapiens,* nondividing body cells contain 46 chromosomes. Table 8.6 lists the chromosome numbers of a variety of primate species, varying from 34 in the spider monkey to 62 in the woolly monkey.

Chromosome number is not necessarily consistent within any given taxonomic group such as a family; closely related species may have differing chromosome numbers. For example, the white-handed gibbon has 44 chromosomes, while the crested gibbon has 52, yet both species belong to the same genus. On the other hand, widely differing species may share the same number of chromosomes. The Old World patas monkey and the New World owl monkey both have the same chromosome number, 54. It therefore follows that chromosome number is not evidence of evolutionary relationships. All the great apes, however, share the same chromosome number of 48.

The Nature of Chromosome Evolution

As we saw in Chapter 2, chromosomes differ in size and position of the centromere. On the basis of these characteristics, chromosomes may be classified and arranged in a standard way; this standardized arrangement of chromosomes is a *karyotype.* Human karyotypes are shown in Figure 2.8.

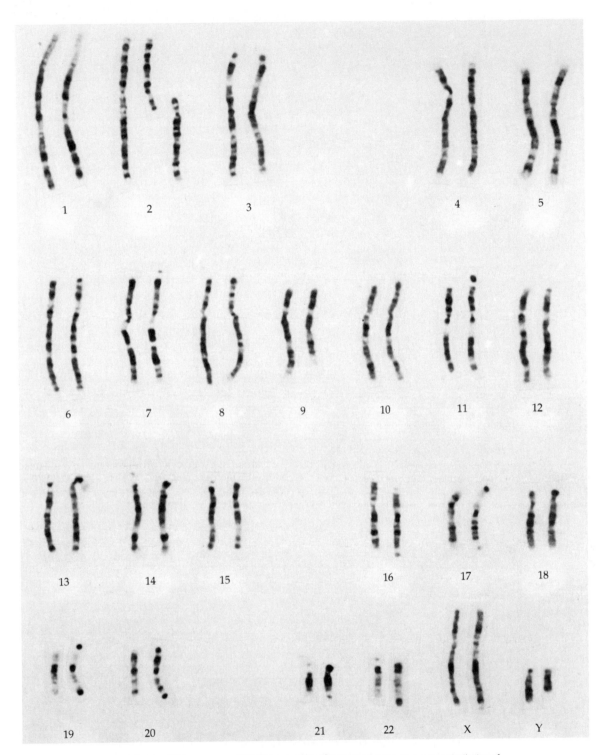

Figure 8.23 Comparison of Human and Chimpanzee Chromosomes The great similarity of human and chimpanzee chromosomes is shown in this composite karyotype. For each pair, the human chromosome is shown on the left and the chimpanzee chromosome on the right.

Figure 8.23 shows a composite karyotype comparing chimpanzee and human chromosomes. Although the chromosome numbers differ, the chromosomes exhibit a high degree of similarity in their appearance. Hypothetically, their similarity is the result of a common inheritance; in other words, these chromosomes are homologous. Through gene mapping, homologous genes are being found in the same position on human and chimpanzee chromosomes.

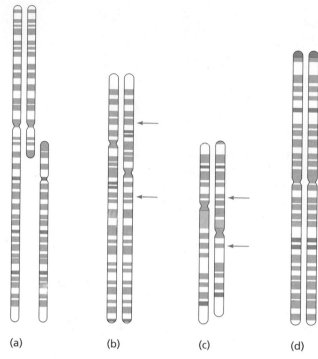

(a)　　　　(b)　　　　(c)　　　　(d)

Figure 8.24 Schematic Representation of Selected Human and Chimpanzee Chromosomes Human chromosomes are on left. (a) Human chromosome 2 shows similarities with two chimpanzee chromosomes. (b) Chromosome 4 shows an inversion; breaks (shown by arrows) occur on either side of the centromere, and the center piece becomes turned around. (c) Chromosome 9 shows an inversion plus chromosomal material, indicated by lighter shading, that is not thought to contain any actual genes. (d) Chromosome 3 shows virtually no variation between human and chimpanzee. Reprinted with permission from Yunis, J. J., J. R. Sawyer, and K. Dunham, "The Striking Resemblance of High-Resolution G-Banded Chromosomes of Man and Chimpanzees," *Science,* 208 (1980), 1145–1149. Copyright 1980 by the AAAS. Courtesy J. J. Yunis.

pericentric inversion A type of inversion whereby two breaks occur in a chromosome, one on either side of the centromere, and the center piece becomes turned around and rejoined with the two outside pieces.

constitutive heterochromatin Chromosomal material that is not thought to contain any actual genes.

The chromosomes seen in Figure 8.23 are giemsabanded. Detailed analysis of the banding patterns leads to the conclusion that "essentially every band and subband observed in man has a direct counterpart in the chimpanzee chromosome complements."[1] Since the banding pattern is largely a reflection of the genetic content of the chromosomes, this supports the theory of close genetic similarity between chimpanzees and humans.

Human and Chimpanzee Chromosomes Compared Although human and chimpanzee chromosomes are very similar, comparisons of human and chimpanzee banded chromosomes reveal many interesting differences. Figure 8.24b illustrates a **pericentric inversion** in which two breaks occur, one on either side of the centromere. The center piece turns around and rejoins the two outside pieces. Thus, human chromosome 4 and its chimpanzee counterpart both contain the same bands, but their relative positions are different.

Ten other chromosomes, including the X chromosome, differ from their chimpanzee counterparts because they contain extra chromosome material called **constitutive heterochromatin.** Geneticists believe that this material does not contain any actual genes (Figure 8.24c).

We already have noted that the human karyotype contains one less chromosome pair than the chimpanzee karyotype does. When we carefully pair up each human chromosome with a chimpanzee chromosome that appears to be similar, we find that human chromosome 2 does not have a homologous chromosome from the chimpanzee set. Also, two small chimpanzee chromosomes, both possessing centromeres near one end, are left unmatched.

One hypothesis proposes that human chromosome 2 evolved from a fusion of two ancestral chromosomes. Such an event is illustrated in Figure 8.25. The two short arms of the two chromosomes break off. If these small, short arms carry no important genes, their loss would not adversely affect the organism. Then the two centromeres fuse, forming a new, larger chromosome. Once this becomes fixed in the population, the number of chromosomes is reduced from 48 to 46.

We can conclude that the common ancestor of humans and chimpanzees possessed 48 chromosomes, which is the chromosome number of the other great apes as well. Figure 8.24a compares human chromosome 2 with two chimpanzee chromosomes. The matching bands support the hypothesis that this human chromosome arose through a fusion of the two smaller ancestral chromosomes.

Comparative Studies of Proteins and DNA

In the previous sections, we saw how evolutionary relationships can be established upon analysis of the genetic material on the cellular level. In the following sections, we will examine similarities on the molecular level, looking first at protein molecules and then at the DNA molecule itself.

---

[1] J. J. Yunis, J. R. Sawyer, and K. Dunham, "The Striking Resemblance of High-Resolution G-Banded Chromosomes of Man and Chimpanzee," *Science* 208 (1980), p. 1145.

Figure 8.25 The Evolution of Human Chromosome 2 It is hypothesized that human chromosome 2 evolved from a fusion of two small ancestral chromosomes: (a) ancestral chromosomes; (b) short arms broken off; (c) centromeres fused together.

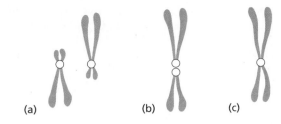

In sickle-cell anemia, the abnormal hemoglobin S differs from the normal hemoglobin A by a single amino acid substitution. This substitution is a reflection of a single base change in the DNA molecule controlling beta-chain synthesis (Chapter 5). However, not all substitutions produce abnormalities. In the course of evolution, occasional substitutions occur that either produce no undesirable changes or, less commonly, produce an improvement.

Thus, in the divergence of two evolutionary lines that begins with common protein structures, successive substitutions will occur. In time, the two divergent populations will possess proteins with similar yet differing structures. The amino acid sequences of the same types of protein or, more accurately, homologous proteins may be compared. Those with the more recent common ancestor should show the greatest similarities in the amino acid sequence; that is, they should show the lowest number of amino acid substitutions.

Early Studies of Protein Structure In the 1960s efficient methods for determining the sequence of amino acids in a protein had not been developed. Vincent Sarich and Alan Wilson performed some of the earliest studies of protein structure by using immunological comparison.[2] They studied the serum albumins, proteins that consist of a single chain of about 570 amino acids, which are found in the blood of all land vertebrates. They took serum albumin samples from various primates and injected them into rabbits. The rabbits responded by manufacturing antibodies against the injected proteins. Those antibodies were used as the test reagent since they reflected the structure of the injected protein.

The antisera that developed from the injection of human serum albumin reacted strongly to human serum albumin. The reaction of antihuman serum albumin to chimpanzee serum albumin, however, was a little weaker, and the reaction to rhesus monkey serum albumin was weaker still. Sarich and Wilson interpreted the strength of the reaction as an indicator of similarity of protein structure. Their work was one of the earliest to demonstrate clearly the very close relationship between humans and the chimpanzee on the molecular level.

Studies of Amino Acid Sequences Since each amino acid is specified by one or more codes in the DNA molecule, the determination of amino acid sequences provides us with a reconstruction of the genetic code. Since some amino acids are determined by more than one code, some changes in the code will not result in an amino acid substitution. Therefore, the amino acid sequence provides us with the minimum number of changes or substitutions in the nucleotide sequence of the DNA molecule.

In 1975 Mary-Claire King and Alan Wilson published an important paper in which they presented an analysis of 12 proteins that are found in both humans and chimpanzees.[3] Taken together, they represent a combined sequence of 2633 amino acids. Among those sequences,

---

[2] V. M. Sarich and A. C. Wilson, "Rates of Albumin Evolution in Primates," *Proceedings of the National Academy of Sciences* 58 (1967), pp. 142–148.

[3] M.-C. King and A. C. Wilson, "Evolution at Two Levels in Humans and Chimpanzees," *Science* 188 (1975), pp. 107–116.

Table 8.7 Differences in the Amino Acid Sequences of Human and Chimpanzee Proteins

Protein	Number of Amino Acid Differences	Number of Amino Acids in Protein
Fibrinopeptides A and B	0	30
Cytochrome c	0	104
Lysozome	0*	130
Hemoglobin α	0	141
Hemoglobin β	0	146
Hemoglobin ^{A}γ	0	146
Hemoglobin ^{G}γ	0	146
Hemoglobin δ	1	146
Myoglobin	1	153
Carbonic anhydrase	3*	264
Serum albumin	6*	580
Transferrin	8*	647
Total	19	2633

* Approximation based on methods other than analysis of known amino acid sequences.

Source: Reprinted from M.-C. King and A. C. Wilson, "Evolution at Two Levels in Humans and Chimpanzees," *Science* 188 (1975), p. 108. Copyright 1975 AAAS.

19 were different in human and chimpanzee proteins (Table 8.7). Like the earlier study, the new data again showed the very close relationship between humans and chimpanzees.

Phylogenetic Trees and Molecular Clocks Similar studies were conducted on a significant number of primates, and from those data anthropologists began to construct **phylogenetic trees,** graphic representations of the evolutionary relationships among animal species.

A phylogenetic tree appears as a series of points connected by lines to form a branching pattern. The single most ancestral point is the root of the tree, and each ancestral point produces two, and only two, descendants. Earlier we noted that changes in amino acids can be accounted for by more than one pattern of change in the genetic code; therefore, alternative branching patterns can be constructed. An important principle in the construction of phylogenetic trees is the **maximum parsimony principle.** Simply stated, the most probable phylogenetic tree is the one based on the fewest changes in the genetic code.

These studies reinforced the idea that humans and chimpanzees are very closely related, more so than is the case with gorillas and orangutans. In other words, humans and chimpanzees had a last common ancestor in the not too remote past, at least in geologic terms. The question was: Just how long ago did this last common ancestor live?

Some molecular biologists have proposed the existence of a "molecular clock." This concept proposes that changes in the structure of a protein or a stretch of DNA take place at a relatively constant rate when averaged over a period of time. This rate varies for different molecules and different groups of animals. The calibration of the clock depends on the existence of a relatively good dated fossil record for a particular lineage. If you know the difference in molecular structure between two species and, from the fossil record, can estimate when the last common ancestor lived, you can estimate the rate of molecular change. Once calibrated, the clock can be used to estimate the time when a common ancestor for other closely related species lived. While there is some debate over the accuracy of the clock, it has proved useful in providing estimates of divergence times that have guided further research. This has been particularly important in working out the evolutionary history of the apes and their relationship to humans.

Studies of Primate Genomes Once the human genome had been sequenced, interest turned to sequencing the genomes of animals that are of importance in medical research and in the understanding of human evolution. This included the chimpanzee genome.

See the Online Learning Center for an Interactive Exercise on the molecular clock.

phylogenetic tree A graphic representation of evolutionary relationships among species.

maximum parsimony principle The principle that the most accurate phylogenetic tree is one that is based on the fewest changes in the genetic code.

This is a rapidly moving area of research, and as such, it presents a major problem for any textbook since by the time these words are read, our knowledge may have increased many-fold. However, in mid-2004 it is generally believed that the DNA code of humans is about 98.8 percent identical to that of the chimpanzee. But it is much more than simply a matter of comparing the two genomes nucleotide by nucleotide and locating differences in the codes. A great deal of the difference between the two genomes consists of tens of thousands of repetitions and deletions of segments of the code. We do not yet know what this means.

Of course, a most interesting question is: What exactly are the genes that are different in the two genomes? Here lies the key to understanding the evolutionary divergence of chimpanzees and humans. In other words, what makes humans unique at the gene level? The work in this area is extremely preliminary, but it appears that genetic differences lie in the areas of smell, hearing, and speech, as well as in several biochemical operations.

Summary

Since the genes are located within the chromosomes, comparative analysis of human and nonhuman chromosomes has provided information for determining evolutionary relationships. When we examine human and chimpanzee karyotypes, we can easily pair up each human chromosome with a chimpanzee counterpart. The only exception is human chromosome 2, which appears to have evolved from the fusion of two smaller chromosomes.

In recent years, detailed biochemical studies of protein molecules have added a valuable perspective to evolutionary studies. By a comparison of protein and DNA molecules from various living species, the evolutionary closeness of these species can be estimated. From these data, phylogenetic trees can be drawn to illustrate the most probable evolutionary relationships among species.

Key Terms

abductors, *188*

allometric growth, *194*

bilophodont, *200*

brachial index, *188*

branch running and walking, *178*

cerebral cortex, *193*

cheek teeth, *197*

chin, *202*

comparative cytogenetics, *204*

comparative molecular biology, *204*

constitutive heterochromatin, *206*

cranial capacity, *196*

crural index, *188*

cusps, *197*

dental arcade, *200*

dental formula, *198*

diastema, *200*

encephalization quotient (EQ), *195*

endocranial cast, *196*

erect bipedalism, *179*

extensor, *187*

folivores, *198*

foramen magnum, *191*

forebrain, *193*

frugivores, *198*

gluteus maximus, *187*

gluteus medius, *187*

gluteus minimus, *187*

ground running and walking, *178*

heel-toe stride, *179*

hindbrain, *193*

insectivores, *198*

intermembral index, *186*

knuckle walking, *179*

lumbar curve, *187*

masseter, *202*

maximum parsimony principle, *208*

midbrain, *193*

neocortex, *193*

New World semibrachiation, *179*

nuchal crest, *191*

nuchal muscle, *191*

occipital condyles, *191*

Old World semibrachiation, *179*

omnivores, *198*

orthograde, *178*

pericentric inversion, *206*

phylogenetic tree, *208*

See the Online Learning Center for additional study questions.

Study Questions

1. How does an anthropologist use data from comparative anatomy to determine evolutionary relationships?

2. In what ways can the primate skeleton be said to be generalized?

3. What is meant by the term *suspensory behavior?* Discuss the evidence for the hypothesis that hominins evolved from a generalized suspensory ancestry.

4. Some hominin fossils show the presence of crests, ridges, and pronounced brow ridges on the skull. How can these features be interpreted?

5. Compare the dentition of modern humans with that of modern apes.

6. What are the major features of the evolution of the primate brain?

7. Describe the evolution of the human karyotype from an ancestral ape karyotype.

8. As animals evolve, so do protein molecules. Discuss the use of comparative biochemical studies in the determination of evolutionary relationships.

Critical Thinking Questions

1. Most comparisons of the genetics of humans and chimpanzees conclude that there is about a $1\frac{1}{2}$ percent genetic difference between humans and chimpanzees. How can that be? Don't you perceive that the difference between you and a chimpanzee is considerably more than that? From what you might know about genetics, explain how such a small genetic difference can exist in animals that seem to be phenotypically much more different.

2. The human body is the result of millions of years of evolution. If you could redesign the human body, what changes would you make? Could you make movement, eating, reproduction, communication, and other behaviors and activities more efficient by redesigning human anatomy? If you were to change one anatomic structure or system, how would that change potentially affect other anatomical and behavioral traits?

3. You are a physician in a small town that has a small zoo. You are asked to examine a chimpanzee that has just died even though you have had no experience with ape anatomy. What parts of the chimpanzee body would you have the greatest ease and difficulty dissecting? Why?

Suggested Readings

Aiello, L., and C. Dean. *An Introduction to Human Evolutionary Anatomy.* London: Academic, 1990. A detailed description of human anatomy, this book emphasizes the anatomical evidence for human evolution.

Katzenberg, M. A., and S. R. Saunders (eds.). *Biological Anthropology of the Human Skeleton.* New York: John Wiley & Sons, 2001. This volume describes methods of skeletal analysis, age changes in the skeleton, prehistoric health and disease, and a variety of other topics.

Martin, R. D. *Primate Origins and Evolution: A Phylogenetic Reconstruction.* Princeton, NJ: Princeton University Press, 1990. This book contains several detailed chapters summarizing comparative primate anatomy.

Napier, J., revised by R. H. Tuttle. *Hands.* Princeton, NJ: Princeton University Press, 1993. This book includes discussions of the anatomy, evolution, and social and cultural aspects of the hand.

Swindler, D., and C. D. Wood. *An Atlas of Primate Gross Anatomy.* Melbourne, FL: Krieger, 1982. This book contains a series of detailed line drawings illustrating the comparative anatomy of the baboon, chimpanzee, and human.

Zihlman, A. L. *The Human Evolution Coloring Book,* 2nd ed. New York: Barnes & Noble, 2001. This "coloring book" is not a children's book but a very complete workbook written by a noted physical anthropologist. It includes important "lessons" on human evolution, including anatomy and molecular genetics.

Suggested Websites

Comparative Mammalian Brain Evolution
http://brainmuseum.org

The eSkeleton Project
www.eSkeletons.org

Overview of Human Genome Sequencing Center
www.hgsc.bcm.tmc.edu

Chapter 9

Nonhuman Primate Behavior

Primatologist Sarah Blaffer Hrdy observes langurs on Mt. Abu, India.

tudies of nonhuman primates form an important part of a scientific enterprise that is giving us increased understanding of the world about us, of the evolutionary processes that gave rise to it, and of our place within it. Beyond that, however, nonhuman species, and especially nonhuman primates, provide an important source of data for understanding many aspects of human behavior and physiology in terms of causation, developmental processes, function, and evolution. ●

—*Robert A. Hinde*

Chapter Outline

See the Online Learning Center for a chapter summary, chapter outline, and learning objectives.

After Reading This Chapter, You Should Be Able to Answer These Questions:

1. What are the six different types of social groups formed by various species of primates?
2. What are some of the methods for studying primate behavior?
3. How would you describe the social behavior of gibbons?
4. How would you describe the social behavior of the gelada?
5. What are some of the characteristics of the savanna baboon's social life?
6. What are some of the characteristics of the social life of chimpanzees?
7. Describe tool making and hunting behavior among chimpanzees.
8. What are some similarities in the behaviors of the various species of primates discussed in the chapter?
9. What are unique features of the behavior of each of the four populations of primates discussed in this chapter?

From casual observers at a zoo to scientists engaged in research, people are fascinated with animal behavior. The physical anthropologist is most interested in the nonhuman primates since all primates, including humans, are united by a common ancestry.

Millions of years have passed since all primates had a common ancestor, or even since humans and apes did. Yet studies of nonhuman primate behavior throw light on current human behaviors—such as the need for physical contact. By studying contemporary nonhuman primate behavior, we can develop ideas on what some of the selective pressures operating on early hominin populations might have been.

Although there are many similarities between human and nonhuman primate behavior, humans have taken a different evolutionary path from any other primate. This chapter considers the behavior of the nonhuman primates, while the next chapter discusses human behavior from the perspective of the behavior of nonhuman primates.

PRIMATE BEHAVIOR

A majority of mammals do not live in large social units; many are solitary or live as mated adults with offspring. Of course, even solitary mammals have to engage in some social activity for mating, and the mother usually spends time feeding and protecting her infants. However, primates, including humans, do tend to form social groups.

Why Primates Form Groups

Why do primates form groups? No single variable explains why this occurs. Many ideas, however, have been proposed.

One hypothesis is the **resource-defense model.** This model is based on the idea that a group of individuals can defend access to resources such as food and keep other animals and other groups away from these resources better than an individual can. The importance of defending resources depends on the nature of the resource. For example, leaves tend to be plentiful and are spread fairly evenly through the forest. On the other hand, fruit is not as plentiful. In a tropical forest, only a few trees will produce fruit at any one time, yet at that time a tree may be loaded with enough fruit to satisfy the needs of all the members of a group. Primates that emphasize fruit in their diets tend to live in larger social groups than primates that emphasize leaves or insects in their diet.

Another model is the **predation model.** This hypothesis emphasizes the risk that primates face from predators. The presence of a large group and defense behavior often associated with such groups help protect individuals from the dangers of carnivores. Semi-terrestrial primates are perhaps the most vulnerable to predation; such primates tend to form large groups.

Neither model explains all the variation and complexity of primate social organization. Both may be operating together and other, as-yet-unknown factors may be present.

Kinds of Primate Social Organization

In studying primate social groups, we see great variation not only among the various primate species but also within a particular species. **Primatologists** have conducted studies about what factors determine the form that a primate group takes. From these studies, we can make some generalizations.

Several factors appear to determine to some degree the size of a particular primate social group. As predicted by the predation model, more terrestrial primates tend to live in larger groups than more arboreal ones. Nocturnal primates, those who are active at night, often develop strategies where single animals or small groups are able to successfully prevent being seen by predators. Diurnal primates, those that are active during the day, are more easily seen. Here there is an advantage of living in a larger group since predators have a much more difficult time approaching such a group without being seen by at least one animal.

resource-defense model A model that gives an explanation of why primates form groups based on the hypothesis that a group of individuals can defend access to resources such as food and keep other animals and other groups away from those resources better than an individual can.

predation model A model that gives an explanation of why primates form groups based on the hypothesis that a group of individuals can protect themselves better or even ward off attacks from predators better than an individual animal could.

See the Online Learning Center for an Internet Activity on primatology.

primatologist A person who studies primates.

Diet also appears to be related to group size. Folivores (leaf eaters) tend to live in smaller groups, probably because leaves are plentiful and can be exploited by several small groups spread out through the forest. As we saw in the discussion of the resource-defense model, frugivores (fruit eaters) tend to live in larger groups.

Primate groups also vary greatly in terms of group membership. One way of making sense of group organization is to think of different primate groups in terms of relationships among females. Since females carry the developing fetus, nurse the infant, and generally carry and care for the young offspring, we would expect that their success in producing offspring will be closely related to the state of their health and nutrition. The latter is closely related to their access to food. Essentially, all females do mate, but the differences in reproductive success among females are related to the female's ability to bring a fetus to term and to raise the newborn. This contrasts with the reproductive success of males, which is related to their access to females for purposes of mating.

One way of looking at variation among primate social groups is to examine the relationship of adult females to food resources. Since the reproductive success of a female is related to her access to food, we would assume that females generally compete for food. Many females forage for food on their own, establishing individual control over resources. However, there are some situations in which a female may enhance her ability to procure food by forming alliances with other females, especially female kin. Groups that are based on associations among related females are termed **female-bonded kin groups.**

Types of Groups A relatively simple form of social grouping is found in many small nocturnal prosimians, such as the galagos, mouse lemurs, and dwarf lemurs, as well as in the orangutan (Table 9.1). The basic social unit is the female and her immature offspring. Each female–offspring unit occupies a specific space termed a **home range.** The ranges of females may overlap extensively, and, among prosimians, females with their young often share the same nest. Males occupy larger ranges that overlap several ranges occupied by females. Males and females do not interact with each other on a regular basis; for example, they do not feed together. They do have periodic contact, and when the female is sexually receptive, mating occurs. The social unit of the dwarf lemur is described in Box 9-1.

The **monogamous pair** is a relatively simple unit that consists of an adult female–male pair, usually mated for life, and their offspring. The young normally leave the group when they reach puberty. This type of social unit is characteristic of some lemuriformes, some New World monkeys, and the gibbons.

Among the marmosets and tamarins, males play major roles in the rearing of offspring. Twins are usually born, and the father carries the infants, transferring the young to the

female-bonded kin groups Primate social groups that are based on associations of females.

home range The area occupied by an animal or animal group.

monogamous pair A social group, found among small-bodied apes and other primates, consisting of a single mated pair and their young offspring.

Table 9.1 Primate Social Groups

Group	Description	Examples
Female–offspring unit	Range overlaps ranges of other female–offspring groups and the larger ranges of the males	Dwarf lemurs, galagos, orangutans
Monogamous pair	Male–female pair and preadult offspring	Gibbons
Polyandrous group	Female with one or more males and offspring	Tamarins
One-male–several-females group	Male with several females; called a harem when the group is a subunit of a larger unit	Hamadryas baboons, geladas, langurs
Multimale group	Several males with several females and offspring	Savanna baboons, rhesus macaques
Fission-fusion society	Several groups varying in size and composition	Chimpanzees

Box 9-1   The Behavior of the Dwarf Lemur

While primates are usually thought of as highly social animals, some of the small nocturnal lemuriformes lead relatively solitary lives. One such primate is Coquerel's dwarf lemur, *Mirza coquereli* (See figure). This lemur is 20 centimeters (7.9 inches) long excluding its 33-centimeter (13-inch)-long tail and is nocturnal and arboreal. These lemurs spend their days sleeping in nests that may contain a single female, a male–female pair, or a few females. Their nests are constructed in the fork of a tree off the ground, and a single animal may have several nests to which it returns in the morning. They leave their nests at dusk and return there at dawn. During the first half of the night they feed alone, but then they will engage in some social activities.

An important part of their diet consists of secretions produced by social insects. During some of the summer months this food source makes up about half their diet. Other foods include various types of plant material, such as fruits, flowers, and gums. Important animal foods include insects, spiders, frogs, bird eggs, and small lizards.

Adult dwarf lemurs occupy relatively small core areas that average 1.5 hectares (3.7 acres) for males and 2.5 to 3 hectares (6.2 to 7.4 acres) for females. The core area is surrounded by a larger peripheral area of over 4 hectares (10 acres). There is some overlapping of the home range, especially in the case of a female and her young or a male and a female. Peripheral areas overlap more extensively, allowing adults of the same sex to come into social contact. However, although the core area makes up only 30 percent of the home range, 80 percent of their activity occurs there. Like most lemurs, the dwarf lemur marks its core area with urine, feces, and secretions from specialized glands.

While occupying the core area, the dwarf lemur engages in solitary activities such as self-grooming, feeding, and resting; these activities typically occur during the earlier part of the night. After midnight, the animal may move out into the peripheral area, where it may contact another dwarf lemur. These include

encounters between the sexes and territorial activities between males.

Sources: E. Pages, "Ethoecology of *Microcebus conquereli* during the Dry Season," in P. Charles-Dominique et al., *Nocturnal Malagasy Primates* (New York: Academic Press, 1980), pp. 97–116; Duke University Primate Center at www.duke.edu/web/primate. *Mirza coquereli* is also known by the earlier name *Microcebus coquereli*.

polyandrous group A form of social organization found in primates in which a female has multiple mates.

one-male group A social unit consisting of a single male associated with several females.

harem A subunit of a larger social group consisting of a male associated with two or more females.

female only for feeding (Figure 9.1). The group often contains three sets of twins of successive ages. This social unit, however, is not as simple as it might first appear. Young animals may transfer from one family group to another, and in some groups a second adult male may be present. Among humans, the term *polyandry* is used to refer to a marriage system where a female is married to two or more males. Therefore, this type of primate social organization is sometimes referred to as a **polyandrous group.**

A more common form of group organization consists of several females associated with a single male. This type of group may exist as a small, independent **one-male group,** or it may be a subunit, sometimes called a **harem,** of a larger unit. The social organization of the hamadryas baboon consists of harems and all-male groups bound together in a hierarchy of larger social groupings. This basic type of organization also is found among howler monkeys, langurs, and geladas.

When circumstances lead to the development of larger social units called the **multimale group,** we find that group membership includes many adult males and adult females. The

Figure 9.1 Golden Lion Tamarin Marmosets and tamarins usually produce twins, which are carried by the father and transferred to the mother for nursing.

large number of females requires the presence of several males. Females in such groups tend to form close bonds, while males usually migrate at puberty to neighboring groups. However, the distinction between one-male and multimale groups is not always clear. The social organizations of baboons, macaques, and other Old World monkeys, some colobus monkeys, and some New World monkeys are examples of multimale group societies.

> **multimale group** A social unit consisting of many adult males and adult females.

Finally, there are many primates that exhibit a variety of social groupings. The size and organization of the various types of groups often depend on the activity of the group and the season of the year. This is typical of chimpanzees, whose social organization may be referred to as a **fission-fusion society,** because large groups break into smaller units and smaller groups coalesce into larger ones.

> **fission-fusion society** Constantly changing form of social organization whereby large groups undergo fission into smaller units and small units fuse into larger units in response to the activity of the group and the season of the year.

Methods in the Study of Primate Behavior

Early studies of primate behavior were conducted primarily with caged zoo populations, and data from these studies led to many erroneous conclusions. Today we realize that these data reflect the unnatural and overcrowded conditions in the cage. When a zoo population is given adequate space and a good food supply and is maintained in a natural social grouping, its behavior is very similar to that of wild populations.

Perhaps the most valid type of primate behavior study is the **field study.** The field observer spends enough time with a natural population to recognize individuals. Since animals become familiar with the observer as well, close observation becomes possible. The disadvantages of such studies are that it takes long periods of time to make contact with the animals and the yield of data is relatively low.

> **field study** A study conducted in the natural habitat of an animal with minimal interference in the animal's life.

Box 9-2   The Rhesus Monkeys of Cayo Santiago

Cayo Santiago is a 15.2-hectare (37.6-acre) island located 1 kilometer (0.6 mile) from the southeast coast of Puerto Rico. In 1938, a population of rhesus monkeys (*Macaca mulatta*) from India was established on this uninhabited island. The colony has been maintained continuously since then.

The idea of developing a colony of free-ranging monkeys in the New World was developed by Clarence Ray Carpenter. In 1938, there was much interest in the project because of the possibility that the political situation in Europe might result in the cutting off of the importation of monkeys from Asia, especially the rhesus macaque, commonly used in laboratory studies. Carpenter traveled to India to trap 500 rhesus macaques, including 100 females with infants. All were tested for tuberculosis, a major cause of illness and death among monkeys, and those showing a positive reaction were not shipped. It took 47 days to transport the animals from India to New York. The animals arrived on Santiago Island on November 14, 1938, and, beginning in December, 409 rhesus monkeys were set free.

Before the arrival of the monkeys, Santiago Island was covered primarily with grass and was used as pasture for goats. A variety of trees and shrubs were planted in anticipation of the monkeys. Little was known about the naturalistic behavior of rhesus monkeys. For example, some people thought that rhesus monkeys were cave dwellers, and they constructed many small artificial caves; none were ever used.

By 1941, the colony was firmly established, and many primatologists were using the animals in their research. However, the financial support of the colony was becoming precarious, and large numbers of monkeys were removed from the island and transported to laboratories in the United States. In 1956, the Laboratory of Perinatal Physiology of the National Institute of Neurological Disease and Blindness (NINDB) and the University of Puerto Rico took over administration of the island colony.

Under new management, improvements in the care of the animals were made and major research was initiated on the island. It was at this time that animals were marked so that individuals could

A rhesus mother and her infant rest in the branches of a tree on Cayo Santiago.

be identified. Annual censuses were conducted, and longitudinal studies of specific animals following their development from birth to death were begun. These long-term studies are extremely difficult in natural populations. Although many animals were removed for laboratory studies, the population increased in size annually. In the 1960s, Santiago Island macaques were used to found new monkey colonies on other islands in the area. In 1970, the island became part of what is now the Caribbean Primate Research Center of the University of Puerto Rico School of Medicine.

Source: R. G. Rawlins and Matt J. Kessler, "The History of Cayo Santiago Colony," in R. G. Rawlins and M. J. Kessler (eds.), *The Cayo Santiago Macaques: History, Behavior and Biology* (Albany: State University of New York Press, 1986), pp. 13–45.

provisioned colony
Group of free-ranging primates that have become accustomed to humans because of the establishment of feeding stations.

Many of these problems are solved to a great extent through studies of **provisioned colonies,** which are natural populations in which feeding stations are established. Because the primate group travels to the feeding stations daily, the researcher can observe individuals closely and can collect census data, such as information on births and deaths. Studies conducted away from the feeding stations are made easier by the primate group's increased tolerance of the observer. The yield of data is greater than that achieved with the standard field study of a nonprovisioned group, and new observers can be introduced into the research situation quite readily. Well-known provisioned colonies include those of the Japanese macaque at Takasakiyama, Japan, and the rhesus macaque colony on Cayo Santiago, Puerto Rico (Box 9-2).

While natural and provisioned populations are the most frequently studied, many universities and research stations maintain artificial colonies. In addition, laboratory studies, conducted primarily by psychologists, involve manipulation of the animals in a laboratory situation.

Summary

Most primates live in groups; that is, primates are social animals. Primates that subsist on sparse resources are most likely to live in groups because they can defend resources from other populations better than could a solitary animal. Primates that are vulnerable to predators, like those that spend time on the ground, might form groups as protection from those predators. In both cases, there is power in numbers.

Primates form many different types of groups. The type formed by a particular species varies based on the lifestyle of the group—semiterrestrial or arboreal, diet, how the young are cared for, and other factors. Table 9.1 summarizes the major types of primate groups.

Perhaps the ideal way to study any animal is in the field where the natural behavior of the animal can be observed in the animal's own habitat. However, it is often not possible or practical to conduct a field study. In these cases, provisioned colonies become an alternative to field studies. Primates also are studied in the zoo and in the laboratory.

CASE STUDIES OF PRIMATE BEHAVIOR

This section deals with the social organization and social behavior of the monkeys and apes. We will examine a small series of anthropoids—the gibbon, gelada, baboon, and chimpanzee—by outlining their basic social organizations and discussing selected aspects of their social behaviors. This is not an exhaustive study, but it is one that will provide some understanding of the basic patterns and general nature of primate behavior. A fifth case study, that of humans, will be presented in Chapter 10.

Social Behavior of the Gibbon

The monkeys and apes are generally characterized by relatively large, complex social units, although small social groups do exist. Since many basic concepts are easier to understand in the context of small groups, we will begin our discussion with a description of the monogamous group.

The monogamous group is a relatively small social unit consisting of a single mated pair and their young offspring. It is found among the gibbons (Figure 9.2). In this section, we will examine some aspects of the social behavior of the white-handed gibbon, *Hylobates lar,* which was studied by J. O. Ellefson in the lowland rain forests of the Malay Peninsula.[1]

The Gibbon Social Group In the monogamous group, the adult male and female mate for life. The close relationship between the adult pair is seen in both grooming and sexual activity.

Grooming is a behavioral pattern common to most primates. In grooming, the animal uses its hands to search and comb through the fur, although lemuriformes use their dental comb instead. Grooming involves the search for dirt, dry pieces of skin, and parasites in the fur. The removal of this material keeps the fur relatively clean and groomed. An animal may spend time grooming itself as a part of this cleaning process; this is called **autogrooming.**

See the Online Learning Center for an Internet Activity on gibbons.

grooming In primates, the activity of going through the fur with hand or teeth to remove insects, dirt, twigs, dead skin, and so on; also acts as a display of affection.

autogrooming Self-grooming.

[1] J. O. Ellefson, "A Natural History of White-Handed Gibbons in the Malayan Peninsula," in D. M. Rumbaugh (ed.), *Gibbon and Siamang,* vol. 3 (Basel: Karger, 1974), pp. 1–136.

Figure 9.2 Female Gibbon Rests with Her Offspring

allogrooming Grooming another animal.

The animals also spend a great deal of time grooming one another; this is referred to as **allogrooming.**

Allogrooming in primates is an important form of social behavior, as it aids in the development and maintenance of close social bonds. It is especially common between closely related individuals and is characteristic of close social ties such as those between mother and child. Among gibbons, grooming is important in the maintenance of the adult male–female bond. The adult gibbon pair groom one another several times a day, primarily in the afternoon. This grooming is reciprocal; the male grooms the female for about as long as the female grooms the male.

Sexual behavior is another important aspect of social behavior. An analysis of the spacing of births suggests that sexual behavior in the white-handed gibbon takes place during short periods every two years or so.

The Gibbon Life Cycle The infant stage of gibbon development lasts from birth to approximately 2 to 2½ years of age. Within a few months after birth, the infant begins to eat solid food. At the end of this stage, it is weaned and also stops sleeping with its mother. Even the very young infant can cling tightly to its mother's fur as she rapidly moves through the high branches of the trees. The mother and other members of the group do not pay a great deal of attention to the infant. As the infant grows older, it moves farther away from its mother for longer periods of time and interacts with older siblings if it has any.

play Energetic and repetitive activity engaged in primarily by infants and juveniles.

The juvenile period begins between 2 and 2½ years and ends between 4 and 4½ years. Important during this stage of gibbon development is **play** behavior. Play is difficult to define, yet play behavior is important among primates and occupies a great deal of the waking hours of juveniles. Play often involves intense, repetitive physical activity that results in the development and refinement of physical skills. Ellefson describes the play of the white-handed gibbon as including "chasing, grappling, hitting, kicking, jerking, holding, biting, stretching, pushing and dropping."[2] It is through play that young primates learn rules of objects, that is, the relationship between the body and objects—for example, what objects the juvenile can move and

---

[2] Ibid., p. 84.

how trees respond to jumping on a branch. Play also provides a setting for the development of social skills and the formation of social bonds between specific individuals.

There is a major difference, however, between the play activities of gibbons and those of many other primates. In larger primate groups, several **play groups** may form, each including many animals of similar age. In the small gibbon family, the sole playmate of an older juvenile is its younger sibling. Thus, the older juvenile is always larger and stronger than the younger, and the physical activity of the older must be controlled to avoid injuring the younger. Also, gibbons spend less time playing than do most other primates.

During the juvenile period, the adults become less and less tolerant of the juvenile's feeding close by. When the juvenile is about four years of age, the adults actively threaten it away from many food sources. Their **threat gestures** include staring, shaking a branch, and lunging toward the young animal.

At about 6 years of age, the gibbon attains full adult size and full sexual maturity. This is the period of **peripheralization.** At this time, the adults (more often the adult male) become aggressive toward the adolescent and actively keep it away from the area in which they are eating. Also, the adolescent gibbon begins to move away from the group to forage and feed on its own.

The subadult phase of gibbon development lasts from the age of six until the animal mates, but the age of first mating is variable. As the animal becomes more and more separated from its group of birth, possibilities arise for the formation of a new social unit. Although the exact mechanisms are not known, peripheral subadult males do attract subadult females, and new male–female pairs are established.

Territoriality All animals occupy space. The area in which a group feeds, drinks, grooms, sleeps, plays, and so forth is its home range. The home ranges of gibbon groups measure about 40 hectares (100 acres) in size. We must always keep in mind, however, that primates utilize three-dimensional space and that the actual space occupied in a tropical forest, with its tall trees, is considerably larger than that suggested by the ground measurement. The area that a group defends against other members of its own species is its **territory.** The territory, which is usually smaller than the home range, represents the boundaries at which the animal actively begins to defend an area against another group.

Gibbons are highly territorial animals, and most of the home range is defended territory. Among the white-handed gibbons studied by Ellefson, territories overlap about 20 percent, and so the neighboring group may be found within the overlapping area. Actual conflict between neighboring males takes place, on the average, about every other day. Conflicts always occur in the area of overlapping territories, which is usually about 23 to 69 meters (25 to 75 yards) wide.

Territorial conflict is expressed primarily in terms of vocalization and display (Figure 9.3). Early in the morning, the southeast Asian forest rings with the sound of the great call of the gibbon. These morning calls broadcast the location of the various gibbon groups. Upon hearing the morning call of a nearby group, a male may lead his group over to the vicinity of that neighboring group. A typical conflict period lasts about an hour, the first half of which is spent in vocalizations and displays by adult males. These are usually followed by chases, but the chases rarely penetrate deep into any group's territory. Actual contact between adult males is rare.

Territorial behavior serves several functions. It spreads individual members of a population over a large area, thereby preventing a concentration of animals and overutilization of resources in a relatively small area. A map of gibbon territories shows a mosaic of small territories

play group A group of juveniles within a larger social unit that engages in play behavior.

threat gesture A physical activity that serves to threaten another animal. Some threat gestures are staring, shaking a branch, and lunging toward another animal.

peripheralization Process whereby an adolescent animal encounters aggressive behavior from adults and gradually moves away from the group.

territory The area that a group defends against other members of its own species.

Figure 9.3 Gibbon Vocalizing

throughout a relatively large area. Territoriality also serves to control population size, since an animal cannot begin to produce offspring until it has found a mate and established its own territory. The number of territories available is stable.

Social Behavior of the Gelada

Geladas, *Theropithecus gelada,* are large, primarily terrestrial monkeys. They once ranged over large areas of east Africa, and they are even represented in the fossil record (Figure 12.9). Today, the geladas are found only in a dry, desolate mountainous region of Ethiopia. Although the geladas are not true baboons (baboons belong to the genus *Papio*), they are similar to baboons in many ways.

The social organization found in this hot, dry habitat may be an adaptation to the environment. Primates that spend a great deal of time on the ground searching for food tend to form large groups for protection against predators. Primates that are more arboreal are relatively secure in the trees, and so they tend to form smaller and more loosely organized groups. Although trees are few and far between in the barren wastes where the geladas live, large social units are not always able to locate adequate food supplies in the hot, dry habitat. Thus, when food is scarce, the larger gelada group breaks up into its constituent groups. These smaller units are a better size for foraging for food under the harsh conditions. The following description of gelada social organization is based on the field studies of Robin and Patsy Dunbar.[3]

Age-Sex Categories Different animals behave in different ways within a social group. The most important differences in social behavior are determined by the sex and age of the individual. Therefore, we need to divide the members of the gelada groups into a series of age-sex categories, as we previously did with the white-handed gibbon.

The infant phase lasts from birth to 18 months of age. The young infant is black or dark brown in color, a marked contrast to the reddish coat color of the adult. This distinctive difference in color between infant and adult, which is characteristic of many primate species, makes the infant easily recognizable. The black gelada infant is a focal point of the group, and all members will protect the infant if it is in danger. During infancy, the young gelada stays very close to its mother. Toward the end of this phase, when the coat color begins to change to the adult color, the adults relax their vigilance and the infant is freer to move around and explore its environment.

The 6- to 18-month-old infant is adult in color, yet it still spends considerable time near its mother. At about 1 to 1½ years of age, the infant is weaned. Then the animal is classified as a juvenile, a phase lasting from 1½ to 3½ years of age. During this period, the juvenile becomes increasingly independent of its mother, and most of its social interactions take place in play groups.

The subadult female, age 3½ to 4½ years, is sexually mature but has not quite reached adult size. As the female completes growth, she associates primarily with other adult females and their offspring and is soon bearing offspring of her own.

The male is considered a subadult for a much longer time than the female—from 3½ to 6 years of age. In part, this is because the male continues to grow for a longer period of time than does the female. While the canine teeth erupt early in the subadult period, full growth of the large canines characteristic of males does not take place until the end of the subadult period. Only at this time do the males take their place in adult life. Because of this longer growth period, the adult male is larger than the female. This larger size, plus other distinctive features such as the cape of fur around the shoulders, makes it easy to distinguish the adult male from the adult female (Figure 9.4). Such a difference in the physical appearance between the male and female is an example of sexual dimorphism.

---

[3] R. Dunbar and P. Dunbar, *Social Dynamics of Gelada Baboons* (Basel: Karger, 1975).

Figure 9.4 The Gelada
A male gelada grooms a female, shown here with her infant.

Sexual dimorphism is common among the more terrestrial monkeys. Monkeys spending considerable time on the ground are vulnerable to predation and hence tend to live in larger social units. This means that a greater number of females are in the troop, which leads to an increase in intrasexual selection. As we saw in Chapter 5, increased intrasexual selection is correlated with an increase in sexual dimorphism. In addition, the larger size of the males provides the group with a mechanism for defense against predators.

Instant recognition of individuals is relatively easy in small units such as the gibbon family, but recognition becomes a problem in larger social groups. In case of danger, a gelada female needs to identify an adult male, and the distinctive physical appearance of the male makes this easy.

Social Organization of the Harem Units   The basic social unit of the gelada is the one-male–several-females unit, or harem. Besides harems, small all-male groups also exist.

A typical harem consists of about 11 members: one adult male, five adult females, and five juveniles and infants. The most cohesive bonds in the unit appear to exist between females, who express their closeness in terms of grooming. In many ways, the male is peripheral to the group. The females form a stable unit that maintains itself with little herding by the male. If a female from a neighboring harem comes too close, the females will chase her off. Similarly, males threaten females from other groups that come too close.

One form of behavior that is often seen in social interactions within the harem or between harems is **agonistic behavior.** This is behavior involving "fighting, threats, fleeing and other related displays."[4] Much agonistic behavior takes the form of display and gesture instead of actual fighting. Agonistic gestures and facial expressions include staring, raising the eyebrows, and lunging in space.

The juvenile male spends most of his time in play groups with other young animals within his harem, although juveniles from adjacent harems play with one another. As he grows older, he pays less attention to the members of the harem of his birth and begins to associate with an all-male group consisting of older juveniles, young subadults, and adult males without females. The older subadult male begins to show interest in the harem groups, and he attaches himself to one as a follower. These follower males are peripheral to the unit;

agonistic behavior
Behavior that involves fighting, threats, and fleeing.

---

[4] N. Chalmers, *Social Behavior in Primates* (Baltimore: University Park Press, 1980), p. 63.

Figure 9.5 The Gelada A gelada herd at rest.

they interact primarily with the juveniles and a few females of the group and generally avoid the adult males.

The juvenile female also participates in play groups until the time of puberty. She then begins to show interest in the adult males, mothers, and young infants and spends her time following the infants around and attempting to play with them. As she reaches sexual maturity, she becomes interested in the group leader. Since the adult male usually has little interest in the young female, the possibility arises that the female will become attached to a young male.

New harem units may arise in a variety of ways. Typically, a follower male forms an attachment with a young female. Once this bond becomes established, the young male and female slowly move away from the larger unit to form a new unit. A less frequent possibility is that a young male will attack an older harem male and take over the harem.

band Among geladas, a social group consisting of a number of harems and all-male units.

While the basic social units of the gelada are the harem and the all-male group, these groups do not wander independently of one another. Instead, they gather into **bands** consisting of harems and male groups that share a home range. During certain seasons, the band comes together in areas where food is plentiful. During times when food is less plentiful, the band breaks up and forages as individual harems and all-male groups.

herd Among geladas, a large social unit consisting of several bands that come together under very good grazing conditions.

Under very good grazing conditions, many bands come together to form a **herd** (Figure 9.5). Herds form in areas where band ranges overlap. In the Dunbars' study at Sankaber, Ethiopia, the herd contained 762 animals divided into 6 bands; in all there were 68 harems and 9 all-male groups.

See the Online Learning Center for an Internet Activity on baboons.

Social Behavior of the Savanna Baboon

Perhaps one of the best-studied primates other than humans is the savanna baboon. In large part, this is because savanna baboons live on the open grassland where humans can easily observe them. This contrasts with the very difficult observing conditions in forest areas.

Also, many anthropologists have been intrigued by the fact that both baboons and early hominids are primates that became adapted to life on the savanna.

Baboons range throughout large areas of Africa where they are the most commonly seen monkeys; in some places, they are considered agricultural pests. The baboons are divided into four kinds: olive (or anubis), yellow, chacma, and Guinea baboons. Many primatologists believe that the four groups represent four subspecies of the species *Papio cynocephalus.*

Many populations of savanna baboon have been studied in many parts of Africa. Baboon social organization is quite flexible and varies from one group to another. For example, the baboon troops at Amboseli, Kenya, exhibit intergroup aggression when in close proximity, yet baboons studied in Uganda show frequent movement of individuals from one group to another. In contrast, the baboons of Nairobi Park, Kenya, show much stability.

The conclusion we must draw from the wealth of field observations of baboons and other primates is that primate societies are variable in their adjustments to the environment. Differences in physical habitat, for example, are reflected in differences in the size of the home range, the troop size, and the general nature of intergroup interactions. This variability is a reflection of the fact that in general, primate social behavior is not biologically determined. Through the formation of learned behavioral patterns, each primate population has developed its particular guide for survival.

The following discussion is based on studies of two populations of savanna baboons living in Kenya—the baboons of Nairobi Park, studied by Irvin DeVore and his colleagues, and the baboons of Amboseli, studied by Stuart and Jane Altmann and their associates.[5]

The Baboon Troop Baboons live in a social unit called a **troop.** In both Nairobi Park and Amboseli, troops average about 40 animals. The baboon troop remains within a home range with distinct boundaries, a fact illustrated by the inability of an observer to drive a troop across these boundaries. Boundaries are never defended; hence, territories do not exist. The home ranges of neighboring troops usually overlap extensively (Figure 9.6). In contrast to the territorial behavior of the gibbon, when more than one baboon troop occupies sections of an overlapping area, the troops tend to ignore one another and avoid contact. When contact between baboon troops is unavoidable, such as around a water hole during the dry season, several troops often drink side by side. They ignore one another, or the smaller troop simply gives way to the larger.

The baboons of Kenya occupy ranges of about 23 to 24 square kilometers (8.9 to 9.3 square miles). The size appears to depend on the size of the troop and the concentration of food. Within the home range are certain **core areas,** which may contain a concentration of food, a water hole, a good resting area, or sleeping trees. The core areas are used exclusively by a single troop, which spends more than 90 percent of its time within the two or three core areas that are found in its home range.

Baboons inhabit the savanna, which is essentially a dry grassland with scattered groups of trees. The primary food of the baboon is grass, which makes up about 90 percent of its diet during the dry season. This is supplemented by other vegetable matter, such as seeds, flowers, and fruits. The baboon also consumes insects and some small reptiles and occasionally eats mammalian flesh.

Although food is easily found, the baboon must obtain much of this food on the ground, where danger from predators poses a real threat. The location of sleeping trees is extremely important for safety during sleeping hours, and the troop must reach the safety of these

troop A multimale group found among baboons and other primates.

core area Sections within the home range of a primate population that may contain a concentration of food, a source of water, and a good resting place or sleeping trees, and in which most of the troop's time will be spent.

---

[5] I. DeVore and K. R. L. Hall, "Baboon Ecology," and K. R. L. Hall and I. DeVore, "Baboon Social Behavior," in I. DeVore (ed.), *Primate Behavior: Field Studies of Monkeys and Apes* (New York: Holt, 1965), pp. 20–52, 53–110; S. A. Altmann and J. A. Altmann, *Baboon Ecology: African Field Research* (Chicago: University of Chicago Press, 1970); J. Altmann, *Baboon Mothers and Infants* (Cambridge, MA: Harvard University Press, 1980).

Figure 9.6 Baboon Troop Distribution Home ranges and core areas of nine baboon troops in Nairobi Park, Kenya. The troops vary in size from 12 to 87.

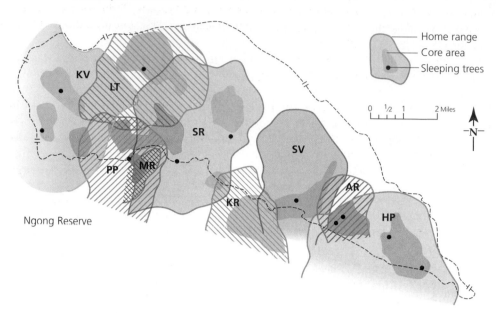

Boundary of Nairobi Park

Ngong Reserve

Home range
Core area
Sleeping trees

0 ½ 1 2 Miles

—N—

trees by nightfall. During the day, the troop depends on the collective protection of the large males, and it relies to an extent on the alarm calls of other animals to warn it of the proximity of predators.

Structure of the Baboon Troop Within the baboon troop, several distinct classes of individuals can be identified. The age-sex categories, similar to those of the gelada, include infants, juveniles, subadult males, adult females, and adult males (Figure 9.7 on pages 228–229).

The adult males play an especially important role in baboon social life, for the troop is dependent upon them for protection when foraging in the open. The baboons show a greater degree of sexual dimorphism than do other monkey species. The very long canine teeth of the male are deadly weapons even against the most powerful carnivores.

The adult males are arranged in a **dominance hierarchy.** While this hierarchy is usually thought of as strictly linear, the relative ranks of the lower-ranking males are not always sharply defined. Also, a pair of males may form an alliance that permits the pair to occupy a position in the system at a higher level than either could occupy alone. The existence of a hierarchy makes it possible for several aggressive adult males to coexist within the same troop.

The most dominant males are usually in good physical condition. They appear to be confident and aggressive, and they are able to attract the support of other males. The most dominant males also seem to be the offspring of the highest-ranking females. The presence of a high-ranking mother enables a male offspring to intimidate other animals higher in rank than himself but lower in rank than the mother, who is quick to back up her young in a conflict situation. Also, the offspring of high-ranking mothers associate more closely with the dominant males than do other offspring.

Once formed, the hierarchy is stable, although changes do occur, especially as members grow old and die. Young males entering the system cannot simply challenge the most dominant male for his position, for the dominant male is likely to be supported by other dominant males. Some high-ranking males are able to maintain their high rank even after they have become old and weak, with their canine teeth worn down to the gums.

Physical aggression is rare, and most aggression is expressed by gesturing rather than by actual fighting. Such agonistic behavior includes staring, raising the eyebrow to expose

dominance hierarchy A system of social ranking based on the relative dominance of the animals within a social group.

See the Online Learning Center for an Internet Activity on dominance and aggression.

the distinctively colored eyelid, slapping the ground, or jerking the head back and forth. When you next visit the zoo and observe a baboon male "yawning," do not feel that he is bored or tired. He is probably displaying his canine teeth as a threat gesture directed toward you, the observer (Figure 9.7(i)).

The dominance system operates in a variety of situations. A dominant male receives his preference of choice food and can monopolize sexually receptive females. A subordinate gives up his sitting place to a more dominant male, a behavior that is termed **displacement.** A subordinate male approaching a more dominant male will **present** his anal region to him and often will be **mounted** by him. The observer uses data on such behaviors as displacement, presenting, and mounting to gain a picture of the dominance system within the troop.

Adult females also form dominance hierarchies, although dominance interactions are not observed as often among females as they are among males. The rank of a female is determined largely by the rank of her mother, and she usually ranks just below her mother. The relative rank of a female baboon with respect to her mother, sisters, and daughters is more significant among females than among males, since a female spends most of her time in the company of family members.

In contrast to females, subadult males leave the troop of their birth and migrate to other troops. These migrations often cover long distances and expose the young males to much danger. This is a major reason why males have a higher death rate than females. As a result, adult males in a given troop have all migrated in from other troops and do not form close kinship bonds as do females.

The relative position of a female varies somewhat depending on whether she is sexually receptive to the male or is associated with a young infant. These changes are related, in part, to the interest of the adult male in receptive females and the concern of the male about the safety of the young. Females in either situation find themselves close to the dominant males, thus elevating their social rank in the troop. In addition, other females show great interest in infants, and they present to or groom the mother in an attempt to come into close association with the infant.

Sexual Relationships The reproductive cycle in the baboon female is about 35 days long. At approximately the midpoint of the cycle, a mature ovum moves from the ovary to the fallopian tube; this event is called ovulation. If sperm are present in the female reproductive tract around the time of ovulation, conception may occur.

Sexual activity in most primates occurs only around the time of ovulation. This period of sexual receptivity is termed estrus. Since sexual behavior functions to ensure the presence of sperm in the female reproductive tract at the time when an ovum is available for fertilization, sexual activity is normally restricted to the estrus period.

During most of her life, the female baboon is not sexually receptive to the male. She is receptive only during estrus, but estrus does not occur during pregnancy or **lactation** (nursing). In addition, sexual activity among many monkey species is restricted to a definite mating season, in which case no sexual activity may take place within a troop for many months of the year. It is therefore apparent that sexual activity is limited among baboons and may be absent for long periods.

Estrus in the savanna baboon is marked by certain physical and behavioral changes, and prominent among them is the swelling of the sexual skin. As the swelling enlarges, the female becomes receptive to the advances of the males. The swelling, in turn, serves as a signal to the males that the female is indeed in estrus. In most mammals, olfactory cues signal sexual receptivity. While this is true to a degree in primates, the prominence of a visual cue underscores the importance of vision to primates.

Early in a female's ovulation period, the more subordinate males make sexual advances; they are short in duration. As the female approaches the time of ovulation, she actively solicits sexual interest from the dominant males. The dominant male and female form a **consort pair,** and they will remain together for several hours to several days. Since the dominant males are copulating around the time of ovulation, they probably will father most of the young.

---

displacement The situation in which one animal can cause another to move away from food, a sitting place, and so on.

presenting A behavior involving a subordinate primate showing his or her anal region to a dominant animal.

mounting A behavioral pattern whereby one animal jumps on the posterior area of a second animal as a part of the act of copulation or as a part of dominance behavior.

lactation Act of female mammal producing milk.

consort pair A temporary alliance between a male and an estrus female.

(a)

Figure 9.7 The Baboons of Tarangire National Park, Tanzania
(a) Adult male and female and juvenile. (b) Adult male. (c) Juvenile. (d) Adult female. Note ischial callosity and sexual skin. (e) Female carrying infant. (f) Grooming cluster. Females grooming in background. (g) Mother grooming offspring. (h) Male showing aggressive behavior toward a female. (i) Canine threat. Note broken canine.

(b)

(c)

(d)

(e)

(f)

(g)

(h)

(i)

Figure 9.7 (Concluded)

Group Cohesion Unlike many mammalian societies, most monkey troops are not held together by herding on the part of the males. The members of the troop appear to prefer to remain with the group of their birth, among familiar individuals with which they have formed social bonds. Consequently, it is difficult to force a member to leave a troop or to introduce a new member into a troop.

Group cohesion appears to be based on the attraction of troop members to three categories of individuals: dominant males, infants, and old females. At rest, the dominant males are surrounded by females and young, which are attracted to their presence. This is especially true of very young animals and mothers of newborns. Infants also become focal points of troop interest. When a newborn appears in a troop, the female members attempt to look at it and handle it and they pay a great deal of attention to the mother.

Lengthy studies of some monkey species have demonstrated a bond that exists between mothers and their adult daughters. A basic subunit of the troop is an old female with her grown daughters and their respective offspring. When the troop is at rest, the females settle down in **grooming clusters** that are composed of several closely related females. As we have seen in other species, grooming symbolizes a closeness between individual primates.

Other close relationships exist among baboons. Barbara Smuts has recognized friendships that occur between adult males and females among the olive baboons in Kenya.[6] Female baboons are wary around the larger adult males, yet females form friendships with specific males in which the relationship is quite different. An adult female is relaxed around

grooming cluster A small group of closely related females that engage in a high degree of grooming.

---

[6] B. B. Smuts, *Sex and Friendship in Baboons* (New York: Aldine, 1985).

Figure 9.8 Baboon Friends An adult male sits with his best friend.

her male friend and often grooms him (Figure 9.8). A male friend appears to protect both the female and her offspring from aggression from other animals. The male may carry the infant as a way of inhibiting aggression against himself on the part of other males. When in estrus, the female is more likely to form a consort pair with her friend, which means that the infant being protected is very likely to be his offspring.

Social Behavior of the Chimpanzee

Perhaps the most extensively studied primate is the chimpanzee, *Pan troglodytes*. The behavior of the chimpanzee in its natural habitat is well known from several long-term studies. The longest-running study is that of the chimpanzees of the Gombe National Park in Uganda, which was begun in 1960 by Jane Goodall and continues today.[7] Other important studies are those in west Africa in the Taï National Park, Ivory Coast, and other sites in the Ivory Coast, Mali, Senegal, Guinea, and Liberia; in central Africa in the Congo and Gabon; and in east Africa at Mahale Mountains National Park, Tanzania, and other sites in Tanzania and Uganda. These studies not only provide us with a great deal of information about chimpanzee behavior but enable us to see the broad spectrum of behavior that differs from group to group on the basis of many factors, such as habitat and, most interesting, differences in traditions of learned behaviors.[8] The description presented here is based largely on the studies at Gombe National Park.

The chimpanzee is primarily arboreal. Its food is found principally in trees, and about 50 to 70 percent of the day is spent feeding and resting in trees. The animals sleep in trees, building new nests each evening. Yet most traveling between trees is done on the ground. Chimpanzees travel many miles each day, with the availability of food determining the length and direction of travel.

The diet of the chimpanzee is primarily vegetarian, including fruits, leaves, seeds, and bark. In addition, the animal occasionally eats insects, such as ants and termites, and sometimes hunts and eats meat. Six to seven hours each day are spent actively feeding.

Like that of the gibbon, gelada, and baboon, the life cycle of the chimpanzee can be divided into stages. The most notable difference between the life-cycle stages of chimpanzees and those of monkeys is that chimpanzees have a longer life span and mature more slowly. The stages in the life of chimpanzees are summarized in Table 9.2. Chimpanzees can live into their 50s.

Chimpanzee Social Organization The chimpanzee social unit is an ever-changing association of individuals that is perhaps best described as a fission-fusion type of society. In contrast to the savanna baboon troop,

Table 9.2 Stages in the Life of Chimpanzees

Stage	Male	Female
Infancy	0–5 years	0–5 years
Juvenile	5–7 years	5–7 years
Adolescence	8–15 years	8–14 years
Maturity	16–33 years	14–33 years
Old age	33 years–death	33 years–death

[7] J. van Lawick-Goodall, *In the Shadow of Man* (Boston: Houghton Mifflin, 1971); J. Goodall, *The Chimpanzees of Gombe: Patterns of Behavior* (Cambridge, MA: Belknap Press, 1986); J. Goodall, "Gombe: Highlights and Current Research," in P. G. Heltne and L. A. Marquardt (eds.), *Understanding Chimpanzees* (Cambridge, MA: Harvard University Press, 1989), pp. 2–21.

[8] J. C. Mitani, D. P. Watts, and M. N. Muller, "Recent Developments in the Study of Wild Chimpanzee Behavior," *Evolutionary Anthropology* 11 (2002), pp. 9–25.

Figure 9.9 Chimpanzee Family Unit

with its relative day-to-day stability and constancy, the chimpanzee **community** consists of a series of small units whose membership is constantly changing. A community consists of individuals which occupy a particular range and which, in the course of a year, have some contact with one another. The size of the community varies depending on births, deaths, and migrations. In 1980, the Gombe Stream community consisted of 42 individuals. Chimpanzee males patrol the boundaries of their communities, and vulnerable males from neighboring communities will be attacked and killed.

An individual chimpanzee may display a great deal of independence as he or she establishes new associations, sometimes on a day-by-day basis; or, on occasion, he or she may travel alone. The typical chimpanzee group usually contains five or fewer adults and adolescents in addition to juveniles and infants, but a number of different kinds of groups can form (Figure 9.9). The eight different kinds of groups are summarized in Table 9.3. Many variables are responsible for the changes in group composition, including the availability of food, the presence of infants, the presence of estrus females, and the invasion of a home territory by neighbors.

community Among chimpanzees, a large group that, through fission and fusion, is composed of a series of constantly changing smaller units, including the all-male party, family unit, nursery unit, consortship, and gathering.

Table 9.3 Composition of Chimpanzee Social Groups

Types of Social Groupings	Description
All-male party	Two or more adults and/or subadult males
Family unit	A mother and her offspring
Nursery unit	Two or more family units; may include unrelated childless females
Mixed party	One or more adult or adolescent males with one or more adult or adolescent females, with or without offspring
Sexual party	A mixed party in which one or more females are in estrus
Consortship	One adult male with one adult female with or without offspring
Gathering	A group including at least half the members of the community and at least half the adult males
Lone individual	A single animal

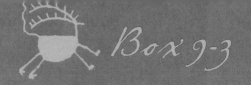

Box 9-3 **The Sexual Behavior of the Bonobo**

The bonobo (*Pan paniscus*) lives in a small, dense tropical forest in Zaire south of the Congo River (Figure 7.23). As early as 1929, the bonobo population had been reduced by the hunting practices of local peoples. Today, few natural groups exist and even fewer captive populations are available for study. Beginning in the 1970s, considerable research has been carried out on the remaining wild populations.

The social behavior of this ape differs in many ways from that of the chimpanzee and bears some interesting resemblances to human behavior. Bonobos live in communities of about 50 animals, but they spend most of their time in smaller groups of 2 to 10 individuals. Compared with chimpanzees, bonobos are more social and more peaceful and spend more of their time in groups.

Bonobo sexual behavior shows some features that are not found in other apes. Bonobos mate face to face (ventroventral) about a quarter of the time. This copulatory position is not found among chimpanzees and is rare among mammals in general; it is found primarily among whales, porpoises, and humans. Female bonobos exhibit a prolonged period of sexual receptivity, with copulations occurring during early phases of the estrus cycle.

Among chimpanzees, males usually initiate sexual behavior; among the bonobos, males and females initiate sexual behavior in an egalitarian manner. Finally, investigators have observed behavior, primarily among females, that has been labeled "homosexual"

Two adult female bonobos in a typical genitogenital rubbing position.

behavior. The behavior observed is described as genito-genital rubbing and is usually seen during feeding sessions or before or after heterosexual mating by one or both of the females.

Sources: B. G. Blout, "Issues in Bonobo *(Pan paniscus)* Sexual Behavior," *American Anthropologist* 92 (1990), pp. 702–714; T. Kano, "The Bonobo's Peaceable Kingdom," *Natural History,* November 1990, pp. 62–70; and R. L. Susman (ed.), *The Pygmy Chimpanzee* (New York: Plenum, 1984).

As with monkeys, social interactions between chimpanzee males can be described by the terms *dominance* and *submission.* Many instances of dominance interactions between two males have been described. For example, if two males go after the same fruit, the subordinate male holds back. Likewise, if a dominant male shows signs of aggression, the subordinate male responds with gestures of submission, such as reaching out to touch the dominant animal and crouching. Although clear-cut dominance interactions do take place, a rigid dominance hierarchy, such as that found among baboons, does not exist.

Much of chimpanzee aggression takes the form of gesture and display, and one animal can achieve dominance over the others by the fierceness of his display activity. One such male, Mike, rose from the bottom of the ladder to the top by incorporating into his display some of Goodall's kerosene cans. He would hurl the cans in front of him as he charged the other males, and they would quickly get out of his way and respond with a submissive gesture. Goodall sees Mike's behavior as evidence of his superior intelligence relative to that of the other chimpanzees in his community.

Goodall and other researchers have discovered that adult male chimpanzees are usually more sociable (interactive) than adult females. In contrast to the baboons, it is the female chimpanzee that usually migrates from one community to another. Thus, closely related males, often brothers, form a close bond within the community in contrast to the females, which often spend time alone with their offspring. Closely related males are more likely to travel and cooperate with one another. Goodall found that males groom each other about twice as long as males and females groom each other (Figure 7.22a). Males also display their affinity for each other by holding and embracing one another much more than they hold and embrace females.

The female reproductive cycle is evidenced in the chimpanzee by the periodic swelling of the sexual skin. The female may initiate sexual contact, but generally sexual behavior is a consequence of male courtship displays. The male leaps into a tree and for about a minute swings from branch to branch with the hair of his head, shoulders, and arms erect. As the male approaches the female, she crouches down in front of him. Consort pairs do not always form, and a female often will mate with several males.

The mother–infant bond is extremely close. At first, the infant is totally dependent on its mother and is constantly held and carried by her. Later, the infant sits upright on her back and begins to move away from her. Mothers frequently play with their babies, and the babies' playmates also include other young and adult animals. After the young stops riding on its mother's back, the juvenile chimpanzee associates more frequently with a play group. Play becomes less important when puberty is reached and the animal begins to enter adult life.

The Use of Tools Of special interest to anthropologists is chimpanzee use of tools. At one time anthropologists defined humans as *the* toolmaking animal. This definition has been revised since chimpanzees and other animals have been observed deliberately manufacturing tools. An example of the employment of tools in obtaining food is the termite stick used by the chimpanzees of Gombe National Park.

Termite feeding becomes an important activity at the beginning of the rainy season. For as many as nine weeks, chimpanzees spend one or two hours each day feeding on termites. This is the time when sexually mature termites grow wings in order to leave the termite mound to found new colonies. Passages within the mound are extended to its surface, but the openings to the outside are sealed over while the termites await ideal flying conditions.

The chimpanzee, upon locating a mound in this condition, scrapes away the thin seal over one of the passages. It then takes a **termite stick** and pokes it down the hole. After a moment, the tool is withdrawn with the termites hanging on it, ready to be licked off by the chimpanzee (Figure 9.10).

termite stick Tool made and used by chimpanzees for collecting termites for food.

In manufacturing a termite stick, the chimpanzee pays attention to the choice of material and the nature of the tool. The termite stick is fashioned from a grass stalk, twig, or vine, and it is usually less than 30.5 centimeters (12 inches) long. If a twig is too long to use, the chimpanzee breaks it to the right length. If a twig or vine is leafy, the animal strips it of its leaves before using it.

Young chimpanzees do not appear to have an interest in collecting termites. Goodall reports that while a mother chimpanzee spends hours termiting, the young become impatient

Figure 9.10 The Termite Stick
Chimpanzees insert a termite stick into a hole in a termite mound.

and attempt to get her to leave. The art of termiting and termite-stick making is learned. When young chimpanzees begin to show an interest, their first termite sticks are poorly made. They have difficulty inserting the stick into the hole and withdrawing it without losing the termites hanging on to it. Through watching their mothers, the young chimpanzees learn, although some are better students than others and are able to make better tools.

Goodall and others describe other examples of tool manufacture. For example, a chimpanzee will make a sponge by chewing a leaf and then use it to sponge up water. One chimpanzee was observed making a series of different tools to extract honey from a dead stump.

Many natural objects are used as tools: sticks as clubs, rocks as missiles, and leaves as towels. Nevertheless, although chimpanzees do make tools in the wild, their inventory of tools does not even begin to approach the complexity of human technology or the degree of human dependence on tools for survival.

Chimpanzees as Hunters Unlike most primates, chimpanzees eat meat. Chimpanzees have been observed killing and eating a variety of animals, including bushbucks, bushpigs, rodents, and young and adult monkeys such as the baboon, but the most common prey is the red colobus monkey. While chimpanzees simply may surprise an animal in the undergrowth and then kill and eat it, they also appear to hunt animals deliberately for food.

Hunting is essentially a male activity. Chimpanzee males hunt frequently, between 4 and 10 times per month, and about half their hunts are successful. The most successful hunts are those that involve groups of males, and the larger the hunting party, the higher the probability of success. Some prey, especially the red colobus monkey, will mount a defense by several males. It takes a large group of male chimpanzees to mob a group of male colobus monkeys. Also, for the hunt to be successful, all the escape routes must be cut off, and this requires several hunters. Actually, hunting is more successful in forests where the canopy is broken rather than continuous, since broken canopies provide far fewer escape routes.

After the kill, other chimpanzees arrive to share the meat. They form temporary groupings called **sharing clusters,** and most members of a cluster eat some of the prey (Figure 9.11). Observations show that the time spent in eating the meat varies from 1 hour and 40 minutes to more than 9 hours. The head seems to be the choicest part of the kill by chimpanzee standards. The animals enlarge the foramen magnum (the large hole in the base of the skull) with their teeth and fingers to get at the brain. They eat the soft tissue together with leaves.

See the Online Learning Center for an Internet Activity on chimpanzee hunting.

sharing cluster Among chimpanzees, a temporary group that forms after hunting to eat the meat.

Figure 9.11 A Sharing Cluster
A small group of male chimpanzees share a monkey carcass.

Some individuals, especially subadults and adult females, simply pick up pieces of meat that have been dropped by other individuals. Other animals tear off a section of a larger piece being consumed by another animal. Often, a particular animal requests meat by the characteristic gesture of holding a hand, open and palm up, under the possessor's chin while making characteristic vocalizations. Any chimpanzee may make such a request, but it is more often ignored than rewarded. However, most meat is shared among males.

Summary

We have just examined some aspects of the social behavior of four primate species: the gibbon, the gelada, the savanna baboon, and the chimpanzee. None of these species is typical, for each represents its own set of adaptations and adjustments to the environments in which it lives. Yet certain themes of behavior emerge from our studies. For example, agonistic behavior appears to be characteristic of each of our groups. In multimale groups, male dominance hierarchies tend to form, yet most dominance behavior is expressed by gesturing rather than actual fighting. Grooming behavior occurs frequently among primates as an expression of close social ties. The protection and care of the infant by the mother and other adults of the social unit also appear to be a universal theme of primate social behavior.

Key Terms

agonistic behavior, *223*
allogrooming, *220*
autogrooming, *219*
band, *224*
community, *231*
consort pair, *227*
core area, *225*
displacement, *227*
dominance hierarchy, *226*
female-bonded kin group, *215*
field study, *217*
fission-fusion society, *217*

grooming, *219*
grooming cluster, *229*
harem, *216*
herd, *224*
home range, *215*
lactation, *227*
monogamous pair, *215*
mounting, *227*
multimale group, *216*
one-male group, *216*
peripheralization, *221*
play, *220*

play group, *221*
polyandrous group, *216*
predation model, *214*
presenting, *227*
primatologist, *214*
provisioned colony, *218*
resource-defense model, *214*
sharing cluster, *234*
termite stick, *233*
territory, *221*
threat gesture, *221*
troop, *225*

Study Questions

1. Describe some of the different kinds of social groups found among primates.
2. What is grooming behavior? How does grooming affect the social relationships of the members of a primate group?
3. Gelada society is organized into a hierarchy of groups. Describe this organization and explain how it relates to changes in the environment.
4. Compare the use of space by the savanna baboon troop with that by the gibbon group. What differences in their habitats would help explain differences in their use of space?
5. Baboon troops are relatively stable and peaceful. Ingroup fighting is rare. How does the existence of the dominance hierarchy promote the stability of the group?

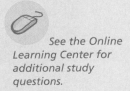

See the Online Learning Center for additional study questions.

6. Periods of sexual activity in primates are usually limited. Describe the sexual cycle of a female monkey and discuss how the period of receptivity in the female affects the social unit.

7. What is meant by a fission-fusion type of social organization? Describe the various types of social groups found among chimpanzees.

8. In the context of hunting, chimpanzees exhibit several behavioral traits that are usually not encountered in other social activities. What are some of these traits?

Critical Thinking Questions

1. Some people have compared nonhuman primates in a traditional zoo (with relatively small cages as opposed to large outdoor displays) to humans in jails. What conditions that a caged (or jailed) population is subjected to might make its behavior different from its typical behavior in the wild?

2. The size and organization of primate social units are the result of the interaction of a great many factors, both biological and environmental. Even within a single species we see different patterns emerging because of differences in the food supply or the presence of predators. Assume that you are looking at a species of African arboreal monkey that lives in moderately large social units. What would you predict would happen under the following circumstances, and why? (*a*) A foreign lumber company has clear-cut sections of the forest but has left "islands" of forest as a conservation method. (*b*) A human village has cleared areas at the periphery of a forest and has turned this area into farmland. (*c*) Global warming has raised the average temperature and lowered the rainfall over time. (*d*) A group of rebels has been using the forest as a staging area. (*e*) Big game hunters have moved into the area and have concentrated on shooting the large males as trophies.

3. In zoos infants must sometimes be taken away from mothers that do not care for them. They are then reared in a nursery. Why would you expect some primate mothers to fail at handling their infants? What do you think some of the problems would be in reintroducing nursery-reared chimpanzee children to the adult group?

Suggested Readings

Boesch, C., and H. Boesch-Achermann. *The Chimpanzees of the Taï Forest: Behavioural Ecology and Evolution.* New York: Oxford University Press, 2000. This is a comprehensive study of the chimpanzees of the Taï Forest in West Africa.

Fleagle, J. G., C. Jenson, and K. Reed (eds.). *Primate Communities.* Cambridge MA: Cambridge University Press, 1999. This book describes and compares communities of living primates from around the world.

Goodall, J. *The Chimpanzees of Gombe: Patterns of Behavior.* Cambridge, MA: Belknap Press, 1986. This book brings together the data gathered from over two decades of research on the chimpanzees of the Gombe.

Heltne, P. G., and L. A. Marquardt (eds.). *Understanding Chimpanzees.* Cambridge, MA: Harvard University Press, 1990. This volume includes 33 papers on chimpanzees.

Richard, A. F. *Primates in Nature.* New York: Freeman, 1985. This is an excellent introduction to the general topic of primate behavior. The author also discusses primate distribution, diet, and communication.

Smuts, B. B., D. L. Cheney, R. M. Seyfarth, R. W. Wrangham, and T. T. Struhsaker. *Primate Societies.* Chicago: University of Chicago Press, 1987. This is a collection of papers covering a variety of topics, including primate socioecology, communication, and intelligence.

Van Lawick-Goodall, J. *In the Shadow of Man.* Boston: Houghton Mifflin, 1971. This is a nontechnical discussion of the behavior of chimpanzees and the early experiences of Jane Goodall in the field.

Suggested Websites

The Bonobo Conservation Initiative:
www.bonobo.org

Budongo Forest Project:
www.budongo.org

Chimpanzee Zoo, a Program of the Jane Goodall Institute:
www.chimpanzee.org

East African Primate Research Sites:
www.indiana.edu/~primate/sites.html

Primate Info Net (Wisconsin Regional Primate Research Center):
http://pin.primate.wisc.edu/

Wild Chimpanzee Foundation:
www.wildchimps.org

Chapter 10

Human Behavior in Perspective

Anthropologist Richard Lee discusses a food plant with the San of southern Africa.

The human condition has led to an open adaptive system based on culture. Culture may have its own set of biological restraints. Mental patterns may be partially shaped by genes, but these can only set the outer limit on the range of possible human behavior. Actual behavior, in specific conditions, can never be understood without an understanding of the cultural and historical process that shapes it. The nature of human nature is essentially cultural. ●

—*Alexander Alland, Jr.*

Chapter Outline

Social Behavior of Human Foragers
The Structure of the Human Band
Age and Diet
Summary

Are Humans Unique?
Culture
Protoculture among Nonhuman Primates

Human Universals
Communication
Language
Skepticism about Ape-Language Studies
Intelligence in Nonhuman Primates
Summary

See the Online Learning Center for a chapter summary, chapter outline, and learning objectives.

After Reading This Chapter, You Should Be Able to Answer These Questions:

1. Although there is much variation, what are some of the general characteristics of a foraging group?
2. What is the grandmother hypothesis, and how does it help explain the high survival rate and the short interval between births that characterize human foragers in comparison to nonhumans?
3. Culture or cultural behavior has been defined in many ways. What are some of the common elements in definitions of cultural behavior?
4. What are the adaptive functions of cultural behavior?
5. What is protoculture? What are some examples?
6. Human behavior varies considerably from society to society. However, there are common elements in all societies. What are some of these human universals?
7. How is language defined? In what ways does language differ from other animal communication systems?
8. Have apes been taught to use language? What skepticism has been expressed about claims that they use language?
9. Does the term *intelligence* only apply to humans? Explain.
10. In general, what behaviors distinguish primates from nonprimates?

Many anthropologists have studied the structure of nonhuman primate society for clues to the origins of human society. They have assumed that human societies were derived from social systems similar to those of the living monkeys and apes. Yet the social systems of modern nonhuman primates also have been evolving through the millennia, and so they do not necessarily represent ancestral patterns.

In this chapter we will examine human hunters and gatherers. Evolutionary forces operating on early foraging societies shaped modern human behavior. As with modern nonhuman primates, modern foraging societies are not fossils; they have changed over time. However, comparative studies of all behavioral systems can provide insights into the limits and possibilities of human behavior and the evolution of that behavior (Chapters 13 through 15).

SOCIAL BEHAVIOR OF HUMAN FORAGERS

See the Online Learning Center for an Internet Activity on human foragers.

In the previous chapter, we examined the social behavior of four primates: the gibbon, the gelada, the baboon, and the chimpanzee. This chapter is a continuation of Chapter 9 and focuses on a fifth primate, the species *Homo sapiens.*

Most humans today live in farming and industrial societies. Yet farming is a recent human development, probably no older than 13,000 years, and industrialism is a product of the eighteenth century. When anthropologists compare humans with other animal societies, they turn to contemporary societies that practice a foraging (hunting-gathering) strategy.

All contemporary foraging societies have been affected by technologically more advanced peoples. In recent centuries, foragers have lived essentially in marginal areas where farming is not practical. Today these societies are rapidly changing as they increasingly come under the influence of neighboring agricultural or industrial peoples. However, although the percentage of the total number of contemporary humans they account for is small, there are still many foraging groups today with varying lifestyles.

The Structure of the Human Band

band Among humans, the basic social unit of hunting and gathering peoples, which typically consists of about 25 members.

The basic social unit of foraging peoples is the **band,** which typically contains about 25 members (about six families). Bands can, however, be much larger, and band membership is often quite variable (see Table 10.1). Small bands may join into larger, multiband units when food is plentiful.

Like the monkey troop and the chimpanzee community, the human band consists of many males and females—adults, subadults, juveniles, and infants. In contrast to the nonhuman primate societies we have surveyed, the adult members of the human band, for the most part, are involved in exclusive male–female relationships. The gibbon social unit consists of a single male and female with their immature offspring, but a third adult normally is not tolerated; within the human band, several male–female partnerships coexist (Figure 10.1).

Table 10.1 Group Size of Nomadic Foragers

San (South Africa)	25 (mean)
Hadza (Tanzania)	20–60
Birhor (India)	27 (mean)
Semang (Indonesia)	20–30
Andaman Islanders (Bay of Bengal)	30–50
Athapaskans (Alaska)	20–75
Copper Inuit (Canada)	About 15
Cape York (Australia)	10–50
Paliyan (India)	About 24

Source: Adapted from R. P. Kelly, *The Foraging Spectrum: Diversity in Hunter-Gatherer Lifeways* (Washington: Smithsonian Institution Press, 1995), p. 211.

(a)

(b)

(c)

Among the many factors related to permanent male–female bonding may be the fact that human females do not exhibit any conspicuous physical indication of estrus, and hence of ovulation, such as the swelling of the sexual skin in baboons and chimpanzees. The lack of estrus in the human female is a feature that clearly defines the human condition, yet anthropologists are not sure why this should be the case. Many hypotheses have been proposed as explanations.

One of the earlier ideas is that the lack of a clearly defined estrus in humans may be related to the development of bonds of cooperation among the males of the band and the lessening of male–male competition over estrus females. Since all females are potentially receptive throughout the year, males do not need to compete for the few females in the band who are near the time of ovulation.

More recent hypotheses center on the role of the female in human society. Some scholars see the lack of estrus as creating a situation where a male must copulate frequently with his mate in order to ensure fertilization. A male's close bonding with a female is also necessary to prevent the female from mating with other males. This increases the probability that a male bonded to a female is the father of her offspring.

On the other hand, other scholars see the hiding of ovulation as a strategy for permitting the female to copulate with a number of males, thus confusing the paternity issue. Therefore, several males would have a vested interest in the female's offspring, which would enhance the protection of the helpless infant. Students of primate behavior have observed that males often kill infants that are not their own; confused paternity would prevent such behavior.

Monkey troops and chimpanzee communities are, to a large degree, closed units. Relationships with adjacent groups are often hostile. Animals of one sex remain with the troop into which they were born for their entire lives and form close bonds with siblings of the same sex. Adolescent animals of the other sex, male baboons and female chimpanzees, for example, leave the group of their birth and migrate to other groups. Once the animal has left the unit of its birth, it no longer has any social relationships with its parents or siblings.

Human bands are similar to baboon troops and chimpanzee communities in that members of one sex, usually females in foraging societies, leave the group of their birth and join—in the case of humans, marry into—a neighboring group. What is different with humans is that they continue to maintain close ties throughout their lives with relatives in other bands. Thus, a woman lives in a band with her husband and children yet maintains close relationships with the bands of her parents and brothers, the band of her sister and her sister's husband, the band of her daughter and her daughter's husband, and so on. She visits these other bands, and may even live with another band for a period of time. As a result, important social and economic relationships are formed among these bands. Kinship is the basic means of social organization in which the relationships of the family extend throughout the society.

The extent of territoriality among hunter-gatherers varies. In many parts of the world, these people do not look upon an area of land as something owned by a particular group, even though some locations, such as particular water holes and sacred areas, are often traditionally regarded as being within the realm of a particular group. In the case of a water hole, other groups show their courtesy by asking permission to use it; this permission is seldom refused. Warfare as we know it in agricultural and industrial societies does not occur among hunter-gatherers, but formalized skirmishes or feuds do occur.

Dominance is a recurrent feature of male–male and female–female social relationships among nonhuman primates. Although there is considerable variation, the typical nature of male–male and female–female relationships in the human band is essentially egalitarian. Although individuals, usually males, may be considered leaders because of their skills and leadership abilities, hunting and gathering societies are generally characterized by cooperation, equal access to resources, and the absence of strict hierarchical systems. Cooperation is essential for successful hunting-gathering.

Age and Diet

As we previously discussed, the membership and organization of humans groups differ in many ways from those of chimpanzees and other primates. A feature of human groups is the presence of a relatively large number of elderly individuals, including females who have lived well beyond the end of their reproductive lives. Postreproductive females are relatively rare among other primates. In fact, very few chimpanzees ever make it to menopause.

Many factors influence the structure of human groups. In human foraging groups there is a sexual division of labor in which men and women have primary responsibilities for certain categories of food. Hunting is almost always a male activity, while females specialize in collecting vegetable food. A complete diet results from the sharing of the foods obtained by both sexes. Food sharing is especially important in humans since juveniles are incapable of procuring adequate food.

The foods consumed by chimpanzees are for the most part easy to obtain and usually can be consumed directly after their collection. (There are a few exceptions, such as the cracking of nuts by the chimpanzees of the Taï Forest.) In contrast to chimpanzees, a large proportion of vegetable foods consumed by humans are difficult to find, acquire, and process. However, such foods can be plentiful in otherwise harsh habitats and often are superior nutritionally. The !Kung San dig deep in the hard ground for large tubers and gather and process nuts; indigenous California peoples gathered acorns that are poisonous unless processed through a difficult, multistep process. Yet nuts in southern Africa and acorns in California are plentiful and are rich in proteins and oils that otherwise might be lacking in the diet.

One problem with a dependence on these types of foods is that young children are incapable of finding, obtaining, and processing much of the food they eat. Among chimpanzees and other mammals, the newly weaned offspring is able to find and eat on its own most of the food it needs. However, human offspring are dependent on adults for food for a lengthy period after weaning. The brain of a human infant is quite small at birth relative to body size. Consequently, the child is very helpless and is dependent on others for an extended time. It is largely because of the immaturity of the brain that humans exhibit an extended infancy and childhood.

Grandmothers and Children Although there are significant differences in the life histories of young humans and chimpanzees, the age at which the last child may be born in both human and chimpanzee females is about the same—45 years of age. This is followed by menopause, which in humans is variable but usually occurs during the fourth or fifth decade of life. It is difficult to estimate an age of menopause for chimpanzees because so few female chimpanzees ever reach menopause, but the meager data we have suggest an age similar to that of humans.

What we see from this last statement is the fact that while human females usually live decades beyond menopause, female apes do not. It is estimated that around 5 percent of chimpanzee females reach menopause, and those who do reach it survive only for a very short time. In human foraging societies about one-third of all adult females reach menopause, and they frequently live for several decades more.

This brings us back to a discussion of kin selection (Chapter 5). Generally speaking, the more adults that attend a child, the greater is the probability that he or she will survive into adulthood since the child will receive additional food and protection. In some animals, such as birds (Figure 5–9), a young female, having just reached puberty, will not mate for a year and will stay with her parents and help raise the next brood. Among humans, post-menopausal females serve the same purpose. This idea is known as the **grandmother hypothesis.**

The diet of human groups focuses on hard-to-get foods that often require processing. The infant is weaned at an age when it cannot possibly have the strength or skills to obtain and process food material and thus is dependent on an overburdened mother. However,

grandmother hypothesis
The idea that the presence of a postmenopausal female in human groups increases the survival rate of children and grandchildren.

the presence of a grandmother changes the picture. Several studies have demonstrated that postmenopausal women are especially efficient at locating and processing food. The mother and the postmenopausal grandmother together are able to provide an adequate diet for the helpless infant. This results in a higher survival rate of children and shorter intervals between the births of successive children, and therefore in a high inclusive fitness (Chapter 5).

A recent study analyzed extensive data from Canada and Finland from the eighteenth and nineteenth centuries.[1] Those data showed that in families where there was a postreproductive grandmother present, there was an increase in the number of children produced. In such families, women began producing children at an earlier age than was the case in families without a grandmother present. There was a shorter interval between the births of successive children and a significantly greater probability of the children surviving to adulthood.

It is frequently stated that foraging peoples have relatively short lives. Indeed, quoted life expectancies are low. However, life expectancy is an average length of life of all people who are born. It averages in not only the old people but also the infants and children who die young. Life expectancy has risen steadily not because older people are living longer (although this has become an important factor in industrial societies in the last few decades) but because fewer infants and children are dying. Once a person reaches adulthood, the probability of living to a relatively old age is pretty much the same in foraging societies as it is in other societies, and foraging communities contain a significant number of older individuals.

Summary

For a significant part of human evolution, people lived as foragers. The current human condition was shaped, in part, by evolutionary forces acting on hunting-gathering groups. The basic social unit of foragers is the band, which consists of adult males and females, subadults, juveniles, and infants. Bands are characterized by exclusive long-term male–female relationships. In human bands, women often leave the band of their birth and marry into a neighboring group. Continuing social relationships function to maintain social and economic relationships between bands. The degree of territoriality and intragroup fighting varies in different hunting-gathering societies. However, the concept of private ownership of land or warfare over territory is foreign to foragers.

Food sharing is an important feature of foraging societies in which males and females perform different economic tasks and pool and share their food. Much vegetable food is difficult to find and process, yet such foods are often plentiful in harsh habitats. Young children are not capable of locating and processing that food and are dependent on adults for a long period of time after they are weaned.

The last child may be borne by human and chimpanzee females at around 45 years of age. This is followed by menopause, which is prevalent in humans but rare in chimpanzees. Postmenopausal women are especially efficient at locating and processing food. Thus, in families in which a postmenopausal female is present, there is a higher survival rate of children, a shorter interval between successive births, and therefore a high inclusive fitness. This idea is known as the grandmother hypothesis.

---

[1] Mirkka Lahdenperä et al., "Fitness Benefits of Prolonged Post-Reproductive Lifespan in Women," *Nature* 428 (2004), pp. 178–181.

ARE HUMANS UNIQUE?

Throughout history, many philosophers have attempted to distance humans from other living organisms. Social scientists have searched for characteristics that mark humanity as unique. On the other hand, modern evolutionary biologists and sociobiologists see continuity in the living world. They see differences, especially differences in closely related species, as quantitative rather than qualitative. In this section, we will explore the question of the uniqueness of the human species.

Culture

The lives of nonhuman animals are controlled primarily by genes. Nevertheless, many animals have been extremely successful in their adaptations to a variety of habitats. Humans, on the other hand, are primarily dependent on learned behavior. In fact, the emergence of the human species and its continuance are dependent on what is called culture.

Culture is one of those words everyone uses but almost everyone uses differently. A person may say, "Those people belong to the Art Society; they certainly are cultured." To the anthropologist, there is one thing culture is not, and that is a level of sophistication or formal education. Culture is not something that one person has and another does not.

Anthropologists have defined culture in hundreds of ways. Fortunately, most definitions have points in common, and these points are included in our definition: Culture is learned, nonrandom, systematic behavior and knowledge and the products that are produced. Culture is transmitted from person to person and from generation to generation.

Culture Is Learned, Patterned, and Transmittable Culture is learned; it is not biologically determined or coded by the hereditary material. When termites emerge from their pupae, workers, soldiers, and queens crawl away to their respective predetermined tasks. They are innately equipped to brave the hazards of their environment. Humans do not function in this manner. A baby abandoned at birth has *no* chance of surviving by itself. In fact, most six- or seven-year-olds would probably perish if left to their own resources. Survival strategies, as well as other behaviors and thoughts, are learned from people such as parents, other relatives, teachers, peers, and friends.

Culture is patterned in two ways. First, it is nonrandom behavior and knowledge; that is, specific actions or thoughts are usually the same in similar situations. For example, in Western societies, when two people meet, they usually shake hands. Second, it is patterned in the sense that it is systematic; that is, one aspect of behavior or thought is related to all others. Taken together, they form a system.

A **system** is a collection of parts that are interrelated so that a change in any one part brings about specifiable changes in the others. For example, in eastern Europe, the change from a communist government to a more democratic one has had repercussions for the educational, economic, moral, and social elements of society. In addition, a group's cultural traditions and the way in which its members relate to one another reflect certain underlying principles about the basic characteristics of people and nature.

Culture is transmittable; it spreads. Information is learned, stored in the cortex of the brain, interpreted, and then transmitted to other people. Knowledge builds on information from past generations. In societies with writing, each generation can continue to influence future generations indefinitely. Therefore, a particular culture is the result of its history as well as its present state. Although there is now evidence that certain nonhuman animals also possess some ability to pass on acquired behavior, in no other animal has this ability evolved to the same degree as it has in humans.

Coping with Change Over time, nonhuman animals usually adapt to changing environments through changes in their physical form. Humans usually adjust to a change in environment with changes in behavior or knowledge (including beliefs, values, and customs).

Of course, physical changes have been important in human evolution, and they account for why we no longer look like our distant ancestors. The size and proportions of the human

system A collection of parts that are interrelated so that a change in any one part brings about specifiable changes in the others.

body and the size and structure of the brain have changed over time. These changes have led to upright posture, which freed the hands from locomotor function; they also have led to the evolution of a brain that is capable of mental functions at a higher level than other animals' brains.

Such changes allow for today's cultural potential. Humans can sometimes substitute cultural innovation for biological alteration. If you were to transplant a group of temperate-zone nonhuman animals to an arctic environment, they might all die. On the other hand, those that were somewhat different from the average, possibly by having more fur, might survive. If you put humans into the same environment, they might make systematic changes in their culture that would lead to appropriate technological and social innovations; they might build an igloo, start a fire, or even kill a polar bear to make a coat.

Humans adapt biologically to changing environments as well as adjusting to environments through the human biological potential for culture. This is one reason why the human species is so widely dispersed. Physical features do not need to change for humans to move into a new environment. Instead, human biological potentials allow for behavioral flexibility, which results in an enormous range of adjustments (Chapter 16).

Protoculture among Nonhuman Primates

Humans have been described as cultural animals who cope with the conditions of their niches largely by means of cultural adjustments. Primatologists are becoming increasingly aware of the fact that not only can nonhuman primates adjust to new situations by means of learned behavior, but also many behavioral patterns are passed down from generation to generation as a type of social tradition. Those who feel that the transmission of learned behavior is common among these forms believe that primates do have a **protoculture;** that is, they are characterized by the simplest, most basic aspects of culture.

protoculture The simplest or beginning aspects of culture as seen in some nonhuman primates.

Protoculture in Monkeys Many behavioral patterns in monkeys are certainly genetically determined. Laboratory studies, in which animals have been reared away from the social unit or reared by a human substitute mother, have shown that certain vocalizations and dominance gestures occur in the isolated monkey. Since the animal had no contact with its natural mother or troop, such similarities between isolated and troop-reared behavior must be interpreted as being genetically determined.

On the other hand, many behavioral patterns are apparently learned. One infant raised with its natural mother never learned to use its cheek pouches for food; its mother never used hers. Later the animal was placed in a cage with another monkey. The second monkey would rush to the food and place much of it in his cheek pouches, leaving little for the first. Very quickly, however, the original animal learned the proper use of the pouches.

Examples of behavioral changes occurred on Koshima Island, Japan, where primatologists introduced sweet potatoes as a food. Normally, macaques rub dirt off food with their hands, but one day a young female took her sweet potato to a stream and washed it (Figure 10.2). Apparently providing greater efficiency in dirt removal, the pattern of sweet-potato washing soon spread to the other members of her play group and then to the mothers of these young monkeys. Four years later, 80 to 90 percent of the monkeys in the troop were washing sweet potatoes. Later, some monkeys began to wash their sweet potatoes in salt water, the salt probably improving the flavor. Often they carried the sweet potatoes a short distance to the shore, and in carrying sweet potatoes, the animals moved bipedally

Figure 10.2 The Japanese Macaque Sweet-potato washing.

Box 10-1

Chimpanzee Culture

In 1948, Alfred Louis Kroeber wrote: "Culture is the special and exclusive product of men, and is their distinctive quality in the cosmos . . ."[1] It wasn't until the 1960s that students of chimpanzee behavior, particularly Jane Goodall, began to describe behaviors among wild chimpanzees that could be labeled "protoculturel" or "culture."

Today primatologists have accumulated data from seven long-term studies of chimpanzees in their natural habitat that represent an accumulation of 151 years of field observation. Analysis of this accumulated field data has revealed a total of 65 distinctive behavioral categories. While some of these behaviors are found in all chimpanzee populations and therefore may be the result of genetic factors, many behaviors are found in some populations and not in others. Where their absence in some populations cannot be explained by ecological factors, it can be assumed that they represent learned traditions. These include using a wood or stone hammer on a wood or stone anvil to crack nuts, termite fishing, using a probe to extract ants, using large leaves as seats, and using leaves to clean the body. Some observers of chimpanzee behavior label these behaviors as cultural (Figures 7.22b and 9.10).

[1] A. L. Kroeber, *Anthropology* (New York: Harcourt, Brace, 1948), pp. 8–9.

Sources: A. Whiten et al., "Culture in Chimpanzees," *Nature* 399 (1999), pp. 682–685; A. Whiten and C. Boesch, "The Cultures of Chimpanzees," *Scientific American*, January 2001, pp. 60–67.

(Figure 10.3). This later development is of interest to students of human evolution since erect bipedalism evolved in the earliest hominins as a dominant form of locomotion.

On Koshima Island, the investigators saw the increased use of this locomotor pattern in response to a new learned behavioral pattern: washing sweet potatoes in salt water. Conceivably, if a behavioral pattern like this had some selective advantage, animals biologically more capable of bipedalism might contribute more genes to the gene pool of the next generation. At any rate, the behavioral changes in the Japanese macaque at least suggest how changes in the frequency of an anatomical trait might result from a change in a behavioral pattern.

See the Online Learning Center for an Internet Activity on protoculture in chimpanzees.

Protoculture in Chimpanzees Protocultural behavior is also present in the chimpanzee. Some of this learned behavior was discussed in Chapter 9 in relation to the use of termite sticks by young chimpanzees and the use of human-made objects to obtain status. In addition, young chimpanzees learn a great deal about chimpanzee society in their play groups. For instance, they learn who the dominant adult females are by the actions taken against them if they get into a fight with another youngster. Chimpanzee females also appear to learn how to be effective mothers from watching their own mothers and taking care of their siblings. Jane Goodall reports that a young female who took care of her orphaned brother seemed to be a more experienced mother when she had her first offspring than were other first-time mothers (Box 10-1).

The point of this discussion is that the beginning of cultural behavior can be seen in monkey and ape societies. Continuing investigations into these phenomena can aid the physical anthropologist in understanding the possible ways in which culture developed in humans.

Human Universals

Many anthropologists, probably most of them, are skeptical of statements that generalize about what all peoples do. But are there not generalizations of that sort that really do hold for the wide array of human populations? There are—and not enough has been said about them.

Figure 10.3 The Japanese Macaque Bipedal transport of sweet potato to the ocean for washing.

This skepticism and neglect of human universals is the entrenched legacy of an era of particularism in which the observation that something *doesn't* occur among the Bongo Bongo counted as a major contribution of anthropology. The truth of the matter is, however, that anthropologists probably always take for granted an indefinite collection of traits that add up to a very complex view of human nature.[2]

Just as all baboons share many behavioral characteristics, all humans share certain behavioral potentials. For instance, except for individuals profoundly affected by disease or injury, all humans can learn a language—baboons cannot. The potential for learning language, and other characteristics of human nature, evolved as a result of evolutionary and cultural forces acting on these behaviors. Just as there is a "prewired" genetic potential for learning language, it is equally true that a specific language, such as English, Chinese, or Navaho, is learned by exposure to an environment in which that language is spoken (or signed). There is no biological propensity to learn one specific language over another. These facts are relatively noncontroversial.

The Sexual Division of Labor The general relationship between nature (biological destiny) and nurture (learning) concerning language abilities may be relatively clear. However, what about other behaviors, say, the division of labor between males and females? Is this behavior a result of nature or nurture or some combination of both factors?

One way this issue has been approached is by asking questions such as this: Are women as a category universally subordinate to men as a category? However, this question is perhaps too loaded with emotion to deal with objectively. Also, a scientific explanation depends on precisely defined concepts, but it is hard to define *subordinate*. James Peoples and Garrick Bailey write:[3]

> So who is right? Are women subordinate to men in all societies or not? Certainly, ethnographers have been biased—but does this bias explain their consistent reports of female subordination? Certainly, the Iroquois and other peoples demonstrate that women in some societies have achieved considerable control over their own lives and even over public decision making—but do such cases represent *full equality* of males and females? Indeed, would we know "full gender equality" if we saw it in a society? What would it look like? Would men and women have to carry out the same kinds of economic tasks before we could say they are equal? Is monogamy necessary, or can a society be polygynous and still qualify? Shall we require that women occupy 50 percent of all leadership roles before we say they have equal rights? How should family life be organized before we can say that husbands in culture X do not dominate their wives?

So perhaps the question about the relationship between the sexes should be phrased something like this: Are there biological differences between the sexes that universally affect behavior in a consistent manner? Besides the most apparent primary sexual differences between men and women, other biologically controlled differences exist. The average man is stronger (more muscular) than the average woman. Many women seem to experience a decrease in fertility if they engage in very heavy exercise; men are not affected in this way. Women not only give birth, but in all societies they care for infants and young children more than men do.

The character of each culture determines the precise way in which the above biological facts are interpreted. For instance, in modern industrial societies, in which machines often substitute for human muscle power and in which the birth rate is low, biological differences between men and women have fewer social consequences than they do in nonindustrial societies. Yet these biological factors are at least partially responsible for the male–female division-of-labor specializations found in societies throughout the world. Hunting, trapping, mining, lumbering, butchering, building boats, and working with stone, bone, shell, and metal seem to

---

[2] D. E. Brown, *Human Universals* (New York: McGraw-Hill, 1991), p.1. Reprinted with permission of The McGraw-Hill Companies.

[3] From *Humanity: An Introduction to Cultural Anthropology* (with Info Trac), 6th edition by Peoples/Bailey. © 2003. Reprinted with permission of Wadsworth, a division of Thomson Learning: www.thomsonrights.com. Fax 800-730-2215.

be overwhelmingly male activities in all societies studied. Gathering wild plant foods, shellfish, and mollusks; collecting resources for use as fuel; fetching water; making clothing; weaving; and taking care of small animals are predominantly female tasks.

There are exceptions to this division of labor. As many as 85 percent of Agta woman hunt. The Agta are a small-stature foraging people of the Philippines. The women hunt the same animals as do men, including wild pigs, deer, and monkeys (Figure 10.4). They hunt while menstruating and when they have nursing children.

Other Human Universals We have been discussing sexual differences in task specialization as an example of a human universal. Donald E. Brown lists hundreds of other possible human universals.[4] There are different degrees of consensus on the universality of the items he lists, but various anthropologists, psychologists, sociologists, sociobiologists, and others have suggested each item as a candidate for universal status.

Some researchers believe that all human societies change through time, have some concept of privacy, have some form of art, practice body ornamentation, distinguish between good and bad behavior (have a moral system), make jokes, have languages that conform to a universal set of grammatical rules, display universal stages of language acquisition, distinguish between general and particular, display ethnocentrism, solve some problems by trial and error, use tools, have kinship terms, have rules about sexual behavior, are aware of the individual self as distinct from others, have a social structure influenced by accumulated information, show collective decision making, have leadership, have some form of play and games, have a world view, and have children who show a fear of strangers. Some people also believe that individuals within all societies have the potential for aggression, hope, anxiety, lying, and feeling loss and grief in respect to the death of close kin; have a sense of duty; and feel boredom.

Figure 10.4 Female Hunter among the Agta of the Northern Philippines

Humans share some of these characteristics with other animals. Chimpanzees make a limited number of tools, and some researchers suggest that they might feel grief when certain other chimpanzees, such as a mother, die. Yet the list of human universals taken as a whole describes only one animal—*Homo sapiens*.

Communication

In his book *Language, Thought and Reality,* the linguist Benjamin Lee Whorf claims, "Speech is the best show man puts on."[5] Indeed, anthropologists consider language to be such an important aspect of our nature that an entire branch of anthropology—anthropological linguistics—is devoted to its description and analysis. The understanding of linguistic behavior is important to the anthropologist's understanding of human adjustments, adaptations, and adaptability.

Language is but one means of communication. **Communication** is a very general term that, in its broadest application, simply means that some stimulus or message is transmitted and received. On more specific levels, communication means different things to the

communication Occurs when some stimulus or message is transmitted and received; in relation to animal life, when one animal transmits information to another animal.

[4] D. E. Brown, *Human Universals,* pp. 157–201.

[5] B. L. Whorf, in J. B. Carroll (ed.), *Language, Thought and Reality: Selected Writings of Benjamin Lee Whorf* (Cambridge, MA: New York Technology Press and Wiley, 1956), p. 249.

physicist, mathematician, engineer, and behavioral scientist. We are concerned with its usage in relation to animals; in this context, communication means that one animal transmits information to another animal. This information can simply convey the presence of the animal, or it can indicate such things as dominance, fear, hunger, and sexual receptiveness. Communication does not necessarily imply thought, but as neurological complexity evolves, so do the methods, mechanisms, and potential of communication.

Methods of Primate Communication Social animals are constantly communicating with one another; even the spatial positions they assume in relation to one another can be forms of communication. Primates communicate through olfactory, tactile, visual, and auditory signals.

Compared with other mammals, the primates, in general, have a reduced olfactory sense. The sense of smell is much more important to prosimians and New World monkeys than to Old World monkeys and apes. Some prosimians, such as the ring-tailed lemur, have specialized skin glands that excrete odoriferous substances. The animal uses this material, along with urine and feces, to mark off territory. Many New World monkeys use the olfactory sense also and, like prosimians, have permanent scent glands.

Although the sense of smell is less important in Old World monkeys and apes, it still serves as a means of communication. Male rhesus monkeys, for example, recognize an estrus female by specific odors originating in the vagina. The importance of deodorants and perfumes emphasizes the role played by olfactory signals in human communication.

The tactile sense is likewise important in primates, and they spend long periods of time touching one another. Grooming, for example, functions not only to remove dirt and parasites from the fur but to communicate affection. Grooming is found among all categories of individuals: between adult males, between a male and an estrus female, and between a female and her infant. The close physical contact between a mother and her infant appears to be essential for the normal development of the individual.

Visual communication is of great importance to primates. The positioning of animals in relationship to one another conveys information about dominance, feeding, sexual behavior, and attitude, and general body posture can signal tension or relaxation. Motivational researchers have concluded that a political candidate, a newscaster, or another person talking to a large group should stand slightly sideways rather than face directly ahead. The latter position, supposedly taken as a dominance display, is said to make an audience nervous.

In addition to the positioning of the body, facial gestures are used extensively among primates to convey information. Various examples of gestures were given in the discussion of the social behavior of the baboon in Chapter 9.

Vocal Communication One thing is certain: Primates, including people, do not have to open their mouths to communicate a wide range of information. Many primate sounds are nonvocal. For instance, the gorilla beats its chest, shakes branches, or strikes the ground to communicate frustration. Likewise, a bit of silence is often as meaningful as noise itself and often indicates danger. Anyone who has been to a zoo, however, and heard the vocalizations of the siamangs or, for that matter, anyone who has visited a schoolyard knows that primates not only vocalize but do so with a great deal of noise. Some arboreal monkeys and apes are among the loudest and most vocal of mammals.

discrete A characteristic of language. Signals, such as words, represent discrete entities or experiences; a discrete signal does not blend with other signals.

call system A system of vocalized sounds that grade one into another.

Nonhuman primates produce a number of vocalized sounds. In prosimians and some monkeys, these sounds tend to be **discrete.** A discrete signal is one that does not blend with other signals; it is individually distinct. Nonhuman anthropoids also produce some discrete calls, but other calls grade into one another, forming a **call system.** This blending makes it difficult to estimate the number of calls, or specific messages, produced, but the number of calls for most species seems to average between 10 and 20.

Although the meaning of different sounds varies a great deal from one species to another, some generalizations can be made. Barking sounds serve as alarm signals among gorillas, chimpanzees, baboons, rhesus monkeys, and langurs. Screeching and screaming sounds often signal distress; growling indicates annoyance. Animals produce different types of grunts while moving around, seemingly to maintain contact between the animals in a group.

One animal can produce sounds that direct the attention of another toward specific objects. Other sounds convey quantitative information, specify a particular type of behavior that should be used, or initiate a whole sequence of related behaviors. Primates also have a great ability to inform one another about their moods at particular moments through subtle changes in their vocalizations.

Language

Nonhuman animals, especially other primates, share many of the features of language. Nevertheless, several characteristics of language are, as far as we know, unique. Other features are developed to a higher degree in language than in any other communication system.

Language is both open and discrete. **Openness** refers to the expansionary nature of language, which enables people to coin new labels for new concepts and objects. The hunter-gatherer who sees an airplane for the first time can attach a designation to it; in the same manner, a biologist who discovers a new species can give it a name.

Most nonhuman primate signals are not discrete. The gibbon who is content one moment and frightened the next simply grades one call into the next. Recently, research has shown that a limited number of nonhuman anthropoid signals do seem to be discrete, such as the two very acoustically different alarm calls of vervet monkeys, one that signals the initial approach of a neighboring group and another that signals a more aggressive approach. However, all the messages of language are discrete. Through language, the human can say, "I am content" or "I am frightened," delivering a distinct message that never blends with any other message.

The discrete units of language are **arbitrary.** A word, for example, has no real connection to the thing to which it refers. There is nothing about a pen that is suggested by the sound "pen." If we all agreed, a pen could be called a "table." Even though the potential for sound formation is innate, the meanings of the arbitrary elements of a language must be learned.

One of the most important and useful things about language is **displacement,** which is the ability to communicate about events at times and places distant from those of their occurrence. Displacement enables a person to talk and think about things not directly in front of him or her. This is the characteristic of language that makes learning from the past, as well as planning for the future, possible. Displacement is to a large degree responsible for creativity, imagination, and illusion.

For a communication system to be called language, it must have a lexicon and a grammar. A **lexicon** is a vocabulary, a set of meaningful units such as words (or hand positions in sign language). A **grammar** is a set of rules used to make up these words and then to combine them into larger utterances such as phrases and sentences. Most rules of a grammar are unconsciously known. If a system has a lexicon and a grammar, it need not be oral to be considered language. Thus, a system such as American Sign Language (ASL) is considered a language, since specific rules govern the combination of the nonvocal signs used.

Symbolic Behavior in Apes As research on primates continues, the uniqueness of humankind diminishes. Research involving several apes—including the chimpanzee Washoe, the bonobo Kanzi, and the gorilla Koko—has cast doubt on the claim that language is exclusively a human characteristic.

The chimpanzee's larynx (voice box) is higher in the throat than is the human larynx. This and other anatomical features of the chimpanzee prevent the animal from producing sounds with the qualities of human speech sounds. Also, chimpanzees do not show development of **Broca's area** of the brain, the area that in humans controls the production of speech (Figure 14.28). However, recent research suggests that chimpanzees may have limited abilities to understand language. For this reason, systems of nonvocal communication, which have a lexicon and a grammar as well as the design features of language not related to speech, have been tried in experimental situations. Washoe and Koko have been taught to use systems of signs based on the American Sign Language for the deaf, and Kanzi has been taught to use a computer that employs arbitrary symbols to represent words or concepts.

By 1991, Washoe had a signing vocabulary of 240 signs (Figure 10.5a). In 1992, Washoe and her chimpanzee family were moved to a new research facility at Central

openness A characteristic of language that refers to the expansionary nature of language, which enables people to coin new labels for new concepts and objects.

arbitrary A characteristic of language. A word or another unit of sound has no real connection to the thing to which it refers; the meanings of the arbitrary elements of a language must be learned.

displacement A characteristic of language. The ability to communicate about events at times and places other than when and where they occur; enables a person to talk and think about things not directly in front of him or her.

lexicon In linguistics, the total number of meaningful units (such as words and affixes) of a language.

grammar A set of rules used to make up words and then to combine the words into larger utterances such as phrases and sentences.

See the Online Learning Center for an Internet Activity on chimpanzee language studies.

Broca's area A small area in the human brain that controls the production of speech sounds.

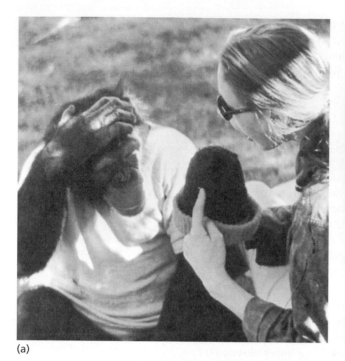

(a)

(b)

Figure 10.5 Attempts at Teaching Apes Language (a) Washoe uses the ASL sign for "hat." (b) Kanzi communicates by pressing symbols on keyboards. (c) Koko is shown making the sign "smoke" for her cat Smoky.

(c)

Washington University. They are participating in many projects, including the study of chimp-to-chimp signing.

In the late 1980s, reports of a young bonobo named Kanzi began to appear. Although raised around chimpanzees who were being taught to use a computer, Kanzi had no training in this skill (Figure 10.5b). The computer had 250 symbols on a keyboard. Each symbol, called a **lexigram**, represented a word. Investigators at the Yerkes Regional Primate Center in Georgia were amazed when Kanzi spontaneously began to use the computer and "asked" to be chased. Kanzi also seems to understand spoken language and responds correctly to certain oral commands.

Some of those who work with Kanzi maintain that he has a simple understanding of grammar. For instance, if a chimpanzee named Matata initiated an action, Kanzi would describe the incident by putting the verbal aspect second—"Matata bite." However, if Matata was acted upon, the verb would go first, as in "grabbed Matata," meaning someone grabbed

lexigram A symbol that represents a word.

Matata. By 1991, Kanzi's custodians said the six-year-old bonobo knew 90 lexigrams and understood 200 spoken words and 650 sentences.

Gorillas were once thought to be less intelligent than chimpanzees, but this is being challenged by the work with the gorilla Koko (Figure 10.5c). By the age of seven years, Koko had an active vocabulary of 375 ASL signs, many more than Washoe or other chimpanzees had acquired at any age. According to her teachers, Koko identifies herself in the mirror and in photographs and invents words and phrases. In 1998, Koko went online in what her handlers called the first interspecies chat over the Internet. Through her tutor Francine Patterson, Koko answered questions posed by humans online. These and other behaviors indicate an intelligence far beyond what was expected before studies of the language ability of apes began.

Skepticism about Ape-Language Studies

"It's about as likely that an ape will prove to have a language ability as that there is an island somewhere with a species of flightless birds waiting for human beings to teach them to fly."[6] This quote from the linguist Noam Chomsky is representative of the general attitude of most linguists and cognitive psychologists toward the language potentials of nonhuman animals.

For a communication system to be called a language, it must have a grammar. A grammar is a set of specific rules that direct the communicator in combining various elements of a language. For instance, in English, modifiers almost always go before what they modify. For example, we say "the big ball rolled down the street" or "a yellow rose was on the vine," not "the ball big rolled down the street" or "a rose yellow was on the vine." Most three-year-old English-speaking children easily learn to put the modifier in front of the word being modified (other languages may have different rules). Yet with the possible exception of Kanzi, none of the apes have even been able to demonstrate an understanding of even the simplest principle of grammar.

However, this is not to say that nonhumans, especially the apes, do not have some of the potentials that are precursors to language. We might call this protolanguage, or as Chomsky and his colleagues label it, the **faculty of language in the broad sense (FLB)**. The FLB includes the motor and neurological systems that allow us to interact with the world around us and the physical and neurological systems that allow us to create sounds and movements that have the potential to communicate. Some nonhuman animals have neurological systems that store knowledge about the world and allow an animal to form a plan of action on the basis of that knowledge. These animals can also act on those plans, as occurs when a chimpanzee in the wild makes a tool to exploit a food source or when a vervet monkey recognizes the dominance ranking of other monkeys and acts accordingly. (The latter is discussed in more detail later in this chapter.) Some psychologists even think that chimpanzees can infer from the actions of others what a person or another chimpanzee is thinking.

Although nonhumans have a large range of intellectual and communicative abilities, some of which are closer to human abilities than others, they still cannot be said to have the potential for language in the full sense of that word. In this regard, Chomsky and his colleagues believe that there are characteristics of language that are unique to humans. They call the unique characteristics of language the **faculty of language in the narrow sense (FLN).** The most important element of the FLN is the idea that all languages are rule-governed (have grammar), and this feature is mostly or completely missing in nonhuman communication.

A primary feature of grammar that is unique to language is called **recursion.** Recursion is the process by which any linguistic unit can be made longer by embedding another unit in it. I can say, "I am going to the store." Or I can say, "My wife and I are going to the store." Or I can say, "My wife, my children, and I are going to the store." In fact, I can add elements to the first sentence endlessly. Notice that I can also add elements to the end of the sentence: "My wife, my children, and I are going to the store, and then we are going

faculty of language in the broad sense (FLB) Shared communicative capabilities of humans and some nonhumans that include motor and neurological systems that allow interaction with the world and physical and neurological systems that allow creation of sounds and movements that have the potential to communicate.

faculty of language in the narrow sense (FLN) Characteristics of language that are unique to humans, such as recursion.

recursion The process by which any linguistics unit can be made longer by embedding another unit in it.

---

6 "Are Those Apes Really Talking?" *Time* (March 10, 1980), pp. 50, 57.

Box 10-2 Bird and Human Communication: Alex the Parrot and the FOXP2 Gene

Alex is an African grey parrot that Irene Pepperberg has been studying for more than 25 years. She believes that Alex does more than just mimic human language and that he is capable of thinking, which includes reasoning and making calculated choices among alternatives. For instance, if Alex is asked to name the color of corn, he replies "yellow" even though he can vocalize the names of six other colors. According to Pepperberg, he can identify 50 objects, count objects up to the number 6, and identify several shapes. She says that Alex can also do mental tasks such as deciding whether something is bigger, smaller, or the same size as something else. Pepperberg does not call Alex's vocalizations language, but she believes that Alex is doing some of the mental tasks made possible in humans by language.[1]

In 2004 researchers identified a gene, called FOXP2, that is present in both birds and humans. This regulatory gene plays a role in the vocalization of both types of animals. Although a mutation in this gene does not alter motor function, people with the mutation lose their ability to understand complex language, pronounce words properly, and string words into grammatical sentences. Researchers determined that in birds that vocalize, the gene "switches on" just before a bird begins to change a song. The researchers hypothesize that the gene allows learning flexibility that permits the bird to imitate the sounds it hears. The study of the Fox2P gene may shed light on the evolution of vocal learning in humans.[2]

[1] D. Smith, "A Thinking Bird, or Just Another Birdbrain?" *The New York Times* (October 9, 1999), section A, p. 1.

[2] S. Haesler et al., "FOXP2 Expression in Avian Vocal Learners and Non-Learners," *Journal of Neuroscience* 24 (2004), pp. 3164–3175.

---

to a movie." The recursiveness of language allows people to compare, analyze, and combine thoughts in a limitless way. To Chomsky and others, the recursive property of language is the main thing that makes language unique to humans.[7]

Herbert Terrace studied a chimpanzee that he named Nim Chimpsky, a play on Noam Chomsky's name. Additional criticisms of ape-language studies are as follows: Nim's utterances did not increase in length over time; 88 percent of Nim's utterances followed the researcher's utterances; Nim's responses were not usually spontaneous; much of the ape's responses were imitations of the human utterances; Nim rarely added information to a "conversation"; and the ape had no concept of turn taking.

Thus, to Terrace, what Nim (and the other apes) was doing did not look like language. Many of the same detractors of ape-language studies have been critical of people who have equated Alex the parrot's vocalizations to language (Box 10-2). For instance, Herbert Terrace believes that Alex's responses are conditioned responses that only minimally involve anything close to thinking. Alex responds to an immediate external stimulus. Humans respond in that way too, but they also respond to mental constructs that exist only in the mind. This displacement is absent in Alex.

Intelligence in Nonhuman Primates

See the Online Learning Center for an Internet Activity on primate intelligence.

The concept of intelligence is an elusive one. Social scientists cannot even form a consensus on the nature of intelligence in humans. Most psychologists see intelligence generally as a capacity to deal effectively with the environment by acting rationally and purposefully. The concept is more problematic when related to nonhumans. For instance, apes have learned to use American Sign Language to some degree. The fact that they can use arbitrary and discrete symbols in an open way to convey displaced information suggests a continuity with human thought processes. Recent research on monkeys also displays this continuity. Does this mean that they are acting rationally or purposefully? Some researchers say yes; others say their actions are simply conditioned by their human handlers.

---

[7] See M. D. Hauser, N. Chomsky, and W. Tecumseh Fitch, "The Faculty of Language: What Is It, Who Has It, and How Did It Evolve," *Science* 298 (2002), pp.1569–1579.

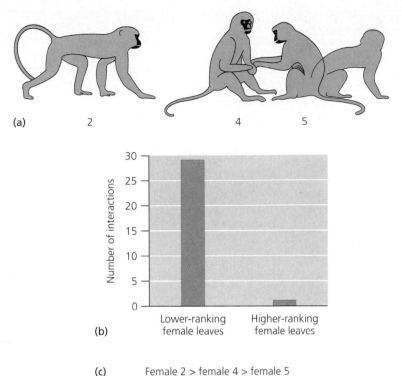

(a)   2   4   5

(b)

(c)   Female 2 > female 4 > female 5

Figure 10.6 Competition over Access to a Grooming Partner in Vervet Monkeys (a) A high-ranking female (2) approaches two lower-ranking females (4 and 5). (b) The lower-ranking female (5) is almost always supplanted. (c) This suggests that the monkeys recognize a rank hierarchy.

What Do Monkeys Know? Dorothy L. Cheney and Robert M. Seyfarth provide insight into the question of monkey intelligence. They designed experiments to see whether African vervet monkeys understand the concept of rank within their dominance hierarchy.

To form powerful alliances, individual vervet monkeys attempt to groom other monkeys that are higher in rank. If a monkey approaches a grooming pair, the invader will displace the monkey it outranks. If the intruder outranks both grooming monkeys, which one will the intruder displace? In 29 out of 30 cases, the more dominant intruder displaced the lower-ranking monkey of the pair (Figure 10.6). Cheney and Seyfarth conclude that the monkey which stays put knows its own rank relative to the invading monkey and knows its rank relative to the monkey which is displaced. The monkey which stays also knows the other two monkeys' relationship to each other. "In other words, she [the monkey who stays] must recognize a rank hierarchy."[8]

Cheney and Seyfarth also explore the extent to which vervets understand their own calls. Vervet monkeys are territorial; when monkeys from one group first sight a neighboring group approaching, they produce a *wrr wrr* warning. If the neighboring group approaches aggressively, the members of the invaded group produce a chuttering sound (Figure 10.7).

The researchers conducted an experiment in which they played a recording of one vervet's *wrr*s to its group when no neighboring group was in sight. The other animals soon learned to ignore the false alarm and also ignored the chutters of the recorded monkey. However, the animals reacted normally to all other calls of the monkey which had "cried wolf." Cheney and Seyfarth conclude that since the *wrr*s and chutters are acoustically dissimilar, the vervets can perceive that *wrr*s and chutters carry similar meaning. Since the recorded monkey was unreliable with one alarm call (*wrr*), the vervets also ignored its other alarm call (chutter).

---

[8] D. L. Cheney and R. M. Seyfarth, *How Monkeys See the World* (Chicago: University of Chicago Press, 1990), p. 82.

**Figure 10.7
Discreteness in Vervet
Monkey Alarm Calls**
The *wrr* and chutter are
both calls that are given in
the presence of another
group. (a) The *wrr* is given
when a neighboring group
has first been spotted. (b)
The acoustically different
chutter is produced under
more aggressive conditions
of contact. Pictured are
spectograms, which are
visualizations of sound.

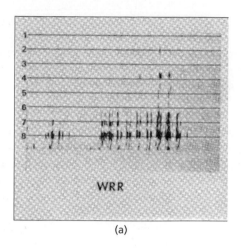

WRR

(a)

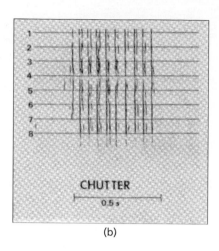

CHUTTER

0.5 s

(b)

Cheney and Seyfarth's work, and the work of several other primatologists, suggests that monkeys generalize about relationships between individuals and represent meaning in their calls. Unlike the case with humans, the monkeys' potential in these areas is very limited. Even if every primate call had meaning, a primate species usually has fewer than 20 calls; the English language contains about 500,000 words. This represents an enormous quantitative difference. Cheney and Seyfarth point out that there are also qualitative differences between monkeys and humans. For instance, monkeys do not know what they know; that is, they do not seem to be aware that they know things. Also, monkeys seem unable to "attribute mental states to others or to recognize that others' behavior is . . . caused by motives, beliefs, and desires."[9]

What Distinguishes Primates? The work with vervet monkeys suggests that intelligence is not an all-or-none characteristic. The developing body of evidence from monkey and ape research projects has led Susan Essock-Vitale and Robert M. Seyfarth to summarize some of the things that set primates apart, at least quantitatively, from most other animals. These behaviors include the facts that primates[10]

> recognize each other as individuals, distinguish kin from nonkin, and behave differently toward those of different dominance ranks. Experiments suggest that these social skills are learned and that they develop with experience. Moreover, primates can remember past interactions, seem able to predict the behavior of others based on prior observations, and discriminate among their own and other individuals' close associations . . . Finally, although primates are not qualitatively different from other animals in this respect, they do seem outstanding in their ability to maintain simultaneously many different kinds of relationships, each finely tuned to the individual characteristics of the participants.

These qualities point to the nonhuman primates' great mental abilities compared with those of other animals. Yet we can only speculate as to the evolutionary meaning of this complex behavior. As with humans, behavior based on learning allows for more behavioral flexibility than does that determined strictly by heredity. This behavioral flexibility allows the animal to choose a variety of strategies, which is especially important when unusual events occur and biologically stereotyped behavior may prove disastrous. In the complexity of the nonhuman primates' social behavior, and in their ability to manufacture tools, we see reflections of what may have been the roots of human culture.

The Evolution of Intelligence Studies of intelligence in nonhuman primates have focused on their ability to solve complex problems. Certainly, problem solving is one aspect of what

---

[9] Ibid., p. 312.

[10] S. Essock-Vitale and R. M. Seyfarth, "Intelligence and Social Cognition," in B. B. Smuts et al. (eds.), *Primate Societies* (Chicago: University of Chicago Press, 1987), p. 452. © 1986 by The University of Chicago Press.

we call intelligence. Several hypotheses have been proposed for the evolution of intelligence and an increase in brain size among primates. These ideals generally fall into two areas. One hypothesis centers on the fact that most primates live in large social units. Successful living in such societies provides situations of conflict, competition, and cooperation. Animals that have the capabilities to form close ties and minimize conflict, for example, are those which are most likely to successfully reproduce.

The other hypothesis centers on the shift to frugavory, the emphasis on fruit in the diet as opposed to leaves and insects. Trees that are producing fruit at a given point in time are widely scattered in the tropical forest, and primates must move from one area to another through the forest to find food. However, particular trees bear fruit in a predictable pattern over time. Unlike grazing for leaves, the successful primate forager must develop a mental map of fruit resources that includes the location of fruiting trees as well as the path to those trees. This map is further complicated by the periodic production of fruit at certain times of the year. Some anthropologists believe that the evolution of the capability of learning such mental maps and timetables is the basis of primate intelligence.

In reality, intelligence is a complex characteristic, and the forces of natural selection that favored its evolution most likely were also complex. Factors that may have led to the evolution of intelligence may have included living in large social units, concentration on the eating of fruits, behaviors to defeat or avoid predators, and behaviors that would allow for increased size of range. In other words, there was most likely a complex interplay of many factors that led to the evolution of greater intelligence.

Summary

Research into primate behavior reveals that many nonhuman primates, especially monkeys and apes, show protocultural behavior. The study of the ways in which behavior is learned and transmitted in nonhuman primates, we hope, will aid in the understanding of the development and nature of human culture.

The terms *communication* and *language* are not synonymous. All organisms communicate in that they transmit and receive messages. These messages need not be symbolic or involve any form of thought; they simply give information. Language has been regarded as a uniquely human form of communication that involves symbolic representations that are arbitrary and discrete. These characteristics, along with openness and displacement, as well as other features not discussed in this text, when taken as a whole differentiate language from the call systems of nonhuman primates and the communication systems of all other organisms.

Nevertheless, experimental work on apes has raised questions regarding the linguistic abilities of nonhuman primates. Can apes be taught human language and then transmit this knowledge to their offspring or other untrained apes? Some investigators believe that the research done with Washoe, Kanzi, Koko, and other apes shows that they have at least rudimentary linguistic ability. Other researchers see the supposed linguistic behavior of apes as nothing more than stimulus–response learning. Still others take a position somewhere between these two conclusions. As new research methods are developed, the early twenty-first century may be a time when more concrete answers are provided to the question of the ape's linguistic abilities.

Perhaps most anthropologists would agree that members of our species are the only living organisms with the capability of asking the questions: What am I? and Why am I? In the search for the answers to these questions, anthropologists are carefully studying the behavior of closely related species. Some nonhuman primates display mental characteristics that once were thought to be distinctly human. These include the ability to categorize experiences and convey distinct and discrete meaning in their calls.

Key Terms

arbitrary, *251*
band, *240*
Broca's area, *251*
call system, *250*
communication, *249*
discrete, *250*
displacement, *251*

faculty of language in the broad sense, *253*
faculty of language in the narrow sense, *253*
grammar, *251*
grandmother hypothesis, *243*

lexicon, *251*
lexigram, *252*
openness, *251*
protoculture, *246*
recursion, *253*
system, *245*

See the Online Learning Center for additional study questions.

Study Questions

1. What is the nature of the human band? What are some points of comparison between the human band and other primate social arrangements?

2. What characterizes male–female relationships in human societies? In what ways do these relationships differ from those of other primates?

3. What is the grandmother hypothesis? How does this hypothesis explain reduced infant and child mortality and a female lifespan decades beyond menopause?

4. Are the words *language* and *communication* synonymous? Explain.

5. In what ways is language different from other animal communication systems?

6. Why is there controversy over the contention made by some researchers that apes can learn human language?

7. Research on vervet monkeys has shown that these animals are capable of behaviors once thought to be unique to humans. What are these behaviors, and in what ways did investigators discover that monkeys were capable of them?

8. What is meant by the term *protoculture*? How do monkeys show protocultural behavior?

Critical Thinking Questions

1. It is very difficult to be objective about our own species, especially to view *Homo sapiens* in the same way we would view another species. Think about or observe a human group—a play group on a playground, students in a class, people at a party. Do you see evidence of play behavior, courtship, dominance and submissive behaviors, presenting, and so forth? Define the behaviors that you observe.

2. In literature these are numerous stories of tribal societies in which women were in charge of both domestic and nondomestic affairs, such as warfare. Why are stories of "Amazon women" fiction? Why in the twenty-first century are women becoming more involved in what used to be exclusively men's activities such as warfare, police work, national and international politics, and big business? What has changed to make this possible?

3. Language is an essential means of communication for humans. Could human culture and society exist without language; that is, with only nonhuman animal calls? Is human thought possible without language?

Suggested Readings

Cheney, D., and R. Seyfarth. *How Monkeys See the World.* Chicago: University of Chicago Press, 1990. This book explores such questions as: What do monkeys know about the world? Are they aware of what they know? It presents the results of research into these and other questions dealing with the issues of primate intelligence and cognition.

De Waal, F. (ed.). *Tree of Origin: What Primate Behavior Can Tell Us about Human Social Evolution.* Cambridge, MA: Harvard University Press, 2001. Nine of the world's leading primatologists discuss what we can learn about human social and cultural evolution from studying contemporary primate behavior.

De Waal, F., and P. L. Tyack. *Animal Social Complexity: Intelligence, Culture, and Individualized Societies.* Cambridge, MA: Harvard University Press, 2003. This volume is a collection of articles on innovation and tradition in a variety of nonhuman animals. It shows how protocultural behavior contributes to fitness and therefore the survival of many different species.

Deacon, D. W. *The Symbolic Species: The Co-Evolution of Language and the Brain.* New York: W. W. Norton, 1997. Deacon brings together recent information from linguistics, neurophysiology, anatomy, and evolutionary studies to paint a picture of the evolution of the brain and language over the last 2 million years.

Fouts, R., and S. T. Mills. *Next of Kin: What Chimpanzees Have Taught Me about Who We Are.* New York: Morrow, 1998. This is the fascinating story of Roger Fouts's 32-year relationship with Washoe, the signing chimpanzee.

Kelly, R. L. *The Foraging Spectrum: Diversity in Hunter-Gatherer Lifeways,* Washington, DC: Smithsonian Institution Press, 1995. As the title indicates, this book deals with the diversity in lifestyles of hunters and gatherers. It attempts to correct misconceptions about foraging peoples by showing the often complex social ecologies they display.

Lee, R. *The Dobe Ju/'hoansi.,* 3rd ed. (Belmont, CA: Wadsworth, 2003). This is a classic ethnography of a hunting and gathering people also known as the !Kung San.

Michel, A. *The Story of Nim: The Chimp Who Learned Language.* New York: Knopf, 1980. This is a short book with marvelous photographs explaining how H. S. Terrace attempted to teach language to a chimpanzee.

Suggested Websites

Central Washington University: Chimpanzee and Human Communication Institute:
www.cwu.edu/~cwuchci/

Chimpanzee Cultures Database:
http://chimp.st-and.ac.uk/cultures/database.htm

The Language Research Center:
www.gsu.edu/~wwwlrc

Chapter 11

The Record of the Past

Paleontological field work in Dinosaur National Monument.

Most fossil animals no longer possess soft tissues like muscles, flesh, and brain; their bones are no longer articulated, and some of their bones are broken or destroyed. Their bones and teeth have been mineralized. Fossil animals do not live in social groups; they have no home range or preferred habitat; and they do not move, feed, play, learn, reproduce, fight, or engage in any other behaviors. Their bones are not associated with those of the animals they interacted with in life. In short, through death most evidence of the interesting information about animals—what they look like, what they eat, how they move, where they live, and so on—is lost. Only through indirect evidence and painstaking study can any information about their habits and lifestyle be reconstructed. •

—Pat Shipman

Chapter Outline

See the Online Learning Center for a chapter summary, chapter outline, and learning objectives.

After Reading This Chapter, You Should Be Able to Answer These Questions:

1. What is a fossil, and how does fossilization occur? Why is fossilization a rare event?

2. Why is there a greater probability of fossilization occurring for some organisms than for others?

3. What can fossils tell us about the organisms they represent?

4. Does the term *species* refer to the same thing when it is used to label a type of organism known only from the fossil record and when it refers to a living organism?

5. What is the difference between relative dating and chronometric dating? What are some types of each of these techniques?

6. Why is it so difficult to grasp what a billion years means?

7. What is the geological time scale?

8. What is plate tectonics, and what does it tell us about the past placement and distribution of organisms?

9. What happened during the Pleistocene epoch? By understanding what occurred during the Pleistocene, why do we have a better understanding of the modern distribution and evolution of many types of organisms, including humans?

Box 11-1   Fossils of the Gods

In Greek mythology, Pelops was the son of Tantalus, the king of Sipylus, and a grandson of Zeus, the chief god. Tantalus sacrificed his son to the gods by cutting him into pieces and using the meat to make a stew. The offering was accepted by the goddess Demeter, who ate the cut of honor, the left shoulder. When the other gods realized what was happening, they brought Pelops back to life and replaced his missing left shoulder with one made of ivory.

The story of the adventures of Pelops from that point on becomes very complicated, as Greek myths often do, but Pelops ended up becoming a great king. After his death, Pelops's bones were kept in the Temple of Artemis at Olympia, where the ivory shoulder blade was believed to have special powers. During the Trojan War, Pelops's shoulder blade was brought to Troy because it was prophesied that its presence was required if the Greeks were to win the war, which of course they did.

The area surrounding Olympia contains many sites in which Pleistocene fossils, including fossilized mammoth bones, are found. The Greeks of mythical times were thought to have been very large—many were said to be giants. Thus, isolated mammoth bones frequently were seen as the remains of ancient Greek heroes and gods. Also, polished fossilized bones often take on the appearance of ivory. Thus, it is quite probable that the ivory shoulder blade of Pelops that was displayed in the temple at Olympia was indeed a mammoth bone. The bone probably no longer exists in the ruins of the temple, since over time the bone would have deteriorated when exposed to the elements.

The area that is Greece today contains abundant fossil sites, and the fossils the ancient Greeks recovered were thought not only to be the remains of the ancients and the gods but also to provide evidence of the existence of many mythological and contemporary creatures, such as griffins, creatures with the bodies of lions and the heads and beaks of eagles.

Source: A. Mayor, *The First Fossil Hunters: Paleontology in Greek and Roman Times* (Princeton, NJ: Princeton University Press, 2000).

Confucius wrote, "Study the past, if you would divine the future." Through the ages, people have pondered their history. The anthropologist is interested in the past for what it will reveal about the nature and development of humans as biological, social, and cultural beings. The anthropologist believes, as Confucius did, that a knowledge of the events leading to the present human condition is an important tool for coping with the problems that confront us.

The past reflects a type of biological immortality. Life begets life, and through the processes of reproduction, the present becomes a slightly modified reconstruction of the immediate past. There is, however, still another type of immortality—that of the fossilized remains of an organism. It is through the preservation of body parts that the anthropologist can see into the past and attempt to reconstruct the history of life.

FOSSILS AND THEIR INTERPRETATION

fossil Remains or traces of an ancient organism preserved in the ground.

See the Online Learning Center for an Internet Activity on fossils.

A **fossil** is the remains or traces of an ancient organism preserved in the ground. Fossils have interested people for thousands of years; in fact, prehistoric societies may have attached magical or religious significance to fossils. The Greeks and Romans not only knew of fossils but also made some assumptions about their meaning. About 500 B.C., some believed that fossil fish represented the ancestors of all life (Box 11-1). During the Middle Ages, knowledge and theories about fossils changed. Fossils were considered remnants of attempts at special creation, objects that had fallen from the heavens, and even devices of the devil.

In the fifteenth century, Leonardo da Vinci wrote: "The mountains where there are shells were formerly shores beaten by waves, and since then they have been elevated to the heights we see today." From that time on, debate has raged over the true meaning of geological formations and the fossils found in them. Only in the past few hundred years have scholars agreed that fossils are the remains of ancient organisms and that they can tell us much about the history of life.

The Nature of Fossils

The "immortality" of the body is limited; most organisms have left no traces of their existence on our planet. Their dead bodies were consumed by other organisms and eventually, through the process of decay, were absorbed into the soil.

Taphonomy is the study of the processes that affect an organism after death, leading in some cases to fossilization. Fossilization is actually a rare event, since several conditions must be met for an organism to be preserved.

First, the remains of the organism must be suitable for fossilization. Different parts of the body decay at different rates. It is therefore not surprising that the vast majority of fossils uncovered are those with hard tissues such as teeth, bones, and shell. These decay more slowly than soft tissues such as skin, brain, and muscles. Vast numbers of ancient organisms that lacked hard material probably will never be known.

Second, a deceased organism must be buried very quickly after death, before it is consumed by scavengers or destroyed by natural elements. However, some types of material, such as shell, can survive for quite some time before burial. The probability of fossilization is greatly increased when the body settles in stagnant water. The lack of oxygen discourages bacterial decay, and the lack of currents in the water minimizes movements of the body. More unusual are volcanic eruptions or violent storms that quickly cover the body with layers of volcanic ash or mud.

Finally, the material in which the remains are buried must be favorable for fossilization. Some soils, such as the acidic soils of the tropics, actually destroy bone. Minerals must be present that will infiltrate the bone, teeth, or shell and replace the organic matter. This is the process of fossilization.

On occasion, preserved soft tissue is found. In 1991, a partially freeze-dried body of a man was found at an elevation of 3200 meters (10,500 feet) in the Italian Alps near the Austrian border. The corpse was not the victim of a recent skiing accident; an arrowhead embedded in his shoulder indicates he was murdered 5300 years ago. Even the man's internal organs, clothing, and tools had been preserved (Figure 11.1).

Mummified remains are known from the hot, dry regions of Egypt, the American Southwest, and the western coastal deserts of South America. Other preserved bodies have been discovered in the peat bogs of northern Europe. These rare finds are extremely valuable because they provide direct evidence of skin, hair, stomach contents (for diet analysis), and much more.

taphonomy The study of the processes of burial and fossilization.

Figure 11.1 The "Ice Man" The partially freeze-dried body of a man who died about 5300 years ago.

mold A cavity left in firm sediments by the decayed body of an organism.

cast A representation of an organism created when a substance fills in a mold.

The vast majority of vertebrate fossils exist in the form of mineralized bone (Figure 11.2a). As the bone lies buried in the ground, minerals replace the organic matter in the bone. Traces of ancient life forms also may be found as molds and casts. A **mold** is a cavity left in firm sediments by the decayed body of an organism; nothing of the organism itself is left. This mold, if filled with some substance, becomes a **cast** that reflects the shape of the fossil (Figure 11.2b). Tracks and burrows of animals have been preserved this way (Figure 11.2c). Materials that were ingested and excreted by animals also can be preserved; they tell us much about the diet of the animals. These forms of preservation, however, are rarely found in the primate fossil record; ancient primates are best known by their fossilized bones and teeth.

Biases in the Fossil Record

The fossil record is not a complete record of the history of living organisms upon the face of the earth. It is but a sample of the plants and animals that once lived. Charles Darwin wrote:[1]

> I look at the natural geological record, as a history of the world imperfectly kept, and written in a changing dialect; of this history we possess the last volume alone, relating only to two or three countries. Of this volume, only here and there a short chapter has been preserved; and of each page, only here and there a few lines.

Sampling Error in the Fossil Record Because the probability of preservation varies from region to region, some organisms are better represented in the fossil record than others, while still others are totally unknown. Species living under conditions in which the odds of fossilization are good, such as freshwater lakes and ponds, will be common as fossils. Birds, however, are not preserved as frequently as mammals, and so the fossil record shows a scarcity of bird species. In reality, birds may have been a predominant life form in a particular area at a particular time.

Another factor in sampling is the accessibility of sites. In some areas, important fossil beds may have formed, but they are not exposed at the surface. Another major reason for geographical sampling error is politics. Some governments have been hostile to anthropological research, and military activity has made visits to other areas impossible. On the other hand, many governments and governmental institutions, such as the National Museums of Kenya, have been extremely active in this type of research. The result has been an uneven sampling of sites in various regions of the world.

Another factor that affects geographical sampling is money. Fieldwork can be very expensive, and the research interests of a scientist must be mirrored by the agencies financing the project. Several factors affect the cost of paleoanthropological research. A low-paid graduate student working in his or her own country may be able to conduct a short-term project for relatively little money. On the other hand, a full-scale overseas multidisciplinary operation may cost several hundred thousand dollars.

An important factor determining the locations excavated is the individual interests of paleoanthropologists. Most excavations occur in deposits representing geographical areas and geological periods that are considered important at the time the research is planned. As time goes on and our knowledge of human paleontology grows, new areas and new periods are considered critical.

Gaps in Fossil Sequences It is sometimes possible to follow the evolution of successive populations for millions of years, only to encounter a period characterized by an absence of fossils. This, in turn, may be followed by the reemergence of the population or by the appearance of a descendant of that population. Such gaps are common, and we will see many examples in subsequent chapters.

Several factors can cause gaps to appear in the fossil record. For one thing, organisms do not necessarily stay in the same habitat or niche. If a species moves into a new habitat, the probability of fossilization may change. Although the population seems to have disappeared, in reality it simply may not have been preserved during the time it resided in that habitat.

---

[1] C. Darwin, *On the Origin of Species* (London: J. Murray, 1859), pp. 310–311.

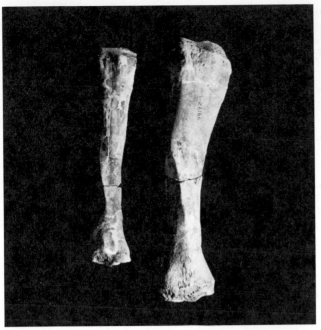

(a)

(b)

Figure 11.2 Fossils The remains of prehistoric life may take the form of (a) fossilized bone (limb bones of *Baluchterium*), (b) cast (internal chambers of an ammonite, (c) tracks (dinosaur).

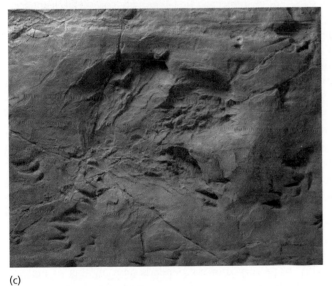

(c)

Another factor bringing about gaps in the fossil record is a change in **sedimentation,** which is the deposition of materials carried in water, wind, or glaciers. Most fossils are found in sedimentary deposits. If sedimentation ceases in a particular area, preservation also may cease and a gap in the fossil record will result. In addition, erosion may destroy sedimentary beds that already have been laid down.

Sampling of Populations Within a given species, the collection of actual specimens recovered represents a sample of the individual organisms that once lived. Anna K. Behrensmeyer estimates that only 0.004 percent of the hominins once living at Omo, Ethiopia, are represented in the fossil record.[2]

sedimentation The accumulation of geological or organic material deposited by air, water, or ice.

---

[2] A. K. Behrensmeyer, "Taphonomy and Paleoecology in the Hominid Fossil Record," *Yearbook of Physical Anthropology 1975* (Washington, D.C.: American Association of Physical Anthropologists, 1976), pp. 36–50.

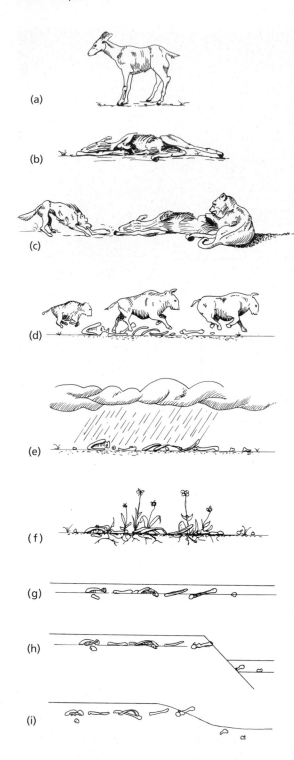

(a)

(b)

(c)

(d)

(e)

(f)

(g)

(h)

(i)

Figure 11.3 The Process of Fossilization (a) A living animal. (b) The carcass of the recently dead animal. (c) Predators feed on the carcass, destroying and disarticulating many bones. (d) Trampling by other animals further breaks up the bones.(e) Weathering by rain, sun, and other elements cracks and splits many of the bones. (f) The roots of plants invade many bones. (g) The bones are fossilized. (h) Faulting displaces and further breaks bones. (i) Fossils are exposed on surface by erosion.

Source: Reprinted by permission of the publisher from *Life History of a Fossil: An Introduction to Taphonomy and Paleoecology* by Pat Shipman, p. 14, Cambridge, MA: Harvard University Press. Copyright © 1981 by the President and Fellows of Harvard College.

Fossilization is a chance phenomenon; it represents a sample of individuals of a given population. This forces us to question if a specific individual is an average member of the population, especially if a species is known only from fragmentary remains or from a single individual. Since the probabilities for fossilization are so low, it is very difficult to know the range of variation of a species, and we often must define a species on the basis of a single specimen.

In situations in which a species is defined on the basis of a reasonable sample of individuals, some unrepresentative fossils are known. For example, the first relatively complete Neandertal skeleton to be discovered is the one from La Chapelle-aux-Saints, France. This skeleton became the prototype of the Neandertals. The Neandertals were pictured as creatures with an unusual posture, hunched over and bowlegged, with massive brow ridges and bestial features.

The specimen from La Chapelle-aux-Saints is not an average Neandertal, however, but the skeleton of an old man suffering from an advanced case of arthritis of the spine (Box 14-3). If a number of Neandertals are compared, this particular individual is one of the least modern in appearance. Today we know that the term *Neandertal* is a general designation for a group of hominins that show a great deal of intraspecific variation.

Differential Preservation

As we have seen, whether a particular organism or parts of an organism are preserved or not depends on a number of factors. The probability of a bone being preserved after death is known as that bone's **preservation potential.** By observing the fate of dead bodies in the field and by conducting many laboratory experiments, taphonomists have gathered data showing that the preservation potential of a particular bone depends on its size, shape, composition, and behavior in water.

Bone size can be thought of in terms of volume. Very large bones, such as skulls and mandibles, are preserved more frequently than are small bones. Bone composition is also a factor. Because carnivores prefer spongy bone, compact bones are more frequently left to be incorporated into the fossil record. Also important is the shape of the bone. Relatively thin, flat bones, such as the innominate and scapula, tend to break easily. These bones are infrequently found as fossils and, when recovered, are often broken and fragmented.

The **hydraulic behavior** of a bone refers to its transport and dispersal in water. Most fossils are derived from bodies that have been deposited in water environments; the fossils are found in sedimentary beds that are formed in water. A bone's composition, its size, and its shape are all important factors in determining what will happen to the bone in water. Ribs and

preservation potential
The probability of a bone being preserved after death.

hydraulic behavior The transport and dispersal of bones in water.

vertebrae are easily transported by water, and so they are frequently moved by water considerable distances from the rest of the skeleton. As they move, they often are abraded by the gravel beds of the stream or river. On the other hand, skulls and mandibles are transported only by rapidly moving streams. Figure 11.3 summarizes the forces that act to destroy bones after the death of an organism.

What Can Fossils Tell Us?

The fossil record is like a puzzle with many pieces missing and still others distorted. Yet a picture, although incomplete, does emerge. Often the image is only an outline of the past; sometimes it is a well-documented history.

With a few exceptions, the fossil record consists solely of skeletal remains, but much can be inferred about the body from the skeleton. For example, areas of muscle attachment can be seen on the surface of bone, often as ridges or roughened areas. From this information, the shape, size, and function of various muscles can be reconstructed. This is important in the reconstruction of locomotor patterns.

Once the musculature has been reconstructed, we can get some idea of what the organism might have looked like by placing a skin over the musculature (Figure 11.4). The fossil record, however, gives no indication of the color of the skin or of the amount of hair on the body.

The relative size of the eye socket, nasal cavities, and hearing apparatus can tell us a great deal about which senses were most important when the animal was alive. The evolution of vision in the primates can be seen in the formation of the eye socket and the frontal position of the eyes on the skull.

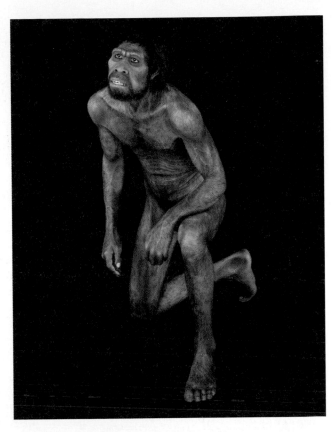

Figure 11.4 Flesh Reconstruction A flesh reconstruction of *Homo erectus.*

Brains are never fossilized, although brain matter has been found from fairly recent times in bodies preserved in wet sites such as bogs. However, some inferences about brain size can be made from the brain case. An examination of the inside surface of the brain case, which conforms to the general size and shape of the brain, gives some idea of the gross structure of the brain itself. In addition, grooves in the brain case, which are clearly seen in an endocranial cast, are indications of arteries, veins, and nerves. While such data have led to inferences regarding intelligence, the development of culture, and the presence or absence of speech, one must view these conclusions with a great deal of skepticism.

Patterns of growth and development are mirrored in the fossil record when one discovers a sequence of specimens representing individuals of different ages. **Computerized tomography** and other medical technologies are being used by paleoanthropologists to discover features such as nonerupted teeth that are embedded within the fossil jaw. These findings provide evidence for reconstructing age at death and patterns of dental development and maturation, as well as for reconstructing life expectancies and population structure. **Paleopathology** deals with investigations of injuries and disease in prehistoric populations, such as arthritis and dental caries (cavities in teeth) in Neandertal skeletons.

In addition to information about the individual and the species, the presence of fossil remains of animals in association with human remains, the remains of human activity, and the geological context all tell us much about the living patterns and ecological relations of the early hominins. Figure 11.5 shows the interrelationships of various types of data and interpretations that can be used to build a picture of the early hominins.

Hominin fossils and **artifacts,** the material remains of human behavior, are the primary data used in the reconstruction of technology, subsistence activities and diet, land-use patterns, and even, to a limited extent, group social structure. **Paleoanthropology,** the interdisciplinary

computerized tomography A technology used in medicine that permits visualization of the interior of an organism's body.

paleopathology The study of injuries and disease in prehistoric populations.

artifact Any physical remains of human activity.

paleoanthropology Scientific study of fossils and artifacts and the context in which they are found.

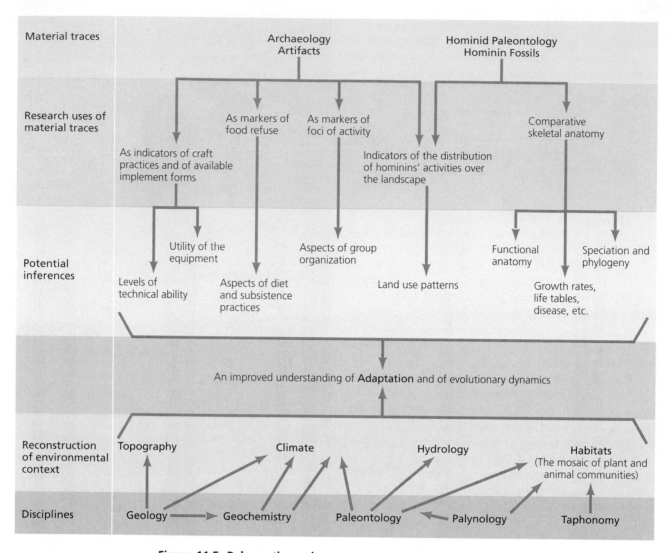

Figure 11.5 Paleoanthropology

paleontology The study of fossils.

palynology The study of fossil pollen.

paleoecology The study of the relationship of extinct organisms or groups of organisms to their habitats.

study of prehistoric hominins and related forms, combines data from many disciplines, such as geology, **paleontology** (the study of fossils), **palynology** (the study of fossil pollen), **paleoecology,** and taphonomy, to reconstruct the environment in which the hominins functioned. Of course, the most important information anthropologists derive from the fossil record is evidence of evolutionary processes, for it is in the fossil record that the actual remains of early forms are found.

Taxonomy and the Fossil Record

In 1963, George Gaylord Simpson wrote:[3]

> Men and all recent and fossil organisms pertinent to their affinities are animals, and the appropriate language for discussing their classification and relationships is that of animal taxonomy. . . . It is notorious that [hominin] nomenclature, particularly, has become chaotic.

[3] G. G. Simpson, "The Meaning of Taxonomic Statements," in S. C. Washburn (ed.), *Classification and Human Evolution,* Viking Fund Publications in Anthropology, No. 37 (New York: Wenner-Gren Foundation for Anthropological Research, 1963), pp. 4–5.

Taxonomic issues are still being debated over 40 years later. Prerequisite to any discussion of the fossil record is an understanding of the problems of the taxonomy of fossils.

The Species Concept in the Fossil Record Fossil taxonomy is one of the most provocative areas in paleoanthropology. With each new find, a new debate begins over the fossil's placement in the evolutionary scheme, and a major problem is the definition of species when applied to fossils. Since the definition of species for living populations is based on the criterion of reproductive success, the difficulties of applying this concept to the fossil record are obvious.

There are two schools of thought concerning the definition of species in the fossil record, and they are diametrically opposed to each other in philosophical outlook. The **typological viewpoint** embodies the ancient philosophy developed by Plato, which holds that basic variation of a type is illusory and that only fixed ideal types are real. According to this concept of the archetype, which was introduced in the discussion of taxonomy in Chapter 6, two fossils that differ from each other in certain respects represent two types and, hence, are two different species. Typologists are sometimes called "splitters."

The typological viewpoint has dominated human paleontology for what are probably psychological reasons more than anything else. The discovery of a new fossil is a highly emotional experience, and a new find becomes more significant if it can be said to represent a new species rather than simply being another specimen of an already known species.

The **populationist viewpoint,** on the other hand, maintains that only individuals have reality and that the type is illusory. More precisely, the populationists argue that since no two individuals are exactly alike, variation underlies all existence.

Let us consider an example of the populationist viewpoint. The heights of four individuals are 155 centimeters (5 feet 1 inch), 160 centimeters (5 feet 3 inches), 170 centimeters (5 feet 7 inches), and 178 centimeters (5 feet 10 inches). Their average height is 166 centimeters (5 feet 5 inches). First, note that the individuals in the sample vary by 23 centimeters (9 inches), and second, note that no one individual in the sample is average. According to this reasoning, variation in fossil finds can be explained as divergence from a statistical average. If this variation is no greater than that which might be found within a related living species, the populationist sees no reason to separate the finds into different taxonomic categories. Populationists are sometimes called "lumpers" because they often lump together into the same taxon specimens that splitters consider to be in different taxa.

To illustrate this point, Figure 11.6 shows a series of skulls that display a fair degree of variation in appearance. How many species are represented here? In this case, they are all modern gorillas, members of the species *Gorilla gorilla*. Yet a series of hominid fossils

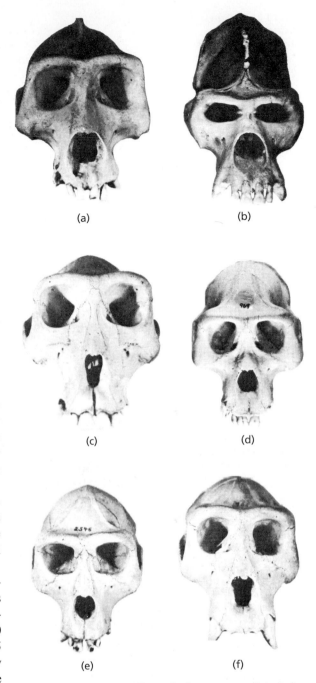

(a) (b)

(c) (d)

(e) (f)

Figure 11.6 Intraspecific Variation A series of six skulls, all members of the same species, *Gorilla gorilla*. Note the degree of variation: (b) and (f) are males, (a) and (c) are probably males, and (d) and (e) are probably females.

typological viewpoint
The viewpoint that basic variation of a type is illusory and that only fixed ideal types are real; two fossils that differ from each other in certain respects represent two types and, hence, are two different species.

Figure 11.7 Age Differences in Chimpanzee Skulls The skulls of an infant and an adult chimpanzee.

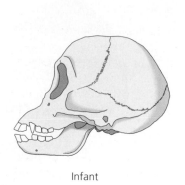

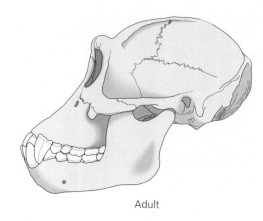

Infant   Adult

populationist viewpoint The viewpoint that only individuals have reality and that the type is illusory; since no two individuals are exactly alike, variation underlies all existence.

paleospecies A group of similar fossils whose range of morphological variation does not exceed the range of variation of a closely related living species.

chronospecies Arbitrarily defined divisions of an evolutionary line.

that show this degree of variation would be broken up by many paleoanthropologists into a number of distinct species.

The Paleospecies Among living organisms, the species is defined in the objective terms of reproductive isolation, yet neither reproductive isolating mechanisms nor gene frequencies can be seen in the fossil record. At best, geographical isolation can be inferred in some situations. In dealing with the fossil record, the taxonomist is restricted to an analysis of morphological variation, and, as has already been noted, variation within a species can be great.

Many anthropologists have concluded that since reproductive criteria cannot be applied to the fossil record, the species concept cannot be legitimately applied to fossil forms. Instead, we must speak of the **paleospecies,** which resembles the species but is defined in terms of morphological variation rather than in terms of genetic isolation and reproductive success. (Some paleoanthropologists speak of **chronospecies,** which are arbitrarily defined divisions of an evolutionary line.) A paleospecies is a group of similar fossils whose range of morphological variation does not exceed the range of variation within a closely related living species. Determination of a paleospecies requires detailed statistical analysis of both the fossil series and the living species being used for comparison.

Reasons for Variability in the Fossil Record Many differences among fossil specimens represent the emergence of new species and higher taxonomic groups. Nevertheless, much of the variation that often is interpreted as interspecific actually is intraspecific.

One form of intraspecific variation is that of age. Figure 11.7 shows the skulls of an infant and an adult chimpanzee; note the absence of a prominent brow ridge and the generally more "human" appearance of the infant's skull. One must be extremely careful when using anything other than adult material in interpreting the fossil record.

Sexual dimorphism was discussed in Chapter 7. We saw that the male adult baboon is larger than the female, has longer canines, and has a mantle of fur over his shoulder. Thus, the sex of an adult baboon is easy to determine even from a skull alone. On the other hand, the gibbon shows little sexual dimorphism; unless the female is nursing a child, male and female gibbons cannot be distinguished at a distance. Evidence suggests that the early hominins showed a greater degree of sexual dimorphism than *Homo sapiens* do today.

Finally, variation within a species can be due to the simple fact that, as we saw in the discussion of genetics, no two individuals are phenotypically identical. One cannot expect any two fossil specimens to be exactly alike. Consider, for example, the tremendous variation within the species *Homo sapiens* with respect to stature, body build, and cranial capacity.

Summary

The remains and traces of ancient organisms make up the fossil record, yet this record is far from being a complete history of life on earth. The process of fossilization is the subject matter of taphonomy. Fossilization is a rare event, because it depends on an organism's having hard parts, such as bones, teeth, or shells, and being buried immediately after death. The work of predators and scavengers and the weathering effects of rain, heat, cold, and wind often serve to destroy most or all of an organism before burial takes place.

Because of the nature of fossilization, the fossil record is a biased sample of the totality of life that once existed. Fossilization is more apt to occur in some areas, such as the bottom of lakes, than others, such as tropical rain forests. Aquatic animals are preserved more frequently than those living in terrestrial habitats. Some parts of the world and some geological time spans have been more thoroughly explored for fossils than have others. A major problem of sampling is the realization that a fossil is a single individual. Is that individual typical of the species, or does it represent a deviation from the norm?

Fossils provide a great deal of information if they are studied carefully. From skeletal remains, the musculature can be reconstructed; from the musculature, one can get a good picture of the physical appearance of the animal when it was alive. The brain case provides some information about the brain itself. In addition, fossils provide data on growth and development patterns and injury and disease. The associated remains of animals, artifacts, and the geological context tell us much about ecological relationships and even, to some extent, the behavior of prehistoric populations.

A major problem in paleoanthropology is the application of taxonomic principles to the fossil record. The species concept as defined in terms of reproductive success cannot be applied to the fossil record. Instead, we must speak of paleospecies, which are defined in terms of morphological similarities and differences.

GEOLOGICAL TIME

It is somewhat paradoxical that in order to learn more about the earth, scientists have investigated the nature of the moon. Yet both bodies, along with the sun and the other planets, are thought to have been formed at about the same time. Because the crust of the moon has not undergone as much alteration as that of the earth, the examination of moon rocks may give a better estimate of the age of the earth than an examination of the earth itself. This estimate now stands at about 4.6 billion years.

When people believed that the earth was only about 6000 years old, it was impossible to conceive of evolutionary theory in both the biological and the geological senses. While microevolution can be observed within a human life span, as we saw in the case of Darwin's finches, macroevolution requires an extremely long time span. Because the concept of deep time is so central to paleoanthropology, we must attempt to gain a feeling for long periods of time (Box 11-2). This section looks at methods for determining the age of fossils and the way in which geologists and paleontologists organize geological time.

Stratigraphy

If a glass of river water sits for a period of time, a thin layer of material soon appears on the bottom of the glass; this layer consists of dirt and other debris that were suspended in

Box 11-2   **What Is a Billion?**

The earliest recognizable fossils date to about 3½ billion years ago. The Cenozoic era, or the Age of Mammals, began about 65½ million years ago. Part of the student's task is learning these dates, as they are approximations of when the major events of evolution took place. It is one thing to memorize a date; it is quite another to comprehend that date, which is so many times greater than the human life span.

Yet failure to comprehend this vastness of time is failure to understand a major aspect of evolutionary history. Macroevolutionary changes are slow changes that take place over vast durations of time. Even relatively fast changes, such as those postulated by the concept of punctuated equilibrium, occur over enormous stretches of time.

A million is 1000 thousand; a billion is 1000 million. A trillion is 1000 billion. These are huge numbers. The late astronomer Carl Sagan tells us how long it would take to count to these numbers if we were to count one number per second, night and day, starting with 1: it would take 17 minutes to count to a thousand, 12 days to count to a million, and 32 years to count to a billion![1]

To get a better feel for the depth of time, we can equate time with distance. Let us say that the history of the earth is represented by a highway stretching from New York to Los Angeles and that New York represents 4½ billion years ago, the age of the earth, and Los Angeles represents today. As we travel along this highway from east to west, the first forms of life appear in Indianapolis, the first animal life in Phoenix, and the first primates around Disneyland. The hominins are evolving on the shores of the Pacific Ocean.

[1] C. Sagan, "Billions and Billions," *Parade Magazine*, May 31, 1987, p. 9.

---

sediment Material that is suspended in water; in still water, it will settle at the bottom.

sedimentary beds Beds or layers of sediments called strata.

stratigraphy The investigation of the composition of the layers of the earth, used in relative dating; based on the principle of superposition.

superposition Principle that under stable conditions, strata on the bottom of a deposit were laid down first and hence are older than layers on top.

the moving water of the river. The atmosphere, through wind and corrosive activities, and bodies of water, through their movements, erode away the land. When the water stops moving, the eroded material, called **sediment,** settles to the bottom under the influence of gravity, and a thin layer forms. In lakes, this process occurs on a much greater scale. Dead animals wash into lakes, where many settle into the bottom mud and become a part of the sedimentary deposit.

Over time, many layers develop, one on top of another. These layers, called **sedimentary beds,** or strata, are said to be stratified. Eventually, a lake will dry up, leaving a series of strata that, at some later point in time, may give up their fossils to the paleontologist. The investigation of the composition of the layers of the earth and their relationship to one another is the study of **stratigraphy.**

The basis of stratigraphic studies is the principle of **superposition.** Simply stated, this principle says that under stable conditions, the strata on the bottom of a deposit are older than the ones on top. The reasoning behind the principle of superposition is relatively straightforward: The materials from a given point in time are deposited on top of materials deposited earlier. Since the compositions of these materials differ at different times, the various layers often can be identified visually (Figure 1.6). In excavating a paleontological or archaeological site, one encounters progressively older remains at increasingly deeper levels. In general, an object that is found deeper in the ground is older than one located closer to the surface. Fossil and cultural remains can be relatively dated based on their position in a deposit (Figure 11.8).

In practice, stratigraphic sequences are not easy to interpret. Neat layers are not always present, and intrusions, such as burials, can place more recent fossils at the same level as much older material (Figure 11.9). Careful analysis of the soil often can reveal such intrusions. Earthquakes, volcanic eruptions, and other cataclysmic events also can alter stratigraphic sequences.

In addition, if long periods of time elapsed during which deposits did not form or deposited sediments were eroded away, long gaps in time will occur between a particular stratum and the layer just above and/or below it. The surfaces of layers that represent such breaks in the geological record are called **unconformities.** For a particular stratigraphic sequence, unconformities may represent more unrecorded time than the time represented by the strata that are present.

unconformity The surface of a stratum that represents a break in the stratigraphic sequence.

Index Fossils In the late eighteenth century, the English geologist, William Smith (Chapter 1), noted that particular combinations of fossil animals and plants occurred together in certain sedimentary formations (Box 1-2). He realized that if these combinations of fossil species were found in areas other than the original, the periods in which the sedimentary layers were laid down in the two areas must be approximately the same. Therefore, strata from one area could be correlated with strata from another.

In this way, certain fossils or combinations of fossils become markers for particular periods of time; certain key fossils are known as **index fossils.** An index fossil is a species that had a very wide geographical distribution but existed for a short time. The appearance of an index fossil in a particular stratum immediately provides the investigator with a relative date for that stratum. If a date is established for an index fossil, any other fossil found in association with it is given the same date.

Fluorine Dating Paleontologists have developed several ways to test whether objects in a site are contemporary. As bones and teeth lie in the ground, they absorb fluorine and other minerals dissolved in the groundwater. On the other hand, the nitrogen content of the bones decreases as the material ages. The amount of minerals absorbed and the amount of nitrogen lost can be used to calculate the relative chronology of the material in a site. Since the rates of absorption and loss depend on the specific nature of the groundwater, however, these methods can be used only for fossils found in the same area.

The most frequent application of these methods is in determining whether bones found in association are indeed of equal age. If one could show that a human skull and a mammoth rib lying next to it contained the same amount of fluorine, then it follows that both creatures were alive at the same time. On the other hand, if the mineral contents of the two bones differ, with the skull containing less fluorine, one could conclude that the human skull was placed at the

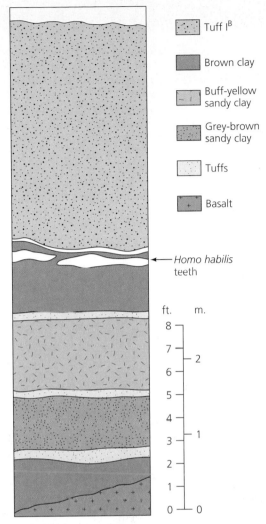

Tuff I^B

Brown clay

Buff-yellow sandy clay

Grey-brown sandy clay

Tuffs

Basalt

← *Homo habilis* teeth

Figure 11.8 Stratigraphic Cross-Section of MK Site, Olduvai Gorge, Tanzania Note the location of teeth belonging to the extinct hominin species *Homo habilis,* to be discussed in Chapter 14.

index fossil A paleospecies that had a very wide geographical distribution but existed for a relatively short period of time, either becoming extinct or evolving into something else.

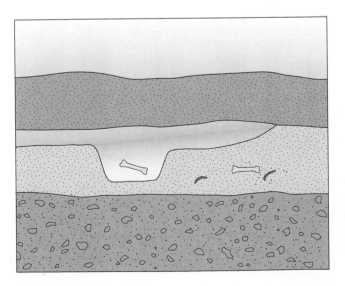

Figure 11.9 Stratigraphic Cross-Section In this hypothetical cross-section of an archaeological site, a hole has been dug into a lower layer. An object lying at the bottom of the hole is therefore found at the same level as much older material.

Box 11-3   The Piltdown Skull

In 1912, Charles Dawson found a skull in a site on Piltdown Common, England, which became known as *Piltdown Man*. The find consisted of a brain case, which was very much like that of a relatively modern human, and a lower jaw, which was similar to that of an ape (see figure). Some additional material was discovered later at a nearby site (Site II).

In the years that followed, paleontologists discovered other transitional forms that differed considerably from Piltdown. Piltdown showed a large, developed brain case associated with a modified apelike jaw. More recently discovered forms showed a relatively small brain case associated with essentially modern teeth and jaws.

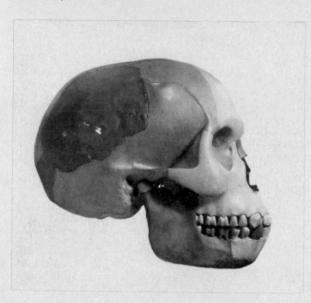

In 1953, the Piltdown skull was declared a hoax. When paleontologists subjected the fossils to fluorine analysis, they found that many of the different fossils contained different percentages of fluorine. The "hominin" material contained less fluorine than did the bones of other extinct animals found with it, indicating that the Piltdown brain case was more recent than the estimates made on the basis of soil analysis.

Fluorine analysis also revealed that the jaw did not belong to the rest of the skull. Although the brain case appeared to be a real fossil of fairly recent date, the jaw was a modified orangutan mandible. The culprit who had masterminded the hoax had filed down the canine teeth and stained the bones to make them appear to be of the same age as known prehistoric animals. These diverse fragments were then placed secretly in the sites.

Not until 1996 was it finally announced that the perpetrator had been unmasked. The hoax had been created by Martin A. C. Hinton, a curator of zoology at the Natural History Museum in London, who specialized in the study of fossil rodents. A canvas traveling trunk belonging to Mr. Hinton was discovered in the southwest tower of the museum. Inside were several bones and teeth, all carved and stained in the same manner as the bones placed in the Piltdown site. It is believed that Mr. Hinton, a well-known practical joker, created the hoax to embarrass Arthur Smith Woodward, Keeper of Geology at the museum, as revenge over a pay issue.

Sources: C. Blinderman, *The Piltdown Inquest* (Buffalo, NY: Prometheus, 1986); F. Spencer, *Piltdown: A Scientific Forgery* (London: Oxford University Press, 1990); J. S. Weiner, *The Piltdown Forgery* (London: Oxford University Press, 1955); and H. Gee, "Box of Bones 'Clinches' Identity of Piltdown Palaeontology Hoaxer," *Nature* 381 (May 23, 1996), pp. 261–262.

---

fluorine dating A method for determining whether two fossils found in the same level of the same site are contemporary by measuring the amount of fluorine absorbed by the fossils.

See the Online Learning Center for an Internet Activity on dating techniques.

lower level through burial. Box 11-3 describes a famous hoax that was resolved through the use of **fluorine dating.**

Chronometric Dating Techniques

Used alone, the study of stratigraphy, index fossils, fluorine, and other mineral analyses can yield only a **relative date.** A relative date only indicates whether one object is older or younger than another object. **Chronometric dates** refer to specific points in time and are noted on specific calendrical systems. **Calendrical systems** are based on natural recurring units of time, such as the revolutions of the earth around the sun or the appearance of the new moon; they note the number of such units that have preceded or elapsed with reference to a specific point in time. For instance, *On the Origin of Species,* by Charles Darwin, was first published in 1859. This date is based on the Gregorian calendar, and it refers to 1859 revolutions of the earth around the sun since the traditional date of the birth of Christ. The same book was published in 5620 according to the Hebrew calendar and in the year 1276 according to the Muslim calendar. The former date is based on the biblical origin of the world; the latter, on the flight of Mohammed from Mecca.

A chronometric date is often given as 10,115 years ago or 10,115 B.P., in which B.P. stands for "before the present." The problem with this type of designation is that one must know the year in which the date was determined. For example, if a date was determined to be 780 B.P. in 1950, it would have to be changed to 840 B.P. in the year 2010. Many anthropologists use 1950 as the reference point for all B.P. dates.

Chronometric dates in paleontology are often given in the following form: 500 B.P. ± 50 years. The "plus or minus 50 years" does *not* represent an error factor. It is a probability statement that is necessary when certain types of determinations are made. This probability is expressed as a **standard deviation.** For example, a standard deviation of 50 years means that the probability of the real date's falling between 550 and 450 B.P. is 67 percent. The probability of the real date's falling between two standard deviations, in our example between 600 and 400 B.P., is 95 percent.

Often the paleontologist must use both chronometric and relative dates together. For example, if one fossil is dated at 30,000 ± 250 B.P. and another at 30,150 ± 250 B.P., it is not possible to tell which of the two fossils is older since the ranges of most-probable date overlap (29,750 to 30,250 B.P. and 29,900 to 30,400 B.P.). Deciding which fossil is older would be impossible with only the chronometric dates, but a relative dating technique might solve the problem.

Radiometric Dating Techniques

A number of dating methods exist that produce chronometric dates. Examples are **tree-ring dating,** or **dendrochronology,** in which the age of a wood sample is determined by counting the number of annual growth rings, and amino acid racemization, which we will discuss later. Nevertheless, the development of **radiometric dating methods,** based on the decay of radioactive materials, has brought about a major revision of the age of the earth and the fossils it contains.

As we saw in Chapter 2, all matter is composed of one or more elements. The elements carbon, oxygen, nitrogen, and hydrogen are important constituents of all plants and animals, while the elements potassium, silicon, and oxygen are important elements in rocks and minerals.

Although most elements are stable, that is, one element does not change into another, many are unstable, or **radioactive.** Also, an element often occurs in more than one form; the different forms of an element are called **isotopes.** Some isotopes of a particular element may be radioactive, while other isotopes may not.

Radioactivity means that the atom is unstable and will decay into another type of atom. Predicting when a particular atom will decay is impossible, but we can express the rate of decay as a probability statement. If we have a given number of atoms, we can say that one-half of those atoms will have decayed in a specified number of years. This number is known as the **half-life.**

Radioactive decay is uniform throughout time and is unaffected by external conditions such as temperature, pressure, and the presence of other elements. Figure 11.10 plots the rate of decay of radioactive carbon; the level of radioactivity is shown on the horizontal axis. In one half-life, exactly one-half of the original atoms have decayed and one-half are left. In two half-lives, three-quarters (one-half plus one-half of one-half) of the original atoms have decayed and one-quarter remain.

Radiocarbon Dating **Radiocarbon dating,** developed by Willard F. Libby in the late 1940s, was the first radiometric

relative dating Any dating technique that places two fossils or artifacts in time relative to one another, where one is older than, younger than, or the same age as the other.

chronometric dates Dates that refer to a specific point or range of time.

calendrical system A system of measuring time based on natural recurring units of time, such as the revolutions of the earth around the sun; they note the number of such units that have preceded or elapsed with reference to a specific point in time.

standard deviation A statistical measurement of the amount of variation in a series of determinations; the probability of the real number falling within plus or minus one standard deviation is 67 percent.

tree-ring dating Chronometric dating method that determines the age of a wood sample by counting the number of annual growth rings.

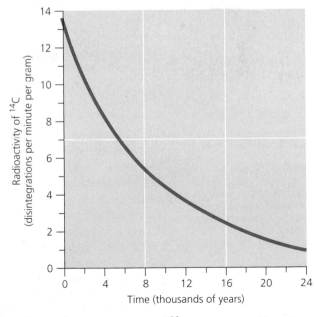

Figure 11.10 Decay Curve of ^{14}C At time 0, the ^{14}C in the animal tissue is in equilibrium with ^{14}C in the atmosphere, with the radioactivity of ^{14}C in the tissue sample measured at 13.56 ± 0.07 disintegrations per minute per gram (dpm/g). When the animal dies, no new ^{14}C is incorporated into the tissue, and the radioactivity decreases over time.

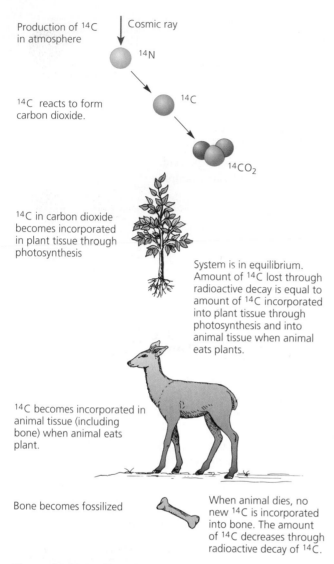

Production of ^{14}C in atmosphere | Cosmic ray

^{14}N

^{14}C reacts to form carbon dioxide.

^{14}C

$^{14}CO_2$

^{14}C in carbon dioxide becomes incorporated in plant tissue through photosynthesis

System is in equilibrium. Amount of ^{14}C lost through radioactive decay is equal to amount of ^{14}C incorporated into plant tissue through photosynthesis and into animal tissue when animal eats plants.

^{14}C becomes incorporated in animal tissue (including bone) when animal eats plant.

Bone becomes fossilized

When animal dies, no new ^{14}C is incorporated into bone. The amount of ^{14}C decreases through radioactive decay of ^{14}C.

Figure 11.11 Radiocarbon Dating

dendrochronology Tree-ring dating.

radiometric dating techniques Chronometric dating methods based on the decay of radioactive materials; examples are radiocarbon and potassium-argon dating.

radioactivity The phenomenon whereby an atom that is unstable will radioactively decay into another type of atom and in the process emit energy and/or particles.

isotopes Atoms of the same element but of different atomic weight.

dating technique. One isotope of carbon, carbon 14 (^{14}C), is radioactive and eventually will decay into nitrogen 14 (^{14}N). The half-life of ^{14}C is 5730 ± 40 years.

Carbon 14 forms in the upper atmosphere by the bombardment of nitrogen by cosmic radiation. The amount of ^{14}C formed in the atmosphere is relatively constant over time; although variations in the amount of solar radiation produce fluctuations in the amount of ^{14}C, it is possible to correct for these fluctuations.

The ^{14}C in the atmosphere combines with oxygen to form carbon dioxide. Carbon dioxide, in turn, is incorporated into plants by photosynthesis and into animals by consumption of plants or other animals (Figure 11.11). As long as the organism is alive, the proportion of ^{14}C to nonradioactive ^{12}C in the body remains constant since the amount of new ^{14}C being incorporated into the body balances the amount being lost through decay. When the organism dies, no new ^{14}C atoms are incorporated into the body, and the atoms present at death continue to decay. The age of the organism at death is calculated by comparing the proportion of ^{14}C to ^{12}C in the prehistoric sample with that in a modern sample.

In the conventional method of radiocarbon dating, the ^{14}C is measured by means of a special counter that measures the emissions given off by carbon-14 atoms when they decay. Another method of radiocarbon dating uses accelerator mass spectrometry to measure the ratio of ^{14}C to ^{12}C directly.

Radiocarbon dating can be used to date any organic material, including, but not limited to, wood and charcoal, cloth, seeds and grasses, bones, ivory, pollen, hair, paper, horn, and shell. Unlike the case with other methods of dating, carbon 14 dates the actual material. The material that is being dated is consumed in the process. The maximum age that can be determined by the conventional method at the present time is 50,000 to 60,000 years.

Potassium-Argon Dating **Potassium-argon dating** is based on the radioactive decay of potassium 40, which has a half-life of 1250 million years. One out of about 10,000 potassium atoms found in rocks is the radioactive isotope potassium 40 (^{40}K). Over time, ^{40}K decays into calcium 40 (^{40}Ca) and argon 40 (^{40}Ar); the latter is a gas that is trapped within certain minerals.

To make use of this technique, the mineral must meet two criteria. First, although potassium is a common constituent of minerals, the method can be used only on material with a sufficiently high potassium content. Second, the material must arise in association with volcanic activity. Under the very high temperatures that accompany volcanic activity, the argon gas is expelled. When the material cools and solidifies, it contains a certain amount of potassium 40 but no argon 40. As time goes on, the amount of ^{40}K decreases while the amount of ^{40}Ar increases. These two variables are used in the determination of the chronometric date.

Another form of the potassium-argon technique is **argon 40/argon 39** ($^{40}Ar/^{39}Ar$) dating. The material is radiated so that the nonradioactive ^{39}K is transformed into ^{39}Ar. The argon gas is extracted, and the amounts of ^{40}Ar and ^{39}Ar are measured. A variation of this technique involves the use of a laser to melt individual crystals to release the argon. This

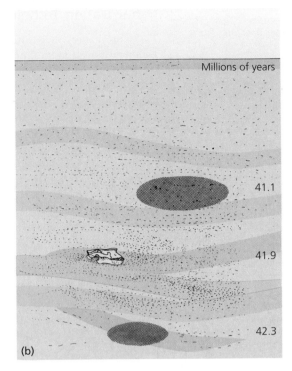

Millions of years

41.1

41.9

42.3

(a)

(b)

Figure 11.12 Potassium-Argon Dating (a) Hypothetical live animal. (b) After death, the body of the animal becomes incorporated into a sedimentary bed (lake deposit). Periodic volcanic eruptions have created volcanic lenses in this bed, and the volcanic material can be dated by the potassium-argon technique. The age of the fossil is inferred from its context in relationship to the dated volcanic lenses.

is termed **single crystal fusion.** This method reduces the effects of contamination and reduces the size of the sample needed.

The potassium-argon technique is limited, with few exceptions, to volcanic ash falls and lava flows. The technique is seldom used to date an actual object, but it is used to date fossilized bones with respect to their placement in relationship to volcanic layers in the surrounding material (Figure 11.12).

Similar techniques can be used with other radioactive isotopes. Table 11.1 lists some of the radioactive isotopes used in radiometric dating. In practice, several different isotopes are used; if similar dates result from the application of two or more techniques, the determined date is considered reliable.

half-life The time in which one-half of the atoms of a radioactive isotope have decayed.

radiocarbon dating A method of chronometric dating based on the decay of carbon 14.

potassium-argon dating Chronometric dating technique based on the rate of decay of potassium 40 to argon 40.

argon 40/argon 39 dating A method of chronometric dating based on making measurements of the relative amounts of argon 40 and argon 39 in a sample.

single-crystal fusion A form of potassium-argon dating that uses a laser to melt individual crystals to release the argon.

Table 11.1 Some Isotopes Used in Radiometric Dating

Letters stand for the following elements: C, carbon; Ar, argon; U, uranium; Pb, lead; Th, thorium.

Parent Isotope	Daughter Isotope	Half-Life	Useful Dating Range
^{14}C	^{14}N	5730 years	50,000–60,000 years
^{40}K	^{40}Ar	1.3 billion years	100,000–4.6 billion years
^{238}U	^{206}Pb	4.5 billion years	10 million–4.6 billion years
^{235}U	^{207}Pb	713 million years	10 million–4.6 billion years
^{232}Th	^{208}Pb	14.1 billion years	10 million–4.6 billion years

Other Dating Techniques

There are many other dating techniques that are based on principles different from the ones we have looked at so far. Here we will briefly review a few of them.

fission-track dating The determination of a chronometric date by counting the proportion of atoms of a radioactive isotope such as uranium 238 that have decayed, leaving visible tracks in a mineral, relative to the total number of atoms of the isotope.

Fission-Track Dating Like potassium-argon dating, **fission-track dating** dates the minerals in a deposit. Minerals are crystalline in nature, which means that their atoms form an orderly three-dimensional structure based on the repetition of modular units. As the nucleus of a heavy isotope such as uranium 238 breaks apart, its decay particles rip holes in the orderly crystal structure of the mineral. In so doing, the particles leave tracks in these crystals.

The tracks can be used to determine a chronometric date. After being chemically treated to make them larger, such tracks can be seen under magnification and counted. The number of atomic disintegrations is directly related to the number of tracks produced. If the concentration of the isotope under study is known, a count of the tracks left will indicate the age of the mineral being dated. This method can give us dates as far back as the beginning of the solar system.

thermoluminescence dating A chronometric dating method based on the fact that when some materials are heated, they give off a flash of light. The intensity of the light is proportional to the amount of radiation to which the sample has been exposed and the length of time since the sample was heated.

Thermoluminescence Dating When some materials, such as crystals, are heated, they give off a flash of light, a phenomenon known as **thermoluminescence.** Minerals in the ground are constantly exposed to radiation from naturally occurring radioactive elements. The radioactivity causes some electrons to separate from the atoms; these electrons then fall into defects in the structure of the crystal, where they remain, accumulating through time. When the material is exposed to heat, the trapped electrons are liberated and, in the process, give off characteristic wavelengths of light at particular temperatures.

If the mineral has been exposed to constant radiation through time, the amount of light will be proportional to the age of the material. In addition, immediately after heating, no more light is seen until the mineral has been exposed to new radiation. Thus, the zero point for determining a date is the last heating of the material or the point at which the mineral was crystallized.

Thermoluminescence can be used to date archaeological finds, such as ceramics, burnt stones (such as those that make up a fire pit), and burnt flint tools, as well as geological material, such as volcanic material. This technique can be used to date fairly young objects, as well as objects from as far back as 300,000 years ago, depending on the nature of the material being dated.

electron spin resonance (ESR) dating A chronometric dating technique based on the behavior of electrons in crystals exposed to naturally occurring radioactivity; used to date limestone, coral, shell, teeth, and other materials.

Electron Spin Resonance Dating In our discussion of thermoluminescence, we saw that naturally occurring radioactivity causes some electrons to separate from the atoms and then fall into defects in the structure of the crystal. Most of the time, these electrons are trapped as pairs, but when an odd number of electrons become trapped, they behave like small magnets. In **electron spin resonance (ESR) dating,** an analysis of this property is used to establish a chronometric date. The method can be used to date many materials, including limestone, coral, shell, and teeth. This method can be used to date materials up to 300,000 years old.

amino acid racemization Chronometric dating method based on change in the three-dimensional structure of amino acids from one form to its mirror image over time.

Amino Acid Racemization Another example of chronometric dating is **amino acid racemization.** Many organic molecules, such as amino acids, occur in two forms that are identical in structure but are mirror images of each other. The amino acids found in proteins in living organisms, by convention, are called left-handed or L-amino acids; the L refers to *levo-*, or "left." Mirroring them are the right-handed or D-amino acids; the D refers to *dextro-*, or "right." When an organism dies, the L-amino acids slowly turn into D-amino acids, a process known as racemization.

coprolite Fossilized fecal material.

Amino acid racemization is used to date fossil material that contains amino acids; such material includes bone, teeth, **coprolites** (fossilized fecal material), corals, and sea shells. The process can be used to determine the age of material up to 200,000 years old. Its reliability decreases with age, however, and some types of material can be dated more accurately than others.

Amino acids are found in fossils since only 40 to 70 percent of the amino acids in datable material decompose. Each amino acid is associated with a characteristic speed of racemization at a given temperature. This is expressed as the racemization rate, which is the time it takes for half of the molecules to change to the D form. Problems occur with the use of this method, however, since many variables can affect the speed of racemization. The most significant variables are temperature and acidity of the soil. Because of this, calibrated ratios can be used only in a specific geographical area, and the consistency of temperatures over long periods of time needs to be demonstrated.

The Geomagnetic Time Scale

The invention of the compass made possible long-distance ocean voyages of exploration. The needle of a compass points toward the north magnetic pole. However, this is not the same as the true north that defines the axis on which the earth spins. At any particular point on the earth the angle made by a line pointing to true north and a line pointing to magnetic north is known as the **declination angle.**

The location of the magnetic north pole wanders over time, and as a result, the declination angle changes. Geologists have reconstructed the changes that have occurred over the last 10,000 years. **Archeomagnetism** is a dating technique that is based on the position of magnetic north as recorded in archaeological samples. When materials are heated to a high enough temperature, the individual crystals line up with magnetic north as it existed at the point in time when the materials were heated, thus creating a record of the location of magnetic north at that time. If the position of magnetic north is known over a period of time, the reconstruction of the declination angle can be used to estimate the date. This method is especially useful in dating hearths that are subject to high temperatures.

Geological studies have revealed the fact that over long periods the polarity of the earth's magnetic field completely reverses so that a compass needle that at one point in time points north might at a later point in time point south. No one has ever observed the occurrence of reversals in the polarity of the earth. Geologists, however, have found crystals in rock that act as small magnets. In molten rock, these crystals orient themselves to the poles before the rock solidifies. Once "frozen," they leave a record of the polarity of the earth at that point in time. The study of the polarity of these materials, both on land and on the sea floor, enables geologists to create a chart showing the sequence of magnetic reversals. When specific reversals are dated by radiometric techniques, a **geomagnetic reversal time scale (GRTS)** can be drawn. If a pattern of normal and reversed polarity is found in a rock formation, the pattern can be matched with the GRTS and dates can be assigned to the formation. Fossils are given approximate dates with respect to their context within the formation.

Figure 11.13 shows a portion of the GRTS. In the figure, intervals of normal polarity, that is, polarity that corresponds to what we find today, are pictured as solid color, while intervals of reversed polarity are seen as white. This scale is constantly being improved as new dates or more detailed profiles are determined. Large divisions of the scale that show primarily a single polarity are called **chrons,** while small subdivisions within a chron are known as **subchrons.** Geomagnetic reversals have been identified in rocks throughout the geologic time scale and have been used to date primate fossils throughout the Cenozoic.

The Geological Time Scale

Large sections of stratigraphic sequences are exposed in many parts of the world. The layers, of various colors and textures, are composed of different types of materials that represent the diverse environmental conditions existing at the time the layers were laid down. In addition, the fossil contents also differ. The study of the stratigraphic sequence of geological features and fossils provides the basis for the geological time scale.

Geologists have divided the history of the earth, as revealed in the stratigraphic record, into a hierarchy of units: the **era, period,** and **epoch.** Each division of geological time is

declination angle The angle formed by a line pointing to true north and a line pointing to magnetic north at a particular point on the surface of the earth.

archeomagnetism A dating technique that uses a determination of declination angle in archaeological samples.

geomagnetic reversal time scale (GRTS) A chart showing the sequence of normal and reversed polarity of the earth's magnetic field.

chron A large division of a geomagnetic time scale that shows primarily a single polarity.

subchron A small subdivision within a chron.

See the Online Learning Center for an Interactive Exercise on the geological time scale.

era A major division of geological time defined by major geological events and delineated by the kinds of animals and plant life it contains. Humans evolved in the Cenozoic era.

period A unit of geological time; a division of an era.

epoch A unit of geological time; a division of a period.

Figure 11.13 The Geomagnetic Reversal Time Scale

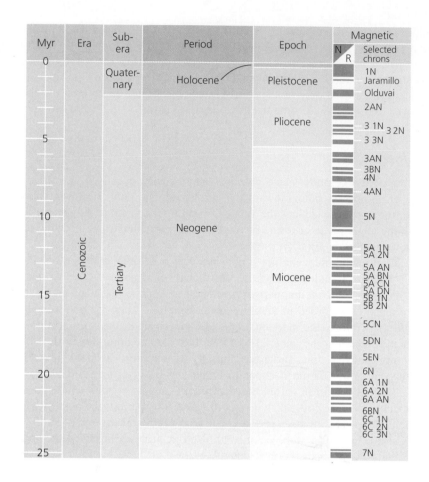

characterized by a distinct fossil flora and fauna and major geological events such as extensive mountain building. In general, the farther back in time we go, the more difficult it is to determine the events that occurred since more recent events often obliterate signs of earlier events. The geological time scale is outlined in Figure 11.14.

Plate Tectonics

See the Online Learning Center for an Interactive Exercise on plate tectonics.

tectonic plate A segment of the lithosphere.

lithosphere The hard outer layer of the earth.

plate tectonics The theory that the surface of the earth is divided into a number of plates that move in relationship to each other. Some of these plates carry the continents.

The surface of the earth can be compared loosely to a cracked eggshell. Like the fractured shell, the earth's surface is made up of several areas separated by distinct boundaries. These areas, called **tectonic plates,** are segments of the **lithosphere,** the hard outer layer of the earth. Unlike the segments of the eggshell, lithospheric plates move relative to one another as they float at about the rate of 2.5 centimeters (1 inch) a year atop a softer, more fluid layer of the earth. This process of constant plate movement, called **plate tectonics,** is in large part responsible for the formation of mountains and valleys, for earthquakes and volcanoes, for the rise of islands out of the sea, and for many other geological occurrences.

Some plates are completely covered by the sea, while others contain landmasses such as the continents and islands. Since the plates move, it follows that continents move, or "drift." Continents may move into each other; "slide" past each other; or break up, with the parts moving away from each other. Except for earthquakes, this movement occurs so slowly in relationship to a human lifetime that it can be detected only with very sensitive equipment.

Yet continents have been mobile for hundreds of millions of years. Approximately 225 million years ago, plates carrying all the major landmasses that existed at the time came together, forming one large continent called Pangaea (which is Greek for "all the earth"). By about 200 million years ago, this single landmass was breaking up.

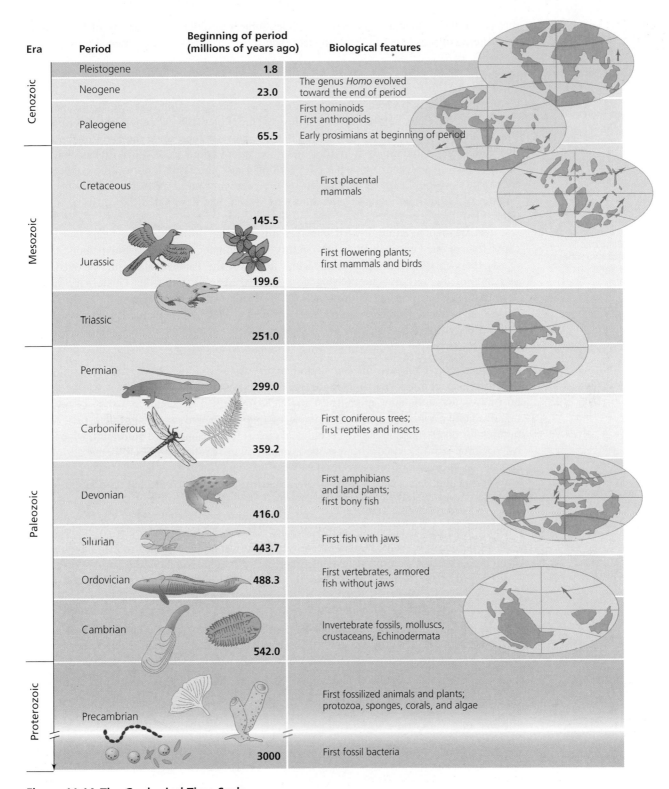

Figure 11.14 The Geological Time Scale

Figure 11.14 illustrates the relationship of the continents to each other at various points in time. An important point about continental drift is that it constantly, but slowly, has established and destroyed migration routes. Therefore, understanding the patterns of continental drift is extremely important in explaining why animals and plants are where they are today, that is, their distribution. The fact that different boundaries existed at different times for a population means that the population was at various times subject to different availability of food, different patterns of predation, different climates, and other changes in environmental pressures.

A Brief History of the Cenozoic

See the Online Learning Center for an Internet Activity on the Cenozoic.

Geological time is divided into three large eras: the Paleozoic, the Mesozoic, and the Cenozoic; the time before the beginning of the Paleozoic is called the Proterozoic. The Cenozoic is called the Age of Mammals because it represents the time of the adaptive radiation of mammals into the numerous and various ecological niches that they occupy today. The Cenozoic began 65.5 million years ago. The dividing line between the Mesozoic and the Cenozoic is marked by the relatively rapid extinction of a very large number of organisms, including the dinosaurs, which had dominated the earth for so long (Box 11-4).

subera A division of an era. The Cenozoic is divided into two suberas: the Tertiary and the Quaternary.

The Cenozoic can be divided into two **suberas,** the Tertiary and the Quaternary, concepts first defined in the eighteenth century. Today, many geologists and paleontologists divide the Cenozoic into three periods: the first two, the Paleogene and the Neogene, are divisions of the Tertiary; the Pleistogene is the only period within the Quaternary subera. As can be seen in Table 11.2, these periods are further divided into epochs: the Paleocene, Eocene, Oligocene, Miocene, Pliocene, Pleistocene, and Holocene (or Recent). In paleoanthropology, the Cenozoic era and its periods and epochs are of major concern since, during this time, the primates, including *Homo sapiens,* evolved.

The Paleogene The most ancient period of the Cenozoic, the Paleogene, contains three epochs: Paleocene, Eocene, and Oligocene. The first mammals evolved in the Mesozoic era, but it was not until the beginning of the Cenozoic, the Paleocene, that they began their major adaptive radiation. At the beginning of this epoch, the mammals found new opportunities for diversification into the ecological niches left vacant by the dinosaurs, which were by that time extinct. Although no modern mammalian families came into being during this epoch, the ancestors of modern families were present.

During the Paleocene, North America and Europe were connected as a single continent. The western and eastern parts of North America were separated by a large sea, and northwestern North America was connected by land to northeastern Asia. Other waterways covered parts of what is now South America, Africa, and Eurasia.

During the Paleocene, climates were warm and wet and mountains rose to new heights. Deciduous broad-leaved forests extended northward to approximately the latitude of today's Oslo, Norway, and Seward, Alaska, and conifer forests extended farther northward. Much of the present-day western United States was covered with subtropical forests and savanna. The early primates evolved within this setting.

During the Eocene, the land bridge between North America and Europe began to separate; the connection was gone by the end of this epoch. Large seas in Eurasia effectively isolated western Europe from the rest of the Old World. South America, Africa, and Australia were all

Table 11.2 The Geological Time Scale: The Cenozoic Era

Subera	Period	Epoch	Beginning Date (millions of years)
Quaternary	Pleistogene	Holocene	0.01
		Pleistocene	1.81
Tertiary	Neogene	Pliocene	5.33
		Miocene	23.03
	Paleogene	Oligocene	33.90
		Eocene	55.80
		Paleocene	65.50

On Thursday, March 18, 2004, at 5:08 P.M. Eastern Standard Time, a small asteroid measuring about 30 meters (100 feet) in diameter passed 43,000 kilometers (26,500 miles) above the surface of the earth. This is the closest encounter of an extraterrestrial object with the earth that has ever been recorded.

The earth's moon and many other moons and planets in the solar system are covered with scars from collisions involving meteors and asteroids from outer space. About 150 "impact structures" left from previous strikes have been identified on the surface of the earth. We may assume that many craters have yet to be found and that others have been obliterated by geological processes such as volcanism, erosions, and sedimentation. The best known impact crater is Meteor Crater in Arizona, which is 1.2 kilometers (4,100 feet) in diameter and 173 meters (570 feet deep) (see figure). The collision occurred about 49,000 years ago. It is probable that asteroids or comets will hit the earth in the future.

Although a dramatic sight, Meteor Crater represents a minor impact compared to that made by an asteroid or comet that may have crashed into the earth 65 million years ago. Some scientists believe that at that time, an extraterrestrial object 10 kilometers (6 miles) or more across struck the planet. The object would have hit the earth with a force 10,000 times more powerful than that of all the world's nuclear weapons. A candidate for the crater that resulted from the impact is located in the area of the Yucatan Peninsula of Mexico. The impact may have been responsible for the extinction of about 75 percent of all animal species living directly before the impact. This mass extinction is one of at least 12 such episodes that have occurred over the last 800 million years.

The discovery that led to the impact-extinction hypothesis dates back to 1978. At that time, a thin layer of iridium-rich clay was discovered in Gubbio, Italy. Since 1978, iridium, a rare element on earth but frequently found in meteorites (the earthly remains of asteroids), has been discovered in 65-million-year-old layers of the earth worldwide. The 65-million-B.P. date corresponds to the boundary between the Cretaceous and Tertiary periods and to the mass extinction.

If an interplanetary object was responsible for the extinctions, the impact may have created an enormous dust cloud of global proportions; as a consequence, sunlight was blocked and plants could not photosynthesize. As plants died out, the animals that were dependent on them for food also perished. Predators became extinct as their herbivorous prey succumbed. Because solar energy reaching the earth's surface was partially blocked, the planet also cooled. After the initial cooling period, a study of plant life suggests that a heating period occurred (the greenhouse effect). Many organisms that initially survived may have been wiped out by these climatic changes.

Another idea is that hot ejecta (objects thrown upward) were thrown into the atmosphere on the impact of the asteroid. On returning to earth, these objects could have caused global wildfires that precipitated a variety of cataclysmic effects, including acid rain that killed off sea, lake, and river life, creating a rippling food chain die-off.

It is probable that a large asteroid or comet will again hit the earth. This possibility has been exploited in such popular movies as the 1998 film *Armageddon.* Some scientists are now discussing the possibility of using the Star Wars Defense System, originally designed to destroy incoming enemy missiles, to divert the course of potentially dangerous interplanetary objects.

Sources: L. W. Alvarez, "Experimental Evidence That an Asteroid Impact Led to the Extinction of Many Species 65 Million Years Ago," *Proceedings of the National Academy of Sciences* 80 (1983), pp. 627–642; H. J. Melosh et al., "Ignition of Global Wildfires at the Cretaceous/Tertiary Boundary," *Nature* 343 (1990), pp. 251–254; V. E. Courtillot, "A Volcanic Eruption," *Scientific American* 263 (October 1990), pp. 82–92; G. S. Paul, "Giant Meteor Impacts and Great Eruptions: Dinosaur Killers?" *BioScience* 39 (1989), pp. 162–172; J. A. Wolfe, "Palaeo-Botanical Evidence of a Marked Temperature Increase Following the Cretaceous/ Tertiary Boundary," *Nature* 343 (1990), pp. 153–156; and NASA Near Earth Object Program, http://neo.jpl.nasa.gov/news/news142.html.

surrounded by water. In the latter part of the Eocene, temperatures began to cool, seasons became more pronounced, glaciers began to form in Antarctica, and climates became drier and more diverse. Nearly all the modern orders of mammals were present by the Eocene. Primates were widespread, and the earliest anthropoids were present by the end of this epoch.

During the Oligocene, climates continued to be characterized by increased cooling, drying, and alternating seasons. Africa and South America were closer than they are today and many islands existed in the southern Atlantic Ocean. Many paleoanthropologists believe that African anthropoids could have rafted across the Atlantic Ocean to South America. Some Oligocene primates are known from South American sites. All Old World primate fossils, which include early anthropoids, come from Africa, which was separated from Europe and Asia.

The Neogene The Neogene period consists of the Miocene and Pliocene epochs. In the early Miocene, we find the ancestors of the Old World monkeys and apes in east Africa; the first hominins may have appeared during this epoch as well. By the middle Miocene, African primates had begun to migrate over a newly formed land bridge into Asia and Europe. In general, climates in the Miocene were somewhat warmer than those in the Oligocene; by the late Miocene, climates were becoming cooler and drier. The continents were pretty much in their present position, but sea levels were higher than they are today and seas still covered large areas of land.

During the Pliocene, climates became cooler and more varied as the Antarctic ice cap continued to expand. Mountain building continued, and the mammals reached their high point in variety and size. During this epoch, the direct ancestors of *Homo sapiens* evolved.

The Pleistogene The epoch comprising all but the last 10,000 years of the Pleistogene period is the Pleistocene, an epoch marked by major fluctuations in the earth's geology and

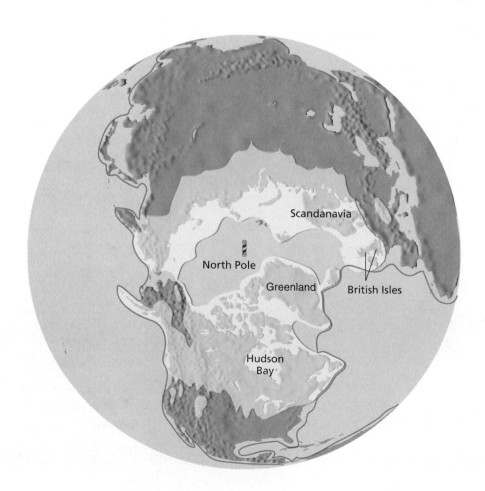

Figure 11.15 Pleistocene Glaciations This map shows the maximum extent of glaciation during the Pleistocene. The blue lines show the shorelines that emerged because of the lowering of the sea level.

climate. The Pleistocene was the time of many giant mammals, such as the giant ground sloths, mammoths and mastodons, and the saber-toothed cat; it was also the time of their extinction. During the Pleistocene, hominins became efficient hunters, and they were probably responsible for the extinction of many of these mammals.

The Pleistocene is noteworthy because during this time, large, long-lasting masses of ice, glaciers, were extensive. Great ice ages had already occurred several times in the history of earth, but the Pleistocene Ice Age is the most recent, and it is certainly the best known. When one speaks of an ice age, the image of a world dominated by freezing temperatures and covered with ice comes to mind, but ice never covered the entire earth. The extent of the continental glaciers is shown in Figure 11.15.

The Pleistocene was not a time of continuous glaciation; rather, it was marked by both **glacial** and **interglacial** periods. During glacials, the glacial ice expanded, but during interglacials, the climates were as warm as or even warmer than those prevailing today. Actually, each of the major glacials and interglacials was a complex event, comprising cooler and warmer episodes.

glacial Period of expansion of glacial ice.

interglacial Period of warming between two glacials.

During the last glacial, sea levels dropped at least 100 meters (330 feet) below their present level, primarily because large amounts of water were "locked up" in glacial ice. Land connections came into existence wherever shallow water had separated two or more landmasses. For example, during the periods of glaciation, Asia was connected by land to North America; thus animals, including humans, were able to cross between the two at the point of connection. The Pleistocene Ice Age also caused changes in vegetation patterns: As glaciers advanced and retreated, forests turned into grasslands. Great herds of mammals flourished, fed by the grasslands at the foot of glacial ice, but as forests again replaced the grasslands, the herds declined.

Summary

The interpretation of the fossil record demands accurate dating of fossils. Relative dating provides information on the sequence of fossils in terms of which are older and which are younger. Stratigraphy is based on the principle of superposition, which states that the lower strata in a deposit are older than those above. One major difficulty with stratigraphy is the possibility that newer material has intruded into older material via burial or cataclysms. Methods such as fluorine analysis can help establish whether two bones are contemporary.

Chronometric dating provides an actual calendrical date. The most important chronometric dating methods are based on the decay of radioactive elements. Carbon-14 dating was the first radiometric technique developed, but it is limited to the last 50,000 to 60,000 years. Potassium-argon dating is based on the radioactive decay of potassium 40, which has an extremely long half-life; consequently, this method can be used to date the age of the earth. Other dating techniques are fission-track dating, amino acid racemization, thermoluminescence, electron spin resonance, and geomagnetism.

The history of the earth is divided, in terms of geological and paleontological events, into four eras. Each era is divided into periods, which, in turn, are divided into epochs. Thus, the Cenozoic era, which is the Age of Mammals, can be discussed in terms of its many subdivisions.

The evolution of life has been greatly affected by earth dynamics. Landmasses move in relationship to each other, thus creating new migratory routes and destroying others. In addition, plate tectonics is responsible for many climatic alternations, and it may have been a prime cause of the cooling that led to the Pleistocene Ice Age. This was a time of fluctuating temperatures and environments, and as such, it presented a series of changing selective pressures that helped to shape human evolution.

Key Terms

amino acid racemization, *278*
archeomagnetism, *279*
argon 40/argon 39 dating, *276*
artifact, *267*
calendrical system, *274*
cast, *264*
chron, *279*
chronometric dates, *274*
chronospecies, *270*
computerized tomography, *267*
coprolite, *278*
declination angle, *279*
dendrochronology, *275*
electron spin resonance
   (ESR) dating, *278*
epoch, *279*
era, *279*
fission-track dating, *278*
fluorine dating, *274*
fossil, *262*
geomagnetic reversal time
   scale (GRTS), *279*

glacial, *285*
half-life, *275*
hydraulic behavior, *266*
index fossil, *273*
interglacial, *285*
isotopes, *275*
lithosphere, *280*
mold, *264*
paleoanthropology, *267*
paleoecology, *268*
paleontology, *268*
paleopathology, *267*
paleospecies, *270*
palynology, *268*
period, *279*
plate tectonics, *280*
populationist
   viewpoint, *269*
potassium-argon
   dating, *276*
preservation
   potential, *266*

radioactivity, *275*
radiocarbon dating, *275*
radiometric dating
   techniques, *275*
relative dating, *274*
sediment, *272*
sedimentary beds, *272*
sedimentation, *265*
single-crystal fusion, *277*
standard deviation, *275*
stratigraphy, *272*
subchron, *279*
subera, *282*
superposition, *272*
taphonomy, *263*
tectonic plate, *280*
thermoluminescence
   dating, *278*
tree-ring dating, *275*
typological viewpoint, *269*
unconformity, *272*

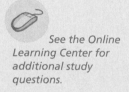

See the Online Learning Center for additional study questions.

Study Questions

1. What does the field of taphonomy tell us about the development of the fossil record? Why is fossilization a relatively rare event?

2. Why are some animals better represented in the fossil record than others? What are the various "sampling errors" found in the fossil record?

3. Although the fossil record is fragmentary, paleontologists are able to reconstruct a great deal about once-living animals. Describe some of the types of information that can be deduced from fossil evidence.

4. Species are defined in terms of reproductive isolation. Since evidence for this cannot be inferred from the fossil record, how does the paleontologist handle the concept of prehistoric species?

5. Individual fossils that were considered representatives of different species have sometimes turned out to belong to a single species. What factors are responsible for variation within species as represented in the fossil record?

6. Distinguish between relative dating and chronometric dating. What are some examples of each type of dating method?

7. Geological events often have a profound influence on the evolution of living organisms. Briefly describe the impact of continental drift on the evolution of plants and animals.

Critical Thinking Questions

1. How can we be confident that certain events took place millions of years ago when no one was around to see them? We reconstruct fossil and archaeological events through inference based on geological and paleontological evidence. What evidence is there that convinces us that now-extinct forms really did live millions of years ago?

2. Although there are limitations on what we can learn from a fossil, the popular media frequently produce reconstructions of what organisms looked like in life. A new fossil hominin has been discovered. You have been hired by a major news magazine to paint a cover illustrating how the hominin looked in life. How would you go about producing the painting? What features would you be confident of? What features would remain speculation?

3. You are an explorer from outer space landing on earth some 200,000 years in the future. The earth is devoid of living hominins. You excavate a site dated 200,000 years old (that is, dated to the year 2006). How would the location of the site affect your reconstruction of human life and culture? As you excavate more and more sites, would your conclusions about hominin life on earth in the year 2006 continually change? Why?

Suggested Readings

Donovan, S. K., and C. Paul. *The Adequacy of the Fossil Record.* New York: John Wiley & Sons, 1999. The authors and 12 contributors discuss why the incomplete nature of the fossil record does not mean that the fossil record is inadequate for answering a wide range of paleontological, geological, and biological questions.

Fowler, B. *Iceman: Uncovering the Life and Times of a Prehistoric Man Found in an Alpine Glacier.* Chicago: University of Chicago Press, 2001. This book describes the scientific research on the 5300-year-old "Ice Man" and the artifacts found with him.

Gould, S. J. *Time's Arrow and Time's Cycle: Myth and Metaphor in the Discovery of Geological Time.* Cambridge, MA: Harvard University Press, 1988. In this book, Stephen Jay Gould discusses the history of the discovery of deep time, particularly the writings of Thomas Burnet, James Hutton, and Charles Lyell.

Prothero, D. A. *Bringing Fossils to Life.* New York: McGraw-Hill, 2nd edition, 2003. This is a general introduction to paleobiology with chapters on the nature of the fossil record, variation in fossil populations, and dating methods.

Shipman, P. *Life History of a Fossil: An Introduction to Taphonomy and Paleoecology.* Cambridge, MA: Harvard University Press, 1981. This book can serve as an introductory text on taphonomy.

Taylor, R. E. *Radiocarbon Dating: An Archaeological Approach.* Orlando, FL: Academic, 1987. This volume discusses the history, methodology, and problems of carbon-14 dating.

Suggested Websites

International Commission on Stratigraphy (ICS):
www.stratigraphy.org/index_top.htm

Minnesota State University Museum:
http://emuseum.mankato.msus.edu/archaeology/dating/

UC Berkeley Museum of Paleontology:
www.ucmp.berkeley.edu

United States Geologic Survey Geologic Time Online Edition:
http://pubs.usgs.gov/gip/geotime

Virtual Courseware for Earth and Environmental Sciences: Virtual Dating:
http://vearthquate.catstatela.edu/VirtualDating

Chapter 12

The Early Primate Fossil Record and the Origins of the Hominins

The Paris Basin in the Late Eocene. The diurnal *Adapis parisiensis* feeds on leaves, while at night the tiny *Pseudoloris* hunts an insect and *Necrolemur* (left) and *Microchoeruis* (right) cling to branches.

If we are to place our origins in proper perspective, we must . . . be concerned not only with identifying our immediate and processional ancestors, but also with developing an appreciation of the true extent of primate diversity in the past, for it is from amidst this diversity that we emerged. ●

—*Russell L. Cicochon and Dennis A. Etler*

Chapter Outline

See the Online Learning Center for a chapter summary, chapter outline, and learning objectives.

After Reading This Chapter, You Should Be Able to Answer These Questions:

1. What is the earliest fossil evidence of the primates? What were the earliest primates like?

2. What were the early true Eocene primates like?

3. What were the earliest anthropoid fossils like? Where were they found and how old are they?

4. What is the fossil evidence for the evolution of New World monkeys and Old World monkeys?

5. What are some of the paleospecies that paleontologists consider to be early hominoids? How do they resemble and differ from living apes?

6. What geological and ecological changes occurred in the Miocene that influenced the evolution of the hominids?

7. What were some of the better-known hominid genera of the Miocene? Which are the best candidates for ancestors of the living hominids?

8. What are the most important characteristics that define the early hominin genera *Sahelanthropus, Orrorin,* and *Ardipithecus?*

See the Online Learning Center for an Interactive Exercise on the nonhominid primate fossil record.

A dominant theme in evolutionary studies is that of origins—the origins of humans, of primates, of animals, and, indeed, of life itself. Yet evidence of origins is difficult to identify since the earliest members of a taxonomic group often lack many of the characteristics of the later and better-known members of that group. Perhaps they resemble more closely the members of the group from which they evolved. Certainly in our search for the earliest primates, we would hardly expect to find a monkeylike or an apelike creature with a fully evolved set of features like those that characterize contemporary animals.

EVOLUTION OF THE EARLY PRIMATES

Overshadowed by the dinosaurs, the earliest mammals evolved during the Mesozoic era. By Paleocene times at the beginning of the Cenozoic era, all the dinosaurs, as well as many other forms of life, were extinct and mammals had begun their adaptive radiation into numerous orders. By the start of the Eocene most of the modern orders of mammals had appeared, including the order Primates.

At the end of the Mesozoic, great forests evolved with flowering trees that provided protection and food for early primates. Some of the early primates, which were quite unlike the primates of today, became extinct without leaving ancestors; others eventually evolved into modern species. This chapter describes what we know about the complex evolutionary history of the early primates.

The Earliest Primates

While there is some disputed paleontological evidence for the existence of very early primates in the Cretaceous, the earliest well-documented primate fossils date from the Early Paleocene—at least they are thought to be primates by some. Yet most investigators believe that the origins of the primates lie in the Cretaceous.

The molecular data suggest that the last common ancestor of all the primates lived some 90 million years ago. Since the features that define the primates evolved after that point in time, one would expect that the earliest recognizable primate fossils would date some time later than the date suggested by the molecular data. In fact, the earliest securely dated fossils that may be thought of as primate (some researchers disagree) date from the Early Eocene, some 55 to 54 million years ago. Using a statistical model, a group of paleontologists reconstructed from the fossil record a date for the last common ancestor of the primates of 81.5 million years ago. They also concluded that only 7 percent or less of all primate species that have ever lived have been found as fossils.[1]

Primates are tropical and subtropical animals found primarily in Africa, southern and southeastern Asia, the southern regions of North America, and parts of South America. Yet when one takes into consideration extinct species, almost half the known primate fossil species have been found in North America and Europe. As we discussed in Chapter 11, North America and Europe had a subtropical climate during the early part of the Cenozoic. The two continents were also connected by a land bridge, which explains the existence of similar forms in both regions.

The Plesiadapiformes The earliest primates belong to the Plesiadapiformes, at least according to those who accept those animals as primates. They were discovered over 100 years ago, and more than 75 paleospecies are recognized from North America and Europe. They were a highly successful group of mammals that underwent a considerable adaptive radiation during the Paleocene; some survived into the early Eocene.

Plesiadapiforms were small arboreal quadrupeds. Their limbs were relatively short and ended in claws; they lacked a grasping big toe. An impression in limestone shows a long

---

[1] S. Tavaré et al., "Using the Fossil Record to Estimate the Age of the Last Common Ancestor of Extant Primates," *Nature* 416 (2002), pp. 726–729.

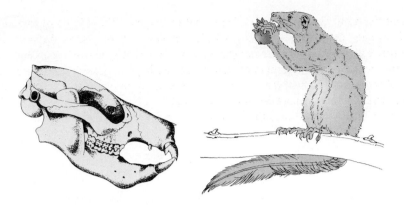

Figure 12.1
Plesiadapis A Paleocene
plesiadapiform.

bushy tail. The snout is long, and the lower incisors lie in a horizontal position and act as pincers against the specialized upper central incisors. There is a large diastema in both the upper and the lower jaws. The skull lacks a postorbital bar, and the brain is relatively small.

Because of these characteristics, many primatologists believe that the plesiadapiformes were not direct ancestors of the later primates but were an early offshoot from the group that included the actual primate ancestor. Many primatologists do not place them in the primate order at all. At one time they were thought to be closely related to the "flying lemurs," or colugos, of the Philippines (order Dermoptera), but the discovery of new postcranial bones has demonstrated that the plesiadapiformes lack the gliding membrane found in the colugos.

Purgatorius, named after the Purgatory Hills of Montana, lived in the Early Paleocene in North America and Europe and is the earliest of the plesiadapiformes. As is the case with so many species from this epoch, all we know of this animal are its teeth. However, from this evidence we know that *Purgatorius* was a small rat-sized animal that had an insectivorous diet but also may have consumed fruit. One of the better-known genera is *Plesiadapis,* which is known from several skulls and postcranial material (Figure 12.1).

The Early True Primates and the Origins of the Prosimians

The Eocene began about 56 million years ago, and it lasted about 22 million years. At the start of the Eocene, North America and Europe were still joined, but they had separated by the end of the epoch. This separation isolated animals that had evolved on what had previously been a single landmass.

The Early and Middle Eocene were very warm and wet with less seasonality than is found at other times. This changed in the Late Eocene, when climates became more diverse with marked seasons. Whales, rodents, bats, horses, and numerous other types of mammals were present by the end of the Eocene.

Primates that show anatomical features of living primates first appear at the beginning of the Eocene. There are no reasonable candidates among the plesiadapiformes or other Paleocene mammals for the direct ancestor of the Eocene primates. There are a few Paleocene fossils that might be early representatives of these primates, but the evidence is not conclusive. Two distinct groups of primates appeared at the beginning of the Eocene in both North America and Eurasia. They make up the families Adapidae and Omomyidae.

The Adapidae and the Origin of the Lemuriformes Members of the Adapidae resemble in many ways the modern lemurs and lorises. They are generally larger than the omomyids; many are as large as the larger lemurs living today. Nails are present on fingers and toes. The several relatively complete skeletons exhibit long torsos, legs, and tails, along with grasping feet with divergent big toes; these were adaptations for leaping and grasping behavior (Figure 12.2).

See the Online Learning Center for an Internet Activity on the Eocene.

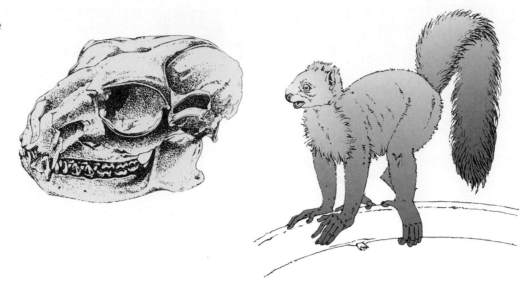

Figure 12.2
Smilodectes An Eocene
adapid.

The adapid skull exhibits an elongated snout. The size of the brain case relative to the size of the facial skeleton is larger than in most mammals, and studies of the brain case show an enlargement of the frontal portion of the brain. A complete bony ring encircles the eye, and the forward position of the eyes results in overlapping fields of vision; the relatively small orbits suggest that the animal was diurnal.

The adapid incisors are short and spatulate and are vertically implanted in the jaw. The upper and lower canines interlock and show a marked sexual dimorphism; the anterior lower premolar is sectorial. Most adapids retained four premolars in each quadrant of the jaw. Various adapid dentitions show differing dietary adaptations, including specializations for eating insects, fruits, and leaves.

The living lemuriformes are divided into two superfamilies. The earliest fossils that can be said to belong to the superfamily Lorisoidea were recovered in 2001 from the Fayum of Egypt. Two species are represented: *Karanisia clarki* is a loris-like primate, and *Saharagalago misrensis* resembles the galagos. They date from the Middle Eocene, between 41 and 37 million years ago. The lower jaw of *Karanisia* provides the earliest evidence of the dental comb that characterizes the lemuriformes.

The usually encountered scenario is that the lemurs (Lemurioidea) migrated from Africa to the island of Madagascar. Yet the earliest known lemur is actually from Pakistan. This is *Bugtilemur mathesoni* from the Early Oligocene deposits of the Bugti Hills. This fact complicates the puzzle of lemur origins and migrations.

The Omomyids and the Origin of the Tarsiers The members of the family Omomyidae appear in the fossil record at about the same time as the adapids, in the Early Eocene. They have been found in North American and Europe, but fossils also have been recovered in Africa and Asia. These were small, nocturnal primates that bear close resemblances to the living tarsiers. In fact, some of the Oligocene forms are actually thought of as tarsiers. As in the tarsiers, the tarsal bones are elongated.

The Omomyid skull exhibits a short snout with a V-shaped jaw. The orbit is encircled by a complete bony ring, and some species possess the beginning of a postorbital closure. The large size of the orbits relative to the length of the skull suggests that the omomyids were nocturnal.

The lower incisors protrude and are moderately or sharply pointed. The canine teeth are relatively small; they are not interlocking, nor do they show marked sexual dimorphism. The anterior lower premolars are not sectorial. Most omomyids show a reduction in the number of teeth, and most show a dental formula with fewer than four premolars in each

Figure 12.3 *Shoshonius* Reconstruction of the omomyid *Shoshonius cooperi.*

quadrant of the mouth. Details of their dentition suggest an insectivorous diet. The omomyids were generally smaller than the adapids.

One of the best known of the Omomyidae is *Shoshonius,* which shows many features that closely resemble the living tarsier (Figure 12.3). This fossil genus was first recovered during the mid-1980s in Wyoming; it dates to the Early Eocene, about 50.5 million years ago. Its orbits are large relative to skull length, and it possesses a postorbital bar; however, a postorbital plate is not present.

Many fossils from this time are known exclusively from teeth. However, the teeth of the early tarsiers are rather unspecialized, and the essential feature of the tarsiers is their method of locomotion: vertical clinging and leaping. This is why the discovery in 1997 of a tibiofibula belonging to *Afrotarsius* in the Fayum of Egypt is so important. The tarsiers are characterized by very long legs relative to the arms and the trunk. Modern tarsiers have an intermembral index of 55. Two bones of the ankle are similarly elongated. The two bones of the lower leg, the tibia and fibula, are fused, hence the name *tibiofibula*. The bone from the Fayum is very similar to that of a living tarsier and can be placed in the family Tarsiidae. Teeth from Jiangsu Province in China are so similar to those of living tarsiers that this fossil has been placed into the genus *Tarsius*. This means that the modern tarsier has the oldest fossil record of any living primate.

Summary

Although the fossil and molecular data suggest that the last common ancestor of all the primates lived in the Cretaceous, the earliest securely dated primate fossils date from the Early Eocene, some 55 to 54 million years ago. Almost half the known living and fossil primate species have been found in North America and Europe, which were subtropical during the early part of the Cenozoic.

The earliest possible primates belong to the Plesiadapiforms that lived in North America and Europe during the Paleocene and Early Eocene. Their limbs are short and end in claws; they lack a grasping big toe, the snout is long, there is a large diastema in both the upper and the lower jaws, the skull lacks a postorbital bar, and the brain is small. Because of these characteristics, many primatologists believe that the plesiadapiforms were not direct ancestors of the later primates but were an early offshoot from the group that included the actual primate ancestor; many primatologists do not place them in the primate order at all.

Primates that show anatomical features of living primates first appear in at the beginning of the Eocene. They belong to two distinct groups that are found in North America and Eurasia. The members of the Adapidae resemble the modern lemurs and lorises; the Omomyidae resemble the modern tarsiers. The earliest loris-like and galago-like primates were discovered in Egypt and date from the Middle Eocene. The earliest lemur is from the Early Oligocene in Pakistan. Middle and Late Eocene fossils from Egypt and China represent the earliest tarsiers.

EVOLUTION OF THE ANTHROPOIDEA

The suborder Anthropoidea is the division of the order Primates that includes the living monkeys, apes, and humans. The earliest anthropoids in the fossil record date from the Middle Eocene and are known from sites in Africa and Asia. Elwyn Simons and Tab Rasmussen list the major specialized features that the Late Eocene and Oligocene anthropoids share with living anthropoids that distinguish the early anthropoids from the prosimians and tarsiers.

> These include (1) complete bony "eye sockets" or postorbital closure; (2) a fused metopic suture (i.e., there is a single frontal bone rather than a right and a left); (3) an annular ecto-tympanic bone attached to the lateral bullar margin (the ear drum is supported by a bone hoop tightly anchored to the bony wall of the ear); (4) lower molars that have reduced trigonids and are bunodont in structure (having rounded puffy cusps for crushing and grinding); and (5) deep mandibles with broadly curved angular regions, steep ascending rami, and fused midline symphyses (indicating a chewing system capable of generating great forces).[2]

---

[2] E. L. Simons and T. Rasmussen, "A Whole New World of Ancestors: Eocene Anthropoidean from Africa," *Evolutionary Anthropology* 3 (1994), pp. 128–139. Copyright © 1994 Wiley-Liss, Inc. Reprinted by permission of John Wiley & Sons, Inc.

In 1927, G. E. Pilgrim described a jaw fragment from the Late Eocene of Myanmar (formerly Burma). Since that time several jaws have been recovered from Myanmar and Thailand belonging to *Amphipithecus, Pondaugnia,* and *Siamopithecus.* However, in the late 1990s new material was recovered that included, for the first time, cranial and postcranial material. Analysis of the new fossils has led to conclusion that these are not anthropoids at all but are related to the adapids. The dental features that suggested anthropoid affinities were the result of convergent evolution. Other, smaller forms were also found in Asia in the 1990s, including *Bahinia, Myanmarpithecus,* and *Eosimias.* These genera also exhibited anthropoid features.

Over several decades many paleontologists have attempted to make a case for an early diversification of anthropoids in the Eocene of Asia and perhaps an Asiatic origin for the anthropoids. Today, however, it is widely believed that Africa is the most likely center of the early anthropoid evolution that took place in the Late Eocene. The anthropoids most likely did not reach Asia until the Late Oligocene.

The Anthropoids of the Fayum

The richest fossil site from the Late Eocene and Early Oligocene is the Fayum in Egypt. During the Eocene and Oligocene, the Fayum was a tropical forest bordering on a large inland sea. The dense forests, swamps, and rivers were the homes of rodents; insectivores; bats; crocodiles; rhinoceros-size herbivores; miniature ancestors of the elephants; water birds such as herons, storks, and cranes; and many species of primates. Today the once-lush tropical forest is a desert with little plant or animal life.

The rich deposits of fossil primates are a part of a series of sedimentary beds that make up the Jebel Qatrani Formation. This formation, some 350 meters (1150 feet) thick, spans the period from 36 to 33 million B.P., which includes the Late Eocene and Early Oligocene. Figure 12.4 (p. 296) shows a cross-section of the Jebel Qatrani Formation and the location of the discoveries of several genera.

The Parapithecidae The fossils discovered before 1988 were found in the upper levels of the Jebel Qatrani Formation, and they are referred to as the *upper-sequence primates.* They are classified into two families, the Parapithecidae and the Propliopithecidae. These primates are listed in Table 12.1.

Table 12.1 Some Fossils from the Fayum, Egypt

Quarry*	Epoch	Age (myr)	Species	Family
Quarries I, M	Early Oligocene	33.1–33.4	*Aegyptopithecus zeuxis*	Propliopithecidae
			Propliopithecus chirobates	Propliopithecidae
			Apidium phiomense	Parapithecidae
			Parapithecus grangeri	Parapithecidae
			Qatrania fleaglei	Parapithecidae
Quarries V, G	Early Oligocene	33.8–34.0	*Propliopithecus haecheli*	Propliopithecidae
			Propliopithecus ankeli	Propliopithecidae
			Apidium moustafai	Parapithecidae
Quarry E	Late Eocene	34.0–35.1	*Oligopithecus savagei*	Propliopithecidae
			Qatrania wingi	Parapithecidae
Quarry L-41	Late Eocene	35.6–35.9	*Catopithecus browni*	Propliopithecidae
			Proteopithecus sylviae	Propliopithecidae
			Serapia eocaena	Parapithecidae

* Quarries refer to specific deposits where fossils have been excavated.
Dates from E. L. Simons and T. Rasmussen, "A Whole New World of Ancestors: Eocene Anthropoidean from Africa," *Evolutionary Anthropology* 3 (1994), pp. 128–139.

**Figure 12.4
Anthropoids of the
Jebel Qatrani
Formation, Fayum,
Egypt**

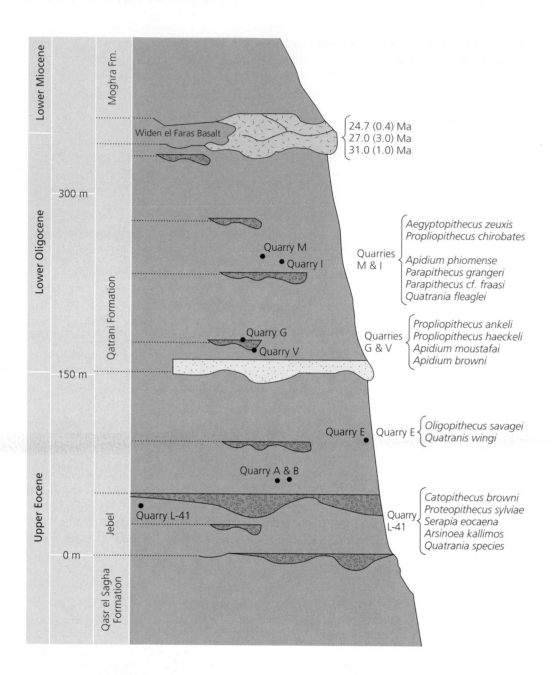

The parapithecids are very small and are similar in size to the living marmosets and tamarins. One species, weighing about 300 grams (0.7 pound), is the smallest known living or extinct Old World anthropoid. The few postcranial bones recovered suggest that they were probably branch runners and walkers and leapers. One genus of this group, *Apidium*, is known from hundreds of individual fossils, and it is one of the most common mammals in the Fayum beds (Figure 12.5).

The parapithecids display several anthropoid features, yet they resemble the tarsiers in some details of dentition and other features. The mandible is V-shaped, and the canines show a marked sexual dimorphism. The molars show low, rounded cusps characteristic of living fruit eaters, and the thick enamel of the molars suggests the inclusion of hard nuts in the diet as well. Their dental formula is 2.1.3.3/2.1.3.3. This is the dental formula found today among New World monkeys, and it may represent the primitive dental formula of all anthropoids.

The Parapithecidae are most likely a branch that split off as part of the early anthropoid radiation. Although they possessed many features found in living anthropoids, the lineage probably became extinct.

The Propliopithecidae The best known propliopithecid is *Aegyptopithecus*. Although the first sparse fossil remains of *Aegyptopithecus* were discovered in 1906, today we are able to study many skulls and some postcranial material (Figure 12.6). The *Aegyptopithecus* male probably weighed about 6 kilograms (13 pounds) and is the largest of the Fayum primates.

Aegyptopithecus is a good example of a transitional form. Its long snout and relatively small brain case remind us of the adapids. The dentition points to an affinity with the hominoid line. Details of the teeth and jaw are similar to those of the Miocene and Pliocene hominoids. The size of the eye sockets suggests that *Aegyptopithecus* was diurnal. The relative expansion of the visual areas of the brain and the relative decrease in the olfactory areas, as seen in the endocranial cast, provide evidence for the importance of vision over smell.

The locomotor behavior of *Aegyptopithecus* is known from the analysis of several postcranial bones (Figure 12.7). It was probably an arboreal quadruped capable of some degree of leaping and suspensory behavior.

The large number of *Aegyptopithecus* specimens makes it possible to analyze the material for variation within the species. Differences in tooth size suggest a marked sexual dimorphism. Living primates that live in

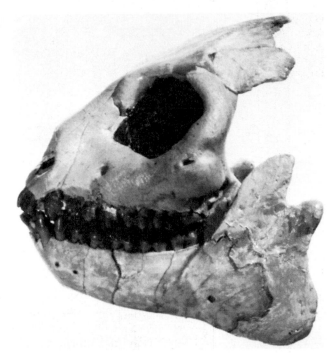

Figure 12.5 *Apidium* A reconstruction of *Apidium*, a member of the family Parapithecidae from the Fayum.

large social units containing several adults of both sexes (such as the baboons) exhibit a high degree of sexual dimorphism. In contrast, primates that live in small social units (for example, the gibbons) show very little difference in size and proportions between the male and female. The fact that *Aegyptopithecus* shows a marked sexual dimorphism suggests that these primates lived in complex social groups.

The many similarities between *Aegyptopithecus* and modern apes have led some paleoanthropologists to view it as an early member of the Hominoidea. Yet recent studies have emphasized the many features that are more similar to those of the New World and Old World monkeys. It is very likely that the propliopithecids represent a group of primates ancestral to both the cercopithecoids and the hominoids.

An area of the Fayum known as Locality 41 is located in the lower strata of the Jebel Qatrani Formation. Several nearly complete skulls of *Catopithecus,* an early member of the family Propliopithecidae, were recovered in 1992 and 1993. These were small animals about the size of a modern marmoset. The dentition suggests a diet of insects and fruits. The diameter of the eye socket falls within the smaller numbers characteristic of living diurnal primates. Analysis of the few known postcranial bones suggests that *Catopithecus* was a branch runner and walker and leaper, moving through its habitat in a way that resembles that of the smaller living New World monkeys today.

The Evolution of the New World Monkeys

The New World monkeys most likely evolved from the early African anthropoids. Throughout most of the Cenozoic, South America was separated from North America. Although there was never a land connection between South America and Africa during that era, a major lowering of

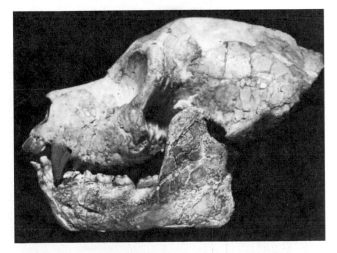

Figure 12.6 *Aegyptopithecus* The reconstructed skull of *Aegyptopithecus zeuxis* from the Oligocene of the Fayum.

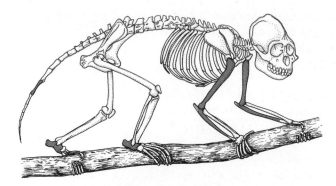

Figure 12.7 *Aegyptopithecus* The reconstructed postcranial skeleton of *Aegyptopithecus zeuxis*. Bones shown in color and the skull have been recovered.

sea levels occurred in the Middle Oligocene. This event would have exposed much of the African continental shelf, and many islands would have surfaced above the South Atlantic waters. Aided by these islands, the ancestral ceboid monkeys could have crossed the Atlantic Ocean on naturally formed rafts.

Although the New World monkeys and Old World monkeys evolved independently, the fact that they are descended from a common ancestor and that they occupy similar ecological niches has led to many similarities in their appearances. This is an example of parallelism.

The oldest fossil member of the superfamily Ceboidea is *Branisella*. It lived in Bolivia about 27 million years ago, during the Late Oligocene. This and another Late Oligocene fossil, *Dolichocebus,* which was found in Patagonia in southern Argentina, show little similarity with any contemporary primate population.

It appears that the differentiation of New World monkeys into their present subfamilies had occurred by Middle Miocene times. Known fossils include possible ancestors of the subfamily Cebinae (the modern squirrel and capuchin monkeys), the subfamily Alouattinae (the modern howler monkeys), and the subfamily Pithecinae (the modern sakis and uakaris). The similarity between the fossil and the modern owl monkey (subfamily Aotinae) is so close that they have been placed in the same genus, *Aotus* (Figure 12.8). Finally, an early representative of the marmosets, family Callitrichidae, also may be present.

The Evolution of the Old World Monkeys

The earliest fossils of the Old World monkeys belong to the genera *Prohylobates* and *Victoriapithecus;* they make up the family Victoriapithecidae. Specimens have been found in fossil beds from the Early and Middle Miocene in north Africa, Kenya, and Uganda.

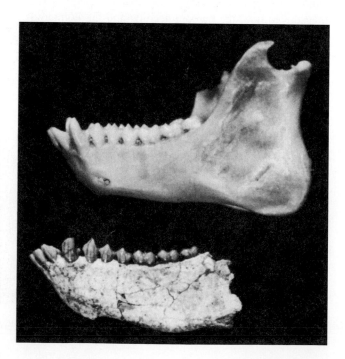

Figure 12.8 *Aotus* The mandible of *Aotus dindensis* from the Middle Miocene (below) and of the modern *Aotus trivigatus* (above).

Both genera are known primarily from dental remains that are more primitive than the teeth of the later monkeys. Discoveries of dental, cranial, and postcranial material on Maboko Island in Kenya suggest that *Victoriapithecus* was a small primate weighing about 3.5 to 4 kilograms (7.7 to 8.8 pounds). It moved quadrupedally in the trees and on the ground.

The origin of the Cercopithecoidea is uncertain. Some paleoanthropologists view the Old World monkeys as a very specialized primate group that evolved as part of an earlier and more generalized anthropoid radiation. Certainly, the anthropoids had undergone a major adaptive radiation, and by Early Miocene times they had become very diverse and numerous. Yet at that time the cercopithecoids, represented by the victoriapithecids, were fairly uncommon. Hominoids occupied many of the ecological niches that would later be occupied by the monkeys. Only later, when the diversity and number of hominoids diminished, did the cercopithecoids assume a dominant role in the mammalian fauna.

There is a gap of 10 million years between the last record of the Victoriapithecidae and the next-oldest known fossil evidence of the Old World monkeys. The monkeys became more numerous in the Late Miocene fossil record. By this time, the Old World monkeys had divided into the two subfamilies seen today: the Cercopithecinae and the Colobinae.

The fossil cercopithecines closely resemble living populations to which they were undoubtedly ancestral or closely related. The earliest macaques lived in the Late Miocene or Early Pliocene of northern Africa. *Parapapio,* from the Lower Miocene of eastern and southern Africa, is probably close to the origin of the baboons and the mangabeys. The geladas, found today in a small range in the Ethiopian desert, were once widespread throughout Africa and extended eastward to India. One species belonging to the genus that includes the living gelada, *Theropithecus oswaldi,* is the largest known monkey (100 kilograms, or 220 pounds) (Figure 12.9). The guenons, today one of the most common monkeys in Africa, are represented by fragmentary dental remains found in Pliocene and Pleistocene beds in east Africa.

While the prehistoric cercopithecines are very similar to extant populations, this is not true for the colobines. Fossil members of the subfamily Colobinae are quite different from modern forms, and they also are found throughout a greater range. They were present in

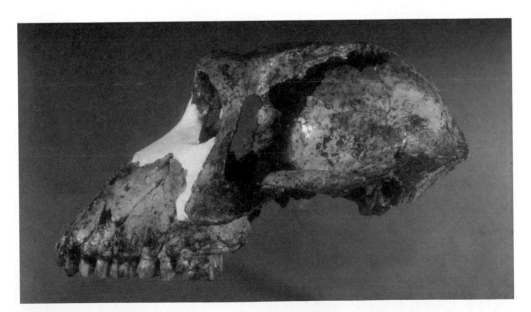

Figure 12.9 *Theropithecus* The skull of *Theropithecus oswaldi,* an extinct species of gelada from the Pleistocene.

Late Miocene and Pliocene Europe. While they also were present in Asia, the fossils have been fragmentary.

Summary

The suborder Anthropoidea includes the living monkeys, apes, and humans. They are characterized by complete bony eye sockets, a fused metopic suture, lower molars that have rounded puffy cusps, deep mandibles with fused midline symphyses, and other features.

The Jebel Qatrani Formation, of the Fayum of Egypt, dates from the Late Eocene and Early Oligocene. The primates of the upper levels belong to the families Parapithecidae and Propliopithecidae. The Propliopithecidae, which includes *Aegyptopithecus,* may represent a group of primates ancestral to both the cercopithecoids and the hominoids.

The ceboids, or New World monkeys, are probably derived from early African anthropoids that traveled across the then-narrower Atlantic Ocean on natural rafts. The earliest-known ceboid dates from the Late Oligocene of Bolivia. The evolution of the ceboids into their present subfamilies took place by the Middle Miocene.

The cercopithecoids, or Old World monkeys, were relatively scarce in the Miocene, yet by the Pliocene and Pleistocene cercopithecoids they became common animals, especially in Africa. The earliest-known fossil cercopithecoids belong to the family Victoriapithecidae, which dates from the Early and Middle Miocene. Beginning in the Late Miocene, the monkeys underwent a divergence into the two subfamilies, the Cercopithecinae and the Colobinae.

EVOLUTION OF THE HOMINOIDEA

The living members of the superfamily Hominoidea include the living apes and humans. Fossil hominoids are well known from the Miocene, during which time they underwent a major adaptive radiation.

Paleoanthropologists have known of the Miocene hominoids for well over a century; the first was described in 1856, three years before Charles Darwin published *On the Origin of Species.* Today they are well represented in the Miocene fossil record. The Miocene was characterized by major geologic events, including the uplifting of the Ethiopian highlands and the development of the East African Rift Valley, areas that have yielded many hominin fossils (Chapter 13). The new highland regions affected the flow of winds coming off the ocean, creating dry regions on the side of the mountains that does not face the sea. At one time Africa was covered by a continuous rain forest, but climatic change brought about the breakup of the forest, which was becoming interspersed with open woodlands, grasslands, and even deserts. Those changes influenced the evolution of the primates, and many anthropologists conclude that the origin of the hominids, the group that includes the living apes and humans, was driven by those climatic changes.

Hominoids of the Early Miocene

The Early Miocene lasted from about 23 to 16 million years ago. The Early Miocene hominoids have been found in Africa and range in size from that of small monkeys to that of chimpanzees. Although there are a number of genera and species, they tend to fall into two

See the Online Learning Center for an Internet Activity on the Miocene.

major groups, represented by the genera *Proconsul* and *Afropithecus*.

Perhaps the best known of the Early Miocene African hominoids are the several species of *Proconsul*. The cranial remains show many primitive features that characterize the early Old World anthropoids, such as a slender mandible and a robust zygomatic arch. Dental features include incisors and canines that are more vertically implanted than they are in modern apes, slender canines, semisectorial lower anterior premolars, and thin enamel on the molars. Analysis of the teeth indicates that they were frugivores. The relative width of the jaw between the canines is less than that in modern apes; this results in a more V-shaped dental arcade (Figure 12.10). The V shape contrasts with the U-shaped dental arcade of the modern chimpanzee and gorilla. The skull of *Proconsul africanus* is shown in Figure 12.11; note the prognathous face and the lack of brow ridges. The skull appears more delicate in build than the skulls of contemporary apes.

Some *Proconsul* postcranial material is known, but the fossils are primarily unassociated fragments rather than articulated skeletons. One exception is a small juvenile *P. africanus* skeleton representing an animal that weighed 15 to 20 kilograms (33 to 44 pounds). Its postcranial anatomy lacks the specializations that characterize the posture and locomotion of the living apes. Its hindlimbs are relatively longer than its forelimbs, which is more typical of monkeys than of apes (Figure 12.12). This animal was probably an arboreal quadruped that lacked the specializations for suspensory behavior that are found in modern apes. *Proconsul* is associated with forest habitats. The discovery of a last sacral vertebra shows that *Proconsul*, like all contemporary apes, had no tail.

Although *Proconsul* and other related genera became extinct toward the end of the Early Miocene, one form seems to have survived. It is represented by *Afropithecus*. Members of this genus appeared late in the Early Miocene and exhibited adaptations to drier habitats. The robust structure of the facial and jaw musculature and the teeth, especially the large molars and premolars, suggests a diet of hard, tough foods that had to be processed before they could be digested. *Afropithecus* also showed a more terrestrial way of life. Many paleontologists believe that *Afropithecus* survived and gave rise to the hominoids of the Middle Miocene.

Continents in Collision

In general, the hominoids of the Early Miocene are found in east Africa. During the Early Miocene, the continent of Africa was isolated by water from Europe and Asia. The fossil record clearly shows that animals that were evolving in Africa were distinct from those evolving in Europe and Asia.

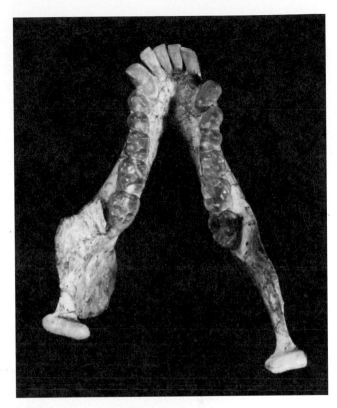

Figure 12.10 *Proconsul* The lower jaw of *Proconsul africanus* from Kenya.

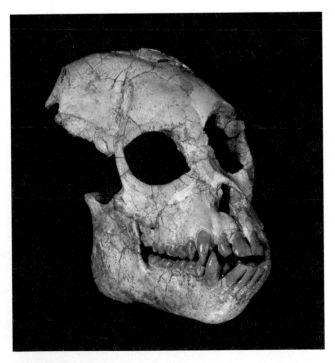

Figure 12.11 *Proconsul* The skull of *Proconsul africanus* from Kenya.

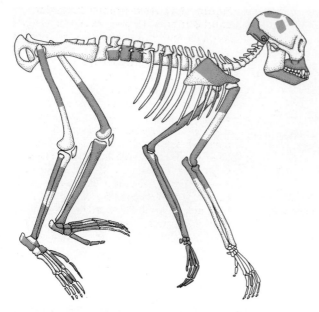

Figure 12.12 *Proconsul* A reconstruction of the skeleton of *Proconsul africanus*. Bones shown in color have been recovered.

See the Online Learning Center for an Internet Activity on plate tectonics.

In the Middle Miocene, the Afro-Arabian tectonic plate came into contact with the Eurasian plate, and a land connection developed between the two continents (Figure 12.13). The fossil record reveals migrations of Asiatic species into Africa and migrations of African species, including hominoids, into Asia between 16 and 14 million B.P.

The forces produced by the coming together of the two large tectonic plates, along with volcanic and earthquake activity, led to the development of mountainous regions. Those mountain ranges had a profound effect on climatic patterns. On the side of the mountains farthest from the sea, the land lay in a rain shadow and received little precipitation. In addition, the average annual temperature gradually lowered during the Miocene.

As a result of these geological and climatic changes, glacial ice expanded in the areas known today as Antarctica and Iceland. Across the wide expanses of Africa, Europe, and Asia, the once-low-lying landscape, which had been covered by a continuous tropical forest, developed into a mosaic of discontinuous and contrasting habitats. The tropical forests diminished in size, and they were replaced in many areas by woodlands (with their lower density of trees), woodland savannas (grasslands dotted with trees), true savanna grasslands, and semiarid regions (Figure 12.14). Many animals that were adapted to forest niches remained in the diminishing forests, but as the area occupied by tropical forests decreased, competition for forest niches became more intense. Meanwhile, other populations entered the newly developing habitats. Thus, the scene was set for an adaptive radiation of the evolving hominoids.

The Miocene Hominid Radiation

By the end of the Early Miocene, most of the African hominoids had become extinct. However, migration from Africa into Europe and Asia had become possible. In Eurasia, the hominoids underwent an extraordinary diversification or adaptive radiation. That proliferation of species probably occurred in response to climatic changes that included increasingly cooler and drier habitats with marked seasons. *Griphopithecus* lived $16\frac{1}{2}$ million years ago in Germany and Turkey and may represent an early member of the family Hominidae, the family that includes the living great apes and humans, that is, all the hominoids except the gibbons.

The list of Middle and Late Miocene hominids is vast, and the details of many of them are still obscure. Generally speaking, they fall into two groups: those with thick enamel on their molars and those with thin enamel on their molars. Thick enamel is associated with drier habitats characterized by clearly defined wet and dry seasons. This type of molar functions to process small, hard, tough food items such as seeds, nuts, and grasses. Molars with thin enamel are associated with wetter tropical conditions. The wear patterns on such teeth help maintain relatively sharp ridges and cusps that are useful in the processing of softer food items such as fruits. *Afropithecus* had relatively thick molar enamel.

Dryopithecus Perhaps the best-known Middle-Late Miocene hominids belong to the genus *Dryopithecus*. This genus was first discovered at St. Gaudens in southern France in 1856, three years before the appearance of *On the Origin Species* by Charles Darwin. Since that time a number of fossils have been recovered in several European sites that have been placed in a number of species.

Postcranial material was found between 1992 and 1994 at Can Llobateres, in northeastern Spain. Those fossils arc about $9\frac{1}{2}$ million years old (Late Miocene). The available bones

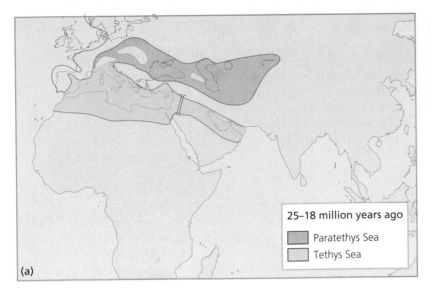

(a)

25–18 million years ago

Paratethys Sea
Tethys Sea

Figure 12.13 Afro-Arabian/Eurasian Land Bridge (a) Between 25 and 18 million years ago, the Afro-Arabian Plate came together with the Eurasian Plate. The initial land bridge (II) permitted the interchange of African and Eurasian mammals. Interference with the currents of the Tethys Epicontinental Seaway brought about major climatic changes. (b) Between 18 and 15 million years ago, a major land corridor was established and the first hominoids appeared in Europe. During that time, woodland and woodland savanna habitats began to replace the tropical forest. (c) Between 15 and 12 million years ago, these open-country habitats expanded, as did the number of hominoid species. These maps are based on the work of Raymond L. Bernor.

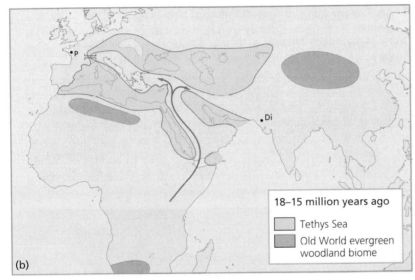

(b)

18–15 million years ago

Tethys Sea
Old World evergreen woodland biome

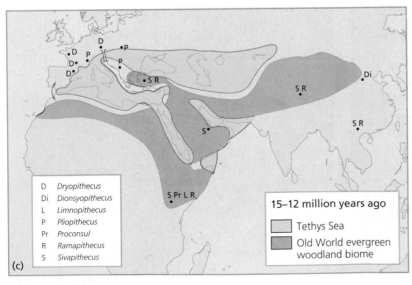

(c)

D	Dryopithecus
Di	Dionsyopithecus
L	Limnopithecus
P	Pliopithecus
Pr	Proconsul
R	Ramapithecus
S	Sivapithecus

15–12 million years ago

Tethys Sea
Old World evergreen woodland biome

Figure 12.14 *Miocene Habitats* During the Miocene, the once-low-lying tropical forest gave way to a mosaic of habitats including woodland savanna, true savanna, and semiarid regions.

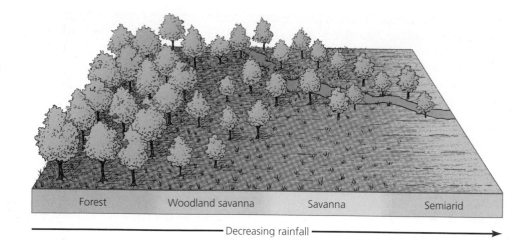

Forest | Woodland savanna | Savanna | Semiarid

⟵—————————————— Decreasing rainfall ——————————————⟶

resemble those of the living apes, including elongated forelimbs and reduced mobility in the lumbar region of the vertebral column. This suggests that this species of *Dryopithecus* was characterized by suspensory behavior and orthograde posture (Chapter 8).

Pliopithecus A group of hominids belonging to the family Pliopithecidae first appeared around 16 million years ago in Europe. They lived during the Middle and Late Miocene, and they were the earliest Eurasian hominoids. The pliopithecids disappeared from the European fossil record about 12 million B.P., but they survived in China until 8 million B.P.

See the Online Learning Center for an Internet Activity on fossil hominoids in China.

Members of genus *Pliopithecus*, which belong to the family Pliopithecidae, were small, gibbon-sized primates that weighed between 6 and 10 kilograms (13 and 22 pounds). The possession of a robust mandible and a large temporalis muscle, as indicated by the skull, suggests that *Pliopithecus* was primarily a leaf-eating primate capable of consuming tough vegetation (Figure 12.15). An analysis of the postcranial skeleton shows that *Pliopithecus*

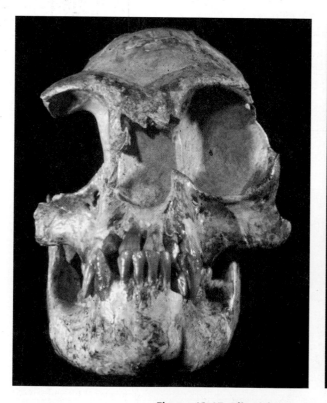
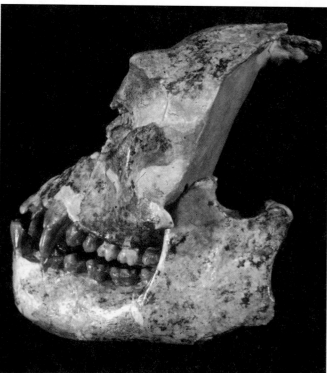

Figure 12.15 *Pliopithecus* Front and side view of *Pliopithecus* from the Miocene of Europe.

was an arboreal quadruped adapted for suspensory behavior in the manner of the New World semibrachiators such as the spider monkeys, although it lacked a prehensile tail. However, *Pliopithecus* does not show anatomical adaptations for the true-brachiation type of locomotion characteristic of modern gibbons and siamangs.

Sivapithecus One of the best-known Late Miocene hominids is *Sivapithecus* (Figure 12.16). *Sivapithecus* dentition is characterized by thick dental enamel on the molars, with the relatively low cusps of the large premolars and molars wearing flat; by relatively small canines with pronounced sexual dimorphism; and by broad central incisors. The mandible is relatively deep, the zygomatic arches are flaring, and the face is **orthognathous** (nonprojecting).

This dental pattern has been associated with the small-object-feeding complex, which is a dental adaptation to coarse materials such as grasses and seeds that are characteristic of drier and more open habitats. Similar dental patterns have been observed in the living gelada and panda. The diet of the gelada emphasizes grasses and seeds, while that of the panda consists of bamboos, which are members of the grass family. However, this view is not shared by all anthropologists. For example, some believe that this dentition was adapted for the processing of fruits with hard rinds.

Figure 12.16 *Sivapithecus* The skull of *Sivapithecus*.

Similar problems exist in the interpretation of posture and locomotion in *Sivapithecus*. Fossilized bones of the limbs, hand, and foot lack the specializations found in the semibrachiators and knuckle walkers. The suggested pattern of locomotion has been described as arboreal quadrupedalism with a degree of climbing and suspension.

orthognathous Describes a face that is relatively vertical as opposed to being prognathous.

Oreopithecus The first fossil to be assigned to the genus *Oreopithecus* was a juvenile mandible first described in 1872. Throughout the years, several *Oreopithecus* fossils have been found, primarily in Italy. In 1958, a badly flattened partial skeleton of a young adult male was discovered in an Italian coal mine. The material in which the skeleton was found is lignite, which is a soft form of coal that originated in a swampy forest habitat. Some fossils that may be related to the European *Oreopithecus* have been found in Africa.

Oreopithecus possesses large canines, a high degree of sexual dimorphism, teeth adapted to processing leafy materials, and a short, wide face (Figure 12.17). The postcranial

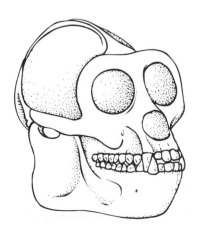
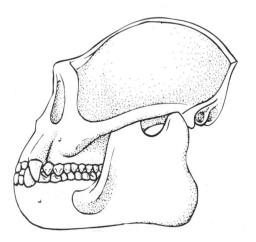

Figure 12.17 *Oreopithecus* Drawing of the reconstructed skull of the "Italian Swamp Ape."

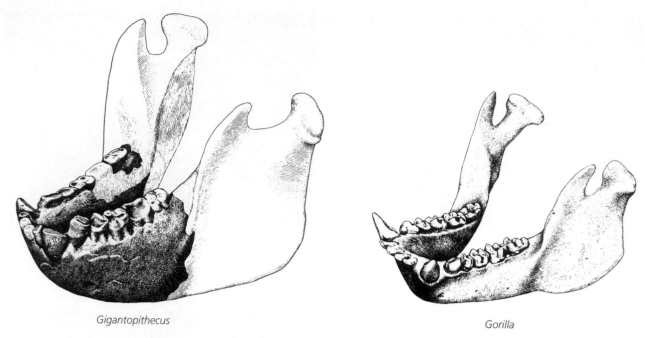

Gigantopithecus

Gorilla

Figure 12.18 Mandibles of *Gigantopithecus* and *Gorilla*

skeleton exhibits longer forelimbs than hindlimbs and several features related to flexibility of the shoulder, elbow, and wrist. The ankle is very flexible, and the primate had a powerful grasping foot. Some paleoanthropologists interpret the skeleton as belonging to a primate that could climb vertical tree trunks and moved by means of suspensory behavior. This suite of locomotor patterns would have been adapted to movement in a swampy forest region.

Gigantopithecus Another important Late Miocene hominid is *Gigantopithecus*. As its name implies, *Gigantopithecus* was a rather large primate; in fact, it was probably the largest primate that ever lived. Although there is disagreement about its actual size, *Gigantopithecus* may have been as tall as 2.75 meters (9 feet) and may have weighed as much as 272 kilograms (600 pounds).

In traditional China, fossilized teeth known as "dragons' teeth" once were used as medical ingredients. In 1935, Ralph von Koenigswald found teeth of *Gigantopithecus* in a Chinese pharmacy in Hong Kong. In the late 1950s and the 1960s, three mandibles and over a thousand teeth were discovered in caves in Kwangsi Province in southern China. These remains belonged to *G. blacki,* which inhabited China and Vietnam during the Pleistocene. *Gigantopithecus* survived to be contemporary with members of the genus *Homo.* An earlier species, *G. giganteus,* is known from the Late Miocene of India and Pakistan.

Figure 12.18 compares the mandible of *Gigantopithecus* with that of *Gorilla.* Dental features of *Gigantopithecus* include relatively small and vertically implanted incisors, reduced canines worn flat by the chewing of coarse vegetation, lack of a diastema, crowding of the molars and premolars, and so forth—all of which contrast markedly with the dentition of the gorilla. Note also the extremely heavy mandible in the region of the molars (Box 12-1).

The Origins of the Modern Hominids

It is apparent that a great number of hominids were present during the Miocene. It would be nice if we could present a diagram showing the exact relationships of the modern primates to their Miocene ancestors. When the number of fossils was few, many paleoanthropologists did just that, but as more and more specimens are recovered, we are seeing that the Miocene radiation represents a great diversification of primates. Virtually all became extinct; some left no descendants, while others left descendants that evolved through time into modern populations.

See the Online Learning Center for an Internet Activity on Gigantopithecus.

were able to obtain images of the inside of the femur and study the thickness of the cortical bone. Many of the differences in structure between the chimpanzee femur and the human femur are related to the stresses generated by erect bipedalism, in this case resulting from the repositioning of the gluteus medius and glueteus minimus (Chapter 8). The fossil femur resembles the hominin pattern. Based on this evidence, the authors conclude that *O. tugenensis* was indeed an erect biped and clearly was a hominin as well. Of course, as is common in this field, not everyone agrees, and the debate continues.

Ardipithecus kadabba

The Middle Awash region and the surrounding areas of Ethiopia have yielded extremely important fossils, many of which will be discussed in Chapter 13. Beginning in 1997, a series of specimens were recovered from the Middle Awash. They were found in five separate areas and dated between 5.8 and 5.2 million years ago. The fossils include cranial, dental, and postcranial specimens (Figure 12.23). Because of their similarities with the later *Ardipithecus ramidus* from Aramis, described in the next section, they were originally placed into a new subspecies of the same species. However, in 2004, they were reclassified as a separate species, *Ardipithecus kadabba. Kadabba* means "basal family ancestor" in the language of the Afar people.

Much of the analysis has focused on the structure of the teeth, especially the shearing pattern involving the upper canine and lower anterior or sectorial premolar (Chapter 8). This dental pattern is found in all living and fossil apes but is absent from living hominins. Not surprisingly, this dental complex in *A. kadabba* is intermediate between that of the apes and that of humans.

Ardipithecus ramidus

In 1992 and 1993, paleoanthropologists Tim White, Gen Suwa, and Berhane Asfaw excavated a site in the Middle Awash area of Ethiopia known as Aramis. Seventeen hominin fossils were collected at that site, including a fragment of a mandible, the remains of a cranial base, many teeth, and two fragmented pieces of limb bones (Figure 12.24). Early in 1995, a new find was announced that consisted of more than 90 fragments that represented about 45 percent of an adult skeleton. These fragments include parts of the skull, arms, vertebral column, pelvis, and legs. The fossils were placed into a new genus and species, *Ardipithecus ramidus. Ramid* is the word for "root" in the language of the Afar people who live in the region. The name suggests that this species lies near the point in hominid evolution where the hominins split off from the line leading to the apes. (More recent discoveries place the time of this split further back in time.)

Figure 12.23 *Ardipithecus kadabba* Fossils from the Middle Awash, Ethiopia, dated between 5.8 and 5.2 million B.P.

Figure 12.24 *Ardipithecus ramidus* Jaw fragment with teeth found at Aramis, Ethiopia.

Table 12.2 Late Miocene and Earliest Pliocene Hominins

Species	Locality	Date
Sahelanthropus tchadensis	Toros-Menalla, Chad	7–6 million B.P.
Orrorin tugenensis	Tugen Hills, Kenya	6.2–5.6 million B.P.
Ardipithecus kadabba	Middle Awash, Ethiopia	5.8–5.2 million B.P.
Ardipithecus ramidus	Aramis and Gona, Ethiopia	4.4 million B.P.

Figure 12.25 Middle Miocene–Early Pliocene Hominids

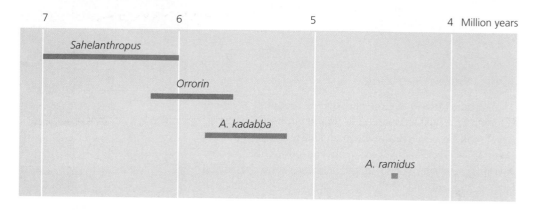

At Aramis, carnivore tooth marks are commonly found on the bones, and the bones appear to have been fragmented before fossilization. At the time the bones were deposited, the area was a flat, wooded plain on which the carcasses of many mammals, including hominins, were torn apart by carnivores.

The geology of this area is characterized by sedimentary beds layered between volcanic **tuffs,** layers of volcanic ash that have been solidified by the pressure of being buried in the earth. The lower Gàala Tuff Complex (*gàala* means "camel" in the Afar language), located just beneath the fossil bed, has been dated by radiometric techniques to 4.4 million B.P. This date represents the maximum age of the fossils. Between 1999 and 2003, the skeletal remains of at least 9 individuals were discovered at Gona in the Afar region of Ethiopia. They have been dated between 4.5 and 4.3 million B.P.

The teeth found at Aramis are hominin-like in any ways. For example, they exhibit a reduced incisor-like canine. Other dental features are more apelike. The canine, although incisor-like in form, is larger than the postcanine teeth. Other dental features are intermediate. The Aramis fossils possess tooth enamel of a thickness intermediate between that of the later hominins and that of the chimpanzee.

tuff Geological formation composed of compressed volcanic ash.

Summary

At one time the period extending from the Late Miocene into the Early Pliocene was a blank on the chart of hominin fossils. Beginning in the early 1990s, several important fossils were recovered, representing three genera and four species. They are listed in Table 12.2. Their placement is time is shown in Figure 12.25.

There is considerable ongoing debate over the significance of this material and how each species fits into the picture of early hominin evolution. We are not likely to see a resolution of this fascinating problem any time soon.

Key Terms

orthognathous, *305*
tuff, *312*

Study Questions

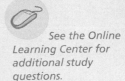

See the Online Learning Center for additional study questions.

1. How long ago did the earliest true primates appear? Where were the early fossils found?

2. Two distinct morphological patterns existed in the Eocene: the adapids and the omomyids. Describe the general features that distinguish one pattern from the other.

3. Describe the fossil evidence for the origins of the anthropoids. Did the anthropoids first evolve in Africa or Asia?

4. How did the evolution of the New World monkeys differ from that of the Old World monkeys? What is the evolutionary relationship between these two groups of primates?

5. Contrast the relative diversity and frequency of hominoid and cercopithecoid fossils in the Early Miocene in the Late Miocene. What is the relationship between the early hominoids and the early cercopithecoides?

6. What features define *Proconsul* as an ape? How did *Proconsul* differ from living apes?

7. What geological events of the Miocene influenced the evolution of the hominids? What were the most important changes in the landscape that affected hominid evolution?

8. Most of the species making up the Miocene Hominid Radiation can be divided into those with thick molar enamel and with thin molar enamel. What are the probable relationships between these features and diet?

9. Several fossils that date from the Late Miocene and Early Miocene might be considered hominin. Why is it difficult to classify these forms accurately?

10. It is frequently stated that the hominins evolved from apes. What "apelike" features do we see in the early hominin genera, *Sahelanthropus, Orrorin,* and *Ardipithecus*? What features place them into the hominins?

Critical Thinking Questions

1. The Eocene forests were filled with early primate forms. In your mind go back in time and visualize what the Eocene forests were like. What kinds of primates were present?

2. While many people talk about humans as having descended from apes, apes are contemporary creatures. The Miocene hominoids, one of which probably gave rise to the hominid lineage, resembled apes in some ways but differed in others. What were these late Miocene "apelike" species like?

3. While we often try to visualize fossil populations by using images of living primates, long-extinct species probably do not resemble closely any living form. Using the two best-known fossil primates, *Aegyptopithecus* and *Proconsul,* write a short description of the animal as if it were living and being observed by you.

4. Many early primate fossil species are known by relatively few specimens—a small number of teeth, for example—and others are known by a considerably larger catalog of fossils. What kinds of information can be gleaned from an analysis of a larger collection of fossils, such as those that exist for *Aegyptopithecus*?

Suggested Readings

Ciochon, R., J. Olsen, and J. James. *Other Origins: The Search for the Giant Ape in Human Prehistory.* New York: Bantam, 1990. This nontechnical book describes the search for *Gigantopithecus* fossils in Vietnam and reviews the evidence of hominoid prehistory in Asia.

Conroy, G. C. *Primate Evolution.* New York: Norton, 1990. This volume contains a very detailed and well-illustrated discussion of the fossil primates, and it includes discussions of the paleoclimates and biogeography of each period of time.

Fleagle, J. G. *Primate Adaptation and Evolution,* 2nd ed. New York: Academic, 1999. This book surveys primate evolution from 65 million years ago to the present.

Suggested Websites

Pondang Fossils Expedition:
www.myanmar.com/primates/

The Primate Fossil Gallery:
www.bergen.org/Smithsonian/prigal.html

Chapter 13

The Early Hominins

The origins of toolmaking as visualized in the 1968 film *2001: A Space Odyssey.*

N o matter what kind of clothes were put on Lucy, she would not look like a human being. She was too far back, out of the human range entirely. That is what happens going back along an evolutionary line . . . . Her head, on the evidence of the bits of her skull that had been recovered, was not much larger than a softball. Lucy herself stood only three and one-half feet tall, although she was fully grown. That could be deduced from her wisdom teeth, which were fully erupted and had been exposed to several years of wear. My best guess was that she was between twenty-five and thirty years old when she died. She had already begun to show the onset of arthritis or some other bone ailment, on the evidence of deformation of her vertebrae. If she had lived much longer, it probably would have begun to bother her. •

—Donald C. Johanson and Maitland A. Edey

Chapter Outline

Discoveries of the Early Hominins
The Early Hominins of South Africa
The Fossils of Olduvai Gorge
The Fossils of the Lake
   Turkana Basin
The Fossils of the Afar
The Fossils of Chad
Drawing a Family Tree
Summary

Early Hominins: Interpretations of the Evidence
Australopithecines as Erect Bipeds
Early Hominin Tool Use
Early Hominin Dentition
The Early Hominin Brain
The Early Hominin Skull
Ecology and the Early Hominins
Summary

See the Online Learning Center for a chapter summary, chapter outline, and learning objectives.

After Reading This Chapter, You Should Be Able to Answer These Questions:

1. What contribution did the early hominin finds in South Africa by Raymond Dart, Robert Broom, and others make to our understanding of hominin evolution? How would you describe these South African hominins?

2. What are the important east African sites? What kinds of early hominins were found there, and who found them?

3. In what ways did the early hominins from South Africa differ from those from east Africa?

4. Have early hominins been found anyplace else other than South Africa and east Africa?

5. What do the hominin footprints at Laetoli tell us about the hominins that made them?

6. What evidence is there that *Australopithecus* and *Paranthropus* were erect bipeds? What might have been some of the adaptive advantages of bipedalism over quadrupedalism for the evolving hominins?

7. What evidence is there that the early hominins used tools?

8. In what ways does the dentition of *Australopithecus* and *Paranthropus* differ from that of earlier hominins, modern apes, and the genus *Homo*?

9. What where some of the changes that evolved in the brains of *Australopithecus* and *Paranthropus* in comparison to earlier forms?

10. What types of habitats did *Australopithecus* and *Paranthropus* occupy, and how might those habitats have influenced their behavior?

The 1977 television miniseries *Roots* was the most-watched series of its time. People seem to be fascinated with tracing their line of descent back through several hundred years of time. Many are drawn to physical anthropology by their curiosity about even deeper roots. The exploration of the origins of humanity raises many interesting questions: With what other contemporary animals do we have a close common ancestry? Why did the hominin line go off in the direction it did? At what point should we use the word *human* to describe our ancestors? What made those ancestors human? What makes us unique?

In Chapter 12 we explored the early hominin fossils from the Late Miocene and Early Pliocene, although the hominin status of some of those finds is still in question. By 4 million years ago the relatively well-known genus *Australopithecus* appears on the scene. Around 2½ million years ago we see the appearance of the genus *Homo,* which coexists until about 1 million years ago with the genus *Paranthropus.* Both of these genera very likely arose from a species of *Australopithecus.* The two genera *Australopithecus* and *Paranthropus* (along with *Kenyanthropus*) are frequently referred to as the **australopithecines.**

australopithecines
Members of the genera *Australopithecus* and *Paranthropus,* who lived in Africa approximately 4 to 1 million years ago.

We will begin the exploration of the australopithecines with the history of discoveries, many of which have captured the imagination of the world. Many of the sites and the names of the associated paleontologists are well known to subscribers to *National Geographic* and viewers of *Nova* and the Discovery Channel. Several have even appeared on the cover of *Time* and *Newsweek.* The section that follows the history of discovery will discuss the anatomy and significance of those fossils.

DISCOVERIES OF THE EARLY HOMININS

The fascinating story of the discovery of the australopithecines begins in late 1924 in South Africa. Like many important early discoveries, it was not accepted immediately because it contradicted many cherished hypotheses held by the prominent paleontologists of the time. However, beginning in 1936, the eventual discovery of hundreds of australopithecine fossils established those species as important elements in the story of hominin evolution. All the fossils have been found in Africa. It was not until the evolution of the genus *Homo* that the hominins moved out of Africa and into other parts of the world. That story will be covered in Chapters 14 and 15.

The Early Hominins of South Africa

Much of South Africa rests on a limestone plateau. Limestone is often riddled with caves, and many of the more ancient ones have become completely filled in with debris. The 1920s was a period of tremendous growth in South Africa, and the need for limestone, a constituent of cement, brought about an increase in quarrying activities. The blasting activities of workers in limestone quarries often expose the ancient cave fills. The material that fills these caves is **bone breccia,** which consists of masses of bone that have been cemented together with the calcium carbonate that has dissolved out of the limestone.

bone breccia Cave fill consisting of masses of bone cemented together with calcium carbonate that has dissolved out of limestone.

In 1924, fossil material from the quarry at Taung was delivered to Raymond A. Dart (1893–1988) of the University of Witwatersrand in Johannesburg, South Africa (Figure 13.1). Embedded within the bone breccia was a small skull. Dart spent 73 days removing the limestone matrix from the skull; he spent four years separating the mandible from the rest of the skull. The fossil that emerged from the limestone matrix consisted of an almost complete mandible, a facial skeleton, and a natural endocranial cast (Figure 13.2). The jaws contained a set of deciduous teeth along with the first permanent molar (Figure 13.3). Dart called the find the "Taung baby"; he named it "Taung" after the quarry in which it was found, and he called it "baby" because it was a child.

Box 13-1 Naming Fossils

Fossils are given designations that include an abbreviation for the site (and sometimes the museum housing the specimens) and an acquisition number. The latter is usually given to fossils in the order in which they are discovered. The site abbreviations used in this book are AL (Afar Locality), BOU-VP (Bouri Vertebrate Paleontology), DNH (Drimolan), ER (East Rudolf, the former name for East Turkana), KNM (Kenya National Museums), KP (Kanapoi), KT (Koro Toro), LH (Laetoli Hominid), MLD (Makapansgat Lime Deposit), OH (Olduvai Hominid), OL (Olorgesailie), SK (Swartkrans), Sts (Sterkfontein), Stw (Sterkforten West Pit), and WT (West Turkana).

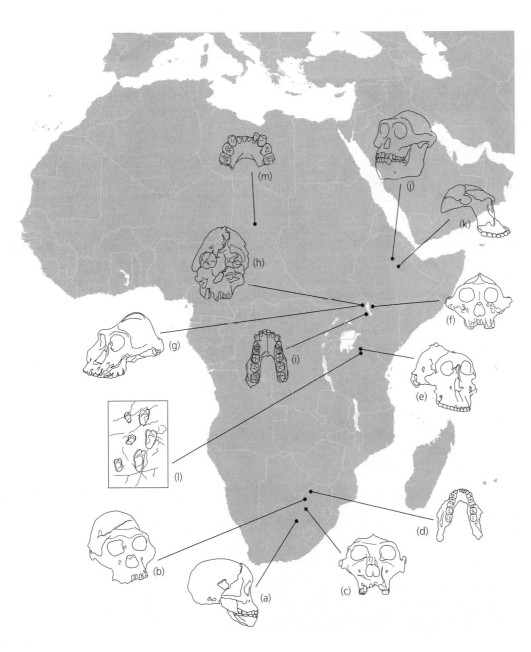

Figure 13.1 Distribution of Early Hominins in Africa See Box 13-1 for the meaning of the abbreviations. (a) *A. africanus,* Taung; (b) *A. africanus,* Sts5, Sterkfontein; (c) *P. robustus,* SK 48, Swartkrans; (d) *P. robustus,* DNH 7, Drimolen; (e) *P. boisei,* OH 5, Olduvai Gorge; (f) *P. boisei,* KNM-ER-406, Koobi Fora; (g) *P. aethiopicus,* WT 17000, Lomekwi; (h) *K. platyops,* WT 40000, Lomekwi; (i) *A. anamensis,* KNM-KP-29281, Kanapoi; (j) *A. afarensis,* reconstructed skull, Hadar; (k) *A. garhi,* BOU-VP-12/130, Middle Awash; (l) *A. afarensis,* footprints, Laetoli; (m) *A. bahrelghazalia,* KT 12/H1, Bahr el Ghazal.

{}

Figure 13.2 *Australopithecus africanus*
The mandibular fragment, facial skeleton, and
natural endocranial cast of the "Taung Baby"
found at Taung, South Africa, in 1924.

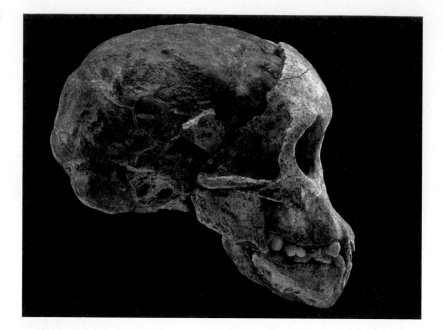

*See the Online
Learning Center for an
Internet Activity on
Australopithecus
africanus.*

Figure 13.3 *Australopithecus africanus* (Top) Taung
mandible; (middle and bottom) mandibles from Makapansgat,
South Africa (MLD 2 and MLD 18).

Dart published his find on February 7, 1925.[1] He named
the skull *Australopithecus africanus,* from *Australo,* meaning "southern," and *pithecus,* meaning "ape." Dart saw in
this skull the characteristics of a primitive hominin, the
most primitive of humankind's known ancestors. Dart based
his opinion on the homininlike structure of the teeth, the
nature of the endocranial cast, and the forward position of
the foramen magnum, which was consistent with erect
bipedalism.

Other paleoanthropologists, however, were not convinced. Some noted the difficulties of making valid
comparisons using an incomplete juvenile skull; some
paleoanthropologists argued that the skull showed close
affiliations to the skulls of apes. Others were convinced
that the earliest hominins would be characterized by
apelike features associated with a large brain, which was
precisely what was seen in the later-discredited Piltdown
skull (Chapter 11). Yet Dart persisted in his contention that
the Taung baby was a bipedal hominin; the years have
proved him correct.

Australopithecus africanus* and *Paranthropus robustus In
his day, Dart's interpretation of *Australopithecus africanus*
was not accepted by most paleoanthropologists and he had
very little support for his ideas. One exception was the
Scottish physician and paleontologist Robert Broom
(1866–1951). After retiring from his medical practice at age
68, Broom began an investigation of three caves in the

---

[1] R. A. Dart, "*Australopithecus africanus,* the Man-Ape of South Africa," *Nature* 115 (1925), p. 195; see
also R. A. Dart, "Recollections of a Reluctant Anthropologist," *Journal of Human Evolution* 2 (1973),
pp. 417–427.

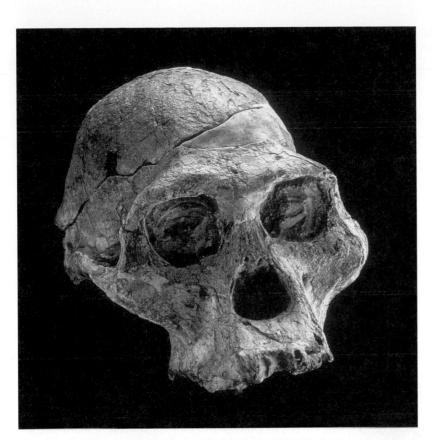

Figure 13.4 *Australopithecus africanus,* Sts 5, from Sterkfontein, South Africa

Sterkfontein Valley. He excavated the first cave, Sterkfontein, between 1936 and 1939 and almost immediately uncovered the first adult specimens of *A. africanus* (Figure 13.4). In 1938, Broom excavated at the site of Kromdraai. There he found a specimen that, unlike *A. africanus,* possessed a sagittal crest on the top of the cranium, a large mandible, and very large premolars and molars (Figure 13.5). He placed that fossil in the new species *Paranthropus*

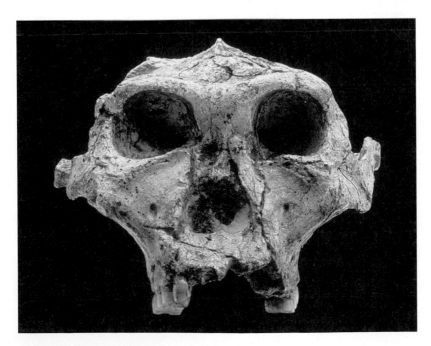

Figure 13.5 *Paranthropus robustus,* SK 48, from Swartkrans, South Africa

Figure 13.6 Reconstruction of the Cave at Swartkrans Diagrammatic section through the Swartkrans hillside. The upper reconstructed part has been removed by erosion since the accumulation of the fossil deposit.

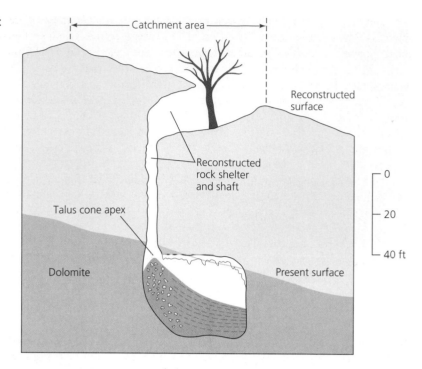

robustus. Paranthropus means "parallel to man." He recovered additional specimens at the site of Swartkrans. Stratigraphically, *A. africanus* is older than *P. robustus.*

C. K. Brain, who began his excavations in 1965, has reconstructed what the cave at Swartkrans was like when the fossils were deposited (Figure 13.6). At that time, the cave was an underground cavern connected to the surface by a vertical shaft. Because of a concentration of moisture in the relatively treeless region, trees were found in the region of the shaft. Leopards are known to drag their prey into trees, where the carcass is relatively safe from scavengers and other carnivores. For this reason, the remains of the animals of prey would have found their way down the shaft and into the cave. This accounts for the relative lack of postcranial remains, which would have been destroyed to a large extent by chewing. *A. africanus* and *P. robustus* would have been among the leopard's prey (Figure 13.7).

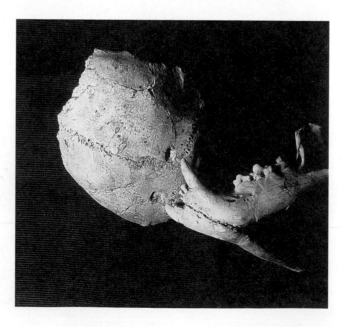

Figure 13.7 Evidence of Leopard Predation This photograph shows part of the skull (parietal) of a juvenile hominin from Swartkrans (SK 54). The two holes in the skull match the lower canines of a leopard. The fossil leopard mandible (SK 349) comes from the same deposit.

The dating of the South African sites has been difficult because of the lack of volcanic material. Most estimates are based on a comparison of the remains of fossil animals with those of similar animals at other dated sites. The material at Sterkfontein covers a vast period of time. It is divided into five stratigraphic layers that are named Member 1 through Member 5. The youngest, Member 5, contains fossils of *Homo* and *Paranthropus robustus;* Member 4 contains fossils of *Australopithecus africanus.* The oldest hominin-bearing layer, Member 2, contains fossils of *Australopithecus,* but the species has not been determined. Recent dating using the radioactive materials aluminum 26 and beryllium 10 have yielded a date of about 4 million years for Member 2, much older than has previously been thought.

These sites are still being excavated and studied. Sterkfontein is probably the richest known hominin fossil site, having yielded over 500 fossils. Excavations in the Sterkfontein area have been enhanced by the discovery of Jacovec Caverns, an extension of the Sterkfontein site.

Not all fossils are discovered in the ground, however. Paleoanthropologists announced in 1994 that they had recovered four bones of a left foot from a box of mammalian bones that originally had been excavated in 1980 at the site of Sterkfontein. The fossils are dated between 3.5 and 3.0 million B.P. These bones (Stw 573), nicknamed "Little Foot," fit together to form an arch that extends from the heel of the foot to the beginning of the big toe. Workers then returned to the cave in an attempt to recover additional bones. In 1997, they found eight more foot and lower leg bones. Further work uncovered leg and arm bones as well as a skull. This skeleton is among the oldest australopithecine fossils, dating from around 4 million B.P., which is contemporary with the oldest australopithecine material in East Africa belonging to the species *Australopithecus anamensis.* It is also one of the few finds in which the skulls have been found in association with postcranial material.

The site of Drimolen, discovered in 1992 just north of Sterkfontein, had yielded 79 hominin fossils by 2000. They are placed into the species *Paranthropus robustus,* although a few specimens are thought to belong to a species of *Homo.* This is not surprising since we know that *Paranthropus* and *Homo* were contemporary. Perhaps the most important fossil is DNH 7, which is the most complete australopithecine skull that has been recovered to date. It is relatively small, lacks a sagittal crest, and is thought to be a female. Evidence of significant sexual dimorphism can be seen in Figure 13.8, which compares the mandible of DNH 7 and that of DNH 8, a mandible thought to be that of a male.

Figure 13.8 Possible Male Mandible (DNH8) (left) and Female Skull (DNH7) (right) of *Paranthropus robustus* from Drimolen, South Africa

Figure 13.9 Olduvai Gorge, Tanzania

The site of Gladysvale, near Sterkfontein, was excavated beginning in 1995. Discoveries included hominin phalanges and teeth of *A. africanus.* Finally, mention should be made of the site of Makapansgat, where 35 hominin fossils have been recovered beginning in 1947.

The Fossils of Olduvai Gorge

See the Online Learning Center for an Internet Activity on Olduvai Gorge and the Leakeys.

Olduvai Gorge, in east Africa, is a 25-kilometer (15½ mile)-long canyon cut into the Serengeti Plain of Tanzania (Figure 13.9). The sedimentary beds, some 100 meters (328 feet) thick, have yielded bones of ancient hominins along with the tools that they made, as well as the remains of the animals they ate.

Geologically, the sequence of sedimentary layers at Olduvai is divided into a series of beds. Bed I and the lower part of Bed II show a continuous sequence of sediments that were deposited when a large lake existed on what is now part of the Serengeti Plain. Bed I and Lower Bed II span the time from 1.9 to 1.5 million B.P. (Figure 13.10).

Hominin sites are located at what were once lake margins or stream banks. These areas provided the early hominins with a source of water as well as a concentration of animal food. In addition, fossilization more frequently occurs in these habitats as opposed to the savanna grasslands and tropical forests. The oldest hominin site is located just above a layer of basalt with a potassium-argon date of 1.9 million B.P. Hominin material also has been recovered from Middle and Upper Bed II, dated between 1.5 and 1.1 million B.P. During that time, the freshwater lake became smaller, and much of the landscape became a dry grassland.

The story of Olduvai Gorge is the story of Louis and Mary Leakey. Louis Leakey was predisposed to think of the early South African hominins as a side branch of the hominin line that played no role in the evolution of modern humans. He saw the genus *Homo* as a lineage of great antiquity whose major features were a large brain and the ability to manufacture tools.

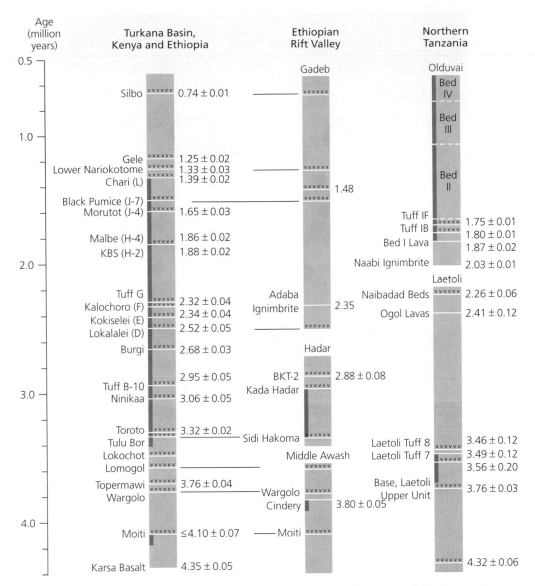

Figure 13.10 Stratigraphic Beds in the Turkana Basin, the Ethiopian Rift Valley, and Northern Tanzania Dated units are shown in each stratigraphic column. The colored line on the left edge of each column indicates an interval in which hominin fossils have been found. (Fossils have been lumped into 0.1-million-year intervals.)

Although he and Mary later went on to make several important discoveries of early *Homo*, their earliest significant find was a hominin that did not belong to the genus *Homo*.

Louis Leakey began his work in Olduvai in 1931; Mary arrived on the scene in 1935. Although the discoveries of animal fossils and important archaeological material were made early, the first significant hominin find did not appear until 1959. In that year, Mary Leakey found an almost-complete skull (the mandible was missing) of a hominin, designated OH 5 (nicknamed "Nutcracker Man"), who lived at Olduvai Gorge around 1.75 million B.P. (Figure 13.11). This date was the first to be determined by the then-new potassium-argon dating technique. At a time when most anthropologists considered hominin evolution to be confined to the last 1 million years, this new information almost doubled the time span estimated for human evolution. The find originally was named *Zinjanthropus boisei*, after *Zinj*, an ancient name for east Africa, and in honor of Charles Boise, a London businessman who financed the excavations at Olduvai Gorge in the 1950s. It is now designated *Paranthropus boisei*.

See the Online Learning Center for an Internet Activity on Paranthropus boisei.

Figure 13.11 *Paranthropus boisei,* OH 5, from Olduvai Gorge, Tanzania

The Fossils of the Lake Turkana Basin

The African Rift Valley runs southward from the Ethiopian highlands into northern Kenya and the Lake Turkana Basin. The Omo River, which drains the Ethiopian highlands, forms a large river delta where it enters Lake Turkana. The lake is 155 miles long with a maximum width of 35 miles.

On the eastern shore is the Koobi Fora region, an area of sediments that covers approximately 1000 square kilometers (386 square miles) and extends some 25 kilometers (15½ miles) inland from the shore of the lake. The Koobi Fora Formation is some 560 meters (1837 feet) thick and is divided into members by a series of tuffs. The fossils all occur between the Tulu Bor tuff dated at 3.3 million B.P. and the Chari tuff dated at 1.4 million B.P. The date of the KBS tuff is of major importance in interpreting the fossils from East Turkana. The fossils fall into two groups, those above and those below the KBS tuff, which is dated at 1.8 million B.P. Although not as extensive, important sedimentary beds have been found on the western shore as well. The Lake Turkana Basin has revealed an excellent fossil record of pollen, freshwater shellfish, and many mammalian groups, including prehistoric members of the pig, cattle, horse, and elephant families.

Over 200 hominin fossils have been recovered from the both sides of the lake since work started in 1968. The fossils represent seven species. Here we will look at those species that are not part of the genus *Homo: Paranthropus boisei, Paranthropus aethiopicus, Australopithecus anamensis,* and *Kenyanthropus platyops.*

Paranthropus boisei* and *Paranthropus aethiopicus Several well-preserved specimens of *Paranthropus boisei* have been recovered from Koobi Fora. KNM-ER 406, shown in Figure 13.12, is of special interest since it was found in the same deposits as a fossil assigned to the genus *Homo.*

Figure 13.12 *Parathropus boisei* Side, front, and top views of KNM-ER 406 from East Lake Turkana, Kenya.

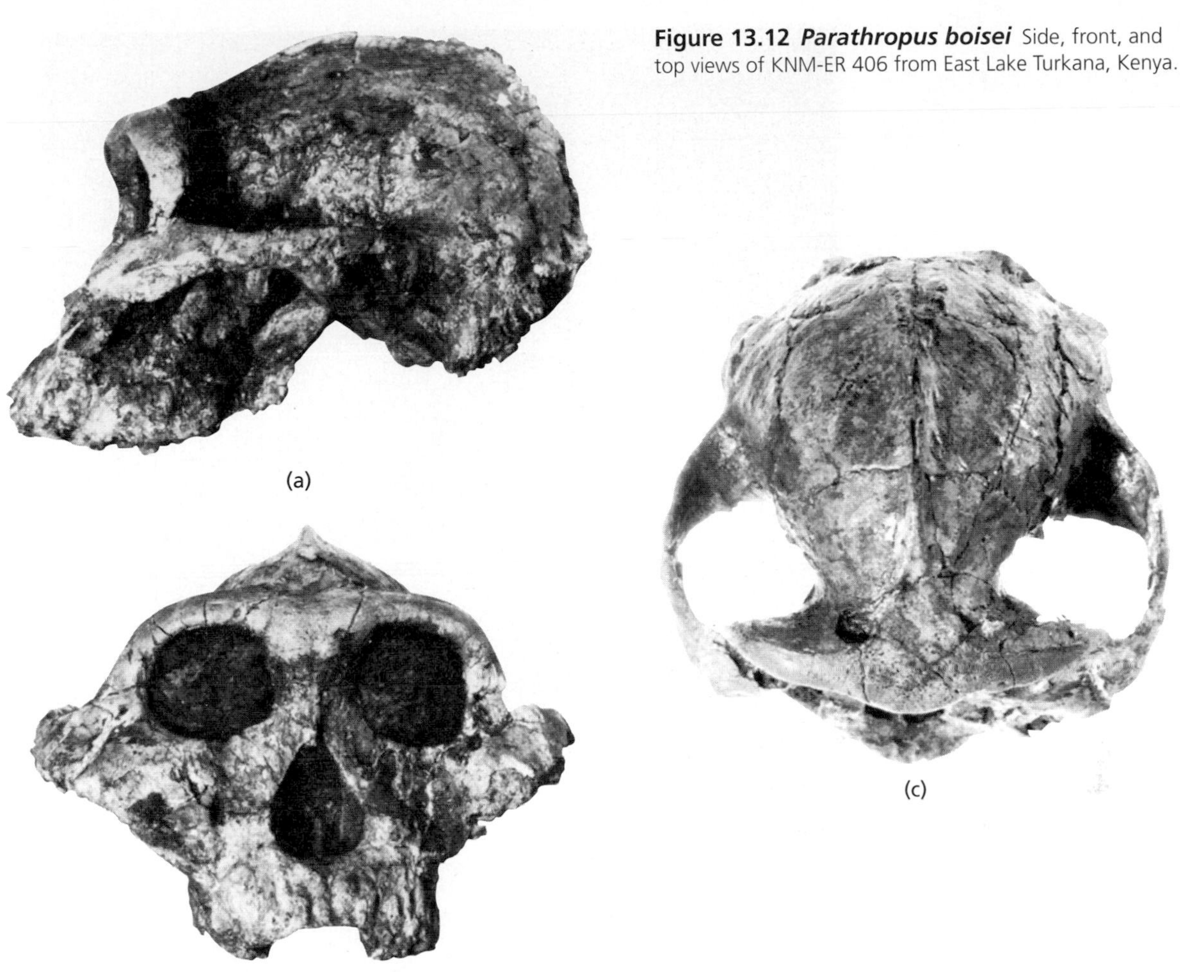

(a)

(b)

(c)

In 1984, excavations began west of Lake Turkana, where the Nachukui Formation extends 5 to 10 kilometers (3 to 6 miles) inland along the western shore of the lake. Investigators found a cranium, KNM-WT 17000, at the site of Lomekwi (Figure 13.13). The find was named the "Black Skull" because of its black color; the color was derived from the manganese-rich sediments in which it was found. WT 17000 appears to resemble *P. boisei*, yet this particular specimen is characterized by a small cranium and retention of some ancestral features from the earlier *Australopithecus*. The skull is dated at 2.5 million B.P., somewhat earlier than the age range for *P. boisei*. Some paleoanthropologists place this find in its own species, *Paranthropus aethiopicus*.

Australopithecus anamensis In 1995, Meave G. Leakey, Richard Leakey's wife, and her colleagues published the description of a new species of *Australopithecus*. It was named *Australopithecus anamensis*. The name *anamensis* comes from *anam,* which means "lake" in the language of the Turkana people. The fossils were found at the site of Kanapoi, southwest of Lake Turkana in Kenya. Additional material also has been found 48 kilometers (30 miles) away at Allia Bay on the eastern side of Lake Turkana. The sediments at both sites were once a part of an ancient lake of which Lake Turkana is a remnant. The habitat may have been one characterized by dry open woods or brush with gallery forest along the rivers.

The fossil beds at Kanapoi have been known for some time; a humerus was recovered at Kanapoi in 1965. The new material, discovered beginning in 1994, includes an incomplete mandible with all its teeth intact, a partial left temporal, additional jaw fragments and isolated teeth, sections of a humerus, and sections of a tibia (Figure 13.14).

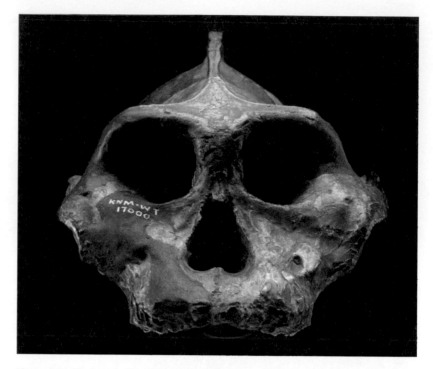

Figure 13.13 *Paranthropus aethiopicus* WT 17000, the "Black Skull," from Lomekwi, West Lake Turkana, Kenya.

The Kanapoi beds also include fossil fish, aquatic reptiles, and many terrestrial mammals.

The Kanapoi fossils have been dated by ^{40}Ar/^{39}Ar dating and by correlation with dated sediments at other east African sites. The fossils found in the lower horizon, dated by the ^{40}Ar/^{39}Ar method, date between 4.17 and 4.07 million years ago. The upper horizon, which contains the postcranial material, is not as precisely dated, but it is thought to date from between 4.1 and 3.5 million B.P. The Allia Bay fossils, which consist mainly of teeth, were found within and below the Moiti tuff, which has been dated at 3.9 million B.P.

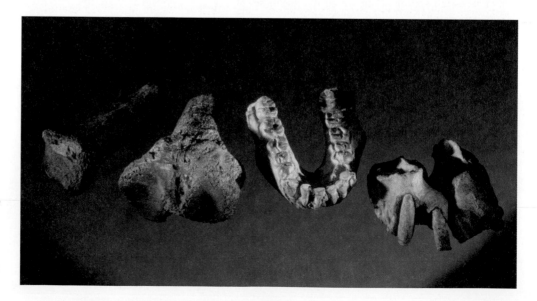

Figure 13.14 ***Australopithecus anamensis*** From the site of Kanapoi, Kenya, left to right are: Section of a right tibia that articulates with the foot; part of the knee of a right tibia; a mandible; and a maxilla.

Figure 13.15 *Kenyanthropus platyops* WT 40000 from Lomekwi, Lake Turkana, Kenya, dated at 3.5 million B.P.

One of the most striking observations about this species has to do with the jaws and teeth; in many ways, they are similar to those of Miocene hominins, yet they are associated with postcranial material similar in many ways to that of early *Homo*. Since at Kanapoi the dental and cranial materials have been found primarily in the lower horizon and the postcranial materials in the upper horizon, the assertion that they belong to the same species will remain open to question until additional material is found.

Kenyanthropus platyops In 1999, paleoanthropologists, including Meave Leakey, were working at Lomekwi on the western shore of Lake Turkana, where hominin material had been found earlier. The sediments are dated between 3.5 and 3.2 million B.P. Several new fossils representing parts of skulls were discovered, including a reasonably complete but distorted cranium. The cranium, WT 40000, is dated at 3.5 million years old (Figure 13.15).

WT 40000 was contemporary with *Australopithecus afarensis,* known from Hadar and Laetoli. Although WT 40000 shares many characteristics with *A. afarensis,* it also exhibits some features found in the chimpanzee but not in *A. afarensis,* such as a small ear opening. WT 40000 also has a number of unique features, such as a flat plane beneath the nose bone, giving the appearance of a flat face. In fact, it is the flat face that is the most distinctive feature of the cranium, and this feature gives rise to its name, *Kenyanthropus platyops,* "flat-faced man of Kenya."

The presence of two distinct species living side by side means that they were probably not competing with each other. The differences in facial morphology suggest that they were specialized for different diets and that they exploited different habitats. Analysis of the fossil remains of other animals and plants suggests that the habitat was fairly wet and vegetated, probably woodland. The habitat at Lomekwi was wetter and more forested than that at Hadar.

The Fossils of the Afar

The Afar Triangle of Ethiopia is a very interesting place for geologists. It is a triple junction where the East African Rift Valley splits in two, with one part going northwest and the other part going northeast. The Awash River flows through this very hot, dry, and desolate landscape, but the sedimentary rocks interspersed with ancient lava flows and tuffs, found in the river valley, are of the time period in which fossils of early hominins were expected to be found.

Australopithecus afarensis In 1973, the International Afar Research Expedition, led by Yves Coppens, Maurice Taieb, and Donald Johanson, began working at Hadar, which is located in the Afar Basin in northern Ethiopia. Because of the special conditions of burial and fossilization, some fossils are very well preserved. Between 1973 and 1977, more than 240 hominin fossils were recovered. The stratigraphic beds date from between 3.6 and 2.9 million B.P.

The first hominin find, consisting of four leg bones, was made in the fall of 1973. A partial femur and tibia fit together to form a knee joint; this provided skeletal evidence of fully developed erect bipedalism. In 1975, the team discovered a collection of 197 bones representing at least 13 individuals, both adults and immatures. Some believe that these individuals, called the "First Family," all died at the same time; they possibly were killed and buried by a sudden flood or another catastrophe. This material has been placed into the species *Australopithecus afarensis* (Figure 13.16).

Perhaps the best-known fossil is "Lucy" (AL 288-1), which was found in 1974 (Figure 13.17). This remarkable find consists of 40 percent of a skeleton. "Lucy" provided the first opportunity for anyone to study the skull and postcranial remains from the same individual of this antiquity.

See the Online Learning Center for an Internet Activity on Hadar and "Lucy."

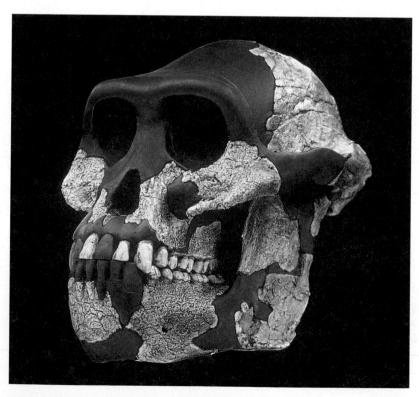

Figure 13.16 *Australopithecus afarensis* **from East Africa, Reconstructed Skull**

After a break in time, paleoanthropologists returned to Hadar in 1990. Since then they have recovered 53 new specimens that are attributed to *A. afarensis*. Among these is a cranial fragment dated at 3.9 million B.P., which makes it the oldest known specimen of this species.

In 1994, the team announced the discovery of three-quarters of a skull that was pieced together from more than 200 fragments. This specimen (AL 444-2) is dated at approximately 3.0 million B.P., which is about 200,000 years younger than "Lucy." The skull is larger than that of "Lucy"; in fact, it is the largest known cranium outside the genus *Homo*. Many paleoanthropologists believe that it probably represents a male. Other important finds include an ulna and a partial humerus.

Laetoli is located in Tanzania, near Lake Eyasi; it is approximately 50 kilometers (31 miles) south of Olduvai Gorge. Mary Leakey and Tim White excavated the remains of several hominins dated between 3.8 and 3.6 million B.P. These fossils have been placed into the species *A. afarensis* (Figure 13.18).

One day at Laetoli about 3.6 million years ago, a light fall of volcanic ash fell over the land, and a light drizzle moistened the ash; later, hominins walked across the ash field. A day or so later, another ashfall covered their tracks; the remaining impressions were discovered in 1978. The site consists of two footprint trails more than 27.5 meters (90 feet) long. Thirty-eight footprints of a small hominin make up the western trail, and 31 footprints make up the eastern trail.

The eastern trail is not as well defined as the western trail. Some see the western trail as having been made by a female and the eastern trail as having been made by a large male. The trails are so close together that Ian Tattersall sees the hominins as "walking in step and accommodating each other's stride."[2] The eastern trail is not as distinct as the western one because, as some paleoanthropologists believe, a third hominin was stepping in the large male's footprints as the three hominins walked over the sticky ash flow. The footprints exhibit specializations of the human foot, which include a well-developed arch and a nondivergent big toe (Figure 13.19).

Australopithecus garhi In 1996 through 1998, a series of fossils were recovered from the Hata Member of the Bouri Formation from the Middle Awash of Ethiopia. One of those finds was an incomplete cranium (BOU-VP-12/130), which has been dated to 2.5 million B.P. (Figure 13.20). Characterized by large anterior dentition and other distinctive details of dental anatomy, the cranial remains were placed in a newly created species, *Australopithecus garhi*. (The word *garhi* means "surprise" in the language of the Afar people.) The postcranial fossils are not associated with the cranial remains and therefore cannot be placed with certainty within the new species at this time. Associated bones of other animals show clear evidence of butchering activity in association with isolated stone tools.

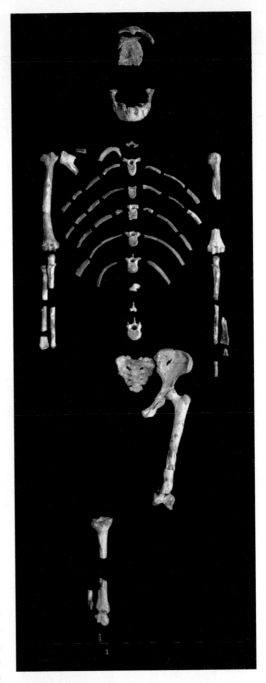

Figure 13.17 *Australopithecus afarensis* "Lucy" (AL 288-1), a female *A. afarensis* skeleton from Hadar, Ethiopia.

[2] I. Tattersall, "The Laetoli Diorama," *Scientific American* 279 (September 1988), p. 53.

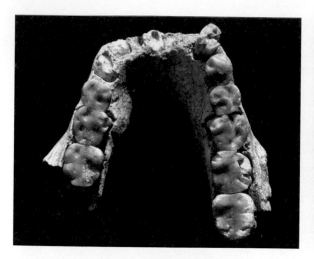
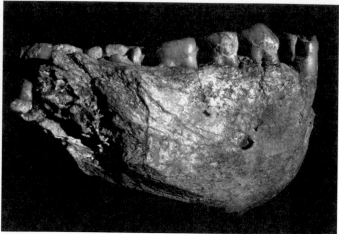

Figure 13.18 *Australopithecus afarensis* Top and side views of the mandible LH 4 from Laetoli, Tanzania.

The Fossils of Chad

The distribution of known specimens of *Ardipithecus, Australopithecus,* and *Paranthropus* has led many paleontologists to conclude that these early hominins existed only in the eastern and southern regions of the African continent. Yet this apparent distribution of early hominin populations may simply be a reflection of the distribution of known fossil sites from this time. The announcement in 1995 that a fossil had been recovered in northern Chad, some 2500 kilometers (1550 miles) west of the Rift Valley, suggests that the distribution of the early hominins may be greater than that suggested by the better-known south and east African sites.

In 1993, several sites were discovered in the region of Bahr el Ghazal near Koro Toro in northern Chad. A fragment of an adult hominin mandible, which contains the crowns of several teeth, was recovered from the site known as KT 12; the fossil is known as KT12/H1

Figure 13.19 Hominid Footprints at Laetoli, Tanzania

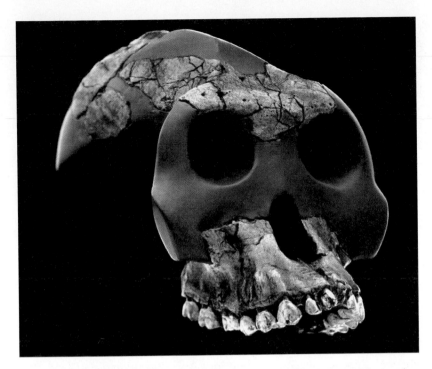

Figure 13.20 *Australopithecus garhi* BOU-VP-12/130 from the Middle Awash, Ethiopia.

(Figure 13.21). The find is associated with other animal fossils that have been dated between 3.5 and 3.0 million years B.P.

The Chad mandible resembles *A. afarensis* in many ways yet differs from other specimens of that species in some features. In 1996, the discoverers placed the specimen into the new species *Australopithecus bahrelghazalia*.

Drawing a Family Tree

Paleoanthropologists see a significant amount of diversity among the early hominins. The question arises: Does this variable assembly of specimens represent a few highly variable species or does it represent a larger number of different species?

Some paleoanthropologists argue that the range of variation among the early hominins may have been greater than that found among contemporary apes. For example, the degree of sexual dimorphism may have been considerably greater than that found among living humans and apes.

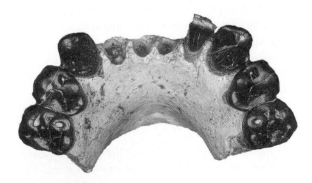

Figure 13.21 *Australopithecus bahrelghazalia* Fragment of an adult mandible (KT12/H1) from northern Chad.

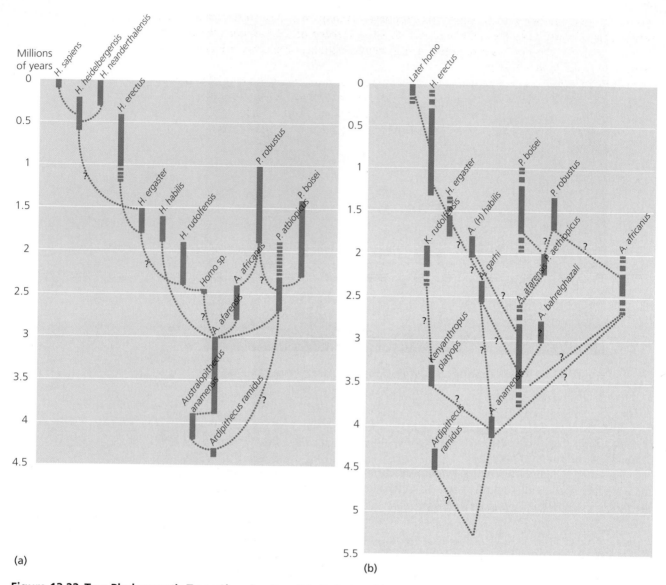

Figure 13.22 Two Phylogenetic Trees Showing Possible Relationships among Fossil Hominin Species (a) Published in 1994 and (b) published in 2001. (a) B. Wood, "The Oldest Hominid Yet," *Nature* 371 (1994), p. 280. (b) D. E. Lieberman. "Another Face in Our Family Tree," *Nature* 410 (2001), pp. 419–420. © 1994, 2001 *Nature* (www.nature.com).

The specimens from Hadar and Laetoli provide a good example of this dilemma. Many paleoanthropologists see these fossils as representing a single species, *A. afarensis*. The smaller specimens, such as "Lucy," would represent females, while the larger, more robust material, represented by AL 444-2, would represent males. If there is only one species present at this time, then *A. afarensis* could be the common stock from which the later *Australopithecus, Paranthropus,* and *Homo* evolved.

Other paleoanthropologists see the Hadar and Laetoli populations as presenting two different species. One population shows robust features that would later lead to *Paranthropus;* the other population includes "Lucy" and leads to *A. africanus* and *Homo.*

The picture is further complicated by the recent discoveries of many new fossils. These differ sufficiently from one another and from known specimens that several new species and genera have been proposed. All or some of these may not be valid.

As each new find is published, a new interpretation of the fossil record is proposed. We, however, must see each new scheme as tentative, for a new discovery in the not-too-distant future could bring about yet another proposal. Perhaps it is best to remember what was said in Chapter 11 and think about each fossil as a piece of a large, complex puzzle. As more and more fossils are discovered, and as newer methods of analysis are developed, the puzzle will become clearer.

For these reasons we are reluctant to show the relationship among the known fossils as a certain reconstruction of our evolutionary history. However, to illustrate the complexity of this task, we present in Figure 13.22 two evolutionary trees, one published in 1994 and the other in 2001. Of course, the earlier one contains fewer species since many were not yet proposed at the time it was developed.

Summary

The fossil evidence of hominins that fall outside of the genus *Homo* are found on the African continent: South Africa; the east African countries of Ethiopia, Kenya, and Tanzania; and the north central African country of Chad. Figure 13.1 is a map of many of the African sites that have yielded the material discussed in this section. No evidence has been found to suggest that *Ardipithecus, Australopithecus,* or *Paranthropus* existed outside the African continent. It appears that Charles Darwin was correct when he stated that human ancestors originated in Africa.

The first of the fossils to be discovered was at Taung, South Africa, in 1924. Raymond Dart placed the juvenile skull in the species *Australopithecus africanus*. Today we have many fossils from several South African caves that are placed into two species: *A. africanus* and *P. robustus*.

Early hominins are well known from several east African sites associated with extensive sedimentary deposits. Prehistoric volcanic activity associated with these beds provides material for chronometric dating. The most significant sites are those of Olduvai Gorge, Koobi Fora, west Lake Turkana, Kanapoi, Hadar, the Middle Awash, and Laetoli. The fossils have been assigned to several species. They are listed in Table 13.1.

Table 13.2 lists the sites that we have discussed. The table also lists for each site the hominin species found; however, there are many controversies surrounding the placement of particular fossils in particular species. The dates for many hominin sites are also tentative.

Table 13.1 Summary of Early Hominin Species

Species	Time Period (million years B.P.)	Distribution
Australopithecus anamensis	4.2–3.9	East Africa
Australopithecus afarensis	3.9–3.0	East Africa
Kenyanthropus platyops	3.5	East Africa
Australopithecus bahrelghazalia	3.5–3.0	North Central Africa
Australopithecus africanus	3.5–2.5	South Africa
Australopithecus garhi	2.5	East Africa
Paranthropus aethiopicus	2.5	East Africa
Paranthropus boisei	2.3–1.4	East Africa
Paranthropus robustus	1.9–1.0	South Africa

Table 13.2 Summary of Major Early Hominin Sites

Site	Estimated Age (million years B.P.)	Species Present
South Africa		
Taung	2.6–2.4	Australopithecus africanus
Sterkfontein and Jacovec Caverns	4.0–2.5	Australopithecus africanus
Swartkrans	1.7–1.1	Paranthropus robustus
Kromdraai	?	Paranthropus robustus
Makapansgat	3.0–2.6	Australopithecus africanus
Gladysvale	?	Australopithecus africanus
Drimolen	2.0–1.5	Paranthropus robustus
Tanzania		
Olduvai Gorge	1.75	Paranthropus boisei
Laetoli	3.7–3.5	Australopithecus afarensis
Peninj	1.3	Paranthropus boisei
Kenya		
Koobi Fora	3.3–1.4	Paranthropus boisei
Lomekwi	2.5	Paranthropus aethiopicus
	3.5	Kenyanthropus platyops
Lothagam	5.5–5.0	?
Kanapoi	4.2–4.1	Australopithecus anamensis
Allia Bay	3.9	Australopithecus anamensis
Tabarin	4.2	Australopithecus afarensis
Ethiopia		
Omo	3.3–2.1	Australopithecus afarensis Paranthropus aethiopicus Paranthropus boisei
Hadar	3.6–2.9	Australopithecus afarensis
Maka	3.4	Australopithecus afarensis
Bouri	2.5	Australopithecus garhi
Konso	1.4	Paranthropus boisei
Chad		
KT 12	3.5–3.0	Australopithecus bahrelghazalia

EARLY HOMININS: INTERPRETATIONS OF THE EVIDENCE

The genera *Australopithecus* and *Paranthropus* together form a group of hominins, often referred to as the australopithecines, that contrast with the hominins belonging to the genus *Homo*. *Australopithecus* existed earlier in time than *Homo;* however, *Paranthropus* was contemporary with early members of the genus *Homo*. Most likely a species of *Australopithecus* gave rise to *Homo*.

Australopithecus and *Paranthropus* are characterized by a small cranial capacity, a relatively large projecting facial skeleton, large premolars, molars with thick enamel, and postcranial features that suggest that their primary means of locomotion was erect bipedalism. Other than these general features, these genera are quite variable. The vast length of time during which these genera existed, their considerable geographical variation, and the fragmentary nature of much of the fossil material make it difficult to make broad generalizations. What follows are descriptions and interpretations of the evidence. The ideas presented here are hypotheses that will be modified as new evidence is uncovered and as new ways of interpreting the evidence are developed.

The major landmarks of hominin evolution are the evolution of habitual erect bipedalism, the development of tool use and tool manufacture, reduction in the size of the dentition,

Table 13.3 Estimated Sizes of Hominin Paleospecies

Paleospecies	Body Weight (kilograms)			Stature (centimeters)		
	Male	Female	Female as % of Male	Male	Female	Female as % of Male
A. afarensis	45	29	64	151	105	70
A. africanus	41	30	73	138	115	83
P. robustus	40	32	80	132	110	83
P. boisei	49	34	69	137	124	91
H. sapiens	65	54	83	175	161	92

Source: Adapted from H. M. McHenry, "How Big Were Early Hominids?" *Evolutionary Anthropology* 1 (1992), p. 18.

and enlargement of the brain. Generally, it is assumed that these landmarks evolved in the order listed. We will discuss the evidence in the same order.

Australopithecines as Erect Bipeds

The anatomical evidence for erect bipedalism is found in the postcranial skeleton. Also, as Raymond Dart observed, the forward position of the foramen magnum in the base of the skull also can be used to infer upright posture. A modest number of early hominin postcranial bones are known.

The size of the early hominins can be estimated from the dimensions of the postcranial bones. They were relatively small compared with modern humans and the great apes. The average reconstructed weight for the four best-known species *(A. afarensis, A. africanus, P. robustus,* and *P. boisei)* ranges from 40 to 49 kilograms (88 to 108 pounds) for males and from 29 to 34 kilograms (64 to 75 pounds) for females (Table 13.3). The average reconstructed stature ranges from 132 to 151 centimeters (52 to 59 inches) for males and from 105 to 124 centimeters (41 to 49 inches) for females. The degree of sexual dimorphism is greater than that found in the genus *Homo.*

Fossil Evidence for Erect Bipedalism The postcranial skeletons of *Australopithecus* and *Paranthropus* are those of erect bipeds. The pelvis, which is bowl-shaped and shortened from top to bottom, is similar in basic structure to that of *H. sapiens* (Figure 13.23); the spine shows a lumbar curve. Erect bipedalism also is deduced from analysis of the footprints discovered at the site of Laetoli in Tanzania.

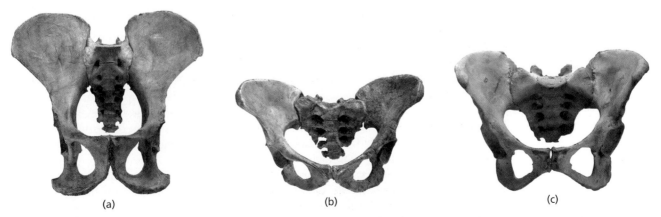

(a)   (b)   (c)

Figure 13.23 Early Hominin Pelvis The pelvis of (b) *Australopithecus africanus* compared with the pelvis of (a) a modern chimpanzee and (c) a modern human.

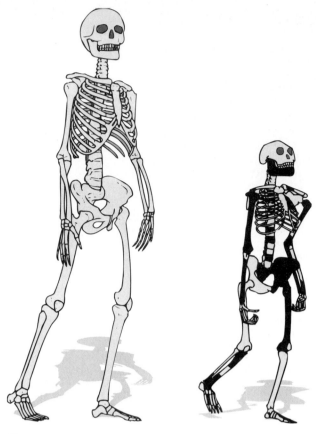

Figure 13.24 Reconstruction of "Lucy" The drawing on the right represents a reconstruction of AL 288-1 from Hadar. The original fossils are shown in black except in the skull. The remainder of the reconstruction is based on construction of mirror images of known parts of the skeleton and reconstructions based on other fossils. Note the long arms and curved fingers. A modern human skeleton is shown for comparison.

There is other evidence for erect bipedalism. Four bones of a left foot belonging to *A. africanus* (Stw 573) fit together to form an arch that extends from the heel of the foot to the beginning of the big toe. The bones show a mixture of humanlike as well as apelike features; the apelike features are more evident in the bones closer to the toe. The investigators concluded that the foot with its grasping big toe was adapted for arboreal climbing as well as for bipedal locomotion.

The postcranial skeleton of *A. afarensis* is of special interest because it exhibits several features that illustrate its transitional status (Figure 13.24). The skeleton exhibits a number of specializations for erect bipedalism. The blade of the ilium is short and broad, the foot possesses a humanlike arch, and the big toe is nongrasping.

Hominins maintain their center of gravity over their legs when standing and walking. This is made possible, in part, by the femur angling in toward the knee, as seen in Figure 8.6. When standing, the knees are positioned close together. In part of the walking cycle, the weight of the body is centered over one leg while the other leg is moving. This balance on one leg is possible because the center of gravity of the body remains over the one knee while the opposite leg is raised off the ground. The short legs of *A. afarensis* suggest that it had a significantly shorter stride than modern humans; this means that its speed on the ground was likely to have been slower than that seen in humans today.

Other features of the postcranial skeleton suggest that *A. afarensis* engaged in some arboreal locomotion in addition to erect bipedalism. The curved, slender fingers and the curved toes are intermediate in relative length between those of apes and those of humans. These features show a degree of grasping that could have functioned as part of an arboreal locomotor pattern. The ability to sleep in trees and to use trees for protection from predators may have been an important factor in the survival of early hominin populations. In addition, these populations may have exploited arboreal food resources.

We can examine the postcranial remains of *A. anamensis* from Kanapoi, Kenya. The region where the fibula articulates with the tibia is reduced; this suggests that the fibula and the associated flexors of the big toe were reduced in size. This implies a loss of mobility of the big toe. In general, the bones strongly support the conclusion that these hominins were erect bipeds.

Many paleoanthropologists have concluded that erect bipedalism is very ancient in the hominins and may have been the most significant factor that distinguished hominins from ape ancestors around the time of the divergence of the two lineages. In 2005 investigators reported bones found at the site of Mille I the Afar region of Ethiopia. These postcranial remains, yet to be attributed to a specific species, walked upright at about 3.8 million B.P. Paleoanthropologists are especially interested in the postcranial material of *Orrorin tugenensis* and *Ardipithecus kadabba* (Chapter 12). Evidence from this material suggests the attainment of erect bipedalism well before the emergence of *Australopithecus*.

Many hypotheses have been put forth over the years to explain why erect bipedalism evolved in the hominins. Erect bipedalism permits hominins to walk on the ground and reach up into the trees for food. It permits them to transport food, tools, and relatively helpless infants in their hands while moving from one place to another. The emancipation of the hands from locomotor functions permits the evolution of the hands into highly

Box 13-2

What Is a Tool?

Anthropologist Joseph S. Eisenlauer notes that the term *tool* as it appears in the anthropological literature frequently is applied to such a broad range of objects that the true significance of this functionally distinct category of implements is largely obscure. He suggests a more focused definition. Specifically, he regards as "tools" only those implements that are used to make, maintain, repair, and/or modify other objects or to process raw materials. The termite stick of the chimpanzee would not be a tool under this definition, whereas a hammerstone used in making a flint projectile point would be.

Another anthropologist, Wendell Oswalt, suggests the name *subsistant* for implements such as the termite stick. The difference between the termite stick and the hammer is more significant than it first might appear. The termite stick is simply an implement used in helping to secure food. The hammerstone is used to manufacture something else.

Eisenlauer believes that the mental step from simply using or even making with one's hands or teeth an object to help get food to using one object to manufacture another was one of the most significant steps in the evolution toward modern hominins. The use of a hammerstone presupposes mental processes by its user that are not necessary to the user of the termite stick. The reason one makes a hammerstone is to use it to modify something else, the finished form of which is only an idea in the maker's head. The termite stick is simply used to secure termites as food.

In the case of humans and chimpanzees, anatomy affords a limited range of technological capabilities. For instance, neither species can effectively carve wood with its teeth. Conceiving of the idea that one implement could be used to produce others is a hallmark of human evolution. This step was never taken in the evolutionary line leading to chimpanzees.

Although we continue to use the word *tool* in its general sense, Eisenlauer's point is well taken. There was an evolution in the use of implements. Perhaps the earliest stage was simply to use an unmodified object for some reason, for example, throwing a rock at another individual. Then implements may have been modified specifically for food getting or other direct survival reasons. Next, objects would be fashioned to make other objects. In the process the human body would become a manipulator of tools rather than being a tool itself. This may have been the point where protocultural behavior at the technological level evolved into the unique technological cultural behavior of hominins.

Sources: J. S. Eisenlauer, Personal Communication, 1999; J. S. Eisenlauer, *Hunter-Gatherer Tools: A Cross-Cultural Ethnoarchaeological Analysis of Production Technology* (Ann Arbor: UMI Dissertation Services, 1993); W. H. Oswalt, *An Anthropological Analysis of Food-Getting Technology* (New York: Wiley, 1976).

developed organs of manipulation that are better for the manufacture of tools. Erect bipeds can walk a greater distance using less energy than quadrupeds can and, with their eyes elevated above the ground, can see over grasses and see a longer way into the distance; this is critical for an animal that emphasizes vision. The air is slightly cooler off the ground, and erect bipedalism exposes less surface area of the body to the hot midday sun. It also may have something to do with phallic display. Perhaps each of these hypotheses contains an element of truth, since erect bipedalism allows for a complete integration of several functions.

Early Hominin Tool Use

Raymond Dart noted the presence of many broken bones in the deposits at Makapansgat. He concluded that they were a result of the deliberate manufacture of bone tools. He termed this an **osteodontokeratic culture,** from *osteo,* meaning "bone"; *donto,* meaning "tooth"; and *keratic,* meaning "horn" (keratin is a main constituent of horn) (Figure 13.25). He saw a femur as a club, a broken long bone as a sharp cutting tool, and a piece of mandible as a tooth scraper. However, later studies by C. K. Brain of the bone material from Swartkrans demonstrated that the features of the bones that suggest deliberate toolmaking to Dart were more likely the result of carnivore activity.

osteodontokeratic culture An archaeological culture based on tools made of bone, teeth, and horn.

In spite of the difficulties in interpreting the bone material in South Africa, paleoanthropologists still believe that tool use and tool manufacture are an important element of early hominin behavior (Box 13-2). The report that modern chimpanzees manufacture tools suggests that such behavior could have characterized the early hominins. Although the earliest hominins may have used their hands for some degree of arboreal locomotion, the fact that they were erect bipeds means that they would have had their hands freed from

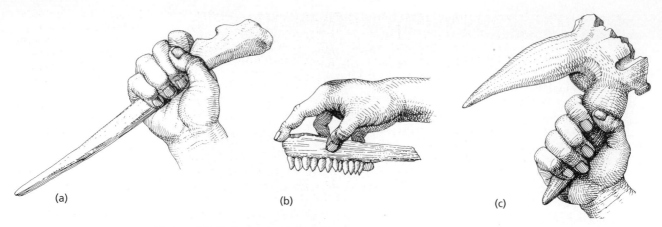

(a)   (b)   (c)

Figure 13.25 Osteodontokeratic Tools Raymond Dart proposed that broken bones were used by the early hominins as tools. He proposed that (a) an antelope ulna was used as a dagger, (b) part of a small antelope mandible was used as a knife blade, and (c) horn cores and a portion of the cranium of a fossil reedbuck were used as a piercing instrument. Today paleoanthropologists believe that these fragmented bones are the result of leopard predation.

primary locomotor functions. These facts lead us to expect an early expression of culture in these prehistoric populations.

The earliest hominin tools most likely were made of perishable materials such as wood, bark, leaves, and fibers. However, the evidence for tool use in the archaeological record consists primarily of stone objects. Early stone tools were probably nothing more than fortuitously shaped natural objects. An example is a small, rounded stone that would fit comfortably in the hand and could be used to crack open a nut to obtain the meat or to break open a bone to obtain the marrow. Such unaltered stones were probably used as tools by early hominins for a long period of time before stones were deliberately altered to achieve a specific shape. It is very difficult to interpret stones found in a site in association with hominin fossils, since such stones may have been unaltered stones used as tools or simply stones deposited in a site through geological activity.

The first concrete evidence of the manufacture of stone tools comes from a site near the Gona River in Ethiopia; this site is dated at 2.6 million B.P. (Figure 14.21). Another early location is the Shungura Formation at Omo, which is dated between 2.5 and 2.4 million B.P. Stone tools also are known from many sites dated between 2.5 and 1 million B.P. However, all these examples of early stone tools are probably associated with early members of the genus *Homo*.

Bones of mammals found at Bouri, which are associated with the remains of *A. garhi,* exhibit evidence of cut marks made by stone tools as well as scars made by the impact of stone tools against the bone (Figure 13.26). The alterations of the bone provide evidence of several food extraction behaviors, including the disarticulation of body parts, removal of flesh from the bones, and the breaking open of bones to extract the marrow. In contrast with the concentration of stone tools at Gona, relatively few, isolated artifacts were recovered at Bouri, probably because of the lack of raw materials at the site for the manufacture of stone tools. The landscape at Bouri was that of a grassy plain associated with the delta of a river as it entered a shallow lake.

The Early Hominin Hand Further evidence for early hominin toolmaking lies in the anatomy of the hand. Randall Susman has compared the hand bones of *A. afarensis, P. robustus, H. erectus,* and fossil *H. sapiens* with those of contemporary humans, chimpanzees, and bonobos.[3] He observes that ape hands are characterized by long curved fingers, narrow fingertips, and relatively small thumbs. The ape hand is most frequently used in a power grip, where an object is held against the palm of the hand by the fingers.

---

[3] R. L. Susman, "Fossil Evidence for Early Hominid Tool Use," *Science* 265 (1994), pp. 1570–1573.

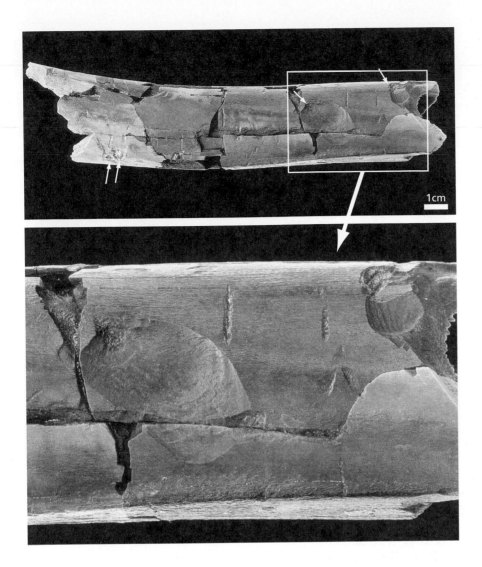

1cm

Figure 13.26 Evidence of Tool Use This is a photograph of the midshaft of a right tibia of a large bovid (cattle-like animal) from the Middle Awash, Ethiopia. The arrows indicate the direction of the impact of a hammerstone. In the enlargement we can see large flakes produced by the impact of a hammerstone and adjacent cut marks. The goal of this activity was probably to extract the marrow from the interior cavity of the bone.

Humans, in contrast, have relatively short, straight fingers. The human thumb is relatively long; this results in a ratio of thumb to finger length that makes it possible to rotate the thumb so that the tip of the thumb can oppose the tip of each finger in turn. The thumbs and fingers possess broad fingertips. This thumb is well adapted for a precision grip (Figure 13.27).

There are no stone tools associated with fossil remains of *A. afarensis*. The hand bones of this species show many apelike features, such as a short thumb with curved phalanges in the other fingers. In contrast to the hand skeleton of *A. afarensis,* the hand of the later *P. robustus* is consistent with a precision grip. The precision grip is considered to be a requirement for complex toolmaking.

The humanlike anatomy of the *P. robustus* hand and the presence of stone tools at the site of Swartkrans suggest that the later *Paranthropus* made tools. Yet tools may have played very different roles in *Homo* and non-*Homo* populations. The importance of tool technology to human evolution is discussed in the next chapter.

Early Hominin Dentition

The majority of known early hominin fossils are isolated teeth and jaw fragments with teeth. In general, the dentition of *Australopithecus* and *Paranthropus* resembles that of *Homo*. Yet the early species of *Australopithecus* show many nonhominin features, while *Paranthropus* evolved rather specialized dentition.

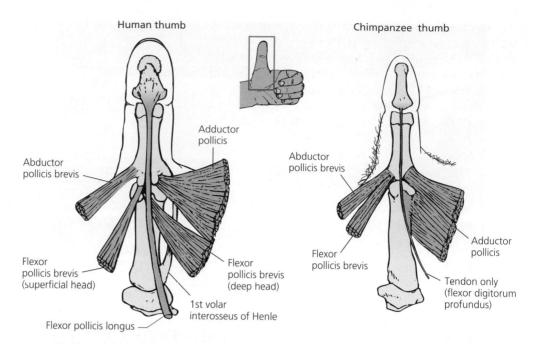

Human thumb

Chimpanzee thumb

Adductor pollicis

Abductor pollicis brevis

Flexor pollicis brevis (superficial head)

Flexor pollicis brevis (deep head)

1st volar interosseus of Henle

Flexor pollicis longus

Abductor pollicis brevis

Flexor pollicis brevis

Adductor pollicis

Tendon only (flexor digitorum profundus)

Figure 13.27 Muscles of the Thumb In this diagram, we are looking at the bottom of the human and chimpanzee thumb. We can observe the various muscles that cross over the joint between the metacarpal and proximal phalanges (i.e., the phalanges closest to the palm). When we compare the anatomy of the two thumbs, we observe the following: (1) Humans possess a deep head of the flexor pollicis brevis muscle; chimpanzees do not. (2) Humans possess a first volar interosseous muscle of Henle; chimpanzees do not. (3) Humans have a flexor pollicis longus muscle. This muscle lies in a bony groove formed by a pair of small sesamoid bones located at the joint between the metacarpal and proximal phalanges. Chimpanzees have only a tendon that mimics this muscle. The sesamoid bones that form a bony groove are absent. Reprinted with permission from R. L. Susman, "Fossil Evidence for Early Hominid Tool Use," *Science* 265 (1994), p. 1570. Copyright 1994 AAAS.

The dental arcade of *A. afarensis* is intermediate in shape between that of modern humans and that of apes (Figure 13.28a). The posterior teeth lie in a fairly straight line, except for the third molar, which is positioned inward. The upper incisors are relatively large and project forward. The canines project above the tooth row, and they are conical in shape, in contrast to the spatulate shape of the modern human canine. A small diastema frequently occurs between the upper canine and incisor.

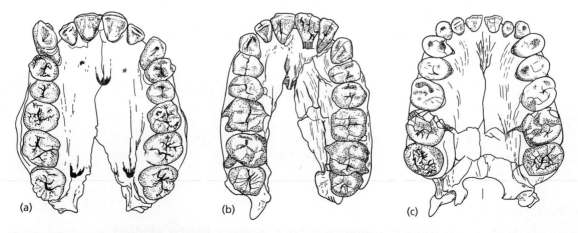

(a)   (b)   (c)

Figure 13.28 Early Hominin Dentition Upper dentition of (a) *Australopithecus afarensis* (AL 200-1a), (b) *Australopithecus africanus* (Sts 52b), and (c) *Paranthropus boisei* (OH 5). Reprinted by permission of Waveland Press, Inc., from Clark Spensor Larsen, Robert M. Matter, and Daniel L. Gabo, *Human Origins: The Fossil Record,* 3rd ed. (Prospect Heights, IL: Waveland Press, 1998). All rights reserved.

The anterior lower premolar is of special interest. As we saw in Chapter 8, the ape premolar is sectorial; it consists of a single cusp that hones against the upper canine. This contrasts with the modern human bicuspid premolar. The anterior lower premolar in *A. afarensis* appears to be transitional between those of apes and those of modern humans. It shows a slight development of the second cusp (Figure 13.29).

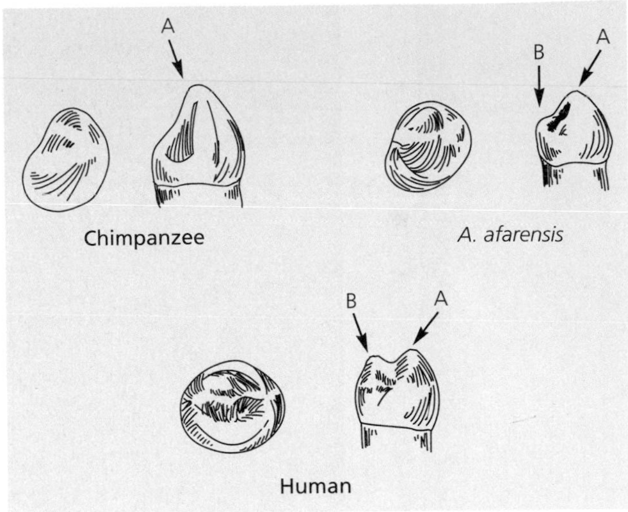

The apelike character of *A. afarensis* is no longer seen in the more recent *A. africanus* (Figure 13.28b). Although the teeth are relatively larger than those of later *Homo*, now the dentition is basically humanlike. However, the dentition of *Paranthropus* shows many specialized features (Figure 13.28c). These include thickened tooth enamel and an expansion in the size of the surface area of the premolars and molars. These and other changes may be related to a specialized diet that consisted of tough, fibrous materials.

Deciduous Dentition The early hominin fossils include dentition from infants and juveniles, including the "Taung baby." This jaw contains a complete set of deciduous teeth and first adult molars in the process of erupting. In modern humans, these features would characterize the dentition of a six-year-old child.

Because of the Taung fossil, many paleoanthropologists see evidence of a long childhood period in *Australopithecus*. One feature of modern humans is a lengthened childhood period compared with that of apes. This prolonged maturation is related to the development of learned behavior as a major mode of hominin adaptation.

Recent analyses of the dentition of *Australopithecus*, apes, and modern humans contradict the idea that the length of the early hominin childhood was more like the human pattern than the ape pattern. In one study, the development of the dental crowns and roots of several fossil specimens were plotted against the development standards of both modern humans and apes. The dental pattern of *Australopithecus* best fits the ape pattern. For example, in the apes the canine erupts after the eruption of the first molars; this contrasts with the earlier eruption of the canine in contemporary humans. In *Australopithecus*, the eruption of the canine is delayed in the same way as it is in the apes. This fact suggests that these forms had a relatively short maturation period, which is similar to those of chimpanzees and gorillas today. On the other hand, the dental pattern of *Paranthropus* does not appear to closely resemble the dentition of either humans or apes.

New medical technology, in particular the computerized axial tomography (CAT) scan, has been used to visualize the juvenile skull from Taung. Investigators scanned the Taung skull and compared it with scans of both a human and a chimpanzee at the same stage of first-molar eruption. The scans revealed that the *Australopithecus* dentition growth and eruption pattern more closely resembled that of a three- to four-year-old chimpanzee than that of a five- to seven-year old human. Studies of bone growth in the Taung facial skeleton show a pattern similar to that of the chimpanzee. All these studies suggest that the prolongation of childhood may be a relatively late development in hominin evolution.

Figure 13.29 The Hominin Premolar The anterior lower premolar from *A. afarensis* is compared with the premolars from a chimpanzee and a modern human. The human premolar is characterized by two cusps, A and B, while the chimpanzee sectorial premolar has only one cusp. Note that the premolar of *A. afarensis* is intermediate with a small development of cusp B.

The Early Hominin Brain

An important part of hominin evolution is the story of the development of the brain. Brains are not normally preserved in the fossil record. However, brain size and some very general features of brain anatomy are reflected in the size and structure of the cranium, or brain case.

Table 13.4 Cranial Capacities of Early Hominin Paleospecies

Species	Specimen	Site	Cranial Capacity (cubic centimeters)
A. afarensis	AL 333-45	Hadar	500
A. afarensis	AL 162-28	Hadar	400
A. africanus	Sts 5	Sterkfontein	485
A. africanus	Sts 60	Sterkfontein	428
A. africanus	MLD 37y38	Makapansgat	435
A. garhi	BOU-VP-12/130	Bouri	450
P. aethiopicus	WT 17000	West Lake Turkana	410
P. robustus	Skw 1585	Swartkrans	530
P. boisei	OH 5	Olduvai Gorge	530
P. boisei	KNM-ER 406	Koobi Fora	510
P. boisei	KNM-ER 13750	Koobi Fora	475
P. boisei	KNM-ER 407	Koobi Fora	506

The size of the brain can be estimated by measuring the volume, or cranial capacity, of the brain case (Chapter 8). The cranial capacities of specimens of *Australopithecus* and *Paranthropus* vary from 400 to 530 cubic centimeters (Table 13.4). These cranial capacities reflect a small brain compared with that of modern *H. sapiens,* which averages about 1350 cubic centimeters. In general, the smallest cranial capacities belong to *A. afarensis,* while the largest are found in *Paranthropus.* Not enough of the cranium of *A. ramidus* has been recovered to estimate its cranial capacity.

Some insights into the mentality of the early hominins might be revealed by an analysis of the structure of the brain. As we saw in Chapter 8, it is possible to make an endocranial cast that represents the shape and features of the inside of the brain case. Several natural endocranial casts also have survived. These casts provide some information about the pattern of convolutions and the location of grooves on the surface of the brain. Although this line of research is controversial, the early hominin brain appears to exhibit a simpler pattern of convolutions with fewer grooves than are found in the modern human brain. It is, however, very difficult to make behavioral interpretations of this evidence.

Erect Bipedalism and the Brain Although the evolution of a large brain is one of the most striking features of the hominins, brain size remained relatively small for a long period of time. Why did the increase in brain size occur late in hominin evolution?

In Chapter 8 we saw that in the evolution of the human pelvis a repositioning of the sacrum in hominins created a complete bony ring through which the birth canal passes. In the chimpanzee, the articulations of the sacrum to the innominate bones and the pelvis to the femur are farther apart than in humans, which mean that the birth canal has a bony roof at one point and a bony floor at another. In humans, the bony roof has moved over the bony floor, creating a complete bony ring through which the head of the child must pass at birth (Figure 13.30). The flexibility of the human infant's skull, however, allows for a certain degree of compression as the child passes through the birth canal, and for a great deal of growth after birth.

Other animals' brains are almost completely developed at birth. For instance, the rhesus money at birth has a brain that is approximately 75 percent of its adult size, and the brain of a chimpanzee newborn is 45 to 50 percent of its adult size. In contrast, the human newborn has a brain less than 30 percent of its adult size, attaining over 90 percent of its adult size by the fifth year of age. Because the human brain grows and matures more slowly than the brains of other mammals, the human child is dependent upon others for a long

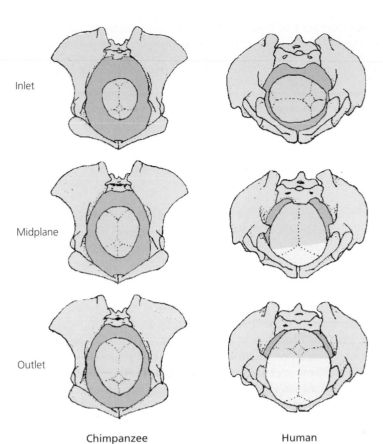

Inlet

Midplane

Outlet

Chimpanzee   Human

Figure 13.30 Pelvis and Fetal Head This diagram shows a female pelvis of a chimpanzee and that of a human from below. Note the size of the head of the fetus in childbirth at the level of the pelvic inlet, midplane and pelvic outlet.

period of time, and it is during this extended period that learning occurs and mental abilities develop.

The enlargement of the brain in hominin evolution took place long after the attainment of erect bipedalism. One hypothesis is that the early hominins were still utilizing the trees to some extent, as suggested by the reconstruction of locomotor patterns in *Australopithecus afarensis*. This would have made it difficult to transport an infant who had to be carried by its mother. It is also possible that they had not developed a technology for caring for helpless infants—such as carrying slings. Since the evolution of a large brain is associated with an increased period of infant helplessness, any extensive brain expansion would have been selected against until the early hominins had become complete terrestrial bipeds and the appropriate technology had developed. It is interesting to note that the enlargement of the brain occurred after the appearance of the first stone tools in the archaeological record.

The Early Hominin Skull

The structure of the early hominin skull is a reflection of the relatively small cranium associated with a large dentition and powerful chewing apparatus. The skull of *A. afarensis* shows a marked prognathism (projecting forward) of the lower part of the facial skeleton. Air spaces, normally present within some bones of the skull, are enlarged **(pneumatized),** which reduces the weight of the skull. The temporalis muscle, an important muscle in chewing, is large. Its expansion is reflected in the development of a **temporal-nuchal crest,** which provides an expanded surface area for the attachment of the muscle to the skull (Figure 13.31).

The cranium of *A. africanus* is somewhat larger than that of *A. afarensis*. The skull of *A. africanus* is less heavily pneumatized, and the temporal and nuchal lines do not meet to

See the Online Learning Center for an Interactive Exercise on the comparative anatomy of the skulls of Australopithecus *and* Paranthropus.

pneumatized The presence of air spaces within some bones of the skull.

temporal-nuchal crest A crest on the back of the skull, forming on the occipital and temporal bones.

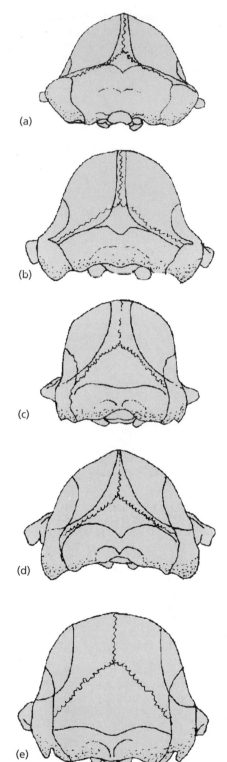

(a)

(b)

(c)

(d)

(e)

Figure 13.31 Development of Crests on Early Hominin Skulls The relatively small size of the brain case and the relatively large size of the muscles of the jaw and neck may result in the development of crests to allow adequate surface area for the attachment of these muscles. The nuchal muscle of the neck attaches to the nuchal crest at the back of the skull. The temporalis muscle of the jaw attaches to the sagittal crest along the top of the skull. These two crests may meet and fuse to form a compound temporal-nuchal crest. Cresting can be seen in these occipital views of the skulls of (a) chimpanzee, (b) *A. afarensis* (AL 333-45), (c) *A. africanus* (Sts 5), (d) *P. boisei* (KNM-ER 406), and (e) *H. habilis* (KNM-ER 1813), an early member of the genus *Homo* (Chapter 14).

form a temporal-nuchal crest. The face is somewhat shorter because of a reduction in the size of the anterior dentition, and it has a very characteristic concave, or "dish-shaped," profile. The nasal bones are relatively flat. The forehead, behind the moderately large brow ridges, is low and flat. The top view shows a very marked **postorbital constriction.** When the skull is viewed from the rear, the lowest part of it is the point of greatest width.

The increase in size of the posterior dentition in *A. africanus* is related to a heavily built mandible. In these forms, chewing created powerful stresses on the bones of the skull, and bony struts evolved to withstand those stresses. For example, two bony columns, called **anterior pillars,** occur on both sides of the nasal aperture in *A. africanus* (Figure 13.32).

Paranthropus is characterized by a specialized chewing apparatus that includes large premolars and molars associated with a thick, deep mandible. Many features of the skull are related to the development of powerful chewing muscles that resulted in powerful forces being placed on the posterior teeth. The zygomatic arch is long and powerfully built for the attachment of the masseter muscle. It flares away from the skull to accommodate the temporalis muscle, which passes between it and the side of the skull. A small anterior sagittal crest appears on top of the skull in most specimens for attachment of the powerful temporalis muscle.

Ecology and the Early Hominins

As is true for all animal populations, hominin evolution represents a continuous adaption to a series of ecological niches. Evolutionary modifications are responses to changes in the environment or to competition with other populations. A challenge of paleontological studies is the great difficulty in determining the environmental factors associated with populations that are exclusively known from fossilized bones. Yet fossils do occur in a context along with the fossils of other animals and plants, archaeological material, and geological features. This allows us to develop some hypotheses regarding the lifeways of ancient populations.

Late Pliocene Habitats Paleoanthropologists search for environmental factors that help explain evolutionary change. Specifically, they are looking for possible explanations for the emergence of the various hominin species. It is significant that east Africa, an area associated with early hominin populations, is also an area that experienced major physical changes from Late Eocene through Late Pliocene times. Major episodes of faulting, warping, uplifting, and volcanic activity dramatically changed the east African landscape. The escarpments and gorges of the East African Rift System were formed, as were new mountains and highland areas. River systems, lakes, and deltas were created, changed, and destroyed. Associated with many of these geological changes were profound changes in climate.

postorbital constriction
As seen from a top view, a marked constriction in the skull immediately behind the orbits and brow ridge.

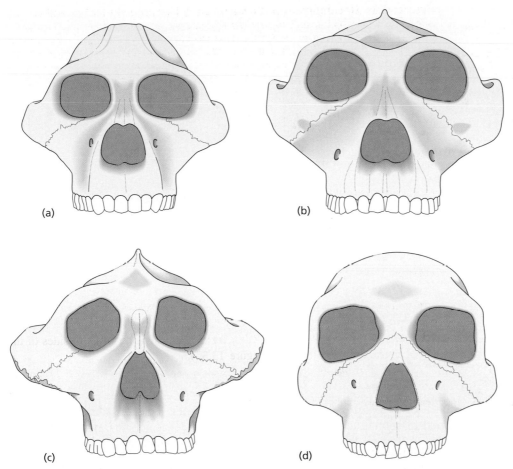

(a)

(b)

(c)

(d)

Elizabeth Vrba identifies a major cooling event that took place approximately 2.5 million years ago.[4] This was a global climate change associated with the first widespread glaciation of the North Pole. This cooling event is associated with the spread of arid and open habitats in east and south Africa.

From the analyses of known dates for various fossil finds, it appears that this cooling event is associated with the appearance of the new hominin genera, *Paranthropus* and *Homo.* It is not known if the cooling event was the main factor that brought about the origins of the two lineages or whether they had already evolved before 2.5 million years ago and the cooling event was responsible for their rapid evolution into new forms.

Several reconstructions of the paleohabitats associated with early hominin remains provide us with a picture of several types of habitats. Table 13.5 lists the results of several of these studies. Nancy E. Sikes tells us that "available paleoenvironmental evidence from Plio-Pleistocene [hominin] fossil and archaeological localities in Africa . . . portrays a diversity of vegetation communities similar to today's topical savanna mosaic, from swamps to treeless or wooded grasslands, woodland, gallery forest, and mountain forest. Very few early [hominin] localities are reconstructed as open grasslands."[5]

The evidence for the extinction of *Paranthropus,* the lastest hominin not placed in the genus *Homo,* is not clear. The youngest known fossil is SK 3 from Swartkrans, South Africa.

anterior pillars Bony columns located on both sides of the nasal aperture of some fossil hominins that help withstand the stresses of chewing.

---

[4] E. S. Vrba, "Late Pliocene Climatic Events and Hominid Evolution," in F. E. Grine (ed.), *Evolutionary History of the "Robust" Australopithecines* (New York: Aldine de Gruyter, 1988), pp. 405–426.

[5] N. E. Sikes, "Early Hominid Habitat Preferences in East Africa: Paleosol Carbon Isotope Evidence," *Journal of Human Evolution* 27 (1994), p. 26.

Table 13.5 Plio-Pleistocene Hominin Habitat, Resource, Geographical Preference*

Habitat Resource or Context	P.r./P.b.	P.b.	H.h./P.b.
Montane forest[†]	x		
Gallery forest/riparian woodland[‡]		x	x
Closed habitat		x	
Closed/mesic[§]		x	
Groves of trees			x
Dambo (wet grassland)			x
Open savanna			x
Open/xeric[‖]	x	x	
Riverine		x	
Stream channel margins		x	x
Fresh water			x

* *P.r.* refers to *Paranthropus robustus; P.b.* to *Paranthropus boisei; H.h.* to *Homo habilis.*
[†] Mountain forests.
[‡] Forests and woodlands along rivers.
[§] Associated with a moderate amount of moisture.
[‖] Associated with a small amount of moisture.
Source: Adapted from N. E. Sikes, "Early Hominid Habitat Preferences in East Africa: Paleosol Carbon Isotopic Evidence," *Journal of Human Evolution* 27 (1994), pp. 25–45.

This specimen of *P. robustus* dates from about 900,000 B.P. There is some evidence for another period of cooling at about this time, but the evidence for this event is not very clear. The fate of *P. boisei* from east Africa is uncertain since fossil evidence from between 1.2 million and 900,000 B.P. is scarce in that region.

The Reconstruction of Diet Associated with varying habitats are different patterns of exploitation of those habitats. For example, *Paranthropus* was adapted for a diet of tough, fibrous material. Specific anatomical adaptations for such a diet include thickened tooth enamel, expansion in size of the surface area of the premolars and molars, and an increase in the mass of the chewing muscles as seen in the robust and flaring zygomatic arch and the development of a sagittal crest. These anatomical changes parallel those of other mammals that feed on such material.

Analysis of the surfaces of the posterior teeth by the electron scanning microscope confirms this hypothesis. Richard Kay and Frederick Grine note that the wear pattern on the molars of *Paranthropus* resembles those of living primates that eat hard food items.[6]

Another approach to the reconstruction of diet is based on the ratio of two of the isotopes of carbon, ^{13}C to ^{12}C, in tooth enamel. Differences in this ratio are a result of the process of photosynthesis in plants that utilize carbon dioxide in the atmosphere. Some of the carbon in carbon dioxide is the isotope ^{13}C, and some is ^{12}C. Different kinds of plants utilize one or the other isotope more frequently. Thus, trees, bushes, and shrubs, characteristic of more forested habitats, incorporate more ^{12}C than do tropical grasses and associated plants that are found in more open habitats. The former are referred as C_3 plants, while the latter are referred to as C_4 plants.

When animals eat plant material, they incorporate the carbon found in the plant into their tooth enamel. Animals that consume primarily C_{3-} plants end up with a different ^{13}C

---

[6] R. F. Kay and F. E. Grine, "Tooth Morphology, Wear and Diet in *Australopithecus* and *Paranthropus* from Southern Africa," in F. E. Grine (ed.), *Evolutionary History of the "Robust" Australopithecines* (New York: Aldine de Gruyter, 1988), pp. 427–447.

to ^{12}C ratio in their tooth enamel than animals that eat primarily C$_{4-}$ plants. Animals that eat both kinds of plants show a ratio that falls between the two; meat eaters show a ratio similar to that of their prey.

An analysis of the tooth enamel from several fossil animals found at Makapansgat, South Africa, falls into several categories. Grassland feeders had relatively high ratios of ^{13}C to ^{12}C. A second group had low ratios and probably emphasized trees, bushes, and shrubs found in the forest in their diet. Two animals—scavenging hyenas and *A. africanus*— had intermediate ratios. This suggests that the hominins had a mixed diet that included forest plant products as well as plant material from the more open areas. However, the microwear pattern on the *A. africanus* teeth is not that of a grass eater. This leads us to the conclusion that the C$_4$ pattern was obtained not from eating grasses but from eating animals that subsisted on grasses. *Australopithecus* may have periodically left the forest to hunt for small animals and scavenge available carcasses.

Summary

Four of the most significant features of the Hominini are erect bipedalism, manufacturing of tools, reduction in the size of the dentition, and enlargement of the brain. All hominin genera were clearly erect bipeds, as evidenced by their postcranial skeletons and the footprints preserved at Laetoli. Although the *A. afarensis* was clearly an erect biped, it was characterized by some features, such as relatively long arms and long, curved fingers and toes, suggesting that it had some proficiency in moving around in the trees.

The earliest known stone tools date from about 2.6 to 2.4 million B.P. Many researchers attribute the tools exclusively to *Homo.* However, the facts that some stone tools may predate the origin of *Homo* and that the hands of hominins other than *Homo* were quite capable of manufacturing tools lend credibility to the idea that *Paranthropus* made crude stone tools. Members of all three non-*Homo* genera also very likely manufactured objects of perishable materials.

Many dental features of *A. afarensis* are intermediate between those of modern humans and those of apes. For example, the canines project above the tooth row and a small diastema frequently occurs between the upper canine and premolar. The dentition of the earlier *A. anamensis* shows even more similarities to the Miocene "dental apes."

Although the teeth are relatively larger than those of later *Homo,* the dentition of *A. africanus* is basically humanlike. The dentition of *Paranthropus,* however, shows many specialized features. These include thickened tooth enamel and an expansion in the size of the surface area of the premolars and molars. These and other changes may be related to a specialized diet consisting of tough, fibrous materials.

The cranial capacities of *Australopithecus* and *Paranthropus* ranged from 400 to 530 cubic centimeters. This number is similar to that of the larger apes, and it is significantly smaller than the 1350-cubic-centimeter average for modern *H. sapiens.*

Key Terms

anterior pillars, *346*
australopithecine, *318*
bone breccia, *318*

osteodontokeratic culture, *339*
pneumatized, *345*

postorbital constriction, *346*
temporal-nuchal crest, *345*

See the Online Learning Center for additional Study questions.

Study Questions

1. Where have the fossils of *Australopithecus* and *Paranthropus* been found? Are different species associated with different areas?

2. How does the skull of the genus *Australopithecus* compare with the skull of the genus *Homo?*

3. The architecture of the skull is, in part, a reflection of the dentition and the jaw. In regard to *Paranthropus,* what are some of the features of the skull of these hominins that can be associated with their large posterior dentition?

4. What evidence suggests that *Australopithecus* was an erect biped? How did the locomotor pattern of *A. afarensis* differ from that of *H. sapiens?*

5. Some paleoanthropologists consider *A. afarensis* as an intermediate between the Miocene dental apes and the hominins. What are some of the apelike characteristics of the skeleton of *A. afarensis?*

6. What are the main differences between the genera *Australopithecus* and *Paranthropus?*

7. What occurred in the Late Pliocene that may have been responsible for the appearance of the genera *Paranthropus* and *Homo?*

Critical Thinking Questions

1. We can ask the question: "What does it mean to be hominin?" The answer to this question can be approached from biological, sociological, psychological, philosophical, and evolutionary perspectives. What would be your answer to this question?

2. The evolution of bipedalism was central to hominin evolution. If humans were quadrupedal but in other ways were similar to today's humans, how would human behavior be different? How would a house, a school, and an office building have to be different? In what ways might interpersonal relationships be different? What other differences would there be?

3. The popular press speaks of the "ape-men" and the "missing link." This conjures up a picture of a prehistoric creature that exhibited a mixture of ape and human features. Yet today we know that an animal ancestral to both apes and humans would be characterized by many features that are no longer found in living apes and humans. Similarly, this creature would lack many features that evolved later in living apes and humans. Examine the fossils attributed to *Australopithecus afarensis*. How would you characterize this species in light of this question? In what ways can we think of *A. afarensis* as a transitional species leading to *Homo?*

Suggested Readings

Dart, R. A. *Adventures with the Missing Link.* New York: Viking, 1959. This is Raymond Dart's autobiographical account of his work with the early hominids of south Africa.

Day, M. *Guide to Fossil Man,* 4th ed. Chicago: University of Chicago Press, 1986. This guide consists of entries detailing important fossil finds.

Hart, D., and R. W. Sussman. *Man the Hunted: Primates, Predators, and Human Evolution.* New York: Westview Press, 2005. This book presents the hypothesis that early hominins were the prey of many animals which shaped much of hominin evolution.

Johanson, D., and E. Blake. *From Lucy to Language.* New York: Simon & Schuster, 1996. This is a beautifully illustrated book on human evolution with detailed descriptions of the major hominin fossils.

Johanson, D. C., and M. A. Edey. *Lucy: The Beginnings of Humankind.* New York: Simon & Schuster, 1981. This is a fascinating behind-the-scenes account of paleoanthropology. The book focuses on the fossil nicknamed "Lucy" and the change in thinking about human evolution that this find has prompted in many circles.

Johanson, D. C., and J. Shreeve. *Lucy's Child: The Discovery of a Human Ancestor.* New York: Morrow, 1989. This sequel tells the story of the discovery of new hominin fossils in Olduvai Gorge.

Morell, V. *Ancestral Passions: The Leakey Family and the Quest for Humankind's Beginnings.* New York: Touchstone, 1996. This book discusses the scientific contribution of the Leakey family with interesting bibliographic information on each of them.

Reader, J. *Missing Links: The Hunt for Earliest Man,* rev. ed. Boston: Little, Brown, 1995. This book tells the story of the hunt for and discovery of many important fossil hominins.

Willis, D. *The Hominid Gang.* New York: Viking, 1989. This easy-to-read book describes the lives and work of the paleoanthropologists responsible for our knowledge of the early hominins.

Suggested Websites

Becoming Human:
http://becominghuman.org

Institute of Human Origins:
http://asu.edu/clas/iho

Koobi Fora Research Project:
www.kfrp.com

The Leakey Foundation:
http://leakeyfoundation.org

Minnesota State University eMuseum
www.mnsu.edu/emuseum

National Museums of Kenya:
www.museums.or.ke

Chapter 14

Early Species of the Genus *Homo*

Homo erectus skull between modern *Homo sapiens* skull (left) and *Paranthropus skull* (right).

Seeing Neandertals in context, in the broad sweep of human evolution, is a valuable perspective. But we must not forget that they were neither "new and improved" versions of *Homo erectus* nor crude prototypes of modern *Homo sapiens*. They were themselves; they were Neandertals—one of the more distinctive, successful, and intriguing groups of humans that ever enriched our family history. •

—*Erik Trinkaus and Pat Shipman*

Chapter Outline

The Early *Homo* Fossil Record

The Genus Homo
Homo habilis *and* Homo rudolfensis
Homo erectus *and* Homo ergaster
Homo antecessor
Homo heidelbergensis
Homo neandertalensis
Summary

The Culture of Early *Homo*

Interpreting the Archaeological Evidence
The Culture of the Earliest Homo
Hunting, Scavenging, and Gathering
The Brain and Language in Prehistoric
*   Populations*
The Culture of the Neandertals
Summary

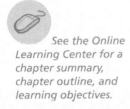

See the Online Learning Center for a chapter summary, chapter outline, and learning objectives.

After Reading This Chapter, You Should Be Able to Answer These Questions:

1. What defines the genus *Homo*? How does *Homo* differ from *Australopithecus* and *Paranthropus*?

2. What are the earliest named species of *Homo*? What characterizes these species, and where are they found?

3. What is the distribution of the fossils that are placed in the species *Homo heidelbergensis*? In what ways to they differ from *Homo erectus* and *Homo ergaster*?

4. In what areas of the world do we find remains of *Homo neandertalensis*? What are some of the physical characteristics of Neandertals that differentiate them from other hominin species?

5. What does the term *Paleolithic* refer to? What are the divisions of the Paleolithic? What do we know about early stone tools and their use?

6. When did hominins first use fire? What functions might fire have served for early hominins?

7. How did early members of the genus *Homo* get food?

8. What changes in brain structure and function evolved in the genus *Homo* that differentiated it from earlier hominins?

9. What features describe the culture of the Neandertals?

10. What are some ways in which the hominins described in this chapter might have been related to each other?

All modern human beings belong to the genus *Homo, Homo* being the Latin word for "human being." While anthropologists use the term *human* in many of their discussions, *human* is not a technical term. We will leave the question of what it is to be human to the philosophers and cultural anthropologists.

The origins of our "humanity," however, lie in the origins and evolution of the genus *Homo.* What, then, are the essential characteristics that define this genus? Since hominin adaptations are often behavioral, we must look beyond the fossil record and examine the archaeological record as well. This chapter will examine both the paleontology and the archaeology of those members of the genus *Homo* that arose before the evolution of *Homo sapiens.*

THE EARLY *HOMO* FOSSIL RECORD

Between 2.5 and 2.3 million years ago, the fossil record reveals the emergence of several new hominin species that anthropologists place into the genera *Paranthropus* and *Homo.* Both genera most likely evolved from a late species of *Australopithecus.* Members of the genus *Homo* coexisted with *Paranthropus* until the latter became extinct some 900,000 years ago. *Paranthropus* was a subject of the last chapter; this chapter discusses the evolution of the genus *Homo.*

The Genus *Homo*

Homo shares many features with *Australopithecus* and *Paranthropus.* Yet *Homo* is characterized by many features that contrast with the other genera, some of which are listed in Table 14.1.

The size of the *Homo* cranium reflects an increase in cranial capacity. Cranial capacities in *Australopithecus* and *Paranthropus* generally fall between 400 and 530 cubic centimeters, while the various known representatives of *Homo* range between about 500 and 2300 cubic centimeters (Table 14.2). The lower values are found in the earlier species.

Table 14.1 The Genera *Australopithecus, Paranthropus,* and *Homo* Compared

Australopithecus/Paranthropus	Homo
Cranial capacity of 400–530 cubic centimeters.	Cranial capacity of 500–2300 cubic centimeters.
Bones of brain case thin.	Bones of brain case very thick to thin.
Crests may develop on brain case.	Crests never develop on brain case.
Point of maximum width of brain case near bottom.	Point of maximum width of brain case bottom to top.
Moderate to large brow ridge.	Large to slight brow ridge.
Marked postorbital constriction.	Moderate to slight postorbital constriction.
Flaring of zygomatic arch.	Zygomatic arch not flared.
Facial skeleton large relative to size of brain case.	Facial skeleton small relative to size of brain case.
Facial skeleton often dish-shaped.	Facial skeleton never dish-shaped.
Suture between nasal and frontal bones upside-down V.	Suture between nasal and frontal bones horizontal.
Anterior pillars alongside nasal aperture.	No anterior pillars.
Relatively large prognathous jaw.	Jaw less massive.
Lack of chin.	Chin may develop.
Premolars and molars large to extremely large.	Smaller premolars and molars.
Thin postcranial bones.	Thick to thin postcranial bones.

Table 14.2 Cranial Capacities of *Homo*

Species	Specimen	Site	Cranial Capacity (cubic centimeters)
Homo habilis	OH 7	Olduvai Gorge	674
Homo habilis	OH 16	Olduvai Gorge	638
Homo habilis	OH 24	Olduvai Gorge	594
Homo habilis	KNM-ER 1813	East Lake Turkana	509
Homo rudolfensis	KNM-ER 1470	East Lake Turkana	752
Homo ergaster	KNM-ER 3733	East Lake Turkana	850
Homo ergaster	WT 15000	West Lake Turkana	900
Homo erectus	OH 9	Olduvai Gorge	1067
Homo erectus	BOU-VP-2/66	Bouri (Middle Awash)	995
Homo erectus	Skull III	Zhoukoudian	918
Homo erectus	Skull X	Zhoukoudian	1225
Homo erectus	Skull XI	Zhoukoudian	1015
Homo heidelbergensis	Kabwe	Kabwe	1285
Homo heidelbergensis	Steinheim	Steinheim	1100
Homo heidelbergensis	Swanscombe	Swanscombe	1325
Homo neandertalensis	Neandertal	Neander Valley	1525
Homo neandertalensis	La Chapelle	La Chapelle-aux-Saints	1625
Homo sapiens	Cro-Magnon	Cro-Magnon	1600

Compared with those of *Australopithecus* and *Paranthropus,* the *Homo* cranium is more delicate and rounded; the zygomatic arch is more slender; a sagittal crest never develops on the brain case; and the cranium lacks developed muscular crests and prominent anterior pillars. In general, *Homo* is characterized by a smaller facial skeleton, including smaller teeth and jaws. Some of the earlier specimens, however, exhibit front teeth that are approximately the same size as those of *Australopithecus,* but the premolars and molars show the beginning of size reduction that is characteristic of *Homo.* There is variation in the dimensions of the facial skeletons; some specimens retain some features found in the australopithecine face, such as facial and mandibular bone characteristics related to powerful chewing.

Erect bipedalism is a diagnostic feature of all hominins. From the known postcranial bones, individuals of the genus *Homo* are larger in body size and exhibit less sexual dimorphism than is seen in the other genera.

***The Early Species of the Genus* Homo** Many paleoanthropologists have suggested that *Homo* originated in Africa around 2.5 million years ago. Some scholars see a cooling of the earth's climate around that time that led to drier climates, more open habitats, and the development of marked seasons; others have not found convincing evidence of such changes.

A mandible from the Chiwondo Beds of Malawi and a temporal bone from the Chemeron Formation of Kenya, both in east Africa, may be the oldest known members of the genus *Homo.* However, the dating of these specimens is far from certain. A maxilla (AL 666-1) from the Hadar region of Ethiopia, found in 1994, most likely belongs to the genus *Homo.* This find, which is associated with stone tools, dates to 2.33 million B.P.

In recent years, there has been a trend toward the recognition of several species of the genus *Homo.* Only one of these species ultimately gave rise to *H. sapiens.* This view is in marked contrast with the earlier idea that the hominins belonging to *Homo* were divided into only a few species. These species were seen as representing a more or less single evolutionary line.

Today there is considerable debate over the number of species within the genus *Homo* as well as the assignment of specific specimens to these species. For purposes of organization, we will describe the fossils of *Homo* in terms of the following species that have been proposed: *H. habilis, H. rudolfensis, H. ergaster, H. erectus, H. antecessor, H. heidelbergensis, H. neandertalensis,* and *H. sapiens.*

Figure 14.1 *Homo rudolfensis*
Skull (KNM-ER 1470) from East Lake
Turkana.

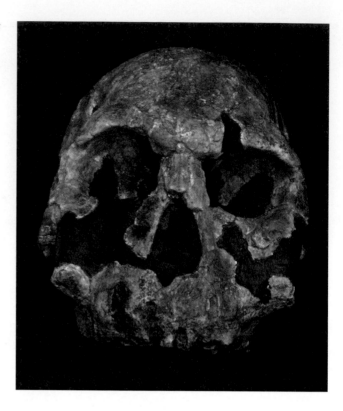

Homo habilis and Homo rudolfensis

The early fossils belonging to the genus *Homo* were originally placed into a single species, *Homo habilis* ("handy human being"). The first specimen of *H. habilis* (OH 7) was discovered by Louis and Mary Leakey in 1960 at Olduvai Gorge. The original specimen consists of a damaged mandible and parts of the brain case of a juvenile; the bones of several adult specimens were later recovered. In 1964, these specimens and others were placed into the newly defined species *H. habilis.*

In 1986, Tim White discovered another specimen of *H. habilis* (OH 62) at Olduvai Gorge. This find is significant because it includes not only parts of the skull but also bones of the right arm and leg that belong to the same individual. For the first time, cranial and postcranial remains attributed to *H. habilis* were found in association. The association, however, is puzzling. Aspects of the skull appear to be rather *Homo*-like, yet some of the postcranial bones resemble those of *Australopithecus* and modern apes. For example, the fragmentary evidence suggests that *H. habilis* had short legs. In fact, its arms may have been almost as long as its legs.

Several hominin fossils were recovered from Koobi Fora, East Lake Turkana, between 1969 and 1976. This material shows well-defined variation. KNM-ER 1470 is an example of one of the larger specimens (Figure 14.1). It has a relatively large brain case with a cranial capacity of about 752 cubic centimeters, the face is broad and flat, the teeth and jaws are large, and it exhibits a slight brow ridge. In contrast to this fossil, KNM-ER 1813 has a smaller cranial capacity of approximately 509 cubic centimeters; the face, jaws, and teeth are small; and it displays more prominent brow ridges (Figure 14.2).

While some paleoanthropologists place all these early fossils into the species *H. habilis,* others divide the material into two species: *H. habilis* and *H. rudolfensis.* The latter species is named after Lake Rudolf, the early name for what is now called Lake Turkana. *H. rudolfensis* includes the larger individuals, including KNM-ER 1470. *H. habilis* consists of the smaller individuals, including KNM-ER 1813 and the material from Olduvai Gorge. KNM-ER 1470, the best-known specimen of *H. rudolfensis,* dates from 1.9 to 1.8 million B.P.; the *H. habilis* fossils fall between 1.9 and 1.75 million B.P.

See the Online Learning Center for an Internet Activity on Homo habilis.

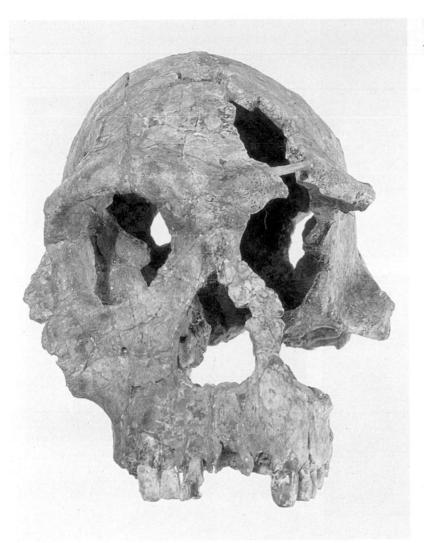

Figure 14.2 *Homo habilis,* **KNM-ER 1813, from Koobi Fora, East Lake Turkana, Kenya**

Homo erectus and *Homo ergaster*

Physical anthropologists are not in agreement over what to call the earliest species of hominin found outside of Africa. The Dutch anatomist Eugène Dubois first described the species *Homo erectus* in the 1890s based on fossils he found in Java. Since then specimens described as *H. erectus* have been found in Africa, China, and the Republic of Georgia (a part of the former Soviet Union).

Beginning in 1975, some paleoanthropologists proposed a new species, *Homo ergaster.* They placed some of the early African representatives of *H. erectus,* along with several new specimens found outside of Africa, into this new species. This is an example of the difference between lumpers and splitters, which was discussed in Chapter 11. Splitters see a significant difference between what they classify as *H. erectus* and *H. ergaster.* For example, they point to the thinner bones of the skull and the reduction of the depression behind the brow ridge in *H. ergaster.* To these anthropologists, *H. ergaster* appears to resemble later *Homo* species more closely than it resembles *H. erectus. H. ergaster* therefore would be a possible direct ancestor of modern humans, with *H. erectus* being a sideline and a dead-end species. On the other hand, lumpers see the differences between the two groups of fossils as relatively minor. They see the two groups as subspecies of the same species.

This issue becomes important when we begin to search for the oldest presence of *Homo* outside of Africa and how this find relates to early African forms as well as later Eurasian populations. The earliest possible hominin fossils outside of Africa are a jaw fragment and

See the Online Learning Center for an Internet Activity on Homo ergaster.

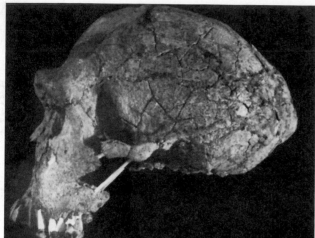

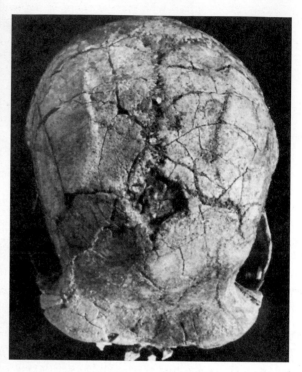

Figure 14.3 *Homo ergaster* Side, front, and top views of KNM-ER 3733 from East Lake Turkana.

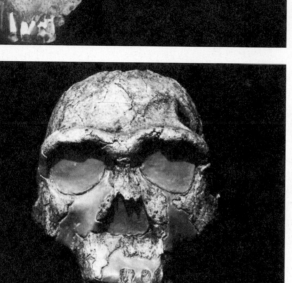

two molars from Longgupo Cave in China that may be 1.9 million years old. However, many anthropologists are not sure if these bones are hominin.

Homo ergaster *from Europe* Another early date for the presence of hominins outside of Africa comes from the site of Dmanisi, in the Republic of Georgia, where hominin fossils and simple stone tools have been found dating to 1.75 million years ago. In May 1999, scientists found two hominin skulls, one of a young male and the other of an adolescent female, along with simple stone tools. The cranial capacities of these two skulls (about 650 and 780 cubic centimeters) are among the smallest in *Homo ergaster* and *Homo erectus* specimens.

The team that excavated the skulls that were found in 1999 assigned them to the species *H. ergaster* rather than to *H. erectus*. This was done in part because the skulls resembled the long-legged *Homo ergaster*. However, in 2001 a third skull was found with traits consistent with the short-legged *Homo habilis*. Then, in 2003, it was announced that leg bones had been found. The analysis of the leg bones has not been published. However when it is, it may clarify the position of the Dmanisi fossils in the hominin family.

Homo ergaster *from Africa* The fossils that are attributed to *Homo ergaster* are found in the Turkana Basin of east Africa and date from about 1.9 to 1.5 million B.P. A very complete skull (KNM-ER 3733), pictured in Figure 14.3, is from an individual who lived about 1.8 million years ago. The remains of KNM-ER 3733 were found together at the same level of the same site with KNM-ER 406, a specimen of *Paranthropus boisei*.

A very exciting find was made in 1984 on the western side of Lake Turkana, dated at about 1.6 million B.P. This find, KNM-WT 15000, from the site of Nariokotome, consists of an almost-complete skeleton of a subadult male close to 12 years of age (Figure 14.4). It is estimated that the "Turkana Boy," if he had lived, would have reached about 183 centimeters (6 feet) in height. Until this discovery, it was generally believed that these early populations were composed of individuals who were relatively short compared with many modern *H. sapiens*. Also, the small pelvis of "Turkana Boy" suggests a small birth canal, a more helpless infant, and a longer childhood period compared with earlier hominins.

H. ergaster resembles in many ways the fossils of *H. erectus* but does vary in some ways, such as in the absence of thick cranial bones and a distinct depression behind the browridges (Figure 14.5). Some of the more important finds of *H. ergaster* and *H. erectus* are located on the map in Figure 14.6 and listed in Table 14.3. The evolutionary relationships of the species of the genus *Homo* are pictured in Figure 13.22 in the previous chapter.

Homo erectus *from Indonesia* One of the major arguments in the late nineteenth and early twentieth centuries centered on the location of the place where the hominins first evolved. Charles Darwin believed that hominin evolution began in Africa primarily because Africa was the homeland of our closest living primate relatives, the chimpanzee and gorilla. Other scholars, however, placed the center of hominin origins in southeast and eastern Asia.

Eugène Dubois, a nineteenth-century Dutch anatomist, was convinced that Asia was the place of human origin. To prove his point, he traveled to the Dutch East Indies (now Indonesia), and there, in 1890 at Kedung Brubus, he discovered a hominin jaw fragment. Dubois continued his work; in 1891, he discovered a small skullcap at Trinil, Java, and a year later he found a femur from a hominin that walked bipedally. Dubois's material is part of the Kabuh Beds of Java, which have been dated at approximately 700,000 to 500,000 B.P.

Dubois's work in Java and the discovery of a "primitive" cranium associated with a relatively modern femur excited the anthropological community. Soon paleoanthropologists traveled to Java to search for the remains of early hominins, and additional specimens of *H. erectus* were found at Sangiran, Modjokerto, Ngandong, and Sambungmachan. The latest specimen was discovered in 1993 at Sangiran.

Until about 10 years ago, the oldest Asian *Homo* fossils were generally thought to be less than 1 million years old. Then, in 1994, Carl Swishen and Garniss Curtis, using a new dating method, redated the finds from Sangiran and Modjokerto to 1.8 and 1.6 million B.P., respectively.[1] (This latter date has been questioned. It may be closer to 1.5 million years old.) This opens up the possibility that *Homo* populations may have migrated from Africa into Eurasia at a very early time. The *H. ergaster* finds from Dmanisi confirm this.

Archaeological evidence suggests that early hominins, either *H. erectus* or *H. ergaster*, spread throughout southeast

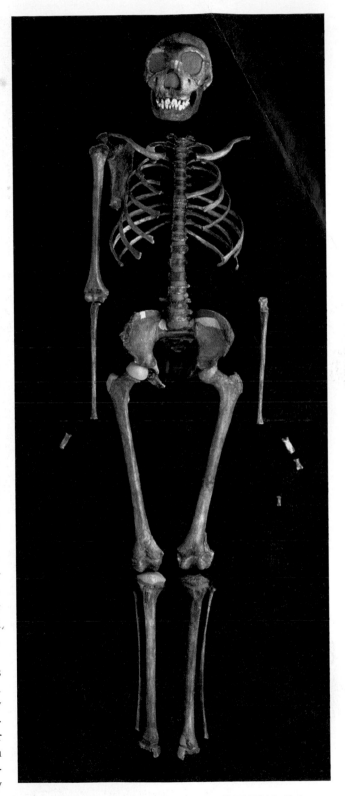

Figure 14.4 *Homo ergaster* Skeleton of WT 15000, "Lake Turkana boy," from Nariokotome, West Turkana.

---

[1] C. C. Swisher III et al., "Age of the Earliest Known Hominids in Java, Indonesia," *Science* 263 (1994), pp. 1118–1121.

Figure 14.5 *Homo ergaster*
Skull of WT 15000, "Lake Turkana boy," from Nariokotome, West Turkana.

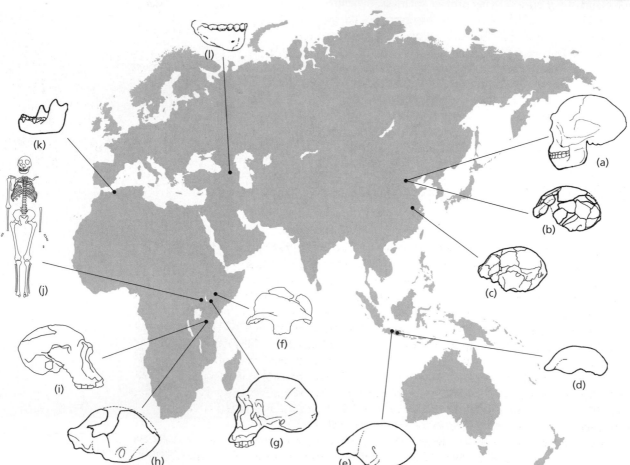

Figure 14.6 Variation and Distribution of the Early Species of the Genus *Homo* (a) *H. erectus*, Skull XII, Zhoukoudian, People's Republic of China; (b) *H. erectus*, Skull XI, Zhoukoudian, People's Republic of China; (c) *H. heidelbergensis*, Hexian, People's Republic of China; (d) *H. erectus*, Sangiran, Java; (e) *H. erectus*, Trinil, Java; (f) *H. erectus*, KNM-OL-45500, Olorgesailie, Kenya; (g) *H. ergaster*, KNM-ER 3733, Lake Turkana, Kenya; (h) *H. erectus*, OH 9, Olduvai Gorge, Tanzania; (i) *H. habilis*, OH 24, Olduvai Gorge, Tanzania; (j) *H. ergaster*, WT 15000, "Turkana Boy," West Lake Turkana, Kenya; (k) *H. erectus*, Ternifine II, Algeria; (l) *H. erectus*, Dmanisi, Republic of Georgia.

Table 14.3 Early Species and Representative Sites of the Genus *Homo*

Species	Approximate Dates (million years B.P.)	Some Important Sites
Homo rudolfensis	2.3–1.9	Lake Turkana, Kenya
Homo habilis	1.9–1.6	Olduvai Gorge, Tanzania Lake Turkana, Kenya
Homo ergaster	1.9–1.5	Lake Turkana and Nariokotome, Kenya Dmanisi, Republic of Georgia
Homo erectus	1.8–0.4	Sangiran, Modjokerto, Ngandong, Sambungmachan, Java Zhoukoudian, Lant'ien, China Olduvai Gorge, Olorgesailie, Kenya Bouri (Middle Awash), Ethiopia Swartkrans, South Africa Ternifine, Algeria
Homo antecessor	0.9–0.7	Gran Dolina, Spain
Homo heidelbergensis	0.8–0.25	Kabwe, Zambia Bodo d'Ar, Omo, Ethiopia Buia, Eritrea Lake Ndutu, Tanzania Saldanha, South Africa Heidelberg, Steinheim, Bilzingsleben, Germany Boxgrove, Swanscombe, England Vértesszöllös, Hungary Petralona, Greece Arago Cave, Moutmaurin, France Salé, Morocco Dali, Lontangong Cave, Yunxian, China
Homo neandertalensis	0.3–0.03	Neander Valley, Germany Spy, Belgium La Chapelle-aux-Saints, Le Moustier, La Quina, La Ferrassie, France Krapina, Yugoslavia Tabūn, Skhūl, Israel
Homo floresiensis	0.04–0.02	Liang Bua, Flores Island, Indonesia

Asia. Although the Indonesian islands of Java and Bali were connected to what is today the mainland of southeast Asia as falling sea levels exposed the lands lying beneath the shallow sea, islands laying to the east of these islands were not connected to Asia because they were separated by deep water. Even when the level fell to its lowest level, 19 kilometers of open water separated the eastern islands from the continental area of southeast Asia. Such a journey would have required some type of water craft. Archaeologists working on the island of Flores have fission-track-dated deposits containing archaeological material to 880,000 B.P.[2]

The island of Java not only has given up early evidence of *H. erectus* outside of Africa, it may have yielded the remains of the most recent *H. erectus* specimens as well. A group of 12 hominin calvaria and partial calvaria and two tibiae were discovered between 1931 and 1933 at Ngandong, which is located on the Solo River. Additional hominin material, including two partial calvaria and pelvic fragments, was recovered between 1976 and 1980.

Some investigators have concluded that *H. erectus* survived to a late date in southeast Asia and was contemporary there with *H. sapiens*. Using a series of bovid teeth from

---

[2] M. J. Moorwood, P. B. O'Sullivan, F. Aziz, and A. Raza, "Fission-Track Ages of Stone Tools and Fossils on the East Indonesian Island of Flores," *Nature* 392 (1998), pp. 173–176.

Box 14-1   The Little Hominins of Flores Island

The field of paleoanthropology is an exciting one, in part because it changes constantly as new fossils are discovered and old ones are reanalyzed. A book or article represents the state of our knowledge at a specific point in time. This means that by the time any book or article appears in print, new ideas and new data may have appeared. Often new fossils fill in the blanks and are, to some degree, anticipated by the various hypotheses that exist, but occasionally a new discovery comes out of left field, totally unanticipated. This is the case with a find that was made in September 2003 and announced to the world in October 2004.

The new discovery on Flores is that of a hominin skeleton. It has been quite well dated by a variety of dating methods to about 18,000 B.P. What is especially remarkable about this find is the very small size of the skeleton and the smallest cranial capacity ever seen in an adult hominin.

Paleontologists are well aware of the phenomenon of miniaturization of mammalian populations living on islands. Perhaps it is the limited resources or the lack of predators that is responsible for this. For example, one of the commonly found fossil species found on Flores is a dwarf species of *Stegodon*, a member of the elephant order close to the ancestors of the mammoths and modern elephants. The discoverers of the skeleton have proposed that this is a miniaturized hominin.

The skeleton, identified as LB 1, was found during archaeological excavations at Liang Bua, a limestone cave. LB 1 actually is not a fossil since it has not been mineralized. The skull is fairly complete; some of the postcranial elements are also fairly complete while others are mere fragments. Various lines of evidence, including the pattern of tooth wear, epiphyseal union, and the

closure of cranial sutures, indicate that it is an adult. The anatomy of the pelvis suggests that it is a female. Reconstruction of stature from various limb bones suggests a height of a little over 1 meter (3½ feet), which places it in the height range of the early australopithecines.

Perhaps the most unusual anatomical feature is its extraordinarily small cranial capacity, measured at 380 cubic centimeters. This is the size of the cranial capacity of a living female chimpanzee. Both the stature and the cranial capacity fall at the lower end of the hominin range; the ratio of cranial volume to body height is outside the hominin range.

In spite of its size and small brain, this is not an australopithecine. The structure of the skull and pelvis places the skeleton into the genus *Homo*. Yet the investigators feel that it is not a diminutive *Homo sapiens* but a direct descendent of *Homo erectus*. We do know that *H. erectus* survived in Southeast Asia longer than any other place. The investigators hypothesize that a small population of *H. erectus* was isolated on Flores, where they underwent miniaturization in the manner of other mammalian island species. Because of these circumstances, the skeleton has been placed in a new species, *Homo floresiensis*.

The validity of this find as a new species and as a descendent of *Homo erectus* is the center of a vigorous debate. Perhaps by the time you read this report, it will have been sorted out.

Sources: P. Brown et al., "A New Small-Bodied Hominin from the Late Pleistocene of Flores, Indonesia," *Nature* 431 (2004), pp. 1055–1061; M. Morwood et al., "Archaeology and Age of a New Hominin from Flores in Eastern Indonesia," *Nature* 431 (2004), pp. 1087–1091.

museum collections and fresh excavations, Carl Swisher and his associates used electron spin resonance (ESR) and uranium-series dating techniques to date the tooth enamel. (The latter technique measures the decay of uranium to thorium in tooth enamel.) The results of the analysis provide a series of mean dates between 53,300 ± 4000 and 27,000 ± 2000 years ago.[3] These dates are much younger than any earlier estimates. The investigators contend that the Ngandong hominins belong taxonomically to *Homo erectus*. An even later find was reported in 2004 on Flores Island in Indonesia, where a population of small hominins existed up until about 18,000 years ago. Placed in a new species, they are thought to be late descendants of *Homo erectus* (Box 14-1).

Homo erectus *from China*   In 1927, a molar tooth was discovered in a cave at the site of Dragon Bone Hill near the village of Zhoukoudian, near Beijing, China. The next 10 years saw the recovery of more than a dozen skulls and almost 150 teeth, but these fossils were lost at the time of the Japanese invasion of China during World War II (Box 14-2). Except for two teeth from the first excavation, all we have today of the original material are meticulous descriptions and casts (Figure 14.7). Beginning in 1979, new excavations have

---

[3] C. Swisher III et al., "Latest *Homo erectus* of Java: Potential Contemporaneity with *Homo sapiens* in Southeast Asia," *Science* 274 (1996), pp. 1870–1874.

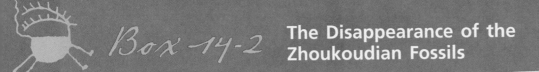

Box 14-2 The Disappearance of the Zhoukoudian Fossils

The discoveries of *Homo erectus* fossils at Dragon Bone Hill near the village of Zhoukoudian, China, caused great excitement among anthropologists, paleontologists, and the general public. The fossils represented a wealth of information about prehistoric humans and their culture.

The invasion of China by Japan at the beginning of World War II created difficulties for the project, and the excavations were suspended in 1937. The fossils continued to be studied at the Peking Union Medical College, however, for at this time the United States was not at war with Japan and the Japanese invaders were respecting foreign interests in China. The project participants, though, expecting an eventual conflict between Japan and the United States, were concerned about the safety of the fossils.

In late November 1941, the fossils from Zhoukoudian were carefully packed into two redwood crates and placed in the college vault. From the vault, they were transported by car to the Marine headquarters in Beijing, where they were transferred to regulation footlockers. These footlockers were then transported by train to Camp Holcomb, 140 miles away, where they were stored. They were to remain in the barracks until the arrival of the USS *President Harrison,* which would transport the fossils to the United States for the duration of the war.

The Japanese attacked Pearl Harbor on December 7, 1941; in China, lying west of the international date line, it was Monday morning, December 8. The Japanese immediately took over the Peking Union Medical College and began searching for the fossils.

The fossils, however, were no longer at the college, having been moved to Camp Holcomb. The Japanese took over the camp; there were no casualties. The Americans at the camp were placed under arrest and led away from the camp; the fossils have never been seen again.

Many hypotheses have been proposed about the fate of the Zhoukoudian fossils. Some believe that they were simply destroyed by the Japanese invaders, who may not have understood their value. Others believe that they were transported to Japan, southeast Asia, or Taiwan. They may even have eventually arrived in the United States. Whatever the case may be, in spite of many attempts to discover their fate, to this day the mystery of the fossils' disappearance remains unsolved.

Exacting measurements and descriptions of the fossils were published, and fine plaster casts were made. Yet many modern analytical techniques, such as the use of x-rays and CAT scans on fossil material, did not exist in the 1930s. The rediscovery of the fossils would provide the scientific community with important new knowledge for the understanding of human evolution.

Sources: For detailed information on the disappearance of the Zhoukoudian fossils and the attempts to recover them, see C. G. Janus, *The Search for Peking Man* (New York: Macmillan, 1975); H. L. Shapiro, *Peking Man* (New York: Simon & Schuster, 1974); and N. T. Boaz and R. L. Ciochon, *Dragon Bone Hill: An Ice-Age Saga of Homo erectus* (Oxford: Oxford University Press, 2004).

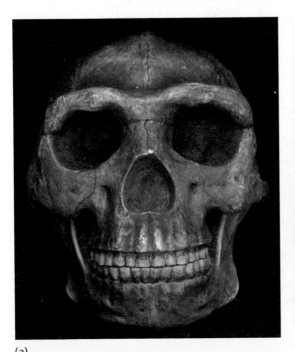
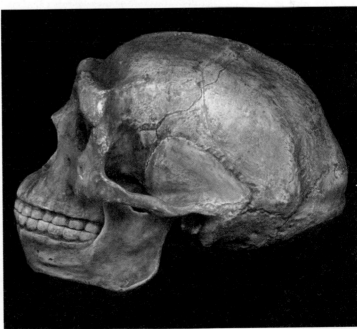

(a)   (b)

Figure 14.7 *Homo erectus* Reconstructed male skull from Zhoukoudian, China. (a) front view; (b) side view.

Figure 14.8 *Homo erectus* Skull (OH 9) from Olduvai Gorge.

been conducted at Zhoukoudian. Abundant stone tools and remains of nonhominin animals have been found, but *H. erectus* material has been fragmentary.

The dating of the Zhoukoudian fossils has been difficult. In 1996, the first radiometric dates were announced; these date the finds to at least 400,000 years ago. The fossils were found in an archaeological context associated with the remains of butchered animals and many stone chopper tools.

A number of other sites have been excavated in China. In 1965, a skull was recovered in Lant'ien County, Shensi Province, China, that appears to be older than those from Zhoukoudian. Dated at approximately 800,000 to 730,000 B.P., it may be the oldest *H. erectus* find in China. The skull has a small cranial capacity, which is estimated at 780 cubic centimeters, and some of the bones of the skull are thicker than those of any other *H. erectus* yet discovered.

Homo erectus *from Africa* Several fossils that can be attributed to *Homo erectus* are known from Olduvai Gorge. The first to be discovered (OH 9) was found by Louis Leakey in 1960 and consists of a partial cranium; it was found at the top of Bed II and is around 1.5 to 1.4 million years old (Figure 14.8). OH 9 is one of the largest known specimens of *H. erectus*. Other, younger fossils include a small, fragmented, and incomplete skull (OH 12); partial mandibles; and a few postcranial bones. A mandible, associated with isolated teeth and stone tools, was discovered in 1991 at Konso-Gardula, Ethiopia, and is dated at about 1.4 million B.P.

In 1997, a partial skull and some postcranial remains were recovered from the Dakanihylo Member of the Bouri Formation, Middle Awash, Ethiopia (Figure 14.9). The find has been dated to about 1.0 million B.P. The associated nonhominin fossils suggest that the hominins at this time were living in an open grassland habitat with lakes or rivers nearby. Many stone tools were found in these beds, and signs of butchering were found on many of the nonhominin skulls. This find shows features that characterize both African and Asian *H. erectus*.

Figure 14.9 *Homo erectus* Partial skull (BOU-VP-2/66) from the Bouri Formation, Middle Awash, Ethiopia.

In 2003, a partial cranium (KNM-OL 45500) of an older juvenile or small adult with an estimated cranial capacity of 800 cubic centimeters was found at a site in Olorgesailie, Kenya. The specimen was dated to about 900,000 to 970,000 years ago. It exhibits a mosaic of characteristics that make it appear close to other African *Homo erectus* finds from that period in some of its anatomic characteristics but not in others. "The stratigraphic position of this small-sized individual at the same level as large Acheulean cutting tools [discussed later in this chapter], which required powerful detachment of massive flakes from outcrops, suggests that both large and small adults occurred in the local hominin population."[4]

In the early excavations at Swartkrans, South Africa, some bones were found that differed from those of *Paranthropus;* many now consider them to be *H. erectus.* Unfortunately, the remains are fragmentary. Other,

---

[4] Richard Potts et al., "Small Mid-Pleistocene Hominin Associated with East African Acheulean Technology," *Science* 305 (2004), p. 77.

less-well-known fossils are from north Africa, with the oldest from Ternifine, Algeria, dating from about 700,000 to 500,000 years ago. This material consists of three mandibles, a piece of skull, and a few teeth, all of which show many similarities to the *H. erectus* specimens from Zhoukoudian.

***The Anatomy of* Homo erectus** The cranial capacity of *H. erectus* averages about 1000 cubic centimeters and generally ranges between about 750 and 1250 cubic centimeters (Table 14.2). The size of the brain case of most specimens falls within the lower range of variation of modern *H. sapiens,* but the distinctive shape of the *H. erectus* cranium betrays major differences in the development of various parts of the brain housed within it.

Most specimens of *H. erectus* have cranial bones that are thick compared with the thin cranial bones of *H. sapiens*. The brow ridges are thick and continuous, and behind the brow ridges there is a pronounced postorbital constriction (Figure 14.10). The skull is low and relatively flat, or **platycephalic,** and in some specimens a bony ridge, the **sagittal keel,** is found along the midline at the top of the brain case. Unlike the sagittal crest found in *Paranthropus,* the sagittal keel is a thickening of bone along the top of the cranium. The profile of the cranium as seen from the side clearly shows the angularity of the occipital; above this angularity is a horizontal bar of bone, the **occipital torus.** In the rear view, the greatest width of the skull is toward the bottom. The facial skeleton of *H. erectus* is comparatively large and broad compared to that of modern *H. sapiens,* with large orbits and nasal openings. The brow ridge extends as a bar of bone across the nasal root and both orbits.

The genus *Homo* is characterized by a reduction in the size of the dentition through time. It is not surprising, therefore, that the teeth of *H. erectus* are smaller than those of *Australopithecus* and larger than those of *H. sapiens*. In general, the dentition in *H. erectus* and that in *H. sapiens* appear very similar. Looking down upon the tooth row, we see that it diverges toward the back, with the greatest distance between the teeth occurring between the third molars. In *H. sapiens,* the greatest distance is between the second molars because the ends of the tooth rows turn slightly inward.

The reduction in size of the molars and premolars and the contrast in relative tooth size between *H. erectus* and *Australopithecus* and *Paranthropus* suggest that the incisors and canines of *H. erectus* were more involved in the processing of food. This may be related to major changes in diet, with an increasing emphasis on meat, and to new ways of preparing food for eating that were made possible by the development of cooking and more effective tools. The mandible lacks a chin but does have a **mandibular torus,** which is a thickening of bone on the inside of the mandible.

Although the number of postcranial bones is few, several parts of the postcranial anatomy, especially the femur, have been studied. Externally, the *H. erectus* femur resembles that of *H. sapiens,* but x-rays reveal that the outer wall of the shaft of the femur is twice as thick as that of *H. sapiens*. Although other relatively minor differences exist in the postcranial skeletons of the two species, both *H. erectus* and *H. sapiens* show an identical or very similar form of erect bipedalism. While the size of *H. habilis* remained relatively small, it appears that the evolution of large body size, characteristic of *Homo,* took place during the transition from *H. habilis* to *H. ergaster* and *H. erectus*.

Homo antecessor

A find from northern Spain has become a new piece in the tangled puzzle of hominin relationships. In 1990, paleoanthropologist Juan Luis Arsuaga and his coworkers found primitive stone tools at the cave site of Gran Dolina in the Atapuerca Hills. The tools were found in a stratum thought to be about 1 million years old. This was an astonishing report at the time, since the earlier evidence of hominins in Europe was only half that old. In 1994, close to 80 hominin fossils were found at Gran Dolina, including teeth, limb bones, a skull, and a jaw fragment. Also in 1994, an incomplete calvarium was found at the site of Ceprano in southern Italy.

platycephalic Having a low, relatively flat forehead.

sagittal keel A bony ridge formed by a thickening of bone along the top of the skull; characteristic of *H. erectus.*

occipital torus A horizontal bar of bone seen above the angularity in the occipital.

mandibular torus A thickening of bone on the inside of the mandible.

**Figure 14.10
A Comparison of the
Skulls of (A)** *Homo
erectus* **and (B)** *Homo
sapiens*

Homo erectus
(a) Low, flat forehead
(b) Prominent brow ridges extending as a bar
(c) Occipital torus
(d) Relatively large facial skeleton with large orbits and large nasal opening
(e) Angular occipital
(f) Relatively large teeth
(g) Large mandible
(h) Sagittal keel
(i) Widest point low on brain case
(j) Pronounced postorbital constriction

Homo sapiens
Vertical forehead
Brow ridges slight or absent

Relatively small facial skeleton

Rounded occipital
Relatively small teeth
Small mandible (sometimes with chin)

Widest point high on brain case
Pronounced to minor postorbital constriction

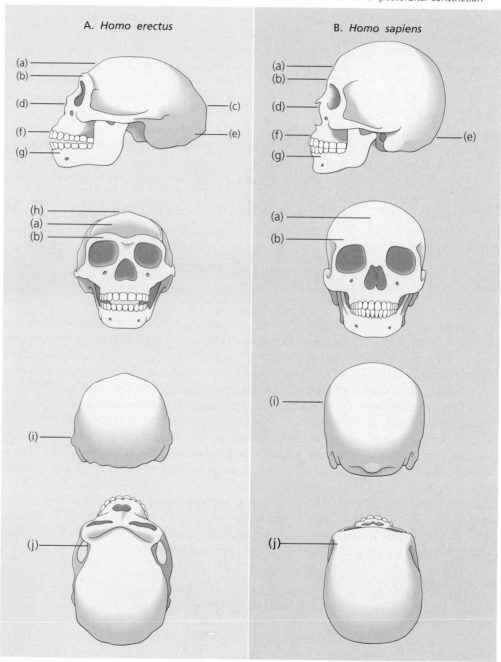

The fossils from Spain and Italy have been dated to about 800,000 B.P. Analysis of the morphology of the Spanish finds suggests that these hominins are more modern than the *H. erectus/H. ergaster* fossils, but they are not as modern as the next youngest population found in Europe, *Homo heidelbergensis*. The species name *Homo antecessor* has been proposed for the new fossils.

Homo heidelbergensis

The fossil record of the past million years is a very incomplete one. This is due in large part to the ebb and flow of the large continental glaciers that covered much of northern Europe and alpine areas. Conditions for fossilization were less than ideal, and the scraping action of the glaciers and the large volume of water from melting glaciers did much to destroy those fossil-bearing sedimentary beds that did exist.

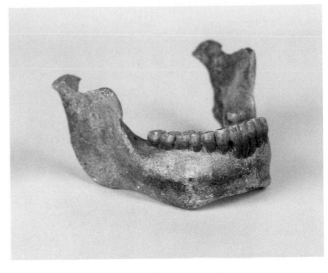

Figure 14.11 *Homo heidelbergensis* The Mauer jaw from Heidelberg, Germany.

Among the early hominin fossils discovered in Europe was a mandible that was found almost 24 meters (79 feet) below the surface in a quarry of river sand near the village of Mauer, not far from the city of Heidelberg, Germany (Figure 14.11). The year was 1907. The jaw did not clearly resemble the other hominin fossils known at that time: *H. erectus* from Java, the Neandertals of Europe, and early *H. sapiens*. More recently, the Mauer jaw has become the type specimen for a group of African, European, and Asian fossils dating between 800,000 and 250,000 years ago, which have been brought together into the species *Homo heidelbergensis*. However, there is not a complete consensus among anthropologists about what fossils should be placed within this species.

See the Online Learning Center for an Internet Activity on Homo heidelbergensis.

Homo heidelbergensis *from Africa* Several well-preserved fossils were recovered between 1921 and 1925 at Kabwe (Broken Hill), Zambia, as part of a mining operation; the cave was subsequently destroyed. The fossils include a nearly complete skull, upper jaw, pelvis, femur, tibia, and humerus; however, the postcranial material may not be contemporary with the cranium. The dating of the fossils is difficult, but they may be 300,000 years old.

The Kabwe cranium has a large cranial capacity of 1280 cubic centimeters, but it possesses massive brow ridges, probably among the thickest of any known Pleistocene hominin (Figure 14.12). It has a very long and broad facial skeleton with a sloping forehead; the teeth had dental caries (cavities), and there was an abscess (infection) in the jaw.

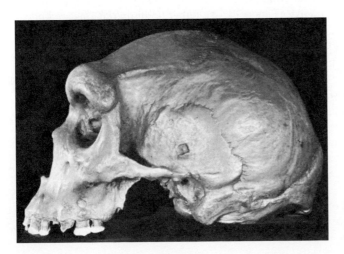

Figure 14.12 *Homo heidelbergensis* Skull from Kabwe (Broken Hill), Zambia.

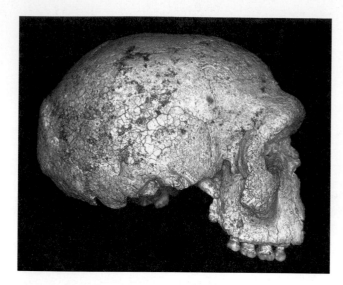

Figure 14.13 *Homo heidelbergensis* Skull from Steinheim, Germany.

The skull from Bodo d'Ar, Ethiopia, is about 600,000 years ago and resembles the remains from Kabwe. Bodo has a very large, broad face with thick brow ridges. Cut marks on the skull suggest that this individual was butchered around the time of his death.

Other fossils from Africa are considered by some paleoanthropologists to belong to this group. These include a recent discovery from Buia, Eritrea, which is discussed in Chapter 15, and the remains from Lake Ndutu in Tanzania, Omo II in Ethiopia, and Saldanha in South Africa.

Homo heidelbergensis *from Europe* Near the end of 1993, a human tibia and, in 1995, a tooth were discovered at Boxgrove, England. Both ends of the very robust limb bone arc missing. The fossils appear to represent hominins living during a warm interglacial that has been dated by faunal analysis to between 524,000 and 478,000 B.P., which is roughly contemporary with the Mauer mandible from Germany. Although very little can be determined about the individual from a tibia shaft, the find does place hominins in England at this early time.

In the mid-1960s, a few broken teeth and an occipital were found near the village of Vértesszöllös, not far from Budapest, Hungary. The skull is represented only by the occipital region, which is less angular and more rounded than that in *H. erectus*. It dates to between 475,000 and 250,000 B.P. The reconstructed skull has a cranial capacity of 1400 cubic centimeters.

A skull from Steinheim was found near Stuttgart, Germany, in 1933 and is dated to about 240,000 to 200,000 B.P. (Figure 14.13). Remains from Swanscombe, England, are of approximately the same age. This latter find consists of an occipital, discovered in 1935; a left parietal, discovered in 1936; and a right parietal, discovered 19 years later. All of these remains belong to the same individual.

The most complete of the two finds is Steinheim. The skull possesses many features that are reminiscent of *H. erectus,* including a low, sloping forehead and large brow ridges. Yet in other ways, the Steinheim skull resembles that of the later hominins, especially the Neandertals. For example, the facial skeleton is relatively small, the face and upper jaw are not prognathous, and the teeth are relatively small. The place of greatest width of the skull is higher than it is in the typical *H. erectus.*

Several other finds known from Europe, including a very complete skull from Petralona in northern Greece and several fossils from Arago Cave in the Pyrenees Mountains of France, are placed into *H. heidelbergensis* (Figure 14.14). Other hominin remains are known from the Second Interglacial, but knowledge of the material is limited. They include four skull fragments and a molar tooth from Bilzingsleben, Germany; a skull recovered at Salé, Morocco; and a mandible from Montmaurin, France.

Homo heidelbergensis *from Asia* A well-preserved cranium that was recovered in 1978 from Dali, in Shaanxi Province, China, is considered by some to belong to *H. heidelbergensis.* The skull is about 200,000 to 100,000 years old and has a cranial capacity of 1120 cubic centimeters. The skull and facial features resemble those of earlier hominins; these archaic characteristics include a sloping forehead and large brow ridges. The skull also has a small face that is flatter than those found in other areas of the world.

A skull found in 1980 in Lontandong Cave, Hexian County, is the first cranium to be discovered in eastern or southeastern China. It dates to between 280,000 and 240,000 B.P. Two fossil skulls, recovered in 1989 and 1990 in Yunxian, China, are considered to be

Box 14-3

How Do You Spell and Pronounce "Neandert_l?"

Certainly, the main controversy about the Neandertals revolves around their place in the human evolutionary tree. A much more trivial concern is how one should spell and pronounce their name. The currently preferred spelling is *Neandertal* as opposed to *Neanderthal*. The latter spelling was used in the past because the 1856 find was made in the Neander Thal of Germany; *Thal* means "valley" in German. However, the "h" in *Thal* is not pronounced in German. At the turn of the twentieth century, spelling reformers in Germany were successful in having most silent h's dropped from the German spelling system; the exception was the retention of silent h's in religious words. The accepted pronunciation of the last syllable of *Neandertal* has always been like that of the word "tall."

350,000 years old or younger based on the analysis of other fossil animals (Figure 14.15). The taxonomic placement of these fossils is being debated.

Homo neandertalensis

The Neandertals are named after a specimen found in 1856 in the Neander Valley near Düsseldorf, Germany (Box 14-3). Europeans of the Victorian age were totally unprepared to accept the Neander Valley fossils as the remains of one of their ancestors. The thought

See the Online Learning Center for an Internet Activity on Homo neandertalensis.

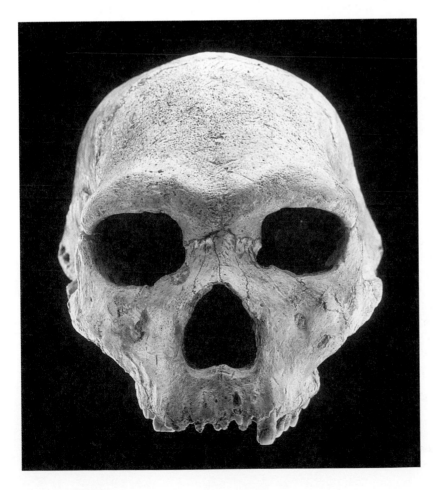

Figure 14.14 *Homo heidelbergensis,* **Petralona 1, from Petralona, Greece**

Figure 14.15 *Homo heidelbergensis* Skull from Yunxian, China.

that this primitive-looking creature could have been related to modern people was repugnant to all but a few scholars. One Englishman considered the creature to be a "half-crazed, half-idiotic [type of man] with murderous propensities." Others considered it to be a freak, a stupid Roman legionnaire, or a victim of water on the brain.

Then, in 1886, two skeletons were removed from a cave in Belgium near the town of Spy. With the discovery of still more Neandertals, such as those at La Chapelle-aux-Saints, Le Moustier, La Quina, and La Ferrassie, all discovered in France in 1908 and 1909, the Neandertal pattern of features began to emerge (Figures 14.16 and 14.19). Today, the

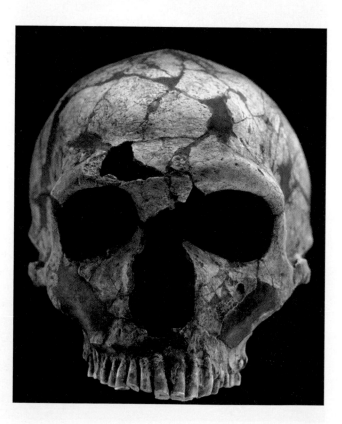

Figure 14.16 *Homo neandertalensis* Neandertal skull from La Ferrassie, France.

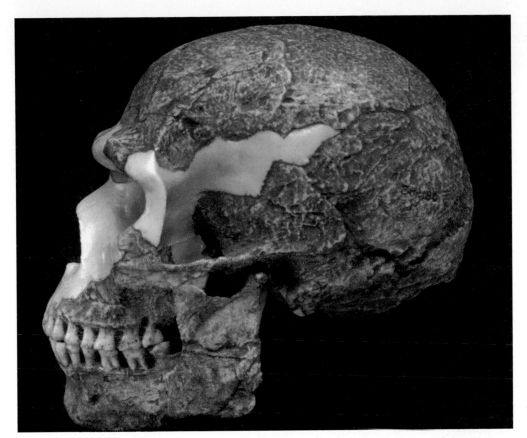

Figure 14.17 *Homo neandertalensis* Skull V, Skhūl, Mount Carmel, Israel.

remains of about 400 Neandertal individuals, found in Europe and western Asia, have been collected.

The Neandertals: Time and Place Clear indications of the Neandertal pattern appear approximately 130,000 years ago. However, partial skulls that display elements of this pattern have been discovered in the Atapuerca Mountains of northern Spain dated to at least 300,000 B.P.

One of the earliest sites to yield skeletons that display what might be the complete Neandertal pattern is Krapina, in Yugoslavia, which contained fragmentary remains of at least 45 and perhaps more individuals. The site may be as much as 120,000 years old. Unfortunately, the site was first excavated by dynamite, and so the remains of the individuals are highly fragmentary. From about 120,000 years ago to about 35,000 years ago, the Neandertal pattern, which had taken tens of thousands of years to develop, remained relatively stable.

The Neandertal pattern also is found in western Asia, including Israel, Iraq, Russia, and Uzbekistan. Fossils recovered at the sites of Tabūn and Skhūl on Mount Carmel, Israel, display a surprising range of variation (Figure 14.17). Some specimens reflected the essential features of Steinheim; others showed more modern characteristics; and still others exhibited a mixture of more modern and Neandertal features. Skhūl has been dated at between 101,000 and 81,000 B.P. Some of the Neandertal fossils are located on the map in Figure 14.18.

Neandertal Anatomy "With slouched posture, a Neandertal man clothed in a leopard skin and carrying a crude wood club walks toward his cave. He stops, appearing dazed and confused, for he is lost. The cave he stands before is not his."

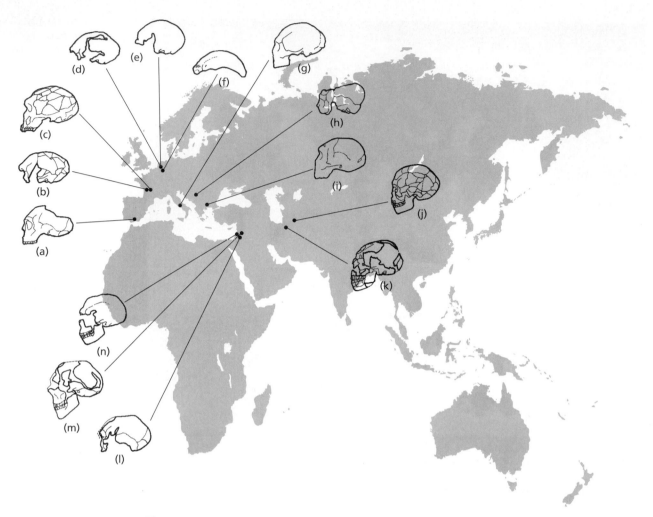

Figure 14.18 Variation and Distribution of Neandertal Fossils (a) Gibraltar; (b) La Quina, France; (c) La Ferrassie, France; (d) Neandertal, Germany; (e) Spy I, Belgium; (f) Spy II, Belgium; (g) Monte Circeo, Italy; (h) Krapina, Yugoslavia; (i) Petralona, Greece; (j) Teschik Tasch child, Uzbekistan; (k) Shanidar 1, Iraq; (l) Skhūl IX, Israel; (m) Skhūl IV, Israel; (n) Tabūn, Israel.

This portrait of a "caveman" is a common way of picturing Neandertals. In fact, healthy Neandertals were not slouching or bent at the knee, nor were they necessarily any less intelligent than modern peoples. Anatomically, people called Neandertals displayed several unique physical characteristics, but some paleoanthropologists believe that if transported to the present time and dressed in modern clothing, Neandertals might not elicit a second glance (Box 14-4). Yet details of their anatomy do contrast in several important ways with the anatomy of modern humans.

The Neandertal skull is characterized by a suite of distinctive features that clearly separate the Neandertals from other prehistoric populations. Neandertals are "flat-headed," or platycephalic. The distance from the top of the head to the level of the eye sockets, the area thought of as the forehead, is less than that in modern *H. sapiens*. Several interesting features of the Neandertal skull are seen from the side and back. The maximum breadth of the Neandertal skull is higher than that in *H. erectus* but lower than that in modern populations; this gives the skull a "barrel" shape when seen from behind. In the side view, the great length of the skull can be seen. The backward projection of the occipital region forms what is called a "bun." The Neandertal face is projecting in contrast to the flat face of modern *H. sapiens*. The forward-projecting face of the Neandertal may be due in part to the

Box 14-4 La Chapelle-aux-Saints

One of the great misfortunes of paleoanthropology is that one of the earliest reasonably complete skeletons of a Neandertal was that of La Chapelle-aux-Saints, found in 1908. The bones, discovered as part of a burial, were sent to Paris, where the entire skeleton was reconstructed (see figure in box and Figure 14.19).

Between 1911 and 1913, Marcellin Boule described La Chapelle-aux-Saints as representing a brutish, apelike population whose members walked with a shuffling, slouched gait. These descriptions colored people's perception of Neandertals for decades, as Boule and Henri V. Vallois's description of the La Chapelle-aux-Saints specimen shows:

> We are impressed by its bestial appearance or rather by the general effect of its simian [apelike] characters. The brain-box, elongated in form, is much depressed; the orbital arches are enormous; the forehead is very receding; the occipital region very projecting and much depressed; the face is long and projects forward; the orbits are enormous; the nose, separated from the forehead by a deep depression, is short and broad; owing to the prolongation of the malar bones, the upper jaw forms a kind of muzzle; the lower jaw is strong and thick; the chin is rudimentary.[1]

The above description was published in 1957, several years after it was discovered that the fossil from La Chapelle-aux-Saints was that of an old man with a severe case of arthritis of the jaw, the spine, and possibly the legs. In addition, this find is not representative of the population and appears rather extreme even by Neandertal standards. It is a good example of sampling error in the fossil record. Yet this one individual has been called the "classic" Neandertal. Although Boule and Vallois's list of traits is generally correct, their interpretation of Neandertals as bestial and apelike is not.

[1] M. Boule and H.V. Vallois, *Fossil Men* (New York: Dryden, 1957), p. 214. Printed with permission of Holt, Rinehart, and Winston, Inc.

Neandertal's greatly enlarged **facial sinuses** and the positioning of the teeth. (A facial sinus is an air-filled space that is lined by a mucous membrane in the bones of the front of the skull.) The nasal region of the Neandertal skull projects forward and is larger than that of modern *H. sapiens*.

The massive skull encases a large brain. In fact, the average cranial capacity of all known Neandertals is a little larger than the average capacity of contemporary *H. sapiens*. It ranges between about 1300 and 1750 cubic centimeters, with an average of about 1400 cubic centimeters (Table 14.2). However, the slightly greater size of the Neandertal brain compared with the brain of anatomically modern humans is not indicative of greater mental ability. Paleoanthropologists believe that the amount of neocortex in the *H. sapiens* brain is greater than that in the Neandertal brain. The slightly greater average cranial capacity in the Neandertals is more likely due to sampling error or to the fact that the musculature of the Neandertals was heavier than that of modern humans, requiring a larger surface area for the attachment of facial and cranial muscles (Figures 14.19 and 14.20).

facial sinus An air-filled space in the bones of the front of the skull.

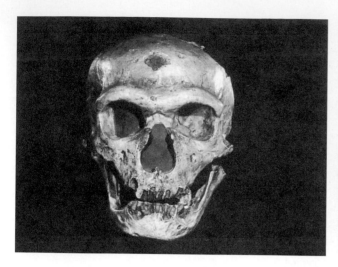
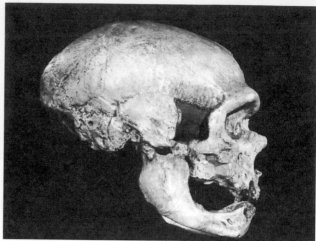

Figure 14.19 *Homo neandertalensis* Cast of La Chapelle-aux-Saints, France.

The teeth project forward. From the side view, one sees a gap between the last molar and the edge of the ascending branch of the mandible (Figure 14.21). Neandertal incisors are, on average, larger than those of modern populations, and sometimes they are as large as those of *H. erectus.* The molars and premolars are no larger than those of modern *H. sapiens,* and the third molar sometimes is very small.

The larger sinuses are also characteristic of earlier hominins, including Steinheim, but the forward dentition pattern of the Neandertal is rare in other hominins. Neandertals, with their forward projection of the jaw, have sufficient room behind the dental arcade for an internal buttress reminiscent of the simian shelf of apes. Neandertals show varying development of a chin: in some, it is completely absent; while in others, it is slightly developed.

Many Neandertal specimens show signs of arthritis in the **temporomandibular joint,** where the mandible articulates with the rest of the skull. The presence of arthritis may be an indication of excessive strain on the joint. Could it be that the Neandertals used their teeth as tools? There is some evidence for this in the wear patterns on teeth, which suggest that Neandertals used their teeth for such tasks as softening skins.

How Can We Explain the Neandertal Facial Configuration? Until the mid-1980s, the most frequently mentioned selective agent used to explain the Neandertal face was cold. One suggestion proposed that the forward projection of the face was a means of keeping the nasal cavities away from the brain, which is sensitive to low temperatures. One function of the nasal cavities is to warm the air that moves through the head to the lungs; for people living in extremely cold climates, maximum warming means a minimum chance of damaging the brain. In addition to the projecting face, Neandertals' nasal cavities are very large, providing a greater surface area for the warming of the air.

Although the Neandertal face may have served well for cold adaptation, this hypothesis does not provide a complete explanation of the Neandertal face. For one thing, the Neandertal facial morphology is found in populations that existed before the onset of the Würm Glacial and during the glacial itself in latitudes not affected by the drops in temperature.

Yoel Rak has proposed an explanation for the Neandertal facial configuration in terms of the biomechanics of the skull.[5] The Neandertal has a robust face with large canines and incisors. The structure of the Neandertal face may have been an adaptation to withstand the

temporomandibular joint
The joint formed at the point of articulation of the mandible and the base of the skull.

---

[5] Y. Rak, "The Neandertals: A New Look at an Old Face," *Journal of Human Evolution* 15 (1986), pp. 151–164.

Figure 14.20 A Comparison of the Skulls of (A) *Homo neandertalensis* and (B) *Homo sapiens*

Homo neandertalesis

(a) Low, flat (platycephalic) forehead
(b) Large, continuous brow ridge
(c) Large orbits
(d) High, large nasal opening
(e) Projecting face
(f) Large front teeth
(g) Chin absent or weak
(h) Large, wide, low cranium
(i) Occipital "bun"
(j) Gap between third molar and ascending branch of mandible

Homo sapiens

Vertical forehead
Brow ridges slight or absent
Smaller orbits
Small, lower nasal opening
Relatively small, flat facial skeleton
Relatively small teeth
Well-developed chin
Large, rounded, high cranium

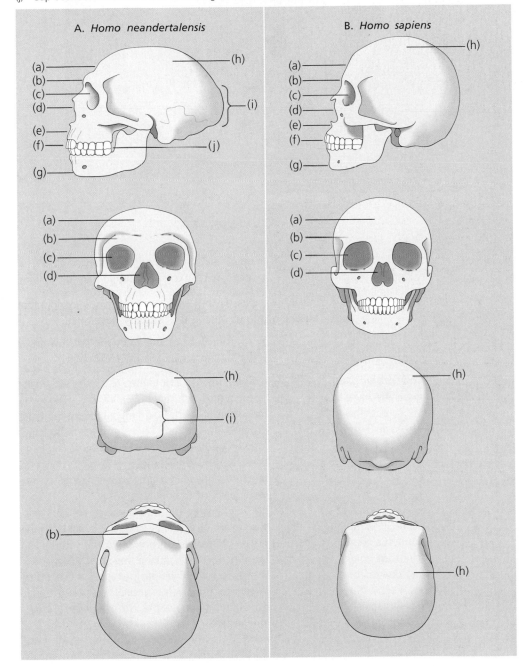

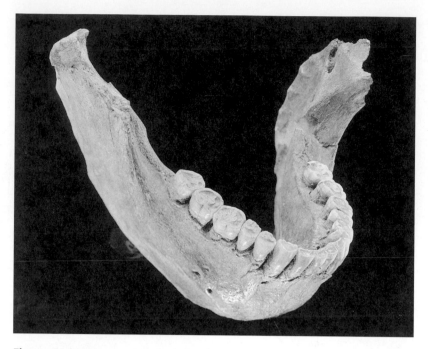

Figure 14.21 *Homo neandertalensis* Mandible from a female Neandertal from Tabūn, Israel.

considerable stresses that developed between the upper and lower teeth. The front teeth of the Neandertals often show considerable wear, indicating that, like some Inuit, they used their front teeth to chew hides and other nonfood materials.

We should not expect a single cause for a complex anatomical pattern. Rak concludes that "the unique Neandertal facial configuration is more probably the result of a combination of factors; a highly complex interaction of forces from the chewing apparatus, a response to climatic conditions and a variety of other factors as yet undetermined."[6]

The Neandertal Postcranial Skeleton Compared with the modern human skeleton, the Neandertal skeleton is generally more robust and the musculature is heavier. Neandertals, who averaged a little over 152 centimeters (5 feet) tall, were generally shorter than most modern humans. Neandertals possess massive limb bones compared with the thin limb bones of modern humans. The long bones are generally curved, with larger areas for the attachment of muscles. The morphology of the finger bones indicates that Neandertals were capable of a grip more powerful than that of modern humans. Taken together, the entire Neandertal postcranial pattern is one that allowed for great power while permitting fine control of the body.

The Neandertal scapula is characterized by a deep groove on the back surface. This suggests strong development of the teres minor muscle, which extends from the scapula to the upper end of the humerus (Figure 14.22). In modern humans, a groove is usually found on the inside (rib side) of the scapula. The Neandertal pattern indicates a powerful teres minor muscle, which functions to rotate the humerus outward while helping to keep the head of the humerus in its socket during movement. A powerful teres minor muscle working to balance other arm muscles that pull the arm down allows for powerful throwing and pounding activities while permitting fine control of movement.

Although Neandertals often have been portrayed as bowed over with their heads hung forward, capable only of an "apelike" walk, this description has no basis in fact—Neandertals were completely bipedal. However, scholars disagree about whether Neandertal

---

[6] Ibid., p. 157.

posture and locomotion were identical to those of modern humans. Like other parts of the Neandertal skeleton, and in contrast to those of modern humans, the pelvic bones are quite robust. There is an exception to this generalization, however, in the upper portion of the pubis, which is thinner and longer in Neandertals. The consequence of this feature for locomotion and posture has not been resolved.

Neandertal DNA In some circumstances, DNA remains in ancient bone, but only bone of relatively recent derivation. A 3.5-gram sample of bone was removed from the right humerus of the original Neandertal material discovered in 1856 in the Neander Valley of Germany. Using extremely careful laboratory procedures, the investigators were able to isolate a sequence of mitochondrial DNA consisting of 360 base pairs. Because this region is associated with fairly rapid mutation rates, differences in the sequence of nucleotides will show up in relatively closely related populations.

Next, the mtDNA sequence was compared with modern human and chimpanzee sequences. The average number of differences among the modern human mtDNA lineages was 8.0; between Neandertal and modern human mtDNA lineages it was 25.6; and between modern human and chimpanzee mtDNA lineages it was 55.0. From these data, we see that the average number of differences in the mtDNA sequences between modern humans and Neandertals is three times that among modern humans. Also, the average number of differences between modern humans and chimpanzees is about twice that of modern humans and Neandertals. Another analysis was done on a sample from a 29,000-year-old Neandertal from Mezmaiskaya Cave in the northern Caucasus. It showed essentially the same result as the Neander Valley sample. Other mtDNA studies indicate that Neandertals and modern humans could not interbreed.

One of the major areas of disagreement among paleoanthropologists is whether the Neandertal gene pool contributed to the gene pool of modern *H. sapiens*. If this were true, we would expect the number of substitutions between the Neandertal and European mtDNA to be significantly greater than that between the Neandertal and other mtDNA lineages. When the Neandertal sequence is compared with modern human sequences from different continents, the data clearly show that this is not the case.

One of the more controversial aspects of DNA studies is the dating of the divergence of two DNA lineages. Determining the timing of the molecular clock is based on the idea that substitutions in the DNA sequence occur on a regular basis, and that time is directly proportional to the number of nucleotide substitutions. The problem is that the rates of substitutions, and hence the molecular clock, differ in various segments of the genome and in different species.

Paleoanthropologists generally agree that the divergence between modern humans and chimpanzees occurred around 6½ to 5½ million years ago. Using that date in association with the number of substitutions between modern human and chimpanzee mtDNA, the

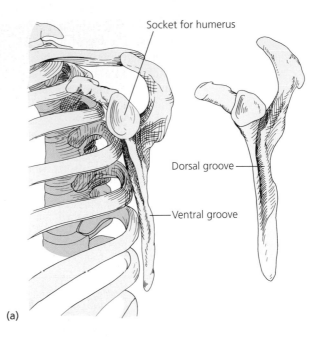

(a)

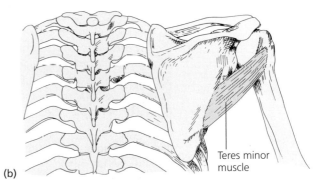

(b)

Figure 14.22 The Neandertal Scapula (a) Side view of the left scapula of Shanidar I (right) and of a modern *H. sapiens* (left). The ventral-groove pattern is found in 80 percent of modern humans and is related to the development of a shoulder muscle, the teres minor, that connects the upper arm to the scapula by attaching to a small portion of the dorsal surface of the scapula. In more than 60 percent of the Neandertal scapulas, we see a single, large groove on the dorsal side of the outer border. All of the outer edge and part of the dorsal surface provided attachment for the teres minor muscle, indicating that it was well-developed. (b) When the teres minor muscle contracts, it pulls the humerus in toward the scapula, thus strengthening the shoulder joint. At the same time, it turns the upper arm, forearm, and hand outward.

investigators estimate that the divergence between Neandertal and modern human mtDNA, that is, the date of the most recent common sequence, falls between 853,000 and 317,000 years ago. Using the same molecular clock, the common ancestor of all modern human mtDNA falls between 200,000 and 120,000 years. Of course, we have to be very careful about these dates, for they are only as good as the estimated divergence date of humans and chimpanzees.

The study of Neandertal mtDNA is very interesting and seems to support the contention of those paleoanthropologists who propose that the Neandertals are a distinct species that did not contribute to the gene pool of modern *Homo sapiens*.[7] However, a fossil discovered in Portugal seems to contradict the genetic information. This 24,500-year-old individual appears to be a hybrid of Neandertal and modern human characteristics. Many paleoanthropologists do not agree with this interpretation, yet the role of the Neandertals in human evolution remains a topic of debate.

Summary

One of the appeals of physical anthropology is the light paleoanthropological research sheds on the evolution of modern humans. The past century and a half of paleontological discoveries have provided a general outline of hominin evolution. Yet the specifics of the story are still elusive. Instead of a simple linear route from, let us say, *Australopithecus africanus* to *Homo habilis* to *Homo erectus* and finally to *Homo sapiens*, the route appears to be tangled and complex.

Starting around 2½ million years ago, the earliest members of our genus, *H. habilis* and *H. rudolfensis*, arose in Africa at about the same time as the early populations of *Paranthropus*. Both *Homo* and *Paranthropus* likely evolved from a late species of *Australopithecus*. At around 1.9 million years ago, we begin to see a new grade of hominins, *H. ergaster* and *H. erectus*. The former may have been the first hominin to range outside of Africa. Many fossil hominins dating from about 1 million to 250,000 years ago show more *H. sapiens*–like characteristics than *H. erectus/H. ergaster*–like characteristics; these are placed into the species *H. heidelbergensis*. However, populations of *Paranthropus* survived until about 900,000 B.P.; some populations of *H. erectus* survived as late as 27,000 B.P.

The Neandertals existed between about 130,000 and about 30,000 years ago. They have been seen as a direct ancestor to modern Europeans by some, and a side branch of humanity that genetically contributed little or nothing to modern populations by others. Today, details of Neandertal anatomy, such as the unique shape of the nasal region, strong upper limb bones, and heavy upper body musculature, have convinced a number of paleoanthropologists that Neandertals should be placed into their own species, *Homo neandertalensis*. (The anatomy of the Neandertals is summarized in Table 14.4.) Recently, this idea has been reinforced by a study of Neandertal DNA that suggests that Neandertals are genetically distinct from modern peoples. However, a recently described fossil from Portugal suggests that modern humans and Neandertals may have interbred. A list of the hominin species discussed in this chapter is presented in Table 14.3 on page 361.

---

[7] D. Caramelli et al., "Evidence for Genetic Discontinuity between Neandertals and 24,000-year-old Anatomically Modern Europeans," *Proceedings of the National Academy of Sciences* 100 (2003), pp. 6593–6597.

Table 14.4 *Homo neandertalensis* and *Homo sapiens* Compared

Homo neandertalensis	Homo sapiens
Flat-headed (platycephalic) brain case.	Higher and rounder brain case.
Cranial capacity of 1300–1750 cubic centimeters.	Cranial capacity of 900–2300 cubic centimeters.
Well-developed brow ridges with continuous shelf of bone.	Brow ridges moderate to absent; never a continuous shelf of bone.
Backward extension of occiput into a "bun."	Rounded occiput; no "bun."
Relatively flat basicrania.	Bent basicrania.
Maximum skull breadth at about midpoint (viewed from rear).	Maximum skull breadth higher on skull (viewed from rear).
Forward projection of face.	Flatter face (nose and teeth more in line with eye sockets).
Variably developed chin.	Well-developed chin.
Relatively large incisors.	Relatively small incisors.
Taurodontism (molars and premolars with enlarged pulp cavities and fused roots).	No taurodontism.
Bones thinner than in *H. erectus*.	Bones thinner than in Neandertals.
Sockets for femurs farther back.	Sockets for femurs farther forward.
Dorsal groove on side of outer border of scapula (in about 60% of specimens).	Ventral groove on side of outer border of scapula (in most specimens).
Long bones more curved with large areas for muscle attachments.	Long bones straighter with smaller articular surfaces.
More powerful muscles to flex fingers.	Less powerful grip.

THE CULTURE OF EARLY *HOMO*

Earlier we saw that behavioral adaptability provides important ways by which humans cope with the requirements of their varied habitats. When did learned behavior begin to replace innate behavior as a major means of coping with environments? The evidence for this change is even more fragmentary than the fossil evidence of physical evolution.

Early hominins very likely made tools of perishable materials such as wood and hides long before they learned to work stone; even chimpanzees make tools out of sticks. It was not until about 2.6 million years ago that stone tools begin to appear in archaeological sites. The **Paleolithic** begins with the appearance of stone tools. *Paleo* means "old," and *lithic* means "stone"; thus, the Paleolithic is the "Old Stone Age." The hominins of old stone age cultures continued to make tools out of perishable materials, but they also chipped away at stone. As time went on, they manufactured an increasing variety of durable stone tools.

The **Lower Paleolithic** begins with the manufacture of the first stone tools. The **Middle Paleolithic** refers to the stone tools of the Neandertals and their contemporaries. Finally, the **Upper Paleolithic,** which will be discussed in the next chapter, includes the stone tools of anatomically modern peoples. Human adaptations are to a large extent behavioral. Some evidence of the behavior of early *Homo* can be seen in the archaeological record, which is the subject of this section.

Interpreting the Archaeological Evidence

Artifacts are the physical remains of human activities. A carefully chipped arrow point and a highly decorated piece of pottery are in themselves works of art worthy of our admiration. In addition to their artistic merit, however, artifacts make up the evidence from which human behavior can be deduced.

An archaeological **site** is any location where manufactured objects are found. All the artifacts from a given site make up an **assemblage,** which in turn can be divided into a series of **industries.** Each industry contains all the artifacts made from one type of material, for example, a **lithic (stone) industry** or a **bone industry.** Because stone is preserved better than are materials such as bone and wood, most ancient sites contain only a stone

See the Online Learning Center for an Internet Activity on the Paleolithic.

Paleolithic A type of culture called the "Old Stone Age."

Lower Paleolithic A cultural stage that begins with the manufacture of the first stone tools.

Middle Paleolithic Refers to the stone tools of the Neandertals and their contemporaries.

Upper Paleolithic Refers to the stone tools of anatomically modern peoples.

site A location where artifacts are found.

assemblage All the artifacts from a given site.

industry All artifacts in a site made from the same material, such as bone industry.

lithic (stone) industry All artifacts in a site that are made of stone.

bone industry All of the bone artifacts from a particular site.

tool An object that appears to have been used for a specific purpose.

utilized material Pieces of stone that have been used without modification.

debitage Waste and nonutilized material produced in the process of tool manufacture.

manuport An unmodified, natural rock, brought into a site by human agency, that shows no sign of alteration.

industry. Nevertheless, we must constantly keep in mind that all hominins probably utilized bone, wood, horn, and other perishable materials as well.

An artifact that appears to have been used for a specific function is a **tool;** examples of tools are choppers, scrapers, burins, and hand axes. Natural objects that are used without further modification are called **utilized material.** They include anvils, hammerstones, and utilized flakes. The word **debitage** refers to the waste and nonutilized material produced in the process of tool manufacture. Unmodified rocks brought into a site by human agency that show no signs of use are termed **manuports.**

A **core** is a nodule of rock from which pieces, or **flakes,** are removed. The individual flakes can be further altered by **retouch,** the further removal of tiny flakes, to create **flake tools.** Two examples of flake tools are the **scraper,** a flake with a scraping edge on the end or side, and the **burin,** a tool with a thick point. The remaining core can be fashioned into a **core tool,** such as a **hand ax.** A cutting edge is created by flaking on one or both ends; the little flakes are produced by hitting a **hammerstone** or a bone hammer against the core. The edge itself is often jagged, but it is quite effective in butchering animals.

Interpreting the archaeological record is often extremely difficult. Ideally, we would like to know the functions of each artifact type, but usually we must be content merely to describe its shape or to place the tool into one of a number of standardized categories such as chopper or scraper. The archaeologist must be careful not to interpret these categories as proven functions, since a scraper, for instance, may have functioned as a knife rather than as an instrument for scraping flesh off a hide.

Figure 14.23 An Early Stone Tool Among the earliest-known stone tools in the archaeological record is this 2.6-million-year-old Oldowan flake tool from the Gona River basin, Ethiopia.

The Culture of the Earliest *Homo*

The earliest-known stone tools were discovered between 1992 and 1994 in the Gona River drainage of the Awash Basin of Ethiopia. These objects were found within the Hadar formation, which has been securely dated by radiometric dating techniques and by studies of the periodic reversal of the earth's magnetic poles to about 2.6 million B.P. Other stone tools were recovered from Bouri, also in the Awash Basin.

Several sites in the Gona region have yielded more than 3000 artifacts. These artifacts include cores, flakes, and flaking debris (Figure 14.23). These well-preserved tools are similar to those first identified by Mary Leakey at Olduvai Gorge. The degree of sophistication, although primitive compared with later artifacts, strongly suggests that the roots of stone tool manufacture extend even further back in time.

Several thousand artifacts have been recovered from the site of Lokalakei in west Turkana, northwestern Kenya, dated at 2.34 million B.P. This archaeological site has yielded well-preserved artifacts and fossil bones representing 12 mammalian species, reptiles, and fish, inhabiting a grassy plain with forest along the river. The stone tools are associated with tortoise bones and fragments of ostrich shells, which suggests that these animals formed an important element in the hominin diet. Analysis of the stone tools, which included the fitting together of flakes with the cores from which they were removed, suggests that the manufacture of stone tools took place at Lokalakei. The process of tools manufacture indicates fine motor precision and coordination more advanced than previously believed.

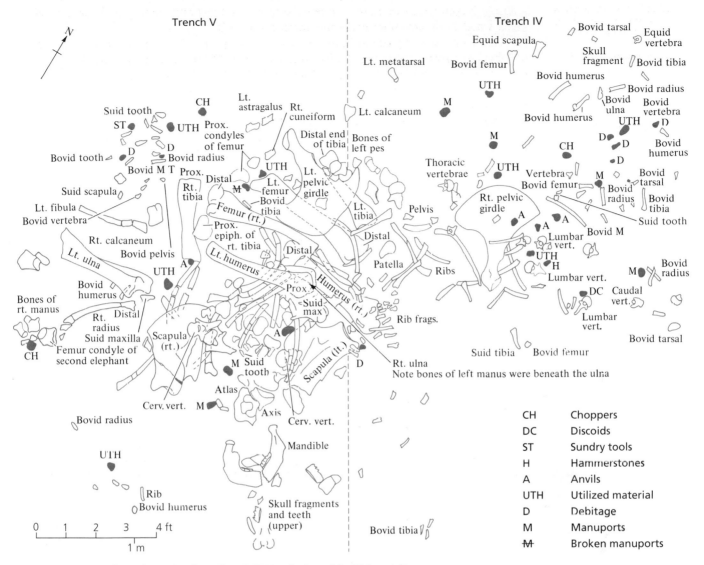

Figure 14.24 Plan of Butchering Site, FLK North, Level 6, Olduvai Gorge

CH	Choppers
DC	Discoids
ST	Sundry tools
H	Hammerstones
A	Anvils
UTH	Utilized material
D	Debitage
M	Manuports
M̶	Broken manuports

The Archaeology of Olduvai Gorge The best-known early archaeological assemblages are those of Olduvai Gorge. These artifacts are assigned to the Lower Paleolithic, or Lower Old Stone Age.

Site FLK in Upper Bed I contains about 2500 artifacts and 60,000 bones, including the disarticulated remains of an extinct form of elephant (Figure 14.24). Of the 123 recovered artifacts associated with the elephant, all but 5 can be classified as tools; most of these are choppers.

The DK site from Bed I is older than 1.75 million B.P.; like most sites of this period, the DK site was located close to water. A large number of crocodile bones have been found, as well as bones from extinct forms of tortoise, cattle, pig, elephant, hippopotamus, horse, and giraffe; all these animals may have played some role in the early hominin diet. The DK lithic industry includes a number of tools, among them various forms of choppers (Table 14.5).

The tools known as choppers are made from round stones shaped by the tumbling effects of stream water. Once collected, a hammerstone is used to create a core with a sharp edge. The resulting core tool can be used for many functions, such as chopping and cutting, while the flakes knocked off the core can be used as knives and puncturing tools.

core A nodule of rock from which flakes are removed.

flake A small piece of stone that is removed from a core when the core is struck by a hammerstone or bone hammer.

retouch Further refinement in the manufacture of stone tools by the removal of additional small flakes.

flake tool A tool manufactured from a flake.

scraper A tool manufactured from a flake with a scraping edge on the end or side.

Table 14.5   Stone Industry from DK, Olduvai Gorge

	Number	%	Number	%
Tools			154	12.9
Choppers	47	3.9		
Scrapers	30	2.5		
Burins	3	0.3		
Others	74	6.2		
Utilized material			187	15.6
Anvils	3	0.3		
Hammerstones	48	4.0		
Flakes	37	3.1		
Others	99	8.3		
Debitage			857	71.5

Data from M. D. Leakey, *Olduvai Gorge, Vol. 3, Excavations in Beds I and II, 1963–1969* (Cambridge, Cambridge University Press, 1971), p. 39.

burin A stone tool with a chisel-like point used for engraving or manufacturing bone tools.

core tool A tool that is manufactured by the removal of flakes from a core.

hand ax Large core tool with a sharp cutting edge, blunted at one end so it can be held in the hand.

hammerstone A stone that is used to remove flakes from a core by striking the hammerstone against the core.

awl A type of tool that is used to puncture a hole in a soft material such as wood or skin.

cleaver A large core tool with a straight, sharp edge at one end.

Paleoanthropologists assume that objects are tools if certain conditions are met. They look for regularity in shape among the objects and whether the objects are found in association with the things on which they may have been used, such as butchered animals. Also, tools often are found at a distance from where the material to make them is located. Many of the stones from FLK and DK display all these features and are therefore considered to be tools.

The tools described above are characteristic of the *Oldowan culture* (Figure 14.25). This assemblage of tools is widespread during this time period throughout eastern and southern Africa. Later in time (Middle and Upper Bed II at Olduvai Gorge), we find a group of tools labeled *Developed Oldowan,* which includes new tool types such as the **awl, cleaver,** and crude hand ax.

One of the most interesting features at Olduvai Gorge is the stone circle of the DK site (Figure 14.26). This circle, about 3.7 to 4.3 meters (12 to 14 feet) in diameter, is formed of basalt blocks loosely piled up to just under 30 centimeters (1 foot) high. Associated small piles of stones may have been supports for branches, while the circle itself may have been a

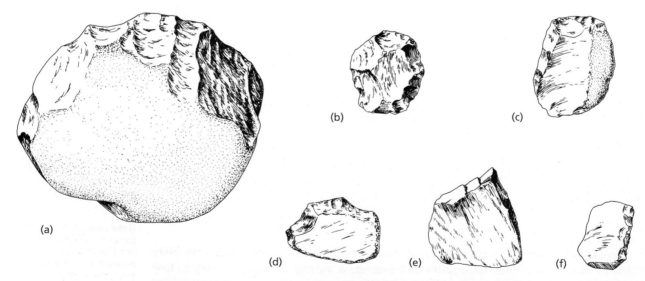

Figure 14.25 Stone Artifacts from the Oldowan Culture of Olduvai Gorge (a) Side chopper; (b) discoid; (c) end scraper; (d) side scraper; (e) burin; (f) utilized flake.

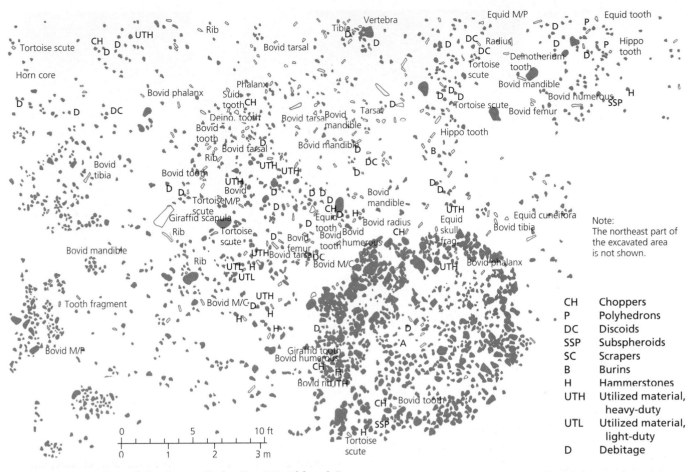

The labels in the figure include:

Tortoise scute, Horn core, Bovid phalanx, Bovid tooth, Bovid tibia, Bovid mandible, Tooth fragment, Bovid M/P, Rib, UTH, Suid tooth, Deino. tooth, Bovid tarsal, Phalanx, Tortoise M/P scute, Giraffid scapula, Bovid femur, Bovid M/C, Giraffid tooth, Bovid humerous, Bovid rib, Tibia, Vertebra, Bovid tarsal, Tarsal, Hippo tooth, Bovid mandible, Equid tooth, Bovid radius, Bovid humerous, Equid skull frag, Equid M/P, Radius, Tortoise scute, Deinotherium tooth, Bovid mandible, Bovid femur, Hippo tooth, Equid cuneiform, Bovid tibia, Bovid phalanx, Polyhedrons, Hippo tooth, Bovid humerus, Bovid tooth

Note:
The northeast part of the excavated area is not shown.

CH	Choppers
P	Polyhedrons
DC	Discoids
SSP	Subspheroids
SC	Scrapers
B	Burins
H	Hammerstones
UTH	Utilized material, heavy-duty
UTL	Utilized material, light-duty
D	Debitage

Scale:
0   5   10 ft
0 1 2 3 m

Figure 14.26 Plan of the Stone Circle, Site DK, Olduvai Gorge

base to support a living structure made of brush. If this stone circle is the support of some type of hut, it would represent the earliest known human habitation structure. Other interpretations, however, have been made. The circle simply may be the result of fractured basalt having been forced up from an underlying layer of lava by the radiating roots of an ancient tree.

The Archaeology of Lake Turkana Several different kinds of sites have been identified in the Koobi Fora area of east Lake Turkana. One type of site is that in which a single large animal is found associated with stone artifacts. The HAS site, which is dated at around 1.6 million B.P., consists of a hippopotamus lying in a stream channel that was part of a delta system. Paleoanthropologists believe that hominins found the animal already dead and that they used the site for their scavenging activity. Scattered among the animal bones and on the nearby bank are 119 artifacts, most of which are small, sharp flakes that could be held between the fingers and used as knives to carve up the carcass (Figure 14.27).

The KBS site at Koobi Fora presents a different behavioral picture. This site contains hundreds of stone artifacts, along with a large number of bones from many animal species: pig, gazelle, waterbuck, giraffe, and hippopotamus. The site was once the sandy bed of a stream, and perhaps a small group of hominins regularly gathered there to cut up small pieces of game. The large variety of animals represented suggests that the hominins transported game to this central location.

The Acheulean Tradition The most frequent cultural manifestation of the Lower Paleolithic is the **Acheulean tradition,** which is characterized by a number of highly diagnostic tool types, including the hand ax. The hand ax may have been used for butchering animals, working wood, cracking bones, digging for roots, and many other purposes.

Acheulean tradition The most frequent cultural manifestation of the Lower Paleolithic; characterized by several highly diagnostic tool types, including the hand ax.

Figure 14.27 The Use of Flake Tools
Archaeologists Kathy Schick and Ray Dezzani are shown using a stone flake to cut through the thick skin of an elephant that died of natural causes.

Throughout this period, archaeologists can trace the development of finer technological control in the manufacturing of hand axes. The earlier types were produced with hammer-stones, and the flakes removed were large and thick; this resulted in a finished product that was large and had a ragged cutting edge. Later, the use of hammers of bone or other similar material produced thinner, more regular flakes; this resulted in a thinner tool with a fairly straight cutting edge.

While hand axes are often considered diagnostic of the Lower Paleolithic, they make up only a small percentage of all the tool types from Lower Paleolithic sites; in fact, some sites lack hand axes altogether. Cores also were transformed into hammers and choppers, while the flakes were made into a variety of tools, such as scrapers, awls, and knives (Figure 14.28).

Figure 14.28 Early Paleolithic Tools (a) Abbevillean hand ax from Olduvai Gorge; (b) chopping tool from Zhoukoudian; (c) cleaverlike tool from Zhoukoudian.

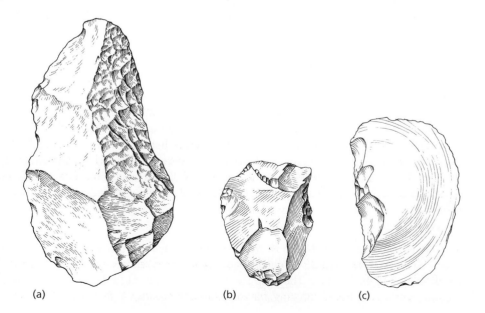

(a)   (b)   (c)

The First Use of Fire The earliest controlled use of fire has been a highly debated topic in anthropology for decades. One of the problems is that it is difficult to distinguish between objects burned by naturally caused fire and those burned by hominin-made fire. Also, it is difficult to determine if fire used by hominins was started by them or captured from a wild-fire and then used. The earliest suggested date for the purposeful use of fire is about 1.5 million years ago in Africa, but that date has received little support. Perhaps the earliest proposed date for the controlled use of fire that has received a consensus is 790,000 years ago. The evidence for this use of fire comes from a site at Gesher Benot Ya'aqov in northern Israel where archaeologist Naama Goren-Inbar and her colleagues discovered groupings of burned flint that they believe are the remains of hearths (fire pits).[8] Near the flint they found burned seeds and wood. If we are seeing the deliberate and controlled use of fire at this time, it is possible that fire use extends farther back in time.

Although the evidence suggests the purposeful use of fire, it is possible that hominins captured the remains of wildfire for their use. However, evidence for the deliberate use of fire at Gesher Benot Ya'aqov fits well with the hypothesis that the controlled use of fire was necessary for hominins to move out of the warm tropical and Middle Eastern climates into the cooler Europe.

Gesher Benot Ya'aqov is in an area of the world that was a crossroads between Africa and Europe. Perhaps it was the use of fire, which most likely originated in Africa and then spread to the Middle East, that allowed people to move into Europe.

The controlled use of fire is considered one of early hominins' major cultural innovations. It was important for many reasons. In addition to warmth, fire provides light. The use of fire for light meant that people did not have to stop their activities at sunset. Around a campfire, discussions could take place, tools could be made, and stories could be told. The use of fire extended the day and increased the possibilities for different types of social interaction. Cooked food killed microorganisms and thereby cut down on the incidence of disease. The hominins that cooked their food might have been on the average healthier than the ones that did not and therefore had a competitive edge in exploiting resources. Fire could also be used for hunting. For instance, fires could run animals into swamps or off cliffs. In addition, fire provided protection from predators and perhaps gave a feeling of control of nature. Fire would later become the basis for much of technology. The manufacturing of most things—metals, plastics, and ceramics, for example—depends on heating processes.

Habitations The site of Terra Amata, in the city of Nice in southern France, is approximately 400,000 years old. When excavated in 1966, this site, once a part of the beach, was interpreted as containing several dwellings. If this interpretation is correct, the huts measure 6 by 12 meters (20 by 40 feet) and are characterized by oval floors. A study of what some interpret as postholes, stone supports, and hearths suggests that the hut was made of saplings or branches.

Archaeologist Paola Vila studied Terra Amata and discovered that about 40 percent of the cores and flakes could be put together to reconstruct the original stones from which these cores and flakes were manufactured.[9] Surprisingly, these pieces came from different stratigraphic levels. A specific tool was manufactured at a specific point in time, but the pieces of the tool were widely distributed at what first appear to be different time levels. This fact suggests that there has been significant disturbance at Terra Amata and that natural processes have moved artifacts made at one point in time into levels that seem to represent different points in time. Perhaps, then, the spatial arrangements of stones and postholes originally interpreted as dwellings are also the result of natural disturbances, not of human activity.

---

[8] N. Goren-Inbar, "Evidence of Hominin Control of Fire at Gesher Benot Ya'aqov, Israel," *Science* 304 (2004), pp. 725–727.

[9] P. Vila, "Conjoinable Pieces and Site Formation," *American Antiquity* 47 (1982), pp. 276–290.

Figure 14.29 Evidence of Butchering This photograph, taken by a scanning electron microscope, shows cut marks made with a stone tool on the surface of a fossilized bone. The cut marks are seen crossing a weathering crack (indicated by the arrow). Within the groove of each cut mark are many fine, parallel striations, features typical of such marks. The scale bar is 0.5 mm long.

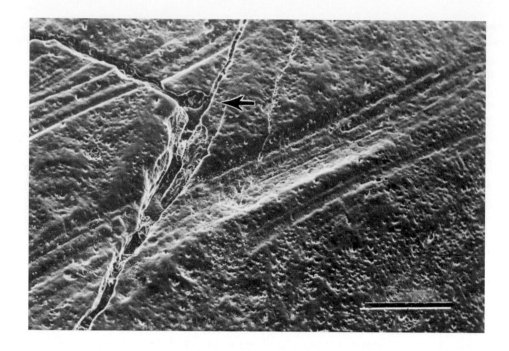

Hominins of this period probably made use of a variety of dwelling types. Some of those dwellings may have been in the open or up against a cliff, perhaps under a cliff overhang. Few habitations were constructed in caves, contrary to the popular notion of prehistoric peoples as "cavemen." Because of the good preservation of cave sites, archaeologists have tended to concentrate on their excavation.

Hunting, Scavenging, and Gathering

The classic description of early hominin subsistence patterns was that of Lower Paleolithic hominins as big-game hunters. Today, new finds and reanalyses of previously found fossils and artifacts place some doubt on this traditional interpretation.

Not so long ago, tools found in association with bones that have cut marks on them were assumed to have been used by hominins for hunting, killing, and butchering animals. Detailed microscopic studies of bones and hominin tooth-wear patterns, however, tell a different story. Paleoanthropologist Pat Shipman has studied cut marks on bones associated with tools and has found several interesting facts (Figure 14.29).

First, many bones that were processed by hominins have carnivore tooth marks in addition to cut marks from tools. In some cases, the cut marks overlay the tooth marks, indicating that the prey animal had been killed by a carnivore before it was butchered. Second, Shipman found that tool cut marks are often not near joints but occur on the shafts of bone. This suggests that the hominins did not have the whole carcass to butcher and that perhaps they cut off meat that remained after carnivores had left the scene or had been chased off. Hominins also could have eaten the marrow.

It is likely that the hominins of the Lower Paleolithic were predominantly scavengers and gatherers of wild plants. They may have performed some hunting, but many anthropologists now believe that hunting of large mammals did not become a major part of any human subsistence pattern until the emergence of later hominins.

Scavenging and hunting are two quite different activities. However, all nonprimate mammalian scavengers also hunt, and this may have been the case among early hominins. In searching for dead animals that still have some food value, animals that are primarily scavengers have to cover larger ranges than do those that are primarily hunters. On the other hand, scavenging does not require as much speed as hunting, although it is aided by endurance. Shipman points out that human bipedalism is not the best locomotor pattern for speed, but it is an efficient method of movement in terms of endurance. Bipedalism may have evolved, at least in part, in response to the selective pressures involved in a scavenging lifestyle.

The Brain and Language in Prehistoric Populations

Beginning about 1.6 million B.P., brain size began to increase over and beyond that which can be explained by an increase in body size. Some researchers point to evidence that suggests that from 1.6 million to about 300,000 B.P., the brain not only dramatically increased in size but also was being neurally reorganized in a way that increased its ability to process information in an abstract (symbolic) way. This symbolism allowed complex information to be stored, relationships to be derived, and information to be efficiently retrieved and communicated to others.

In modern people, an area, usually located on the left hemisphere of the frontal lobe of the cerebral cortex, controls the muscles for speech. This area of the brain, known as Broca's area, may have been present as early as 1.8 million B.P. in KNM-ER 1470, a specimen of *H. rudolfensis* (Figure 14.30). The presence of Broca's area does not necessarily mean that *H. rudolfensis* could speak, or at least not in a modern sense. The other neural features needed for fully developed language and speech, as well as the anatomical prerequisites needed for speech, may not have evolved this early. It is not possible to know exactly when the reorganization of the brain reached its modern state; many investigators believe this occurred around 300,000 years ago.

The neural prerequisites of speech may have begun to evolve well before there was any recognizable evidence of language-type communication. The **motor hypothesis of language** holds that the complicated motor skills needed to manufacture tools lead directly to the motor skills needed to produce speech. In modern humans the area of an infant's brain that corresponds to Broca's area controls hand movements used for manipulating objects and for using the muscles that control the speech apparatus. At about two years of age, about half of this area becomes specialized for language. Thus, the evolution of the ability to manufacture tools and in other ways to manipulate the environment may have been one of the

motor hypothesis of language One of many ideas about the origin of language; holds that the sophisticated motor coordination needed for the production of language as well as complex patterns of grammar evolved from preexisting complex motor patterns used for the manipulation and manufacture of objects.

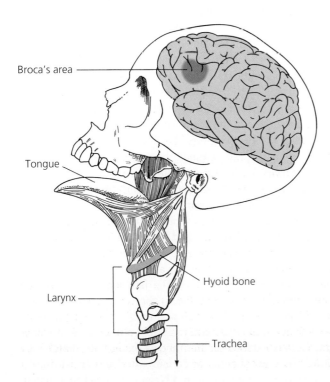

Broca's area

Tongue

Hyoid bone

Larynx

Trachea

Figure 14.30 Broca's Area and the Hyoid Bone The position and shape of the hyoid bone are important indicators of the potential for speech. The hyoid bone anchors muscles connected to the jaw, larynx, and tongue. Broca's area of the brain controls these muscles as they function to produce speech sounds.

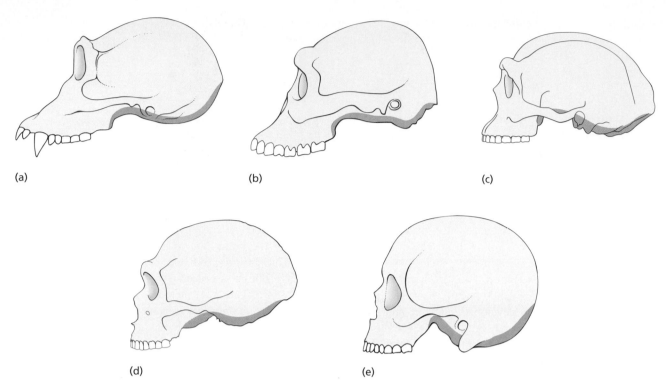

Figure 14.31 Comparison of Basicrania The shape of the base of the cranium in living forms is correlated with the position of the larynx. The flatter the basicranium, the higher the larynx in the neck. In turn, the position of the larynx in the throat influences the types of vocalizations that can be produced. The figure shows a series of composite representations of (a) the chimpanzee, (b) *Australopithecus africanus,* (c) *Homo erectus,* (d) *Homo neandertalensis,* and (e) *Homo sapiens.* (Skulls are not drawn to scale.)

early events that led to the modern motor capacity for language. This ability to manipulate the environment evolved to a much greater degree in the hominin line than it did in the evolution of the apes. As humans learned to use symbols, the previously evolved ability to combine hand movements in a complex series of actions to make tools requiring numerous sequential steps contributed to the ability to combine the symbols of language (such as words) in complex grammatical patterns.

If the brain's reorganization was basically modern by about 300,000 or more years ago, and if this reorganization was a prerequisite for full language abilities, who were the first people to speak in a modern way? One type of evidence for speech comes from the examination of the shape of the **basicranium,** the floor of the brain case (Figure 14.31). A straight basicranium indicates that the larynx (voice box) is positioned high in the neck; such a vocal tract would be unable to produce many human speech sounds. In modern humans, the basicranium is flexed, or bent, indicating a larynx low in the neck; this creates an acoustic situation favorable for speech sounds. The *Australopithecus* and *Paranthropus* basicrania are straight and are similar to those of modern apes. The basicranium of *H. erectus* is more flexed than the basicranium of *Australopithecus* but not quite as bent as that of a modern adult human skull. This may mean that the position of the larynx, and hence the shape of the vocal track, may have been approaching the modern configuration as early as 1.6 million years ago.

The other anatomical indication for speech is found in the analysis of the hyoid bone, a delicate bone in the neck that anchors muscles connected to the jaw, larynx, and tongue. This bone is so fragile that we have only one fossil specimen, that of a 60,000-year-old Neandertal found in Kebara Cave in Israel.

According to some reconstructions, the Neandertal basicranium is straighter than that of the modern human or *H. erectus,* and this has led to computer models of the Neandertal vocal apparatus that indicate that Neandertals could not pronounce certain vowel sounds, such as *a, i,* and *u.* Since *H. erectus* has a quite modern basicranium, even if Neandertals lacked articulate

basicranium The floor of the brain case.

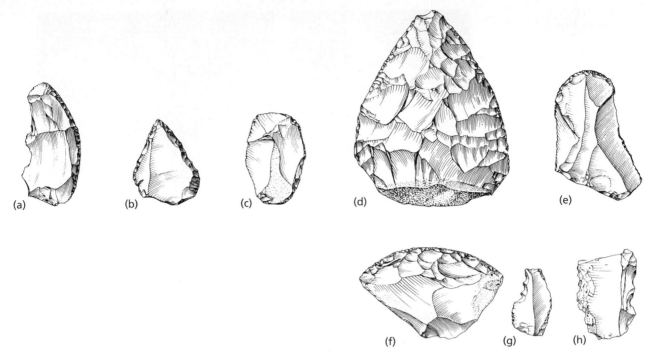

Figure 14.32 Mousterian Industries (a) Typical Mousterian, convex side scraper; (b) typical Mousterian, Mousterian point; (c) Mousterian of Acheulean, backed knife; (d) Mousterian of Acheulean, hand ax; (e) Mousterian of Acheulean, end scraper; (f) Quina-type Mousterian, traverse scraper; (g) and (h) denticulate Mousterian tools.

speech in the modern sense, it would not necessarily mean that more modern humans living at the same time as or before Neandertals could not speak as we do. For some researchers, the Kebara hyoid contradicts the basicranial data on Neandertals. It is seen by some as being almost identical in size, shape, and anatomical position to the hyoids of contemporary humans and thus indicates that the Neandertals *could* talk like modern humans.

The Culture of the Neandertals

The cultural tradition associated most frequently with Neandertals is the **Mousterian,** named after the cave of Le Moustier in France. Some non-Neandertals also are found in association with Mousterian assemblages, and non-Mousterian cultural traditions existed during the time period of the Neandertals.

The Mousterian is a Middle Paleolithic cultural tradition. It is a continuation and refinement of the Acheulean tradition and is characterized by an increase in the number and variety of flake tools and an ultimate deemphasis of the hand ax. For example, in some early Neandertal sites, hand axes make up as much as 40 percent of the stone tools, whereas in later assemblages, they drop to less than 8 percent. In some Mousterian sites, bone tools are predominant.

The sites of the Middle Paleolithic show great variability in tool types and their frequencies (Figure 14.32). However, the interpretation of the originality and meaning of Neandertal technology varies greatly. Some researchers see Neandertal artifacts as being totally utilitarian and having little or no symbolic value. These anthropologists also tend to believe that much of later Neandertal technology is the result of imitation as a result of contact with modern people. In this view, expressed by archaeologist Richard Klein, "Neandertals were only interested in a point or an edge."[10] According to Klein, Neandertals did not conceptualize a particular tool, they just were creating a sharp point or cutting edge to perform a particular task.

Mousterian tradition A Middle Paleolithic cultural tradition associated with the Neandertals, characterized by an increase in the number and variety of flake tools and an ultimate deemphasis of the hand ax.

See the Online Learning Center for an Internet Activity on the culture of the Neandertals.

[10] Quoted in C. Holden, "How Much Like Us Were the Neandertal," *Science* 282 (1998) p. 1456.

Figure 14.33
Neandertal Artifacts
These artifacts, found at the Neandertal site of Arcy-sur-Cure, are made of teeth and ivory. Dated at about 45,000 years old, they indicate to Francesco d'Errico and others that late Neandertals were capable of the same behavior seen in early *Homo sapiens sapiens*. (left) Perforated fox canine. (right) Part of an ivory ring, exterior diameter 29 millimeters (1.1 inches).

 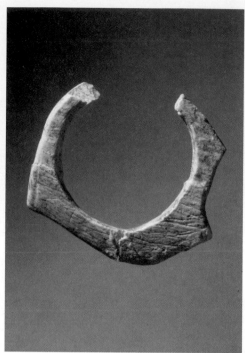

However, Francesco d'Errico and his colleagues believe that bone tools and jewelry found at the site of Arcy-sur-Cure in France show that Neandertals were capable of creating pieces that communicated meaning and were not the result of contact.[11] In addition to having possible aesthetic value to Neandertals, many of these pieces had regular patterns of notches and incisions. These patterns may have had some symbolic meaning (Figure 14.33). D'Errico concludes that the biological differences between Neandertals and modern people did not necessarily mean that there were differences in intellectual capacities.

Were Neandertals "Cavemen"? Caves are among the best places in which fossils and artifacts can be found. In many areas, the cycle of wetting due to rain and drying out occurs less frequently in caves than in open sites, and hence the chance of rapid deterioration is reduced. Because of the buildup of garbage and the flaking off of material from the roof and floor, caves often provide the researcher with a well-preserved stratigraphy. Since preservation is somewhat better in caves than in open sites, caves have been extensively investigated for signs of human occupation, and most Neandertal sites have been found in this context.

Humans are not by nature cave-dwelling animals, as caves are dark, often damp, and quite uncomfortable. People did inhabit the mouths of caves, but rarely did they venture into the deep interiors. In fact, most often what are called "caves" are not caves at all but rock shelters or rock overhangs. Yet there is evidence of Neandertals using the deep interior of the cave at Bruniquel, in southern France, at around 47,600 B.P. Hundreds of meters from the cave entrance, archaeologists found a complex quadrilateral structure of unknown function. Since only Neandertals inhabited Europe at this time, we can postulate the existence of portable light sources and complex patterns of communication and social organization.

Neandertals also may have spent a great deal of their time in open-air sites, but these have not been preserved with as great a frequency as have cave sites. This is an example of how differential preservation influences the data.

However, some open-air sites are known; among the most famous is Molodova I in the western part of Ukraine. At this site, mammoth bones served as the support for animal hides

---

[11] F. d'Errico et al., "Neanderthal Acculturation in Western Europe? A Critical Review of the Evidence and Its Interpretation," *Current Anthropology* 39 (1998), pp. S1–S44.

that created a house with an inside area 5.4 meters (18 feet) in diameter. Fifteen hearths have been found in the floor of this ancient home.

Was the Life of Neandertals Harsh? In a word, yes. At least it was very hard compared with the lives of most people living in the more technologically developed nations today. However, the life of Neandertals may have been no more severe than that of modern *H. sapiens* living in similar habitats 2500 years ago.

Anthropologist Debbie Guatelli-Steinberg and her colleagues compared the teeth of Neandertals with those of 2500-year-old Inuits (Native Americans) of Alaska. They studied small defects in tooth enamel that indicate periods during childhood development when food was insufficient for the normal development of tooth enamel. Their examination found that Neandertals had periodic episodes of inadequate nutrition but that "while other indicators may eventually demonstrate that Neandertal populations were more stressed than those of modern foragers [such as the Inuit], and that this stress resulted from foraging inefficiency relative to them, the evidence from this study does not lend support to this conclusion."[12]

Some anthropologists have thought that the ultimate demise of the Neandertals was due, at least in part, to the fact that the more technologically advanced people that moved into their territories had a competitive advantage in securing and processing food. Guatelli-Steinberg and her colleagues' analysis throws some doubt on this hypothesis, since it appears that Neandertals were no worse off nutritionally than were modern humans with more advanced technologies living in harsh Arctic habitats.

Burial of the Dead and Symbolic Thought Throughout historical time, burials have been a behavior associated with symbolic behavior. Symbolic behavior permits one thing, such as a word, an object, or a behavior, to represent something else. The ability to use symbols (Chapter 12) lies at the base of most complex modern human behaviors, including language, art, mathematics, economics, kinship relationships, and religion and other belief systems. Evidence of symbolic behavior is found infrequently in the fossil and archaeological record. Possible burials that are unearthed that contain not only bones but also possible symbolic objects have great significance to anthropologists.

The first suggested dates for purposeful burials that might indicate symbolic behavior date from within the time range of *Homo heidelbergensis* about 350,000 years ago. Spanish researchers found a pink hand axe at Atapuerca, Spain, in a pit along with the remains of 27 people (Figure 14.34).

Some of these researchers believe that the stone ax has symbolic significance. It was the only artifact found in the pit, and although quartz hand axes like the one found in Spain are common, the color is not. Perhaps the people responsible for placing the ax in the pit had to search for it and the striking color had some ritual significance. Eudald Carbonell,

Figure 14.34 Hand Ax from Atapuerca, Spain This hand ax was the only artifact found with the skeletal remains of 27 people who might have been buried purposefully. It is dated at about 350,000 B.P., and the association of the ax with the skeletal remains and its unusual pink color suggest that it had symbolic significance to those who made it.

Source: Marina Mosquera, Area de Prehistòrica, Department d'Històrica i Geografia, Universitat Rovira i Virgili Plaça, Imperial Tàrraco 1 43005 Tarragona, Spain.

---

[12] D. Guatelli-Steinberg, C. S. Larsen, and D. L. Hutchinson, "Prevalence and the Duration of Linear Enamel Hypoplasia: A Comparative Study of Neandertals and Inuit Foragers," *Journal of Human Evolution* 47 (2004), p. 80.

Figure 14.35 Neandertal Burial An adult male burial from Mount Carmel, Israel.

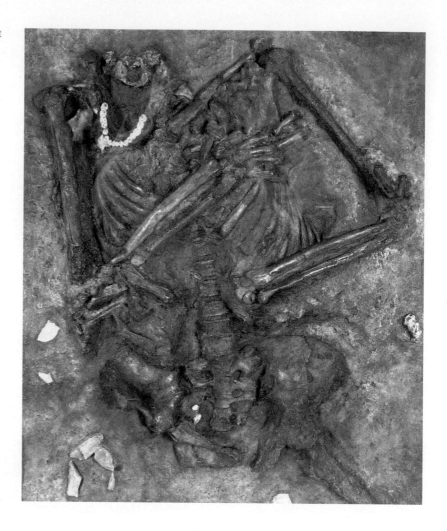

who was on the team that found the ax, told BBC News: "It's a great discovery. This is an interpretation, but in my opinion and the opinion of my team, the axe could be the first evidence of ritual behaviour and symbolism in a human species. . . . We conclude it could be from a funeral rite."[13] Not everyone agrees with this interpretation. Some people believe that the fossils wound up in the pit as a result of the flow of water or mud that pushed them into the pit along with the hand ax.

Homo heidelbergensis is thought by some anthropologists to have ultimately given rise to both Neandertals and anatomically modern *Homo sapiens* (Chapter 15). For a long time it was thought that Neandertals were the first to bury the dead systematically and ritualistically, starting perhaps 100,000 years ago. Over 30 Neandertal sites show evidence of such burials (Figure 14.35). From pollen analysis it has been suggested that flowers might have been put in Neandertal graves along with stone tools and animal bones. Perhaps the flowers showed grief or another emotion, the grave goods might have indicated a need for the tools in an afterlife, and the animal bones might have been some type of offering. Yet for each one of these conclusions, some researchers see alternative explanations. The pollen might have been in the soil to begin with or have been blown into the grave; the stone tools might represent accidental associations with the skeletal material or have wound up in the graves for another, nonsymbolic reason; and predators might have deposited the animal bones.

If the *H. heidelbergensis* find from Spain and the Neandertal material turn out not to represent ritualistic burials, the first such burials might be confined to our own species,

---

[13] Paul Rincon, "Scientists Claim They Have Found the Oldest Evidence of Human Creativity: A 350,000-Year-Old Pink Stone Axe," BBC News, March 23, 2003.

Box 14-5

Who Are We Having for Dinner? The Roots of Cannibalism

Anthropologists have debated for decades whether some of our ancestors were cannibals. In the late 1800s some paleontologists thought that the bones of about 20 Neandertals from the Krapina rock shelter in Croatia were cannibalized. By the 1930s most anthropologists doubted that cannibalism ever existed in prehistoric times.

We know that cannibalism has occurred in modern times. There have been pathological criminals such as Jeffrey Dahmer, who received a sentence of 1070 years in prison for murdering and cannibalizing 17 victims. We know of the occurrences of survival cannibalism such as the famous case of the Donner wagon train party in 1846–1847. These stranded people were starving and resorted to cannibalism to survive in the Sierra Nevada during a severe winter. We also know that some tribal peoples consumed body parts of slain enemies, and some, such as the Fore of New Guinea and the Wari' of the western Amazon, practiced ritual cannibalism when they ate their dead relatives during mortuary rites. Anthropologists have wondered whether prehistoric peoples also practiced some type of cannibalism.

New techniques of analysis that include the use of the scanning electron microscope and biochemical analysis show that our ancestors indeed ate one another. Recent reanalysis of the bones at Krapina, as well as hominin bones from another Croatian site and a Neandertal site in France, has shown strong indications of cannibalism. But cannibalism goes back much further than that. More than 780,000 years ago, the fossils designated by some as *Homo antecessor* were dining on others of their species. Six *H. antecessor* individuals from the Gran Dolina in the Atapuerca Hills of northern Spain carry scars from having been butchered. The cut marks on the hominin bones match those on nonhuman animal bones in the same area.

Closer to home and to the present time, Richard A. Marlar and his associates have found biochemical evidence of cannibalism at an Anasazi site dated to about 850 years ago. The Anasazi were a Native American group who lived in the Four Corners area of the American Southwest. Marlar found traces of human myoglobin on ceramic pots from the site of Cowboy Wash in southwestern Colorado. Myoglobin is a protein that is found in heart and skeletal muscles. Its presence in the ceramic vessels indicates that humans were cooked in the pots. Fossil human feces found at the site also tested positive for myoglobin, confirming that the person producing the feces had eaten human flesh.

The growing evidence that cannibalism was widely distributed throughout the world and goes back in time at least 780,000 years shows that this practice, which is repugnant to almost everyone today, has deep roots in the past.

Sources: A. Defleur et al., "Neanderthal Cannibalism at Moula-Guercy, Ardèche, France," *Science* 286 (1999), pp. 128–131; R. A. Marlar et al., "Biochemical Evidence of Cannibalism at a Prehistoric Puebloan Site in Southwestern Colorado," *Nature* 407 (2000), pp. 74–78; and T. White, "Once Were Cannibals," *Scientific American,* August 2001, pp. 58–65.

H. sapiens. There is evidence of burials by anatomically modern people in Israel at two sites: Qafzeh and Skhūl (Chapter 15). At one excavation at Qafzeh a child was buried with a deer antler, and at another 71 pieces of red ocher, used as a pigment, were found. The researchers who found the ocher alongside the bones believe it had ritual significance. At Skhūl, the buried individual is holding the jawbone of a wild boar. All this evidence is dated to between 90,000 and 100,000 years ago.

How Neandertals Behaved The interpretation of paleoanthropological evidence is difficult. Often a find can be seen as evidence for two or more competing ideas. Nowhere is this more the case than with the Neandertals. Anthropologists today believe that Neandertals and modern people did coexist in several parts of the world for thousands of years. Yet their relationship to each other is debatable.

One question is whether Neandertals and modern people mated successfully. That is, did they have offspring that in turn were fertile? Some see the 24,500-year-old child found in Portugal as evidence of hybridization between Neandertals and modern people. The child has the short arms and broad trunk of a Neandertal, but a modern-looking mandible including a well-developed chin and modern-appearing pubic bones. Others see the child as a stocky modern *Homo sapiens* child and point to genetic evidence that seems to suggest that Neandertals were genetically too different from modern humans to have reproduced successfully.

The evidence is growing that at least some Neandertals practiced cannibalism and purposely buried their dead. If this is true, perhaps Neandertals were not the dimwitted individuals incapable of planning and symbolic thought that some anthropologists, mostly in the past, pictured them as being. Cannibalism and the placing of goods in graves may indicate ritualistic behavior (Box 14-5).

We have already discussed the fact that the artifacts of late surviving Neandertals show little difference from the technology of the more modern people that coexisted with them. Some see this similarity as imitation of modern people's technology on the part of Neandertals. Other researchers view Neandertal technology as independent innovation and therefore as evidence of the Neandertal ability to think creatively.

In the last half decade or so, the idea of Neandertals as prehumans that could not speak in the modern sense, could deal only with the present situation, lacked artistic and other creative abilities, and in other ways were behaviorally inferior to modern humans has subsided. It has been replaced with the idea that although Neandertals may have differed to some degree biologically and behaviorally from totally modern people, they were a highly sophisticated population that for more than 100,000 years successfully exploited the environments that they occupied. What became of the Neandertals as a population will be dealt with in the next chapter.

Summary

The oldest-known archaeological material dates from around 2.6 million B.P. from the Gona River basin. Other important east African archaeological sites include the Omo River basin, Hadar, Olduvai Gorge, and east Lake Turkana. While both *Paranthropus* and *Homo* were for the most part contemporary at these sites, it is assumed that the development of technology was largely an adjustment of *Homo* and that the artifacts recovered represent the behavior of this genus.

The earliest stone tools are predominantly choppers and flakes. Later Paleolithic tools, attributed to *H. erectus,* are associated with hand-ax traditions such as the Acheulean. The degree to which *H. erectus* depended on hunting for subsistence is debated. Today, many researchers believe that gathering wild vegetation and scavenging for meat and marrow were important methods of obtaining food.

Neandertals used tools made of stone, bone, wood, and shell. Their cultural tradition, called the Mousterian, continued the use of hand axes, but the number and variety of flake tools increased throughout the Neandertal period. Neandertals lived in both rock shelters and open-air sites, and although some groups were probably more settled than others, most groups were probably nomadic.

To some, Neandertals seem to show a consciousness that we can recognize as "human." They may have buried their dead and placed artifacts and flowers in the graves, although this view has been challenged. Some anthropologists believe that the Neandertals may have differed from modern people in many ways. Some investigators believe that the Neandertals evolved into *H. sapiens* in Europe, while others think they are a side branch of human evolution that did not contribute to the gene pool of contemporary peoples.

Key Terms

Acheulean tradition, *383*	bone industry, *379*	core tool, *380*
assemblage, *379*	burin, *380*	debitage, *380*
awl, *382*	cleaver, *382*	facial sinus, *373*
basicranium, *388*	core, *380*	flake, *380*

Study Questions

1. Compare the anatomical characteristics of the genera *Homo* and *Australopithecus*.
2. What was the distribution of *H. erectus* and *H. ergaster*? Briefly describe the finds made in each major geographical area.
3. List the members of the species *H. heidelbergensis* mentioned in this chapter. Tell where they were discovered and explain how this group of fossils differs from both earlier and later species of the genus *Homo*.
4. What are some of the major anatomical differences between Neandertals and modern humans?
5. What evidence exists to justify the idea that *H. erectus* was primarily a gatherer of wild plant material and a scavenger of already killed animals as opposed to an efficient big-game hunter?
6. Summarize what is known about the origins of the Neandertals.
7. What type of evidence is used to construct models for the potential for language and speech abilities in fossil populations?
8. Discuss assumptions that have been made about the Neandertals' worldview.

See the Online Learning Center for additional study questions.

Critical Thinking Questions

1. Today, there is only one species of hominin in existence, *Homo sapiens*. About 2 million years ago, there might have been several species in the genus *Homo* as well as a couple of *Paranthropus* species living at the same time. What models can you come up with for the possible relationships among these varied hominins?
2. You have read the material on the Neandertals. Do some additional research on them. On the basis of your reading, what do you believe is the evolutionary relationship of Neandertals to modern people? Are they archaic *Homo sapiens* or a different species of *Homo*? Did they contribute to the modern human gene pool, or were they a dead-end side branch of the hominin evolutionary tree? Support your conclusions.
3. Many of the material things that you or your parents own are not necessary for survival. Early hominins and modern hunters and gatherers get along with much less. What would be the minimum tool kit you would need to survive in a temperate environment?

Suggested Readings

The following handbooks list individual fossils along with pertinent information:

Day, M. *Guide to Fossil Man: A Handbook of Human Paleontology,* 4th ed. Chicago: University of Chicago Press, 1986.

Larsen, C. P., R. M. Matter, and D. L. Gebo. *Human Origins: The Fossil Record,* 3rd ed. Prospect Heights, IL: Waveland, 1998.

Also recommended are the following:

Arsuaga, J. L., and A. Klatt (translator). *The Neanderthal's Necklace: In Search of the First Thinkers.* New York: Four Walls Eight Windows, 2004. The codirector of the largest Neandertal dig explains what we know about how Neandertals lived, why they "disappeared," and their relationship to modern people.

Boaz, N. T., and R. L. Ciochon. *An Ice-Age Saga of Homo erectus.* Oxford: Oxford University Press, 2004. This book is about the extensive excavation of *Homo erectus* fossils at a site near Zhoukoudian, China, and about *Homo erectus* in general.

Klein, R. G. *The Human Career: Human Biological and Cultural Origins,* 2nd ed. Chicago: University of Chicago Press, 1999. This is a comprehensive, readable book detailing current research in paleontology and archaeology.

Reader, J. *Missing Links: The Hunt for Earliest Man,* rev. ed. Boston: Little, Brown, 1995. This book tells the story of the hunt for and discovery of many important fossil hominids.

Shipman, P. *The Man Who Found the Missing Link: Eugène Dubois and His Lifelong Quest to Prove Darwin Right.* New York: Simon & Schuster, 2001. A highly readable and entertaining biographical account of the work of Eugène Dubois, the discoverer of "Java Man."

Whitehead, P. F., W. K. Sacco, and S. B. Hochgraf. *A Photographic Atlas of Physical Anthropology.* Englewood, CO: Morton Publishing, 2005. Chapter 8 of this book has numerous photographs and drawings of the fossils mentioned in this chapter.

Suggested Websites

The Fossil Evidence for Human Evolution in China:
www.cruzio.com/~cscp/index.htm

Human Evolution at the Smithsonian Institution:
www.mnh.si.edu/anthro/humanorigins/ha/a_tree.html

The Hominid Index:
www.modernhumanorigins.com/hominids.html

The Neandertal Museum:
http://217.160.110.111/neanderthal/

Chapter 15

The Evolution of *Homo sapiens*

4,000-year-old cave painting from Tassili n'Ajjer, Algeria, shows a weary hunter returning from the hunt.

Few topics in anthropology have generated more interest and debate over the past few years than the biological and behavioural origins of fully "modern" human populations. The debates have arisen partly from new discoveries and the application of new dating methods, and partly from the use of more sophisticated approaches to the modelling of human evolutionary processes, both in terms of biological evolution, and the associated (and inevitably interrelated) patterns of cultural change. A central factor in much of this rethinking has of course been the recent developments in molecular genetics, which are now opening up an entirely new perspective on the evolutionary origins of modern human populations. •

—*Paul Mellars and Chris Stringer*

Chapter Outline

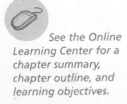

See the Online Learning Center for a chapter summary, chapter outline, and learning objectives.

After Reading This Chapter, You Should Be Able to Answer These Questions:

1. Where have fossils of early modern humans been found?

2. What are the two main competing concepts of the evolution of modern humans? What are the strengths and weaknesses of each one?

3. What is the "Out of Africa Again and Again Model" of human evolution?

4. When did hominins first migrate to Australia? What is the evidence for this?

5. When did hominins first arrive in the New World? What type of evidence is there for that expansion?

6. What are some of the characteristics of Upper Paleolithic technology? What technological advances did Upper Paleolithic peoples make compared with Middle Paleolithic peoples?

7. Other than technology, what do we know about Upper Paleolithic culture?

8. What do we know about the early culture of people in the Americas?

9. What do the terms *Mesolithic* and *Neolithic* refer to?

10. Where did the first civilizations arise, and what were some of their characteristics?

Anthropocentrism is the belief that humans are the most important elements in the universe and that everything else exists for human use and fancy. This belief runs counter to modern scientific thought. Yet since the nineteenth century, scientists have debated what it is to be human. These discussions often seem to be anthropocentric or, if we may coin a new term, *sapiencentric.*

As an example, some scholars see the origins of creative thought and behavior, such as that seen in pictorial art, as occurring only after the origins of modern humans. Although the Neandertals and their contemporaries do not appear to have expressed themselves through pictorial art, they may have developed other creative outlets, such as storytelling. We just don't know!

As we will see shortly, anatomically modern peoples may have originated at the same time as or even before the time of the Neandertals, yet *H. sapiens* may not have developed pictorial art until about 30,000 years ago. Why? Perhaps art and other new behaviors originated because of changes in the environment or as a result of cultural exchanges, not because of any physical or mental changes. This chapter will focus on what it means to be modern, and it will examine the debate over modern human origins and evolution.

HOMO SAPIENS

Today, modern *H. sapiens* populations are distributed widely over the globe. This section will survey the earliest appearances of modern *H. sapiens* in various areas of the world (Figure 15.1).

The Distribution of Fossil *Homo sapiens* in the Old World

Asia Two early modern hominins from Israel, one from Jebel Qafzeh and the other from Tabūn, place anatomically modern humans well back into the Neandertal time range. The Jebel Qafzeh fossil has been dated by electron spin resonance dating to between 115,000 and 96,000 B.P. (Figure 15.2). The dating of Tabūn is less certain, but it is probably older than 100,000 B.P.

Although many paleoanthropologists believe that Jebel Qafzeh and Tabūn are about 100,000 years old, the earliest reliable dates for *H. sapiens* in eastern Asia are much more recent. One of these early reliable dates is associated with an anatomically modern human from Niah Cave in north Borneo; the fossil has been dated by radiocarbon dating at about 41,500 B.P. The adult female found in the cave is delicately built; the skull lacks brow ridges, the forehead is high, and the back of the head is rounded. The Niah Cave individual resembles modern populations of New Guinea.

Many finds have been made in China, but perhaps the best known is a series of skulls from the Upper Cave of Zhoukoudian. They are relatively recent, dating to between 18,000 and 10,000 years ago. The skulls are all modern, but they are interesting in that each one differs in some respects from the others; they provide a good example of intrapopulation variability. One skull shows a forward-jutting zygomatic arch and **shovel-shaped incisors** similar to those of present Asian populations. Shovel-shaped incisors are incisors that have a scooped-out shape on the tongue side of the tooth. These skulls also closely resemble many Native American skulls.

Europe Early modern humans often are seen in terms of a population called Cro-Magnon, which lived about 28,000 years ago or later (Figure 15.3). In 1868, several partial skeletons were discovered in a rock shelter in southwestern France. They became the prototype of *H. sapiens.* Early scholars envisioned Cro-Magnon people as light-skinned, beardless, upright-walking individuals who invaded Europe and destroyed the bestial Neandertals. In general, Cro-Magnon people are characterized by broad, small faces with high foreheads and prominent chins and cranial capacities as high as 1590 cubic centimeters. Their height has been estimated at 163 to 183 centimeters (5 feet 4 inches to 6 feet), but their skin color and amount of body hair can only be surmised.

shovel-shaped incisors
Incisors that have a scooped-out shape on the tongue side of the tooth.

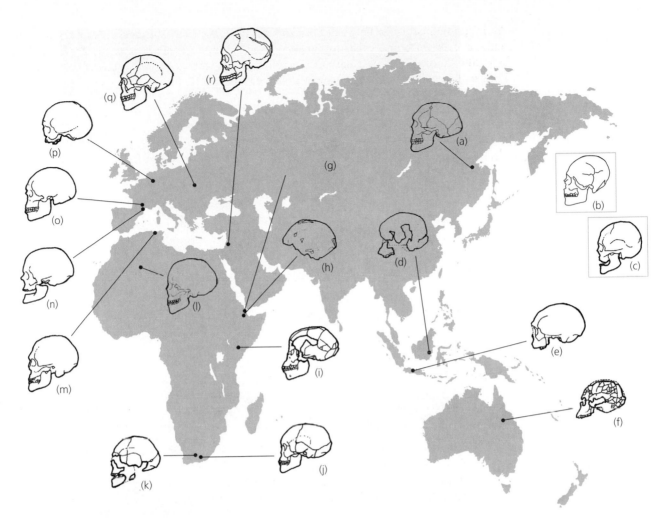

Figure 15.1 Variation and Distribution of *Homo sapiens* (a) Upper Cave 101, Zhoukoudian, People's Republic of China; (b) Kennewick, Washington, United States; (c) Tepexpan, Mexico; (d) Niah Cave, Borneo; (e) Wadjak, Java; (f) Talgai, Australia; (g) and (h) Omo, Ethiopia; (i) Lothagam Hill, Kenya; (j) Fish Hoek, South Africa; (k) Cape Flats, Cape Peninsula, South Africa; (l) Asselar, Mali; (m) Afalou, Algeria; (n) Cro-Magnon, France; (o) Combe Capelle, France; (p) Oberkassel, Germany; (q) Predmost, Czechoslovakia; (r) Jebel Qafzeh IX, Israel.

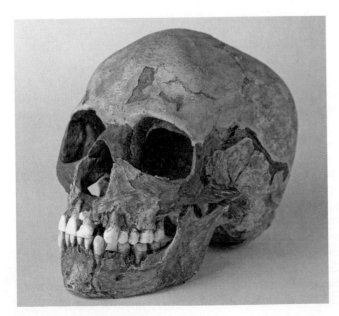

Figure 15.2 *Homo sapiens*
Jebel Qafzeh skull, Israel.

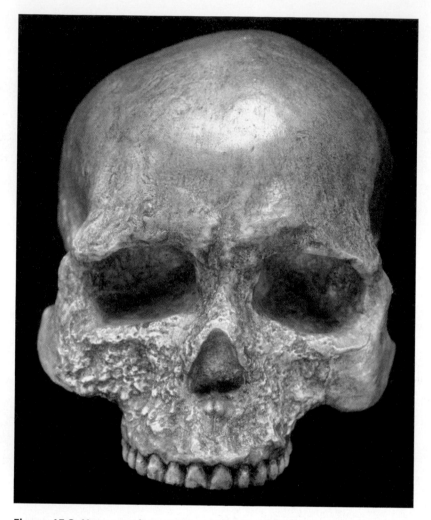

Figure 15.3 *Homo sapiens* Skull from Cro-Magnon, France.

In other parts of Europe, even older fossil populations of modern people exist. At the 38,000-year-old site of Mladeč in the Czech Republic, paleontologists found a cranium that was quite robust yet basically modern in appearance. It and other finds in eastern, central, and southern Europe show modern features, yet these specimens also exhibit characteristics, such as brow ridges, that are intermediate in size between those of the Neandertals and those of modern humans.

Africa The oldest modern *Homo sapiens* fossils come from Africa. Fossils found in the Kibish formation of Ethiopia near the Omo River are dated to about 195,000 years ago. Omo 1 (Figure 15.4) is a partial skull and skeleton and Omo 2 is a skull without a face. Richard Leakey found the bones in 1967, but a reliable date for the fossils based on the ^{40}Ar/^{39}Ar dating method was not published until 2005.

Fossils from another Ethiopian site, Herto in the Afar region, are dated to about 156,000 years ago. The find includes three skulls, pieces of skulls and teeth from seven other individuals, over 600 stone tools, and hippopotamus bones with stone tool cut marks.

The most complete of the skulls has an estimated cranial capacity of 1450 cubic centimeters, larger than that of the average modern human. One of the more fragmentary skulls may be even larger. The third skull is that of a child who was about six or seven years old at the time of his or her death. Most of the measurements of the skulls are within the range of modern human anatomy. The most obvious modern features are a less prominent brow ridge than in Neandertals and other premodern people and a higher forehead (cranial vault). Some researchers see the fossils as modern enough to be placed in the same taxonomic category as fully modern people; others see differences significant enough to merit a subspecies name. The latter group calls the fossils from Herto *Homo sapiens idaltu*. *Idaltu* means "elder" in the language of the Afar people and refers to the possible position of the Herto fossils close to the base of the modern human family tree and to the fact that the most complete skull was "old" in the sense that it had heavily worn teeth.

The oldest sub-Saharan fossils that show a greater number of modern characteristics than the Ethiopean fossils are fragmentary finds from the Klasies River mouth in South Africa. This material is about 120,000 years old as dated by electron spin resonance dating. Also in South Africa, finds from Border Cave that have many modern features have been dated to between 115,000 and 100,000 B.P. However, the dating from both sites has been questioned, as has the degree to which they exhibit modern features. What appear to be modern human footprints have been found at Langebaan Lagoon, South Africa, and date to about 117,000 years ago.

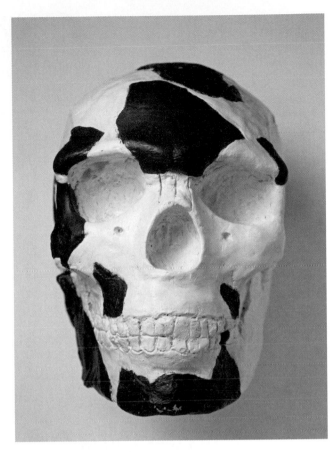

Figure 15.4 *Homo sapiens* Omo I skull, Ethiopia.

The Anatomy of *Homo sapiens*

Modern humans have a distinctly round head that contains a large brain that averages 1350 cubic centimeters. From front to back, the cranial arch, or vault, is short but high. The occipital bone is delicate; it lacks the large bony crests that in other anthropoids function as surface areas for the attachment of large neck and jaw muscles.

Compared with earlier hominins, the modern human face and eye sockets are smaller; the front of the upper jaw and the mandible are also small. The modern human has a strong chin, which is the bony projection of the lower part of the mandible. Compared with the earlier hominin skeletons, the modern human skeleton is generally less robust and the musculature is lighter (Figure 14.20).

See the Online Learning Center for an Interactive Exercise on the comparative anatomy of the skulls of Homo sapiens, Homo neandertalensis, and Homo erectus.

Ideas on the Origins of *Homo sapiens*

During the last two decades, paleoanthropologists have uncovered new evidence and have developed new hypotheses to explain the origins of *Homo sapiens*. Although there are several competing models, most are variations of two basic models, labeled the replacement model and the regional continuity model (Figure 15.5).

In the **replacement model,** which anthropologist William Howells calls the "Noah's Ark" model, *H. sapiens* are seen as having evolved in Africa some 200,000 years ago. They then radiated out of that area and spread throughout Asia and Europe. These *H. sapiens* ultimately replaced earlier hominin populations, including the Neandertals.

replacement model The hypothesis that states that modern *H. sapiens* evolved in Africa and radiated out of this area, replacing archaic hominin populations.

This replacement occurred because *H. sapiens* either killed off archaic forms or exploited the resources of the environment into which they moved more effectively than other hominins could. The inability of the indigenous hominins to compete with *H. sapiens* for such resources as food may have led to their decline. Or both processes may have operated. At any rate, the proponents of the replacement model, in its original form, believe that the earlier forms did not interbreed with *H. sapiens* populations; therefore, they did not

Figure 15.5 The Origins of Modern Humans These two diagrams represent two views of the origins of modern *H. sapiens*. The regional continuity model assumes that modern human populations are direct descendants of local *H. erectus* populations. The replacement model assumes that local non-*H. sapiens* populations were replaced by migrations of *H. sapiens* that originated in Africa.

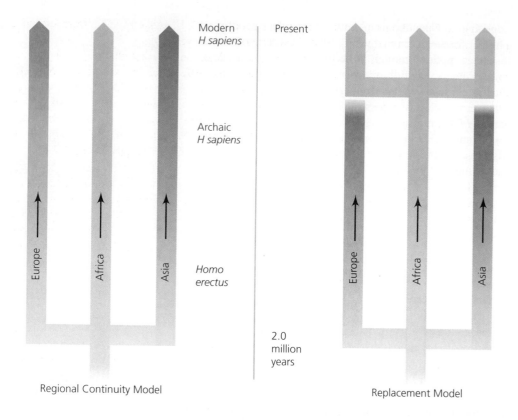

Regional Continuity Model

Replacement Model

contribute genes to contemporary *H. sapiens*. Gene flow did not occur between existing hominin populations, and there are no transitional forms outside of Africa. Physical variation in modern populations would have evolved only after the origin of modern humans.

The **regional continuity model** assumes multiple origins of *H. sapiens* from existing local populations. For example, Neandertals gave rise to modern European populations. This is not to say that each regional *H. sapiens* population evolved in total isolation. On the contrary, enough gene flow and migration between these populations would have occurred to maintain a single species, *H. sapiens*. This gene flow and similar selective forces in the different regions are seen as reasons for parallel evolution in the direction of modern humanity.

regional continuity model The hypothesis that states that modern *H. sapiens* had multiple origins from existing local populations; each local population of archaic humans gave rise to a population of modern *H. sapiens*.

According to this latter model, modern-population differences in physical characteristics are deeply rooted. They point to possible physical features, especially in Asia, that characterize specific regions that are seen in both modern and fossil forms. Such similarities suggest the existence of transitional forms. Proponents of the regional continuity model believe that modern *H. sapiens*'s last common ancestor existed perhaps 1.9 million years ago.

The Story of "Mitochondrial Eve" The "mitochondrial" in "Mitochondrial Eve's" name refers to mitochondrial DNA (mtDNA). Mitochondrial DNA is found in the cytoplasm of the cell, and it is inherited exclusively from the mother's sex cell. Since there is no recombination of the two parents' mtDNA, the only difference in a child's mtDNA and that of its mother, grandmother, great-grandmother, or any other direct female relative is due to mutation. Alan Wilson, Rebecca Cann, and Mark Stoneking proposed that the mtDNA of all modern populations can be traced back to a population of African women who became known collectively as "Mitochondrial Eve."[1] By assuming a mutation rate of 2 percent per

---

[1] R. L. Cann, M. Stoneking, and A. C. Wilson, "Mitochondrial DNA and Human Evolution," *Nature* 325 (1987), pp. 31–36.

million years, they believe that the current variation in mtDNA suggests a common ancestral population to all current people that lived about 200,000 years ago.

Led by Milford Wolpoff, paleoanthropologists have pointed out that in order for the geneticists' model to work, the only thing affecting the differences in the structure of mitochondrial DNA would be random mutation. However, any genes entering the gene pool of "Eve's" descendants from other populations would create a different degree of variation than would be expected if random mutation were the only cause for such variation. There *were* people before "Eve"; thus, if all modern people are the descendants of "Eve's" gene pool only, all the people not of her line would have died off without breeding with any of "Eve's" descendants.

When the "Mitochondrial Eve" hypothesis was presented in the mid-1980s, the earliest agreed-upon fossil evidence for the first appearance of modern humans was placed at about 40,000 years ago, although some suspected the existence of much older dates. The idea that modern humans existed in the age of Mitochondrial Eve some 200,000 or more years ago did not match the fossil evidence. However, the fossils from Herto show the existence of anatomically modern people at about 156,000 years ago. In 2005 the revised dating of the Omo fossils pushed the possible date for the earliest fossil evidence of the first modern humans back to 195,000 B.P.

Genetic studies done since the 1980s, including more recent mtDNA studies and comparative studies of the Y chromosome, continue to place the origin of modern humans at about the same time as the Omo and Herto fossils. These fossils, along with the mtDNA and Y-chromosome data, are seen by some anthropologists as providing strong support for the replacement model. Yet some studies of nuclear DNA indicate a more ancient common ancestor for *Homo sapiens,* and these studies seem to support the regional continuity model. Perhaps the answer lies in a complex combination of the two models.

Like other scientific controversies, the debate between proponents and opponents of the "Mitochondrial Eve" hypothesis illustrates the self-correcting nature of science. As the research used to compile the data for a hypothesis is constantly repeated and reanalyzed, the new research either validates the old hypothesis or invalidates it. The construction of specific phylogenetic trees showing an African origin for *H. sapiens* is questioned by some, but the research did illustrate that there is greater mtDNA variation in African populations. This reinforces the idea inferred from the fossil record that hominins have existed in Africa longer than they have on any other continent.

A More Complex Model of the Origin of Anatomically Modern Humans The replacement model for the origin of anatomically modern people also is called the "Recent African Origins Model." It suggests that the last common ancestors of all modern humans existed in Africa about 200,000 years ago. This date is recent compared with that suggested by the regional continuity model, which sees the last common ancestor of modern humans as existing in Africa almost 2 million years ago. Both models propose that Africa was the home of the common ancestors of all modern people.

A more complex model has been proposed. This model, sometimes referred to as the "Out of Africa Again and Again Model" or the "Mostly-Out-of-Africa Model," sees regional continuity infused with minor and major gene flow between regions.[2] The proponents of this model see several major expansions of hominins out of Africa as well as later major expansions out of other areas of the world. As one group expanded into another, various scenarios became possible. They could have freely interbred or interbred on rare occasions, the expanding group could have replaced or mostly replaced the indigenous group, or the indigenous group could have maintained its gene pool to varying degrees if it prevailed in any conflicts or other types of competition with the entering group. Figure 15.6 illustrates this idea.

---

[2] A. R. Templeton, "Out of Africa Again and Again," *Nature* 416 (2002), pp. 45–51; J. H. Relethforth, *Reflections of Our Past: How Human History Is Revealed in Our Genes* (Boulder, CO: Westview), 2003.

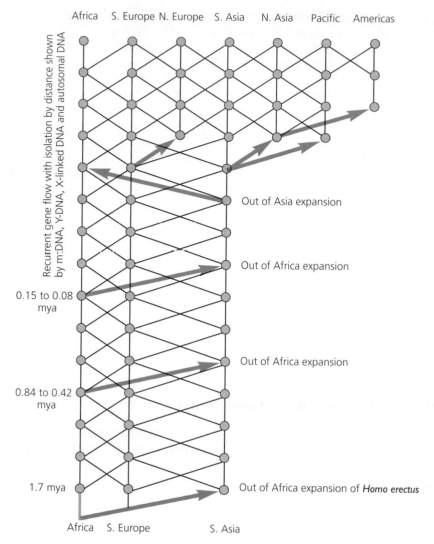

Figure 15.6 Out of Africa Again and Again This diagram represents Alan Templeton's picture of the evolution of modern humans, using mtDNA, Y-chromosome, X-chromosome, and autosomal chromosome data to construct the evolutionary "tree." The diagram shows the primary influence of Africa's contribution to the modern gene pool and the more recent contributions of other gene pools through gene flow. The vertical lines represent regional continuity from one period to the next, diagonal black lines represent minor gene flow between regions, and diagonal red arrows represent large-scale gene flow between regions. The illustration does not estimate the possibility of different degrees of genetic contributions from indigenous regional groups and groups expanding into an area. Reprinted from A. Templeton, "Out of Africa Again and Again," *Nature* 416 (2002), pp. 45–54 (www.nature.com).

DNA evidence for whether regional populations of modern and nonmodern people interbred and, if they did, the degree of interbreeding is inconclusive. There are some fossils that have been interpreted as providing evidence of interbreeding by some but not all researchers. One is a 24,500-year-old skeleton found in Portugal that according to one interpretation has physical characteristics of both Neandertals and anatomically modern *H. sapiens*. The prominent chin looks very modern, yet the stocky truck and short arms and legs are reminiscent of the Neandertals. Some paleoanthropologists see this skeleton of a four-year-old child as the product of interbreeding (perhaps several generations earlier) of Neandertal and modern human populations. Some anthropologists interpret the Mladeč cranium from the Czech Republic and other fossils in Europe and the Middle East as showing the mixing of Neandertal and modern human gene pools.

The Migrations of *Homo sapiens* to Australia and the New World

There is evidence of modern-looking populations in Africa as early as 195,000 years ago, in Asia somewhat after that, and in Europe at 38,000 B.P. and perhaps earlier. Except for the mysterious Kow Swamp fossils, to be discussed shortly, all hominins in Australia and the New World are modern in appearance. No representatives of *Australopithecus, Paranthropus,* or *Homo* other than *H. sapiens* have been found.

Australia People reached the islands of Indonesia from the mainland of southeast Asia by crossing over land connections formed by the lowering of ocean levels associated with glacial periods. Australia was never connected by land to the mainland of Asia, yet humans may have reached Australia more than 195,000 years ago or even earlier. Although Australia was separated from Asia, the periodic lowering of the sea level may have made migration by watercraft from Asia to Australia possible at an early date.

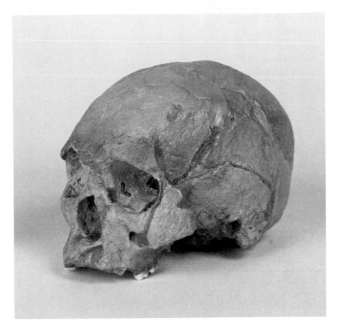

Figure 15.7 *Homo sapiens* Skull from Wadjak, Java.

Many of the skeletal finds from southeast Asia resemble the modern Australian aborigine. The Wadjak skulls from Java, discovered in 1890, show large brow ridges, a receding forehead, a deep nasal root, and large teeth (Figure 15.7). A find from Lake Mungo in New South Wales, Australia, dated at 40,000 B.P., represents the oldest skeletal remains in Australia. It is also the earliest evidence of cremation burial anywhere in the world. Large fragments of bone remain after cremation. The remains of the Lake Mungo individual, whose bones had been broken and placed in a depression, are those of a person of fully modern appearance.

One of the mysteries of prehistory concerns a second population from Australia. This population, from Kow Swamp in the state of Victoria, displays a low, retreating forehead; large brow ridges; and other features reminiscent of earlier forms. The surprising thing is that the Kow Swamp finds are dated between 13,000 and 9000 B.P. This is thousands of years after earlier patterns ceased to be recognizable elsewhere in the world. Since 40 burials have been excavated, we cannot attribute this to sampling error. However, some anthropologists have suggested that some of the morphological features may be due to artificial cranial deformation (see Figure 17.4).

The New World Most anthropologists believe that the Americas were populated by Asian big-game hunters who followed their prey across the Bering Strait to North America. American aborigines show similarities to Asian populations in body build, head shape, eye and skin color, hair type, dentition, presence of the Diego blood antigen, and many other physical characteristics. They also share many features of their languages.

When did the first migrants arrive in the New World? Today, on a clear day, the shore of Siberia is visible from Cape Prince of Wales, Alaska. At times in the past, Siberia and Alaska were connected by a landmass, as much as 2000 kilometers (1250 miles) from north to south, called **Beringia.** Beringia was exposed during the Pleistocene when large amounts of water were trapped in glacial ice, causing a drop in sea level (Figure 15.8).

Current geological and biological evidence suggests that Beringia existed at 80,000 B.P. or before. Before that time, North America and Asia had not been connected for about 15 million years. A warm period from 35,000 to 27,000 years ago flooded Beringia. During that time, people may have crossed the open water during the winter when the channel froze, or they even may have used simple watercraft. From approximately 27,000 to 11,000 years ago, Beringia again provided a wide grassy plain to those moving between Asia and North America. This plain was exposed as dry land for the last time about 11,000 years ago.

See the Online Learning Center for an Internet Activity on the paleoanthropology of Australia.

Beringia The landmass, some 2000 kilometers (1250 miles) from north to south, that connected Siberia and Alaska during the glacials.

Figure 15.8 Beringia
During the Pleistocene, large amounts of water were taken up in glaciers, and sea levels dropped, exposing what previously had been the sea floor. The Bering Sea floor between Siberia and Alaska was exposed, creating a large unglaciated area known as Beringia. The last time Beringia existed was from about 27,000 to 11,000 years ago. It was during that time that people first entered the New World from Siberia.

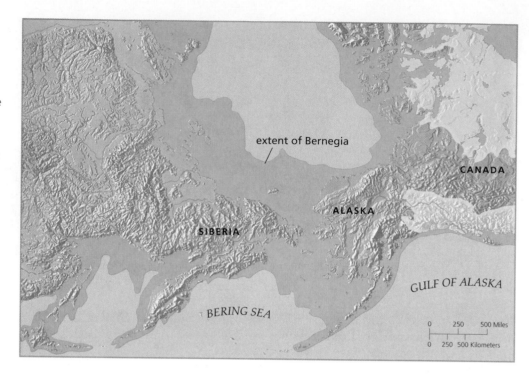

The firmest dates for the first presence of people in the New World are about 13,200 to 12,800 B.P., but dates of up to 27,900 years ago have been suggested. Most of the evidence for the early presence of humans in the New World is archaeological rather than paleontological; we will discuss this archaeological evidence in a later section of this chapter.

There is little skeletal evidence of early hominins in the New World. An electron spin resonance date of 15,400 B.P. has been proposed for human bones found in Kansas, and a date of around 13,000 B.P. has been suggested for a woman found on one of the Channel Islands of southern California. In 2004, investigators announced that three skeletons had been found in submerged caves along the Caribbean coast of Mexico's Yucatan Peninsula. They might be 13,000 years old. If these dates are correct, those remains would be the oldest yet found in the Americas. Fossils with dates of about 11,000 to 10,000 years have been recovered in North, Central, and South America. All fossil hominins found in the Americas possess Asian characteristics, and they also appear similar to modern Native American populations.

A recent study based on a series of cores from the floor of the Bering and Chukchi seas indicates that Beringia was a tundra similar to that of Arctic Alaska today. Instead of a rich grassland supporting a high density of herd animals, this tundra was relatively unproductive and required the development of a specialized technology for survival, not unlike that seen among the Inuits of the Arctic in this century. Since Beringia existed for thousands of years at a time, the migration from Asia to North America could have been a very slow one.

Kennewick Man In 1996, a 7880-year-old skeleton called Kennewick Man was found along the banks of the Columbia River in Washington State. With about 90 to 95 percent of the skeleton found, Kennewick Man is the most complete and the oldest skeleton found in the Pacific Northwest (Figure 15.9).

Because of the 1990 Native American Graves Protection and Repatriation Act (NAGPRA), the Army Corps of Engineers, which has jurisdiction over the land where the skeleton was found, locked it away. NAGPRA specifies that Native American remains are to be given to the Native American group that can best show an ancestral link to the remains. The problem with the Kennewick Man skeleton is that its affiliation is unclear. Anthropologists who initially were able to study the remains note that it exhibits many "Caucasoid"

See the Online Learning Center for an Internet Activity on Kennewick Man.

features and that it could not be shown to be connected to any existing Native American group. In July 2004, a decision by the Ninth U.S. Circuit Court of Appeals would have made the fossils available for study. However, new proposed federal legislation might block the implementation of the court's ruling.

The discovery of Kennewick Man raises many questions about the origins of New World populations. An analysis of 2000 skulls from 19 populations around the world has led anthropologist C. Loring Brace and his colleagues to the conclusion that there were at least two migrations to the New World.[3] The first migration consisted of Eurasians, populations that show a great deal of admixture between European and Asian populations. They entered the New World about 15,000 years ago and were the presumed ancestors of Kennewick Man. These populations were similar to the living Ainu, the aboriginal "Caucasoid" population of Japan. These early Americans moved south and were the ancestors of most native populations south of the U.S.–Canadian border. The second major wave entered the New World about 5000 years ago and represented Asian populations that had fewer admixtures with Europeans than the first migrants. This second wave became the ancestors of the modern Inuit (Eskimo) and some other populations, including the Na-Dene speakers such as the Navaho. Genetic, linguistic, and archaeological evidence seems to support this hypothesis.

Figure 15.9 *Homo sapiens* Kennewick Man from the State of Washington.

Summary

We cannot say exactly when fossils classified as *H. sapiens* first appeared; the precise point in time is a relative and arbitrary matter. However, the earliest *H. sapiens* may be from Africa at about 195,000 years ago. The "Mitochondrial Eve" hypothesis proposes a similar date for an African origin of modern humans. Modern *H. sapiens* may have been present in Asia as early as 115,000 years ago, and they were in Australia and Europe about 60,000 and 38,000 years ago, respectively. The only hominin populations found in Australia and the New World are classified as *H. sapiens*. Although considerably older dates have been proposed, firm dates for people in the New World go back to only about 13,200 years ago (Table 15.1).

Two models have been proposed to account for the appearance and spread of *H. sapiens*. According to the replacement model, modern *H. sapiens* evolved in a limited area, such as Africa, and then moved into other areas of the world; they completely replaced the Neandertals and other non–*H. sapiens* populations. Proponents of the regional continuity model believe that the Neandertals contributed to the origin of modern Europeans while other populations evolved into *H. sapiens* in other geographical areas. Intermediate models see different degrees of interbreeding between archaic hominins and *H. sapiens* populations. By about 30,000 years ago, *H. sapiens* was the only type of hominin existing on earth.

[3] C. L. Brace et al., "Old World Sources of the First New World Human Inhabitants: A Comparative Craniofacial View," *Proceedings of the National Academy of Sciences* 98 (2001), pp. 10,017–10,022.

Table 15.1 The Peopling of the Americas: A Sample of the Evidence Mentioned in This Chapter

Location	What Was Found	Possible Earliest Date*
Meadowcroft Rockshelter, Pennsylvania	Flakes, projectile points, possible basket fragments	19,000 B.P.
Monte Verde, Chile	Primitive structures, fire pits, stone and wood tools	14,000 B.P. or older
Folsom and Clovis, New Mexico	Folsom and Clovis points	13,200 B.P.
Submerged site, Yucatan Peninsula	Three skeletons	13,000 B.P.
Columbia River, Washington State	Skeleton	7880 B.P.

* Scholars disagree on these dates. See text.

THE CULTURE OF *HOMO SAPIENS*

During the Upper Paleolithic, human cultural development achieved a level of complexity that had never before existed. The cultural traditions associated with the Upper Paleolithic are found throughout Europe, northern Asia, the Middle East, and northern Africa.

Humans' Relationship to the Environment

tundra A type of landscape where the ground is frozen solid throughout most of the year but thaws slightly during the summer.

The development of the Upper Paleolithic must be seen in relation to the nature of the environment during that time. The period comprises the latter part of the last glaciation. Northern and western Europe was essentially a **tundra.** This was a land that was frozen solid throughout most of the year with the top several feet thawing during the summer months. A proliferation of plant life in the summer was capable of supporting large herds of animal life. The tundra of Canada today teems with animal life, such as the moose and caribou, but the Pleistocene European tundra was a low-latitude tundra that received more solar radiation than that received by the Canadian tundra today; thus, it was able to support a huge mass of herd animals.

Upper Paleolithic peoples hunted the large herd animals, often specializing in one or two types. This was in contrast to the scavenging or perhaps more individualistic hunting techniques of the Neandertals. This shift in orientation toward cooperative hunting of herd animals with improved projectile technology may have been responsible for the development of the Upper Paleolithic complex. Among the more important animals hunted were reindeer, horse, and bison; fish, such as salmon, were also important.

Unfortunately, humans' growing mastery in the utilization of these natural resources may have been matched by the disruption of ecological balances. During the Late Pleistocene, more than 50 genera of large mammals became extinct. Yet the extinction of large animals was not accompanied by the extinction of large numbers of smaller animals or plants, and an analysis of the record has shown no evidence of droughts in most areas. One factor does correspond with these extinctions: *H. sapiens.* Most extinctions can be correlated with the movements of people into an area. It seems very possible that human technology and social efficiency had developed to a point at which the environment could have been endangered.

One thing humans may have done when they entered an area was to alter the vegetation by burning it. New information on the use of fire by Australia's earliest inhabitants indicates that their use of fire contributed to the extinction of at least 60 species, including all animals larger than people. The use of fire may have led to mass extinctions elsewhere in the world.

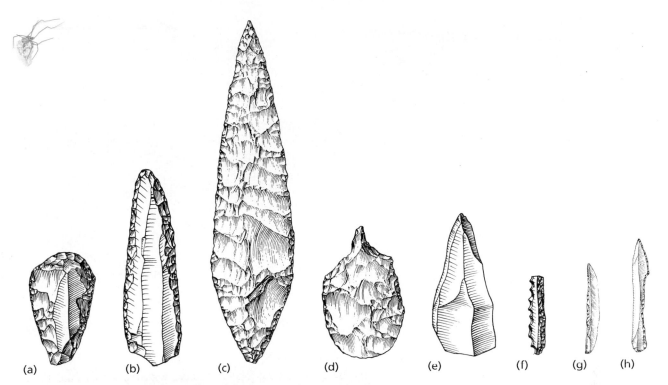

Figure 15.10 Upper Paleolithic Tool Types (a) Aurignacian, scraper on retouched blade; (b) Aurignacian, Aurignacian blade; (c) Solutrean, laurel-leaf point; (d) Solutrean, borer end scraper; (e) Perigordian, burin; (f) Perigordian, denticulated backed bladelet; (g) Magdalenian, backed bladelet; (h) Magdalenian, shouldered point.

The Upper Paleolithic of Europe was characterized by alternating periods of very cold and mild climate; people had to develop the technology to survive in such an environment. The archaeological record contains evidence of tailored clothing. Humans in a cold environment also need housing. In southwestern France, they used rock shelters, but many open settlements also have been found. Villages in this area were built in the river valleys, where they were somewhat protected from the cold of the plateau.

Upper Paleolithic Technology

The Upper Paleolithic is often defined in terms of the stone **blade.** Blades are not unique to this period, but the high frequency of their use is.

    Blades are stone flakes with roughly parallel sides and extremely sharp edges that are generally about twice as long as they are wide. They are manufactured from carefully prepared cores, and they can be made quickly and in great numbers. The manufacture of blades represents an efficient use of a natural resource—in this case, flint. François Bordes points out that from a pound of flint, the Upper Paleolithic blade technique could produce 305 to 1219 centimeters (10 to 40 feet) of cutting edge, whereas the early Mousterian flake technique could produce only 102 centimeters (40 inches).[4]

    From the basic blade, a wide variety of highly specialized tools can be manufactured. Unlike humans of the Lower Paleolithic, who used the general-purpose hand ax, humans of the Upper Paleolithic used tools designed for specific purposes. The primary function of a number of these tools was the making of other tools. Figure 15.10 illustrates some of the Upper Paleolithic tool types.

blade Flakes with roughly parallel sides and extremely sharp edges; blades are frequently found in Upper Paleolithic sites.

---

[4] F. Bordes, *The Old Stone Age* (New York: McGraw-Hill, 1968).

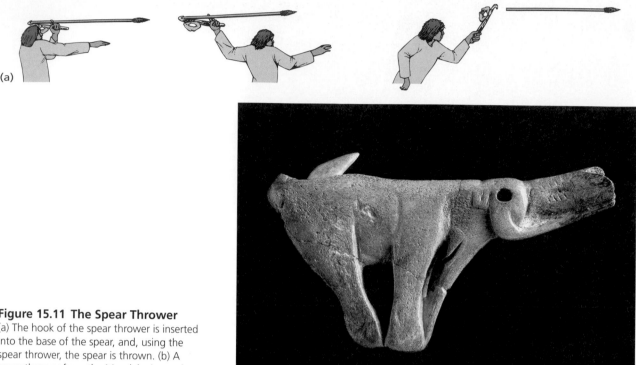

Figure 15.11 The Spear Thrower
(a) The hook of the spear thrower is inserted into the base of the spear, and, using the spear thrower, the spear is thrown. (b) A spear thrower from the Magdalenian rock shelter of Montastruc, Tarn-et-Garonne, France, carved as a mammoth.

Figure 15.12 Upper Paleolithic Eyed Needles Magdalenian bone needles.

Bone, along with antler, horn, and ivory, became a very common raw material. Bone has many advantages over stone; for example, it does not break as easily. The widespread use of bone resulted from the development of the burin, which had a thick point that did not break under pressure when used to work bone. Some of the later Upper Paleolithic cultures became very dependent on bone implements, and stone points practically disappeared.

One of the major reasons for the success of Upper Paleolithic populations was the development of new projectile weapons. These are **compound tools,** that is, tools composed of several parts. Hafting appears in the archaeological record; the ax is no longer a hand ax but an ax with a handle. Although some compound tools may have been produced as part of the Late Middle Paleolithic, they became more common in Upper Paleolithic cultures.

A spear was made by hafting a bone point to a shaft, and to add to the force of penetration, it was often used with a spear thrower (Figure 15.11). A harpoon consisted of a barbed bone point that detached from the shaft after entering the animal yet remained tied to the shaft by a cord; the dragging of the shaft behind the animal would impede its flight. The shaft could be retrieved and used again. In glacial climates, long pieces of wood were rare and the shafts were valuable; the points were easily made from antler or bone. Later in the period, the bow and arrow appeared. Several types of fishing gear, such as barbed fishhooks and fish spears, also are known.

Another innovation of the Upper Paleolithic is the eyed needle, which first appeared about 25,000 years ago (Figure 15.12). It usually was made of bone or ivory. Many presume that the needle was used to make waterproof tailored clothing similar to that commonly worn by contemporary people living in high northern latitudes. Evidence of European Upper Paleolithic clothing also comes from images of clothed humans found in some cave paintings and in sculptures, beads that were probably sewn onto shirts and pants, and the presence of stone tools that appear to have been used for working hides. The impression of woven material made in wet clay reveals the existence of weaving 27,000 to 25,000 years ago. Woven materials may have been used for clothing or flexible baskets.

Figure 15.13 Venus Figurine
The Venus of Willendorf, from Austria, 11.1 centimeters (4.3 inches) high.

compound tool A tool that is composed of several parts, for example, a harpoon.

Art of the Upper Paleolithic

The Upper Paleolithic is characterized by a variety of artistic methods and styles. Paintings and engravings can be seen developing from early beginnings to the colorful and skillful renderings of the Magdalenian peoples. Realistic, stylized, and geometric modes were used.

Paleolithic art also found its expression in the rare modeling of clay; sculpturing in rock, bone, ivory, and antler; and painting and engraving on large surfaces such as cave walls, as well as on small objects. Utensils were decorated, but perhaps the most interesting works are the statues and cave paintings.

Some of the most famous statuaries are the statues called **Venus figurines,** which were carved in the round from a variety of materials. Although they are only a few centimeters high, some figures have extremely exaggerated breasts and buttocks and very stylized heads, hands, and feet (Figure 15.13). Perhaps they represent pregnant women, motherhood, or fertility. Upper Paleolithic artists also made models of animals, including the famous set of clay figures of a bison, a bull, a cow, and a calf that were found deep in a cave in France. The earliest Upper Paleolithic sculptures date to about 32,000 B.P. Painting was developing at about the same time.

Upper Paleolithic cave art is found in France, Spain, Italy, the south Urals, Australia, and other parts of the world. Dates of older than 32,000 years have been proposed for some cave art.

For the most part, the subject matter of cave art is animals, although humans also are depicted. These were hunting peoples, and we might suppose that the art expressed their relationship to the fauna that supported them (Figure 15.14). Several hypotheses have been suggested to explain the meaning of cave art.

Some researchers believe that most representations of nature served magical purposes. This conclusion is based on several facts. First, some cave paintings are found in almost

See the Online Learning Center for an Internet Activity on Paleolithic art.

Venus figurines Small Upper Paleolithic statues characterized by exaggerated breasts and buttocks and very stylized heads, hands, and feet.

See the Online Learning Center for an Internet Activity on the cave art of France.

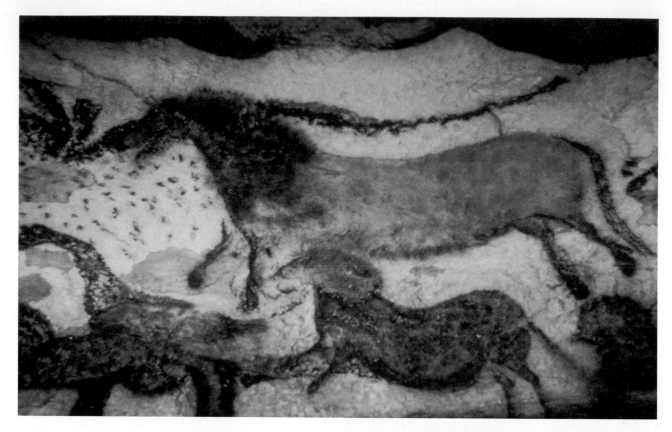

Figure 15.14 Cave Art Herd of horses, Lascaux Cave, Perigord, Dordogne, France.

imitative magic A type of magic that is based on the belief that one can affect an actual entity such as a person or animal by manipulating the image of that entity.

inaccessible areas of caves. Perhaps rituals, not open to the majority of the people, were performed using the paintings and engravings. For example, some modern societies believe that if a person harms an image of an animal or a person, the act will have a similar effect on the real animal or person. This is called **imitative magic.** An Upper Paleolithic shaman may have performed similar rituals so that the animal depicted would be weakened and therefore would be easier to capture and kill.

Other investigators see no evidence of imitative magic. They suggest that the cave may have acted as a meeting place where people shared information on hunting. A cave, Grotte Chauvet, contains hundreds of animal images, many of which are not of food animals (Box 15-1). Thus, at least for the people who created these images, some of the art seems to have had no relation to hunting, magical or otherwise. Still other caves contain ancient footprints of men, women, and children. This suggests that entire groups, not just specific individuals such as shamans, visited the galleries. Perhaps the artworks served primarily aesthetic purposes.

The decoding of the meaning of ancient pictures and other symbols may prove to be illusive. If archaeologists 20,000 years from now were to find evidence of late twentieth century objects, would they be able to determine what these objects mean to us today? A logo representing a company performing tune-ups on automobiles might be interpreted as an important religious symbol. One thing does seem likely. The people who made the paintings were attempting to develop symbolic and descriptive ways of transmitting and storing information. This would be manifested later in the development of writing systems.

Upper Paleolithic Cultural Traditions

The Upper Paleolithic tool technologies of Europe often are divided into five traditions, which are, from earliest to most recent, Châteperronian, Aurignacian, Gravettian,

Until 1995, the most spectacular of the approximately 300 caves known to contain Upper Paleolithic paintings was Lascaux Cave in France. In 1942, the Lascaux cave paintings were accidentally discovered by four boys searching for hidden treasure. One of the boys, Jacques Marsal, was so impressed by the cave's 80 multicolored paintings and 1500 engravings that as an adult he became the curator of the cave, one of France's major tourist attractions. Marsal held this position until his death in 1989. Because of the deterioration of the paintings due to problems created by tourism, however, the cave is now closed to the public. In its place, a full-scale replica of the main hall, dubbed Lascaux II, has been built by the French government.

In January 1995, the French government announced that Jean-Marie Chauvet and other explorers had found an underground limestone cavern that contained about 300 Upper Paleolithic paintings and engravings. The cavern, known as Grotte Chauvet, which is located near the town of Vallon-Pont-d'Arc, is about five times larger than the cave at Lascaux, with four larger chambers yet to be explored.

The cave at Vallon-Pont-d'Arc appears to be undisturbed, and it is interesting in several ways. It contains murals of about 50 extinct mammalian species, which is more than twice as many as in all other Paleolithic caves combined. Many large animal groupings are portrayed. In other caves, animals are usually depicted individually. Hyenas, bears, lions, owls, and a panther are depicted here; they are less common in other Paleolithic caves. In other caves, the animals pictured are usually not carnivores but herbivores, which are generally harmless to people. Grotte Chauvet also contains about 40 rhinoceros paintings (see figure). Both carnivores and rhinoceroses were not food animals. Archaeologists are attempting to explain why they, and not food animals such as reindeer, are depicted on the cave walls.

The cave's explorers also found ancient human footprints, tracings of human hands, brushes, pigments, pieces of flint, evidence of the use of controlled fire, and the skeletal remains of bears. Geometric shapes such as dots and bars are found associated with the paintings.

In addition to human-made images, the cave contained a bear skull that appears to have been carefully placed on a stone slab. Was the slab an altar of some type? Some investigators have characterized the cave as a sacred place. Yet perhaps what looks sacred to a modern Westerner was something entirely different to the people who used and decorated the cave. The cave was occupied an estimated 32,000 years ago.

Sources: J.-M. Chauvet et al., *Dawn of Art: The Chauvet Cave* (London: Thames and Hudson, 1996); J. Pfeiffer, "The Emergence of Modern Humans," *Mosaic* 21 (1990), p. 20; A. Marshack, "Images of the Ice Age," *Archaeology* 48 (July/August 1995), pp. 28–39.

Cave Painting of Rhinoceros at Grotte Chauvet, France

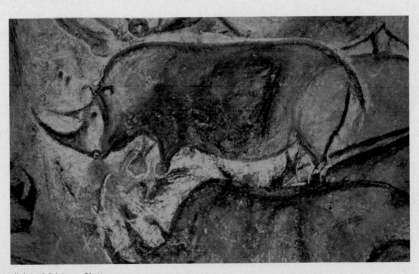

cliché n° 34 Jean Clottes

Solutrean, and Magdalenian. Much of the archaeological evidence of these traditions comes from France. We will briefly survey how these traditions manifested themselves in France.

The Châteperronian (also called the Lower Perigordian) is in many ways a transitional combination of industries. Beginning about 32,000 years ago, it contains many tools that are characteristic of the Mousterian tradition of the Neandertals. Yet mixed with these older tool types are tools that are found in the next tradition, the Aurignacian. The Aurignacian is associated only with modern peoples such as the Cro-Magnon. Beginning about 28,000 years ago, these people began making tools of bone and antler.

Bone became a very important material for the manufacture of tools. This is seen in the Gravettian tradition, beginning about 25,000 years ago. They made bone awls, punches, and points. The Solutrean, beginning about 20,000 years ago, took flint working to a high level of sophistication. The Solutreans were replaced about 17,000 to 16,000 years ago by the Magdalenians, who at first made very poorly crafted stone tools. Although the Magdalenians were not the best stone tool makers, they excelled in the use of bone and antler. They also developed Upper Paleolithic art to its peak.

Non-European Upper Paleolithic Cultures European-type assemblages are found in the Middle East, India, east Africa, the Crimea, and Siberia. On the other hand, some African traditions differed from those in Europe, and the hand ax remains the most commonly found tool. The retention of the hand ax in some parts of Africa was not an indication of backwardness; rather, it was an adjustment to forest conditions. The hand ax has a long history of development in some parts of Africa.

Recently it has been suggested that some people who lived in Africa as long as 90,000 years ago developed certain tool types, such as bone harpoon points, that are not seen in Europe until 14,000 B.P. At Katanda in Zaire, archaeologists found barbed and unbarbed bone points. These points may have been hafted to a wood shaft and used to spear fish. The Katanda people also used materials such as ocher pigment and stones that were brought in from distant localities. They may have developed a semisettled lifestyle based on fishing tens of thousands of years before people did in other parts of the world.

In east and southeast Asia, simple chopping tools were used until the end of the Paleolithic. According to one suggestion, this was the result of reliance on materials other than stone, such as bamboo, for tool manufacture.

Similarly, chopping tools and crude flake tools made up most of the stone artifacts of the natives of Australia. When the first inhabitants reached the continent about 60,000 to 40,000 years ago, they found an environment whose largest animal was the kangaroo. Australia also lacked the types of raw materials needed for producing good blade tools. Although they did have resources of bone and wood and made a variety of tools out of those materials, their overall technology was restricted by the lack of resources and by their isolation from ideas that were developing elsewhere.

Archaeology of the New World

Early inhabitants of the New World entered Alaska from Asia. Once in Alaska, where did the earliest inhabitants of the New World go? Southern Alaska, much of Canada, and the northwestern United States were covered with glacial ice, but ice-free routes were open during most of the Pleistocene through central Alaska, along the eastern foothills of the Rocky Mountains, and along the West Coast. Like Beringia, these routes provided large game for migrating hunters.

Most likely, the migrants entered the New World in very small groups. Since there was no competition for food from other human groups, the first populations in the New World increased rapidly in size and range. According to some estimates, the founding population in America could theoretically have been as small as 25 people. Such calculations are interesting, but they are not direct evidence of what actually occurred. Some evidence does exist that people moved across Beringia more than once. Each migration may have been very small, but every time a new group entered the New World, its members would have brought with them a new influx of genes and gene combinations.

Most New World sites contain cultural remains only; skeletal material dated before 11,500 B.P. is extremely rare. One of the many candidates for a pre-13,200-year-old date is Meadowcroft Rockshelter in Pennsylvania. This site contains flakes, a projectile point, and other tools from a level that has been dated by radiocarbon dating to 16,000 to 11,000 B.P. A possible basket fragment comes from an even lower level; it is dated at 19,000 ± 2400 years. The dates have been questioned because of possible contamination of the site by naturally occurring coal. The coal is derived from ancient trees, and it has lost all of its radioactive carbon. The nonradioactive carbon from these trees, dissolved in water, may have mixed with the carbon in the basket and other organic material in the level. If this occurred, the older carbon would make the artifacts appear older than they really are.

Another possible early site is Orogrande Cave in southern New Mexico, which is dated at 27,000 B.P. The evidence includes what archaeologist Richard MacNeish believes is a human palm print on a piece of fire-baked clay. Other archaeologists are not yet convinced of the antiquity of the print or even that it was made by a human. Recently, dates of 18,000 to 12,260 B.P. have been suggested for sites in the Mojave Desert and the Petrified Forest in Arizona. While finds from Kansas, Pennsylvania, New Mexico, California, Arizona, Virginia, and other areas of the New World suggest the possibility of pre–13,200 B.P. dates for humans in the New World, archaeological finds from Clovis, New Mexico, provide the oldest agreed-upon dates for people in the New World. The finds from Clovis and surrounding sites date from 13,200 to 12,800 B.P.

Early sites also are known from South America. In general, the great tropical forests of South America are seen as having been uninhabitable until the advent of horticulture, yet recently archaeologists located stratified Paleoindian deposits in association with a painted sandstone cave at Caverna da Pedra Pintada in the state of Monte Alegre, Brazil. They recovered 24 tools and more than 30,000 flakes, which included triangular, stemmed bifacial points. Both conventional dating and the accelerator mass spectrometry method of radiocarbon dating were used to date many plant samples, from which the investigators estimate that the site was first occupied from about 11,200 to 10,500 B.P. Thousands of carbonized fruits and wood fragments also were found. These provide evidence as to the food resources of the occupants of the site. One familiar food resource is the Brazil nut. Remains of bone and shell testify to a diverse diet obtained from animal sources.

A very important South American site is Monte Verde, in south-central Chile. Dated at about 14,000 B.P., the site contains primitive structures, stone and wood tools, and fire pits. The date for Monte Verde is accepted by most New World archaeologists, but not by all.

Folsom and Clovis Points Just as fossils are not found in the chronological order in which they were deposited, neither are artifacts. In 1926, a cowboy discovered "arrowheads" near the town of Folsom, New Mexico; these and similar artifacts are now called Folsom points. These artifacts are associated with an extinct type of bison (Figure 15.15). Radiocarbon dating places the bison and artifacts at between 13,200 and 12,800 B.P. In the light of current speculation on relatively early dates for the first Americans, a date of about 13,000 years ago might not seem startling. Yet in the 1920s, the belief was that humans had not been in North America anywhere near that long.

In 1932, another important "arrowhead" find was made in New Mexico when blade tools were discovered near the town of Clovis; these Clovis points are larger than the later Folsom points. The term "arrowhead" is placed in quotation marks because neither the Folsom nor the Clovis points were really arrowheads, nor were they spearheads; they were used to tip lances. A lance is a weapon that is held and repeatedly thrust into the prey. On the other hand, a spear is made to be thrown, not held, and it often has barbs to keep it from falling out of the prey animal.

Both the Folsom and Clovis points are **fluted;** that is, each type has a rounded groove in the shaft of the point (Figure 15.16). This furrow made hafting of the wood lance shaft to its point easier. With the possible exception of a point found in Siberia, fluted points are not found in other parts of the world, and they are assumed to be an American invention. Clovis and Folsom assemblages are the most common tool types

fluted Referring to fluted points where a rounded groove has been made in the shaft of the point, most likely to facilitate hafting.

Figure 15.15 Folsom Point A Folsom point in association with ribs of extinct bison, Folsom, New Mexico.

Figure 15.16 Clovis Points This is a sample of Clovis points from sites in Arizona. These sharp points, made from minerals such as chert and quartzite, could penetrate even the thick hides of the mammoths that were hunted by the Clovis people.

found from about 13,200 to 9000 B.P. Clovis and similar kinds of points have been found in all U.S. states except Hawaii, and their distribution extends from the Arctic to South America.

The Clovis and Folsom people were basically hunters of large game. The Clovis people, whose remains first appeared in the western United States, hunted mammoths. They appear to have followed the herds eastward, ultimately reaching the northeast coast. However, the mammoth declined to the point of extinction, perhaps due to overhunting, and in the Great Plains and the Rocky Mountain valleys, the Folsom tradition replaced that of the Clovis people. Bison were the mainstay of the Folsom hunters.

Summary

The Upper Paleolithic traditions generally represent an increase in the percentage of blade tools over time; sometimes these blades were hafted to ax or spear handles. In addition to stone tools, tools of bone, antler, horn, and ivory became more varied and complex than those of earlier times. *H. sapiens* may have been the first big-game hunters.

In the Upper Paleolithic, artistic development showed mastery of both painting and sculpting, as well as the use of complex symbols. Large cave paintings were expertly executed in western Europe and east to the Urals; small objects also were decorated, and numerous small statues were produced. Although some art may have been created for its own sake, most of this early art may have had symbolic significance. Some "decorations" may actually be calendrical, mathematical, or even writing systems.

The earliest established New World lithic industries are the Folsom and Clovis, which have been dated to about 13,200 and 12,800 B.P. These unique fluted points are not found in other parts of the world. The Clovis people were hunters of mammoth, while the later Folsom hunters relied on bison. Many pre-Clovis dates have been suggested. One of the firmest is that for Monte Verde in Chile. It is dated at 14,000 B.P. or slightly earlier.

POST-PLEISTOCENE *HOMO SAPIENS*

The Pleistocene ended about 10,000 years ago. A few thousand years before, human populations in some parts of the world entered a period of rapid sociocultural change. Paleolithic cultures were replaced by other types of cultures and, ultimately, modern agricultural and industrial societies.

The Mesolithic: Transition from Hunting-Gathering to Farming

The changes from a hunting-gathering existence to a farming economy did not occur overnight. The dependence on group living, along with the biological and technological developments, created a potential for new systems of subsistence. This potential began to be expressed at an increased pace in the period between the retreat of the last glaciers and the advent of agricultural communities, a period known as the **Mesolithic.**

During the Mesolithic, societies began to utilize the land around them more intensively. The last part of the Upper Paleolithic was characterized by enormous herds of large mammals in the grasslands of Eurasia, but about 12,000 years ago, climatic changes began to occur that ultimately converted these grasslands into forests. With the advance of the forests came the disappearance of the herds; they were replaced by less abundant and more elusive animals such as elk, red deer, and wild pigs.

Mesolithic A cultural stage characterized by generalized hunting and gathering and the advent of farming.

Box 15-2   "Man's Best Friend"

In the United States today there are about 50 million domesticated dogs. Some of these dogs fulfill utilitarian functions: guide dogs, guard dogs, police dogs, and hunting dogs. Most dogs, however, are pets and companions. Dogs are so much a part of our culture that there is now a Dog Genome Project similar to the Human Genome Project discussed in Chapter 3. A goal of this project is to learn how the different breeds of dog evolved.

Domestic dogs derived from gray wolves, which can still breed with domesticated dogs. In fact, most experts classify dogs in the same species, *Canis lupus,* as wolves; dogs are placed in the subspecies *Canis lupus familiaris.*

Why were dogs domesticated? There are many ideas on this. One scenario is that in areas where forestation had occurred,

hunters had to play hide-and-seek with well-hidden animals. The domestication of the dog may have been the result of the increased pressures of hunting in dense, dark forests. As we discussed in the chapters on primates and the fossil record, the development of a refined visual sense in primates was accompanied by a decrease in the sense of smell. The wolf's nose seems to have been employed by people to sniff out nonvisible prey. By 14,000 to 10,000 years ago, the wolf already had been domesticated in such widespread places as southwestern Asia, Japan, Iran, England, Illinois, and Idaho.

Source: R. Mestel, "Ascent of the Dog," *Discover,* October 1994, pp. 90–98.

Along with changes in hunting patterns came an intense exploitation of aquatic resources, and Mesolithic sites often are found near seas, lakes, and rivers. A characteristic type of site is the **shell midden,** a large mound composed of shells, which provides evidence of the emphasis on shellfish as a food resource. Fishing was an important activity, and remains of boats and nets from this period have been recovered. Waterfowl also made up an important part of the diet in many areas.

shell midden A large mound composed of shells, which provides evidence of the emphasis on shellfish as a food resource.

In addition, people began to exploit the plant resources of their habitats intensively. Much of this exploitation was made possible by the development of a technology for processing vegetable foods that cannot be eaten in their natural state; for example, the milling stone and the mortar and pestle were used to break up seeds and nuts. Storage and container vessels found in Mesolithic sites allowed for easy handling of small and pulverized foods (Figure 15.17). Out of this utilization of plant resources, farming developed.

The Origins of Farming

domestication The control of the reproductive cycle of plants and animals.

Domestication involves the control of the reproductive cycle of plants and animals. Through the use of farming techniques, people were able to plant and harvest large quantities of food in specific areas; in time, they selected the best food-producing plants to breed. Domestication thus led to selection initiated by humans, which over the centuries has created new varieties of plants. Many theories have been proposed regarding the origins of plant domestication, but the important point to note is that farming was probably not a deliberate invention. It most likely arose from an intensive utilization of and dependence on plant material, a pattern that developed out of Mesolithic economies.

Current evidence suggests that hunter-gatherers first domesticated rye in the Near East as long as 13,000 years ago. However, people living in the Near East did not become dependent on farming until about 10,000 years ago. In addition to its development in this Near East location, plant and animal domestication developed in other areas of the Old World and in Mexico and Peru. Domestication occurred independently in the Near East and the New World, and perhaps in southeast Asia and west Africa as well.

Although the development of farming has been seen as the great revolution leading to modern civilization, we must emphasize that farming was a revolution in potential only. Many hunting-gathering peoples rejected farming because it would have brought about a decline in their standard of living. For example, even in a semiarid region during a drought, the food supply of the San of South Africa is reliable and plentiful (Chapter 10). The farming and pastoral communities are the ones that suffer the most in such times.

Origins of Domestication in the New World The origins of domestication always have been thought to have been much earlier in the Old World than in the New World. Old World plant domestication has been placed at about 13,000 years ago; plant domestication in the New World has been thought to have begun between 6000 and 3500 years ago. However, evidence suggests a date for squash seeds and stems as early as 10,000 B.P. These squash parts, from a cave at Oaxaca, Mexico, show signs of domestication, such as thicker stems than are found in wild squash.

If the antiquity of this sample is correct, domestication in the New World started thousands of years before the currently accepted date. Yet there is little evidence that any plants other than squash were domesticated at this time; beans and maize were domesticated much later. Perhaps the transition from hunting and gathering to farming in the New World was somewhat longer than in the Old World. In the latter areas, farming was in full swing by about 2700 years after initial domestication. Of course, a perceived gap in time between initial domestication and full-scale farming in either the Old World or the New World may be simply due to a lack of evidence rather than an actual delay.

The Neolithic

Ultimately, in some areas over a period of thousands of years, and sometimes quickly, food production came to dominate hunting and gathering in many parts of the world. With farming came an increase in the frequency of village life. This stage of human history is called the **Neolithic.**

The Neolithic was a time of great change in both technology and social organization. Although some people who were predominantly hunters and gatherers cultivated some crops or altered the terrain to encourage the growth of wild plants, it was the shift to full-scale farming that ushered in great changes. By producing food in one place rather than searching for it, societies developed a more settled pattern of existence. Farming meant that more food could be acquired in less space, and as a result, population densities increased. This led to the interaction of greater numbers of people, and thus it brought about a greater exchange of ideas and an increase in innovation, which is dependent on such exchanges.

The Neolithic was characterized by the elaboration of tools for food preparation: querns, milling stones, mortars, and pestles. Pottery, used only rarely by nonfarming peoples, became refined and varied, and the techniques of weaving and spinning cloth were developed (Figure 15.18).

Most Neolithic villages were small, self-sufficient farming communities. During the Neolithic, many technological and social systems were being developed that would later be important in the first civilizations. This can be seen at the settlement of Çatalhüyük in Turkey, which dates from 8500 to 7700 B.P.

At Çatalhüyük, timber, obsidian, marble, stalactite, and shell all were imported, and skillfully made artifacts attest to the development of occupational specialization. Wooden bowls and boxes, jewelry, bone awls, daggers, spearheads, lance heads, arrowheads, ladles, spoons, spatulas, hooks and pins, and obsidian mirrors, as well as other beautifully made

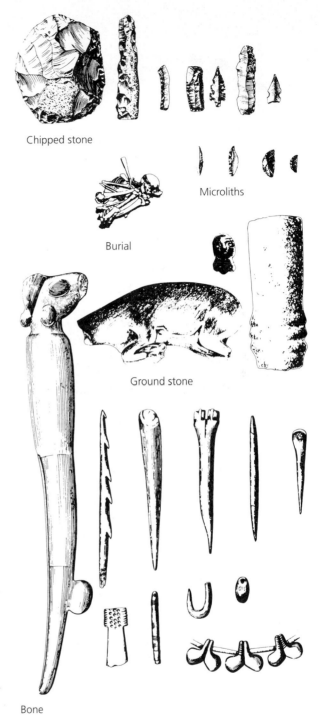

Chipped stone

Microliths

Burial

Ground stone

Bone

Figure 15.17 Mesolithic Artifacts Various artifacts from the Mesolithic of Palestine (Natufian), ca. 10,000 B.P.

Neolithic A cultural stage marked by established farming.

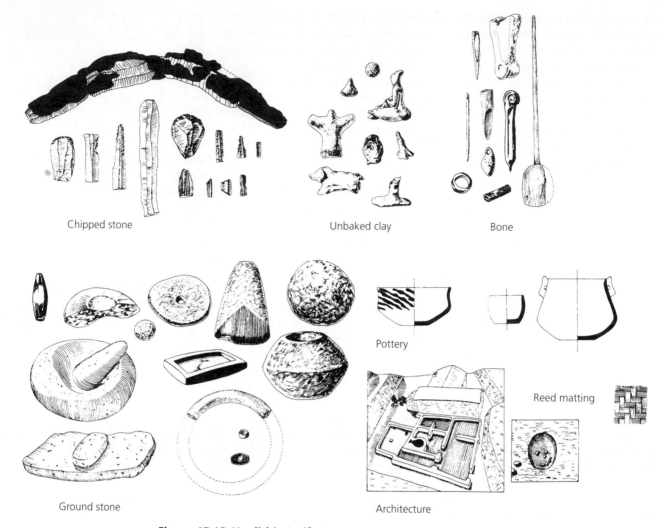

Chipped stone

Unbaked clay

Bone

Ground stone

Pottery

Reed matting

Architecture

Figure 15.18 Neolithic Artifacts Various artifacts from the Neolithic of Jarmo, Iraq, ca. 8750 B.P.

See the Online Learning Center for an Internet Activity on Çatalhüyük.

objects, contributed to a rich material inventory. The residents at Çatalhüyük lived in plastered mud-brick houses that were contiguous to one another; they entered them from the roof. Murals painted on the walls depicted animals, hunters, and dancers, and statues portrayed gods and goddesses, as well as cattle.

Because Çatalhüyük may have had a population as high as 10,000 people, early research saw it as a highly organized community with centralized authority. New archaeological investigations, which began in the 1990s, question the nature of the social organization at Çatalhüyük. The data suggest that Çatalhüyük was made up of groups of extended families that were relatively autonomous. This view would place this settlement in a transitional phase between the more or less autonomous social pattern of hunters and gatherers and that of the more centralized farming societies. Excavations on this site continue and perhaps will provide a clear picture of the life at this Neolithic village.

The Rise of Civilization

For the vast majority of prehistory, that time before the first true writing, hominins lived in small bands. Their population densities were generally under one person per square mile. Leaders led by example and reputation. The bands' subsistence depended on combinations of hunting, fishing, gathering, and scavenging.

Then, about 13,000 years ago, evidence of the first domestication of plants appears. Beginning in the Middle East, plant and animal domestication gradually came to dominate earlier subsistence patterns, and the first civilizations arose. A **civilization** is a society in which the population density is higher than in earlier systems. The right to lead is often hereditary and absolute. There are considerable differences in access to power, wealth, and prestige. Technology is far advanced from that of band societies.

There are many thoughts on the origins of civilization, but one of the major factors involved was the increase in population. Techniques such as irrigation and flood control made farming possible in special areas such as the floodplain of the Tigris and Euphrates rivers, and this supported large populations. Once populations reached a certain number, which was dependent on environmental and social variables, the older patterns of social organization broke down and new ones developed. In the older systems, each individual participated in food production, and all members maintained a similar standard of living. Kinship served as the cornerstone of social organization. These patterns were replaced by the occupational division of labor, class systems, political and religious hierarchies, public works such as road and public building construction, codes of law, markets, new forms of warfare, and urban centers. Allied with these important sociological traits were material traits such as monumental architecture, the development of science, and, in many cases, metallurgy and writing systems.

The earliest civilization, Sumer, developed in the Middle East. During this period, known as the **Bronze Age** of the Old World, people first developed the art of metallurgy. Civilizations also arose in other parts of the Old World: first in Egypt, China, and India and later in Europe and sub-Saharan Africa. In addition, civilization also developed independently in the New World—in Mexico, Peru, and adjacent areas.

Because of increased food supplies and the increased number of children a family could take care of, populations increased rapidly with the development of the Neolithic and Bronze Age cultures. A couple living in a mobile society usually can deal with only one infant at a time because the mother has to carry the infant everywhere and the child normally nurses until five years of age or later. Until the infant walks and is weaned, a second child would be a great burden. In contrast, a farming couple can usually support a large family with babies born only a year apart. Even today, it is not unusual for an Amish farming family in the United States to have 10 or more children; these children become valued farmworkers.

In the Old World, the Bronze Age was followed by the **Iron Age.** This period saw the rise and fall of great empires, as well as the shift of power from the Middle East to Greece and Rome, and then to western Europe. The 1700s marked the beginning of the **Industrial Age,** which led directly to the modern civilizations of today.

civilization A type of society with relatively high population density; based on the de-emphasis of kinship as a method of social control and the rise of central authority in the form of a government and powerful priesthood. Civilizations often also include monumental architecture, writing, mathematics, public works, and full-time armies.

Bronze Age The stage of cultural history that includes the earliest civilizations and the development of metallurgy.

Iron Age A cultural stage characterized by the use of iron as the main metal.

Industrial Age A cultural stage characterized by the first use of complex machinery, factories, urbanization, and other economic and general social changes from strictly agricultural societies.

Summary

Humans were exclusively foragers and scavengers for the vast majority of prehistory. About 13,000 years ago, domestication of plants and animals became a subsistence option for the people in the Near East. Plant and animal domestication spread widely throughout the Old World; it was independently developed in the New World. In most parts of the world, the foraging way of life was gradually replaced by farming. Some foraging societies, however, still exist.

In the places where farming and raising animals occurred, settlement patterns changed, sometimes gradually, from nomadic to settled, and population size increased dramatically. Ultimately, the kinship-based organization of society was supplemented by government control. Cities arose to produce goods, to distribute those goods and farm products, and to ship excesses to other societies. Cities also served as religious and political centers. Writing, mathematics, science, and metallurgy became features of most developing civilizations. In addition, animals were "drafted" to do farmwork such as pulling plows. Eventually, beginning in the eighteenth century, human power and animal power were joined by machine power, and the Industrial Age was born.

Key Terms

Beringia, *407*
blade, *411*
Bronze Age, *423*
civilization, *423*
compound tool, *412*
domestication, *420*
fluted, *417*

imitative magic, *414*
Industrial Age, *423*
Iron Age, *423*
Mesolithic, *419*
Neolithic, *421*
regional continuity
   model, *404*

replacement model, *403*
shell midden, *420*
shovel-shaped incisors, *400*
tundra, *410*
Venus figurines, *413*

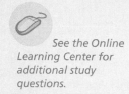

*See the Online
Learning Center for
additional study
questions.*

Study Questions

1. What are some of your ideas on where and when *H. sapiens* appears in the fossil record?

2. How do the replacement model and the regional continuity model of the origin of *H. sapiens* differ from each other? What is the evolutionary role of the Neandertals in each of these models?

3. What is the "Out of Africa Again and Again Model"? How does it differ from the earlier models?

4. What are the current ideas about the migration of *Homo sapiens* into North and South America?

5. Who is Kennewick Man? What does the debate over the fossils involve?

6. Discuss the cultural innovations of the Upper Paleolithic.

7. To what do the terms *Mesolithic* and *Neolithic* refer? What characterizes each of these cultural stages?

8. In what area of the world did plant domestication first originate? Where else did it develop independently?

9. How did the first civilizations differ from the Neolithic farming societies?

Critical Thinking Questions

1. Think about what it means to be human. What do you believe differentiates you from your pet dog or cat? What physical and behavioral characteristics make you different not only from the dog or cat but from archaic hominins? Or are the differences between us and other animals, both living and extinct, matters of relative distinction only?

2. You have read about the regional continuity concept and the replacement concept. Does one of these make more sense to you than the other? If so, why? What might be other alternatives to these two ideas?

3. Hominins can be defined on the basis of anatomical as well as behavioral features, as revealed in the archaeological record. Does there appear to be a correlation between specific fossil hominin species and particular behavioral traits? Do different hominin species differ solely in their biology, or do they also differ in their behavior?

Suggested Readings

The following handbooks list individual fossils along with pertinent information:

Day, M. *Guide to Fossil Man: A Handbook of Human Paleontology,* 4th ed. Chicago: University of Chicago Press, 1991.

Larsen, C. S., R. M. Matter, and D. L. Gebo. *Human Origins: The Fossil Record,* 3rd ed. Prospect Heights, IL: Waveland, 1998.

Whitehead, P. F., W. K. Sacco, and S. B. Hochgraf. *A Photographic Atlas of Physical Anthropology.* Englewood, CO: Morton Publishing, 2005. Chapter 8 has numerous photographs and drawings of the fossils mentioned in this chapter.

Also recommended are the following:

Brace, C. L. *The Stages of Human Evolution,* 5th ed. New York: Prentice Hall, 1995. This edition of a book first published in 1967 is a detailed inventory of hominin fossils with chapters on evolutionary theory.

Conroy, G. C. *Reconstructing Human Origins: A Modern Synthesis.* New York: Norton, 1998. This text presents an overview and synthesis of our current knowledge of the human fossil record.

Fagan, B. M. *Seventy Great Inventions of the Ancient World.* London: Thames & Hudson, 2005. This book is a celebration of hominin inventiveness, starting with the first stone tool.

Tattersall, I. *Human Odyssey: Four Million Years of Human Evolution.* Lincoln, NE: iUniverse, 2002. This volume is based on the displays at the American Museum of Natural History and includes over 125 illustrations.

Williams, S. *Fantastic Archaeology: The Wild Side of North American Prehistory.* Philadelphia: University of Pennsylvania Press, 1991. This book explores the misinterpretations of North American archaeological data as well as outright hoaxes, followed by an up-to-date summary of the prehistory of the Americas.

Suggested Websites

Great Archaeological Sites:
www.culture.gouv.fr/culture/arcnat/en

The Hominid Index:
www.modernhumanorigins.com/hominids.html

Human Evolution at the Smithsonian Institution:
www.mnh.si.edu/anthro/humanorigins/ha/a_tree.html

Institute for Ice Age Studies (Paleolithic Art):
www.insticeagestudies.com/library.html

Kennewick Man Virtual Interpretive Center:
www.kennewick-man.com

The Leakey Foundation:
www.leakeyfoundation.org

Chapter 16

The Biology of Modern *Homo sapiens*

Taking anthropometric measurements of the Efe Pygmies of the Ituri Forest, Democratic Republic of Congo.

The genetic basis of man's capacity to acquire, develop or modify, and transmit culture emerged because of the adaptive advantages which this capacity conferred on its possessors. •

—Theodosius Dobzhansky (1900–1975)

Chapter Outline

Human Adaptability: Adjustments
Behavioral Adjustments
Acclimatory Adjustments
Developmental Adjustments
Summary

Human Adaptation
The Nature of Skin Color
Adaptation and Body Build
Summary

The Nature of Human Growth and Development
Growth and Development of the Human Body
Puberty
Control of Growth and Development
The Secular Trend in Growth and Development
The Adult Skeleton
Summary

See the Online Learning Center for a chapter summary, chapter outline, and learning objectives.

After Reading This Chapter, You Should Be Able to Answer These Questions:

1. What is the difference between an adjustment and an adaptation?

2. What are the three basic types of adjustments, and how do they differ from one another?

3. How does the body adjust to Arctic habitats, desert habitats, and high-altitude habitats?

4. "Differences in skin color evolved as a means of adapting to different environments." How would you explain this statement?

5. How do certain aspects of body build represent adaptations to different environments?

6. What is the difference between the concept of growth and that of development?

7. How does bone growth occur?

8. How is puberty defined? What are some of the landmarks of growth and development that occur during puberty? What are the differences in the growth and development of males and females during puberty?

9. Why are there differences in the patterns of growth and development from person to person? In other words, what affects growth and development?

A common dream, which has served as the plot of more than one novel, involves viewing or meeting an exact duplicate of oneself who lives in another place or time. This "second self" can be no more than illusory. Except for identical twins and the possibility of clones, genetic variables alone reduce the probability that two people can be exactly the same to all but zero. Even identical twins show variation due to differences in their environments.

There are three principal mechanisms that bring about variation among individuals and populations. The first is nongenetic means of coping with the environment called adjustments: Behavioral adjustments are cultural responses to environmental stress, acclimatory adjustments are reversible physiological responses to such stress, and developmental adjustments are alterations in the pattern of growth and development. The second mechanism that brings about variation is microevolutionary change or adaptation. Finally, there are genetic differences in the processes of growth and development. These mechanisms are the subjects of this chapter.

HUMAN ADAPTABILITY: ADJUSTMENTS

Physiologically, humans are animals who evolved under conditions in the tropics. Yet today human populations occupy a wide range of habitats, from the equatorial deserts of north Africa to the icy wastelands of the Arctic.

adjustment The ability of humans to survive in stressful environments by nongenetic means.

One reason that the human species survives in a wide diversity of habitats is nongenetic changes termed **adjustments.** However, the genetic potentials that allow for nongenetic adjustments are themselves the products of the evolutionary process. A major problem facing researchers in this area is the determination of the relative importance of genetic and nongenetic forms of adaptability, which we have termed here adaptation and adjustment, respectively. In fact, in most situations, both processes are working together.

Behavioral Adjustments

behavioral adjustment Survival in a stressful environment made possible by cultural means, primarily technology.

Behavioral adjustments are cultural responses to environmental stresses. Because these adjustments are nongenetic, they may be continuously altered to meet new environmental situations.

An example of how culture allows people to survive in stressful habitats is housing. The type of housing that is used in an area is influenced by such factors as temperature, humidity, wind, rain, and light. A classic example of the use of housing in a stressful habitat is the igloo of the Inuit (Figure 16.1). The igloo consists of a dome-shaped structure connected to the outside by a tunnel. The construction material is snow, which is an excellent

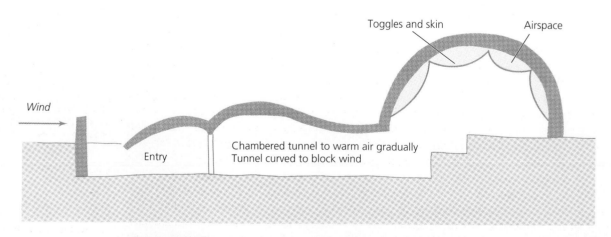

Figure 16.1 The Igloo The Inuit igloo is designed to permit people to survive in the extremely hostile Arctic environment.

insulator because air is trapped within the snow itself. Heat within the structure is produced by a small seal-oil lamp. The heat of this lamp causes the snow to melt slightly during the day and refreeze at night, forming an icy reflective layer on the inside. This reflective layer and the dome shape serve to reflect the heat throughout the igloo. Relatively little heat is lost to the outside, since the dome shape minimizes the surface area from which heat can radiate. A long entryway helps warm the air gradually as one enters the structure, and it also serves to block the entry of wind into the habitation area.

Habitation structures are only one aspect of a people's technology. It is through all aspects of technology that people can survive under difficult environmental conditions. In fact, through behavioral adjustments, humans have been able to spend limited periods of time deep under the ocean and in outer space.

Acclimatory Adjustments

Acclimatory adjustments are reversible physiological changes to environmental stress. Examples of acclimatization may be seen in three particularly stressful environments: the Arctic, the desert, and high altitudes.

accliatory adjustment Reversible physiological adjustments to stressful environments.

Arctic Habitats Perhaps one of the more stressful habitats occupied by humans is the Arctic. Not surprisingly, people occupied the Arctic regions late in human prehistory, and humans can become acclimatized to the climate only to a very limited degree.

The primary environmental stress in the Arctic is very low temperatures. Cold stress can lead to frostbite, an actual freezing of the tissues, which usually occurs in exposed, high-surface-area parts of the body such as fingers, toes, and earlobes. Another result of cold stress is **hypothermia,** or lowered body temperature. Normal body temperature, as measured in the mouth, averages 37°C (98.6°F). When the body temperature falls below 34.4°C (94°F), the ability of the hypothalamus of the brain to control body temperature is impaired. Temperature-regulating ability is lost at 29.4°C (85°F), and death may result.

hypothermia Lowered body temperature induced by cold stress.

Unlike other animals that occupy the Arctic, humans are not well adapted to cold stress; this fact is probably a reflection of people's tropical origins. Humans do not possess thick layers of subcutaneous fat or thick fur; in fact, the human body has remarkably little in the way of insulation. The most important factor for survival in the hostile Arctic climate is responding with behavioral adjustments, such as specialized housing, clothing, and other technologies.

While clothing and shelter provide insulation for humans in the Arctic, it is interesting to see what happens when a human is exposed to cold without the necessary behavioral adjustments. The nude human body at rest must begin to combat a lowering of body temperature when the air temperature stands at approximately 31°C (87.8°F). This temperature is known as the **critical temperature.**

critical temperature The temperature at which the body must begin to resist a lowering of body temperature; occurs in the nude human body at approximately 31°C (87.8°F).

The subject of this experiment must both increase the heat produced by the body and reduce the loss of heat to the air. Two short-term methods of producing additional body heat are exercise and shivering. As any jogger knows, a high degree of muscle activity yields heat, but such exercise can be maintained only for limited periods. More important is shivering. Low body temperature causes the hypothalamus of the brain to stimulate increased muscle tone, which, when it reaches a certain level, results in shivering. At the height of shivering, the increase in muscle metabolism can raise body heat production to five times normal, but, as with exercise, shivering cannot continue indefinitely. A major mechanism for conserving heat is peripheral **vasoconstriction.** Constriction of the capillaries in the skin prevents much of the warm blood from reaching the surface of the skin, where much of the body's heat would be lost to the air.

vasoconstriction Constriction of the capillaries in the skin in response to cold temperatures that prevents much of the warm blood from reaching the surface of the body where heat could be lost.

People living in Arctic conditions for long periods are less affected by the cold as time passes. Perhaps the most important acclimatory adjustment is in the **basal metabolic rate.** The basal metabolic rate, which represents the total energy used by the body in maintaining those body processes necessary for life, is a measure of the minimum level of heat produced by the body at rest. Under cold stress, individuals are able to acclimatize by

basal metabolic rate The measure of the total energy utilized by the body to maintain those body processes necessary for life; the minimum level of heat produced by the body at rest.

increasing their basal metabolic rate; this increase can be as much as 25 percent in adults and 170 percent in infants. The increased basal metabolic rate results in the production of additional body heat, but the production of this heat requires that individuals consume a great quantity of high-energy food sources. The native diet in Arctic regions, which consists largely of protein and fat, provides the necessary types of food.

Desert Habitats In some ways, humans are better able to survive in the hot and arid climates of the world than in the Arctic regions. This ability is due to the general lack of body hair, which, if present, would act as insulating material.

In desert habitats, the human body must get rid of excess heat that is being absorbed by the body. In general, a nude human body loses heat in any one of four ways (Figure 16.2). The first is **conduction,** which occurs when heat appears to move from a warmer object to a cooler object by direct contact. Thus, if you touch an object cooler than yourself, heat will move from your body to the cooler object. The second is **convection,** in which the warm object is surrounded by a cooler fluid, either liquid or air. A person who is hot from absorbing solar radiation will lose heat as the heat from the body is transferred to the cooler air. As the air next to the body warms up, it expands, and expanding air rises. As the warm air rises from the skin, cooler air flows down to replace it. Thus, currents set up in the air carry away heat.

The third way in which an object can rid itself of heat is by **radiation.** Radiation represents electromagnetic energy that is given off by an object as electromagnetic waves of a characteristic wavelength. Other forms of electromagnetic waves include visible light, ultraviolet radiation, and radio waves.

The fourth way in which an object can lose heat is through **evaporation.** When water is turned from a liquid to a gas, in this case water vapor, a certain amount of energy, in the form of heat, is required. Therefore, when you get out of the swimming pool on a warm day, you feel cool because some of your body heat is being used in the process of transforming the pool water left on your skin into water vapor.

While conduction, convection, radiation, and evaporation are used by the human body to rid itself of excess heat in warm climates, in air temperatures above 35°C (95°F), body heat is lost primarily through evaporation. Therefore, **sweating** is the most important method of controlling body temperature in warm climates. Humans have a greater capacity to sweat than does any other mammal.

Humans have a high density of sweat glands over their bodies, although the number of sweat glands per square centimeter does differ in different parts of the body. Interestingly, people who go to live in desert environments do not develop additional sweat glands; the number of sweat glands does not differ significantly between desert- and nondesert-dwelling populations.

Acclimatizing to desert life is not well understood, but within a few weeks, people living in hot, arid climates seem to reach some type of acclimatory adjustment. In time, the sweat glands become more sensitive and produce more sweat. Of course, sweat is not all water; it also contains salts, and much sodium is lost through sweating. With time,

conduction The movement of heat from one object to another by direct contact.

convection Movement of heat from an object to the surrounding fluid, either gas or liquid; heat causes the gases and fluid to move away from the object.

radiation Electromagnetic energy that is given off by an object.

evaporation Liquid is transformed into a gas utilizing energy.

sweating The production of a fluid, sweat, by the sweat glands of the skin; the evaporation of the sweat from the skin leads to a cooling of the body.

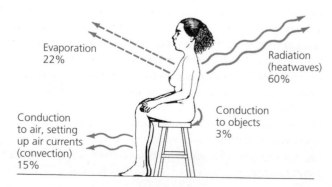

Figure 16.2 Heat Loss in a Nude Human Figure This figure illustrates the various mechanisms by which heat is lost from a nude human body at rest. The percentages refer to the contribution of each mechanism to the total heat loss.

Evaporation 22%

Radiation (heatwaves) 60%

Conduction to air, setting up air currents (convection) 15%

Conduction to objects 3%

the concentration of salt in sweat is reduced, and the relatively high salt concentrations found in desert water usually compensate for salt loss. Urine volume is also reduced, thus helping the body conserve the water so badly needed for sweating. The same acclimatization ability has been found in peoples from all parts of the world. It appears to represent a basic ability of the human species instead of an adaptation of certain populations.

In addition, there are other short-term responses to increased heat loads. A physiological response is **vasodilation** of the capillaries of the skin. In vasodilation, the bloodstream brings more heat to the body's surface as the capillaries of the skin dilate; then the heat is removed by sweating. People also can make a number of behavioral adjustments to hot climates. In desert regions people reduce physical activity during the heat of the day, thereby reducing heat production by the body. Also, desert-dwelling people adopt a relaxed body posture that increases the surface area of the body from which sweat may evaporate.

> **vasodilation** Opening up of the capillaries of the skin in response to warm temperatures, increasing the flow of blood to the surface of the body and thereby increasing the loss of body heat.

Adjustment to hot climates is aided by cultural factors such as clothing and shelter. Desert dwellers cover their bodies to protect the skin from sunlight and reduce the amount of heat from the sun that directly heats the body. Their clothing is designed to permit the free flow of air between the clothing and the body. This airflow is necessary to carry off the water vapor formed by the evaporation of sweat.

It is interesting to note that the color of clothing does not seem to make much difference in hot climates. An experiment involving black and white Bedouin robes showed that the black robes gained about $2^1/2$ times as much heat as the white robes. Yet the temperature of the skin under black robes is the same as that under white robes. Most likely, the greater convection currents between the black robe and the skin are responsible for this phenomenon.

See the Online Learning Center for an Internet Activity on high-altitude habitats.

High-Altitude Habitats Many people experience **high-altitude,** or **mountain, sickness** when they travel into the mountains. The symptoms of high-altitude sickness may include "shortness of breath, respiratory distress, physical and mental fatigue, rapid pulse rate, interrupted sleep, and headaches intensified by activity. There may also occur some slight digestive disorders and in some cases a marked loss of weight. In other cases the individual may feel dyspnea, nausea, and vomiting."[1] Although most people eventually become acclimatized to high altitude, many do not. They continue to suffer from chronic mountain sickness as long as they remain at high altitude.

> **high-altitude (mountain) sickness** Includes shortness of breath, physical and mental fatigue, rapid pulse rate, headaches; occurs in persons not acclimatized to high altitudes.

Less than 1 percent of the world's population lives at high altitude, yet these people are of great interest to anthropologists. High-altitude environments pose many stresses on human populations, including low oxygen levels, high levels of solar radiation, cold, high winds, and, often, lack of moisture, rough terrain, and limited plant and animal life.

Our previous discussions of Arctic and desert environments stressed the great importance of culture as a means of adjustment to stressful environments. Culture plays a major role at high altitudes as well, and it helps people adjust to many of the environmental problems that they face. However, a major situation in which culture plays virtually no role is **high-altitude hypoxia.**

> **high-altitude hypoxia** Low oxygen pressure due to being at high altitude.

Hypoxia refers to low oxygen pressure, which occurs when low levels of oxygen are supplied to the tissues of the body. High-altitude hypoxia is one of the few environmental stresses that cannot be adjusted to by some cultural means. Although the use of oxygen tanks provides limited adjustment, this solution is available only in high-technology cultures and is practical only for short periods (Box 16-1).

The earth's atmosphere exerts an average of 1.04 kilograms of pressure on every square centimeter (14.7 pounds per square inch) of surface area at sea level. At sea level, this

---

[1] A. R. Frisancho, "Functional Adaptation to High Altitude Hypoxia," *Science* 187 (1975), p. 313. The term *dyspnea* refers to difficult or painful breathing.

Box 16-1

How High Can People Live without Bottled Oxygen?

The highest human settlement in the world is Aucanquilcha, located at an elevation of about 6000 meters (20,000 feet) in the Andes of northern Chile. It is possible for some individuals to perform at higher altitudes for short periods. "While the well-adapted climber can survive and function adequately for months at 19,000 feet, at 26,000 feet this is possible only for days, if no artificial oxygen is used."[1]

The highest place on earth is the summit of Mount Everest, which lies 8848 meters (29,028 feet) above sea level. The first humans known to stand atop Mount Everest were Edmund Hillary and Tenzing Norgay on May 29, 1953. Since then, several expeditions have reached the summit with the aid of bottled oxygen. In fact, it was believed that it was impossible for humans to climb that high without the use of bottled oxygen.

On May 9, 1978, two members of an Austrian expedition, Peter Habeler and Reinhold Messner, were the first humans to reach the top of Mount Everest without the use of bottled oxygen.[2] In 1981, the American Medical Research Expedition moved into the Himalayas to conduct research on human physiology at extreme altitudes. Research stations were established at several altitudes, and two members of the team reached the summit of Mount Everest without bottled oxygen and were able to take a limited number of physiological measurements.[3]

The symptoms of high-altitude sickness become exaggerated at extremely high altitude, even in those who have become acclimatized to some degree. Reinhold Messner describes his feelings on route to Mount Everest:

My rucksack weighed between 12 and 16 kilos [26 and 35 pounds], and to carry it was such an effort for me that it took all my strength and all the oxygen in my muscles, simply to thrust out my chest to take in air, and then to let it out again . . . I could only manage 30 or 40 steps without oxygen, and they cost me so much strength, that the possibility of my climbing Everest without oxygen didn't even enter into the question.[4]

At high altitude, mental functions begin to become impaired, as described by Peter Habeler:

Our altitude was now 28,500 feet, and we had obviously reached a point at which normal brain functions had broken down, or at least were severely limited. Our attentiveness and concentration declined; our instinct no longer reacted as reliably as before; the capacity for clear logical thinking had also apparently been lost.[5]

[1] O. Ölz, "Everest without Oxygen: The Medical Fundamentals," in P. Habeler, *The Lonely Victory* (New York: Simon & Schuster, 1979), p. 220.

[2] P. Habeler, *The Lonely Victory;* R. Messner, *Everest: Expedition to the Ultimate* (New York: Oxford University Press, 1979).

[3] J. B. West, "Human Physiology at Extreme Altitudes on Mount Everest," *Science* 223 (1984), pp. 784–788.

[4] Messner, *Everest,* p. 156.

[5] Habeler, *The Lonely Victory*, p. 183.

---

pressure raises a column of mercury in a closed tube to an average height of 760 millimeters (29.92 inches). Therefore, we say that the average air pressure at sea level is 760 millimeters (29.92 inches) of mercury.

The atmosphere is composed of many gases. Approximately 21 percent of air is oxygen; that portion of the total atmospheric pressure that is due to the pressure of oxygen is the **partial pressure** of oxygen. At sea level, the partial pressure of oxygen is 159 millimeters (6.26 inches) of mercury. As one gains altitude, the total air pressure and the partial pressure of oxygen decrease (Figure 16.3). At 4500 meters (14,765 feet), the partial pressure of oxygen decreases by as much as 40 percent, thus substantially reducing the amount of oxygen that can reach the tissues of the body.

partial pressure The pressure exerted by a particular gas in the atmosphere.

The actual entry of oxygen into the bloodstream takes place in the approximately 300 million **alveoli** of the lungs. The alveoli are small air sacs that are richly endowed with blood capillaries. Although the partial pressure of oxygen at sea level is 159 millimeters (6.26 inches) of mercury, the partial pressure of oxygen in the alveoli at sea level is 104 millimeters (4.16 inches) of mercury. This is because not all the air in the lungs is replaced with each breath. The partial pressure of oxygen in the arteries and capillaries of the circulatory system is 95 millimeters (3.80 inches) of mercury, while the partial pressure of oxygen in the tissues is 40 millimeters (1.60 inches) of mercury.

alveoli Small air sacs, located in the lungs, that are richly endowed with blood capillaries. Oxygen is absorbed by the blood in the alveoli.

Oxygen diffuses from the higher to the lower partial pressure; therefore, oxygen moves from the blood into the tissues. At high altitudes, however, where the partial pressure of

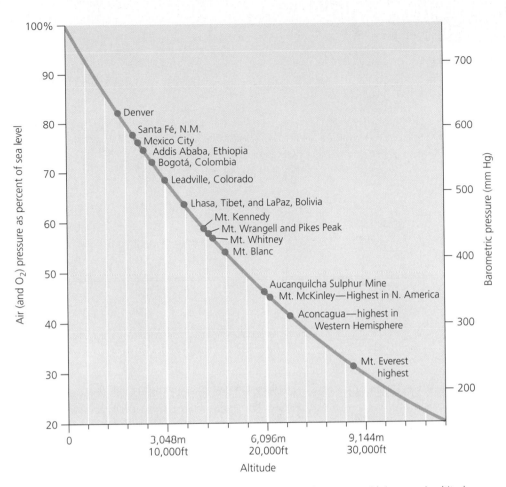

Figure 16.3 Air Pressure This graph shows the decrease in air pressure with increase in altitude.

oxygen in the atmosphere is low, the partial pressure of oxygen in the blood would be too low to allow diffusion of oxygen from the blood to the tissues unless special physiological adjustments took place. These are the adjustments that make possible human habitation of high-altitude environments.

Moving into High Altitudes When a person who normally lives near sea level first travels into high mountains, he or she will probably notice an increase in the breathing rate, which may reach twice that at sea level. The increased breathing rate brings more oxygen into the alveoli, and it helps increase the partial pressure of oxygen in the blood. This **hyperventilation,** or increased breathing rate, eventually is reduced, and it levels off as the person becomes acclimatized to the high altitude.

About 97 percent of the oxygen in the blood is carried in chemical combinations with hemoglobin in the red blood cells; the other 3 percent is dissolved in the plasma and may be ignored. The chemical association of oxygen and hemoglobin is loose and reversible. When the partial pressure of oxygen is high, as in the alveoli of the lungs, oxygen will combine with hemoglobin. When the hemoglobin reaches the capillaries, where the partial pressure of oxygen is low, the oxygen is released from the hemoglobin molecule and is free to diffuse into the cells.

When the blood leaves the lungs, the hemoglobin is about 97 percent saturated; that is, oxygen has combined with about 97 percent of the hemoglobin molecules. Some of the oxygen then is given up in the capillaries of the tissues. As a result, the hemoglobin in the veins returning to the heart and lungs is only about 70 percent saturated. At high altitudes,

hyperventilation
Increased breathing rate producing a high level of oxygen in the lungs.

Figure 16.4 Average Partial Pressure of Oxygen This chart shows the partial pressure of oxygen in the lungs and in various parts of the circulatory system, comparing individuals living at sea level (Lima, Peru) and at high altitude [Morococha, Peru, at 4540 meters (14,891 feet)].

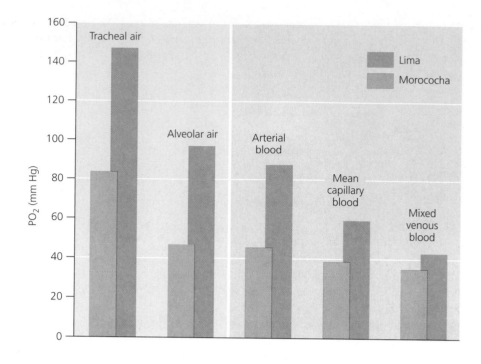

developmental adjustments Alterations in the pattern of growth and development resulting from environmental influences.

several factors operate to alter these percentages, thereby permitting the hemoglobin molecules to carry more oxygen to the tissues. For example, because of hyperventilation, the concentration of carbon dioxide in the blood decreases, thus altering the blood chemistry in such a way as to increase the amount of oxygen carried in the blood.

Many other acclimatory adjustments take place. In time, the number of capillaries in the body increases, thereby shortening the distance that the oxygen must be carried by the blood to the tissues. In addition, the number of red blood cells increases, and hence the amount of hemoglobin being carried by the blood also increases. Therefore, although the partial pressure of oxygen as it enters the lungs differs at sea level and at high altitude, the partial pressure of oxygen in the blood is not very different by the time it reaches the capillaries (Figure 16.4). Many changes also occur at the cellular level that enable cells to carry out their metabolic functions at lower oxygen levels.

While the factors discussed above permit people to live at high altitudes, people cannot overcome all the negative biological effects from high-altitude living. For example, high altitude affects reproduction; birth weights are lower, and infant mortality is greater. In addition, as we will discuss in the next section, the growth and development of children are slower.

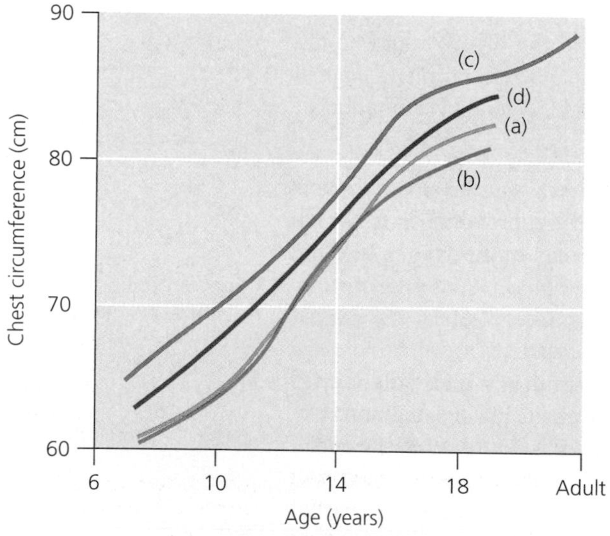

Developmental Adjustments

Some variations in the pattern of growth and development provide a means of adjustment to environmental stress. Those variations are called **developmental adjustments.** A good example of developmental adjustment can be seen in differences in growth rates involving chest circumference.

It has been known for some time that individuals who grow up at high altitudes develop greater chest circumferences than do those who grow up at lower elevations (Figure 16.5).

Figure 16.5 Chest Circumferences This graph compares the growth of chest circumference of three Peruvian populations found at (a) sea level, (b) moderate altitude of 2300 meters (7544 feet), and (c) high altitudes between 4000 and 5000 meters (13,120 and 18,040 feet). A growth curve from the United States is included for comparison (d).

This is related to greater lung volume, primarily in what is termed the **residual volume,** the amount of air remaining in the lungs after the most forceful expiration. Greater residual volume in children growing up at high altitude appears to develop as a result of a rapid and accelerated development of the lungs in childhood.

residual volume The amount of air remaining in the lungs after the most forceful expiration.

Summary

Although *Homo sapiens* is physiologically a tropical species, human populations today occupy a great variety of habitats and are able to survive under stressful environmental conditions. Adjustments are nongenetic mechanisms by which animals can survive in specific habitats.

Behavioral adjustments are cultural responses to environmental stress. The utilization of technology, such as specialized clothing, housing, and tools, and the development of particular forms of social behavior are cultural ways in which humans are able to adjust to hostile conditions.

Humans also can adjust in physical ways by means of reversible physiological responses to environmental stress; these are termed acclimatory adjustments. For example, under conditions of extreme Arctic cold, the basal metabolic rate of the body increases, resulting in an increased production of body heat. Under desert conditions, the sweat glands become more sensitive and produce more sweat; urine volume is reduced. Changes in blood chemistry permit humans to survive the dangers of hypoxia at high altitudes. Through such mechanisms, human populations have been able to spread over the earth and have come to terms with some of the earth's most difficult habitats.

A third way of coping with stressful environments is called developmental adjustments. The human body is capable of some alterations in the patterns of growth and development due to environmental conditions, as when children living at high altitude develop larger lungs to cope with low oxygen pressure.

HUMAN ADAPTATION

Microevolutionary change, or **adaptation,** is an important factor bringing about variation within and among populations. Here we will discuss two examples of adaptation in human populations: skin color and body build.

The Nature of Skin Color

People are commonly referred to as red, white, black, yellow, or brown. Yet in spite of this apparent rainbow of humanity, only one major pigment, **melanin,** is responsible for human coloring. Skin color also is affected by hemoglobin: The small blood vessels underlying the skin give lighter-skinned persons a pinkish cast. The larger the number of blood vessels, the greater the influence of hemoglobin on skin color.

Melanin is produced in the outermost layers of the skin, the **epidermis** (Figure 16.6). The pigment is produced in specialized cells called **melanocytes.** People with dark skin and people with light skin have, on the average, the same number of melanocytes in the same area of the body. Skin color is determined by the amount of melanin produced, the size of the melanin particles, the rate of melanin production, and the location of the melanin in the skin.

See the Online Learning Center for an Internet Activity on skin color.

adaptation Changes in gene frequencies resulting from selective pressures being placed on a population by environmental factors; results in a greater fitness of the population to its ecological niche.

melanin Brown-black pigment found in the skin, eyes, and hair.

epidermis The outermost layer of the skin.

melanocyte Specialized skin cell that produces the pigment melanin.

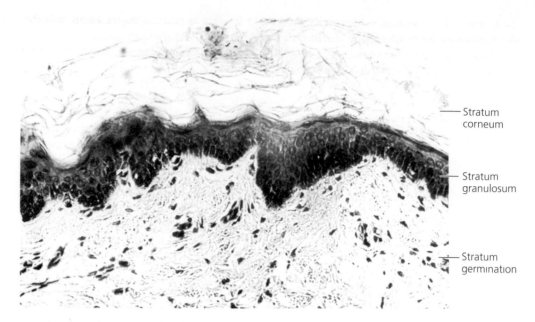

Stratum corneum

Stratum granulosum

Stratum germination

Figure 16.6 Human Skin A photograph of the outermost layer of the skin (epidermis) as seen through the microscope. In this cross section of dark skin, the concentration of melanin can be seen in the stratum granulosum.

Skin Color as an Adaptation People with dark skin are often found in more equatorial regions, while persons with light skin are found farther from the equator. Why would darker skin color be adaptive in equatorial regions?

Sunburn and sunstroke certainly can affect mortality, especially in open tropical habitats. Skin cancer is less of an issue since skin cancers tend to develop late in life, when a person is not likely to reproduce. However, other factors may be related to skin color. For example, a possible correlation has been suggested between ultraviolet radiation and one of the B complex vitamins, folic acid. Bright sunlight reduces the amount of folic acid in the body. Low levels of folic acid may lead to birth defects in which the brain or spinal cord is not completely developed. Low levels of folic acid also inhibit sperm production. This would be a direct link between sunlight and lowered fertility that would explain the existence of dark-skinned persons in tropical areas.

Another hypothesis links skin color with production of vitamin D, which is vital for calcium absorption in the intestines. Calcium is necessary for normal bone development, and the lack of this mineral leads to bone diseases such as **rickets.** Although some vitamin D comes from digested foods, most is manufactured within the skin, and this biochemical reaction requires ultraviolet radiation. The amount of ultraviolet radiation that reaches those layers of the skin where vitamin D synthesis takes place is influenced by the concentration of melanin in the skin. In northern regions where sunlight is limited by sunlight striking the earth at an angle and extensive cloud cover, light skin is adaptive in that it maximizes vitamin D production. People such as the Inuit who have migrated into Arctic regions in fairly recent times are not as light as one might expect. However, their survival depends on foods that are rich in vitamin D, such as raw fish. Although it was at one time believed that excessive amounts of vitamin D could bring about abnormalities, this hypothesis has been disproved. Thus, vitamin D is not a factor that explains dark skin in equatorial regions. Folic acid does.

Differences in skin color are due in part to the latitude of the earth where a person's ancestors evolved. Of course, people often have mixed ancestry. However, there is a general principle called **Gloger's rule** which states that within the same species of mammals, there is a tendency to find more heavily pigmented forms near the equator and lighter forms

rickets A bone disease that usually is caused by a lack of calcium, phosphate, or vitamin D.

Gloger's rule Within the same species of mammals, there is a tendency to find more heavily pigmented forms near the equator and lighter forms away from the equator.

away from the equator. The correlation between latitude and skin color was stronger before the mass migrations of people that began in the 1500s.

Ultraviolet radiation is not only a function of latitude. The geographical areas of most intense ultraviolet radiation are the grasslands of the equatorial regions. People in these areas often have extremely dark skin that always remains dark, as we can see in the Nilotic peoples of the grasslands of east Africa (Figure 16.7b) and the aboriginal populations of the Australian desert. Extremely dark skin is not characteristic of indigenous tropical-forest dwellers, since the heavy vegetation filters out much of the solar radiation. The pygmies of the Congo Basin of Africa, for example, are lighter than the people who entered the forest some 2000 years ago from the Cameroons, which lies northwest of the Congo. On the other hand, peoples living in the Arctic are darker than one might expect. Snow reflects ultraviolet radiation, thereby increasing the amount of such radiation that ultimately reaches their skin.

Another hypothesis about the distribution of human skin color revolves around the chances that one might be injured by cold temperatures. It has been noticed for decades that soldiers with dark skin suffer from frostbite more frequently than do light-skinned troops. For instance, there were up to six times as many frostbite-related deaths among African American troops during the Korean War than among soldiers of European descent. Thus, cold would have selected against people with heavily pigmented skin in early European populations that were living under glacial conditions, thus establishing light skin in the area.

Cultural factors also may affect skin color. For instance, light-skinned people who wear little clothing or make a practice of sunbathing will appear darker in the summer than genetically similar people who protect themselves from tanning. Suntan lotions also alter the color of the skin. Of course, darkened skin produced by exposure to ultraviolet radiation or tanning lotions will not be passed on to the next generation. However, if there is an advantage or disadvantage in the ability to tan, natural selection will increase or decrease the frequency of this trait.

Adaptation and Body Build

Natural selection plays a major role in determining the size and shape of the human body. The effects of natural selection are greatest under the most stressful conditions. Thus, if people live in a generally mild climate that is frigid for three months of the year, they must be adapted to the harsh conditions as well as to the mild ones. Each time the stressful conditions arise, the genes of those individuals who do not survive will be eliminated. Their nonadaptive genes will not be transmitted to the next generation. Over time, the population will become increasingly adapted to its local circumstance.

Radiation of Heat and Body Build We have already discussed some aspects of the problem of heat loss in desert habitats. Radiation is the most significant mechanism for heat loss in the nude human body at rest, accounting for 67 percent of the heat loss at an air temperature of 24°C (75.2°F). The efficiency of radiation as a heat-reducing process depends largely on body build.

The amount of heat that can be lost from an object by radiation depends on the ratio of surface area to body mass. Suppose two brass objects of identical weight, a sphere and a cube, are heated to the same temperature and then left to cool. Which object cools faster? The cube cools faster. Although both objects have the same weight, the cube has more surface area from which the heat can radiate. On the other hand, the sphere has the smallest surface per unit weight of any three-dimensional shape.

While weight increases by the cube, surface area increases only by the square. This is generally true of human beings as well. As seen in Table 16.1, the ratio of body weight to surface area of skin is higher in cooler northern regions and decreases toward the equator. Just as a sphere has the smallest surface area per unit weight, a short, stocky human body also has a low surface area per unit weight. Thus, we would expect that people in Arctic regions, in order to reduce heat loss, would be short and stocky, with short limbs. When the Inuit's body is examined, this expectation is confirmed. In contrast, the Nilotes live in

Table 16.1 Ratio of Body Weight to Body Surface Area in Males*

Population	Median Latitude	Ratio (kilograms per square meter)
China		
North		36.02
Central		34.30
South		30.90
North Europe to north Africa†		
Finland	65°N	38.23
Ireland	53°N	38.00
France	47°N	37.78
Italy	42½°N	37.15
Egypt (Siwah)	26°N	36.11
Arabs (Yemen)	15°N	36.10

* Women show ratios different from men's. This may be due to differences in the mechanisms of heat regulation between men and women. For example, the ratio for France (women) is 38.4, compared with 37.78 for men, as seen above.
† There is some discontinuous variation in the north Europe to north Africa range. For example, the ratio for Germany is 39.14, even though it is south of Finland.
Source: Eugene Schreider, "Variations morphologiques et différences climatiques," *Biométrie Humaine* 6 (1971), pp. 46–49. Used with permission of Dr. Schreider.

the hot equatorial regions of east Africa and have long, linear trunks with long arms and legs. Such linearity provides a large surface area for the radiation of heat (Figure 16.7).

Two principles describe the general relationships discussed above between surface area of the body and mass of the body in mammals, including humans. The first is **Bergmann's rule.** This rule states that within the same species, the average weight (mass) of the members of a population increases and the surface area of the body decreases as the average environmental temperature decreases. The second is **Allen's rule.** This rule states that within the same species, the relative size of protruding parts of the body, such as the nose and ears, and the relative length of the arms and legs increase as the average environmental temperature increases. Longer arms and legs have a greater surface area relative to mass compared with shorter arms and legs and therefore are better suited to remove heat from the body quickly.

Variability extends to other parts of the anatomy. Anthropologists have studied variation of many features, including the nose, hair texture, and hair color, but the reasons for variability in these features are poorly known. Variation also occurs in various physiological traits, in molecular traits such as blood types, and in the frequencies of genetic disease.

Bergmann's rule Within the same species of mammals, the average weight of the members of a population increases and the surface area of the body decreases as the average environmental temperature decreases.

Allen's rule Among mammals, populations of the same species living near the equator tend to have body parts that protrude more and to have longer limbs than do populations farther away from the equator.

Summary

Adaptation refers to microevolutionary changes. This section has examined two examples of adaptation in human populations: skin color and body build.

Human skin color is due primarily to the pigment melanin. In general, people living in equatorial regions tend to have darker skin than do those living at higher latitudes. In this case, melanin may be acting to protect the body from the harmful ultraviolet rays of the sun and also to regulate the production of vitamin D. People living in equatorial regions also tend to be tall and linear, a body build that maximizes the amount of surface area per unit of body weight. This body shape maximizes the efficiency by which excess heat can be removed from the body.

(a)

(b)

Figure 16.7 Body Build
The body builds of an
(a) Inuit of the Arctic and
(b) Nilote of the African
savanna.

THE NATURE OF HUMAN GROWTH AND DEVELOPMENT

The patterns of growth and development differ among human groups. These patterns also differ among individuals within groups due to variations in heredity, nutrition, disease, and health care.

Growth can be defined as an increase in the size or mass of an organism. For example, we may observe growth by measuring the increase in a child's height and weight over time. On the other hand, **development** is change over time from an immature to a mature or specialized state. The appearance of the specialized tissues that make up the various organs of the body from the undifferentiated cells of the early embryo and the changes in the sex organs and other features that occur as an individual passes through puberty are both examples of development.

Each of the estimated 100 trillion cells of the adult human is ultimately derived from a single fertilized ovum. The process of growth from this single cell occurs in three ways: increase in the number of cells, which is accomplished by the process of mitosis (**hyperplasia**), increase in cell size (**hypertrophy**), and increase in the amount of intercellular material (**accretion**).

The different rates at which various types of cells divide are largely responsible for the differences in body proportions and in body composition that develop with age. As we see in Figure 16.8, the tonsils, the thymus gland, and the lymph nodes are composed of lymphoid tissue that grows very rapidly in early childhood. Lymphoid tissue traps foreign particles in the body and plays a major role in the development of immunity to diseases. By

See the Online Learning Center for an Internet Activity on embryo development.

growth Increase in the size or mass of an organism.

development The process whereby cells differentiate into different and specialized units; change over time from an immature to a mature or specialized state.

hyperplasia Growth by virtue of increase in the total number of cells resulting from mitosis.

hypertrophy Growth by virtue of increase in the size of cells.

accretion Growth by virtue of an increase in intercellular material.

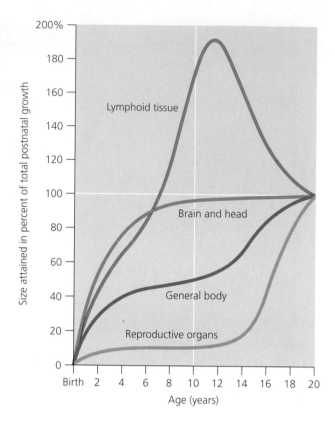

Figure 16.8 Growth Curves of Different Parts and Tissues of the Body This graph illustrates the differences in growth of different tissues and parts of the body, expressed in terms of percent of total growth attained after birth.

the end of five or six years, the nervous system has reached 90 percent of its adult size; after this, the growth rate is extremely slow. In contrast, the elements of the reproductive system grow very slowly until puberty, when their growth accelerates. Growth rates of fatty tissues will be discussed when we examine puberty.

Growth and Development of the Human Body

Anthropologists study the process of human growth most extensively in the skeleton. Interest in **osteology,** the study of bones, stems from archaeological and paleontological fieldwork that involves careful study of skeletal remains. Information about populations, including sex ratios, age at death, and diseases, provides insights into the biology of prehistoric populations. Methods of burial and artificial deformation of the skeleton tell us much about the cultural practices surrounding life and death.

The Growth of Bones Initially, a fetal limb bone is formed of cartilage. The actual bone first appears at the center of this cartilage, an area that is called the **primary center of ossification;** in many bones, this center appears before birth. The process of **ossification** soon turns most of the cartilage into bone.

The formation of other centers of ossification occurs most frequently near the ends of long bones such as the humerus. Although considerable variation exists, primary and **secondary centers of ossification** generally appear in a characteristic order at particular ages. Figure 16.9 shows examples of ages at which centers of ossification appear, from birth to age five years, in females. As ossification continues, bone replaces the remaining cartilage and ultimately the centers of ossification unite to form a single bone.

Growth of mammalian long bones does not occur at the ends, but in very narrow areas between the centers of ossification. As the individual increases in size, these areas, called **growth plates,** become increasingly thinner and eventually disappear as the centers of

---

osteology The study of bones.

primary center of ossification Area of first appearance of bone within the cartilage model of a long bone.

ossification Process of bone formation.

See the Online Learning Center for an Interactive Exercise on sexing and aging skeletal material.

secondary center of ossification Area of bone development, usually near the end of a long bone.

growth plate Narrow zone on a bone where bone growth occurs.

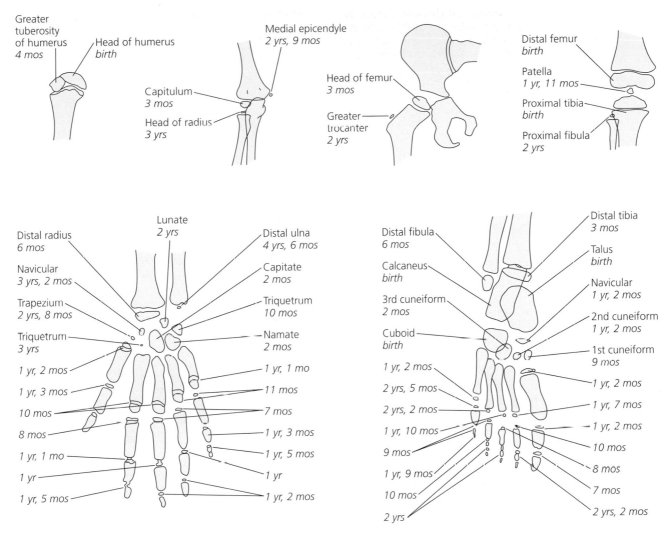

Figure 16.9 Dates of Appearance of Centers of Ossification, Birth to Five Years of Age, in Females of European Ancestry

ossification fuse. Once fusion occurs, growth stops. As is true with the appearance of centers of ossification, fusions of growth plates generally occur in a characteristic order and at certain average ages, although individuals vary. Figure 16.10 shows the average ages of fusion for selected growth plates in males.

The appearance of a center of ossification or the fusion of a growth plate may be used to define a standard **bone age.** These standards vary among populations and between males and females. The standard bone age represents the average chronological age at which these events take place. In contrast, **chronological age** is the time since birth. For example, Figure 16.11 shows the x-rays of the wrists of two boys, each with a chronological age of 15 years. The x-ray on the left shows more unfused growth plates than does the x-ray on the right. The boy on the left has a bone age of 12¹/₂ years; the boy on the right has a bone age of 15¹/₂ years.

The Development of Dentition Like other mammals, humans develop two sets of teeth. The first is a set of **deciduous,** or baby, teeth; the second is a set of **permanent teeth.** Humans have 20 deciduous teeth and 32 permanent teeth.

In humans, teeth begin to develop in the five-month-old fetus, and the first deciduous tooth erupts (appears through the gum) about six months after birth. By the average age of

bone age A standard age based on the appearance of centers of ossification and fusion of growth plates.

chronological age Period of time since birth.

deciduous teeth The first set of teeth that develop in mammals; also known as the baby or milk teeth.

permanent teeth The second set of teeth that erupts in mammals; humans have 32 permanent teeth.

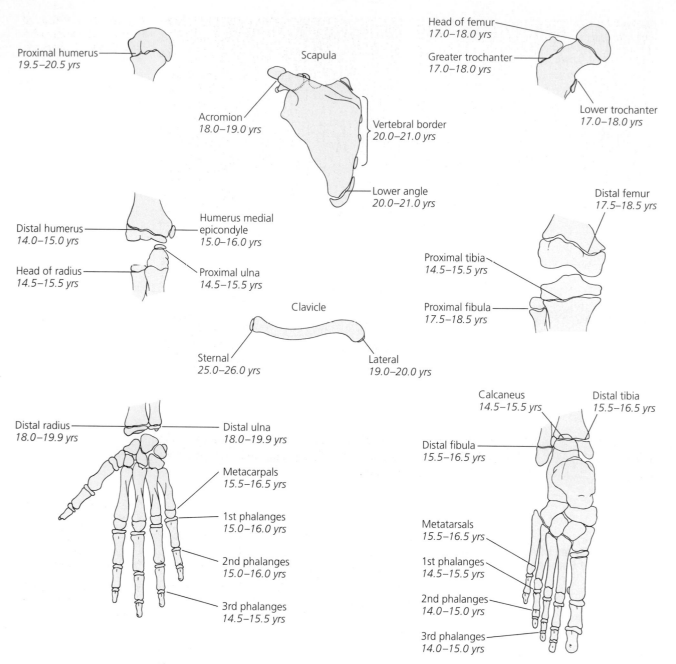

Figure 16.10 The Average Age at Which Fusion of Growth Plates Occurs in Males of European Ancestry

three years, all 20 deciduous teeth have fully erupted and the permanent teeth are developing in the jaws. At six or seven years of age, the deciduous teeth begin falling out, to be replaced by the permanent teeth.

Although variation does occur, most of the deciduous and permanent teeth erupt in a fairly consistent order at particular ages. For example, the second permanent molar erupts at an average age of 12 years. (In England the eruption of the second molar was formerly used to decide when a child was old enough to go to work.) Other teeth are not so regular: third molars, the "wisdom teeth," may erupt between the ages of 18 and 80 years and in some individuals may never erupt at all.

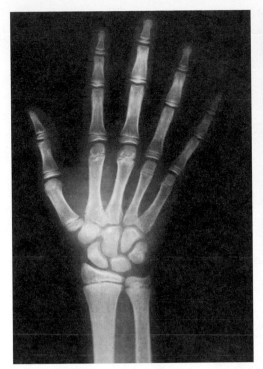
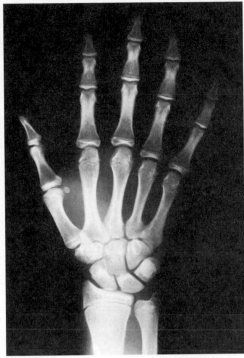

Figure 16.12, developed by the American Dental Association, shows the status of the different teeth at various ages. This chart depicts the "typical" sequence and average age of tooth eruption; there is considerable variation in both.

Puberty

Of all the events in an individual's life cycle, one of the most significant both biologically and socially is **puberty.** In most human societies, the onset of puberty occasions a ritual that marks a major transition in the social life of the individual.

One of the major physical changes that occurs in puberty is a rapid increase in stature. If we plot the height of a child on a series of dates (on the child's birthday, for example), we obtain what is called a **distance curve.** An example of a distance curve for a male is shown in Figure 16.13a. At about 14¹/₂ years of age, there is a major increase in the growth rate known as the **adolescent growth spurt.** This is most clearly seen in a **velocity curve,** which plots the height gained for each year (Figure 16.13b). Females experience a similar growth spurt, but it occurs earlier than in males. Also, the increase in stature and the speed of growth are less in girls than in boys.

The later onset of puberty in males may account for their greater stature as adults. The hormones involved in the sexual changes at puberty also bring about the end of bone growth in the long bones. Thus, the later onset of puberty gives males a longer time to grow.

The earliest signs of puberty in males are the enlargement of the testes and changes in the texture and color of the scrotum; these are soon followed by the enlargement of the penis and the growth of pubic hair. Individuals vary in the age at which these events occur. Growth of the penis begins at 12¹/₂ years on the average, but it may begin as early as 10¹/₂ or as late as 14¹/₂. A problem of social adjustment at this time is that some boys may be just beginning puberty after their peers have completed it.

The earliest sign of puberty in the female is the development of the **breast bud,** which is an elevation of the breast as a small mound. Also, there is a slight enlargement of the **areolar area,** the dark area surrounding the nipple. In the female, there is a sudden and

puberty An event in the life cycle that includes rapid increase in stature, development of sex organs, and the development of secondary sexual characteristics.

distance curve A graph that shows the total height (or other measurement) of an individual on a series of dates.

adolescent growth spurt A rapid increase in stature and other dimensions of the body that occurs during puberty.

velocity curve A curve that illustrates the velocity or rate of growth over time by plotting the degree of growth per unit of time.

breast bud An elevation of the breast as a small mound; the earliest sign of puberty in the female.

areolar area The dark area surrounding the nipple of the breast.

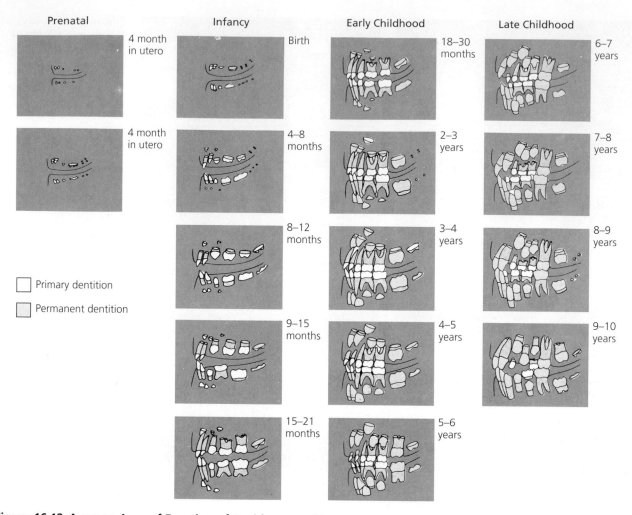

Figure 16.12 Average Ages of Eruption of Deciduous and Permanent Dentition The deciduous teeth are shown in white.

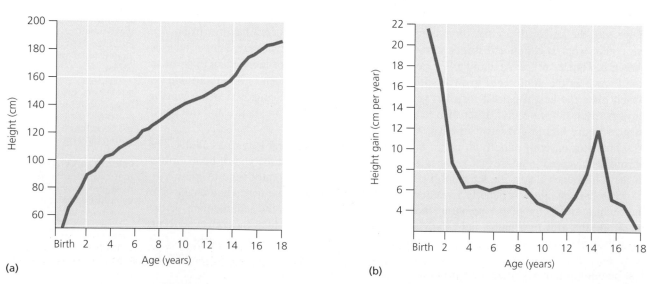

(a)

(b)

Figure 16.13 Count Philibert Guéneau de Montbeillard Published a Record of the Growth of His Son to the Age of 18 Beginning in 1759 (a) This is an example of a distance curve that shows total height on each of several dates. (b) This is an example of a velocity curve that shows the total height gained in each year.

visible event known as **menarche** (rhymes with "monarchy"), the first menstrual flow. Menarche actually appears late in puberty; it represents a mature stage of development of the uterus. It does not, however, mark the development of full reproductive functions. These occur a year or so later.

Within a given population, the age at menarche is quite variable. In addition, when *averages* from different populations are compared, great variation is apparent as well. In some populations, the average age at menarche may be under 13, whereas in other populations, the average age may exceed 18 (Table 16.2).

In addition to changes in the reproductive organs, other changes that differentiate males and females occur at puberty. These are the **secondary sexual characteristics.** An example found in males is the development of facial hair and of a deeper voice. The voice change is due to lengthening of the vocal cords, which, in turn, results from the growth of the larynx. Voice change also occurs in the female. Perhaps more important for both sexes, however, are changes in body proportions and body composition.

Dimensions of the Body One of the oldest studies within physical anthropology is **anthropometry,** the "systematized art of measuring and taking observations on man, his skeleton, his brain, or other organs, by the most reliable means and methods for scientific purposes (see chapter opening)."[2]

Anthropometric measurements can be plotted as growth curves. Different parts of the body grow at different rates, and many differences that characterize the sexes after puberty simply represent differences in relative growth rates. For example, Figure 16.14 plots two anthropometric measurements against age in the form of velocity curves. The first plots **biacromial width,** a measurement of the width of the shoulders. At puberty, males develop relatively broad shoulders. The second graph plots **bitrochanteric width,** a measurement of hip width. Here the greatest growth at puberty is in the female.

Dimensions of the body may vary from population to population as a result of different selective pressures in the different environments in which those populations live. The human skeleton is very malleable in its early stages of development. For instance, chest circumference increases with the low oxygen pressure found at high altitude. This was discussed earlier in this chapter in the section "Developmental Adjustments."

Changes in Body Composition Along with the adolescent growth spurt is a change in the composition of the body.

Table 16.2 Median Age at Menarche (First Menstruation) in Several Populations

Population or Location	Median Age (years)
Wealthy Chinese (Hong Kong)	12.5[*]
Wroclaw (Poland)	12.6[*]
California (United States)	12.8[*]
Moscow (Russia)	13.0[*]
Tel Aviv (Israel)	13.0[†]
Burma (urban)	13.2[*]
Oslo (Norway)	13.5[*]
Wealthy Ibo (Nigeria)	14.1[*]
Transkei Bantu (South Africa)	15.0[*]
Tutsi (Rwanda)	16.5[*]
Hutu (Rwanda)	17.1[‡]
Bundi (New Guinea)	18.8[*]

[*] J. M. Tanner, "The Secular Trend towards Earlier Physical Maturation," *Trans. Soc. Geneesk* 44 (1966), pp. 524–538.
[†] A. Ber and C. Brociner, "Age of Puberty in Israeli Girls," *Fertility and Sterility* 15 (1964), pp. 640–647.
[‡] J. Hiernaux, *La Croissance de écoliers Rwandais* (Brussels: Outre-Mer, Royal Academy of Science, 1965).

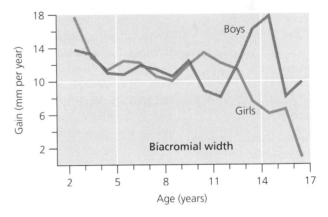

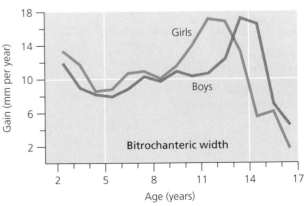

Figure 16.14 Annual Change in Shoulder (Biacromial) Width and Hip (Bitrochanteric) Width in Boys and Girls

---

[2] A. Hrdlička, *Practical Anthropology* (Philadelphia: Wistar Institute of Anatomy and Biology, 1939), p. 3.

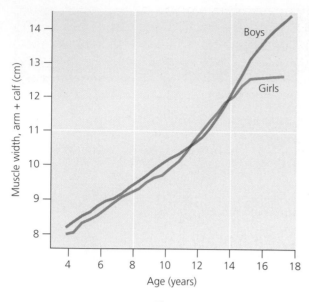
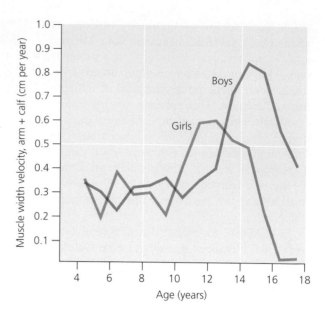

Figure 16.15 Muscle Growth Distance and velocity curves showing the sum of widths of upper arm and calf muscles as seen in x-rays.

The amount of muscle tissue increases, especially in males. Apart from the large muscles, males develop larger lungs, larger hearts, and a greater capacity for carrying oxygen in the blood in comparison with females. These differences are associated with greater speed, strength, and physical endurance (Figure 16.15).

Changes also occur in the amount of **subcutaneous fat,** the fat deposited under the skin. These changes are observed especially in the limbs. With the onset of the growth spurt, the relative proportion of subcutaneous fat decreases. Because this decrease is greatest in males, females enter adulthood with relatively more subcutaneous fat, especially over the pelvis and on the breasts, the upper back, and the upper arms.

Control of Growth and Development

The nature and rates of growth and development are controlled by the complex interaction of many factors. Among these are the endocrine glands, nutrition, and heredity.

The **endocrine glands** produce a special group of chemicals called **hormones,** which are secreted directly into the bloodstream and are carried throughout the body. A number of hormones have an effect on growth and development. For example, **growth hormone,** produced by the pituitary gland, is essential for normal growth, particularly the growth of bone. Children deficient in this hormone reach an average adult height of only 130 centimeters (51 inches) although they have normal body proportions.

Sex hormones play major roles in growth and development, especially at puberty. **Testosterone** is manufactured by cells of the testes. At puberty, testosterone stimulates the growth of the testes and the male sex organs, such as the penis and the prostate, and also stimulates the development of secondary sexual characteristics such as facial hair. In the female, **estrogens** are produced by the ovaries. Estrogens stimulate the growth of the female sex organs, such as the vagina and the uterus, and cause secondary changes such as breast development. Other hormones, produced by other glands, also influence the pattern of growth and development in the individual.

The Effects of Nutrition and Disease on Growth and Development The processes of growth utilize the raw materials taken into the body as food. Nutrients help sustain growth and development, repair damage, and maintain vital processes, and they provide energy for bodily activities. The lack of proper nutrition can seriously retard normal growth and development.

menarche First menstruation.

secondary sexual characteristic Physical feature other than the genitalia that distinguishes males from females after puberty.

anthropometry The study of measurements of the human body.

biacromial width A measurement of the width of the shoulders.

bitrochanteric width A measurement of hip width.

subcutaneous fat The fat deposited under the skin.

endocrine glands Organs that produce hormones.

hormones Complex molecules produced by the endocrine glands that regulate many bodily functions and processes.

growth hormone A hormone produced by the pituitary gland; essential for normal growth.

testosterone A male sex hormone.

estrogen Hormone produced in the ovaries.

Figure 16.16 Marasmus Children facing starvation in Liberia in 1996.

Protein-caloric malnutrition is a broad term covering many nutritional problems. Malnutrition is especially prevalent in developing nations, primarily those undergoing the transition to urbanized societies. Severe malnutrition is also common during war.

One form of protein-caloric malnutrition is **kwashiorkor,** a Ghanaian word meaning "second-child disease." Kwashiorkor is usually associated with the period immediately after weaning, which often takes place when a second child is born. In many parts of the world, especially in the tropics, the child moves from its mother's milk to a diet of carbohydrates and little protein. The main food is usually a starchy gruel made from yams, taro, corn, rice, or millet; animal protein is scarce and, when available, expensive. Thus, the child may receive enough food to satisfy hunger but does not receive the proteins vital to normal health, growth, and development.

Several symptoms characterize kwashiorkor. **Edema,** or water retention, occurs in the feet and lower legs and may occur in other parts of the body. Growth is retarded. Muscle wasting occurs, as seen in the thinness of the upper arms and by the child's difficulty in holding up its head when pulled from a lying to a sitting position. Because the diet is high in carbohydrates, a relatively thick layer of subcutaneous fat and a distended belly often are seen. Many psychomotor changes occur, including retarded motor development. The child is apathetic, miserable, withdrawn, and indifferent to its environment.

Marasmus results from a diet low in both protein and calories (Figure 16.16). It occurs in all ages, but usually in children soon after weaning. Symptoms of marasmus include extreme growth retardation, wasting of muscles and subcutaneous fat, diarrhea, and severe anemia. Since vital nutrients are absent during a critical time for brain growth, mental retardation often occurs. Early death is the rule.

Kwashiorkor and marasmus represent extreme examples of malnutrition and growth retardation. In addition to these, less severe forms of malnutrition and the lack of specific nutrients, or an excessive amount of many nutrients, in the diet also can lead to problems.

Growth and development are affected by many diseases. Many genetic abnormalities, such as PKU, and chromosomal abnormalities, such as Down syndrome (Chapter 3), clearly affect growth. Likewise, nongenetic diseases, such as those caused by bacteria, viruses, fungi, and parasites, also can influence growth.

Many childhood diseases may retard normal growth and development. Although measles and chicken pox may have no lasting effect on well-nourished children, severe and prolonged nongenetic diseases inevitably impair growth, especially in malnourished populations.

protein-caloric malnutrition A class of malnutrition that includes kwashiorkor and marasmus.

See the Online Learning Center for an Internet Activity on malnutrition.

kwashiorkor A form of protein-caloric malnutrition brought about by a protein-deficient diet that contains a reasonable supply of low-quality carbohydrates.

edema Retention of water in the tissues of the body.

marasmus A form of protein-caloric malnutrition caused by a diet deficient in both protein and carbohydrates.

Table 16.3 Average Differences between Monozygotic and Dizygotic Twins and Pairs of Siblings

Difference in	Monozygotic Twins	Monozygotic Twins Reared Apart	Dizygotic Twins	Same-Sex Siblings (Not Twins)
Stature (centimeters)	1.7	1.8	4.4	4.5
Weight (kilograms)	1.9	4.5	4.5	4.7

Source: H. H. Newman et al., *Twins: A Study of Heredity and Environment* (Chicago: University of Chicago Press, 1937), p. 72.

Table 16.4 Average Difference in Menarche

Relationship	Difference (months)
Monozygotic twins	2.8
Dizygotic twins	12.0
Pairs of sisters	12.9
Pairs of unrelated women	18.6

Source: E. Petr, "Untersuchungen zur Erbbedingtheit der Menarche," *Zeitschrift für Morphologie und Anthropologie* 33 (1935), pp. 43–48.

Heredity and Growth and Development Growth is a complex process involving the interaction of cultural, environmental, and genetic factors. The exact role of heredity is not precisely known, but it is certainly polygenic (Chapter 3). Tall parents tend to have, on the average, tall children, but genetic factors are complex and difficult to analyze.

One method of estimating the relative influence of heredity and environment is through twin studies, which were discussed in Chapter 2. Tables 16.3 and 16.4 present data on growth from such twin studies. The similarities between monozygotic twins in stature, weight, and age at menarche, together with the differences between dizygotic twins and pairs of nontwin siblings, suggest a strong genetic influence on these traits. Yet the differences between monozygotic twins, especially when twins are reared apart, show that environmental influences are also present.

Twin studies suggest that genes strongly influence growth, primarily by establishing optimal limits for growth. Thus, an individual may have the genetic potential for a particular stature, yet that stature may not be reached because of malnutrition or childhood disease. The nature of the genetic mechanism, however, is unknown.

The Secular Trend in Growth and Development

secular trend The tendency over the last hundred or so years for each succeeding generation to mature earlier and become, on the average, larger.

Occasionally we read a newspaper or magazine article that reports that people are getting larger each generation. Scientists have long been aware of this phenomenon, which is called the **secular trend.** The secular trend is the tendency over the last hundred or so years for each succeeding generation to mature earlier and grow larger (Figure 16.17). This trend has occurred worldwide. In the twentieth century, the change in mean body height per decade was about 0.6 centimeter (0.25 inch) in early childhood, about 1.3 centimeters (0.5 inch) in late childhood (8 years old for girls and 10 years old for boys), and about 1.9 centimeters (0.74 inch) at mid-adolescence (age 12 for girls and age 14 for boys).[3]

What causes secular trends? No one knows for sure. Some researchers believe that a general improvement in nutrition, better sanitation, better health services, and less tedious lifestyles are responsible. These factors have permitted individuals to more closely approach their genetically determined potential weight and stature. Today, a leveling off of the secular trend appears to be occurring among the higher socioeconomic urban population.

---

[3] H. V. Meredith, "Findings from Asia, Australia, Europe, and North America on Secular Change in Mean Height of Children, Youths, and Young Adults," *American Journal of Physical Anthropology* 44 (1976), pp. 321–322.

Box 16-2   Aging

Someday, genetic-engineering techniques may be used to arrest the aging process, although today the idea is a fantasy of science fiction. All people age. *Aging* is the uninterrupted process of normal development that leads to a progressive decline in physiological function and ultimately to death.

It has been suggested for decades that certain groups of people age at a much slower rate and live considerably longer lives than other groups. Russians from the Caucasus Mountains, Hunzas from the Karakoram Mountains in Pakistan, and Ecuadorans have been represented in the popular literature as including within their populations a very high percentage of people who are well over 100 years old. However, when these cases are carefully examined, these people usually turn out to be in their 70s and 80s.[1] In fact, these populations do not show average life expectancies any greater than that of the general U.S. population.

So, then, why do people exaggerate age? One reason may be that the society is attempting to show that its culture is better than others or even to display a biological superiority. In some groups, a man of draftable age customarily takes the identity of his father in order to avoid military service. In many societies, great age brings with it increased prestige or fame.

The rates of aging and the time of death are influenced by both genetic and cultural factors. *Life expectancy* is how long a person can, on the average, expect to live. Although average life expectancies differ considerably from population to population, the oldest ages that people attain in different cultures are very similar. For humans, as for each other animal species, there seems to be a theoretical maximum age determined by genetic predestiny. This is called the *life span*. The life span for humans is about 120 years. A French woman, Jeanne Calmut, lived longer than any other person for whom we have a record. At the time of her death in 1997, she was 122 years and 164 days old.[2]

Many investigators of the aging process believe that the maximum life span of a species is due to a developmental "clock." The timing of this clock is controlled, in part, by regulatory genes. These genes determine the appearance and disappearance of biochemical products that control the aging process. Recent studies indicate that another aspect of the genetic developmental clock might involve mitochondrial DNA. As mutations accumulate in mtDNA, the body might age. These models of aging, as well as others that have been proposed, are hypothetical. As of yet, aging is inadequately understood.

Many developmental events contribute to old age. The following will or may occur as one gets older: loss of bone density, gain of fat but loss of muscle tissue, loss of teeth, dry skin, menopause, decline in sperm count, decline in near and far vision, diminished senses of hearing and taste, rise in cholesterol levels, and increase in susceptibility to many diseases, including heart disease, cancer, cerebrovascular disease, chronic pulmonary disease, diabetes, and chronic liver disease. The occurrence and degree of these events are highly variable among individuals within a population as well as variable among populations.

[1] A. Leaf, "Long-Lived Populations: Extreme Old Age," *Journal of American Geriatrics* 30 (1982), pp. 485–487.

[2] J-M. Robine and M. Alland, "The Oldest Human," *Science* 279 (1998), pp. 1834–1835. *See also* T. Overfield, *Biologic Variation in Health and Illness: Race, Age, and Sex Differences* (Menlo Park, CA: Addison-Wesley, 1985), and J. S. Olshansky, B. A. Carnes, and C. Cassel, "In Search of Methuselah: Estimating the Upper Limits to Human Longevity," *Science* 250 (1990), pp. 634–640.

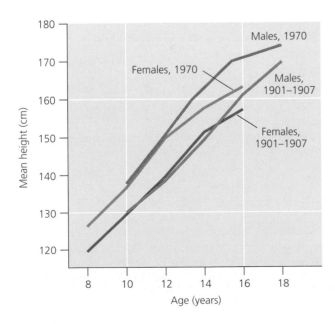

Figure 16.17 Secular Trend This graph shows the mean height of "white" Australian males and females measured in 1901–1907 and in 1970.

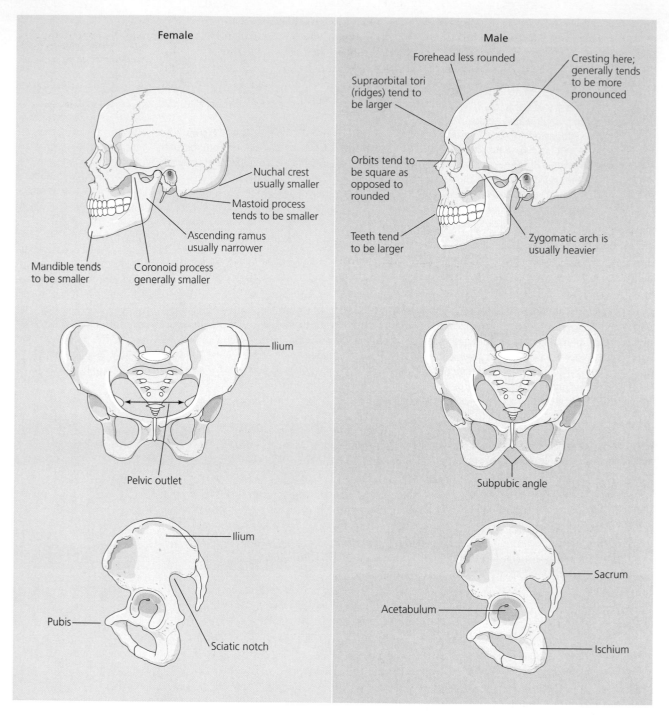

Figure 16.18 Sex Determination of the Skeleton Comparison of the stereotypic female and male skull and pelvis.

The Adult Skeleton

By the early 20s, most of the growth plates have closed and all the teeth, with perhaps the exception of the highly variable third molars, are fully erupted. Age-related changes in the adult skeleton are generally degenerative changes such as the closure and obliteration of sutures in the skull, loss of teeth, and degeneration of bone in the skull and other parts of the anatomy.

An example of age-related changes in the postcranial skeleton may be seen in the analysis of the **pubic symphysis,** which is the part of the pelvis where the two innominates join. (The pelvis consists of two halves, the innominates, that in turn are divided into sections. The front section is the pubis.) Age can be estimated by separating the two innominates and carefully examining the **symphyseal face,** or the surface where one pubis joins the other. Using analysis of the skull and the postcranial bones in the adult, a reasonable estimate of age at death can be made.

The adults of many mammalian and primate species show marked differences in size and structure between males and females, a feature referred to as sexual dimorphism. Sexual dimorphism is relatively slight in humans, yet various parts of the male and female skeleton do show noticeable differences.

In Figure 16.18, which compares the male pelvis with the female pelvis, adaptations for childbearing can be seen in the female pelvis. Note, for example, that the female pelvis is characterized by a U-shaped and broader subpubic angle; a smaller acetabulum; a larger, wider, and shallower sciatic notch; a circular or elliptical pelvic inlet; and many other features.

Many sexual differences in the human skeleton reflect the male's greater size and heavier musculature. Areas where muscles attach to bone are seen as roughened areas and projections, and the size of these areas and projections is a reflection of the size of the attached muscle.

The study of bones is called osteology. The application of the methods and techniques of osteology to identifying skeletal remains in criminal investigations is called **forensic anthropology.** Forensic anthropology is discussed in Chapter 18.

pubic symphysis The area of the pelvis at which the two innominates join.

symphyseal face The surface of the pubis where one pubis joins the other at the pubic symphysis.

See the Online Learning Center for an Interactive Exercise on sexing and aging skeletal material.

forensic anthropology Application of the techniques of osteology and skeletal identification to legal problems.

Summary

Growth is an increase in the size of an organism; development is a change from an undifferentiated to a highly organized, specialized state. There are three ways in which growth occurs: Hyperplasia is an increase in the number of cells, hypertrophy is a general increase in cell size, and accretion is an increase in the amount of intercellular material.

Bone growth begins with the appearance of primary and secondary areas of ossification, areas where bone is replacing cartilage. In long bones, growth takes place in growth plates that close when growth ceases in a fairly regular order at characteristic ages. Bone age is the average chronological age at which these events occur. The pattern of tooth formation and eruption serves a similar purpose.

Growth can be charted in distance and velocity curves that plot the increase in stature, or some other variable, over time. When examining a growth curve, we notice a period known as the adolescent growth spurt. This is an aspect of puberty, which also includes changes in the reproductive organs and the secondary sexual characteristics. Specific anthropometric measurements also can be plotted against age and illustrate aspects of sexual dimorphism. Differences in patterns of growth and development may be seen in children growing up in stressful environments; these are known as developmental adjustments.

The nature and rates of growth and development are controlled by the complex interaction of internal and external factors. These factors include the hormones, which are particularly involved in the control of puberty; environmental factors, including the availability and usage patterns of food; diseases, both those that are genetic and those caused by disease organisms; and heredity, which plays a major role by setting the potential limits to growth measurements such as stature. Improvement in nutrition, better sanitation, and better health services may be responsible for an increase in average stature and weight over the years, a tendency referred to as the secular trend.

Key Terms

acclimatory adjustment, *429*
accretion, *439*
adaptation, *435*
adjustment, *428*
adolescent growth spurt, *443*
Allen's rule, *438*
alveoli, *432*
anthropometry, *445*
areolar area, *443*
basal metabolic rate, *429*
behavioral adjustment, *428*
Bergmann's rule, *438*
biacromial width, *445*
bitrochanteric width, *445*
bone age, *441*
breast bud, *443*
chronological age, *441*
conduction, *430*
convection, *430*
critical temperature, *429*
deciduous teeth, *441*
development, *439*
developmental
   adjustments, *434*
distance curve, *443*

edema, *447*
endocrine glands, *446*
epidermis, *435*
estrogen, *446*
evaporation, *430*
forensic anthropology, *451*
Gloger's rule, *436*
growth, *439*
growth hormone, *446*
growth plate, *440*
high-altitude hypoxia, *431*
high-altitude (mountain)
   sickness, *431*
hormones, *446*
hyperplasia, *439*
hypertrophy, *439*
hyperventilation, *433*
hypothermia, *429*
kwashiorkor, *447*
marasmus, *447*
melanin, *435*
melanocyte, *435*
menarche, *445*
ossification, *440*

osteology, *440*
partial pressure, *432*
permanent teeth, *441*
primary center of
   ossification, *440*
protein-caloric
   malnutrition, *447*
puberty, *443*
pubic symphysis, *451*
radiation, *430*
residual volume, *435*
rickets, *436*
secondary center of
   ossification, *440*
secondary sexual
   characteristic, *445*
secular trend, *448*
subcutaneous fat, *446*
sweating, *430*
symphyseal face, *451*
testosterone, *446*
vasoconstriction, *429*
vasodilation, *431*
velocity curve, *443*

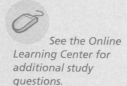

See the Online Learning Center for additional study questions.

Study Questions

1. How does *adaptation* differ from *adjustment*?
2. Why would one expect peoples living in hot equatorial grasslands to be very tall and linear and to have dark skin?
3. How are skin color and general body build related to each other?
4. A human wearing little clothing sets out into the Arctic winter. Another, similarly dressed, sets out into the Sahara Desert. Describe the physiological events that will take place in each situation.
5. Very high altitude presents what is perhaps the most difficult habitat for human habitation. Describe the various stresses found at high altitude and the human responses to those stresses.
6. What is the major difference between *growth* and *development*?
7. What factors are responsible for differences in the patterns of growth and development among individuals or groups of individuals?
8. What is the secular trend?

Critical Thinking Questions

1. In this chapter we used the igloo as an example of one ingenious way in which humans have adjusted behaviorally to the extremely harsh Arctic environment. An even more hostile environment is outer space. What behavioral adjustments have the people who have lived on the International Space Station had to make? What situations do you think

might have been the hardest to adjust to? Do you think that any acclimatory adjustments might have taken place for those who spent long periods in zero gravity? Can you imagine what types of developmental adjustments might occur with children who might in the future be conceived and raised in a zero-gravity environment?

2. Modern humans cope with different environments or changes in an environment primarily through adjustments. However, humans also have adapted biologically to different environments, as was exemplified by the description of the evolutionary relationship of skin color, body build, vitamin D, folic acid, and ultraviolet radiation. Write a science fiction scenario that proposes some major change in either a local environment or the worldwide environment and then hypothesize how the affected population might adapt to the change.

3. Females generally grow and develop somewhat faster than do males, reaching puberty earlier than males do. What adaptive function might this have? What biological and behavioral consequences might be the result? How might human social relationships be different if males grew and developed faster than females and reached puberty sooner?

Suggested Readings

Bogin, B. *Cambridge Studies in Biological Anthropology, No. 23: Patterns of Human Growth.* Cambridge: Cambridge University Press, 1999. This book provides a basic introduction to the topic of human growth and development from an anthropological perspective.

Bogin, B. *The Growth of Humanity.* New York: John Wiley & Sons, 2002. This is a synthesis of human demographics, human ecology, and human biology as they relate to population dynamics and human patterns of growth and development.

Cameron, N. *Human Growth and Development.* San Diego: Academic Press, 2002. This is an advanced treatment of the subject with essays by 21 experts in the field of growth and development.

Frisancho, A. R. *Human Adaptation: A Functional Interpretation,* rev. ed. Ann Arbor: University of Michigan Press, 1993. This book discusses human adaptations to stressful environments, including heat and cold stress, high-altitude hypoxia, and malnutrition.

Sinclair, D., and P. Dangerfield. *Human Growth after Birth,* 6th ed. Oxford: Oxford University Press, 1999. This book is a basic text on human growth and development.

Tanner, J. M. *Foetus into Man: Physical Growth from Conception to Maturity,* 2nd ed. Cambridge, MA: Harvard University Press, 1990. This is a general introduction to the study of human growth and development.

Thompson, J. L., G. E. Krovitz, and A. J. Nelson. *Patterns of Growth of Development in the Genus Homo.* Cambridge: Cambridge University Press, 2004. This is a comprehensive volume on growth and development.

Suggested Websites

Princeton University Outdoor Safety Information:
www.princeton.edu/~oa/safety/

State of the World's Children:
www.unicef.org/

Chapter 17

The Analysis of Human Variation

The diversity of humankind.

Biological race assumes that our customary races—the people we customarily classify as black or white—are divided by genes or heritable traits, but most biologists now understand that no cluster of genes or heritable traits divide them. Though there are heritable differences between us, they do not cluster and do not pick out the classes we call "races." So, for example, we differ in skin color, and these differences are heritable, but skin color is inherited independently of other traits like blood type or eye color. Moreover, differences in color are continuous rather than sharp and vary as much within as between racial groups, and differences in skin color divide us into subgroups that cut across rather than match the groups we call races. ●

—Michael Root

Chapter Outline

See the Online Learning Center for a chapter summary, chapter outline, and learning objectives.

After Reading This Chapter, You Should Be Able to Answer These Questions:

1. What is meant by the terms *clinal distribution* and *discontinuous variation*?

2. What is a folk taxonomy of human variation? Are folk taxonomies scientifically accurate?

3. What are some of the early "scientific" classifications of race, and why are they considered invalid today?

4. Today human biological variation is measured mostly in terms of genetics. What have genetic studies of human variation told us about the concept of race?

5. Racial classifications still are used in medicine. Why are such classifications suspect?

6. What is meant by the statement "race is a social construct with little biological basis"?

7. What are some of the sociocultural factors that influence scores on intelligence and achievement tests?

Physically, humans are different from one another. Siblings vary from one another, members of related families vary significantly from one another, and people of different geographical ancestry vary from one another. Important questions for biological anthropologists include the following: How much do they vary? and What is the significance of that variation?

Current research tells us that no two humans genetically vary from one another by more than about one-tenth of a percent, and the majority of that small degree of variation is within groups perceived to be different "races," not between them. This has led investigators of human variation to conclude that the concept of race as it is used by the general public, government agencies, and some scientists (such as some medical researchers) is not valid. In a sense race is real; however, it is real as a social concept but not as a biological one, at least not in the way most people perceive it to be. This chapter studies the complex topic of human variation and the concept of race.

THE DISTRIBUTION OF VARIABILITY

Adjustments and adaptations are responses to particular environmental conditions. Many of those environmental conditions are associated with particular habitats. For example, dark skin color and linear body build are associated with hot, open, tropical climates. Since such climates are found near the equator, it follows that there will be a characteristic distribution of these traits when they are plotted on a map. This section will examine the distribution of variable features of human populations.

Clinal Distributions

The frequencies of a particular trait may vary systematically from place to place, and this can be seen when frequencies are plotted on a map. This is seen in Figure 17.1, which plots the frequencies of blood type B in Europe. Note that the frequencies of blood type B decrease along a line from the upper right-hand corner of the map to the French-Spanish border.

A distribution of frequencies that shows a systematic gradation over space is known as a clinal distribution. Clinal distributions develop in at least two ways. A cline might be determined

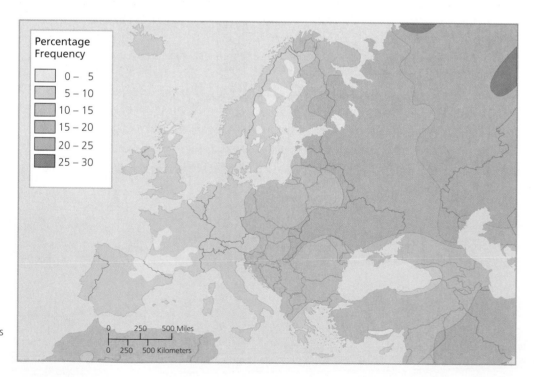

Figure 17.1
Distribution of Blood Type B in Europe This is an example of a clinal distribution.

by a gradual change in some selective pressure. For instance, an increase in the frequency of the allele for sickle-cell anemia may be related to an increase in the prevalence of the malaria-carrying mosquito as one moves from temperate into more tropical areas. As the selective pressure changes, so may the distribution of the trait.

A cline also may develop when a particular trait originates in a specific area and spreads outward by means of gene flow. The farther away one is from the center of origin, the lower the frequency tends to be. The distribution of blood type B may be the result of this process: Blood type B has its highest frequencies in central Asia and may have originated there.

Discontinuous variation occurs when a particular trait appears in high or low frequencies in various areas with little or no gradation between those areas. An example is the frequency of red hair in the United Kingdom (Figure 17.2).

Skin color and body build are generally clinal in nature as described by Gloger's, Bergmann's and Allen's rules (Chapter 16). Since human populations are mobile, discontinuous variation in skin color and body build occurs as peoples with different skin colors and body builds migrate into new areas. Also, the interbreeding of these migratory peoples has produced multiple skin-color variants and a variety of body builds. In the following sections, we will examine the distribution of other factors.

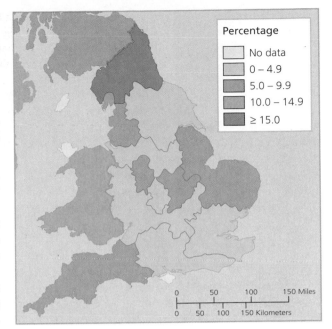

Figure 17.2 Distribution of Red Hair in the United Kingdom This is an example of discontinuous variation.

discontinuous variation
Distribution of alleles, allele combinations, or any traits characterized by little or no gradation in frequencies between adjacent regions.

Distribution of Blood Types In Figure 17.1, we see the clinal distribution of blood type B in Europe. The clinal distribution of many blood-type antigens, coupled with the nonclinal distribution of still other antigens, suggests that considerable variation occurs in the frequencies of particular blood types from population to population.

Some populations are characterized by particular blood-type frequencies. For example, high frequencies of blood type A are found in Scandinavia and among the Inuit; high frequencies of blood type B are found in central Asia, north India, and west Africa (Figure 17.3); and high frequencies of blood type O are found throughout most of North and South America and in Australia. The distribution of blood types and their use in the classification of human variation will be discussed more thoroughly in the next section.

As was discussed in Chapter 5, selective pressures are operating on the ABO blood type system. For example, researchers have hypothesized that smallpox is more severe and mortality rates are higher among peoples of blood types A and AB than among peoples of types O and B. If this hypothesis is correct, smallpox, in areas where it is common, would act as a selective agent tending to eliminate A and AB individuals. O and B individuals would be left to reproduce most of the next generation. Maybe this is why in countries such as India, where smallpox was once common, B is the most common blood type today.

An interesting distributional study focuses on the Diego blood antigen. Table 17.1 shows that this antigen is found only in eastern Asian populations and in the aboriginal populations of the New World which are derived from the peoples of eastern Asia. According to one hypothesis, the Diego antigen is of fairly recent origin. Presumably, the antigen was carried to the New World when the ancestors of the Native Americans migrated across the Bering Strait (Chapter 15).

Variability in Frequency of Genetic Disease

Specific genetic diseases, or high frequencies of genetic diseases, characterize all populations. For example, cystic fibrosis is a recessive genetic abnormality. While the abnormal

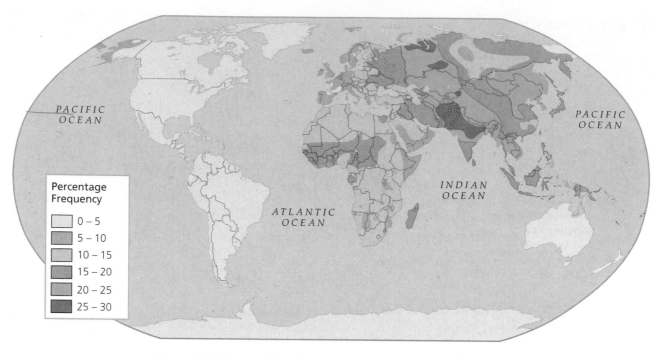

Figure 17.3 The Worldwide Distribution of the Allele I^B

allele is relatively common in European populations, it is rare in Asiatic and African populations. Another example is the allele associated with Tay-Sachs disease among Ashkenazi Jews. Table 17.2 lists some genetic abnormalities associated with particular groups of people.

Why are certain genetic diseases associated with particular populations? Major factors in establishing high frequencies of particular alleles in specific populations include inbreeding in small populations, the preference for consanguineous matings in many societies, and the founder principle operating in small migrant populations.

Balanced polymorphism, or heterozygous advantage (Chapter 5), has been identified as the mechanism responsible for the relatively high frequency of sickle-cell anemia in many populations of Africa and elsewhere. This mechanism also may be involved in the elevated frequencies of cystic fibrosis, phenylketonuria, schizophrenia, Tay-Sachs disease, and other conditions. Modern technology has alleviated the selective advantage of many balanced polymorphisms, and so it may be impossible to discover the nature of the former advantage that a heterozygous genotype bestows on individuals of a population.

Cultural Variation

Different populations have different technologies, marriage patterns, religions, and economies. They possess different ideas of nature, justice, and law. Even body

Table 17.1 Frequencies (Percent) of Diego-Positive Phenotype in Various Populations

Population	Frequency of Diego-Positive
Caingangs (Brazil)	45.8
Carajas (Brazil)	36.1
Caribs (Venezuela)	35.5
Maya Indians (Mexico)	17.6
Guahibos (Venezuela)	14.5
Japanese	12.3
Chippewas (Canada)	10.8
Koreans	6.1
Guajiros (Venezuela)	5.3
Apaches (United States)	4.1
Eskimos (Alaska)	0.8
Lapps (Norway)	0.0
Polynesians	0.0
Aborigines (Australia)	0.0
Whites (United States)	0.0
Asiatic Indians	0.0
Africans (Liberia, Ivory Coast)	0.0
Bushmen (South Africa)	0.0

Source: G. A. Harrison et al., *Human Biology* (New York: Oxford University Press, 1964), p. 275.

Table 17.2 The Ethnic Distribution of Genetic Disease*

Population	Disease	Inheritance Pattern[†]
Europeans in general	Alkapoturnia	AR
	Anencephaly	PG
	Cystic fibrosis	AR
	Oculocutaneous albinism	AR
	Porphyria variegata	AD
	Spina bifida	PG
Ashkenazi Jews	Gaucher's disease	AR
	Hyperuricemia (gout)	AD
	Tay-Sachs disease	AR
Greeks, Italians, and Armenians	G6PD deficiency	XLR
	Thalassemia major (Cooley's anemia)	AR
Northern Europeans	Lactase deficiency	AD
	Pernicious anemia	PG
Irish	Phenylketonuria (PKU)	AR
Amish and Icelanders	Ellis–van Creveld syndrome	AR
Africans	G6PD deficiency	XLR
	Hemoglobinopathies (hemoglobin S, hemoglobin C)	CD
	Polydactyly	PG
Chinese	Alpha thalassemia	AR
	G6PD deficiency, Chinese type	XLR
Japanese	Acatalasia	AR
	Cleft palate	PG
	Wilson's disease	AR

* This table indicates some of the genetic diseases found in high frequencies in particular populations.

† AR, autosomal recessive; AD, autosomal dominant; PG, polygenic; XLR, X-linked recessive; CD, codominant.

Source: V. McKusick, *Mendelian Inheritance in Man: Catalogs of Autosomal Dominant, Autosomal Recessive, and X-Linked Phenotypes,* 5th ed. (Baltimore: Johns Hopkins, 1978).

movements and thought patterns are culturally tempered. Within a group, all these factors are integrated into a functional system, with each element related in some way to the others. The cultural system, in turn, is intimately related to the noncultural environment and to human biology.

Different peoples have different ideas of beauty, based on their cultural traditions. To achieve effects that they consider to be aesthetically pleasing, many groups permanently alter the shape and the structure of the body by artificial means. This alteration often serves to distinguish individuals of high status in cultures in which little clothing is worn. Various societies provide medical and religious justifications for body alterations. Examples of body alterations include circumcision, clitoridectomy (surgical removal of the external portion of the clitoris), scarification, body piercing, and tattooing.

The face and the head are frequently subject to modification. For example, many people bind the heads of infants to create an artificially shaped head (Figure 17.4a). Punan women of Borneo slit their earlobes and insert brass rings, eventually drawing each lobe down to the shoulder.

Societies throughout the world alter the body to enhance beauty, attain status, or become initiated. Several groups pierce the nasal septum, others slit the lips, and, in the United States, many pierce the ear and other parts of the head and body (Figure 17.4b). Each method allows ornaments to be attached. Foot binding, plastic surgery, hair and skin transplants, and many other methods of surgically or cosmetically altering the body are practiced in various parts of the world.

(a)   (b)

Figure 17.4 Deformation of the Head (a) Woman from the Mangbetu of the Democratic Republic of the Congo with an artificially elongated head. This is accomplished by tightly binding cord around the head of an infant; (b) American showing body piercing.

Summary

Human variation is often clinal in nature, that is, expressed as gradations. Yet some traits appear almost exclusively within one or a few populations. These traits are said to show a distribution that is discontinuous.

Humans differ in their anatomy, physiology, ontogeny, and culture. Except for culture, which is by definition learned, all these factors can have a genetic component. In many instances, the environment also plays a powerful role in creating variation. In fact, it would be more accurate to say that human morphology (form) and behavior are products of the dynamic interaction between cultural, biological, and environmental variables. Because the relationship between these variables is dynamic, the differences between human groups are in a constant state of flux. For any particular trait, two groups may become more or less similar to each other at different times, depending on the particular situations.

Box 17-1   Skeletal Evidence of Cultural Practices

While many alterations of the human body are deliberate, many other changes in anatomy are nondeliberate side effects of cultural practices. For example, humans in all cultures habitually assume particular resting postures. In adulthood, the postures learned in childhood have become normal and comfortable. Postures encountered in other cultures may prove difficult and often painful to assume and may permanently affect the anatomy.

D. H. Ubelaker excavated a large number of skeletons at Hacienda Ayalan on the southern coast of Ecuador. On analysis,

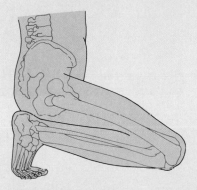

he found that many of the bones of the foot, specifically the metatarsals and the phalanges (see the appendix), showed several unusual features, such as small bony extensions.

Analysis of the Ecuadoran skeletons suggests that the unique features in the foot skeleton developed from the stresses produced from frequent and extreme hyperdorsiflexion of the metatarsophalangeal joints. The figure illustrates this extreme backward movement of the joints between the metatarsal bones of the ankle and the phalanges of the toes. This movement would result from the individual's assuming a kneeling position with the weight of the body pressing down on the joints within the foot. Since these features are found most frequently in female skeletons, Ubelaker suggests that this body position was assumed by women as they ground maize on stone metates. Thus, whether describing skeletal material or a living human body, anthropologists must know whether they are dealing with genetic traits, environmentally produced features, or cultural modifications of some genetically determined trait.

Source: D. H. Ubelaker, "Skeletal Evidence for Kneeling in Prehistoric Ecuador," *American Journal of Physical Anthropology* 51 (1979), pp. 679–686.

THE CLASSIFICATION OF HUMAN VARIATION

People are natural classifiers. They see nature as being composed of types of things rather than individual entities. If every rock, tree, or animal had a unique label attached to it, effective communication would be impossible. Therefore, people speak in categories; they talk of igneous rocks, pine trees, and mammals.

Each group of people classifies the world around it. Any human group has an answer to the question "What kinds of rocks, trees, or animals are there?" but the categories expressed by people do not necessarily describe the world as seen by objective science. These categories reflect specific cultural traditions and differ from society to society. Anthropologists refer to such classifications as **folk taxonomies.**

Categorization or classification is necessary in everyday communication as well as in science. Without the ability to generalize, conversation would be difficult and laws and theories could not exist. Nevertheless, folk taxonomies do not always correspond to reality. When the inaccuracies apply to categorizations of people, they often mirror hatred and mistrust.

folk taxonomy Classification of some class of phenomena based on cultural tradition.

Folk Taxonomies of Race

In coping with the world, people visualize human variation in terms of categories. The simplest type of classification is one in which a particular people will classify themselves as "human" and everyone else as "less than human." For instance, the Navahos of the American Southwest call themselves *diné,* which, roughly translated, means "the people." This label implies that the Navaho see themselves as set apart and distinct from the non-Navahos they encounter. This frequently encountered type of conceptualization also existed among the ancient Greeks, who divided humankind into two categories: Greeks and barbarians. Some Greeks believed that the barbarians just made noises or babbled. Today we play a reversal on the Greeks with the saying "It's all Greek to me."

Figure 17.5 Four American Racial Stereotypes in the Movies (a) Graham Green, born on the Six Nations Reserve in Ontario, Canada, in *Maverick* (1994); (b) Jet Li, born in Beijing, China, in *Hero* (2002), (c) Vivien Leigh, born of British parents in Darjeeling, India, and Hattie McDaniel, born in Wichita, Kansas, in *Gone with the Wind* (1939).

(a)

(b)

(c)

See the Online Learning Center for an Internet Activity on how race and ethnicity are handled by the United States Census Bureau.

In urban centers, and to a lesser degree elsewhere, a person encounters daily a variety of people of different statures, skin colors, and facial features. If people at an American suburban shopping center were asked to list the different types of people in the world, the most frequent answers would probably be Caucasoid, Mongoloid, and Negroid; or Black, Brown, Yellow, Red, and White; or African American, Indian or Native American, Hispanic, and Asian; or some other combination of terms (Figure 17.5).

Such classifications are examples of folk taxonomies that reflect how many Americans perceive human differences. Do they also reflect reality? The answer is both yes and no. Folk taxonomies do have a social reality in that many forms of behavior are determined by them. In a situation requiring interaction with another person, an American of European ancestry may behave differently if the other individual is perceived as "Hispanic" or "African American." On the other hand, physical anthropologists deal with biological reality, and here folk taxonomies do not reflect what we know about human variation.

Few Americans have seen aboriginal peoples from remote regions of the world, such as the Ainu, the Australian aborigine, the San, or the Lapp. Most Americans have contact primarily with peoples whose origins are in Europe, the Middle East, west Africa, Latin America, and parts of Asia, particularly Japan, China, and southeast Asia. A person who looks somewhat different from the people normally encountered is forced into an existing category. Thus, American soldiers during World War II often classified the Melanesians of the western Pacific as "Negro" even though there was no direct genetic link with the peoples of the African continent.

Folk taxonomies tend to mix the concept of race with the concept of ethnicity. In biology, racial differences are differences in heritable (genetic) characteristics. A **race** is a taxonomic division of a species. A race biologically differs in a significant number of genetic characteristics from other races in the same species. To an anthropologist an **ethnic group** is a group of people who share a common culture: traditions, language, religion, and history. A nonanthropologist often mixes racial labels such as white and black with ethnic labels such as Hispanic, African American, and Greek-American.

Attempts at Scientific Classifications of Human Variation

"Races do not exist; classifications of mankind do."[1] Scientific classifications of people, like folk taxonomies of people, are attempts to divide human beings into specific groups, but this is where the similarity ends.

A scientific classification is a means of discovering the processes that create the phenomenon being classified, in this case, human variation. A scientific classification of human variation would be a model serving a function similar to that of other scientific models, such as the Hardy-Weinberg formula. This formula is a way of discovering whether forces of evolution are working on a population. Similarly, a classification of human variation should be a way of discovering the processes involved in creating human genotypic and phenotypic variation.

Folk taxonomies are usually based on ethnocentric ideas about the inherent differences in physical appearance and behavior between groups. Although some of these beliefs may be partially based on observation, most are based on folklore or stereotypes. In contrast, the criteria used in scientific classification must be derived from empirical studies. In other words, the attributing of different characteristics to different populations must be validated through procedures of the scientific method.

Carolus Linnaeus (1707–1778) was perhaps the first person to apply systematic criteria in a uniform way in classifying humans. His contribution, the first scientific taxonomy of the living world, included people. Linnaeus labeled all humans *Homo sapiens,* from *Homo,* meaning "man," and *sapiens,* meaning "wise." He then divided the human species into four groups based on the criteria of skin color and geographical location. These four categories are *H. sapiens Africanus negreus* (black), *H. sapiens Americanus rubescens* (red), *H. sapiens Asiaticus fucus* (darkish), and *H. sapiens Europeus albescens* (white).

Among scientists, this classification did not stand the test of time. For one thing, it excluded many peoples. Where were the peoples of Oceania, India, and other areas to be placed? Could it legitimately be said that all peoples of Africa had the same skin color? North Africans are light-skinned, the San of south Africa are brownish-yellow, and the Bantu are dark. While Linnaeus's general system of classification of plants and animals was readily adopted by the scientific community, his classification of people was not. Nevertheless, his notion of four races is still used by many Europeans and Americans.

Nineteenth-Century Classification Johann Friedrich Blumenbach (1752–1840) was a German physician and student of comparative human anatomy. He divided the human species into five "races": *Caucasian, Mongolian, Ethiopian, Malayan,* and *American.* The term *Ethiopian* was later changed to *Negro.*

Anders Retzius (1796–1860) noted many variations within the five types proposed by Blumenbach. Deciding that the shape of the head was an important criterion for classifying

race A taxonomic division of a species differing biologically in a significant number of genetic characteristics from other races of the same species.

ethnic group A group of people who share a common culture, including traditions, language, religion, and history.

See the Online Learning Center for an Internet Activity on the anthropological approach to race.

---

[1] G. A. Dorsey, "Race and Civilization," in C. A. Beard (ed.), *Whither Mankind: A Panorama of Modern Civilization* (New York: Longmans Green, 1928), p. 254.

cephalic index The breadth of the head relative to its length.

people, Retzius developed the cephalic index as a means of comparing populations. The **cephalic index** is the breadth of the head relative to the length, as given by the formula

$$\frac{\text{Head breadth}}{\text{Head length}} \times 100$$

These early attempts set up two criteria for the classification of human variation: outward physical characteristics and geographical origin. The measurements made and the indices calculated led to classifications that were wholly descriptive in nature. They did not explain the process that created the observed variations. Often the classifications arrived at did not appear to fit the real world, as when members of the same family were placed into different "races" on the basis of the criteria used.

Use of Blood Types in Classification With the development of genetic theory, anthropologists began to question the use of the traditional criteria of classification. Skin color, they argued, was a poor standard, since its mechanism of inheritance is unknown and it is affected by environment and culture. Therefore, some anthropologists turned to the blood-type systems as a basis for classification. Blood type is easy to determine; in most cases, blood typing can be done in the field. A given blood type is either present or absent, and it is not affected by environmental factors. Finally, the mechanisms of inheritance of blood types, for the most part, are known.

William Boyd published in 1950 the following classification based on an analysis of the frequencies of specific blood types: (1) *Early European* (hypothetical category, represented today only by the Basques of Spain), (2) *European* (Caucasoid), (3) *African* (Negroid), (4) *Asiatic* (Mongoloid), (5) *American Indian,* and (6) *Australoid.*[2]

A major problem with the use of blood-type frequencies as the sole criterion for the categorizing of human populations is that most of these frequencies show a clinal distribution. Although major differences may exist in two populations from either end of the cline, this distinctiveness is blurred by subtle differences in frequencies in intermediate populations.

Classification and the Fossil Record To some people, there are a fixed number of categories of people that correspond to basic divisions from the remote past. A classification based on the fossil record is that of Carlton S. Coon, who in his 1962 book *The Origin of Races* divided the human species into five categories: *Australoids, Mongoloids, Caucasoids, Congoids* (dark-skinned Africans), and *Capoids* (the San and Hottentots of southern Africa).[3]

Coon postulated that humankind separated into his five divisions before the evolution of our species, *Homo sapiens.* To him, human fossils represented early stages in this pre-*sapiens* development. An early fossil found in Java would be an early Australoid, while a fossil from China would be an early Mongoloid, and so on. Coon also proposed that hominins in each of the five evolutionary lines evolved into *Homo sapiens* at different times, and, hence, different living races have developed on a *Homo sapiens* level for differing amounts of time, which accounts for differences in cultural development. This clearly racist conclusion is not consistent with the evidence.

In Chapter 15, we discussed the regional continuity model of human evolution that links certain finds with contemporary populations. The problem with such links, however, is that human variation does not follow clear-cut evolutionary lines. Gene flow between adjacent groups and migrations serve to confuse such lines. While distinct populations may have existed among human ancestors, it is extremely unlikely that such groups maintained themselves as distinct entities over long periods of evolution.

Geographical Races Another approach to the classification of human variation is the 1961 scheme of Stanley Garn.[4] He observed that people living in the same large geographical area tend to resemble one another more closely than they do people in different geographical areas (Figure 17.6). Of course, this is a generalization with many exceptions. Garn divided

---

[2] W. C. Boyd, *Genetics and the Races of Man* (Boston: Little, Brown, 1956).

[3] C. S. Coon, *The Origin of Races* (New York: Knopf, 1962).

[4] S. M. Garn, *Human Races* (Springfield, IL: Charles C. Thomas, 1961).

Figure 17.6 The Faces of Human Variation

(a) San, Kalahari Desert, Botswana

(b) Efe, Ituri Forest, Zaire

(c) Somba, Dahomey

(d) Ainu, Hokkaido, Japan

Figure 17.6 *(continued)*

(e) Bagish, China

(f) Bangalore, India

(g) Hmong, Laos

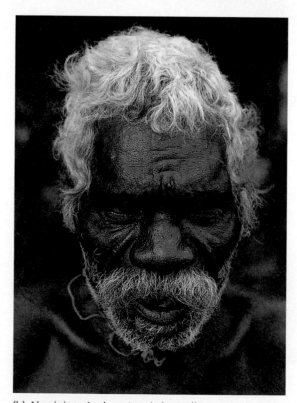

(h) Aborigine, Arnhem Land, Australia

(i) Mendi, South Highlands, New Guinea

(j) Tonga, Polynesia

(k) Hamadan, Iran

Figure 17.6 *(concluded)*

(l) Kauto Keino Lapp, Norway

(m) Tbilisi, Georgia

(o) Taos Pueblo, New Mexico

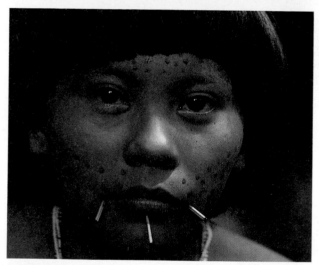

(n) Yanomama, Brazil

geographical race A major division of humankind into large geographical areas wherein people resemble one another more closely than they resemble people in different geographical areas.

the human species into nine large **geographical races.** Geography alone is the major criterion for classification, not an arbitrarily chosen trait such as skin color, blood type, or cephalic index. Since gene flow does take place more frequently within a major geographical zone than between adjacent zones, populations in the same major geographical areas generally show some similar gene frequencies.

The Changing Nature of Human Variation A problem with dividing humanity into any finite number of races, at any level, is that human variation is dynamic, and the shape of clines changes constantly. Old populations are broken down, and new ones are established.

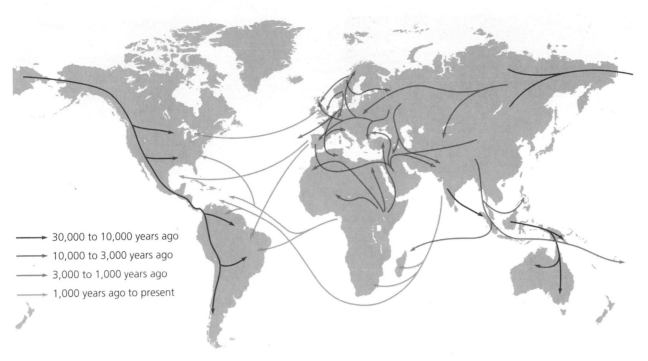

Figure 17.7 Major Movements of Humans in the Last 30,000 Years

- → 30,000 to 10,000 years ago
- → 10,000 to 3,000 years ago
- → 3,000 to 1,000 years ago
- → 1,000 years ago to present

Between 1845 and 1854, 3 million people migrated to the United States. Between 1881 and 1920, 23 ½ million people entered the United States from such countries as Great Britain, Italy, Germany, Spain, Russia, Portugal, and Sweden. Some of these people formed partial isolates, such as Germans in Pennsylvania, Welsh in upper New York, and Scandinavians in Wisconsin and Minnesota.

Data gathered in the last census show that in March 2000, 28.4 million persons residing in the United States were foreign born. Of these individuals, 51.0 percent were born in Latin America, 25.5 percent were born in Asia, 15.3 percent were born in Europe, and 8.1 percent were born in other regions of the world.[5] Data from the U.S. Immigration and Naturalization Service report that in the late 1990s persons who legally immigrated to the United States were predominately from Mexico, the Philippines, India, Vietnam, China, and Nigeria. The balance represented virtually every geographic area of the world. With each migration, the gene pool is reconstituted; hence, a description of the people in a geographical area at one specific time may not hold at another time (Figure 17.7).

The Nature of Human Variation and Its Classification In traditional systems of classification, particular traits are used to divide humankind into a finite number of categories. Most often one or a few traits are used to define each category, one of the most frequently used being skin color. If a classification based on skin color is valid, these categories would be real, natural units. These natural units would differ from one another in a number of ways since natural groups are characterized by clusters of traits. In other words, when a few traits are used in such classifications, the underlying assumption is that groups so classified will be different from each other in traits not used in the classification.

When we plot the distribution of different traits on a map, we are struck by the fact that the patterns of the distribution more often than not do not correspond with one another. For example, the distribution of skin color in Europe changes from light to dark from north

[5] L. Lollock, *Current Population Reports: The Foreign-Born Population in the United States* (Washington, DC: U.S. Census Bureau, 2001). Publication can be found on the Web at www.census.gov/population/www/socdemo/foreign.

Table 17.3 Comparison of Traits in Five Populations*

Trait	Population				
	South American Native	West African	English	Japanese	Greek
PTC nontasting[†]	1.2	2.7	31.5	7.1	
Blood type B[‡]	0–5	15–20	5–10	20–25	10–15
Lactase deficiency[§]	Up to 100	Up to 100	32	90	88
Sickle-cell trait and anemia[¶]	Up to 16	Up to 34	0	0	Up to 32

* Data are expressed in average percentages.
[†] G. A. Harrison et al., *Human Biology* (New York: Oxford University Press, 1964), p. 274.
[‡] A. E. Mourant, A. C. Kopeč, and K. Domaniewska-Sobczak, *The Distribution of the Human Blood Groups and Other Polymorphisms,* 2nd ed. (London: Oxford University Press, 1976).
[§] See Robert D. McCracken, "Lactase Deficiency. An Example of Dietary Evolution," *Current Anthropology* 12 (1971), pp. 479–517; and Norman Kretchner, "Lactose and Lactase," *Scientific American* 277 (October 1972), p. 76.
[¶] Frank B. Livingstone, *Abnormal Hemoglobins in Human Populations* (Chicago: Aldine, 1967), pp. 162–470.

to south, while the frequency of blood type B roughly decreases from east to west. Some populations characterized by very dark skin also are associated with curly hair, and others with straight hair; some are tall, others are short; some have thick lips, others have thin lips. Populations living in Australia, southern India, and Africa may share skin color but differ considerably in other traits. Even in Africa the physical differences among populations differ as much as, or even more than, the populations of Europe.

This point is further illustrated in Table 17.3. Here we see the frequencies of phenyl-thiocarbamide (PTC) nontasting, blood type B, lactase deficiency (an enzyme required to break down lactose, or milk sugar), and sickle-cell trait and anemia. With respect to PTC nontasting and lactase deficiency, west Africans are closest to South American Indians, yet in relation to sickle-cell anemia, west Africans are closest to Greeks.

The Genetic Relationship between Human Populations

Earlier in this chapter, we discussed the work of William Boyd, who used blood-type frequencies in developing a classification of human races. His was an early attempt to employ the study of human variation on the molecular level. Since the 1950s great progress has been made in the analysis of molecular variation. Now both nuclear and mitochondrial DNA can be studied directly. The methodologies that have been developed for such studies have provided scientists with a wealth of data for studying the genetic relationships among populations.

Two important conclusions can be drawn from the molecular data. First, the average genetic differences between geographically separated human populations are fewer than the genetic differences within a single population. Second, because of the relatively small number of genetic differences among geographically separated populations, those populations should not be assigned to separate subspecies. The differences in human populations are fewer than those that zoologists consider significant enough to employ to divide nonhuman species into subspecies.

In 1988, Luigi Luca Cavalli-Sforza and his colleagues collected published data on gene frequencies from 42 aboriginal populations in Africa, North and South America, Oceania, Europe, and Asia.[6] They then constructed a genetic tree that diagrammed those genetic relationships. A tree showing the relationships among 38 populations is shown in Figure 17.8.

---

[6] L. L. Cavalli-Sforza et al., "Reconstruction of Human Evolution: Bringing Together Genetic, Archaeological, and Linguistic Data," *Proceedings of the National Academy of Sciences,* 85 (1988), pp. 6002–6006.

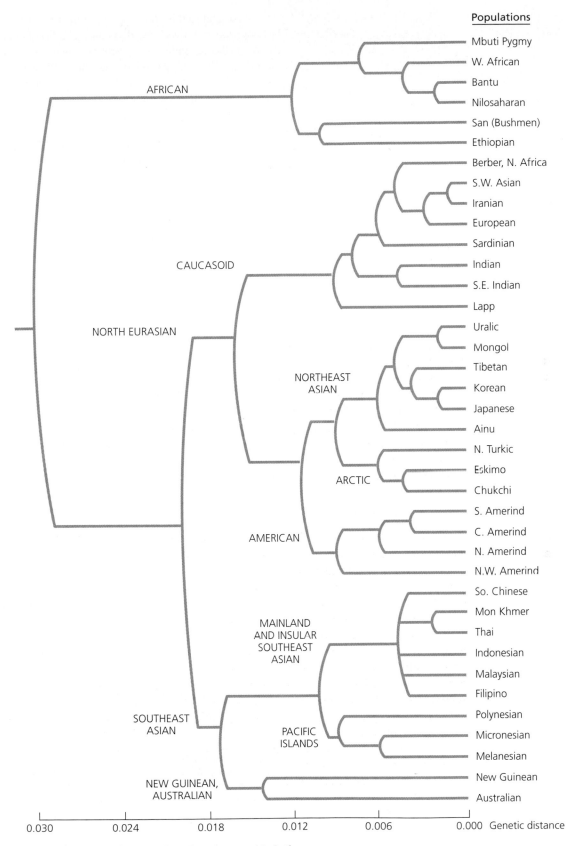

Populations

Figure 17.8 Genetic Tree Showing Human Variation

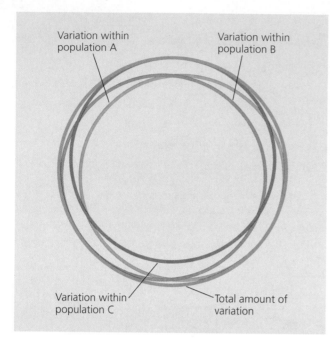

Variation within population A

Variation within population B

Variation within population C

Total amount of variation

Figure 17.9 Nature of Genetic Variation in Human Groups Recent studies have shown that between 85 and 93 percent of all human variation exists within continental populations. The 7 to 15 percent variation between human populations living on different continents falls below what taxonomists use to divide populations into subspecies (races). This is one of the reasons most biological scientists do not believe that dividing humans into races is valid biologically.

genomics The study of the entire genome of a species.

haplotype A group or block of nucleotides that tends to be inherited together.

According to this study, the 42 human populations may be separated into two large divisions. The first contains the Africans; the second may be broken down into two major groupings: the north Eurasians and the southeast Asians.

The north Eurasian "supercluster" includes the Caucasoids, a group that includes the peoples of Europe, north Africa, southwest Asia, and India. A major subdivision includes two further groupings. The first includes the peoples of northeast Asia, such as the Mongols, the Tibetans, the Japanese, the Arctic peoples of Asia, and the Eskimos. The second grouping includes the aboriginal peoples of North and South America.

The second major "supercluster" is that of the southeast Asians. This group includes the peoples of mainland and insular southeast Asia, such as those of Thailand, Indonesia, Malaya, and the Philippines; the peoples of the Pacific islands, including those of Polynesia, Micronesia, and Melanesia; and the peoples of Australia.

This study does not attempt to develop a classification of human populations per se; rather, it attempts to determine the genetic relationships among those populations. Linguistic models for the distance between groups generally correspond to the genetic data. Two linguistic superfamilies show very close correspondence with the two major divisions based on genetic data markers.

Genomics Genomics is the study of an entire genome. A genome is defined as all the genes carried by a single gamete of a specific species. One thing that genomic researchers study is haplotypes. A **haplotype** is a group or block of nucleotides that tends to be inherited together. Genomic studies of human variation have shown patterns in haplotypes for continental populations (close to what Garn called geographical races). In a study that collected haplotype data from Africa, Asia, and Europe, 52 percent of the 928 haplotypes studied were found on all three continents, 72 on two continents, and 28 percent on only one continent (most in Africa).[7] Even though there is a pattern for such groupings of linked genes as well as differences between populations in the frequencies of individual genes, the conclusion of genomic researchers is that fixed groupings of people do not emerge from these studies.

There is more variation for any specific haplotype within a continental group than there is between groups (Figure 17.9). For any haplotype, a person from one continent is likely to be more closely related to a person from another continent than to a person living on his or her own continent. Also, haplotype similarities or differences do not correspond well to phenotypic traits used in western folk taxonomies such as skin color and hair type. Therefore, many genomic researchers, such as Svante Pääbo, believe: "In the future, we . . . need to focus on individuals rather than populations when exploring genetic variation in our species".[8]

Race as Illusion

About 93 percent of allelic variation in human populations occurs within any given continental group.[9] The remaining 7 percent accounts for a very small proportion of human

---

[7] S. B. Gabriel, et al., "The Structure of Haplotype Blocks in the Human Genome," *Science,* 296 (2002), pp. 2225–2229.

[8] S. Pääbo, "The Mosaic That Is Our Genome," *Nature,* 421 (2003), p. 411.

[9] A. Goodman, "Interview with Alan Goodman," in *Race—The Power of Illusion,* PBS, Larry Adelman, series producer, 2003.

variation. Much of this variation has little biological significance, such as differences in the percentages of the various alleles for eye color. Because of this fact, biological scientists consider race a social concept with little biological meaning.

Race as it is used in Western folk taxonomies is a relatively recent concept. Most cultures do not divide people on the basis of supposed differences in what are considered important biological characteristics. For instance, before slavery in the Americas, slaves who were kept by a particular group, such as the ancient Egyptians, were not all of the same physical type. Slaves often looked just like their masters. They were enslaved as a result of warfare among similar groups of people, because they were in debt to the person who became their master, or because they spoke a language different from that of a more powerful group.

Predominately, in the western world, the concept that people who looked different were also different in other ways, such as their level of intelligence, their morality, and their ability to be "civilized," was used to justify unequal treatment of those people. This concept justified slavery; genocidal policies toward Native Americans, Australian Aborigines, Tasmanians, and other indigenous peoples; the exclusion of immigrants from certain areas of the world; and other racist policies.

Since the mid-1950s in the United States, racial policies such as segregation in schools and the exclusion of people from professions on the basis of physical differences have been declared unconstitutional. The advantages of the "white" majority in terms of power, wealth, income, and prestige have declined in recent decades. With this decline, the folk taxonomy that sees a limited number of significantly different races has begun to fade. This is reflected in and is being reinforced by changes in the way the United States government collects data on individuals.

The Office of Management and Budget (OMB) determines how federal agencies, including the United States Census Bureau, collect data on people's perceived ancestral group affiliation. From 1977 to 1997 people were asked to mark whether they were of Hispanic origin or not of Hispanic origin and to mark separately what race they were: White, Black, Asian, Pacific Islander, American Indian, and Other. There are subcategories for some of these types. A respondent could only mark one "race."

Starting in 1997, respondents could mark more than one category. Respondents now can choose any of 126 "races." Therefore, a person could classify himself or herself, for example, as a White–Japanese–American Indian. The number of possible categories will increase in the 2010 and 2020 censuses until no limit is placed on the number of possible categories. The Census Bureau considers these categories to be self-selected social definitions of what it is calling *race*. In reality they are mostly self-estimates of geographical ancestries that mix the concept of perceived biological affinity and that of cultural identity. Yet this approach is certainly more realistic than the concept that there are four races and a Hispanic–non-Hispanic distinction.[10]

Race and Medicine

> Race is no more produced by genes today than was the ancestral condition of being a
> lord or serf an expression of a lord or serf gene five hundred years ago, even though one
> would have been able to locate statistically significant differences of particular DNA
> fragments between serfs and lords.[11]

If the division of humanity into a number of finite groups such as black, white, Asian, Pacific Islander, and American Indian is not valid biologically, why do we read reports that make statements such as "blacks develop high blood pressure and heart failure more than whites"? The answer is simple. Many medical researchers and medical organizations are using these

[10] You can read the American Anthropological Association's statement on the way the OMB determines race and ethnic standards at www.aaanet.org/gvt/ombdraft.htm.

[11] J. Stevens, "Racial Meaning and Scientific Methods: Changing Policies for NIH-Sponsored Publications Reporting Human Variation," *Journal of Health Politics, Policy and Law,* 28 (2003), p.1036.

labels to refer to social categories, not biological ones, or they still believe, contrary to genetic studies, that the concept of biological race based on old folk classifications is valid.

In reality, a person designated as black, white, Asian, Pacific Islander, or American Indian could be a mixture of numerous ancestries and could share little genetically with other people classified under the same racial label. It is true that correlations between people classified by the old racial folk taxonomy and various diseases might hold true statistically. However, in most cases this is the case because people grouped into the same "race" often share similar social behaviors and opportunities, including diet, working conditions, and access to medical care.

In Chapter 3, we observed that certain groups have a higher incidence of certain genetic diseases, such as albinism among the Hopi (a Native American group) and sickle-cell anemia in "black" Americans. In reality, these are not diseases of groups with a specific racial (genetic) identity but of people with a specific ancestry in a specific area of the world. An increased incidence of the allele for sickle-cell anemia is the result of the relationship between the allele for sickle-cell anemia and malaria (Chapter 3). People with one allele for the disease possess a heterozygous advantage that provides protection against malaria. People with ancestry not only in Africa but also in other areas where malaria was a problem, such as the Mediterranean and southern India, also have a high incidence of sickle-cell anemia and other similar genetic diseases.

To some degree the Hopi culturally select for albinism. Albinos were thought to have spiritual powers and were therefore valued by the Hopi. Also, the Hopi realized that the sun adversely affects albinos and allowed albinos to stay in the village rather then go into the fields, where they would have greater exposure to ultraviolet radiation. Albino men may have had a greater number of children than did nonalbino men. Therefore, the high incidence of albinism among the Hopi did not occur because the Hopi are genetically dissimilar from other groups that do not have a high incidence of albinism but because the Hopi had cultural practices related to albinos that were different from the practices of other people.

The medical profession is struggling with the question of the value of traditional racial classification in medical research and the diagnosis and treatment of disease. Most medical researchers believe that ancestry is a better diagnostic tool in medicine than is the traditional concept of race. Each patient or research subject should be treated as an individual, but data should be collected about a person's ancestry (which is almost always mixed) as a potential indicator of a correlation to a specific disease found more frequently in a group from a specific continental area or displaying a specific cultural practice.

Human Variation and Intelligence

Alfred Binet (1857–1911) developed the IQ test in France in 1904. Binet never meant for the test to be used to measure something that might be called general intelligence. In fact, he did not believe that there was one thing called intelligence. His test was developed to determine whether schoolchildren needed special education. He did not see a score on his test as being fixed but as changing as educational deficits were remedied. Binet worried that his test would be used to permanently classify a child as dumb. As it turned out, Binet's fears were realized. For most of the twentieth century, the IQ test was seen as establishing a fixed intelligence score for a person. It was used to stigmatize not only individuals but entire groups of people based on a group's average score on the test.

IQ testing began in the United States early in the twentieth century, when members of various ethnic groups, such as Poles, Greeks, Italians, and Jews, were entering the United States in large numbers. Those immigrant groups were consistently found to average about 20 points lower than the national average on IQ tests. Later in the century, people classified as "African American" scored about 15 points lower on average than did "whites."

A question that has received much attention and that has been at the core of much political and educational policy is "Are the differences in IQ scores due to environmental causes or differences in innate potential?" The answer that has been obvious to many social and behavioral scientists is that differences in intelligence scores between groups of people are mostly due to sociocultural factors. For instance, by 1970, the descendants of the immigrants

See the Online Learning Center for an Internet Activity on eugenics.

See the Online Learning Center for an Internet Activity on the differential course of human history on the different continents.

who entered the United States around the time of World War I were scoring at the national level or higher on IQ tests. This was due to obvious social changes in language skills, lifestyle, and education. As more African Americans have reached middle- and upper-class economic status in the United States, their average scores on IQ tests and other standardized tests have increased.

IQ tests use symbols that are common within the particular culture that develops the test. The test is said to be **culture-bound.** This means that if the test has relevance at all, it will have relevance only for members of the culture that uses the language and general concepts employed in the test.

As an example, most Americans may think that the question illustrated in Figure 17.10 is a perfectly logical one to ask. Yet making the correct choice in the time given depends on previous experience. If this question were given to Australian aborigine trackers, for example, who have had little or no contact with the concepts of two-dimensional geometry, they would probably answer it incorrectly because of their lack of experience with the things pictured. On the other hand, if a city-dwelling American were asked to identify if a set of footprints was made by a man or a woman, an adult or a child, he or she would probably fail where the Australian tracker would succeed.

Verbal exams are equally biased. In one of these, a battery of questions is asked, such as the name of the person who wrote *Faust*. The answer to this, Goethe (Gounod wrote the opera), might be familiar to children who emigrated from Germany or who have German parents. Or it might be known by a college student who enrolled in world literature as opposed to one who enrolled in English literature. Going one step further, the upper-middle-class teenager who does not have to work after school to help support his or her family may spend leisure time reading. A person from a poor family who must work may have no time or motivation to read books. Also, a poor family simply may maintain a household without books.

On the same test, by the way, is the question: What is ethnology? Ethnology is a branch of anthropology, but the answer given as correct for this question conforms to none of the modern anthropological definitions of this term. In other words, an incorrect response might be marked "correct." The point is that these tests are biased toward "white" middle-class experiences; in some cases, the answers expected by the testers are grounded in the middle-class experience.

In the light of the preceding observations, one easily can see why various ethnic groups in the United States tend to score, on the average, lower than "whites" on standard IQ tests. These tests embody questions that are considered important to the "white" middle-class population. In fact, such commonly used tests as the Stanford-Binet were standardized by using "white" subjects only.

IQ tests emphasize mathematical manipulation, a subject to which middle-class children usually are exposed early in life. Their parents may have been to college, and many of these children have had early preschool experience as well. In lower socioeconomic communities, the parents often had to go to work early in life; few have gone to college. Thus, mathematical logic is both less important and less attainable to them. Such parents often do not value the existing educational systems because they do not see the schools as helpful in preparing their children for jobs or in providing social mobility. As a result, children from lower socioeconomic groups often do not attend preschool. In addition, vocabulary and other dialect differences exist between social classes, ethnic groups, and regions of the country. Lower IQ scores often reflect a lack of understanding of the question because of the way in which it is worded.

Another important point is that even when comparisons are made between ethnic groups in the United States with differing lifestyles and experiences, the differences in IQ scores within each group greatly exceed the differences between groups. Whereas the scores of

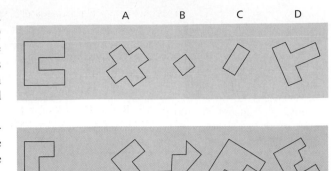

Figure 17.10 Intelligence Testing This is an example of a test for the measurement of spatial ability. The subject is asked to mark the drawing that will make a complete square with the first figure. Speed is important. This type of test would be extremely difficult for members of a society in which geometric shapes are not utilized to the same degree as they are in U.S. society.

culture-bound The state or quality of having relevance only to the members of a specific cultural group.

Box 17-2 — Are the Japanese, on the Average, Smarter Than Americans?

In October of 1986, Yasuhiro Nakasone, prime minister of Japan, offered an explanation of why Japan competes so well against the United States: The Japanese people score higher on IQ tests than Americans do. Indeed, the mean national IQ score in Japan is about 111 compared with 100 in the United States. Nakasone's remark seems to suggest a belief in a connection between race and intelligence. Nakasone seems to be blaming the differences in scores on innate factors. In examining Japanese culture, no innate factors need be postulated to explain the 11-point IQ-score advantage that the Japanese appear to display.

Here are some reasons that could explain the differences in average scores between Japanese and Americans:

1. Japanese children attend school for an average of 240 days a year; American children attend school less than 180 days a year.

2. The quality of education is uniformly high in Japan. Most Japanese are of the same social class, and about 99 percent are of the same ethnic group.

3. Discipline and expectations of students in Japan are much greater than in the United States.

4. Japanese students are assigned heavier course loads and more homework than their American counterparts.

5. Economic success in Japan is absolutely dependent on academic achievement. Although academic achievement increases the chances of economic success in the United States, it is not absolutely essential.

6. Almost all Japanese value education. The consequences of dropping out of school are extremely negative. Only 2 percent of Japanese high school seniors drop out of school compared with 27 percent of high school seniors in the United States.

It is therefore no wonder that mean IQ scores are higher in Japan than in the United States. The Japanese place a greater value on education. As a result, Japanese children take educational goals more seriously and spend more time in school and on homework than American children. The differences in average IQ scores between groups labeled as different races or ethnic groups in the United States most likely are also due to a mix of sociocultural factors rather than innate differences.

Even though the American mean IQ is not as high as that of the Japanese, Americans are responsible for innovating more of this century's new technologies than any other nationality and have won more Nobel Prizes than have the members of any other culture. IQ scores do not test such things as creativity. American society emphasizes creativity.

Sources: E. Brown, "Nakasone's World-Class Blunder," *Time,* October 6, 1986, pp. 66–67; "A Racial Slur Stirs Up a Storm," *Newsweek,* October 6, 1986, p. 35; T. Watanabe, "Cookie-Cutter Education," *Los Angeles Times,* June 24, 1990, pp. D10–D11.

---

people from the same ethnic group might differ by 50 points or more, the averages of two different groups might vary by only about a dozen or so points. This means that many members of one population will individually score either higher or lower than the average score of another population.

Little evidence exists to suggest that the average differences in IQ scores that are observed between groups are due to innate differences. Richard Herrnstein and Charles Murray in *The Bell Curve* state that such innate differences do exist.[12] They point out that African Americans who have attained middle-class or higher economic status on the average score higher than lower-socioeconomic-class African Americans and whites. Yet these middle-class African Americans still on the average score lower than middle-class whites.

People matched for economic status, however, are not necessarily matched for other social dimensions. African Americans as a social group have had very different social experiences in the United States than have whites who have not suffered prejudice and discrimination. The behaviors and values most inducive to creating children with high IQ scores might be found less frequently in African American and other minority groups, even if they have attained middle or higher economic status. Cross-culturally, it can be shown that economic status is correlated with IQ scores (Box 17-2).

IQ scores tell us little or nothing about a person's creative, social, musical, or artistic talents. Intelligence as tested by an IQ test leaves us with an imprecise and culture-bound definition of intelligence. Howard Gardner believes that there are several relatively separate types of intelligence, including linguistic, musical, logical-mathematical, spatial (the perception

---

[12] R. J. Herrnstein and C. Murray, *The Bell Curve* (New York: The Free Press, 1994).

and re-creation of the visual world), bodily kinesthetic (skill in handling objects), and personal (skill, for instance, that gives "access of one's own feelings").[13]

Robert Sternberg believes that intelligence is exercised in three areas. Contextual intelligence guides a person in selecting the appropriate environments in which to be and in adapting to environments. Experiential intelligence is the ability to confront new situations on the basis of previous experiences. Internal intelligence is the ability to plan, monitor, and change an approach to solving a problem.[14] Both Gardner and Sternberg agree that intelligence is more than a single score on a single type of test.

Human Variation and Cultural Capabilities

It's believed by some that the non-European peoples are incapable of developing civilizations. The term *civilization* is like the term *culture:* Everyone has a different idea of what it is. It is beyond the scope of this text to discuss the various schools of thought on the subject. Instead, let us define it in terms of the common elements in most definitions. Civilization usually implies technological complexities, such as a large number and variety of artifacts, often including monumental architecture, metallurgy, and a body of scientific knowledge. Most important, it implies complex social arrangements, such as occupational specialization, centralized governments, religious and political hierarchies, social classes, and codes of law and conduct. In civilizations, the individual becomes subject to the regulations of a state, whereas in noncivilizations, the family (including extensions of the family, such as clans) is the single most important regulating agent.

Civilization arose in areas characterized by a maximum of trade and movement of people, which provided for the diffusion of artifacts and ideas. Because innovation is basically a recombination of things existing in a society into new forms, as the number of elements increases in a society, the rate of innovation increases. The cart could not have been invented if the wheel did not already exist. In his Pulitzer-prize winning book *Guns, Germs and Steel,* Jared Diamond offers an explanation for why it was Eurasians who established colonial empires throughout the world and not Africans or Native Americans.[15] Too often answers to this question resort to racist explanations. Diamond points out that this question should be addressed in terms of both proximate and ultimate explanations.

The proximate, or immediate, answer is that Europeans had guns, germs, and steel, but the question then becomes why they had these things. The first part of the answer is that the Europeans had agriculture. As we discussed in Chapter 15, and will discuss further in Chapter 18, agriculture had a large impact on the pace of development of human culture and the development of disease. To take the question back one more step, why were Europeans more likely to develop agriculture?

Diamond suggests two main reasons. One is that the European continent had more domesticable plants and animals to work with. Only a small fraction of wild mammals have the potential to be domesticated. The other factor has to do with the ability of domesticated plants and animals to spread from the point of domestication. Because Europe is oriented on an east-west axis, plants domesticated in one area could spread easily along the same latitude, where the same general conditions would exist. In contrast, Africa and the Americas are oriented on a north-south axis, which would have made this type of spread more difficult.

Civilizations did not arise in central Africa because the terrain was not suitable for quick movement of people or goods. The rivers of this area are not navigable because of great fault systems that create rapids along their courses. Restricted travel; a hot, humid climate; dense vegetation; and endemic disease, not innate inferiority, hampered the early development of civilization in the Congo Basin. Yet in areas of Africa where these conditions did not exist, early civilizations did arise and spread into the forest areas. The empires of Ghana, Kanem-Bornu,

[13] H. Gardner, *Intelligence Reframed: Multiple Intelligence for the 21st Century* (New York: Basic Books, 2001).

[14] R. Sternberg, *Thinking Styles* (New York: Cambridge University Press, 1999).

[15] J. Diamond, *Guns, Germs, and Steel: The Fates of Human Societies* (New York: Norton, 1997).

Mali, and Songhai rose to greatness when their goods were traded throughout the world. The people involved were not members of the "white race."

Are There "Pure Races"?

The assertion that some races are "purer" than others, which Hitler used to justify the killing of millions of people, is not validated by any factual data. People are spread over an extremely large area, and physical variation exists in all directions without extensive discontinuities. Through gene flow and migration or invasion, all areas of the world are constantly interchanging genes. This may be an extremely slow process, as in the case of the Australian aborigine, or a very dynamic process, as in Europe.

The picture of human variation is a constantly changing one. Since no two people are alike through time and space, the same is true of human populations. If we were to move back in time 10,000 years, the people inhabiting the earth would not fall into the groupings or clinal patterns of today. Even today, certain groups, such as the Ainu and the San, are changing, primarily through intermarriage with other groups. New groups are emerging.

Those Americans labeled as "African American" are in many ways dissimilar to the African populations from which some of their ancestors came. Estimates indicate that today's African American gene pool contains between 20 and 30 percent European and Native American alleles. This is seen in the statistics for such traits as lactase deficiency. The Africans who were brought to America came from such groups as the Yoruba and the Ibo of west Africa, groups that display close to 100 percent lactase deficiency. African Americans, on the other hand, are only 70 percent lactase-deficient. This is partially due to the flow of northern European genes into this population's gene pool. In addition, a limited number of Native American genes have entered gene pools that are derived predominantly from Africa and Europe. On the other side of the coin, the groups in the United States generally classified as "white" have a certain frequency of genes within their gene pools that are derived from African, Native American, Asiatic, and other non-European sources. As we have emphasized throughout this chapter, human gene pools are always being reconstituted; there are no stable divisions of *Homo sapiens*.

Summary

People are socially classified into "races" that do not correspond to biological facts. Folk taxonomies of race are frequently linked to ideas of superiority and inferiority, and they serve as justification for the socioeconomic stratification that benefits the ruling group. It is easier to subject a group to harsh and unjust treatment if the people in it are relegated to a completely different ancestry and if they are portrayed as being inferior.

While anthropologists have become more realistic about the nature of human variability, people in general still use the simplistic division of humankind into a small number of stereotyped "races." This section has discussed the problems that concern "race" as a social category. Human biological differences have often been correlated with differences in intelligence and cultural capabilities. Upon examination, these differences either are not supported by factual data or, where they do exist, are not traceable to genetic components.

In the case of intelligence, an additional problem exists. There is no consensus on just what intelligence is—so how can it be measured? In the 1980s, new ideas about the nature of intelligence were proposed by investigators who were generally critical of IQ-type intelligence tests. We conclude that behavioral differences between peoples are almost always the result of cultural influences. Nevertheless, a genetic component may be involved in such things as the linearity of the Nilotes, which facilitates spear throwing. Researching the heritability of human traits is a legitimate activity of scientists, but as in any research, the variables must be carefully defined and controlled.

Key Terms

cephalic index, *464*
culture-bound, *475*
discontinuous variation, *457*

ethic group, *463*
folk taxonomy, *461*
genomics, *472*

geographical race, *468*
haplotype, *472*
race, *463*

Study Questions

See the Online Learning Center for additional study questions.

1. What factors are responsible for the clinal nature of the distribution of some traits? Why are the distributions of many traits discontinuous?

2. In what ways are folk taxonomies different from scientific classifications?

3. Briefly describe the ideas on racial classification of Carolus Linnaeus, Johann Friedrich Blumenbach, William Boyd, and Carlton S. Coon.

4. Many people classify "races" on the basis of a single criterion, such as skin color. What are the inherent dangers of using only one or a few criteria to classify human populations?

5. What do your textbook authors conclude about the nature of human variation?

6. The traditional concept of race still is used by many medical professionals even though it generally is not considered a valid biological construction. Why is it still used in medicine?

7. A legitimate scientific pursuit is the exploration of possible intellectual differences between groups. Explain why IQ and other standardized tests are not good measures of the comparative intelligence of different populations.

8. Many writers have correlated the origin of civilization with the "white race." Why is this a false correlation?

Critical Thinking Questions

1. We discussed the distribution of skin color, body build, and genetic disease in this chapter. Propose several hypotheses about the distribution of other physical traits. Describe these traits and predict whether they would be distributed in a clinal or nonclinal manner, or in some other way. Then come up with some ideas on what the possible causal factors responsible for the distribution might be.

2. Why is the idea that there are pure races inconsistent with biological and evolutionary facts? What would a pure race be like? Why is the biological and cultural nature of modern humans contrary to the establishment of pure races?

3. Most anthropologists do not believe that the concept of race can accurately be applied to humans or used to describe human variation. Yet the concept of race is a powerful social fact. Why?

Suggested Readings

Some general texts in the field of human biological variation are

Cavalli-Sforza, L. L., and F. Cavalli-Sforza. *The Great Human Diasporas: The History of Diversity and Evolution.* Reading, MA: Addison-Wesley, 1995.

Marks, J. *Human Biodiversity: Genes, Race, and History,* New York: Aldine de Gruyter, 1995.

Molnar, S. *Human Variation: Race, Type, and Ethnic Groups,* 5th ed. Englewood Cliffs, NJ: Prentice Hall, 2002.

The *American Anthropologist,* volume 100 (September 1998), contains a series of articles on the concept of race.

The following books deal with intelligence and intelligence testing:

Gardner, H. *Intelligence Reframed: Multiple Intelligence for the 21st Century.* New York: Basic Books, 2001.

Gould, S. J. *The Mismeasure of Man,* rev. ed. New York: Norton, 1996.

Sternberg, R., and W. M. Williams (eds.). *Intelligence, Instruction, and Assessment: Theory into Practice.* Hillsdale, NJ: Lawrence Erlbaum Associates, 1999.

Sternberg, R., and W. M. Williams (eds.). *The Evolution of Intelligence.* Hillsdale, NJ: Lawrence Erlbaum Associates, 2001.

Additional books that deal with human variation are

Gates, N. E. *The Concept of "Race" in Natural and Social Science.* New York: Taylor and Francis, 1997. E. Nathaniel Gates examines the idea that race is an arbitrary social construct with no scientific basis in fact.

Graves, J. L., Jr. *The Emperor's New Clothes: Biological Theories of Race at the Millennium.* Piscataway, NJ: Rutgers University Press, 2001. This book traces the development of the concept of race and discusses how scientific ideas of race have been inadequate.

Marks, J. *What Does It Mean to be 98% Chimpanzee.* Berkeley: University of California Press, 2002. The author describes the genetic similarity of humans and chimpanzees and uses it to reassess the genetic significance of human variation.

Nicholson, P. Y. *Who Do We Think We Are? Race and Nation in the Modern World.* New York: M. E. Sharpe, 2001. This volume discusses how the concept of race and the growth of modern nations are linked.

Suggested Websites

American Anthropological Association's Statement on Race:
www.aaanet.org/gvt/ombfact.htm

Genetically Speaking, Race Doesn't Exist in Humans:
www.eureka/ert.org/pub_releases/1998-10/WUiS-GSRD-071098.thp

Population Estimates by Age, Sex and Race (National Center for Health Statistics):
http://govinfo.kerr.orst.edu/document/pestimates/peconv.html

Race: The Power of an Illusion:
www.pbs.org/race/000_About/002_4-background-01-03.htm

Chapter 18

The Modern World

The earth as seen from outer space.

W e travel together, passengers on a little spaceship, dependent on its vulnerable resources of air, water, and soil . . . preserved from annihilation only by the care, the work, and the love we give our fragile craft. ●

—*Adlai E. Stevenson (1900–1965)*

Chapter Outline

Cultural Changes and Their Consequences
Urbanization and Industrialization
The Role of Disease in Human Evolution
The Earth at Risk
What Can We Say about the Future?
Learning from Our Mistakes
Summary

Application of Anthropological Knowledge
Darwinian Medicine
Forensic Anthropology
Anthropology and You—A Personal Note to the Student
Summary

See the Online Learning Center for a chapter summary, chapter outline, and learning objectives.

After Reading This Chapter, You Should Be Able to Answer These Questions:

1. What are some of the major sociocultural changes that have taken place in the world in the last two and a half centuries?

2. What have been some of the possible evolutionary consequences of urbanization and industrialization?

3. Has disease played a role in human evolution?

4. Many human activities are damaging the earth's ecosystems. What are some of those activities, and what problems is each one causing?

5. What are some possible solutions to human-caused ecological problems?

6. What is Darwinian medicine?

7. What types of information might a forensic anthropologist be able to supply to a criminal or other type of investigation?

The amount of cultural change that has occurred in the last 10,000 years has been phenomenal. Any adult in a modern industrial society could list numerous technological innovations and social changes that have taken place in his or her own lifetime. It is not possible to notice biological evolutionary changes in such a short period of time. Yet humans are still evolving. All the factors that influence evolution—mutation, sampling error, migration, nonrandom mating, and natural selection—are still operating on human populations.

Domestication of plants and animals created new conditions that affected the human gene pool. More recently, urbanization and industrialization have produced conditions, such as the use of medical x-rays, that, among other effects, have increased mutation rates. A whole array of other factors, such as weapons of modern warfare, the depletion of the ozone layer, acid rain, and the reduction of biological diversity, could affect future human evolution.

CULTURAL CHANGES AND THEIR CONSEQUENCES

Up until about 5000 years ago, the major source of power for *Homo sapiens* was the muscles of their own bodies. With the advent of agricultural societies, draft animals such as oxen did some of the work. It was not until the 1700s that machines began to take over some of the jobs of people and animals. The use of machines ushered in the Industrial Age, and with it an enormous amount of change.

Since 1750 the world population has multiplied 8½ times, from about 725 million to about 6.5 billion in 2005. Where agrarian societies were about 90 percent rural, many industrial societies are now more than 80 percent urban. Many other changes that have occurred in the last 250 years are listed in Table 18.1. The first section of this chapter discusses some of these changes and their consequences.

Table 18.1 The Past Two and a Half Centuries of Change

1. The largest urban communities of the industrial era are nearly 20 times the size of the largest of the agrarian era.
2. Women in industrial societies give birth to only about a third as many children as women in preindustrial societies.
3. Life expectancy at birth is almost three times greater in advanced industrial societies than it was in agrarian societies.
4. The family, for the first time in history, is no longer a significant productive unit in the economy.
5. The role and status of women in the economy and in society at large have changed substantially.
6. The role and status of youth also have changed, and youth cultures have become a significant factor in the life of industrial societies. [In industrial nations, where birth rates have declined, sometimes dramatically, in the last few decades, "gray culture" will become increasingly important as the average age of the citizens of those nations increases.]
7. The average per capita production and consumption of goods and services in advanced industrial societies is at least 10 times greater than in traditional agrarian societies.
8. The division of labor is vastly more complex.
9. Hereditary monarchical government has disappeared in industrial societies, except in ceremonial and symbolic survival, and the proprietary theory of the state has vanished entirely.
10. The functions and powers of government have been vastly enlarged.
11. Free public educational systems have been established and illiteracy has been largely eliminated in industrial societies.
12. New ideologies have spread widely (notably socialism, capitalism, nationalism, and pragmatism), while older ones inherited from the agrarian era have been substantially altered or have declined in influence.
13. The speed of travel has increased 100 times, and the speed of communication 10 million times, rendering the entire planet, in effect, smaller than England in the agrarian era.
14. A global culture has begun to emerge, as evidenced in styles of dress, music, language, technology, and organizational patterns (e.g., factories, public schools).
15. Global political institutions (e.g., the United Nations, the World Court) have been established for the first time.
16. Several societies have acquired the capacity to obliterate the entire human population.

Source: Adapted from G. Lenski, P. Nolan, and J. Lenski, *Human Societies: An Introduction to Macrosociology* (New York: McGraw-Hill, 1995), pp. 270–271. By permission of Gerhard Lenski.

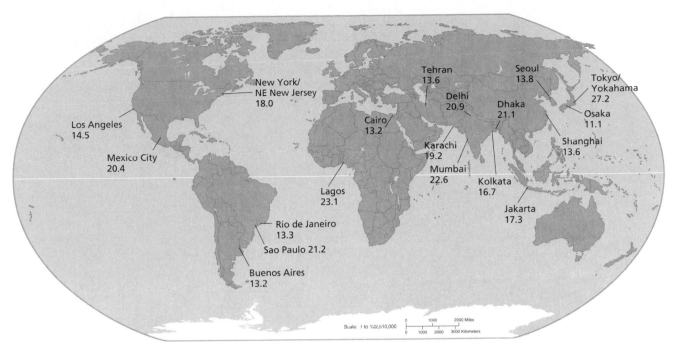

Figure 18.1 The Growth of Cities Population projections for the 19 largest cities in the world in the year 2015. Numbers are in millions.

Urbanization and Industrialization

Cities first arose about 5500 years ago, but they were small and represented nuclei for predominantly rural agricultural societies. **Urbanization** refers to the proportionate rise in the number of people living in cities in comparison to the number living in rural areas. Although early urban centers were economically important, major urbanization did not generally occur until the end of the nineteenth century. Urbanization is correlated with the rise of industrialism since the economic changes caused by industrialism led to the migration of rural populations to the cities. **Industrialism** is the dependence on mechanization—the use of machines—to produce products and render services. The invention and refinement of early steam engines in 1698 and later that were designed to do production work acted as a catalyst for industrialism. Nonindustrial societies depend on human and animal power to do the work of the society.

An **urbanized society** is one in which a majority of the population live in cities. In 1800, less than 5 percent of the world's population lived in cities. In 1900, only Great Britain had a population with more than 50 percent of its citizens living in cities.

Today, the story has changed. Up to 80 percent of the people in the world's more developed countries live in cities, and about 50 percent of the entire world population lives in cities. If the rate of urbanization remains constant, by the year 2025 about 61 percent of the world's population will be living in urban areas of 2500 people or more.[1] Figure 18.1 shows population projections for the 19 largest cities in the world in the year 2015.[2]

For most of human evolution, natural selection operated on scavenging or hunting-gathering societies. In the last 10,000 years, selective pressures associated with farming have had their effect, as can be seen in the relationship of sickle-cell anemia to farming (Chapter 6). Urbanization, on the other hand, is a phenomenon chiefly of the twentieth century. Some parts of the world have been urban for four to five generations, but urbanization for

See the Online Learning Center for an Internet Activity on urbanization.

urbanization A rise in the number of people living in cities in comparison to the number living in rural areas.

industrialism The dependence on mechanization—the use of machines—to produce products and render services.

urbanized society A society in which a majority of the population lives in cities.

---

[1] G. T. Miller Jr., *Living in the Environment,* 10th ed. (Belmont, CA: Wadsworth, 1998), p. 312.

[2] *The World Almanac and Book of Facts, 2004* (New York: World Almanac, 2004), pp. 856–857.

most of the world has been much more recent. Consequently, a close fit to urban life has not had sufficient time to evolve. Also, the nature of urban habitats has changed greatly even in this short period.

Mutations occur, natural selection works, and drift and nonrandom mating operate in urban situations. Therefore, evolution is occurring in cities, but this evolution may be different from that taking place in agricultural areas. Evolutionary forces produce one of two basic results: survival (adaptation) or extinction; thus far, extinction has been the more frequent outcome of evolution.

It is premature to say how the conditions of urbanization will affect humankind. In the next few pages, we will present some of the data and ideas about the effects of both urbanization and industrialization on human evolution. Since all industrial societies today are highly urbanized, the term *industrial society* will be used to denote societies consisting of largely urban populations that engage in manufacturing, commerce, and services.

Industrial Societies, Mutation, and Sampling Error   With industrialism came the use and development of physical and chemical materials that are known or suspected to cause mutation; among these are chemicals added to foods, used in medicines, and used for insect control. These mutagens, along with induced radiation, were discussed in Chapter 5. The long-term effects of the increase in mutagenic substances on human evolution are unknown, but an increase in the mutation rate might increase the genetic load of industrial populations. This, along with the fact that some persons with genetic diseases can today survive to reproduce, could lower the general viability of a population.

While any increase in deleterious mutations within a population will cause human suffering, the benefits of the substances causing mutation may outweigh the suffering. When used properly, some mutagens, such as x-rays, have lengthened lives. Thus, many things that can be harmful in one sense are beneficial in others. As geneticist Curt Stern (1902–1981) said, "When, in prehistoric times, fire was made to serve human purposes it introduced a new danger which, in spite of extensive safe-guards, still kills and maims many people every year."[3] Although mutagenic substances are not directly analogous to fire, further research is needed to determine whether mutagens in the industrial environment, overall, will be advantageous or destructive to our future.

Sampling error is a phenomenon of small population size. As we discussed in earlier chapters, genetic drift occurs easily in societies consisting of small bands, yet demonstrating that genetic drift occurs in large urban centers would be difficult. The founder effect also is limited in industrial societies. For example, when small groups left the cities to establish communes in the 1960s, they did not remain closed; new people entered, and some of the original "settlers" left.

Industrial Societies and Mating Patterns   Industrial societies are characterized by both physical and social mobility. In the last 200 years, the invention of trains, automobiles, and aircraft has increased the ease with which people can travel long distances. Such movement is important in industrial societies, since jobs often become available at distant locations. In the past, for example, numerous engineers were needed in areas where the aerospace and automotive industries were developing, and so many engineers moved to those areas. Today international trade, tourism, and overseas military operations bring people from diverse areas together.

L. L. Cavalli-Sforza and W. F. Bodmer have listed the following genetic consequences of such mobility: First, because of intergroup mating, hybrid groups have tended to develop from populations that were once widely separated (Figure 18.2). Second, a general decrease has taken place in isolated populations, with an accompanying decrease in inbreeding. Third, the number of heterozygotes may increase when genetic isolates break down. Fourth, mating

---

[3] C. Stern, *Principles of Human Genetics,* 3rd ed. (San Francisco: Freeman, 1973), p. 632.

(a)   (b)

Figure 18.2 "Racial Hybrids" Warfare often brings widely separated populations together for more than conflict. For instance, thousands of children were born during the Vietnam War as a result of relationships between American soldiers and Vietnamese civilians. (a) African-American/Vietnamese. (b) European-American/Vietnamese.

that can now take place in a larger group may become more selective and, hence, increase the probability of assortative mating.[4]

Once people become settled in an area, mates often are chosen from within a very close radius. A high percentage of the urban marriages in the last 40 years have been between people who lived very close to each other before they were married. The important factor is that the population density of a large city can be very high. For example, Manhattan has a density of 9275 people per square kilometer (24,021 people per square mile).[5] So even within a small distance, many potential mates are available in a large city. Also, because of mobility, the people who live close to one another in a large city may have diverse origins. Compared with members of hunting-gathering societies, most urbanites choose their mates from among people living close to them. Even so, the chances of marrying someone of a different ethnic background are, of course, much greater.

Industrial Societies and Differential Fertility Each environmental or cultural shift brings new selective pressures and new fitness values for the potential genotypes of a population. The processes of industrialism and urbanization have created many selective situations not found in farming or hunting-gathering societies. We will discuss one of these: pollution. Another selective situation that differs in foraging and industrial societies is the type and distribution of disease. This will be discussed later in this chapter.

Pollution of various types, such as air, water, thermal, and noise pollution, also may be bringing about differential mortality in industrial societies. Hunter-gatherers who move camps usually leave their garbage behind, but as people began to build cities, the amount and persistence of filth increased along with the population.

---

[4] L. L. Cavalli-Sforza and W. F. Bodmer, *The Genetics of Human Populations* (San Francisco: Freeman, 1971), pp. 784–785.

[5] *Statistical Abstract of the United States*, 120th ed. (Washington, DC: U.S. Bureau of the Census, 2000), p. 40.

Figure 18.3 Smog The ingredients in smog cause numerous health and environmental problems.

endocrine disruptors
Natural and synthetic chemicals that affect the endocrine system.

endocrine system A network of glands that, through the production of hormones, control the body's internal functions.

environmental estrogens
Synthetic or natural endocrine disruptors that may find their way into water, soil, air, and food and may affect the endocrine system.

The first urban centers had many kinds of pollution. As early as 5000 years ago, when crude oil was being burned as a fuel, air pollution had started to ravage urbanites' lungs. In 1167 the army of Frederick Barbarossa found that the air of Rome "had become densely laden with pestilence and death." British kings of the Middle Ages decreed that polluting the air by burning coal was punishable by death, but the Industrial Age ushered in new toxins for the atmosphere.

The automobile creates a brownish haze over many cities throughout the world (Figure 18.3). The ingredients in this smog can cause breathing difficulties, chest pain, coughing, and nausea. Some of these substances are known to cause degeneration of the optic nerve, hearing impairment, skin disease, eye irritation, asthma attacks, bronchitis and emphysema, and headaches. Many substances found in smog are known to be cancer-producing agents. Smog also damages crops, forests, and wildlife.

The high population density in cities also has created problems of water pollution. The methods used to provide food for these large populations have created soils saturated with insecticides, which eventually find their way into lakes, rivers, and oceans. Nuclear power plants spill boiling water into the ocean, causing thermal pollution.

Another type of pollution is caused by endocrine disruptors. **Endocrine disruptors** are natural and synthetic chemicals that affect the endocrine system. The **endocrine system** is a network of glands that control the body's internal functions through the production of hormones. Endocrine disruptors can alter hormonal functioning by mimicking the male sex hormones, the androgens, and the female sex hormones, the estrogens. They also can block or alter the functioning of the body's own hormones.

Humans and wildlife have been exposed to natural endocrine disruptors that are found in clover, soybeans, other legumes, whole grains, and a variety of fruits and vegetables throughout prehistory and history. Exposure to synthetic endocrine disruptors arises from numerous sources, including certain pesticides, herbicides, fungicides, products and byproducts associated with plastics, some pharmaceuticals such as birth control pills, certain detergents, various industrial chemicals, and heavy metals such as lead, mercury, and cadmium.

One synthetic estrogen is diethylstilbestrol (DES). At one time physicians used it to prevent miscarriages. Studies have shown that daughters of mothers who took DES have a higher-than-normal rate of vaginal and cervical cancers. Sons of women who took DES have a higher rate of malformed or small penises, undescended testicles, and abnormal sperm. These and other types of reproductive system problems are suspected but have not been conclusively shown to occur in humans exposed to **environmental estrogens**—synthetic estrogens that get into the soil, air, water, and food.

Modern industrial societies differ from nonindustrial societies in terms of the types and quantities of pollution to which people are exposed. This exposure may produce subtle changes in the human gene pool. Since individuals in each population differ from one another, we might expect that natural selection will increase the genotypes that allow individuals to adapt to increased levels of a specific type of pollution. Therefore, we can say that the human species is still evolving, at least in terms of microevolution. As we will discuss later, the specifics of this microevolution are difficult to measure.

As has been stressed in previous chapters, the precise effects of pollutants on human evolution are unknown. We do know that smog kills or contributes to the death of an increasing number of people. Most likely, pollutants affect some people more severely than others. Selective pressures are often very subtle, and a shift of even a fraction of a percent in the fitness value of a genotype may lead to a major shift in gene frequencies over the generations.

The Role of Disease in Human Evolution

Selective factors that act on populations include predation, famine, and disease. All these have helped shape modern peoples physically, emotionally, and psychologically. As the potential for more complex behavior evolved in the hominins, the manufacture of hunting tools and weapons reduced the impact of predation from nonhuman animals on human populations. Today, the major predators of human populations are enemy populations, small organisms, and microorganisms. For example, about 15,375,000 people died in the First World War that ended in 1918; in that same year, an influenza epidemic killed at least 25 million people.

Microorganisms were responsible for the influenza epidemic of 1918. The disease was most lethal to people of reproductive age. Therefore, assuming that resistance to the disease was at least in part genetic, the surviving population and their offspring had a greater chance of surviving another outbreak of the same disease.

Epidemiology is the study of the distribution and causes of disease and injury in human populations. Epidemiologists are interested in the frequency and types of disease and injuries and the factors that influence their pattern of distribution. Anthropological epidemiologists are interested in such questions as: What types of disease were common in prehistoric populations, and how did that affect human evolution? Why are different types of disease common in some populations and not in others? How can an understanding of the evolution of human disease aid contemporary populations in dealing with current patterns of disease?

epidemiology The study of the distribution and causes of disease and injury in human populations.

Disease in Fossil Populations Paleopathology is the study of disease and injuries in fossil specimens. Fossilized bone can display clear indications of bone diseases such as arthritis, joint diseases, bone cancer, and rickets. The use of x-rays, chemical analysis, and other methods of investigation can indicate other types of disease, including soft tissue diseases that leave their mark in bone. For instance, tuberculosis and syphilis can cause skeletal damage. Fossilized bone also can indicate injuries such as broken bones.

See the Online Learning Center for an Internet Activity on paleopathology.

For instance, some Neandertal skeletons have a pattern of fractures consistent with those of modern rodeo bull riders. This indicates that Neandertals might have had serious up-close and personal contact with large game animals. The study of bone and teeth also can give indications of nutrition, patterns of growth and development, and individual workload. In the latter case, for example, the high amount of physical stress on women who grind corn leads to a similar pattern of stress on bone as that found in contemporary bodybuilders.

An example of paleopathology in a fossil population comes from Shanidar Cave in Iraq, where the remains of nine individuals have been found. Besides showing the Neandertal pattern with some more modern overtones, many of the Shanidar individuals are interesting for cultural reasons. From this cave, dated about 60,000 to 46,000 B.P., comes evidence of burial with flowers and, perhaps, the first known incident of successful surgery.

About 17 percent of the Neandertals from Shanidar have a joint disease called calcium pyrophosphate deposition disease.[6] Although fossilized bones are usually all that remains of an ancient organism, soft-tissue diseases and injuries sometimes can be inferred from the evidence found in fossilized bones. One of the nine Shanidar finds, Shanidar I, is a good example of what a paleopathologist can conclude from a fossil specimen. Erik Trinkaus writes:

> Shanidar I was one of the most severely traumatized Pleistocene [hominins] for whom we have evidence. He suffered multiple fractures involving the cranium, right humerus, and right fifth metatarsal, and the right knee, ankle, and first tarsometatarsal joint show degenerative joint disease that was probably trauma related.[7]

---

[6] B. M. Rothschild, "Oldest Bone Diseases," *Nature* 349 (1991), p. 288.

[7] E. Trinkaus, *The Shanidar Neandertals* (New York: Academic, 1983), p. 401.

Figure 18.4 Neandertal Surgery The normal (top) and abnormal (bottom) humeri of Shanidar I. The middle section of the normal humerus was restored in plaster and should be somewhat longer, making the abnormal humerus about 10 percent shorter than the normal one.

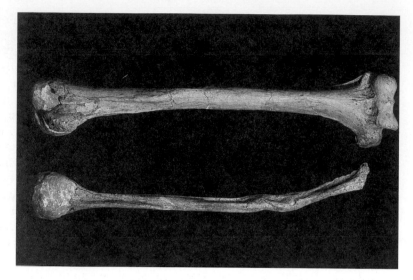

In addition to the injuries listed above, Shanidar I was blind in the left eye, as inferred from a crushed orbit. Because of injuries, his right arm, clavicle, and scapula had never fully grown. The humerus had apparently been cut off slightly above the elbow, and healing of the bone indicates that the individual survived this ordeal (Figure 18.4). If this was an intentional procedure to remove a withered arm, it is the earliest known evidence of successful surgery. An unusually great amount of wear on Shanidar I's front teeth suggests that the teeth were used for grasping in place of the right arm. In addition, analysis of the skull shows that the top right side was damaged and had healed before his death.

Erik Trinkaus offers several possible explanations for Shanidar I's infirmities. What is obvious is that this individual had major debilitating injuries and lived to a relatively old age; he died a few years younger than the average life expectancy for Americans at the end of the nineteenth century. Shanidar I may not have been able to contribute directly to the food supply of his community, yet his longevity perhaps attests to other functions he was able to provide. By analogy with contemporary societies, we may surmise that his wisdom and experience were valued by the community and contributed to the survival of his society.

Disease in Foraging, Farming, and Industrial Populations As hominins evolved physically, they also evolved culturally. They learned to make stone tools approximately 2½ million years ago; sometime later they learned to control the use of fire and at some point to hunt large game. Contact with game animals lead to an increase in the number of zoonoses. **Zoonoses** are infectious diseases that are transmitted to humans from other animals. These diseases include the brain disorder called encephalitis and the intestinal disease called trichinosis, as well as tetanus, rabies, and sleeping sickness. Foragers in some environments also are subject to parasitic diseases such as lice and intestinal worms. These types of disease are more common in foragers than in modern populations.

Epidemics are less common among foragers than among modern peoples. The 1918 influenza outbreak, which was transmitted to humans from pigs, killed so many people because modern people live in close proximity to other people. The virus "played tag," moving from one host to another. Foraging populations are small, mobile, and often isolated from other people for long periods. If an infectious disease took hold in a hunting and gathering band, all the people who were infected might either die or get better before they could pass on the disease to others.

Foraging populations display a lower frequency of the common noninfectious diseases of modern populations. In the United States about 50 percent of deaths each year are due

zoonoses Infectious diseases that are transmitted to humans from animals.

to cardiovascular disease. One in three Americans will get some form of cancer in his or her life. Adult-onset diabetes is now the fourth major cause of death in the United States. One hundred years ago it ranked 100th as a cause of death. All these diseases are rare in modern foragers, and we presume they were so in the past. The question is why.

One reason may be diet. Foragers do not share the high-sodium, high-sugar, and often high-fat diets of modern industrial people. Even in the United States, the large rise in the frequency of diabetes might be in part due to diet. Although some Americans still eat high-fat diets, many have substituted low-fat and nonfat items into their diet. The problem is that a lot of low-fat and nonfat processed food has sugar added to enhance taste. Increased sugar in the diet might be partially responsible for the increase in diabetes. Hunters and gatherers generally have low-sugar diets and hence may be less subject to diabetes.

Probably the main reason foragers do not die as frequently from cardiovascular disease, cancers, and diabetes is that they do not live as long as modern peoples. These diseases can affect people at any age but are most frequently fatal in people past reproductive age. As average life expectancies have risen, even in modern populations, these diseases have become more common.

Between 13,000 and 10,000 years ago, people began to domesticate plants and animals. This period corresponds to the extinction of many large game animals. During the Mesolithic of the Middle East, adult stature declined by about 2 inches and damage to the tooth enamel became more frequent than in foraging populations. Both the loss of stature and the problems with the formation of tooth enamel can be due to starvation or malnutrition. Although domestication of plants and animals is seen as a cause for increased population due to a generally more predictable source of food than hunting and gathering, the variety of food decreased. Many hunters and gatherers had available to them numerous types of meat and vegetable materials. The limited menu of early farmers may have led to various vitamin and mineral deficiencies as well as less than the optimal amounts of protein in their diets. The Mesolithic also saw an increase in infectious disease, perhaps because people were living in larger groups and those groups had more sustained contact with other groups. This would have allowed disease organisms to spread from host to host.

In the Neolithic, population and contact between populations grew, allowing for more rapid spread of infectious disease. As intensive agriculture (the use of the plow and fertilization of soil) developed about 5000 years ago, the standing water in the furrows of plowed fields became the breeding ground of disease-bearing insects. For instance, such an environment was perfect for mosquitoes, some species of which carry malaria. Untreated animal feces, used as fertilizer, enter the drinking water supply as runoff from the fields. This condition leads to the spread of gastrointestinal diseases such as cholera.

As more people moved to cities, a situation that accelerated during the Industrial Revolution, diseases spread even more rapidly than in previous times. The large population density of cities allowed pathogens to move easily from one person to another. Diseases called **zymotics,** or crowd diseases, become common. These diseases include smallpox, measles, and scarlet fever. In modern developed nations, many zymotics have been all but wiped out or controlled by vaccines, but others, such as severe active respiratory syndrome (SARS), have become problems.

zymotics Infectious diseases that spread easily from person to person in crowded areas.

Disease as a Selective Agent Infectious diseases can act as a selective agent on a population. The specific way in which a disease acts on the gene pools of human populations has been demonstrated for malaria. In Chapter 5 we saw how individuals heterozygous for sickle-cell anemia are resistant to malaria. Over many generations the increased fitness of the heterozygous individuals led to a substantial rise in the frequency of the allele for hemoglobin S. Other diseases, including bubonic plague, or the Black Death, and most of the other infectious diseases mentioned in this section have been thought to be strong selective agents. Today, there is increasing evidence that the HIV (human immunodeficiency virus) is acting as a selective agent on some populations.

Box 18-1   Human Technology as a Selective Agent

As we saw in Chapter 6, a selective agent is any factor that brings about a difference in fertility. Three selective agents that affect human populations are predation, famine, and disease. Human activity also has been a major element in the evolutionary formula. Of course, humans can act as a selective agent in the role of predator. For most of human prehistory, humans were hunters and gatherers. Human hunting behaviors selected against the individuals within a hunted population that were more likely to be caught. This box focuses on activities of the last 60 years. For example, modern humans have accelerated the pace of evolution in populations of disease organisms and agricultural pests through the development of chemical and biological agents.

The first use of antibiotics in the 1940s was seen as a miracle of medicine. Indeed, antibiotics have saved millions of lives. When the first antibiotic, penicillin, was used in 1947, it cured most bacterial infections. Today, many bacteria are penicillin-resistant, and many are resistant to even the newest antibiotics. The evolution of many resistant viruses that have been treated with antiviral drugs is even more rapid than is the case with bacteria. Bacteria and viruses have considerable variability within their populations, and high mutation rates continuously create new variants. If an antibiotic or antiviral drug does not eliminate every disease organism it was used against, then, because the survivors might be resistant to the drug, the next generation of organisms might be more resistant than the first. The organisms that survive the initial application of the drug produced this next generation. The same is true of agricultural pests treated with chemical insecticides. Each generation might become more resistant to the insecticide until the insecticide has little effect.

In the United States, the annual cost that results from the increased resistance of disease organisms, agricultural pests, and other problems that have resulted from the human acceleration of evolution approaches $100 billion. The social costs are also high. People die as a result of antibiotic-resistant and antiviral-resistant organisms, and farmers lose crops due to insecticide-resistant insects. Also, the cost of treating disease might be very high and unattainable for many. The scientific community is addressing these problems, and a summary of strategies that have been developed is outlined in the source listed below.

Source: Stephen R. Palumbi, "Humans as the World's Greatest Evolutionary Force," *Science* 293 (2001), pp. 786–790.

Some biologists believe that HIV is at least as powerful a selective agent as malaria.[8] HIV leads to AIDS (acquired immune deficiency syndrome). The average time from infection with HIV to the onset of AIDS symptoms is 7.8 years. Paul Schliekelman and his colleagues have found that a gene called CCR5 that codes for a cell-surface receptor has several alleles. These receptors affect a person's susceptibility to HIV and the time period between HIV infection and the onset of AIDS. One variant of the CCR5 gene might delay the onset of the disease by two to four years. That delay would allow those who have the allele to produce more offspring; hence, the allele would be selected for and would increase in frequency over time. Worldwide, about 11.8 million young people ages 18 through 24 live with HIV/AIDS. With 8.6 million infected, sub-Saharan Africa has the highest number of young adults with AIDS. The lifetime risk of a 15-year-old boy in Botswana, Africa, dying of AIDS is about 90 percent.[9] Selection would favor any genetic advantage that would lead to a greater survival rate through the reproductive years.

Another variant of the CCR5 gene, called the delta-32 mutation, is found in northern European populations, but rarely in Africa. A person homozygous for delta-32 is apparently completely resistant to HIV infection and therefore does not develop AIDS. This allele is thought to have been present in northern European populations for at least 700 years. The frequency of this mutation may have first arisen as a result of the selective advantage it gave to those who possessed it during the Black Death of 1346 to 1352. The advantage it gives to people living in an AIDS environment is an example of preadaptation.

Just as disease organisms act as selective agents on human populations, human technology acts as a selective agent on disease organisms. Box 18-1 addresses this point.

---

[8] P. Schliekelman, C. Garner, and M. Slatkin, "Natural Selection and Resistance to HIV," *Nature* 411 (2001), p. 545.

[9] UNICEF Statistics: www.childinfo.org/eddb/hiv_aids/hyoung.htm.

The Earth at Risk

Pollution and disease are only two of many environmental concerns. Although modern technology has made many people's lives easier and longer, the negative consequences of modern technology could ultimately make the earth uninhabitable. Four consequences of modern practices that are particularly menacing are the weapons of modern warfare and terrorism, the depletion of the ozone layer, acid rain, and the reduction of biological diversity.

Radiation, Chemical, and Biological Warfare In December 1987 the United States and the Soviet Union agreed to destroy 2611 nuclear warheads carrying missiles, eliminating all intermediate-range missiles. In 1991 it was announced that there would be a reduction in short-range nuclear weapons and other military cutbacks. In 1994 the Ukrainian president agreed to destroy all nuclear warheads that Ukraine inherited as a result of the breakup of the Soviet Union. The former Soviet states Belarus and Kazakhstan also gave their nuclear weapons to Russia. South Africa, Libya, Argentina, Brazil, South Korea, Iraq, and Taiwan have also ended their nuclear weapons programs. Even though there has been progress in reducing nuclear proliferation, the world is still left with thousands of megatons of nuclear power in the form of weapons. As of 2005, China, France, Russia, the United Kingdom, the United States, India, Israel, North Korea, and Pakistan possessed nuclear weapons. Together these countries have over 30,000 nuclear warheads. Iran is suspected of working on the development of nuclear weapons, and Syria may have a secret nuclear weapons program.[10] There may be several hundred highly portable nuclear devices that could easily be placed in target areas by states or terrorist groups. However, the existence of those devices, which were supposedly developed first in the United States and then in the Soviet Union, is not certain. If they do exist, their security is unknown to the general public.

Another potential danger from radioactive materials is a radioactive dispersal device (RDD). One type of RDD combines a traditional explosive such as dynamite with radioactive material and is commonly referred to as a dirty bomb. The radioactive material could be stolen from a nuclear power plant or another source. A second type of RDD is a radioactive device that could be placed in a public place such as a mall, train station, or sports stadium. People passing by the device would be exposed to radiation. In either case, the RDD would not kill masses of people outright. Its main health effects would be those associated with radiation exposure. The cleanup of a RDD would be very costly.[11] For this reason, RDDs have been called *weapons of mass disruption* instead of nuclear (and some chemical and biological) weapons, which are called *weapons of mass destruction.*

Concern also exists about chemical weapons. On March 20, 1995, an attack on a Tokyo subway using sarin, a type of nerve gas, killed 12 people and injured 5000. This was not the first incidence of the use of chemicals in warfare or by terrorists. During the First World War (1914–1918), more than 91,000 soldiers, from all involved countries, were killed, and more than 1.2 million were injured by mustard gas and chlorine gas. As of February 12, 2001, 174 countries had ratified or acceded to the Chemical Weapons Convention. The treaty bans the production, acquisition, stockpiling, transfer, and use of chemical weapons. Unfortunately, lack of money and cooperation has prevented the treaty from being enforced effectively.

A third tool of war is biological weapons. Current research attempts to use genetic engineering and other methods to create deadly viruses, bacteria, parasites, and venoms. Although a 1972 treaty, ratified by 144 nations, bans the use and production of biological weapons, research goes on.

---

[10] Arms Control Association, "Nuclear Weapons: Who Has What at a Glance," April 2004, www.armscontrol.org/factsheets/Nuclearweaponswhohaswhat.asp.

[11] United States Nuclear Regulatory Commission, "Fact Sheet on Dirty Bombs," March 2003, www.nrc.gov/reading-rm/doc-collections/fact-sheets/dirty-bombs.html.

On September 11, 2001, an act of terrorism killed 2995 people in New York and Washington, DC. The terrorists turned commercial airliners into weapons of mass destruction. A fear is that the next step might be the use of chemical or biological weapons or, perhaps, even nuclear weapons.

The first bioterrorism attack in the United States actually occurred quite some time ago, in 1984. A Buddhist cult in Oregon, the Rajneeshee, used salmonella to infect food at 10 restaurants and a supermarket. No one died, but 751 people became ill. In 2001, anthrax spores were spread through the U.S. mail. The culprits who carried out this act of terrorism still remain unknown in 2005. It is known that the cost to the terrorists might have been under $2500. This small cost is associated with several deaths and billions of dollars of monetary loss due to declines in postal revenues, costs of decontamination, costs of relocations due to building closures, and so on. The Office of Technology Assessment of the U.S. Congress estimates that the release of 100 kilograms of aerosolized anthrax over Washington, DC, could kill up to 3 million people and cost about $26 billion for every 100,000 people exposed to the spores.[12]

The sarin nerve gas attack, mentioned earlier, is an example of chemical terrorism. Today, there are a variety of extremely toxic chemicals transported from place to place within the United States every day. About 20 of the people arrested in conjunction with the September 2001 terrorist attacks had hazardous materials transport licenses. Bioterrorism could come in the form of smallpox, anthrax, salmonella, *E. coli,* foot-and-mouth disease, and many other agents.

The use of nuclear, chemical, and biological weapons could threaten the survival of the human species. Any of these destructive agents could cause environmental damage that would render the earth uninhabitable.

ozone A molecule composed of three oxygen atoms (O_3). Atmospheric ozone shields organisms from excessive ultraviolet radiation.

stratosphere That part of the atmosphere 20 to 50 kilometers (12 to 31 miles) above the earth's surface where ozone forms.

The Depletion of the Ozone Layer **Ozone,** a molecule composed of three oxygen atoms (O_3), forms in the **stratosphere,** the area of the atmosphere between 20 and 50 kilometers (12 and 31 miles) above the earth's surface. The ozone layer encircles the earth and absorbs 99 percent of the ultraviolet radiation from the sun. High amounts of ultraviolet radiation interrupt normal cell activity, and so without this protection, most life on earth would cease.

The ozone layer is thinning, in part, because of industrial activities, in particular the use of chlorofluorocarbons (CFCs), a class of chemicals used as refrigerants, in plastic foams, and in some spray cans. Natural factors such as volcanic eruptions and the 11-year solar cycle also increase or decrease the amount of ozone. Currently, the depletion of ozone is increasing the frequency of skin cancer in humans. Each 1 percent deletion of ozone may increase skin cancer by about 6 percent. NASA's ozone-measuring satellite indicates that globally ozone is decreasing 2.3 percent per decade. In the northern midlatitudes (roughly between Seattle and New Orleans), ozone losses are between 4 and 5 percent per decade. As of September 2003, there was a hole in the ozone layer larger than North America.[13]

In addition, depletion of ozone could eventually decrease yields of certain food crops, affect food chains, and cause changes in world climatic patterns. If the depletion were to go unchecked, it could ultimately threaten all life on earth. The good news is that a ban on CFCs called the Montreal Protocol might be the first step in "repairing" the ozone layer.

Global Warming The 2004 movie *The Day after Tomorrow* told a story about the rapid appearance of killer tornadoes, hailstorms, tidal waves, severe cold, and other climatic disasters. Although much of the science was fiction and the short time scale was ridiculous, scientists concur that human activities are contributing to a warming of the atmosphere and oceans that could lead to environmental and health disasters.

---

[12] Center for Biodefense Strategies, Johns Hopkins University, 2001, at http://www.hopkins-biodefense.org/pages/agents/agentanthrax.html.

[13] Aldhou, "Ozone Hole Bigger Than America," *Energy and Environmental Management,* 1 (Nov.–Dec. 2003), p. 9.

Global warming refers to the rising average temperature of the earth's atmosphere and oceans. The most significant cause of this warming is **greenhouse gases,** which can be produced naturally and by human activity. These gases permit infrared radiation (sunlight) to enter the atmosphere, which absorbs some of the radiation before it can be reflected back into space. The absorbed radiation heats the atmosphere and oceans.

The main greenhouse gas is water vapor. However, the gas that has increased most significantly because of human activity is carbon dioxide. This increase has been due mostly to the burning of fossil fuels such as oil and coal and to deforestation. Other greenhouse gases include methane and nitrous oxide. Some greenhouse gases are produced exclusively through human activity. Those gases include chemicals used in refrigeration and in aerosol sprays.

Some climate scientists believe that the average global temperature might rise as much as 1.6–5.5 degrees celsius (3–10 degrees fahrenheit) by 2100. Polar ice and glaciers are already melting, and if this continues, coastal cities might eventually wind up under water. Other effects of global warming include droughts in some areas of the world and torrential rain in others, along with a shifting of climatic zones. In addition to these environmental disasters, numerous health crises are arising from global warming. In the summer of 2003, more than 30,000 people died as a result of an extended heat wave that many scientists attribute to global warming. Also, the rise in levels of atmospheric carbon dioxide is causing an increase in respiratory ailments such as asthma.[14]

The Kyoto Protocol is a 1997 agreement to reduce greenhouse gases over time. As of March, 2005, 145 states and regional organizations had ratified or agreed to join the accord. The United States withdrew its support for the accord in 2001.[15]

Acid Rain Some industrial plants, such as those that burn fossil fuel, release sulfur dioxide into the atmosphere; automobile exhaust contains nitrogen oxides that also enter the atmosphere. Sulfur dioxide and nitrogen oxides are carried back to the earth in rain; they oxidize to form sulfuric acid and nitric acid, respectively. **Acid rain,** as this precipitate is called, has acidified lakes to the point where life can no longer exist. In Canada alone, aquatic life has been depleted or threatened in at least 48,000 lakes, mainly because of U.S. industry (Figure 18.5). Acid rain is becoming a problem in areas of the world which are becoming more industrial. Acid rain has changed environments, sometimes drastically, and therefore has created new selective pressures on humans by destroying food, water, and other resources.

The Reduction of Biological Diversity The rain forests contain about 62 percent of the earth's species, and yet by 2020, according to one prediction, human activities will have led to a 95 percent reduction of rain forests. By the year 2035, the remaining rain forests will be gone or greatly disturbed. What does this mean to humans? A partial list of the effects of the loss of the world's rain forests includes reduction in atmospheric oxygen that is created by green plants, loss of plants used in making medicines, loss of fuel plants, loss of as many as 20,000 food plants, possible transformation of tropics into deserts, erosion, major changes in world climates, and crop failures due to the extinction of insects that formerly pollinated the crops. All these things could have enormous negative economic effects. For instance, erosion and desertification can lead to devastating floods that kill thousands of people and can cost billions to clean up. The loss of topsoil, necessary for growing crops, can prevent people from feeding themselves and make them dependent on others.

global warming The rise in average temperature of the earth's atmosphere and oceans.

greenhouse gases Gases that absorb some of the infrared radiation that enters the atmosphere resulting in the heating up of the atmosphere and oceans.

acid rain Rain that carries acids that pollute water systems and soils.

See the Online Learning Center for an Internet Activity on biodiversity.

[14] S. Perkins, "Dead Heat: The Health Consequences of Global Warming Could Be Many," *Science News,* 166 (July 3, 2004), pp. 10–12.

[15] The reader can check the status of the accord at the website called *Ratification of the Kyoto Protocol:* http://environment.about.com/gi/dynamic/offsite.htm?zi=1/XJ&sdn=environment&zu=http%3A%2F%2F www.ems.org%2Fclimate%2Fkyoto_ratify.html.

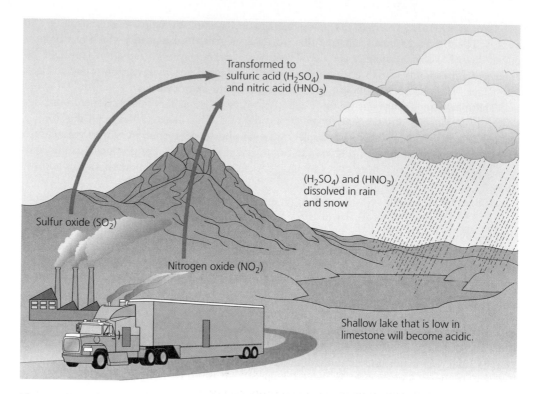

Transformed to
sulfuric acid (H$_2$SO$_4$)
and nitric acid (HNO$_3$)

(H$_2$SO$_4$) and (HNO$_3$)
dissolved in rain
and snow

Sulfur oxide (SO$_2$)

Nitrogen oxide (NO$_2$)

Shallow lake that is low in
limestone will become acidic.

Figure 18.5 Acid Rain One of the effects of acid rain is to acidify lakes to the point where life no longer can exist.

intensive farming
Farming that involves the clearing of a piece of land of all of its natural vegetation and replacing it with one crop that is usually not native to the area.

monoculture A field planted with one crop for a long period of time.

Another factor that has led to a loss of biodiversity is intensive farming. **Intensive farming** involves clearing a pierce of land of all of its natural vegetation and replacing it with one crop, called a **monoculture,** that is usually not native to the area. The entire natural ecosystem is removed and replaced with an artificial ecosystem with limited biodiversity. This reduced biodiversity is lessened further by the use of insecticides, herbicides, fences to keep animals out, and the shooting and trapping of animals that attempt to enter the fields.

Our increasing ability to genetically engineer crops also might lead to a considerable loss of biodiversity. Improving crops through bioengineering could help feed billions of people. At the same time, it would reduce biodiversity even beyond that of a nongenetically engineered monoculture by growing genetically uniform plants.

The Control of Population Many of the world's current problems are directly related to the enormous increase in population (Table 18.2). At its present rate of growth, the human species could eventually crowd everything else off the earth. Of course, before that could happen, widespread disease, mass starvation, and other catastrophic events would come into play. In the early 2000s, up to 20 million people per year died from a lack of food or from normally nonfatal infections worsened by deficiencies in food resources. More than half of those deaths were of children under the age of five.

Many world governments have begun to tackle the problem of population growth (Figure 18.6). In 1994 delegates from about 180 countries met in Cairo for the United Nations International Conference on Population and Development. After nine days of heated debate, the members endorsed a plan to reduce the rate of population growth.[16] However, the United Nations is having a difficult time raising the money to finance these programs.

---

[16] W. Roush, "Population: A View from Cairo," *Science* 265 (1994), pp. 1164–1167.

Table 18.2 Human Population Growth

Years Ago (from 2005)	Years Elapsed*	World Population	Comment
1,000,000		125,000	
300,000	700,000	1,000,000	
10,000	290,000	5,320,000	Domestication begins
6000	4000	86,500,000	
2000	4000	133,000,000	
250	1750	728,000,000	Industrialization
105	155	1,610,000,000	Medical "revolution"
55	50	2,555,078,000	
45	10	3,039,332,000	
(the present) 0	45	6,450,219,000	Information Age
Year 2050	45	9,050,494,000	

* Note that (1) it took 700,000 years to reach the first million from a population of 125,000; (2) it took only 55 years (1950 to 2005) for an increase of about 3.9 billion to occur; (3) it is estimated that between the years 2005 and 2050 more than 2.5 billion people will be added to the world population.

Source: U.S. Bureau of the Census, "Total Midyear Population for the World: 1950–2050" (2004), at http://www.census.gov/ipc/www/worldpop.html.

One of the main elements in this plan is the education of women. In general, as the educational level of women increases, the fertility rate decreases. For instance, in Japan not only are increasing numbers of women working outside the home, many are working as professionals. As a result, the number of children per woman in Japan in 2004 was 1.3. At this rate of reproduction, the Japanese population will be reduced by half by the end of the century. Most of the populations of other industrial nations are also shrinking.

The Cairo conference suggested that governments institute policies to raise the literacy and educational levels among women in third-world countries. The conference also called for world governments to work toward policies that would give equal access to women in jobs, obtaining credit, receiving inheritances, and owning property. Women so empowered are likely to choose to have fewer children than women whose lives revolve exclusively around domestic concerns.

These suggestions have had little effect on nations that are just beginning to develop their industrial economies and on nonindustrial nations. For instance, in the northern areas of India it is not unusual for a woman to have 10 or more children. Although the rate of population increase in the more industrialized southern areas of India has decreased significantly, India's overall rate of increase could lead to a population of 2 billion or more by the end of the century. That is considerably more people than the population of the entire world 100 years ago. Similar increases in population are occurring in most of the poorer areas of the world. The differences in birth rates between the more and the less economically developed nations is creating a world in which a very high percentage of the people in the more developed nations are relatively old, whereas the majority of people in the less developed nations are children and young adults. This trend will continue and will lead to numerous social challenges in both wealthier and poorer areas of the world.

Figure 18.6 An Urban Population

Many ecologists consider the Cairo plan to be too weak. Some countries have adopted much more severe measures to reduce their populations, including mandating sterilization for males who have fathered a specified number of children and imposing economic or other social punishments on people who have what is defined by the country in question as too many children. Family-planning programs reduced the world's population by about 130 million people between the years 1978 and 1983. However, the funds for family-planning programs in many parts of the world have been cut in recent years.

Population reduction policies have not had the predicted effect. The peak population growth rate of about 2 percent annually was registered in the mid-1960s. It is now down to about 1.8 percent. However, the world population still climbed to about 6.5 billion in 2005, and it will reach approximately 7 billion in the year 2013. Two factors account for the increase: people are living longer, and nearly 34 percent of the world's population is below the age of 15.

Along with population control, people must learn to use resources better and recycle those that are scarce. Also, they must use their technological knowledge to prevent, not to create, environmental deterioration.

What Can We Say about the Future?

Ever since modern evolutionary theory originated, people have wondered what is in store for the human species in the future. Some have said that people will lose all their hair and develop hooves or that people's legs will degenerate from lack of use. The type of thinking behind these hypotheses not only is illogical but also could be counterproductive in the search for solutions to contemporary problems.

This pattern of thought is similar to the nineteenth-century Lamarckian theory of evolution. The assumption is that when something becomes unnecessary, it will disappear, and when something becomes necessary, it will appear. Thus, one might reason that body hair will disappear totally because clothes can take its place. This type of thinking becomes dangerous when it is applied to something like smog. Some maintain that smog is not all that bad because eventually people will evolve lungs that can cope with it.

Evolution does not proceed by way of necessity or lack of necessity. A trait appears only if there is genetic potential for it and only if that potential is expressed. The chance that any particular new trait will appear, and appear at the right time and in the right place, is infinitesimally small.

Similarly, a trait disappears only if it is selected against or if it diminishes because of random genetic drift. If it is selectively neutral, there will be no reason for it to vanish. Hair will not become scarcer unless the *lack* of hair has a selective advantage over the retention of hair. Although some people may be less affected by smog and other pollution, lungs will not adapt to smog unless mutations occur that allow this to happen. However, there is no reason to believe that this will happen.

Science provides no crystal balls. The anthropologist or other researcher cannot describe what the human form will be like in the future, nor can anyone predict random change or the effects that unknown environmental conditions of the future will have on the genetic material. Nevertheless, there are some absolutes—existence or nonexistence, for instance. Since we do know some of the requirements that can support life and some of the conditions that can bring about extinction, we can—and should—examine *H. sapiens'* chances for survival.

For the human species to continue, policy makers must realize that certain conditions are necessary for survival. First, certain resources are nonreplenishable, for example, fossil fuels (such as coal and oil) and natural gases (such as helium). Humans depend on these resources and have no guarantee of a substitute should they run out.

Second, the earth is, in effect, a container with the ground acting as the bottom and the atmosphere acting as the sides and lid. Pollution is pumped into the ground, water, and air, where it often becomes trapped. Humans reside in that container, and they require that healthful conditions exist within it.

Figure 18.7 The Homeless Overpopulation is one reason for the large number of homeless people in the world today.

Third, the earth has a finite amount of space. Humans cannot occupy all that space, since the things they depend on for food and environmental stability also must have room to exist (Figure 18.7).

Learning from Our Mistakes

Continued media and educational discussions about population problems and massive pollution of bodies of water, as well as other potentially destructive occurrences, have focused at least some political concern on environmental programs. Yet concern is not enough. Culture—learned, patterned, transmittable behavior is humankind's major tool for survival. The next years will test just how good a tool it is. For what is needed, if humans are not to go the way of the dinosaurs, is a willingness to change basic beliefs and behaviors that have proved to be nonadaptive. Ideas that place humans above nature must be replaced with ideas that see people as a *part* of nature. Rather than subdue the world around us, we should intelligently interact with the environment. Rather than reproduce ourselves into situations of increasing starvation, disease, and general degradation, we should use reproductive restraint.

We also must avoid the trap of thinking that technology will always save us; the misuse of modern technology *is* one cause of the ecological crisis. We must learn to be more selective in the types of technology we use and develop. Why not put our money and effort into technologies such as solid-waste recycling, nonpolluting machinery, and efficient and nondisruptive energy sources instead of innovations that lead to the darkening of our lungs; the poisoning of our food, air, and water; and the possible dehumanizing of the human species?

In your daily life you can help restore the quality of the environment by doing such things as choosing a simpler lifestyle. This would include choosing low-energy alternatives to high-energy ones. Instead of buying a car that gets 8 miles per gallon, consider one that gets the highest miles per gallon. Perhaps walk or bike to work or school, if feasible. Use earth-friendly technologies instead of earth-destructive ones. Learn to avoid needs that are artificially created by advertising. Read an ecology book!

Above all, we must not fall into a gloom-and-doom trap. In many respects, the next 50 or so years may be the most exciting in human history. All of us can be heroes by virtue of our involvement in the social and technological revolution that already has begun. Apathy will be the worst enemy of the struggle to prove that we can efficiently interact with nature.

Summary

With industrialization came problems foreign to foragers. Many products and by-products of factories included mutagens and carcinogens. Industrial cities often were polluted and characterized by disease and crime. The need for more space and resources to support the growth of populations led (and continues to lead) to significant environmental disruptions.

As people transitioned from foragers, to farmers, to industrialists, the nature of disease changed. Epidemiological changes created new selective pressures on human populations. In addition, the weapons of modern warfare and the consequences of recent technologies have led to increased environmental destruction. These factors, as well as new patterns of mating and migration, have created selective pressures on urban and industrial societies that are very different from those that characterized the first 6 million years of hominin evolution.

APPLICATION OF ANTHROPOLOGICAL KNOWLEDGE

The knowledge gained through anthropological investigation is not purely academic. The study of genetics has aided in building theories of inheritance that have been important in recognizing, treating, and—through counseling—preventing genetic disease. In this light, research into genetics and general evolutionary theory has awakened people to the dangers of increasing the genetic load by arresting a genetic disease without curing it. We also have developed hypotheses on the long-range evolutionary effects of artificially increased mutation rates, which are a result of human-caused environmental contamination by radiation and chemicals.

Studies of human variation have put differences among people into an empirical perspective instead of one based on social and biological myths. These studies have very definitely affected policy making as well as the ideas held by the educated public. In fact, the works of an early anthropologist, Franz Boas, were extensively cited in the historic 1954 U.S. Supreme Court decision that legally ended racial segregation in the United States. Anthropological studies have shown that the tendency of some groups within our society to score lower on IQ and other standardized tests is due to social deprivation and environmental deterioration, and to cultural bias in the tests themselves, rather than to supposed innate differences. This has been realized by some educators and administrators. We hope that the implementation of policies aimed at correcting these situations will increase the standard of living for everyone.

Anthropology is an ecological discipline, and one of its main contributions has been the investigation of relationships between humans and their environment. From these studies, it has become clear that people, like all animals, must maintain a proper balance with nature. The great potential of people for cultural behavior provides adaptive flexibility, but it is limited; if this potential is used carelessly, it could create a sterile environment.

The studies of humans' closest relatives, the primates, and of evolutionary prehistory have provided a multidimensional picture of human nature. Through these anthropological studies, many current biological and social problems, such as those that arise in urban situations, are put into understandable perspectives from which solutions can be sought.

There are two other areas of applied physical anthropology that we will examine. These are Darwinian medicine and forensic anthropology.

Darwinian Medicine

The field of **Darwinian medicine** has developed over recent years. Studies in this field attempt to find evolutionary explanations for human vulnerability to various diseases and other medical conditions. Scholars believe that the application of evolutionary insights to

See the Online Learning Center for an Internet Activity on Darwinian medicine.

Darwinian medicine A field of medicine that attempts to understand the human vulnerability to diseases and other medical conditions in terms of evolutionary theory.

medical conditions will help in the treatment, cure, and prevention of illness. A lack of such understanding may lead to a well-meaning physician prescribing a treatment that does more harm than good. For example, in some cases it may be the wrong thing to prescribe anti-nausea drugs to pregnant women. Vomiting may be the way a pregnant woman rids her body of toxins that may injure the fetus. Nausea and vomiting during pregnancy may have been selected for and result in higher fitness than if it did not occur.

One the basic tenets of Darwinian medicine is expressed in this quotation by Randolph M. Nesse and George C. Williams: "The assumption that natural selection maximizes health . . . is incorrect—selection maximizes the reproductive success of genes. Those genes that make bodies having superior reproductive success will become more common, even if they compromise the individual's health in the end."[17]

What appears to be an illness might actually be helping an individual or an individual's offspring live to reproductive age. We already saw how vomiting is one way for a pregnant woman to rid her body of toxins that may kill or disable her fetus. This increases the fetus's chance of living to reproduce, and therefore passing on the mother's genes. Nesse and Williams also point out that coughing helps clear potentially harmful matter from the lungs, pain alerts a person to potential problems of the body, fever indicates an increase in metabolism necessary to defeat pathogens, and anxiety promotes escape from and avoidance of dangerous situations.

Vomiting, coughing, pain, fever, and anxiety are examples of conditions that we might interpret as illness. In reality, they are often defense mechanisms that help our bodies overcome illness. Of course the body sometimes can overreact to a problem and the defense mechanism might become deadly as when people die of dehydration due to sustained vomiting. A person also might cough, vomit, or have pain when nothing harmful is going on in the body. This is called the **smoke-detector principle.** Just as a smoke detector might go off from some insignificant smoke from cooking, the body's defense mechanisms might be triggered from stimuli that pose no real health risk. However, this sensitivity also means that the body will react when something that is potentially dangerous does occur.

smoke-detector principle A defense mechanism that is so fine tuned that even an insignificant stimulus might trigger it.

The body's defense mechanisms against illness have evolved over millions of years. Misunderstanding these defense mechanisms has potential health risks. Many doctors have their patients intervene at the first sign of nausea, fever, or other defense mechanisms. However, since these defense mechanisms are the body's way of defeating the illness, interrupting the process might cause more harm than good. Most people have taken fever reducers or anti-nausea drugs without experiencing any harm. This is because most illnesses that trigger fever, nausea, and other defense mechanisms are not severe, or the defense mechanism was initiated by the smoke-detector principle.

In Chapter 3 we discussed another condition that in some contexts would be considered an illness, and in other contexts a defense against illness. The person homozygous for hemoglobin S ($Hb^S Hb^S$) is said to have the disease sickle-cell anemia. Treatments for sickle-cell anemia are relatively recent, and if untreated the person with sickle-cell anemia usually dies before reproductive age. Hemoglobin A is normal hemoglobin. The individual heterozygous for the two alleles ($Hb^A Hb^S$) has what is known as the sickle-cell trait. The heterozygous individual does not show increased fitness over the $Hb^A Hb^A$ individual in environments lacking malaria but has a significant advantage in a malaria environment.

Heterozygous advantage might exist for other conditions, such as glucose-6-phosphate dehydrogenase deficiency (G6PD), which also has been linked to malaria resistance (Chapter 5). It has been suggested that the individual who has one recessive allele for the deadly recessive disease cystic fibrosis might have increased fitness in environments where typhoid fever or cholera is present. In a like manner, people who have one allele for Tay-Sachs disease may be resistant to tuberculosis, and the person who is heterozygous for phenylketonuria (PKU) seems to have fewer miscarriages on the average than does the homozygous dominant individual.

---

[17] R. A. Nesse and G. C. Williams, "The Evolution and Origin of Disease," *Scientific American*, 44 (November 1998), p. 86.

In the evolution of defense mechanisms against disease, there are trade-offs. The individual might have pain or fever or feel nauseous even when there is nothing dangerous occurring in the body. A population of people might experience high infant mortality from a disease that is fatal in a homozygous genotype, as in the case of sickle-cell anemia, while having a heterozygous advantage against an infectious disease from the allele responsible for the genetic disease.

Understanding the evolution of human anatomy, physiology, and psychology will provide an understanding of human wellness and illness. Such understanding might lead to recommendations about individual and public health that significantly differ from what traditional medicine has supplied so far. Darwinian medicine is a new field that promises some important insights into the human condition.

Forensic Anthropology

See the Online Learning Center for an Internet Activity on forensic anthropology.

Physical anthropologists are specialists in the human skeleton. This is derived, in part, from their studies of comparative primate anatomy and fossilized skeletal remains and the analysis of burials and cemeteries. Forensic anthropology is the applied application of this knowledge. Forensic anthropologists assist medical examiners in the analysis of skeletal remains in investigations of murder, suicide, and accidental death. The results of these analyses often are used in criminal and civil court cases. Forensic anthropologists also work for various international organizations and governments to identify people killed in natural disasters or as a result of human rights violations and genocide. In the latter case, forensic anthropologists have played a major role in helping to identify people placed in mass graves because of reigns of terror by military dictators or warfare in such places as Argentina, Guatemala, Rwanda, and Bosnia. They also have assisted in the identification of remains of servicemen reported as missing in action in Vietnam.

The tasks of a forensic anthropologist are varied. Often the subject of study is a single skeleton, but when several skeletons are intermingled, as would be found in a mass grave or the site of a major disaster, the forensic anthropologist is able to sort out the isolated bones and bone fragments and determine which bones are the remains of which particular individual.

A major task is the identification of the individual represented by a skeleton. What descriptive features can be determined from skeletal material? The sex of an adult skeleton can be determined with a fair degree of accuracy due to the presence of secondary sexual characteristics and the presence of a degree of sexual dimorphism in human anatomy (Figure 16.18). The pelvis shows the greatest differences and the rate of successful determination of sex is estimated at 96 percent, but the rate of success using only a skull is 80 percent. Sex determination from isolated bones or fragments is much more difficult and less accurate. Because secondary sexual characteristics have yet to develop, sex is very difficult or impossible to determine on skeletal material from children.

On the other hand, estimation of age is more accurate on skeletal material from children than on that from adults. The pattern of tooth formation within the jaw and tooth eruption (Figure 16.11) and the development of centers of ossification and fusion of growth plates (Figures 16.8 and 16.9) are indicative of age. Estimation of age in adults is usually based on degenerative changes and tends to be less precise.

"Racial" identification is extremely problematic. As we saw in Chapter 17, "race" is a social concept, not a biological one. While most anthropologists are of the opinion that "races" do not exist as biological categories, the fact that "race" is used in the police and criminal systems means that forensic anthropologists need to make "racial" identifications. In actuality, the forensic anthropologist is making an estimate of population affinity. There has been so much admixture and variability in the human gene pool that dividing the species into a finite number of "races" makes no sense. Yet different populations of people from different areas of the world do differ statistically in some anatomical and genetic characteristics. The forensic anthropologist often can provide an estimate of the ancestry of a specimen or even the degree of admixture from different ancestries.

Stature is usually reconstructed through the use of formulas. These formulas represent the results of analyses of known features found in collections of skeletons. Greater development of limb skeletons on one side of the body can be used to reconstruct whether the victim was right- or left-handed.

Conditions due to malnutrition often can be determined from skeletal material. For example, many Native American skulls show a spongy hyperostosis—lesions on the surface of the cranial vault—that is associated with iron-deficiency anemia. This condition often is associated with malnutrition that comes from an overemphasis on maize, which is deficient in iron. Several diseases also leave signs on bone.

The human body is often subject to cultural modification. While tattooing and body piercing cannot be determined from skeletal material, head-shape modification and the filing of teeth can. Often such modification is identified with particular social groups. A forensic anthropologist may be able to provide a reconstruction of what the person looked like in life, recognition of habitual activities including occupation, and the determination of the approximate time since death (Box 18-2).

The cause of death often can be determined by an examination of the skeleton. Death due to trauma is the easiest to identify. Different types of weapons—guns, knives, blunt instruments—leave different types of wounds.

Anthropology and You—A Personal Note to the Student

You have now come to the end of the text and most likely the end of the course. We suspect that you probably enrolled in physical anthropology because it met some general education requirement, although the course might be a requirement for a major in anthropology or perhaps some other program. Because of the general absence of anthropology in most high schools, the field of anthropology was probably a new one for you. Now that you have completed this course, perhaps you are thinking in the back of your mind about enrolling in further anthropology courses.

As we discussed in Chapter 1, anthropology is a wide-ranging subject. Various aspects of anthropology explore subjects that can best be classified as natural science, social science, or humanities. The best way to explore the breadth of anthropology is to complete a four-fields introduction, introducing yourself to cultural anthropology, archaeology, and linguistics. However, the focus of this text is physical anthropology, and so we will now explore the field of physical anthropology beyond the introductory course for those who are considering majoring in physical anthropology or perhaps considering a career in this field.

The research interests of physical anthropologists are varied and include many areas that are not covered in this text. Table 18.3 presents the results of a survey of the specialties of physical anthropologists. While many research interests are in the areas emphasized in this text—genetics, evolutionary biology, primatology, and paleoanthropology—other interests lie in subfields that more properly belong to biology or medicine. Physical anthropologists are quite visible in the biological and medical world, and researchers often can be found in departments and schools of biology, genetics, molecular biology, public health, medicine, dentistry, and others.

Anthropology has taken its place as an important discipline in universities, liberal arts colleges, and community colleges. Teaching, especially in the latter two venues, can be an exciting and rewarding experience.

Finally, there are many areas where physical anthropologists can apply their expertise to more practical matters. H. Russell Bernard and Willis E. Sibley found that a B.A. degree in anthropology "if it is combined with appropriate personal training [provides] . . . an excellent competitive position for careers in many fields."[18] These fields include various health professions, forensic investigation, public administration, government work, counseling, advertising, market research, journalism, and many others.

---

[18] H. R. Bernard and W. E. Sibley, *Anthropology and Jobs* (Washington, D.C.: American Anthropological Association, 1975), pp. 1–2.

Box 18-2

Flesh Reconstructions in Forensic Anthropology

When the skeletal remains of an individual are found, a forensic anthropologist might be retained to determine the age at death, sex, ancestral affiliations, and cause of death of the person. If DNA analysis and dental records cannot identify the specific individual, a forensic anthropologist working with an artist (one person might play both roles) might attempt to reconstruct the appearance of the person. The flesh reconstruction might help investigators determine the identity of the individual.

The artist and anthropologist start by reconstructing the skull and producing a model of it. Knowledge of how to do the reconstruction comes from detailed studies of anatomy and experience in human dissection. In doing dissections, they look for patterns that exist between bone and the soft tissues that overlay it. These patterns guide the reconstruction.

After reconstructing the skull (a), the face is reconstructed layer by layer. Simulated fat, muscles, skin, and hair are added to the bony foundation (b). The result is an interpretation based on the artist's and anthropologist's skill and knowledge of human anatomy (c). The skull leaves no trace of many facial features, so the reconstruction is only an approximation of what the person looked like in life (d). People seeing the reconstruction might make a connection to it and come forward with information.

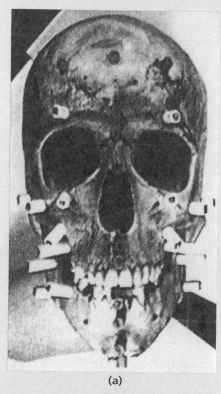

(a)

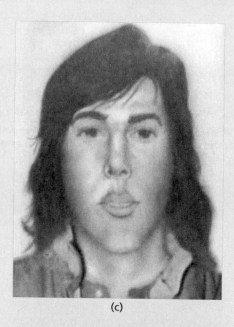

(c)

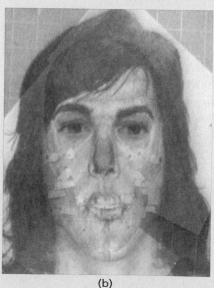

(b)

(d)

Table 18.3 What Physical Anthropologists Study: Teaching and Research Specialties of Physical Anthropologists Ranked by Percentage of Responses

Growth, anatomy, morphology (13.9%)
Growth and development, dental anthropology, anatomy, biomechanics, functional morphology, kinesiology

Evolutionary biology (13.5%)
Paleoanthropology, evolution, paleontology, taxonomy, evolutionary theory, molecular evolution

Population studies (12.8%)
Human variation, human adaptation, demography, population biology, paleodemography, dermatoglyphics, physiological adaptation, serology, population structure

Skeletal biology (12.2%)
General osteology, forensic anthropology, paleopathology, bone biology

Biomedical anthropology and related areas (12.2%)
Biomedical anthropology, epidemiology, nutrition, disease, aging, health/nutrition, human physiology, paleonutrition

Primatology (11.1%)
Behavior, evolution, general primatology, anatomy, ecology, paleontology, morphology, locomotion, dentition, electromyography, field studies, biomechanics

Genetics (8.8%)
Human genetics, population genetics, cytogenetics, biochemical genetics, dental genetics, quantitative genetics, molecular genetics, immunogenetics, primate genetics

Other areas (15.5%)
Statistics, ecology, sociobiology, human ecology, culture and biology, quantitative methods, evolution of behavior, history, archaeology

Source: C. W. Wienker and K. A. Bennett, "Trends and Developments in Physical Anthropology," *American Journal of Physical Anthropology* 87 (1992), pp. 383–393. Copyright © John Wiley & Sons, Inc. Reprinted by permission of John Wiley & Sons, Inc.

Summary

The knowledge gained from physical anthropology research is often applicable to real-life problems. The discipline of physical anthropology has contributed to our understanding of genetic disease, human ecology, and modern social problems associated with racism, ethnocentrism, and urban crises.

Two areas of applied physical anthropology that have received considerable attention recently are Darwinian medicine and forensic anthropology. Researchers in the area of Darwinian medicine investigate how illness and wellness are related to evolutionary processes and overall fitness. One general finding that comes from Darwinian medicine is that sometimes a physical condition that appears to be disadvantageous to an individual might convey selective advantage to that individual or to the breeding population to which the individual belongs. For example, an individual feeling ill from nausea and vomiting might be getting rid of dangerous toxins that could threaten his or her life, or if pregnant, the life or health of a fetus. Or a person carrying an allele that is lethal in the homozygous genotype might be protected from an infectious disease, such as malaria.

Forensic anthropology is involved in skeletal identification and analysis for legal purposes. Forensic anthropologists work with police departments, coroners, government agencies, and human rights groups in investigating deaths. Skeletal investigations often yield information on the age, sex, and cause of death of individuals known only from their skeletons. Bones can sometimes also give indications of ancestry, disease, and the nutritional status of the deceased.

Key Terms

acid rain, 495
Darwinian medicine, 500
endocrine disruptor, 488
endocrine system, 488
environmental estrogens, 488
epidemiology, 489

global warming, 495
greenhouse gases, 495
industrialism, 485
intensive farming, 496
monoculture, 496
ozone, 494

smoke-detector principle, 501
stratosphere, 494
urbanization, 485
urbanized society, 485
zoonoses, 490
zymotics, 491

See the Online Learning Center for additional study questions.

Study Questions

1. What factors differentiate urban life from rural life?
2. What are some of the problems caused by the enormous increase in population in the last 250 years?
3. What can a paleoanthropologist tell about disease and injury in fossil populations?
4. How have the causes and distribution of disease changed as hominins transitioned from forgers to farmers and then to industrialists?
5. What are some of the major problems facing people in the twenty-first century?
6. In your opinion, what should be done to improve the quality of human life?
7. What is the major concept embodied in the field of Darwinian medicine? What contributions to our conceptualization of health and illness has Darwinian medicine made?
8. In what ways can a forensic anthropologist contribute to a criminal investigation?

Critical Thinking Questions

1. What evolutionary effects do you believe might occur from a large-scale biological, chemical, or nuclear terrorist act? Can you think of any science fiction stories based on the effect of any of these types of warfare? How logical are they?
2. Most human predators are microscopic; that is, they are microorganisms. In what ways do you think that disease has contributed to the shaping of modern humans? What would happen if we could cure all infectious and genetic diseases? How might this affect future human evolution?
3. Hominins have been altering their environments for millions of years, but it perhaps has been since the Industrial Revolution that those alterations have been profound. Two types of scientific alterations have been in the news. The first involves the fact that some insecticides and plastics mimic estrogens and these chemicals can get into the water supply and foods. Second, plants and animals are being genetically modified for specific utilitarian reasons. What might be some evolutionary consequences of these events?

Suggested Readings

Bodley, J. H. *Anthropology and Contemporary Human Problems,* 4th ed. Palo Alto, CA: Mayfield, 2001. This book considers current problems such as natural resource depletion, war, hunger, and population growth, and it attempts to put them into an anthropological perspective.

Byers, S. *Introduction to Forensic Anthropology.* Boston: Allyn and Bacon, 2002. This is a general introduction to forensic anthropology.

Halweil, B., et al. *State of the World 2004.* New York: Norton, 2004. This book reports on world ecological and economic conditions. A new volume is published each year, so look for the most current edition.

Miller, G. T., Jr. *Living in the Environment,* 13th ed. Belmont, CA: Wadsworth, 2004. This is an excellent and comprehensive text that outlines environmental problems and presents possible solutions. Thousands of references are listed.

Miller, J., S. Engelberg, and W. J. Broad. *Germs.* New York: Simon & Schuster, 2001. This is a best-selling book on biological warfare.

Roberts, C., and K. Manchester. *The Archaeology of Disease,* 3rd ed. Ithica, NY: Cornell University Press, 2005. This is a general, introductory text on paleopathology.

Ryan, A. S. (ed.). *A Guide to Careers in Physical Anthropology.* Westport, CT: Bergin & Garvey, 2002. This is a collection of essays describing various careers in physical anthropology.

Trevathan, W. R., et al. *Evolutionary Medicine.* New York: Oxford University Press, 1999. This book deals with the evolution of human diseases and how an understanding of this could be useful in modern treatments and cures.

Suggested Websites

Archaeology Magazine:
www.archaeology.org

Darwinian Medicine:
www.darwinianmedicine.org

Human Rights and Forensic Anthropology:
http://garnet.acns.fsu.edu/~sss4407

Society for Medical Anthropology:
www.medanthro.net

Worldwatch Institute:
www.worldwatch.org

Zeno's Forensic Page (extensive list of links in the area of forensic anthropology):
http://forensic.to/forensic.html

An Introduction to Skeletal Anatomy and the Anatomy of the Brain

Important evidence for evolution is found in anatomy. Because of the interest of anthropologists in the skeletons of living primates, the fossil record, and human burials, physical anthropologists have become specialists in the skeleton. Skeletal evidence also is used in studies of growth and development and in forensic anthropology.

Various aspects of the skeleton are discussed in several chapters of this text. Because different readers may study these chapters in different orders, a general introduction to skeletal anatomy is presented in this appendix so that it can be used with any chapter.

To understand the primate skeleton, it is important to constantly refer to the drawings and locate on them the bones and features that are being discussed. Important bones and features that can be seen in the drawings in this appendix appear in bold type. This is a general discussion designed to provide the reader with the tools necessary for understanding the text. More detailed discussions of skeletal anatomy can be found in the Suggested Readings and Suggested Websites at the end of this appendix.

SKELETAL ANATOMY OF PRIMATES

The Postcranial Skeleton

The postcranial skeleton is the part of the skeleton behind the skull or below the skull in bipedal animals such as humans; it is all the skeleton except the skull (Figures A.1 and A.2). The axis of the skeleton is the spine, or **vertebral column,** which consists of a series of interlocking vertebrae. The vertebrae differ in morphology in various regions of the spine. The vertebrae in these regions may be identified as **cervical, thoracic, lumbar, sacral,** and **coccygeal.** The term *articulation* refers to the coming together of two bones at a joint. All ribs articulate with the vertebrae, and most of the ribs articulate in front with the **sternum.**

The forelimbs and hindlimbs are connected to the spine at the **shoulder girdle** and the **pelvis,** respectively. The shoulder girdle consists of two bones: the **clavicle** (collarbone), which articulates with the sternum, and the **scapula** (shoulder blade). The scapula articulates with the clavicle and the **humerus,** the bone of the upper arm. The articulations of the clavicle with the scapula and the scapula with the humerus are close together, providing for movement and flexibility in the shoulder. The humerus articulates with the scapula as a ball in a socket.

The lower arm consists of a pair of bones: the **radius** and the **ulna.** The radius articulates with the humerus in such a way that it can rotate around an axis; in so doing, the wrist and hand rotate. The wrist consists of eight bones, the **carpals;** the palm region of the hand contains the five **metacarpals.** The bones of the fingers are the **phalanges,** two in the thumb and three in each finger. (However, there has been a reduction in the number of bones in the fingers in some primates, such as the potto, spider monkeys, and colobus monkeys.)

A

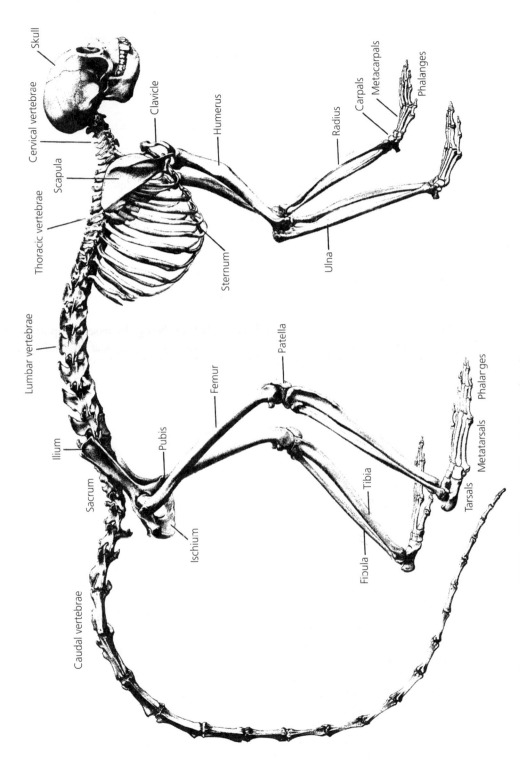

FIGURE A.1 Skeleton of an Old World Monkey, *Miopithecus talapoin*

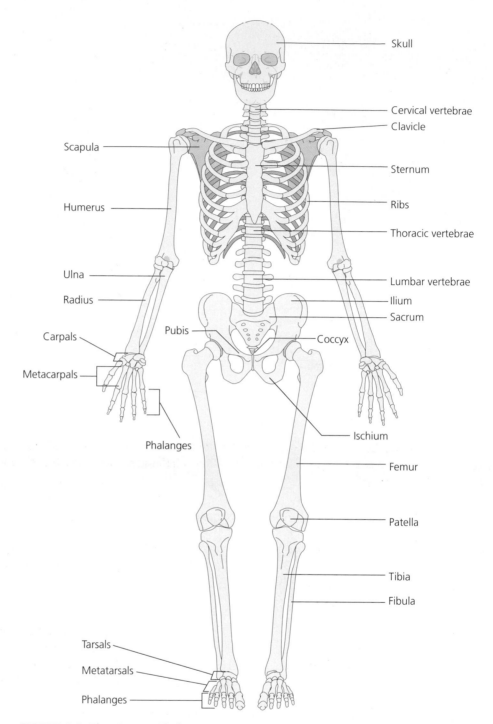

Skull

Cervical vertebrae

Clavicle

Scapula

Sternum

Humerus

Ribs

Thoracic vertebrae

Ulna

Lumbar vertebrae

Radius

Ilium

Sacrum

Carpals

Pubis

Coccyx

Metacarpals

Ischium

Phalanges

Femur

Patella

Tibia

Fibula

Tarsals

Metatarsals

Phalanges

FIGURE A.2 The Human Skeleton

The hindlimbs articulate with the spine by means of the pelvis. The pelvis itself is composed of three units: a pair of **innominate** bones, or os coxae, and the **sacrum.** The latter is made up of fused sacral vertebrae. Each innominate in the adult is divided into three regions corresponding to what are three separate bones in the fetus. These regions are the **ilium,** the **ischium,** and the **pubis.**

The bone of the upper leg is the **femur.** The lower leg, like the lower arm, consists of two bones, the **tibia** and the **fibula;** unlike the lower arm, the lower leg does not rotate. The

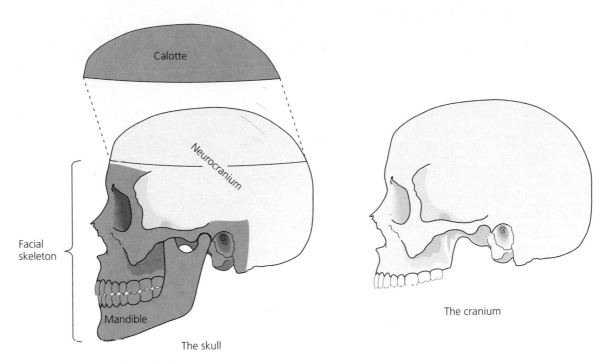

FIGURE A.3 Divisions of the Skull

small **patella** is commonly called the kneecap. The ankle consists of the seven **tarsals;** the arch of the foot, five **metatarsals;** and the toes of the **phalanges,** two in the big toe and three in each of the others.

The Skull

The skull consists of 28 separate bones plus the teeth. The skull has two major parts: the **mandible,** or lower jaw, and the **cranium.** The skull also may be partitioned into a **facial skeleton** and the **neurocranium,** or **brain case.** The top section of the neurocranium is the **calotte** (Figures A.3, A.4, and A.5).

The Brain Case The brain is housed in the brain case, or cranium. The brain case is made up of several separate bones. As we can see from the top or side, the bones of the cranium come together at immovable joints called sutures. The part of the skull surrounding the sides and top of the brain is the **calvarium,** which is composed of the **frontal, parietals, temporals,** and **occipital.**

The cranial base is the floor of the brain case. It consists of the ethmoid and sphenoid, plus parts of the occipital, temporals, and frontal bones. A large hole, the **foramen magnum,** is found in the occipital bone. The spinal cord passes through this opening and enters and merges with the brain. On either side of the foramen magnum are two rounded surfaces, the **occipital condyles,** which fit into a pair of depressions on the top of the uppermost vertebra. This is how the skull articulates with the spine. Finally, the auditory bulla, a balloonlike structure, houses the middle ear.

The Facial Skeleton and Mandible The skeletal supports for the senses of smell, sight, hearing, and taste and the skeletal apparatus for chewing are all parts of the facial skeleton. The facial skeleton is composed of a number of small bones. It can be divided into several regions, including the nasal cavity, upper jaw, and mandible.

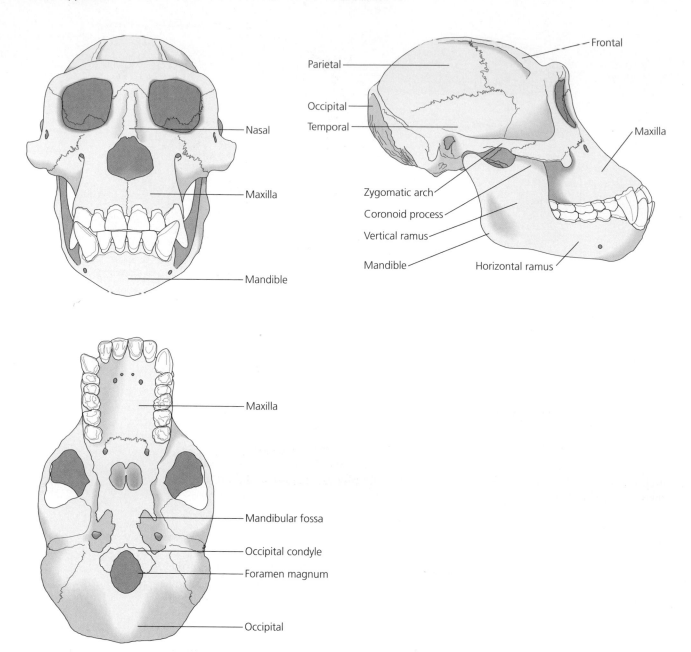

FIGURE A.4 The Chimpanzee Skull

The upper jaw is made up of a pair of bones: the **maxillae.** The top of the nose is formed by the nasal bones. Within the nose itself, the inner surface of the nasal cavity is covered with membranes containing the receptors for the sense of smell. These membranes sit on a series of thin, convoluted bony plates, the turbinals and nasal conchae, which may be extensive in animals with a keen sense of smell.

The mandible, or lower jaw, is composed of two halves fused in the middle in many primates (Figure A.6). The **horizontal ramus** contains the teeth. Behind the molars, the **vertical ramus** rises at an angle and ends in a rounded surface, the **mandibular condyle,** which articulates with the rest of the skull. To the front of the vertical ramus is a projection, the **coronoid process.** There are four types of teeth embedded in the mandible: the incisors, canines, premolars, and molars. In addition, the facial skeleton includes the lacrimals, **palatine,** vomer, and **zygomatics,** as well as part of the frontal.

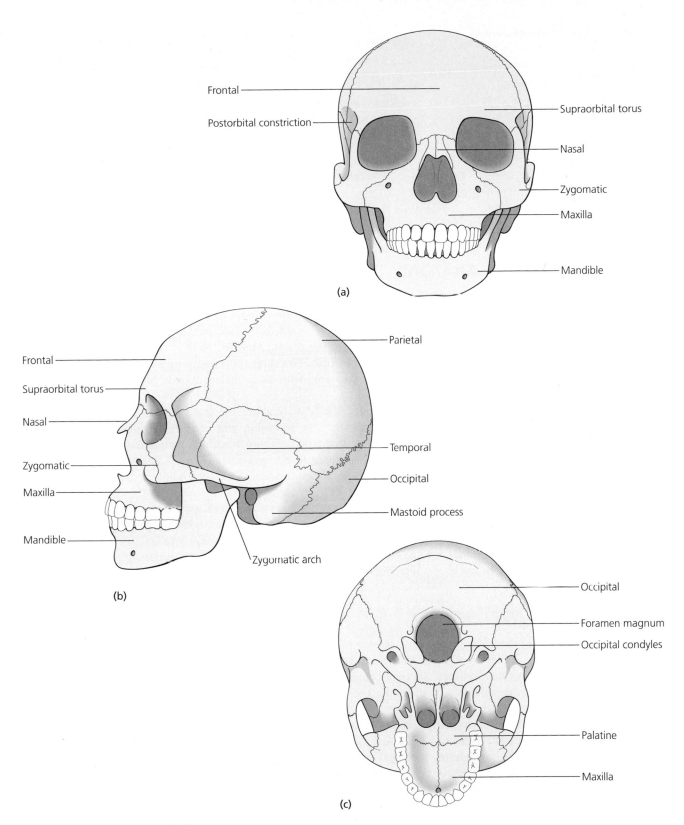

FIGURE A.5 The Human Skull

FIGURE A.6 The Human Mandible

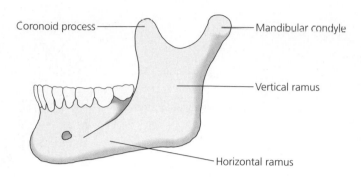

THE ANATOMY OF THE HUMAN BRAIN

We may identify several structures that are parts of the brain. The major parts of the human brain that appear below in bold type are identified in the figures (Figure A.7).

The **brainstem** is involved with certain body functions that are essential to life, such as the regulation of breathing and heartbeat. Attached to the brainstem is a major structure of the hindbrain, the **cerebellum.** The cerebellum has a number of functions, including those that are basic to movement of the body: balance, body position, and position in space.

In the center of the brain, immediately above the brainstem, is a group of cells that make up the limbic system. Like the brainstem and cerebellum, the limbic system is involved with basic functions of the body. These functions include regulating body temperature, blood pressure, blood sugar levels, and more. Sexual desire and self-protection through fight or flight, emotional reactions critical to the survival of the individual, lie within the limbic system.

A critical part of the limbic system is a structure known as the **hypothalamus.** The hypothalamus regulates hunger, thirst, sleeping, waking, body temperature, chemical balances, heart rate, sexual activity, and emotions. It also plays a major role in the regulation of hormones through control of the **pituitary gland.** The pituitary gland regulates the estrous cycle and reproductive behavior.

The Cerebrum

The most prominent structure of the human brain is the **cerebrum,** which is so large that it covers and obscures many structures of the brain. The cerebrum is divided into two halves, or hemispheres; the right hemisphere controls the left side of the body, and the left controls the right side of the body. The two halves are connected by nerve fibers that make up the **corpus callosum.**

The human cerebrum is covered by the **cerebral cortex,** a layer about 3 millimeters (0.125 inch) thick. The human cortex is intricately folded into a series of rounded ridges, or convolutions, separated from one another by fissures. The convolutions increase the surface area of the cerebral hemispheres since a convoluted surface has a greater surface area than does a smooth surface.

Each hemisphere is divided into four lobes by deep grooves, and each lobe is named after the bone of the skull that overlays the lobe. The functions of the cortex in the various lobes have been determined by studies of electrical stimulation of the area, observations of persons with specific brain damage, and animal experimentation. The **temporal lobes** deal with perception and memory, and a section of the temporal lobe, the **auditory cortex,** is responsible for hearing. The **occipital lobes** handle the sense of sight; the cortex in this area

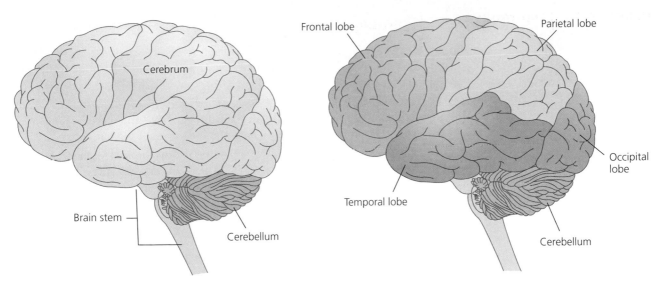

Main parts of the brain

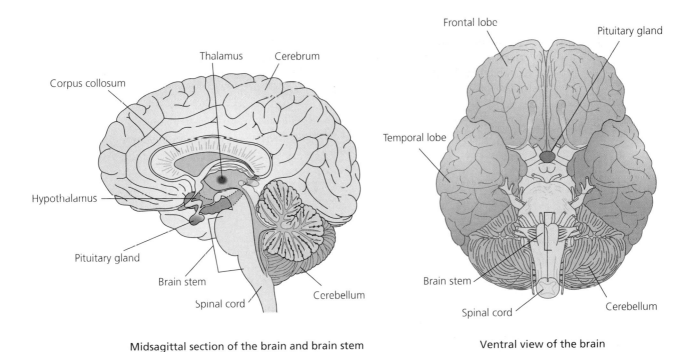

Midsagittal section of the brain and brain stem

Ventral view of the brain

FIGURE A.7 The Human Brain

is often called the visual cortex. The **parietal lobes** receive sensory information from the body. The largest parts of the cerebrum are the **frontal lobes,** which deal with purposeful behavior.

While the two cerebral hemispheres look alike, there are many subtle differences. In general, the left side deals more with language than the right side does; the right is involved more with spatial abilities.

Suggested Readings

Aiello, L., and C. Dean. *An Introduction to Human Evolutionary Anatomy.* London: Academic, 1990. This is a very detailed description of human anatomy from an evolutionary perspective.

Steele, D. G., and C. A. Bramblett. *The Anatomy and Biology of the Human Skeleton.* College Station, TX: Texas A&M University Press, 1988. This book features a large number of excellent carefully labeled photographs of human bones.

Swindler, D., and C. D. Wood. *An Atlas of Primate Gross Anatomy.* Melbourne, FL: Krieger, 1982. This book contains a series of detailed line drawings illustrating the comparative anatomy of the baboon, chimpanzee, and human.

White, T. D., and P. A. Folkens. *Human Osteology,* 2nd ed. San Diego, CA: Academic, 2000. This book is a detailed discussion of the human skeleton for the paleoanthropologist.

Whitehead, P. F, W. K. Sacco, and S. B. Hochgraf. *A Photographic Atlas of Physical Anthropology.* Englewood, CO: Morton Publishing, 2005. This book contains an extensive collection of colored photographs of primate skeletal material.

Suggested Websites

The eskeleton Project:
www.eSkeletons.org/

The Human Brain:
wwwl.vh.org/Providers/Textbooks/BrainAnatomy/BrainAnatomy.html

Glossary

See the Online Learning Center for vocabulary flashcards and audio glossary.

A

abductor A muscle that moves a part of the body away from the midline of the body.

ABO blood-type system A blood-type system that consists of two basic antigens, A and B. Blood type O is the absence of both antigens.

acclimatory adjustment Reversible physiological adjustments to stressful environments.

accretion Growth by virtue of an increase in intercellular material.

Acheulean tradition The most frequent cultural manifestation of the Lower Paleolithic; characterized by several highly diagnostic tool types, including the hand ax.

achondroplastic dwarfism Form of dwarfism in which the individual's head and trunk are of normal size but the limbs are quite short; inherited as a dominant.

achromatopsia A recessive genetic abnormality in which the retina of the eye lacks the cones that are necessary for color vision and for seeing in fine detail. Also called *total color blindness*.

acid rain Rain that carries acids that pollute water systems and soils.

adaptation Changes in gene frequencies resulting from selective pressures being placed on a population by environmental factors; results in a greater fitness of the population to its ecological niche.

adaptive radiation The evolution of a single population into a number of different species.

adenine One of the bases found in DNA and RNA; a purine.

adenosine triphosphate (ATP) The main fuel of cells. ATP is manufactured by the mitochondria.

adjustment The ability of humans to survive in stressful environments by nongenetic means.

adolescent growth spurt A rapid increase in stature and other dimensions of the body that occurs during puberty.

adult The period in an individual's life cycle after the eruption of the last permanent teeth.

agglutination A clumping together of red blood cells in the presence of an antibody.

aging The uninterrupted process of normal development that leads to a progressive decline in physiological function and ultimately to death.

agonistic behavior Behavior that involves fighting, threats, and fleeing.

albinism A recessive abnormality that leads to little or no production of the skin pigment melanin.

alcaptonuria A recessive genetic abnormality that results in the absence of an enzyme that is involved in the breakdown of the amino acid tyrosine, bringing about a buildup of homogentisic acid in the body which is deposited in various organs of the body.

allele An alternative form of a gene.

Allen's rule Among mammals, populations of the same species living near the equator tend to have body parts that protrude more and to have longer limbs than do populations farther away from the equator.

allogrooming Grooming another animal.

allometric growth Pattern of growth whereby different parts of the body grow at different rates with respect to each other.

allopatric species Species occupying mutually exclusive geographical areas.

altruism Behavior characterized by self-sacrifice that benefits others.

alveoli Small air sacs, located in the lungs, that are richly endowed with blood capillaries. Oxygen is absorbed by the blood in the alveoli.

amino acid A type of molecule that forms the basic building block of proteins.

amino acid racemization Chronometric dating method based on change in the three-dimensional structure of amino acids from one form to its mirror image over time.

amniocentesis A medical technique in which amniotic fluid is removed for study of the fetus.

amniote egg An egg with a shell and several internal membranes, which made reproduction on land possible.

amniotic fluid The fluid surrounding the fetus.

analogies Structures that are superficially similar and serve similar functions but have no common evolutionary relationship.

anterior pillars Bony columns located on both sides of the nasal aperture of some fossil hominids that help withstand the stresses of chewing.

anthropocentricity The belief that humans are the most important elements in the universe.

anthropoid A member of the suborder Anthropoidea; includes the New World monkeys, Old World monkeys, apes, and humans.

anthropological linguistics The study of language in cross-cultural perspective; the origin and evolution of language.

anthropology The broad-scope scientific study of people from all periods of time and in all areas of the world. Anthropology focuses on both biological and cultural characteristics and variation as well as biological and cultural evolution.

anthropometry The study of measurements of the human body.

antibody A protein manufactured by the body to neutralize or destroy an antigen.

antigen A substance that stimulates the production or mobilization of antibodies. An antigen can be a foreign protein, toxin, bacterium, or other substance.

ape A common term that includes the small-bodied apes (the gibbons and siamang) and the great apes (the orangutan, chimpanzee, bonobo, and gorilla).

applied anthropology A branch of anthropology devoted to applying anthropological theory to practical problems.

arbitrary A characteristic of language. A word or another unit of sound has no real connection to the thing to which it refers; the meanings of the arbitrary elements of a language must be learned.

arboreal Living in trees.

archaeology The scientific study of the past and current cultures through the analysis of artifacts and the context in which they are found.

archeomagnetism A dating technique that uses a determination of declination angle in archaeological samples.

archetype The divine plan or blueprint for a species or higher taxonomic category.

areolar area The dark area surrounding the nipple of the breast.

argon 40/argon 39 dating A method of chronometric dating based on making measurements of the relative amounts of argon 40 and argon 39 in a sample.

artifact Any physical remains of human activity.

artificial gene A gene that is made in a laboratory and used in place of a defective or undesirable gene.

artificial selection The deliberate breeding of domesticated animals or plants.

assemblage All the artifacts from a given site.

assortative mating Preference for or avoidance of certain people as mates for physical or social reasons.

aster In cell division, the fibers that radiate from the centrosome.

asymmetry of function The phenomenon in which the two hemispheres of the brain specialize in regard to different functions.

atom A building block of matter.

Australopithecines Members of the genera *Australopithecus* and *Paranthropus,* who lived in African approximately 4 to 1 million years ago.

autapomorphic feature A feature that is unique to a particular species.

autogrooming Self-grooming.

autosome A chromosome other than a sex chromosome.

awl A type of tool that is used to puncture a hole in a soft material such as wood or skin.

B

back cross The process of crossing a hybrid with its homozygous recessive parent.

balanced polymorphism Maintenance of two or more alleles in a gene pool as the result of heterozygous advantage.

band Among geladas, a social group consisting of a number of harems and all-male units. Among humans, the basic social unit of hunting and gathering peoples, which typically consists of about 25 members.

basal metabolic rate The measure of the total energy utilized by the body to maintain those body processes necessary for life; the minimum level of heat produced by the body at rest.

base A subunit of a nucleotide that makes up the DNA and RNA molecules: adenine, cytosine, guanine, thymine, uracil.

basicranium The floor of the brain case.

behavioral adjustment Survival in a stressful environment made possible by cultural means, primarily technology.

behavioral thermoregulation Using behavior, such as avoiding or seeking sources of heat, to regulate body temperature.

Bergmann's rule Within the same species of mammals, the average weight of the members of a population increases and the surface area of the body decreases as the average environmental temperature decreases.

Beringia The landmass, some 2000 kilometers (1250 miles) from north to south, that connected Siberia and Alaska during the glacials.

biacromial width A measurement of the width of the shoulders.

bilophodont Refers to a form of molar found in Old World monkeys consisting of four cusps with a small constriction separating them into two pairs.

binocular field The visual field produced by the overlapping of the separate visual fields from each eye when the eyes are located on the front of the face.

binomen A two-part name given to a species; the first name is also the name of the genus. An example of a binomen is *Homo sapiens.*

binomial nomenclature A system of naming species that uses a double name such as *Homo sapiens.* The first name alone names the genus; both names used together name the species.

bioinformatics A new discipline dedicated to the analysis of genetic information and the practical use of that information.

biological environment The living elements surrounding the organism.

biological evolution Change in the frequencies of alleles within a gene pool of a population over time.

bipedalism See **erect bipedalism.**

bitrochanteric width A measurement of hip width.

blade Flakes with roughly parallel sides and extremely sharp edges; blades are frequently found in Upper Paleolithic sites.

blending theory An early and incorrect idea that the inherited characteristics of offspring are intermediate between maternal and paternal genetic characteristics.

bone age A standard age based on the appearance of centers of ossification and fusion of growth plates.

bone breccia Cave fill consisting of masses of bone cemented together with calcium carbonate that has dissolved out of limestone.

bone industry All of the bone artifacts from a particular site.

brachial index The length of the radius relative to the length of the humerus.

brachiation Hand-over-hand locomotion along a branch with the body suspended underneath the branch by the arms.

branch running and walking A form of quadrupedalism in which the animal is walking along a branch, grasping with both hands and feet.

breast bud An elevation of the breast as a small mound; the earliest sign of puberty in the female.

Broca's area A small area in the human brain that controls the production of speech sounds.

Bronze Age The stage of cultural history that includes the earliest civilizations and the development of metallurgy.

brow ridge Ridge of bone above the eye sockets.

burin A stone tool with a chisel-like point used for engraving or manufacturing bone tools.

C

calendrical system A system of measuring time based on natural recurring units of time, such as the revolutions of the earth around the sun; they note the number of such units that have preceded or elapsed with reference to a specific point in time.

call system A system of vocalized sounds that grade one into another.

carbohydrates Organic compounds composed of carbon, oxygen, and hydrogen; include the sugars and starches.

carnivore An animal that eats primarily meat.

carrier A person who possesses a recessive allele in the heterozygous condition.

cast A representation of an organism created when a substance fills in a mold.

catarrhine nose Nose in which nostrils open downward and are separated by a narrow nasal septum; found in Old World monkeys, apes, and humans.

catastrophism Idea that the earth has experienced a series of catastrophic destructions and creations and that fossil forms found in each layer of the earth are bounded by a creation and destruction event.

cell The smallest unit able to perform all those activities collectively called life. All living organisms are either one cell or composed of several cells.

centriole A pair of small bodies found near the nucleus of the cell from which the spindle is formed.

centromere A structure in the chromosome holding the two chromatids together; during cell division, it is the site of attachment for the spindle fibers.

centrosome A body that lies near the nucleus of the cell that contains two centrioles.

cephalic index The breadth of the head relative to its length.

cerebral cortex The "gray matter" of the brain; the center of conscious evaluation, planning, skill, speech, and other higher mental activities.

cheek pouch Pocket in the cheek that opens into the mouth; some Old World monkeys store food in the cheek pouch.

cheek teeth The premolars and molars.

chin A bony projection of the lower border of the outside of the mandible.

chordate A member of the phylum Chordata; chordates are characterized by the presence of a notochord, a dorsal, hollow, single nerve cord, and gill slits at some point in the life cycle.

chromatid One of the two strands of a replicated chromosome. Two chromatids are joined together by a centromere.

chromosomal aberration Abnormal chromosome number or chromosome structure.

chromosomal sex The number of X and Y chromosomes a person has. The chromosomal sex of a person with two X chromosomes is a female. The chromosomal sex of a person with one X and one Y chromosome is a male.

chromosome A body found in the nucleus of the cell containing the hereditary material.

chron A large division of a geomagnetic time scale that shows primarily a single polarity.

chronological age Period of time since birth.

chronometric dates Dates that refer to a specific point or range of time. Chronometric dates are not necessarily exact dates, and they often are expressed as a probability.

chronospecies Arbitrarily defined divisions of an evolutionary line.

civilization A type of society with relatively high population density; based on the de-emphasis of kinship as a method of social control and the rise of central authority in the form of a government and powerful priesthood. Civilizations often also include monumental architecture, writing, mathematics, public works, and full-time armies.

clade A group of species with a common evolutionary ancestry.

cladistics A theory of classification that differentiates between shared ancestral and shared derived features.

cladogram A graphic representation of the species, or other taxa, being studied, based on cladistic analysis.

class Major division of a phylum, consisting of closely related orders.

classification A system of organizing data.

cleaver A large core tool with a straight, sharp edge at one end.

clinal distribution A distribution of frequencies that show a systematic gradation over space; also called continuous variation.

cloning The process of asexual reproduction in an otherwise multicellular animal.

codominance The situation in which, in the heterozygous condition, both alleles are expressed in the phenotype.

codon A sequence of three bases on the DNA molecule that codes a specific amino acid or other genetic function.

coefficient of relatedness A measurement of the degree of genetic relationship or the number of shared genes between two individuals.

communication Occurs when some stimulus or message is transmitted and received; in relation to animal life, when one animal transmits information to another animal.

community Among chimpanzees, a large group that, through fission and fusion, is composed of a series of constantly changing smaller units, including the all-male party, family, unit, nursery unit, consortship, and gathering.

comparative cytogenetics The comparative study of chromosomes.

comparative molecular biology The comparative study of molecules.

competition The situation in which two populations occupy the same or parts of the same niche.

complementary pair A set of two nucleotides, each on a different polynucleotide chain, that are attracted to each other by a chemical bond. In DNA, adenine and thymine, and cytosine and guanine, form complementary pairs.

compound tool A tool that is composed of several parts, for example, a harpoon.

computerized tomography A technology used in medicine that permits visualization of the interior of an organism's body.

conduction The movement of heat from one object to another by direct contact.

cones Cells of the retina of the eye; each of the three types of cones is sensitive to a specific wavelength of light, thereby producing color vision.

consanguineous mating Mating between biological relatives.

consort pair A temporary alliance between a male and an estrus female.

constitutive heterochromatin Chromosomal material that is not thought to contain any actual genes.

control In an experiment, a situation in which a comparison can be made between a specific situation and a second situation that differs, ideally, in only one aspect from the first.

convection Movement of heat from an object to the surrounding fluid, either gas or liquid; heat causes the gas or fluid to move away from the object.

convergence Nonhomologous similarities in different evolutionary lines; the result of similarities in selective pressures.

coprolite Fossilized fecal material.

core A nodule of rock from which flakes are removed.

core area Sections within the home range of a primate population that may contain a concentration of food, a source of water, and a good resting place or sleeping trees, and in which most of the troop's time will be spent.

core tool A tool that is manufactured by the removal of flakes from a core.

cranial capacity The volume of the brain case of the skull.

creation-science The idea that scientific evidence can be and has been gathered for creation as depicted in the Bible. Mainstream scientists, many religious leaders, and the Supreme Court discount any scientific value of "creation-science" statements.

critical temperature The temperature at which the body must begin to resist a lowering of body temperature; occurs in the nude human body at approximately 31°C (87.8°F).

cross-cousin preferential marriage Marriage between a person and his or her cross-cousin (father's sister's child or mother's brother's child).

crossing-over The phenomenon whereby sections of homologous chromosomes are interchanged during meiosis.

crural index The length of the tibia relative to the length of the femur.

cultural anthropology The study of the learned patterns of behavior and knowledge characteristic of a society and of how they vary.

cultural environment The products of human endeavor, including technology and social institutions surrounding the organism.

culture Learned, nonrandom, systematic behavior and knowledge that can be transmitted from generation to generation.

culture-bound The state or quality of having relevance only to the members of a specific cultural group.

cusp A point on a tooth.

cystic fibrosis A recessive genetic abnormality that affects the production of mucus in the lungs.

cytogenetics The study of the heredity mechanisms within the cell.

cytology The study of the biology of the cell.

cytoplasm Material within the cell between the plasma membrane and the nuclear membrane.

cytosine One of the bases found in the DNA and RNA molecule; a pyrimadine.

D

Darwinian medicine A field of medicine that attempts to understand the human vulnerability to diseases and other medical conditions in terms of evolutionary theory.

debitage Waste and nonutilized material produced in the process of tool manufacture.

deciduous teeth The first set of teeth that develop in mammals; also known as the baby or milk teeth.

declination angle At a particular point on the surface of the earth, the angle formed by a line pointing to true north and a line pointing to magnetic north.

deletion A chromosomal aberration in which a chromosome breaks and a segment is not included in the second-generation cell. The genetic material on the deleted section is lost.

deme The local breeding population; the smallest reproductive population.

dendrochronology Tree-ring dating.

dental arcade The tooth row as seen from above.

dental comb A structure formed by the front teeth of the lower jaw projecting forward almost horizontally; found in prosimians.

dental formula Formal designation of the types and numbers of teeth. The dental formula 2.1.2.3/2.1.2.3 indicates that in one-half of the upper jaw and lower jaw there are two incisors, one canine, two premolars, and three molars.

deoxyribonucleic acid (DNA) A nucleic acid that controls the structure of proteins and hence determines inherited characteristics; genes are portions of the DNA molecule that fulfill specific functions.

deoxyribose A five-carbon sugar found in the DNA molecule.

development The process whereby cells differentiate into different and specialized units; change over time from an immature to a mature or specialized state.

developmental adjustments Alterations in the pattern of growth and development resulting from environmental influences.

diabetes Failure of the body to produce insulin, which controls sugar metabolism; has a complex genetic basis influenced by environmental factors.

diaphragm A muscle that lies beneath the lungs. When the diaphragm contracts, the volume of the lungs increases, causing a lowering of pressure within the lungs and movement of air from the outside into the lungs. When the diaphragm relaxes, air is expelled from the lungs.

diastema A space between teeth.

dichromacy The possession of two visual pigments, sensitive to blue and green, in the retina of the eye.

diphyodonty Having two sets of teeth, the deciduous and the permanent teeth.

directional selection A type of natural selection characterized by a generation-after-generation shift in a population in a specific direction, such as toward larger body size. In this example, individuals with smaller body size are being selected against.

discontinuous variation Distribution of alleles, allele combinations, or any traits characterized by little or no gradation in frequencies between adjacent regions.

discrete A characteristic of language. Signals, such as words, represent discrete entities or experiences; a discrete signal does not blend with other signals.

displacement (behavior) The situation in which one animal can cause another to move away from food, a sitting place, and so on.

displacement (language) A characteristic of language. The ability to communicate about events at times and places other than when and where they occur; enables a person to talk and think about things not directly in front of him or her.

disruptive selection A type of natural selection characterized by a generation-after-generation shift in the population away from the average individual, such as, for example, toward both larger and smaller body size. In this example, individuals with average (mean) body size are being selected against.

distance curve A graph that shows the total height (or other measurement) of an individual on a series of dates.

diurnal Active during daylight hours.

dizygotic twins Fraternal twins; twins derived from separate zygotes.

domestication The control of the reproductive cycle of plants and animals.

dominance (behavior)   Behavior in which one animal displaces another and takes preference in terms of sitting place, food, and estrus females.

dominance (genetic)   When in the heterozygous genotype only one allele is expressed in the phenotype, that allele is said to be dominant.

dominance hierarchy   A system of social ranking based on the relative dominance of the animals within a social group.

dorsal   Toward the top or back of an animal.

Down syndrome   Condition characterized by a peculiarity of eyefolds, malformation of the heart and other organs, stubby hands and feet, short stature, and mental retardation; result of extra chromosome 21.

duplication   Chromosomal aberration in which a section of a chromosome is repeated.

dyspnea   Difficult or painful breathing.

E

ecological isolation   Form of reproductive isolation in which two closely related species are separated by what is often a slight difference in the niches they occupy.

ecological niche   The specific microhabitat in which a particular population lives and the way that population exploits that microhabitat.

ecology   The study of the relationship of organisms or groups of organisms to their environment.

edema   Retention of water in the tissues of the body.

electron spin resonance (ESR) dating   A chronometric dating technique based on the behavior of electrons in crystals exposed to naturally occurring radioactivity; used to date limestone, coral, shell, teeth, and other materials.

Ellis–van Creveld syndrome   A rare recessive abnormality characterized by dwarfism, extra fingers, and malformations of the heart; high incidence among the Amish.

empirical   Received through the senses (sight, touch, smell, hearing, taste), either directly or through extensions of the senses (such as a microscope).

encephalization quotient (EQ)   A number reflecting the increase in brain size over and beyond that explainable by an increase in body size.

endocranial cast   A cast of the inside of the brain case.

endocrine disruptors   Natural and synthetic chemicals that affect the endocrine system.

endocrine glands   Organs that produce hormones.

endocrine system   A network of glands that, through the production of hormones, control the body's internal functions.

environment   Everything external to the organism.

environmental estrogens   Synthetic or natural endocrine disruptors that may find their way into water, soil, air, and food and may affect the endocrine system.

enzyme   A molecule, usually a protein, that makes a chemical reaction happen or speeds up a slow chemical reaction. It is not itself altered in the reaction.

epidemiology   The study of the distribution and causes of disease and injury in human populations.

epidermal ridges   The pattern of ridges found on the hands and feet that form "fingerprint" patterns. These ridges are richly endowed with nerve endings that are associated with a refined sense of touch.

epidermis   The outermost layer of the skin.

epoch   A unit of geological time; a division of a period.

era   A major division of geological time defined by major geological events and delineated by the kinds of animals and plant life it contains. Humans evolved in the Cenozoic era.

erect bipedalism   A form of locomotion found in humans in which the body is maintained in an upright posture on two legs while moving by means of a heel-toe stride.

erythroblastosis fetalis   A hemolytic disease affecting unborn or newborn infants caused by the destruction of the infant's Rh+ blood by the mother's anti-Rh antibodies.

erythrocyte   Red blood cell; cell found in blood that lacks a nucleus and contains the red pigment hemoglobin.

estrogen   Hormone produced in the ovaries.

estrus   Time period during which the female is sexually receptive.

ethnic group   A group of people who share a common culture including traditions, language, religion and history.

eugenics   The study of the methods that can improve the inherited qualities of a species.

evaporation   Liquid is transformed into a gas utilizing energy.

evolution   See **biological evolution.**

evolutionary psychology   The study of the role of biology and natural selection on human behavior.

experiment   A test of the predictive value of a hypothesis. A controlled experiment compares two situations in which only one factor differs.

extensor   A muscle that straightens out the bones about a joint.

extinction   The disappearance of a population.

F

facial sinus   An air-filled space lined with a mucous membrane in the bones of the front of the skull.

faculty of language in the broad sense (FLB)   Shared communicative capabilities of humans and some nonhumans that include motor and neurological systems that allow interaction with the world and physical and neurological systems that allow creation of sounds and movements that have the potential to communicate.

faculty of language in the narrow sense (FLN) Characteristics of language that are unique to humans, such as recursion.

familial hypercholesterolemia A rare dominant abnormality controlled by a multiple-allele series of at least four alleles. The disease is caused by a defective protein that can result in extremely high levels of cholesterol in the blood.

family Major division of an order, consisting of closely related genera.

female-bonded kin groups Primate social groups that are based on associations of females.

field study A study conducted in the natural habitat of an animal with minimal interference in the animal's life.

fission-fusion society Constantly changing form of social organization whereby large groups undergo fission into smaller units and small units fuse into larger units in response to the activity of the group and the season of the year.

fission-track dating The determination of a chronometric date by counting the proportion of atoms of a radioactive isotope such as uranium 238 that have decayed, leaving visible tracks in a mineral, relative to the total number of atoms of the isotope.

fitness Measure of how well an individual or population is adapted to a specific ecological niche as seen in reproductive rates.

flake A small piece of stone that is removed from a core when the core is struck by a hammerstone or bone hammer.

flake tool A tool manufactured from a flake.

fluorine dating A method for determining whether two fossils found in the same level of the same site are contemporary by measuring the amount of fluorine absorbed by the fossils.

fluted Referring to fluted points where a rounded groove has been made in the shaft of the point, most likely to facilitate hafting.

folivore An animal that eats primarily leaves.

folk taxonomy Classification of some class of phenomena based on cultural tradition.

foramen magnum A large opening in the occipital bone at the base of the skull through which the spinal cord passes.

foramina Small holes found in bone that permit the passage of nerves and blood vessels.

forebrain The anterior of three swellings in the hollow nerve cord of the primitive vertebrate brain formed by a thickening of the wall of the nerve cord.

forensic anthropology Application of the techniques of osteology and skeletal identification to legal problems.

fossil Remains or trace of any ancient organism preserved in the ground.

founder principle Situation in which a founding population does not represent a random sample of the original population; a form of sampling error.

four-chambered heart A heart that is divided into two sets of pumping chambers, effectively separating oxygenated blood from the lungs from deoxygenated blood from the body.

fovea A depression within the macula of the retina of the eye that contains a single layer of cones with no overlapping blood vessels; region of greatest visual acuity.

frugivore An animal that eats primarily fruits.

G

gamete A sex cell produced by meiosis that contains one copy of a chromosome set (23 chromosomes in humans). In a bisexual animal, the sex cell is either a sperm or an ovum.

gametic mortality Form of reproductive isolation in which sperm are immobilized and destroyed before fertilization can take place.

gene A section of DNA that has a specific function.

gene flow The process in which alleles from one population are introduced into another population.

gene pool The sum of all alleles carried by the members of a population.

gene therapy A genetic-engineering method in which genetic material is manipulated in ways that include removing, replacing, or altering a gene.

generalized species Species that can survive in a variety of ecological niches.

genetic counselor A medical professional who advises prospective parents or a person affected by a genetic disease of the probability of having a child with a genetic problem.

genetic drift The situation in a small population in which the allelic frequencies of the F_1 generation will differ from those of the parental generation due to sampling error.

genetic engineering The altering of the genetic material to create specific characteristics in individuals.

genetic equilibrium A hypothetical state in which a population is not evolving because the allele frequencies remain constant over time.

genetic load The totality of deleterious alleles in a population.

genetic sex In humans, male sex is determined by the presence of the *SRY* gene, which is located on the Y chromosome. Persons who lack the Y chromosome, and hence the *SRY* gene, or who possess an abnormal allele of the *SRY* gene, are genetically female.

genetics The study of the mechanisms of heredity and biological variation.

genome All of the genes carried by a single gamete.

genomics The study of the entire genome of a species.

genotype The genetic constitution of an individual.

genus A group of closely related species.

geographical isolation Form of reproductive isolation in which members of a population become separated from another population through geographical barriers that prevent the interchange of genes between the separated populations.

geographical race A major division of humankind into large geographical areas wherein people resemble one another more closely than they resemble people in different geographical areas.

geomagnetic reversal time scale (GRTS) A chart showing the sequence of normal and reversed polarity of the earth's magnetic field.

gestation The period of time from conception to birth.

gill arches Skeletal elements supporting the gill slit in nonvertebrate chordates and some vertebrates.

gill slits Structures that filter out food particles in nonvertebrate chordates and are used for breathing in some vertebrates.

glacial Period of expansion of glacial ice.

global warming The rise in the average temperature of the earth's atmosphere and oceans.

Gloger's rule Within the same species of mammals, there is a tendency to find more heavily pigmented forms near the equator and lighter forms away from the equator.

gluteus maximus In humans, the largest muscle of the human body; acts as an extensor, extending the leg in running and climbing.

gluteus medius Muscle of the pelvis that in monkeys and apes acts as an extensor, but in humans acts as an abductor.

gluteus minimus Muscle of the pelvis that in monkeys and apes acts as an extensor, but in humans acts as an abductor.

gonad General term used for an organ that produces sex cells; the ovary and testis.

grammar A set of rules used to make up words and then to combine the words into larger utterances such as phrases and sentences.

grandmother hypothesis The idea that the presence of a postmenopausal female in human groups increases the survival rate of children and grandchildren.

great apes The orangutan from Asia and the chimpanzee, bonobo, and gorilla from Africa.

greenhouse gases Gases that absorb some of the infrared radiation that enters the atmosphere resulting in the heating of the atmosphere and oceans.

grooming In primates, the activity of going through the fur with hand or teeth to remove insects, dirt, twigs, dead skin, and so on; also acts as a display of affection.

grooming claw A claw found on the second toes of prosimians that functions in grooming.

grooming cluster A small group of closely related females that engage in a high degree of grooming.

ground running and walking A form of quadrupedalism that takes place on the ground as opposed to in the trees.

growth Increase in the size or mass of an organism.

growth hormone A hormone produced by the pituitary gland, essential for normal growth.

growth plate Narrow zone on a bone where bone growth occurs.

guanine One of the bases found in the DNA and RNA molecules; a purine.

H

habitat The place in which a particular organism lives.

half-life The time in which one-half of the atoms of a radioactive isotope have decayed.

hammerstone A stone that is used to remove flakes from a core by striking the hammerstone against the core.

hand ax Large core tool with a sharp cutting edge, blunted at one end so it can be held in the hand.

haplorhine primates Primates, such as monkeys, apes, and humans, that lack a rhinarium and possess a free upper lip.

haplotype A group or block of nucleotides that tends to be inherited as a unit.

hard palate The bony roof of the mouth that separates the mouth from the nasal cavity, permitting the animal to breath and chew at the same time.

Hardy-Weinberg equilibrium A mathematical model of genetic equilibrium: $p^2 + 2pq + q^2 = 1$.

harem A subunit of a larger social group consisting of a male associated with two or more females.

heel-toe stride Method of progression characteristic of humans where the heel strikes the ground first; the person pushes off on the big toe.

hemochorial placenta Type of placenta found in most anthropoids in which materials pass between the maternal and fetal bloodstreams through a single vessel wall.

hemoglobin Red pigment in red blood cells that carries oxygen to and carbon dioxide from body tissues.

hemoglobin A (HbA) Normal adult hemoglobin whose globin unit consists of two alpha and two beta chains.

hemoglobin A$_2$ (HbA$_2$) A normal variant of hemoglobin A consisting of two alpha and two delta polypeptide chains that is found in small quantities in normal human blood.

hemoglobin C An abnormal variant of hemoglobin A that differs from the latter in having a single amino acid substitution on the beta chain at the same position as the substitution producing hemoglobin S.

hemoglobin F (HbF) A normal variant of hemoglobin, also known as *fetal hemoglobin,* that consists of two alpha and two gamma polypeptide chains found in the fetus and early infant; it is gradually replaced by hemoglobin A.

hemoglobin S (HbS) An abnormal variant of hemoglobin A that differs from the latter in having a single amino acid substitution on the beta chain; known as *sickle hemoglobin.*

hemolytic disease Disease involving the destruction of blood cells.

hemophilia A recessive X-linked trait characterized by excessive bleeding due to a faulty clotting mechanism.

herd Among geladas, a large social unit consisting of several bands that come together under very good grazing conditions.

heterodont Dentition characterized by regional differentiation of teeth by function.

heterozygous Having two different alleles of a particular gene.

high-altitude hypoxia Low oxygen pressure due to being at high altitude.

high-altitude mountain sickness Includes shortness of breath, physical and mental fatigue, rapid pulse rate, headaches; occurs in persons not acclimatized to high altitudes.

higher taxa Taxa above the genus level, such as family, order, class, phylum, and kingdom.

hindbrain The posterior of three swellings in the hollow nerve cord of the primitive vertebrate brain formed by a thickening of the wall of the nerve cord.

home range The area occupied by an animal or animal group.

homeothermic The ability to control body temperature and maintain a high body temperature through physiological means.

hominid Member of the family Hominidae; includes all living great apes and humans, plus several extinct forms.

hominin Member of the tribe Hominini; includes living humans plus several extinct forms that include, among others, members of the genera *Ardipithecus, Australopithecus* and *Paranthropus.*

hominine Member of the subfamily Homininae; includes living chimpanzees, bonobos, and humans, plus several extinct forms.

hominoid Member of the superfamily Hominoidea; includes living small-bodied apes, great apes, and humans, plus many extinct forms.

homodont Situation in which all teeth are basically the same in structure, although they may differ in size, as is found in reptiles.

homologous chromosomes Chromosomes of the same pair containing the same genes but not necessarily the same alleles.

homology A similarity due to inheritance from a common ancestor.

homoplastic Referring to a similarity that is not homologous. Homoplasy can arise from parallelism, convergence, analogy, and chance.

homozygous Having two like alleles of a particular gene; homozygous dominant when the allele is dominant and homozygous recessive when the allele is recessive.

homozygous dominant Having two dominant alleles of the same gene.

homozygous recessive Having two recessive alleles of the same gene.

hormones Complex molecules produced by the endocrine glands that regulate many bodily functions and processes.

Huntington's disease A degenerative neurological disorder caused by the inheritance of a dominant allele.

hybrid Individual that is the result of a cross or mating between two different kinds of parents.

hybrid inviability Form of reproductive isolation in which a mating between two species gives rise to a hybrid that is fertile but nevertheless does not leave any offspring.

hybrid sterility Form of reproductive isolation in which a hybrid of two species is sterile.

hydraulic behavior The transport and dispersal of bones in water.

hyperplasia Growth by virtue of increase in the total number of cells resulting from mitosis.

hypertrophy Growth by virtue of increase in the size of cells.

hyperventilation Increased breathing rate producing a high level of oxygen in the lungs.

hypothermia Lowered body temperature induced by cold stress.

hypothesis An informed supposition about the relationship of one variable to another.

I

imitative magic A type of magic that is based on the belief that one can affect an actual entity such as a person or animal by manipulating the image of that entity.

immutable Unchanging.

inclusive fitness An individual's own fitness plus his or her effect on the fitness of any relative.

incomplete penetrance The situation in which an allele that is expected to be expressed is not always expressed.

independent assortment A Mendelian principle that states that differing traits are inherited independently of each other. It applies only to genes on different chromosomes.

index fossil A paleospecies that had a very wide geographical distribution but existed for a relatively short period of time, either becoming extinct or evolving into something else.

induced mutation Mutation caused by human-made conditions.

Industrial Age A cultural stage characterized by the first use of complex machinery, factories, urbanization, and other economic and general social changes from strictly agricultural societies.

industrialism Industrialism is the dependence on mechanization—the use of machines—to produce products and render services.

industry All artifacts in a site made from the same material, such as a bone industry.

infantile That period in an individual's life cycle from birth to the eruption of the first permanent teeth.

insectivore An animal that eats primarily insects; also a member of the mammalian order Insectivora.

intelligent design theory An essentially religious explanation of the world that assumes the existence of a supernatural force that is responsible for the great complexity of life on earth today.

intensive farming Farming that involves the clearing of a piece of land of all of its natural vegetation and replacing it with one crop that is usually not native to the area.

interglacial Period of warming between two glacials.

intermediate expression The situation whereby a heterozygous genotype is associated with a phenotype that is more or less intermediate between the phenotypes controlled by the two homozygous genotypes.

intermembral index The length of the humerus and radius relative to the length of the femur and tibia.

intersexual selection A form of sexual selection; selection for traits that make males more attractive to females.

intrasexual selection A form of sexual selection. Selection for characteristics that make males better able to compete with one another for sexual access to females.

inversion Form of chromosome aberration in which parts of a chromosome break and reunite in a reversed order. No genetic material is lost or gained, but the positions of the involved alleles are altered.

Iron Age A cultural stage characterized by the use of iron as the main metal.

irreducible complexity Concept that there are processes and structures that are too complex to have arisen through evolutionary mechanisms but must have arisen by the work of a "designer."

ischial callosities A thickening of the skin overlying a posterior section of the pelvis (ischial tuberosity), found in Old World monkeys and some apes.

isotopes Atoms of the same element but of different atomic weight.

J

juvenile That period in an individual's life cycle that lasts from the eruption of the first to the eruption of the last permanent teeth.

K

karyotype The standardized classification and arrangement of chromosomes.

kin selection A process whereby an individual's genes are selected for by virtue of that individual's increasing the chances that his or her kin's genes are propagated into the next generation.

kinetochore Protein structures that form on each side of each centromere in cell division that function in chromosome orientation within the cell.

kingdom A major division of living organisms. All organisms are placed into one of five kingdoms: Monera, Protista, Fungi, Planti, and Animalia.

Klinefelter syndrome A sex-chromosome count of XXY; phenotypically male, tall stature, sterile.

knuckle walking Semierect quadrupedalism, found in chimpanzees and gorillas, with upper parts of the body supported by knuckles as opposed to palms.

kwashiorkor A form of protein-caloric malnutrition brought about by a protein-deficient diet that contains a reasonable supply of low-quality carbohydrates.

L

lactation Act of female mammal producing milk.

lesser apes See **small-bodied apes.**

lethals Alleles that cause premature death.

leukocyte A white blood cell; cell in blood that functions to destroy foreign substances.

lexicon In linguistics, the total number of meaningful units (such as words and affixes) of a language.

lexigram A symbol that represents a word.

life expectancy How long a person, on the average, can expect to live.

life span The theoretical genetically determined maximum age.

linguistics The scientific study of language.

linkage Association of genes on the same chromosome.

linkage groups Sets of genes that are found on the same chromosome.

lipids Class of compounds that includes fats, oils, and waxes.

lithic (stone) industry All artifacts in a site that are made of stone.

lithosphere The hard outer layer of the earth.

Lower Paleolithic A cultural stage that begins with the manufacture of the first stone tools.

lumbar curve A curve that forms in the lumbar region of the spine in humans.

M

macroevolution "Large-scale" evolution; the evolution of new species and higher taxa.

macula The central area of the retina consisting of cones only.

mammals Members of the class Mammalia, a class of the subphylum Vertebrata, that are characterized by a constant level of activity independent of external temperature and by mammary glands, hair or fur, heterodonty, and other features.

mammary glands Glands found in mammalian females that produce milk.

mandible The bone of the lower jaw; contains the lower dentition.

mandibular torus A thickening of bone on the inside of the mandible.

manuport An unmodified, natural rock, brought into a site by human agency, that shows no sign of alteration.

marasmus A form of protein-caloric malnutrition caused by a diet deficient in both protein and carbohydrates.

marsupial A member of the infraclass Metatheria of the class Mammalia; young are born at a relatively less-developed stage than in placental mammals. After birth, the young attaches to a mammary gland in the pouch, where it continues to grow and develop.

masseter A muscle of chewing that arises on the zygomatic arch and inserts on the mandible.

maximum parsimony principle The principle that the most accurate phylogenetic tree is one that is based on the fewest changes in the genetic code.

mechanical isolation Form of reproductive isolation that occurs because of an incompatibility in structure of the male and female sex organs.

meiosis Form of cell division occurring in specialized tissues in the testes and ovaries that leads to the production of gametes or sex cells.

melanin Brown-black pigment found in the skin, eyes, and hair.

melanocyte Specialized skin cell that produces the pigment melanin.

menarche First menstruation.

Mesolithic A cultural stage characterized by generalized hunting and gathering and the advent of farming.

messenger RNA (mRNA) Form of RNA that copies the DNA code in the nucleus and transports it to the ribosome.

metaphase plate During cell division, the central plane of the cell.

microenvironment A specific set of physical, biological, and cultural factors immediately surrounding the organism.

microevolution "Small-scale" evolution; genetic changes within a population over time.

microhabitat A very specific habitat in which a population is found.

midbrain The middle of the three swellings in the hollow nerve cord of the primitive vertebrate brain formed by a thickening of the wall of the nerve cord.

Middle Paleolithic Refers to the stone tools of the Neandertals and their contemporaries.

mitochondria Bodies found in the cytoplasm that convert the energy in the chemical bonds of organic molecules into ATP.

mitochondrial DNA (mtDNA) A double-stranded loop of DNA found within the mitochondria; there can be as few as one or as many as a hundred mitochondria per cell, and each mitochondrion possesses between 4 and 10 mtDNA loops.

mitosis Form of cell division whereby one-celled organisms divide and whereby body cells divide in growth and replacement.

model A representation of a phenomenon on which tests can be conducted and from which predictions can be made.

modifying gene A gene that alters the expression of another gene.

mold A cavity left in firm sediments by the decayed body of an organism.

molecule Unit composed of two or more atoms linked by a chemical bond.

monkey Any member of the superfamilies Ceboidea (New World monkeys) and Cercopithecoidea (Old World monkeys).

monocausal explanation Attributing one cause to the explanation of a phenomenon.

monoculture A field planted with one crop for a long period of time.

monogamous pair A social group, found among small-bodied apes and other primates, consisting of a single mated pair and their young offspring.

monotreme A member of the subclass Prototheria of the class Mammalia; egg-laying mammal.

monozygotic twins Identical twins; derived from a single zygote.

morphology The study of structure.

motor hypothesis of language A hypothesis that holds that the complicated motor skills needed to manufacture tools lead directly to the motor skills needed to produce speech.

mountain sickness See **high-altitude sickness.**

mounting A behavioral pattern whereby one animal jumps on the posterior area of a second animal as a part of the act of copulation or as a part of dominance behavior.

Mousterian tradition A Middle Paleolithic cultural tradition associated with the Neandertals, characterized by an increase in the number and variety of flake tools and an ultimate de-emphasis of the hand ax.

multimale group A social unit consisting of many adult males and adult females.

multiple alleles A situation in which a gene has more than two alleles.

mutagens Factors—such as radioactivity, chemicals, and viruses—that are capable of causing mutations.

mutation An alteration of the genetic material.

N

natural selection Differential fertility and mortality of variants within a population.

negative eugenics Method of eliminating deleterious alleles from the gene pool by encouraging persons with such alleles not to reproduce.

neocortex Gray covering on the cerebrum of some vertebrates; site of higher mental processes.

Neolithic A cultural stage marked by established farming.

New World semibrachiation Locomotor pattern involving extensive use of hands and prehensile tail to suspend and propel the body in species otherwise quadrupedal.

niche See **ecological niche.**

nocturnal Active at night.

nondisjunction An error of meiosis in which the members of a pair of chromosomes move to the same pole rather than moving to opposite poles.

notochord A cartilaginous rod that runs along the back (dorsal) of all chordates at some point in their life cycle.

nuchal crest Flange of bone in the occipital region of the skull that serves as the attachment of the nuchal musculature of the back of the neck.

nuchal muscle The muscle in the back of the neck that functions to hold the head up. In primates with heavy facial skeletons, the large nuchal muscle attaches to a nuchal crest.

nuclear DNA (nDNA) DNA found within the nucleus of the cell.

nuclear membrane A structure that binds the nucleus within the cell.

nucleic acids The largest of the molecules found in living organisms; they are composed of chains of nucleotides.

nucleotide The basic building block of nucleic acids; a nucleotide is composed of a five-carbon sugar (either ribose or deoxyribose), a phosphate, and a base.

nucleus A structure found in the cell that contains the chromosomes.

O

occipital condyles Two rounded projections on either side of the foramen magnum that fit into a pair of sockets on the top of the spine, thus articulating the skull with the spine.

occipital torus A horizontal bar of bone seen above the angularity in the occipital.

Old World semibrachiation Locomotor pattern involving extensive use of hands, but not the tail, in leaping in a basically quadrupedal animal.

olfactory Referring to the sense of smell.

omnivorous Eating both meat and vegetable food.

one-male group A social unit consisting of a single male associated with several females.

oogenesis The production of ova.

openness A characteristic of language that refers to the expansionary nature of language, which enables people to coin new labels for new concepts and objects.

opposable thumb Anatomical arrangement in which the fleshy tip of the thumb can touch the fleshy tip of all the fingers.

order Major division of a class, consisting of closely related families.

orthognathous Describes a face that is relatively vertical as opposed to being prognathous.

orthograde Vertical posture.

ossification Process of bone formation.

osteodontokeratic culture An archaeological culture based on tools made of bone, teeth, and horn.

osteology The study of bones.

outgroup Species used in a cladistic analysis that are closely related to the species being studied and are used to differentiate between shared derived and ancestral derived features.

ovulation The point during the female reproductive cycle, usually the midpoint, when the ovum has matured and breaks through the wall of the ovary.

ovum A female gamete or sex cell.

ozone A molecule composed of three oxygen atoms (O_3). Atmospheric ozone shields organisms from excessive ultraviolet radiation.

P

paleoanthropology Scientific study of fossils and artifacts and the context in which they are found.

paleoecology The study of the relationship of extinct organisms or groups of organisms to their environments.

Paleolithic A type of culture called the "Old Stone Age."

paleontology The study of fossils.

paleopathology The study of injuries and disease in prehistoric populations.

paleospecies A group of similar fossils whose range of morphological variation does not exceed the range of variation of a closely related living species.

palynology The study of fossil pollen.

pangenesis An early and inaccurate idea that acquired characteristics of the parents are transmitted to their offspring.

parallelism Homoplastic similarities found in related species that did not exist in the common ancestor; however, the common ancestor provided initial commonalities that gave direction to the evolution of the similarities.

partial pressure The pressure exerted by a particular gas in the atmosphere.

pedigree A reconstruction of past mating in a family, expressed as a diagram.

penetrance The degree to which an allele is expressed in the phenotype.

pentadactylism Possessing five digits on the hand and/or foot.

peptide bond A link between amino acids in a protein.

pericentric inversion A type of inversion whereby two breaks occur in a chromosome, one on either side of the centromere, and the centerpiece becomes turned around and rejoined with the two outside pieces.

period A unit of geological time; a division of an era.

peripheralization Process whereby an adolescent animal encounters aggressive behavior from adults and gradually moves away from the group.

permanent teeth The second set of teeth that erupts in mammals; humans have 32 permanent teeth.

phenotype The observable and measurable characteristics of an organism.

phenotypic sex The sex that a person is judged to be, based on his or her physical appearance. Phenotypic sex may not correspond to chromosomal sex.

phenylketonuria (PKU) A genetic disease, inherited as a recessive, brought about by the absence of the enzyme responsible for the conversion of the amino acid phenylalanine to tyrosine; phenylalanine accumulates in the blood and then breaks down into by-products that cause severe mental retardation in addition to other symptoms.

phenylthiocarbamide (PTC) An artificially created substance whose main use is in detecting the ability to taste it; ability to taste PTC is inherited as a dominant.

philtrum A furrow in the upper lip that serves to attach the upper lip to the gum.

phosphate unit A unit of the nucleic acid molecule consisting of a phosphate and four oxygen atoms.

phyletic gradualism The idea that evolution is a slow process with gradual transformation of one population into another.

phylogenetic tree A graphic representation of evolutionary relationships among species.

phylogeny The evolutionary history of a population or taxon.

phylum Major division of a kingdom, consisting of closely related classes; represents a basic body plan.

physical anthropology A branch of anthropology concerned with human biology and evolution.

physical environment The inanimate elements that surround an organism.

phytoliths Microscopic pieces of silica that form within plants; the distinctive shapes of phytoliths found in different plants permit their identification when observed imbedded in fossil teeth.

placenta An organ that develops from fetal membranes that functions to pass oxygen, nutrients, and other substances to and waste material from the fetus.

placental mammal A member of the infraclass Eutheria of the class Mammalia; mammals that form a placenta.

plasma membrane A structure that binds the cell but allows for the entry and exit of certain substances.

plate tectonics The theory that the surface of the earth is divided into a number of plates that move in relationship to each other. Some of these plates carry the continents.

platycephalic Having a low, relatively flat forehead.

platyrrhine nose Nose in which nostrils open sideways and are usually separated by a broad nasal septum; characteristic of the New World monkeys.

play Energetic and repetitive activity engaged in primarily by infants and juveniles.

play group A group of juveniles within a larger social unit that engage in play behavior.

pleiotropy Situation in which a single allele may affect an entire series of traits.

pneumatized The presence of air spaces within some bones of the skull.

point mutation An error at a particular point on the DNA molecule.

polar body A cell that develops in oogenesis that contains little cytoplasm and does not develop into a mature ovum.

polyandrous group A form of social organization found in primates in which a female has multiple mates.

polygenic The result of the interaction of several genes.

polymorphism The presence of several distinct forms of a gene or phenotypical trait within a population with frequencies greater than 1 percent.

polypeptide Chain of amino acids.

polyphyodonty The continuous replacement of teeth such as found in reptiles.

population bottlenecking A form of sampling error in which a population is reduced in size, which in turn reduces variability in the population. The population that descends from the reduced population is therefore less variable than the original population.

populationist viewpoint The viewpoint that only individuals have reality and that the type is illusory; since no two individuals are exactly alike, variation underlies all existence.

porphyria A dominant genetic abnormality that results from a defect in the breakdown of hemoglobin in the blood. Symptoms include sensitivity to sunlight and the development of psychiatric symptoms.

positive eugenics Method of increasing the frequency of desirable traits by encouraging reproduction by individuals with these traits.

postmating mechanism Any form of reproductive isolation that occurs after mating.

postorbital bar A feature of the skull formed by an upward extension of the zygomatic arch and a downward extension of the frontal bone that supports the eye.

postorbital constriction As seen from a top view, a marked constriction in the skull immediately behind the orbits and brow ridge.

postorbital septum A bony partition behind the eye that isolates the eye from the muscles of the jaw and forms a bony eye socket or orbit in which the eye lies.

potassium-argon dating Chronometric dating technique based on the rate of decay of potassium 40 to argon 40.

power grip A grip in which an object is held between the fingers and the palm with the thumb reinforcing the fingers.

preadaptation The situation in which a new structure or behavior that evolved in one niche is by chance also suited, in some cases better suited, to a new niche.

precision grip A grip in which an object is held between one or more fingers with the thumb fully opposed to the fingertips.

predation model A model that gives an explanation of why primates form groups based on the hypothesis that a group of individuals can protect themselves better or even ward off attacks from predators better than an individual animal could.

prehensile tail A tail found in some New World monkeys that has the ability to grasp.

premating mechanism A form of reproductive isolation that prevents mating from occurring.

prenatal That period of an individual's life cycle from conception to birth.

presenting A behavior involving a subordinate primate showing his or her anal region to a dominant animal.

preservation potential The probability of a bone being preserved after death.

primary center of ossification Area of first appearance of bone within the cartilage model of a long bone.

primatology The study of primates.

principle of acquired characteristics Concept, popularized by Lamarck, that traits gained during a lifetime can then be passed on to the next generation by genetic means; considered invalid today.

principle of use and disuse Concept popularized by Lamarck that proposes that parts of the body that are used are often strengthened and improved, whereas parts of the body that are not used become weak and ultimately may disappear.

prognathism A jutting forward of the facial skeleton and jaws.

pronograde Posture with the body held parallel to the ground.

prosimians Members of the suborder Prosimii; includes the lemuriforms and tarsiiforms.

proteins Long chains of amino acids joined together by peptide bonds (a polypeptide chain).

protein-caloric malnutrition A class of malnutrition that includes kwashiorkor and marasmus.

protoculture The simplest or beginning aspects of culture as seen in some nonhuman primates.

prototherian Referring to mammals belonging to the subclass Prototheria; a monotreme or egg-laying mammal.

provisioned colony Group of free-ranging primates that have become accustomed to humans because of the establishment of feeding stations.

puberty An event in the life cycle that includes a rapid increase in stature, development of sex organs, and the development of secondary sexual characteristics.

pubic symphysis The area of the pelvis at which the two innominates join.

punctuated equilibrium A model of evolution characterized by an uneven tempo of change.

purine Base found in nucleic acids that consists of two connected rings of carbon and nitrogen; in DNA and RNA, adenine and guanine.

pyrimidine Base found in nucleic acids that consists of a single ring of carbon and nitrogen; in DNA, thymine and cytosine; in RNA, uracil and cytosine.

Q

quadrumanous Locomotor pattern found among orangutans, who often suspend themselves under branches and move slowly using both forelimbs and hindlimbs.

quadrupedalism Locomotion using four limbs, with hands and feet moving on a surface such as the ground or top of a branch of a tree.

R

race A taxonomic division of a species that differs biologically in a significant number of genetic characteristics from other races of the same species.

radiation Electromagnetic energy that is given off by an object.

radioactivity The phenomenon whereby an atom that is unstable will radioactively decay into another type of atom and in the process emit energy and/or particles.

radiocarbon dating A method of chronometric dating based on the decay of carbon 14.

radiometric dating techniques Chronometric dating methods based on the decay of radioactive materials; examples are radiocarbon and potassium-argon dating.

range See **home range.**

recessive An allele that is expressed only in the homozygous recessive condition.

recombination New combinations of alleles on the same chromosome as a result of crossing-over.

recursion The process by which any linguistic unit can be made longer by embedding another unit in it.

regional continuity model The hypothesis that states that modern *H. sapiens* had multiple origins from existing local populations; each local population of archaic humans gave rise to a population of modern *H. sapiens.*

regulatory gene A segment of DNA that functions to initiate or block the function of another gene.

relative dating Any dating technique that places two fossils or artifacts in time relative to one another, where one is older than, younger than, or the same age as the other.

replacement model The hypothesis that states that modern *H. sapiens* evolved in Africa and radiated out of this area, replacing archaic hominin populations.

reproductive isolating mechanism A mechanism that prevents reproduction from occurring between two populations.

reproductive population A group of organisms capable of successful reproduction.

residual volume The amount of air remaining in the lungs after the most forceful expiration.

resource-defense model A model that gives an explanation of why primates form groups based on the hypothesis that a group of individuals can defend access to resources such as food and keep other animals and other groups away from those resources better than an individual can.

restriction enzyme Enzyme used to "cut" the DNA molecule at specific sites; used in recombinant DNA technology.

retina The layer of cells in the back of the eye that contains the cells—rods and cones—that are sensitive to light.

retouch Further refinement in the manufacture of stone tools by the removal of additional small flakes.

Rh blood-type system A blood-type system consisting of two major alleles. A mating between an Rh− mother and Rh+ father may produce in the infant the hemolytic disease erythroblastosis fetalis.

rhinarium The moist, naked area surrounding the nostrils in most mammals; present in the lemuriforms.

ribonucleic acid (RNA) A type of nucleic acid based on the sugar ribose; exists in cells as messenger RNA and transfer RNA.

ribose A five-carbon sugar found in RNA.

ribosome Small spherical body within the cytoplasm of the cell in which protein synthesis takes place.

rickets A bone disease that usually is caused by a lack of calcium, phosphate, or vitamin D.

rods Cells of the retina of the eye that are sensitive to the presence or absence of light; function in black-and-white vision.

S

sagittal crest Ridge of bone along the midline of the top of the skull that serves for the attachment of the temporalis muscle.

sagittal keel A bony ridge formed by a thickening of bone along the top of the skull; characteristic of *H. erectus.*

sampling error In population genetics, the transmission of a nonrepresentative sample of the gene pool over space or time due to chance.

scent marking Marking territory by urinating or defecating, or by rubbing scent glands against trees or other objects.

science A way of learning about the world by applying the principles of scientific thinking, which includes making empirical observations, proposing hypotheses to explain those observations, and testing those hypotheses in valid and reliable ways; also refers to the organized body of knowledge that results from scientific study.

scraper A tool manufactured from a flake with a scraping edge on the end or side.

seasonal isolation Form of reproductive isolation in which the breeding seasons of two closely related populations do not exactly correspond.

secondary center of ossification Area of bone development, usually near the end of a long bone.

secondary sexual characteristic Physical feature other than the genitalia that distinguishes males from females after puberty.

secreter allele A dominant allele of the secretor gene. People who inherit this allele secrete blood type antigens into their body fluids such as semen, saliva, tears, and mucus.

sectorial premolar Unicuspid first lower premolar with a shearing edge.

secular trend The tendency over the last hundred or so years for each succeeding generation to mature earlier and become, on the average, larger.

sediment Material that is suspended in water; in still water, it will settle at the bottom.

sedimentary beds Beds or layers of sediments called strata.

sedimentation The accumulation of geological or organic material deposited by air, water, or ice.

segregation In the formation of sex cells, the process in which paired hereditary factors separate, forming sex cells that contain either one or the other factor.

selective agent Any factor that brings about differences in fertility and mortality.

selective pressure Pressure placed by a selective agent on certain individuals within the population that results in the change of allelic frequencies in the next generation.

semibrachiation A form of quadrupedalism in which an animal makes extensive use of its forelimbs to suspend itself under branches in order to reach food below.

sex chromosomes The X and Y chromosomes. Males usually have one X and one Y chromosome; females usually have two X chromosomes.

sex-controlled trait Non-sex-linked trait that is expressed differently in males and females.

sex-limited gene Non-sex-linked allele that is expressed in only one of the sexes.

sex-limited trait Non-sex-linked trait that is expressed in only one of the sexes.

sexual dimorphism Differences in structure between males and females of the same species.

sexual isolation Form of reproductive isolation in which one or both sexes of a species initiate mating behavior that does not act as a stimulus to the opposite sex of a closely related species.

sexual selection Selection that favors characteristics that increase reproductive success, usually due to male competition or female mate choice.

sexual skin Found in the female of some primate species; skin in anal region that turns bright pink or red and may swell when animal is in estrus.

shared ancestral (symplesiomorphic) feature Compared with shared derived features, a homology that did not appear as recently and is therefore shared by a larger group of species.

shared derived (synapomorphic) feature A recently appearing homology that is shared by a relatively small group of closely related taxa.

sharing cluster Among chimpanzees, a temporary group that forms after hunting to eat the meat.

shell midden A large mound composed of shells, which provides evidence of the emphasis on shellfish as a food resource.

shovel-shaped incisors Incisors that have a scooped-out shape on the tongue side of the tooth.

sickle-cell anemia Disorder in individuals homozygous for hemoglobin S in which red blood cells will develop into a sickle shape, which, in turn, will clog capillaries, resulting in anemia, heart failure, and so on.

sickle-cell trait The condition of being heterozygous for hemoglobin A and S, yet the individual usually shows no abnormal symptoms.

simian shelf A bony buttress on the inner surface of the foremost part of the ape mandible, functioning to reinforce the mandible.

single-crystal fusion A form of potassium-argon dating that uses a laser to melt individual crystals to release the argon.

site A location where artifacts are found.

slow climbing A form of quadrupedalism in which the animal moves very slowly through brushes and trees.

small-bodied (lesser) apes The gibbons and simiangs of Asia. The primate family Hylobatidae, which includes the gibbons and is a diverse group consisting of 13 species placed into four genera.

smoke-detector principle A defense mechanism that is so fine tuned that even an insignificant stimulus might trigger it.

social Darwinism The application of the principles of biological evolutionary theory to an analysis of social phenomena.

social intelligence The knowledge and images that originate in an individual's brain that are transferred by speech, sign language, and in the last 5000 years, writing, to the brains of others.

specialized species A species closely fitted to a specific niche and able to tolerate little change in that niche.

speciation An evolutionary process that is said to occur when two previous subspecies (of the same species) are no longer capable of successful interbreeding; they are then two different species.

species The largest natural population whose members are able to reproduce successfully among themselves but not with members of other species.

sperm Male gamete or sex cell.

spermatids Cells produced by meiosis in the male that are transformed into mature sperm.

spermatogenesis Sperm production.

spindle Structure that appears in the cell undergoing cell division that is responsible for the movement of the chromosomes.

spontaneous generation An old and incorrect idea that complex life forms could be spontaneously created from nonliving material.

spontaneous mutation Mutation that occurs spontaneously, that is, in response to the usual conditions within the body or environment.

stabilizing selection A type of natural selection characterized by a generation-after-generation shift in a population in the direction of the average (mean) individual, such as, for example, toward average body size. In this example, individuals with small and large body size are being selected against.

standard deviation A statistical measurement of the amount of variation in a series of determinations; the probability of the real number falling within plus or minus one standard deviation is 67 percent.

stereoscopic vision Visual perception of depth due to overlapping visual fields and various neurological features.

strata Layers of sedimentary rocks.

stratigraphy The investigation of the composition of the layers of the earth, used in relative dating; based on the principle of superposition.

stratosphere That part of the atmosphere 20 to 50 kilometers (12 to 31 miles) above the earth's surface where ozone forms.

strepsirhine primates Primates, such as lemurs and lorises, that possess a rhinarium and philtrum.

structural gene A segment of DNA that codes for a polypeptide that has a phenotypic expression.

subchron A small subdivision within a chron.

subcutaneous fat The fat deposited under the skin.

subera A division of an era. The Cenozoic is divided into two suberas: the Tertiary and the Quaternary.

subspecies Interfertile groups within a species that display significant differentiation among themselves.

superposition Principle that under stable conditions, strata on the bottom of a deposit were laid down first and hence are older than layers on top.

suspensory behavior Form of locomotion and posture whereby animals suspend themselves underneath a branch.

sweating The production of a fluid, sweat, by the sweat glands of the skin; the evaporation of the sweat from the skin leads to a cooling of the body.

symbol Something that can represent something distant from it in time and space.

sympatric species Different species living in the same area but prevented from successfully reproducing by a reproductive isolating mechanism.

symphyseal face The surface of the pubis where one pubis joins the other at the pubic symphysis.

symplesiomorphic feature See **shared ancestral feature.**

synapomorphic feature See **shared derived feature.**

synthetic theory of evolution The theory of evolution that fuses Darwin's concept of natural selection with information from the fields of genetics, mathematics, embryology, paleontology, animal behavior, and other disciplines.

system A collection of parts that are interrelated so that a change in any one part brings about specifiable changes in the others.

T

tactile pads The tips of the fingers and toes of primates; areas richly endowed by tactile nerve endings sensitive to touch.

taphonomy The study of the processes of burial and fossilization.

taxon A group of organisms at any level of the taxonomic hierarchy. The major taxa are the species and genus and the higher taxa: family, order, class, phylum, and kingdom.

taxonomy The science of classifying organisms into categories.

Tay-Sachs disease Enzyme deficiency of lipid metabolism inherited as a recessive; causes death in early childhood.

tectonic plate A segment of the lithosphere.

temporal-nuchal crest A crest on the back of the skull, forming on the occipital and temporal bones.

temporalis A muscle of chewing that arises on the side of the skull and inserts on the jaw.

temporomandibular joint The joint formed at the point of articulation of the mandible and the base of the skull.

termite stick Tool made and used by chimpanzees for collecting termites for food.

territory The area that a group defends against other members of its own species.

testosterone A male sex hormone.

thalassemia Absence or reduction of alpha- or beta-chain synthesis in hemoglobin; in the homozygous condition (thalassemia major), a high frequency of hemoglobin F and fatal anemia occurs; in the heterozygous condition (thalassemia minor), it is highly variable but usually occurs with mild symptoms.

theory A step in the scientific method in which a statement is generated on the basis of highly confirmed hypotheses and used to generalize about conditions not yet tested.

therian Referring to mammals belonging to the subclass Theria; the "live-bearing" mammals including the marsupials and placental mammals.

thermoluminescence dating A chronometric dating method based on the fact that when some materials are heated, they give off a flash of light. The intensity of the light is proportional to the amount of radiation to which the sample has been exposed and the length of time since the sample was heated.

threat gesture A physical activity that serves to threaten another animal. Some threat gestures are staring, shaking a branch, and lunging toward another animal.

thymine One of the bases found in DNA; a pyrimidine.

tool An object that appears to have been used for a specific purpose.

total color blindness See **achromatopsia.**

trait One aspect of the phenotype.

transfer RNA (tRNA) Within the ribosome, a form of RNA that transports amino acids into the positions coded in the mRNA.

translocation Form of chromosomal mutation in which segments of chromosomes become detached and reunite to other nonhomologous chromosomes.

tree-ring dating Chronometric dating method that determines the age of a wood sample by counting the number of annual growth rings.

trichromacy The possession of three visual pigments, sensitive to blue, green, and red, in the retina of the eye.

trisomy The state of having three of the same chromosome, rather than the normal pair. For example, trisomy 21, or Down syndrome, is a tripling of chromosome number 21.

troop A multimale group found among baboons and other primates.

true brachiation Hand-over-hand locomotion along a branch with the body suspended underneath the branch by the arms.

true-breeding Showing the same traits without exception over many generations.

tuff Geological formation composed of compressed volcanic ash.

tundra A type of landscape where the ground is frozen solid throughout most of the year but thaws slightly during the summer.

Turner syndrome Genetic disease characterized by 45 chromosomes with a sex chromosome count of X–; phenotypically female, but sterile.

twin studies Comparisons of monozygotic twins to dizygotic twins for the purpose of estimating the degree of environmental versus genetic influence operating on a specific trait.

tympanic membrane The eardrum.

typological The viewpoint that basic variation of a type is illusory and that only fixed ideal types are real; two fossils that differ from each other in certain respects represent two types and, hence, are two different species.

U

unconformity The surface of a stratum that represents a break in the stratigraphic sequence.

uniformitarianism Principle that states that physical forces working today to alter the earth were also in force and working in the same way in former times.

uniquely derived feature See **autapomorphic feature.**

Upper Paleolithic Refers to the stone tools of anatomically modern peoples.

uracil One of the bases found in RNA; a pyrimidine.

urbanization A rise in the number of people living in cities in comparison to the number living in rural areas.

urbanized society A society in which a majority of the population lives in cities.

utilized material Pieces of stone that have been used without modification.

V

variable Any property that may be displayed in different values.

vasoconstriction Constriction of the capillaries in the skin in response to cold temperatures that prevents much of the warm blood from reaching the surface of the body where heat could be lost.

vasodilation Opening up of the capillaries of the skin in response to warm temperatures, increasing the flow of blood to the surface of the body and thereby increasing the loss of body heat.

velocity curve A curve that illustrates the velocity or rate of growth over time by plotting the degree of growth per unit of time.

ventral The front or bottom side of an animal.

Venus figurines Small Upper Paleolithic statues characterized by exaggerated breasts and buttocks and very stylized heads, hands, and feet.

vertebrate A member of the subphylum Vertebrata; possesses a bony spine or vertebral column.

vertical clinging and leaping A method of locomotion in which the animal clings vertically to a branch and moves between branches by leaping vertically from one to another. The animal moves on the ground by hopping or moving bipedally.

X

X chromosome The larger of the two sex chromosomes. Females usually possess two X chromosomes; males usually possess one X and one Y chromosome.

X-linked Refers to genes on the X chromosome.

Y

Y chromosome The smaller of the two sex chromosomes. Females usually possess no Y chromosome; males usually possess one X and one Y chromosome.

Y-5 pattern Pattern found on molars with five cusps separated by grooves, reminiscent of the letter Y.

Y-linked Refers to genes on the Y chromosome.

Z

zoonoses Infectious diseases that are transmitted to humans from animals.

zygomatic arch The "cheek" bone; an arch of bone on the side of the skull.

zygote A fertilized ovum.

zygotic mortality Form of reproductive isolation in which fertilization occurs but development stops soon after.

zymotics Infectious diseases that spread easily from person to person in crowded areas.

Glossary of Primate Higher Taxa

Extinct taxa are indicated by a †.

A

Adapidae† Family of Eocene prosimians found in North America, Asia, Europe, and possibly Africa; may be related to lemurs and lorises.

Adapinae† Subfamily of the Adapidae found in Europe and Asia.

Alouattinae Subfamily of the Cebidae; includes the howler monkeys.

Anthropoidea Suborder of the order Primates; includes the New World monkeys, Old World monkeys, apes, and humans.

Aotinae Subfamily of the Cebidae; includes the owl monkeys.

C

Callitrichidae A family of New World monkeys consisting of the marmosets and tamarins.

Catarrhini Infraorder of the suborder Anthropoidea that includes the superorders Cercopithecoidea and Hominoidea.

Cebidae A family of New World monkeys that includes the squirrel, spider, howler, and capuchin monkeys, among others.

Cebinae Subfamily of the Cebidae; includes the capuchin and squirrel monkeys.

Ceboidea A superfamily of the suborder Anthropoidea; includes all the New World monkeys, consisting of the families Callitrichidae and Cebidae.

Cercopithecidae Family of the superfamily Cercopithecoidea; includes the Old World monkeys.

Cercopithecinae Subfamily of the family Cercopithecidae; includes the Old World monkeys that are omnivorous and possess cheek pouches, such as the macaques, baboons, guenons, and mangabeys.

Cercopithecoidea Superfamily of the suborder Anthropoidea; consists of the Old World monkeys.

Colobinae A subfamily of family Cercopithecidae; the Old World monkeys that are specialized leaf eaters, possessing a complex stomach and lacking cheek pouches, such as the langurs and colobus monkeys.

D

Daubentoniidae Family of Madagascar prosimians consisting of the aye-aye.

G

Gorillini Tribe of the subfamily Homininae that includes the gorillas, chimpanzees, and bonobos.

H

Hominidae Family of the superfamily Hominoidea that includes orangutans, gorillas, chimpanzees, bonobos, and humans.

Homininae Subfamily of the family Hominidae that includes the African great apes and humans.

Hominini Tribe of the subfamily Homininae that includes humans.

Hominoidea Superfamily of the suborder Anthropoidea; includes the apes and humans.

Hylobatidae Family of the superfamily Hominoidea; the lesser apes consisting of the gibbons and siamang.

I

Indriidae Family of Madagascar prosimians that includes the indri, sifaka, and avahi.

L

Lemuridae Madagascar lemuriforms; includes the lemurs.

Lemuriformes Infraorder of the suborder Prosimii that includes the lemurs, indris, and aye-aye of Madagascar and the lorises, potto, angwantibo, and galago.

Lorisidae lemuriforms; includes the loris, potto, angwantibo, and galago.

O

Omomyidae† Family of Eocene and Oligocene primates, showing some resemblance to the tarsiers, found in North America, Europe, Asia, and Africa.

P

Parapithecidae† Family of the order Primates consisting of Early Oligocene primates from the Fayum, Egypt.

Parapithecoidea† Suborder of the order Primates that contains the family Parapithecidae.

Pithecinae Subfamily of the Cebidae; includes the titis, sakis, and uakaris.

Platyrrhini Infraorder of the suborder Anthropoidea that includes the New World monkeys and various New World fossil taxa.

Plesiadapiformes† Group of Paleocene fossil mammals that are thought by some paleontologists to be among the earliest members of the Primate order.

Ponginae Subfamily of the family Hominidae that includes the organutans of southeast Asia.

Primates Order of the class Mammalia that includes the living prosimians, tarsiers, New World monkeys, Old World monkeys, lesser apes, great apes, and humans.

Proconsulidae† Family of miocene hominoids from Africa.

Propliopithecidae† Family of the infraorder Catarrhini from the Middle Oligocene to Late Miocene of Africa and Europe; may have given rise to the Old World monkeys and the hominoids.

Prosimii Suborder of the order Primates that includes the lemurs, indris, and aye-aye of Madagascar and the lorises, potto, angwantibo, galagos, and tarsiers of Africa and Asia.

T

Tarsiiformes Infraorder of the suborder Prosimii that includes the tarsiers of southeast Asia.

V

Victoriapithecidae† Family of Early and Middle Miocene Old World monkeys from north and east Africa.

Credits

Illustration Credits

Figures 2.9, 2.10 S. S. Mader, *Biology,* 6th ed. (New York: McGraw-Hill, 1997). Reproduced with permission of The McGraw-Hill Companies.

Figure 2.14 J. H. Postlethwaite and J. L. Hopson, *The Nature of Life* (New York: McGraw-Hill, 1989). Courtesy of the authors.

Figures 2.15, 2.16 J. H. Postlethwaite, J. L. Hopson, and R. C. Veres, *Biology* (New York: McGraw-Hill, 1991). Courtesy of the authors.

Figure 3.7 S. S. Mader, *Biology,* 6th ed. (New York: McGraw-Hill, 1997). Reproduced with permission of The McGraw-Hill Companies.

Figure 4.2 From C. E. Purdom, *Genetic Effects of Radiation.* Copyright © 1963 by Academic Press, Inc. Used with permission of Academic Press and C. E. Purdom.

Figure 4.3 Diagram created with a simulation developed by Kent E. Holsinger, University of Connecticut, http://darwin.eeb.uconn.edu/simulations/simulations.html.

Figure 5.1 Based on data from A. H. Booth, "Observations on the Natural History of the Olive Colobus Monkeys, *Procolobus verus* (van Benedan)," *Proceedings of the Zoological Society of London* 129 (1957).

Figure 5.6 From *Student Atlas of Anthropology,* 1st ed. by John L. Allen/Audrey C. Shalinsky. Copyright © 2004 by The McGraw-Hill Companies, Inc. All rights reserved. Reprinted by permission of McGraw-Hill/Dushkin Publishing. www.dushkin.com.

Figures 5.9, 5.13 J. H. Postlethwaite and J. L. Hopson, *The Nature of Life* (New York: McGraw-Hill, 1989). Courtesy of the authors.

Figure 5.14 David Lack, *Darwin's Finches* (Cambridge: Cambridge University Press, 1947). Courtesy of Dr. Peter Lack on behalf of the estate of David Lack.

Figure 6.1 From *Life: An Introduction to Biology,* 2nd edition, by William S. Beck and George G. Simpson, 1965.

Figures 6.8, 6.9 From G. B. Johnson, *The Living World,* 3rd ed. (New York: McGraw-Hill, 2003). Reproduced with permission of The McGraw-Hill Companies.

Figure 6.10b Clark, W. E. LeGros, *The Antecedents of Man.* Edinburgh University Press, 1959. Reprinted by permission. www.eup.ed.ac.uk

Figure 7.1 Clark, W. E. LeGros, *The Antecedents of Man.* Edinburgh University Press, 1959. Reprinted by permission. www.eup.ed.ac.uk.

Figure 7.2 D. R. Swindler, *Introduction to the Primates* (Seattle: University of Washington Press). Reprinted by permission of University of Washington Press.

Figure 7.5 Schultz, A. H., *The Life of Primates,* © 1969 by Adolph H. Schultz. Reprinted by permission of Weidenfeld & Nicolson, a division of The Orion Publishing Group and A. H. Schultz.

Figures 7.6, 7.20 From *Student Atlas of Anthropology,* 1st ed. by John L. Allen/Audrey C. Shalinsky. Copyright © 2004 by The McGraw-Hill Companies, Inc. All rights reserved. Reprinted by permission of McGraw-Hill/Dushkin Publishing. www.dushkin.com.

Figures 8.3, 8.4 Schultz, A. H., *The Life of Primates,* © 1969 by Adolph H. Schultz. Reprinted by permission of Weidenfeld & Nicolson, a division of The Orion Publishing Group and A. H. Schultz.

Figure 8.5 John Buettner-Janusch, *Origins of Man.* Copyright © 1966 by John Wiley & Sons, Inc. Reprinted with permission of John Wiley & Sons, Inc.

Figure 8.6 Drawing by Luba Dmytryk Gudz in Johanson, Donald C., and Maitland A. Edey, *Lucy: The Beginnings of Humankind.*

Figures 8.12, 8.13 Adapted from Romer, Alfred S., *The Vertebrate Body,* 2nd ed. (Philadelphia: W. B. Saunders, 1955).

Figure 8.15 Reprinted from *An Introduction to Human Evolutionary Anatomy* by Leslie Aiello and Christopher Dean, p. 134. Copyright 1990, with permission of Elsevier.

Figure 8.16 Drawings reprinted from *Primate Adaptations and Evolution,* 2nd ed., by John Fleagle, p. 293. Copyright 1998, with permission of Elsevier.

Figures 8.21, 8.22 Reprinted from *An Introduction to Human Evolutionary Anatomy* by Leslie Aiello and Christopher Dean, pp. 35 and 55. Copyright 1990, with permission of Elsevier.

Figure 8.24 Reprinted with permission from Yunis, J. J., J. R. Sawyer, and K. Dunham, "The Striking Resemblance of High-Resolution G-Banded Chromosomes of Man and Chimpanzees," *Science* 208 (1980), pp. 1145–1149. Copyright 1980 AAAS. Courtesy of J. J. Yunis.

Figure 9.6 Nancy DeVore/Anthro-Photo.

Figure 10.5 D. L. Chaney and R. M. Seyfarth, *How Monkeys See the World.* Copyright © 1990 by The University of Chicago.

Figure 11.5 Glenn L. Isaac, "Early Hominids in Action: A Commentary on the Contribution of Archaeology to Understanding the Fossil Record in East Africa," *Yearbook of Physical Anthropology,* 19. Copyright © 1975 by Alan R. Liss, Inc. Reprinted with permission of John Wiley & Sons.

Figure 11.8 Mary Leakey, *Olduvai Gorge, Volume 3: Excavations in Beds I and II, 1960–1963* (Cambridge: Cambridge University Press, 1971) Reprinted with the permission of Cambridge University Press.

Figure 11.13 W. B. Harland et al., *A Geologic Time Scale 1989* (Cambridge: Cambridge University Press, 1990). Reprinted by permission of Cambridge University Press.

Figure 11.14 J. H. Postlethwaite and J. L. Hopson, *The Nature of Life* (New York: McGraw-Hill, 1989). Courtesy of the authors.

Figures 12.1, 12.2 Art by Rudolph Freund for *Scientific American.*

Figure 12.3 All rights reserved, Photo Archives, Denver Museum of Nature and Science.

Figures 12.4, 12.7 Reprinted from *Primate Adaptations and Evolution*, 2nd ed., by John Fleagle, p. 401. Copyright 1998, with permission of Elsevier.

Figure 12.12 Walker, A., and M. Pickford, "New Postcranial Fossils of *Proconsul africanus* and *Proconsul nyanzae*," in Russell L. Ciochon and Robert S. Corrucini, *New Interpretations of Ape and Human Ancestry,* 1983, figure 2, p. 333. With kind permission of Springer Science and Business Media and Alan C. Walker.

Figure 12.13 Bernor, R. L., "Geochronology and Zoogeographical Relationships of Miocene Hominoidea," in Russell L. Ciochon and Robert S. Corrucini, *New Interpretations of Ape and Human Ancestry,* 1983, figures 2–4, pp. 30, 37, 43. With kind permission of Springer Science and Business Media and R. L. Bernor.

Figure 12.17 Reprinted with permission from Szalay, F. S., and A. Berzi, "Cranial Anatomy of Oreopithecus," *Science* 180 (1973), p. 184. Copyright 1973 AAAS.

Figure 12.18 Illustrations by Tom Prentiss in Simons, E. L., and P. E. Ettel, "Gigantopithecus," *Scientific American* (January 1970), p. 81. Used by permission of N. H. Prentiss.

Figure 13.6 Courtesy of C. K. Brain, Transvaal Museum, Republic of South Africa.

Figure 13.10 "Development of Pliocene and Pleistocene Chronology of the Turkana Basin, East Africa, and Its Relation to Other Sites" by F. Brown in *Integrative Paths to the Past,* edited by Corrucini/Ciochon, © 1994. Reprinted by permission of Pearson Education, Inc., Upper Saddle River, NJ.

Figure 13.25 Courtesy Dr. Owen Lovejoy, Kent State University.

Figure 13.26 Transvaal Museum Memoire No. 10, 1957, *Osteodontokeratic Culture of Australopithecus prometheus.* Used with permission of the Transvaal Museum.

Figure 13.27 Reprinted with permission from R. L. Susman, "Fossil Evidence for Early Hominid Tool Use," *Science* 265 (1994), page 1570. Copyright 1994 AAAS.

Figure 13.29 Drawing by Luba Dmytryk Gudz in Johanson, Donald C., and Maitland A. Edey, *Lucy: The Beginnings of Humankind.*

Figure 13.30 Reprinted from "The Obstetric Pelvis of A.L. 288-1 (Lucy)," by R. G. Tague and C. O. Lovejoy, *Journal of Human Evolution* (1986), pp. 237–255. Copyright 1986, with permission of Elsevier.

Figure 13.31 White, Tim D., Donald C. Johanson, and William H. Kimbel, "*Australopithecus africanus*: Its Phylogenetic Position Reconsidered," South African Journal of Science 77 (October 1981). Used by permission.

Figure 13.32 Reprinted from *The Australopithecine Face* by Y. Rak. Copyright 1983, with permission of Elsevier.

Figure 14.22 Illustrations by Whitney Powell in Trinkaus, E., and W. W. Howells, "The Neandertals," *Scientific American* (December 1979), p. 131, top and bottom. Reprinted by permission of the artist.

Figures 14.24, 14.25, 14.26 Mary Leakey, *Olduvai Gorge, Volume 3: Excavations in Beds I and II, 1960–1963* (Cambridge: Cambridge University Press, 1971). Reprinted with the permission of Cambridge University Press.

Figures 14.28, 14.32 François Bordes, *The Old Stone Age.* Copyright © 1968 by François Bordes. Reproduced with permission of The McGraw-Hill Companies.

Box 14-3 Marcellin Boule and Henri V. Vallois, *Fossil Men* (New York: The Dryden Press, 1957).

Figure 15.8 C. C. Plummer, D. McGeary, and D. H. Carlson, *Physical Geology,* 10th edition (New York: McGraw-Hill, 2005), p. 309. Reproduced with permission of The McGraw-Hill Companies.

Figure 15.10 François Bordes, *The Old Stone Age.* Copyright © 1968 by François Bordes. Reproduced with permission of The McGraw-Hill Companies.

Figure 15.11a C. J. Jolly and R. White, *Physical Anthropology and Archeology,* 5th edition. Copyright © 1995 by McGraw-Hill, Inc. Reproduced with permission of The McGraw-Hill Companies.

Figures 15.17, 15.18 Braidwood, Robert, *Prehistoric Men,* 1st Edition, © 1975. Reprinted by permission of Pearson Education, Inc., Upper Saddle River, NJ.

Figure 16.1 *House Form and Culture* by Rapoport, Amos, © 1969. Reprinted by permission of Pearson Education, Inc., Upper Saddle River, NJ.

Figure 16.3 Folk, G. E., "Barometric Pressures and Oxygen Pressure at High Altitude," *Introduction to Environmental Physiology* (Philadelphia: Lea and Febiger, 1966). Used by permission.

Figure 16.4 Based on chart published in Alberto Hurtado, "Animals in High Altitudes: Resident Man," in D. B Dill (ed.), *Handbook of Physiology: Adaptation to the Environment, 1964* (American Physiological Society).

Figure 16.5 A. R. Friancho & P. T. Baker, "Altitude and Growth: A Study of the Patterns of Physical Growth of a High-Altitude Peruvian Quechua Population," *American Journal of Physical Anthropology* 32 (1970), p. 290. Reprinted with permission of John Wiley & Sons, Inc.

Figure 16.8 Richard E. Scammon, "The Measurement of the Body," in J. A. Harris, et al., *The Measurement of Man* (Minneapolis, MN: University of Minnesota Press, 1930), page 193. © 1930 by the University of Minnesota.

Figures 16.9, 16.10 From W. M. Krogman, *The Human Skeleton in Forensic Medicine,* 1962. Courtesy of Charles C. Thomas Publisher, Ltd., Springfield, Illinois.

Figure 16.12 © American Dental Association.

Figures 16.13, 16.14 Tanner, J. M. *Growth at Adolescence,* 2nd ed., 1962. Reprinted by permission of Blackwell Scientific Publications.

Figure 16.15 From Tanner, 1962, based on the data of Jones, Tanner, J. M. (1962), *Growth at Adolescence,* 2nd Edition, Oxford: Blackwell Scientific Publications.

Figure 16.17 Data taken from tables in H. V. Meredity, "Findings from Asia, Australia, Europe, and North America on Secular Change in Mean Height of Children, Youths, and Young Adults," *American Journal of Physical Anthropology,* 44 (1976), pp. 315–326. Original data published in R. E. Roth and M. Harris, *The Physical Condition of Children Attending Public Schools in New South Wales* (Sidney: Department of Public Instruction, 1908), and D. L. Jones, et al., *Height, Weight and Other Physical Characteristics of New South Wales Children Part I: Children Age Five Years and Older* (Sidney: New South Wales Department of Health, 1973).

Figures 17.1, 17.3 Mourant, A. E., A. C. Kopéc, and K. Domaniewski-Sobezak, *The Distribution of the Human Blood Groups and Other Polymorphisms,* 2nd edition, 1976. By permission of Oxford University Press.

Figure 17.2 E. Sunderland, "Hair-Colour Variation in the United Kingdom," *Annals of Human Genetics* 20 (1955–1956), p. 327.

Figure 17.7 Morton Klass and Hal Hellman, *The Kinds of Mankind: An Introduction of Race and Racism.* J. B. Lippencott, 1971. Courtesy of Morton Klass.

Figure 17.8 L. L. Cavalli-Sforza et al., "Reconstruction of Human Evolution: Bringing Together Genetic, Archaeological, and Linguistic Data," *Proceedings of the National Academy of Sciences* 85 (1988), pp. 6002–6006. Adapted by permission of L. L. Cavalli-Sforza.

Figure 17.9 Copyright ©1999 by the BSCS and Videodiscovery, Inc.

Figure 17.10 Bischof, L. J., *Intelligence: Statistical Concept of Its Nature.* Copyright © 1954 by Doubleday & Company, Inc. Reprinted by permission of Random House, Inc.

Box 17-1 D. H. Ubelaker, "Skeletal Evidence for Kneeling in Prehistoric Ecuador," *American Journal of Physical Anthropology* 51 (1979), p. 683. Reprinted with permission of John Wiley & Sons, Inc.

Photos

Chapter 1 opener: © ENGLISH HERITAGE Photo Library Photographer: Jonathan Bailey; **Figure 1.1:** Jenike/Anthro-Photo File; **Figure 1.2:** The Dian Fossey Gorilla Fund International; **Figure 1.3:** Culver Pictures; **Figure 1.5:** By courtesy of the National Portrait Gallery, London; **Figure 1.6:** Stone/Getty Images; **Figure 1.7:** Logan Museum of Anthropology, Beloit College, Beloit, WI; **Figure 1.8:** © Bettmann/CORBIS ; **Figure 1.9:** Brown Brothers; **Figure 1.10a:** Fred Bavendam/Peter Arnold, Inc.; **Figure 1.10b:** David Cavagnaro/Peter Arnold, Inc.

Chapter 2 opener: M. Freeman/PhotoLink/Getty Images; **Figure 2.1:** Image # 219467 American Museum Natural History; **Figure 2.6:** Ray Simmons/Photo Researchers, Inc.; **Figure 2.7:** Michael Abbey/Photo Researchers, Inc.; **Figure 2.8a, b:** CNRI/Photo Researchers, Inc.

Chapter 3 opener: The Image Bank/Getty Images; **Figure 3.6a:** Biophoto Associates/Photo Researchers, Inc.; **Figure 3.6b:** Lauren Shear/Photo Researchers, Inc.

Chapter 4 opener: Stone/Getty Images

Chapter 5 opener: © Mark Jones/Animals Animals/Earth Scenes; **Figure 5.5a:** Andrew Syred/Photo Researchers, Inc.; **Figure 5.5b:** Omikron/Photo Researchers, Inc.; **Figure 5.7:** Renee Purse/Photo Researchers, Inc.; **Figure 5.8:** Zoological Society of San Diego

Chapter 6 opener: © CORBIS; **Figure 6.11:** B. G. Thomson/Photo Researchers, Inc.; **Figure 6.12:** Mike James/Photo Researchers, Inc.

Chapter 7 opener: Taxi/Getty Images; **Figure 7.4a:** WK Sacco specimen courtesy of Yale Peabody Museum; **Figure 7.4b:** WK Sacco; **Figure 7.4c:** WK Sacco; **Figure 7.7:** © David Haring, OSF/Animals Animals/Earth Scenes; **Figure 7.8:** © Patti Murray/Animals Animals/Earth Scenes; **Figure 7.9:** Norman Myers/Bruce Coleman; **Figure 7.10:** © Ken Lucas/Visuals Unlimited; **Figure 7.11:** Tom McHugh/Photo Researchers; **Figure 7.12:** Ron Garrison/Zoological Society of San Diego; **Figure 7.13:** © Ruth Cole, Animals Animals/Earth Scenes; **Figure 7.14:** Tom McHugh/Photo Researchers, Inc.; **Figure 7.15:** Terry Whittaker/Photo Researchers, Inc.; **Figure 7.16:** © Gallo Images/CORBIS; **Figure 7.17:** © Joe McDonald/Visuals Unlimited; **Figure 7.18:** Art Wolfe/Photo Researchers, Inc.; **Figure 7.19a:** © Theo Allofs/CORBIS; **Figure 7.19b:** © Glenn Vanstrum/Animals Animals/Earth Scenes; **Figure 7.21a:** Wayne McGuire/Anthro-Photo File; **Figure 7.21b:** © Gallo Images/CORBIS; **Figure 7.22a:** © Gerry Ellis/Minden Pictures; **Figure 7.22b:** Tetsuro Matsuzawa; **Figure 7.23:** © M. Colbeck, OSF/Animals Animals/Earth Scenes

Chapter 8 opener: © Bettmann/CORBIS; **Figure 8.1a (left):** © Clem Haagner; Gallo Images/CORBIS; **Figure 8.1a (right):** © The Natural History Museum, London; **Figure 8.1b (top):** Peter Waser/Wisconsin National Primate Research Center; **Figure 8.1b (bottom):** © The Natural History Museum, London; **Figure 8.1c (left):** © Photodisc/Getty Images; **Figure 8.1c (right):** Bones Clones, Inc.; **Figure 8.1d (left):** © Martin Harvey/CORBIS; **Figure 8.1d (right):** © The Natural History Museum, London; **Figure 8.1e (left):** © Frans Lanting/Minden Pictures; **Figure 8.1e (right):** WK Sacco; **Figure 8.1f (left):** WK Sacco; **Figure 8.1f (right):** © Dani Carlo Studio/Animals Animals/Earth Scenes; **Figure 8.1g (left):** © Martin Harvey/ CORBIS; **Figure 8.1g (right):** WK

Sacco specimen courtesy of Yale Peabody Museum; **Figure 8.1h (left):** © Richard Sobol/Animals Animals/Earth Scenes; **Figure 8.1h (right):** Bones Clones, Inc.; **Figure 8.1i (left):** © Jorg & Petra Wegner/Animals Animals/Earth Scenes; **Figure 8.1i (right):** Bones Clones, Inc.; **Figure 8.1j (left):** © Cameron/CORBIS; **Figure 8.1j (right):** Bones Clones, Inc.; **Figure 8.7:** WK Sacco specimen courtesy of Yale Peabody Museum; **Figure 8.8 (left):** © Royalty-Free/CORBIS; **Figure 8.8 (right):** Stone/Getty Images; **Figure 8.9:** WK Sacco; **Figure 8.10a:** Photographs by Robert N. Frankle & Rebecca L. Stein; **Figure 8.10b:** © Gerry Ellis/Minden Pictures; **Figure 8.11Aa:** WK Sacco specimen courtesy of Yale Peabody Museum; **Figure 8.11Ab:** WK Sacco specimen courtesy of Yale Peabody Museum; **Figure 8.11Ac:** WK Sacco specimen courtesy of Yale Peabody Museum; **Figure 8.11Ad:** WK Sacco specimen courtesy of Yale Peabody Museum; **Figure 8.11Ba:** WK Sacco; **Figure 8.11Bb:** WK Sacco; **Figure 8.11Bc:** WK Sacco; **Figure 8.11Bd:** WK Sacco; **Figure 8.11Ca:** WK Sacco; **Figure 8.11Cb:** WK Sacco; **Figure 8.11Cc:** WK Sacco; **Figure 8.11Cd:** WK Sacco; **Figure 8.11Da:** WK Sacco; **Figure 8.11Db:** WK Sacco; **Figure 8.11Dc:** WK Sacco; **Figure 8.11Dd:** WK Sacco; **Figure 8.14:** Photograph by Dodie Stoneburner; **Figure 8.17:** WK Sacco; **Figure 8.18:** WK Sacco; **Figure 8.19:** WK Sacco; **Figure 8.20:** WK Sacco; **Figure 8.23:** Courtesy J. J. Yunis

Chapter 9 opener: Dan Hrdy/Anthro-Photo File; **Box 9-1:** © Konrad Wothe/Minden Pictures; **Figure 9.1:** © Frans Lanting/Minden Pictures; **Box 9-2:** Irven DeVore/Anthro-Photo File; **Figure 9.2:** © Lynn D. Odell/Animals Animals/Earth Scenes, **Figure 9.3:** infocusphotos.com; **Figure 9.4:** © Gallo Images/CORBIS; **Figure 9.5:** Richard Wrangham/Anthro-Photo File; **Figure 9.7a-i:** Photographs by Robert N. Frankle & Rebecca L. Stein; **Figure 9.8:** Barbara Smuts/Anthro-Photo File; **Figure 9.9:** Photodisc/Getty Images; **Box 9-3:** © Frans Lanting/Minden Pictures; **Figure 9.10:** Getty Images; **Figure 9.11:** Jane Goodall Institute

Chapter 10 opener: Stan Washburn/Anthro-Photo File; **Figure 10.1a;** Marjorie Shostak/Anthro-Photo File; **Figure 10.1b:** Bryan & Cherry Alexander Photography; **Figure 10.1c:** Washburn/Anthro-Photo File; **Figure 10.2:** Courtesy of Masao Kawai, Japan Monkey Centre, Kyoto University, Japan; **Figure 10.3:** Courtesy of Masao Kawai, Japan Monkey Centre, Kyoto University, Japan; **Figure 10.4:** Bion Giffin; **Figure 10.5a:** Photo courtesy of R. A. and B. T. Gardner; **Figure 10.5b:** Great Ape Trust of Iowa; **Figure 10.5c:** Ron Cohn, The Gorilla Foundation, Koko.org; **Figure 10.7a:** From Cheney and Seyfarth, *How Monkeys See the World*, p. 152; The University of Chicago Press; **Figure 10.7b:** From Cheney and Seyfarth, *How Monkeys See the World*, p. 152; The University of Chicago Press

Chapter 11 opener: © James L. Amos - Photo Researchers, Inc.; **Figure 11.1:** © Sygma/Corbis; **Figure 11.2a:** Image # 315485 American Museum of Natural History; **Figure 11.2b:** Natural History Museum; **Figure 11.2c:** © The Natural History Museum, London; **Figure 11.4:** American Museum of Natural History; **Figure 11.6a-f:** From John Buettner-Janusch, *Origins of Man*, 1966. Used with permission of John Wiley & Sons, Inc.; **Box 11-3:** E. M. Fulda/Image # 106772 Photo by E. M

Fulda. American Museum of Natural History; **Box 11-4:** © P. Kent/Animals Animals/Earth Scenes

Chapter 12 opener: John Fleagle/Academic Press; **Figure 12.5:** Peabody Museum, Yale University; **Figure 12.6:** Peabody Museum, Yale University; **Figure 12.8:** Courtesy of T. Setoguchi & A. L. Rosenberger; **Figure 12.9:** © and courtesy of Eric Delson, City University of New York/American Museum of Natural History; **Figure 12.10:** National History Museum, London; **Figure 12.11:** © The Natural History Muscum, London; **Figure 12.15:** © and courtesy of Eric Delson, City University of New York/American Museum of Natural History; **Figure 12.16:** © The Natural History Museum, London; **Figure 12.19:** Salvador Moyà-Solà, *Science,* Vol. 306, Issue 5700, 1339–1344, 19 Nov. 2004, figure 1; **Figure 12.21:** © M.P.F.T.; **Figure 12.22:** Gamma Press USA; **Figure 12.23:** David L. Brill; **Figure 12.24:** David L. Brill

Chapter 13 opener: Photofest; **Figure 13.2:** David L. Brill; **Figure 13.3:** Alun R. Hughes; **Figure 13.4:** David L. Brill; **Figure 13.5:** David L. Brill; **Figure 13.7:** Photography by J. F. Thackery, Courtesy of the Transvaal Museum, Pretoria; **Figure 13.8:** National Geographic Society Image Collection; **Figure 13.9:** National Geographic Society Image Collection; **Figure 13.11:** David L. Brill; **Figure 13.12:** Courtesy of R. E. F. Leakey, National Museums of Kenya; **Figure 13.13:** The Human Origins Program, Smithsonian Institution; **Figure 13.14:** National Geographic Society Image Collection; **Figure 13.15:** National Museums of Kenya; **Figure 13.16:** David L. Brill; **Figure 13.17:** David L. Brill; **Figure 13.18:** Tim White; **Figure 13.19:** Anthro-Photo File; **Figure 13.20:** David L. Brill; **Figure 13.21:** © M.P.F.T.; **Figure 13.23a-c:** David L. Brill; **Figure 13.26:** David L. Brill

Chapter 14 opener: National Geographic Society Image Collection; **Figure 14.1:** The Human Origins Program, Smithsonian Institution; **Figure 14.2:** John Reader/Photo Researchers, Inc.; **Figure 14.3:** R. E. F. Leakey, National Museums Kenya; **Figure 14.4:** David L. Brill; **Figure 14.5:** David L. Brill; **Figure 14.7a, b:** The Human Origins Program, Smithsonian Institution; **Figure 14.8:** © The Natural History Muscum, London; **Figure 14.9:** © David L. Brill; **Figure 14.11:** © The Natural History Museum, London; **Figure 14.12:** Image # 410816 American Museum of Natural History; **Figure 14.13:** Milford H. Wolpoff; **Figure 14.14:** © David L. Brill; **Figure 14.15:** Dr. Dennis A. Etler; **Figure 14.16:** David L. Brill; **Figure 14.17:** Erik Trinkaus/Peabody Museum of Archaeology and Ethnology, Harvard; **Figure 14.19:** Image # 327423 and # 327424 American Museum of Natural History; **Figure 14.21:** © David L. Brill; **Figure 14.23:** © David L. Brill; **Figure 14.27:** K. D. Schick and N. Toth; **Figure 14.29:** Courtesy of Pat Shipman; **Figure 14.33:** Randall White; **Figure 14.34:** Museo Nacional de Ciencias Naturales, Madrid; **Figure 14.35:** © The Natural History Museum, London

Chapter 15 opener: Erich Lessing/Art Resource, NY; **Figure 15.2:** © The Natural History Museum, London; **Figure 15.3:** The Human Origins Program, Smithsonian Institution; **Figure 15.4:** © The Natural History Museum, London; **Figure 15.7:** © The Natural History Museum, London; **Figure 15.9:** Dr. James Chatters; **Figure 15.11b:** © The British Museum; **Figure 15.12:** © The Natural History Museum,

Index